The Brown & Benchmark Re

AMERICAN GOVERNMENT, 1992

Edited by

Dr. Jeffrey M. Elliot
North Carolina Central University

 Wm. C. Brown Publishers

Book Team

Editor *Edgar J. Laube*
Project Editor *Roger B. Wolkoff*
Production Editor *Diane E. Beausoleil*
Permissions Editor *Vicki Krug*

 Wm. C. Brown Publishers

President *G. Franklin Lewis*
Vice President, Publisher *Thomas E. Doran*
Vice President, Operations and Production *Beverly Kolz*
National Sales Manager *Virginia S. Moffat*
Group Sales Manager *Eric Ziegler*
Executive Editor *Edgar J. Laube*
Director of Marketing *Kathy Law Laube*
Marketing Manager *Kathleen Nietzke*
Managing Editor, Production *Colleen A. Yonda*
Manager of Visuals and Design *Faye M. Schilling*
Production Editorial Manager *Julie A. Kennedy*
Production Editorial Manager *Ann Fuerste*
Publishing Services Manager *Karen J. Slaght*

WCB Group

President and Chief Executive Officer *Mark C. Falb*
Chairman of the Board *Wm. C. Brown*

Permissions Editor Karen Dorman

Cover Design Kay D. Fulton

Cover Image © Jeffrey M. Spielman/The Image Bank

Printed in the United States of America by Wm. C. Brown Publishers,
2460 Kerper Boulevard, Dubuque, IA 52001

10 9 8 7 6 5 4 3 2 1

Contents

About the Editor

Dr. Jeffrey M. Elliot is a Professor of Political Science at North Carolina Central University, as well as a free-lance writer and editor. He received his Bachelor of Arts degree in 1969 and his Master of Arts in 1970 from the University of Southern California and his Doctor of Arts degree from the Claremont Graduate School in 1978. In 1985, he was awarded an honorary Doctor of Humane Letters degree from Shaw University, and in 1986, California State University, San Bernardino, established The Jeffrey M. Elliot Collection, a permanent archive of his published works. Dr. Elliot is the author of over sixty published books and 500 articles, reviews, and interviews. His work has appeared in more than 250 publications, both in the United States and abroad, and has been nominated for numerous academic and literary awards. In 1991, he was selected as North Carolina Central University's "Most Outstanding Researcher." Recent book titles include: *The Trilemma of World Oil Politics* (Borgo Press, 1991); *Third World* (Dushkin Publishing Group, 1991); *Urban Society* (Dushkin Publishing Group, 1991); *Voices of Zaire: Rhetoric or Reality?* (Washington Institute Press, 1990); *The Arms Control, Disarmament, and Military Security Dictionary* (ABC-Clio, 1989); *The State and Local Government Political Dictionary* (ABC-Clio, 1987); *Fidel Castro: Nothing Can Stop the Course of History* (Pathfinder Press, 1986); *Black Voices in American Politics* (Harcourt Brace Jovanovich, 1985); *The Presidential-Congressional Political Dictionary* (ABC-Clio, 1984); and *Tempest in a Teapot: The Falkland Islands War* (Borgo Press, 1983). Dubbed the "Boswell of Modern America," Dr. Elliot has conducted over 350 interviews, among them: President Jimmy Carter, Nobel Prize winner Bishop Desmond Tutu, Cuban president Fidel Castro, Zairian president Mobutu Sese Seko, UNITA president Jonas Savimbi, PLO chairman Yasir Arafat, Contra leader Adolfo Calero, and Jamaican prime minister Michael Manley. In addition to his academic duties, he serves as Distinguished Advisor on Foreign Affairs to Congressman Mervyn M. Dymally (D-Calif.), editor or contributing editor to six journals, chairperson of the Durham County Youth Services Advisory Board, vice president and a member of the board of directors of the Durham Housing Authority Crime Prevention Board. He is the subject of a book-length study, *The Work of Jeffrey M. Elliot: An Annotated Bibliography and Guide* (Borgo Press, 1986).

To the Reader

This reader reflects the conviction that the abstract discussion of issues, events, and personalities fails to stimulate and arouse student interest. Nearly every day, political developments raise significant questions about the policies, processes, and institutions of government. Indeed, in the past decade, the political system has been plagued by a host of urgent problems, as well as by more subtle, but no less serious, challenges, such as the expansion of government power, the erosion of civil liberties, the politicization of the courts, and the loss of faith in the legal system. These developments underscore the delicate balance between personal rights and public needs that drives a democratic society. This book evinces the editor's and publisher's dissatisfaction with many of the readers on the market, which in our view, fail to provide the student with a basic understanding of the subject. Unlike other books, this reader introduces the student to the "nuts and bolts" of American government. But, unlike the others, they are introduced in the hope that the student will be able to use the information to build an argument, a case, a point for or against.

Amid the welter of readers on the market, precious few seem to satisfy this need. In compiling this book, the editor examined more than 750 articles, culled from over 250 newspapers, magazines, and journals. Obviously, students will not read dull, obtuse, outdated articles. For this reason, the editor has only included articles that are skillfully argued, carefully written, thoughtfully organized, and free of needless jargon. The articles encompass the major topics that are typically covered in the standard introductory course in American government. In all but the first chapter, we have chosen to limit the number of selections to three per topic. The limitation on selections will, we hope, increase the likelihood that students will read all or most of them. In addition, by limiting the selections for each topic, there exists the greater possibility that students will be able to associate an argument with the author who makes it.

In addition to the readings, which are organized around five main themes, each part is prefaced by a section overview, discussion questions, a glossary of key terms, and a selected bibliography. A brief abstract accompanies each article. Students at both the introductory and advanced levels will find this approach helpful in identifying the salient questions addressed in college courses on American government. Instructors will also discover that the book is a useful teaching tool—bringing together in one volume, published on an annual basis—the core themes of the subject, thereby eliminating the need for inconvenient library reserve assignments for students. In many cases, readers provide only topical or entertaining material, at the expense of more scholarly, time-tested selections. For this reason, students are not adequately introduced to a broad cross section of the literature on the subject in question. We have sought to avoid this pitfall, by selecting readings that represent an authoritative treatment of the major topics that comprise the study of American government. As consistently as possible throughout the book, articles are included that offer competing interpretations of the issues under discussion.

Featuring key classic and contemporary readings and cases that introduce students to the underpinnings and currents of American government, the reader is designed to complement standard texts by illustrating and amplifying important issues and concepts. At the same time, the organization and design of the book make it suitable for use as a core text. The sixty-two selections were chosen not only to provide students with basic subject-matter information, but also to heighten their interest and appreciation of the richness and excitement of the political system.

Hopefully, this reader will assist students to understand the relationships between citizens, decision makers, government policies, and the broader environment in which American government functions, as well as human motivations and conflict, official role playing and decision making, and the way politics affects the quality and character of American life. Like any new book, there is always room for improvement. The editor and publisher welcome your ideas and suggestions, knowing that, in the end, its success will depend on how well it serves your purposes.

Dr. Jeffrey M. Elliot
Editor

Acknowledgments

We would like to thank the following people for their expertise as reviewers for this project: Gayle Berardi, Stephen F. Austin State University; Edward Portis, Texas A & M University; Clyde Wilcox, Georgetown University; Laura Woliver, University of South Carolina.

THE AMERICAN EXPERIMENT

The United States is a vast country. Its landscapes and climates vary. Its people come from every part of the world. Over the years, observers of the American scene have asked what factors have held the nation together for more than 200 years. In the late 1700s, J. Hector St. John de Crevecoeur, a Frenchman, asked: How is it possible for immigrants and their descendants from so many backgrounds to be transformed into new men and women who act upon new principles?" Alexis de Tocqueville, a French observer who visited the United States in the 1830s, wondered how recent immigrants, bringing different customs and traditions, could develop loyalty and love for their new country. "What makes everyone take such a keen interest in public life?" he asked. "Why do they feel American?"

In the United States today, one can find Vietnamese, Indian, Korean, Panamanian, Danish, and Croatian communities, 200 Native-American tribes, and hundreds of other ethnic neighborhoods. There are more Cubans in Miami than in any Cuban city except Havana, more Poles in Buffalo than anywhere except Warsaw, more Jews in the United States than in Israel, and more people of Mexican ancestry in Los Angeles County than in any city except Mexico City. Approximately 28 million persons in the United States (two-thirds of whom are native-born Americans) have mother tongues—first languages—other than English or live in households in which another language is spoken.

Although many factors bind America together, one is dominant: shared political beliefs. The United States has attempted to define its identity not by race, religion, ethnicity, or language, but by a set of commonly held ideals, such as liberty, equality, opportunity, and acceptance of diversity. The nation was born of a revolution, which it defended in terms of its expressed ideals. The authors of the Declaration of Independence called upon the world to witness the justice of that revolution against England. Since that time, the nation itself and the composition of its population have undergone many changes. The ideals that shaped the political structure of the country have gone through changes too, taking on new meanings to exert powerful influence on our behavior as a nation and our lives as individuals.

These ideals define our identity; they serve as bonds that unite us in the face of diversity and disagreement; and they provide a framework for public and private action. The United States stands for something to the millions of people who have come to our shores and to those who wish to come here. German-Americans, French-Americans, Jewish-Americans, Black-Americans, Chinese-Americans, Mexican-Americans—all are nonetheless Americans who have access to and can subscribe to these ideals. We work, we play, we sell, we buy, we make peace and war in the name of American beliefs. The ideals of liberty, equality, opportunity, and acceptance of diversity have shaped our history and are essential to our future as a peaceful and prosperous multicultural society.

Chapter 1, *American Democracy,* comprises several historical documents that have shaped our understanding of the American political system, beginning with the Declaration of Independence, authored by Thomas Jefferson in 1776, which presents the case for independence from England, and affirms the essential rights of "life, liberty, and the pursuit of happiness." The second document, the Constitution of 1787, provides the written framework for the United States government that established a strong national government of three branches—legislative, executive, and judicial—and provided for the control and operation of that government. In addition to these two documents, the chapter also includes three selections from the Federalist Papers, a series of letters published in the late 1780s by Alexander Hamilton, James Madison, and John Jay to explain and help bring about ratification of the Constitution. The three papers focus on the dangers of parties and interest groups, the importance of checks and balances, and the role of the federal judiciary.

Chapter 2, *Political Culture,* begins with an examination of American pluralism, the need for a new conservative agenda, the rise of the political Right, and the hypocrisy of the radical Left. The second selection questions the likelihood of a liberal revival, challenging the cyclical theory of American politics. In the third article, the author, who predicts the end of the conservative revolution, calls for a new revolution—one that is rooted in a commitment to democracy, social responsibility, and government action.

Chapter 3, *The Constitution,* starts by asking whether the Bill of Rights is in danger at home, noting that the majority must resist the efforts of special-interest groups to reinterpret its protections to serve their own political agendas. The second article maintains that Americans must be willing to accept a "readjustment" of their basic rights in order to protect public order, combat crime, fight AIDS, and eliminate drugs. The final section, which urges the nation to put human needs before military needs, argues for a bill of economic and social rights that would be funded by cuts in the defense budget.

Chapter 4, *Federalism,* features an article that suggests that federal laws and policies have made it increasingly difficult for the states to promote the well-being of its citizens. The second selection contends that federal mandates, which gathered strength during the Reagan era, have left the states and cities holding the bag, unable to fund much-needed programs. In the final piece, the author suggests that while the federal bureaucracy may be gripped by paralysis, the state governments are demonstrating unprecedented foresight in program development and the allocation of resources.

Chapter 5, *Civil Rights and Civil Liberties,* analyzes the issues that divide blacks and whites, offering several prescriptions for eliminating racial barriers and narrowing the gap between the races. The second article reviews the recent Supreme Court term, concluding the Reagan-Bush court majority has, in the interest of reducing crime, undermined the rights of all Americans. In the final selection, the author discusses the new "political correctness" on college campuses. In their zeal to eliminate racial, sexual, and sexual choice slurs, many colleges have become bastions of neo-Nazism, threatening fundamental liberal values.

DISCUSSION QUESTIONS

1. In what sense, if any, is the Declaration of Independence a radical document?
2. Is the Constitution still relevant to today's problems? If not, why?
3. Do parties and factions undermine national unity? If so, how?
4. Is the present system of checks and balances sufficient to prevent abuses of power?
5. Should the Supreme Court's powers be curtailed by Congress? Why, or why not?
6. Has the New Right succeeded in forcing their particular morality on the nation?
7. Why has liberalism fallen out of favor with the American public?
8. Has the Reagan revolution changed America for the better? Why, or why not?
9. Is the Bill of Rights in danger? If so, from whom?
10. Do Americans have too many rights and too few responsibilities?
11. Has the time come to enact a Bill of Economic and Social Rights? Why, or why not?
12. In what sense, if any, has the federal government abandoned the nation's poor?
13. How have federal mandates, in the form of new programs and regulations, affected the states?
14. To what extent, if any, are state governments responding to the challenges of bureaucratic gridlock at the federal level?
15. Is affirmative action fair to working-class whites? Why, or why not?
16. Do recent Supreme Court rulings threaten the rights of suspects and defendants? If so, how?
17. Does the movement for "politically correct" speech on college campuses pose a threat to the First Amendment?

KEY TERMS

AFFIRMATIVE ACTION   A policy or program that provides special consideration or compensatory treatment to disadvantaged groups in order to remedy past discrimination.

BILL OF RIGHTS   The first ten amendments to the Constitution, ratified in 1791, that set forth such basic protections as freedom of speech, press, religion, and assembly.

BUREAUCRACY   A large, complex organization of appointed officials that is structured hierarchically to carry out specific functions.

CHECKS AND BALANCES   A constitutional provision that divides power among the legislative, executive, and judicial branches of government in the hope of limiting the actions of the others.

CIVIL LIBERTIES   The right of individuals to freedom of expression, together with freedom from arbitrary arrest or prosecution.

CIVIL RIGHTS   The constitutional right of all individuals, especially blacks and other minorities, to equal treatment under the law.

CONSERVATISM   A political philosophy that seeks to limit the role of government in domestic affairs, promote traditional social values, and extend America's power in the international arena.

DEMOCRACY   A system in which ultimate political authority rests with the people.

EXCLUSIONARY RULE   A legal position adopted by the Supreme Court forbidding the admission of illegally seized evidence in court.

FEDERALISM   A system of government in which power is constitutionally shared between a national government and regional, or subdivisional, units of government.

INTEREST GROUP   A body of people acting in an organized fashion to influence government policy.

JUDICIAL REVIEW   The power of the courts to declare acts of the legislature and of the executive to be unconstitutional.

LIBERALISM   A set of beliefs that favor political reform and social change, as well as expanded government programs to promote the public welfare.

LIBERTY   The right of individuals to pursue their lives free from government oppression or tyranny.

MAJORITY RULE   A basic principle of democracy, which asserts that the greater number of citizens in any political unit should select officials and determine policies.

PLURALISM   A theory of government that holds that power is widely dispersed among competing interest groups held in check by various social and political forces.

POLITICAL CULTURE   The pattern of beliefs and attitudes toward government and the political process held by a community or nation.

POLITICAL SOCIALIZATION   The process by which young people acquire their political beliefs, values, and opinions.

REVERSE DISCRIMINATION   The charge that affirmative action programs favoring preferential treatment discriminate against the majority.

SEPARATION OF POWERS   A principle of the American system whereby government power is constitutionally divided among the legislative, executive, and judicial branches.

Chapter 1

American Democracy

Article 1. The Declaration of Independence

This document, which was primarily written by Thomas Jefferson and declares the independence of the American colonies from Great Britain, expresses the American creed of equality under the law, the natural rights of man, the principle of limited government, the recognition of popular sovereignty, and the right of the people to revamp or abolish their government. The Declaration of Independence established the legitimacy of the new nation in the eyes of foreign governments, as well as in the eyes of the colonists themselves. It sealed the colonists' separation from the British Crown and established a free, "united" states of America.

The Unanimous Declaration of the Thirteen United States of America

When in the course of human events, it becomes necessary for one people to dissolve the political bands which have connected them with another, and to assume among the powers of the earth, the separate and equal station to which the laws of Nature and of Nature's God entitle them, a decent respect to the opinions of mankind requires that they should declare the causes which impel them to the separation.

We hold these truths to be self-evident, that all men are created equal, that they are endowed by their Creator with certain unalienable rights, that among these are life, liberty and the pursuit of happiness. That to secure these rights, governments are instituted among men, deriving their just powers from the consent of the governed,— That whenever any form of government becomes destructive of these ends, it is the right of the people to alter or to abolish it, and to institute new government, laying its foundation on such principles and organizing its powers in such form, as to them shall seem most likely to effect their safety and happiness. Prudence, indeed, will dictate that governments long established should not be changed for light and transient causes; and accordingly all experience hath shown, that mankind are more disposed to suffer, while evils are sufferable, than to right themselves by abolishing the forms to which they are accustomed. But when a long train of abuses and usurpations, pursuing invariably the same object evinces a design to reduce them under absolute despotism, it is their right, it is their duty, to throw off such government, and to provide new guards for their future

security.—Such has been the patient sufferance of these colonies; and such is now the necessity which constrains them to alter their former systems of government. The history of the present King of Great Britain is a history of repeated injuries and usurpations, all having in direct object the establishment of an absolute tyranny over these states. To prove this, let facts be submitted to a candid world.

He has refused his assent to laws, the most wholesome and necessary for the public good.

He has forbidden his governors to pass laws of immediate and pressing importance, unless suspended in their operation till his assent should be obtained; and when so suspended, he has utterly neglected to attend to them.

He has refused to pass other laws for the accommodation of large districts of people, unless those people would relinquish the right of representation in the legislature, a right inestimable to them and formidable to tyrants only.

He has called together legislative bodies at places unusual, uncomfortable, and distant from the depository of their public records, for the sole purpose of fatiguing them into compliance with his measures.

He has dissolved Representative Houses repeatedly, for opposing with manly firmness his invasion on the rights of the people.

He has refused for a long time, after such dissolutions, to cause others to be elected; whereby the legislative powers, incapable of annihilation, have returned to the people at large for their exercise; the state remaining in the meantime exposed to all the dangers of invasion from without, and convulsions within.

He has endeavoured to prevent the population of these states; for that purpose obstructing the laws for naturalization of foreigners; refusing to pass others to encourage their migrations hither, and raising the conditions of new appropriations of lands.

He has obstructed the administration of justice, by refusing his assent to laws for establishing judiciary powers.

He has made judges dependent on his will alone, for the tenure of their offices, and the amount and payment of their salaries.

He has erected a multitude of new offices, and sent hither swarms of officers to harass our people, and eat out their substance.

He has kept among us, in times of peace, standing armies without the consent of our legislatures.

He has affected to render the military independent of and superior to the civil power.

He has combined with others to subject us to a jurisdiction foreign to our constitution, and unacknowledged by our laws; giving his assent to their acts of pretended legislation:

For quartering large bodies of armed troops among us:

For protecting them, by a mock trial, from punishment for any murders which they should commit on the inhabitants of these states:

For cutting off our trade with all parts of the world:

For imposing taxes on us without our consent:

For depriving us in many cases, of the benefits of trial by jury:

For transporting us beyond seas to be tried for pretended offenses:

For abolishing the free system of English laws in a neighbouring province, establishing therein an arbitrary government, and enlarging its boundaries so as to render it at once an example and fit instrument for introducing the same absolute rule into these colonies:

For taking away our charters, abolishing our most valuable laws, and altering fundamentally the forms of our governments.

For suspending our own legislatures, and declaring themselves invested with power to legislate for us in all cases whatsoever.

He has abdicated government here, by declaring us out of his protection and waging war against us.

He has plundered our seas, ravaged our coasts, burnt our towns, and destroyed the lives of our people.

He is at this time transporting large armies of foreign mercenaries to complete the works of death, desolution and tyranny, already begun with circumstances of cruelty and perfidy scarcely paralleled in the most barbarous ages and totally unworthy the head of a civilized nation.

He has constrained our fellow citizens taken captive on the high seas to bear arms against their country, to become the executioners of their friends and brethren, or to fall themselves by their hands.

He has excited domestic insurrections amongst us, and has endeavoured to bring on the inhabitants of our frontiers, the merciless Indian savages, whose known rule of warfare is an undistinguished destruction of all ages, sexes, and conditions.

In every stage of these oppressions we have petitioned for redress in the most humble terms: Our repeated petitions have been answered only by repeated injury. A prince, whose character is thus marked by every act which may define a tyrant, is unfit to be the ruler of a free people.

Nor have we been wanting in attentions to our British brethren. We have warned them from time to time of attempts by their legislature to extend an unwarrantable jurisdiction over us. We have reminded them of the circumstances of our emigration and settlement here. We have appealed to their native justice and magnanimity, and we have conjured them by the ties of our common kindred to disavow these usurpations, which, would inevitably interrupt our connections and correspondence. They too have been deaf to the voice of justice and of consanguinity. We must, therefore, acquiesce in the necessary which denounces our separation, and hold them, as we hold the rest of mankind, enemies in war, in peace friends.

WE, THEREFORE, the Representatives of the United States of America, in General Congress, Assembled, appealing to the Supreme Judge of the world for the rectitude of our intentions, do, in the name, and by authority of the good people of these colonies, solemnly publish and declare, That these United Colonies are, and of right ought to be FREE AND INDEPENDENT STATES; that they are absolved from all allegiance to the British Crown, and that all political connection between them and the state of Great Britain, is and ought to be totally dissolved; and that as free and independent states, they have full power to levy war, conclude peace, contract alliances, establish commerce, and to do all other acts and things which independent states may of right do. And for the support of this Declaration, with a firm reliance on the protection of Divine Providence, we mutually pledge to each other our lives, our fortunes, and our sacred honor.

JOHN HANCOCK.

New Hampshire
JOSIAH BARTLETT   MATTHEW THORNTON
WM. WHIPPLE

Massachusetts Bay
SAML ADAMS   ROBT TREAT PAINE
JOHN ADAMS   ELBRIDGE GERRY

Rhode Island
STEP. HOPKINS   WILLIAM ELLERY

Connecticut
ROGER SHERMAN   WM. WILLIAMS
SAML HUNTINGTON   OLIVER WOLCOTT

New York
WM FLOYD   FRANS. LEWIS
PHIL. LIVINGSTON   LEWIS MORRIS

New Jersey
RICHD. STOCKTON   JOHN HART
JNO WITHERSPOON   ABRA CLARK
FRAS. HOPKINSON

Pennsylvania
ROBT MORRIS   JAS. SMITH
BENJAMIN RUSH   GEO. TAYLOR
BENJA. FRANKLIN   JAMES WILSON
JOHN MORTON   GEO. ROSS
GEO. CLYMER

Delaware
CAESAR RODNEY   THO M'KEAN
GEO READ

Maryland
SAMUEL CHASE   CHARLES CARROLL
WM. PACA   of Carrollton
THOS. STONE

Virginia
GEORGE WYTHE   THOS. NELSON Jr.
RICHARD HENRY LEE   FRANCIS LIGHTFOOT LEE
TH JEFFERSON   CARTER BRAXTON
BENJA. HARRISON

North Carolina
WM HOOPER   JOHN PENN
JOSEPH HEWES

South Carolina
EDWARD RUTLEDGE   THOS HEYWARD JUNR.
THOMAS LYNCH JUNR.   ARTHUR MIDDLETON

Georgia
BUTTON GWINNETT   GEO WALTON
LYMAN HALL

Article 2. The Constitution of the United States of America

The document by which the United States is governed and drafted at the Constitutional Convention in 1787, the Constitution defines the basic institutions of the nation, dividing the powers of governing between a national government and the states. It also describes the organization of the central government, which is split into three branches, and spells out their functions. In addition, it includes a Bill of Rights (the first ten amendments), which are designed to protect individual liberty, while striking a proper balance between freedom and authority. Although written in the eighteenth century, the Constitution has proved to be remarkably adaptable. A relatively short document (about 7,000 words), it provides only the basic framework of the government and a set of general principles. For this reason, the meaning of the Constitution has been open to different interpretations.

Preamble

WE THE PEOPLE of the United States, in order to form a more perfect Union, establish justice, insure domestic tranquillity, provide for the common defense, promote the general welfare, and secure the blessings of liberty to ourselves and our posterity, do ordain and establish this Constitution for the United States of America.

Article I

Section 1. All legislative powers herein granted shall be vested in a Congress of the United States, which shall consist of a Senate and House of Representatives.

Section 2. The House of Representatives shall be composed of members chosen every second year by the people of the several states, and the electors in each state shall have the qualifications requisite for electors of the most numerous branch of the state legislature.

No person shall be a Representative who shall not have attained to the age of twenty-five years, and been seven years a citizen of the United States, and who shall not, when elected, be an inhabitant of that state in which he shall be chosen.

Representatives and direct taxes shall be apportioned among the several states which may be included within this Union, according to their respective numbers, which shall be determined by adding to the whole number of free persons, including those bound to service for a term of years, and excluding Indians not taxed, three-fifths of all other persons. The actual enumeration shall be made within three years after the first meeting of the Congress of the United States, and within every subsequent term of ten years, in such manner as they shall by law direct. The number of Representatives shall not exceed one for every thirty thousand, but each state shall have at least one representative; and until such enumeration shall be made, the state of New Hampshire shall be entitled to choose three, Massachusetts eight, Rhode Island and Providence Plantations one, Connecticut five, New York six, New Jersey four, Pennsylvania eight, Delaware one, Maryland six, Virginia ten, North Carolina five, South Carolina five, and Georgia three.

When vacancies happen in the representation from any state, the executive authority thereof shall issue writs of election to fill such vacancies.

The House of Representatives shall choose their Speaker and other officers; and shall have the sole power of impeachment.

Section 3. The Senate of the United States shall be composed of two Senators from each state, chosen by the legislature thereof, for six years and each Senator shall have one vote.

Immediately after they shall be assembled in consequence of the first election, they shall be divided as equally as may be into three classes. The seats of the Senators of the first class shall be vacated at the expiration of the second year, of the second class at the expiration of the fourth year, and of the third class at the expiration of the sixth year, so that one-third may be chosen every second year; and if vacancies happen by resignation, or otherwise, during the recess of the legislature of any state, the executive thereof may make temporary appointments until the next meeting of the legislature, which shall then fill such vacancies.

No person shall be a Senator who shall not have attained to the age of thirty years, and been nine years a citizen of the United States, and who shall not, when elected, be an inhabitant of that state for which he shall be chosen.

The Vice President of the United States shall be President of the Senate, but shall have no vote, unless they be equally divided.

The Senate shall choose their other officers, and also a President pro tempore, in the absence of the Vice President, or when he shall exercise the office of President of the United States.

The Senate shall have the sole power to try all impeachments. When sitting for that purpose, they shall be on oath or affirmation. When the President of the United States is tried, the Chief Justice shall preside: And no person shall be convicted without the concurrence of two-thirds of the members present.

Judgment in cases of impeachment shall not extend further than to removal from office, and disqualification to hold and enjoy any office of honor, trust or profit under the United States: but the party convicted shall nevertheless be liable and subject to indictment, trial, judgment and punishment, according to law.

Section 4. The times, places and manner of holding elections for Senators and Representatives, shall be prescribed in each state by the legislature thereof; but the Congress may at any time by law make or alter such regulations, except as to the places of choosing Senators.

The Congress shall assemble at least once in every year, and such meeting shall be on the first Monday in December, unless they shall by law appoint a different day.

Section 5. Each House shall be the judge of the elections, returns and qualifications of its own members, and a majority of each shall constitute a quorum to do business; but a smaller number may adjourn from day to day, and may be authorized to compel the attendance of absent members, in such manner, and under such penalties as each House may provide.

Each House may determine the rules of its proceedings, punish its members for disorderly behaviour, and, with the concurrence of two-thirds, expel a member.

Each House shall keep a journal of its proceedings, and from time to time publish the same, excepting such parts as may in their judgment require secrecy; and the yeas and nays of the members of either House on any question shall, at the desire of one-fifth of those present, be entered on the journal.

Neither House, during the session of Congress, shall, without the consent of the other, adjourn for more than three days, nor to any other place than that in which the two Houses shall be sitting.

Section 6. The Senators and Representatives shall receive a compensation for their services, to be ascertained by law, and paid out of the Treasury of the United States. They shall in all cases, except treason, felony and breach of the peace, be privileged from arrest during their attendance at the session of their respective Houses, and in going to and returning from the same; and for any speech or debate in either House, they shall not be questioned in any other place.

No Senator or Representative shall, during the time for which he was elected, be appointed to any civil office under the authority of the United States, which shall have been created, or the emoluments whereof shall have been increased during such time; and no person holding any office under the United States, shall be a member of either House during his continuance in office.

Section 7. All bills for raising revenue shall originate in the House of Representatives; but the Senate may propose or concur with amendments as on other bills.

Every bill which shall have passed the House of Representatives and the Senate, shall, before it becomes a law, be presented to the President of the United States; if he approves he shall sign it, but if not he shall return it, with his objections to that House in which it shall have originated, who shall enter the objections at large on their journal, and proceed to reconsider it. If after such reconsideration two thirds of that House shall agree to pass the bill, it shall be sent, together with the objections, to the other House, by which it shall likewise be reconsidered, and if approved by two thirds of that House, it shall become a law. But in all such cases the votes of both Houses shall be determined by yeas and nays, and the names of the persons voting for and against the bill shall be entered on the journal of each House respectively. If any bill shall not be returned by the President within ten days (Sundays excepted) after it shall have been presented to him, the same shall be a law, in like manner as if he had signed it, unless the Congress by their adjournment prevent its return, in which case it shall not be a law.

Every order, resolution, or vote to which the concurrence of the Senate and House of Representatives may be necessary (except on a question of adjournment) shall be presented to the President of the United States; and before the same shall take effect, shall be approved by him, or being disapproved by him, shall be repassed by two thirds of the Senate and House of Representatives, according to the rules and limitations prescribed in the case of a bill.

Section 8. The Congress shall have power to lay and collect taxes, duties, imposts and excises, to pay the debts and provide for the common defense and general welfare of the United States; but all duties, imposts and excises shall be uniform throughout the United States;

To borrow money on the credit of the United States;

To regulate commerce with foreign nations, and among the several States, and with the Indian tribes;

To establish a uniform rule of naturalization, and uniform laws on the subject of bankruptcies throughout the United States;

To coin money, regulate the value thereof, and of foreign coin, and fix the standard of weights and measures;

To provide for the punishment of counterfeiting the securities and current coin of the United States;

To establish post offices and post roads;

To promote the progress of science and useful arts, by securing for limited times to authors and inventors the exclusive right to their respective writings and discoveries;

To constitute tribunals inferior to the Supreme Court;

To define and punish piracies and felonies committed on the high seas, and offenses against the law of nations;

To declare war, grant letters of marque and reprisal, and make rules concerning captures on land and water;

To raise and support armies, but no appropriation of money to that use shall be for a longer term than two years;

To provide and maintain a Navy;

To make rules for the government and regulation of the land and naval forces;

To provide for calling forth the militia to execute the laws of the Union, suppress insurrections and repel invasions;

To provide for organizing, arming, and disciplining, the militia, and for governing such part of them as may be employed in the service of the United States, reserving to the states respectively, the appointment of the officers, and the authority of training the militia according to the discipline prescribed by Congress;

To exercise exclusive legislation in all cases whatsoever, over such District (not exceeding ten miles square) as may, by cession of particular states, and the acceptance of Congress, become the seat of the government of the United States, and to exercise like authority over all places purchased by the consent of the legislature of the state in which the same shall be, for the erection of forts, magazines, arsenals, dock-yards, and other needful buildings;—and

To make all laws which shall be necessary and proper for carrying into execution the foregoing powers, and all other powers vested by this Constitution in the government of the United States, or in any department or officer thereof.

Section 9. The migration or importation of such persons as any of the states now existing shall think proper to admit, shall not be prohibited by the Congress prior to the year one thousand eight hundred and eight, but a tax or duty may be imposed on such importation, not exceeding ten dollars for each person.

The privilege of the writ of habeas corpus shall not be suspended, unless when in cases of rebellion or invasion the public safety may require it.

No bill of attainder or ex post facto law shall be passed.

No capitation, or other direct, tax shall be laid, unless in proportion to the census or enumeration herein before directed to be taken.

No tax or duty shall be laid on articles exported from any state.

No preference shall be given by any regulation of commerce or revenue to the ports of one state over those of another: nor shall vessels bound to, or from, one state, be obliged to enter, clear, or pay duties in another.

No money shall be drawn from the Treasury, but in consequence of appropriations made by law; and a regular statement and account of the receipts and expenditures of all public money shall be published from time to time.

No title of nobility shall be granted by the United States: And no person holding any office of profit or trust under them, shall, without the consent of the Congress, accept of any present, emolument, office, or title, of any kind whatever, from any King, Prince, or foreign state.

Section 10. No state shall enter into any treaty, alliance, or confederation; grant letters of marque and reprisal; coin money; emit bills of credit; make any thing but gold and silver coin a tender in payment of debts; pass any bill of attainder, ex post facto law, or law impairing the obligation of contracts, or grant any title of nobility.

No state shall, without the consent of the Congress, lay any imposts or duties on imports or exports, except what may be absolutely necessary for executing its inspection laws: and the net produce of all duties and imposts, laid by any state on imports or exports, shall be for the use of the Treasury of the United States; and all such laws shall be subject to the revision and control of the Congress.

No state shall, without the consent of Congress, lay any duty of tonnage, keep troops, or ships of war in time of peace, enter into any agreement or compact with another state, or with a foreign power, or engage in war, unless actually invaded, or in such imminent danger as will not admit of delay.

Article II

Section 1. The executive power shall be vested in a President of the United States of America. He shall hold his office during the term of four years, and, together with the Vice President, chosen for the same term, be elected, as follows:

Each state, shall appoint, in such manner as the legislature thereof may direct, a number of electors, equal to the whole number of Senators and Representatives to which the state may be entitled in the Congress; but no Senator or Representative, or person holding an office of trust or profit under the United States, shall be appointed an elector.

The electors shall meet in their respective states, and vote by ballot for two persons, of whom one at least shall not be an inhabitant of the same state with themselves. And they shall make a list of all the persons voted for, and of the number of votes for each; which list they shall sign and certify, and transmit sealed to the seat of the government of the United States, directed to the President of the Senate. The President of the Senate shall, in the presence of the Senate and House of Representatives, open all the certificates, and the votes shall then be counted. The person having the greatest number of votes shall be the President, if such number be a majority of the whole number of electors appointed; and if there be more than one who have such majority, and have an equal number of votes, then the House of Representatives shall immediately choose by ballot one of them for President; and if no person have a majority, then from the five highest on the list the said House shall in like manner choose the President. But in choosing the President, the votes shall be taken by states, the representation from each state having one vote; a quorum for this purpose shall consist of a member or members from two thirds of the states, and a majority of all the states shall be necessary to a choice.

In every case, after the choice of the President, the person having the greatest number of votes of the electors shall be the Vice President. But if there should remain two or more who have equal votes, the Senate shall choose from them by ballot the Vice President.

The Congress may determine the time of choosing the electors, and the day on which they shall give their votes; which day shall be the same throughout the United States.

No person except a natural born citizen, or a citizen of the United States, at the time of the adoption of this Constitution, shall be eligible to the office of President; neither shall any person be eligible to that office who shall not have attained to the age of thirty-five years, and been fourteen years a resident within the United States.

In case of the removal of the President from office, or of his death, resignation, or inability to discharge the powers and duties of the said office, the same shall devolve on the Vice President, and the Congress may by law provide for the case of removal, death, resignation, or inability, both of the President and Vice President, declaring what officer shall then act as President, and such officer shall act accordingly, until the disability be removed, or a President shall be elected.

The President shall, at stated times, receive for his services, a compensation, which shall neither be increased nor diminished during the period for which he shall have been elected, and he shall not receive within that period any other emolument from the United States, or any of them.

Before he enters on the execution of his office, he shall take the following oath or affirmation:—"I do solemnly swear (or affirm) that I will faithfully execute the office of President of the United States, and will to the best of my ability, preserve, protect and defend the Constitution of the United States."

Section 2. The President shall be commander in chief of the Army and Navy of the United States, and of the militia of the several States, when called into the actual service of the United States; he may require the opinion, in writing, of the principal officer in each of the executive departments, upon any subject relating to the duties of their respective offices, and he shall have power to grant reprieves and pardons for offenses against the United States, except in cases of impeachment.

He shall have power, by and with the advice and consent of the Senate, to make treaties, provided two thirds of the Senators present concur; and he shall nominate, and by and with the advice and consent of the Senate, shall appoint ambassadors, other public ministers and consuls, judges of the Supreme Court, and all other officers of the United States, whose appointments are not herein otherwise provided for, and which shall be established by law: but the Congress may by law vest the appointment of such inferior officers, as they think proper, in the President alone, in the courts of law, or in the heads of departments.

The President shall have power to fill up all vacancies that may happen during the recess of the Senate, by granting commissions which shall expire at the end of their next session.

Section 3. He shall from time to time give to the Congress information of the state of the Union, and recommend to their consideration such measures as he shall judge necessary and expedient; he may, on extraordinary occasions, convene both Houses, or either of them, and in case of disagreement between them, with respect to the time of adjournment, he may adjourn them to such time as he shall think proper; he shall receive ambassadors and other public ministers; he shall take care that the laws be faithfully executed, and shall commission all the officers of the United States.

Section 4. The President, Vice President and all civil officers of the United States, shall be removed from office on impeachment for, and conviction of, treason, bribery, or other high crimes and misdemeanors.

Article III

Section 1. The judicial power of the United States, shall be vested in one Supreme Court, and in such inferior courts as the Congress may from time to time ordain and establish. The judges, both of the supreme and inferior courts, shall hold their offices during good behaviour, and shall, at stated times, receive for their services, a compensation, which shall not be diminished during their continuance in office.

Section 2. The judicial power shall extend to all cases, in law and equity, arising under this Constitution, the laws of the United States, and treaties made, or which shall be made, under their authority;—to all cases affecting ambassadors, other public ministers and consuls;—to all cases of admiralty and maritime jurisdiction;—to controversies to which the United States shall be a party;—to controversies between two or more states;—between a state and citizens of another state;—between citizens of different states,—between citizens of the same state claiming lands under grants of different states, and between a state, or the citizens thereof, and foreign states, citizens or subjects.

In all cases affecting ambassadors, other public ministers and consuls, and those in which a state shall be a party, the Supreme Court shall have original jurisdiction. In all the other cases before mentioned, the Supreme Court shall have appellate jurisdiction, both as to law and fact, with such exceptions, and under such regulations as the Congress shall make.

The trial of all crimes, except in cases of impeachment, shall be by jury; and such trial shall be held in the state where the said crimes shall have been committed; but when not committed within any state, the trial shall be at such place or places as the Congress may by law have directed.

Section 3. Treason against the United States, shall consist only in levying war against them, or in adhering to their enemies, giving them aid and comfort. No person shall be convicted of treason unless on the testimony of two witnesses to the same overt act, or on confession in open court.

The Congress shall have power to declare the punishment of treason, but no attainder of treason shall work corruption of blood, or forfeiture except during the life of the person attained.

Article IV

Section 1. Full faith and credit shall be given in each state to the public acts, records, and judicial proceedings of every other state. And the Congress may by general laws prescribe the manner in which such acts, records and proceedings shall be proved, and the effect thereof.

Section 2. The citizens of each state shall be entitled to all privileges and immunities of citizens in the several states.

A person charged in any state with treason, felony, or other crime, who shall flee from justice, and be found in another state, shall on demand of the executive authority of the state from which he fled, be delivered up, to be removed to the state having jurisdiction of the crime.

No person held to service or labour in one state, under the laws thereof, escaping into another, shall, in consequence of any law or regulation therein, be discharged from such service or labour, but shall be delivered up on claim of the party to whom such service or labour may be due.

Section 3. New states may be admitted by the Congress into this Union; but no new state shall be formed or erected within the jurisdiction of any other state; nor any state be formed by the junction of two or more states, or parts of states,

without the consent of the legislature of the states concerned as well as of the Congress.

The Congress shall have power to dispose of and make all needful rules and regulations respecting the territory or other property belonging to the United States; and nothing in this Constitution shall be so construed as to prejudice any claims of the United States, or of any particular state.

Section 4. The United States shall guarantee to every state in this Union a republican form of government, and shall protect each of them against invasion; and on application of the legislature, or of the executive (when the legislature cannot be convened) against domestic violence.

Article V

The Congress, whenever two thirds of both Houses shall deem it necessary, shall propose amendments to this Constitution, or on the application of the legislatures of two thirds of the several states, shall call a convention for proposing amendments, which, in either case, shall be valid to all intents and purposes, as part of this Constitution, when ratified by the legislatures of three fourths of the several States, or by conventions in three fourths thereof, as the one or the other mode of ratification may be proposed by the Congress; provided that no amendment which may be made prior to the year one thousand eight hundred and eight shall in any manner affect the first and fourth clauses in the Ninth Section of the First Article; and that no state, without its consent, shall be deprived of its equal suffrage in the Senate.

Article VI

All debts contracted and engagements entered into, before the adoption of this Constitution, shall be as valid against the United States under this Constitution, as under the Confederation.

This Constitution, and the laws of the United States which shall be made in pursuance thereof; and all treaties made, or which shall be made, under the authority of the United States, shall be the supreme law of the land; and the judges in every state shall be bound thereby, any thing in the Constitution or laws of any State to the contrary notwithstanding.

The Senators and Representatives before mentioned, and the members of the several state legislatures, and all executive and judicial officers, both of the United States and of the several states, shall be bound by oath or affirmation, to support this Constitution; but no religious test shall ever be required as a qualification to any office or public trust under the United States.

Article VII

The ratification of the conventions of nine states shall be sufficient for the establishment of this Constitution between the states so ratifying the same.

Done in convention by the unanimous consent of the states present the seventeenth day of September in the year of our Lord one thousand seven hundred and eighty seven and of the independence of the United States of America the twelfth. In witness whereof we have hereunto subscribed our names,

Go. WASHINGTON—*Presid't*,
and deputy from Virginia
Attest WILLIAM JACKSON *Secretary*

New Hampshire
JOHN LANGDON   NICHOLAS GILMAN

Massachusetts
NATHANIEL GORHAM   RUFUS KING

Connecticut
WM. SAML. JOHNSON   ROGER SHERMAN

New York
ALEXANDER HAMILTON

New Jersey
WIL: LIVINGSTON   WM. PATERSON
DAVID BREARLEY   JONA: DAYTON

Pennsylvania
B FRANKLIN   THOS. FITZSIMONS
THOMAS MIFFLIN   JARED INGERSOLL
ROBT MORRIS   JAMES WILSON
GEO. CLYMER   GOUV MORRIS

Delaware
GEO: READ   RICHARD BASSETT
GUNNING BEDFORD JUN   JACO: BROOM
JOHN DICKINSON

Maryland
JAMES MCHENRY   DANL CARROLL
DAN OF ST THOS.
  JENIFER

Virginia
JOHN BLAIR—   JAMES MADISON JR.

North Carolina
WM. BLOUNT   HU WILLIAMSON
RICHD. DOBBS SPAIGHT

South Carolina
J. RUTLEDGE   CHARLES PINCKNEY
CHARLES COTESWORTH   PIERCE BUTLER
  PINCKNEY

Georgia
WILLIAM FEW   ABR BALDWIN

Amendments

Article I

Congress shall make no law respecting an establishment of religion, or prohibiting the free exercise thereof; or abridging the freedom of speech, or of the press; or the right of the people peaceably to assemble, and to petition the government for a redress of grievances.

Article II

A well-regulated militia, being necessary to the security of a free state, the right of the people to keep and bear arms, shall not be infringed.

Article III

No soldier shall, in time of peace be quartered in any house, without the consent of the owner, nor in time of war, but in a manner to be prescribed by law.

Article IV

Tht right of the people to be secure in their persons, houses, papers, and effects, against unreasonable searches and seizures, shall not be violated, and no warrants shall issue, but upon probable cause, supported by oath or affirmation, and particularly describing the place to be searched, and the persons or things to be seized.

Article V

No person shall be held to answer for a capital, or otherwise infamous crime, unless on a presentment or indictment of a Grand Jury, except in cases arising in the land or naval forces, or in the militia, when in actual service in time of war or public danger; nor shall any person be subject for the same offense to be twice put in jeopardy of life or limb; nor shall be compelled in any criminal case to be a witness against himself, nor be deprived of life, liberty, or property, without due process of law; nor shall private property be taken for public use, without just compensation.

Article VI

In all criminal prosecutions, the accused shall enjoy the right to a speedy and public trial, by an impartial jury of the state and district wherein the crime shall have been committed, which district shall have been previously ascertained by law, and to be informed of the nature and cause of the accusation; to be confronted with the witnesses against him; to have compulsory process for obtaining witnesses in his favor, and to have the assistance of counsel for his defense.

Article VII

In suits at common law, where the value in controversy shall exceed twenty dollars, the right of trial by jury shall be preserved, and no fact tried by a jury, shall be otherwise reexamined in any court of the United States, than according to the rules of the common law.

Article VIII

Excessive bail shall not be required, nor excessive fines imposed, nor cruel and unusual punishments inflicted.

Article IX

The enumeration in the Constitution, of certain rights, shall not be construed to deny or disparage others retained by the people.

Article X

The powers not delegated to the United States by the Constitution, nor prohibited by it to the states, are reserved to the states respectively, or to the people.

Article XI

The judicial power of the United States shall not be construed to extend to any suit in law or equity, commenced or prosecuted against one of the United States by citizens of another state, or by citizens or subjects of any foreign state.

Article XII

The electors shall meet in their respective states, and vote by ballot for President and Vice President, one of whom, at least, shall not be an inhabitant of the same state with themselves; they shall name in their ballots the person voted for as President, and in distinct ballots the person voted for as Vice President, and they shall make distinct lists of all persons voted for as President, and of all persons voted for as Vice President, and of the number of votes for each, which lists they shall sign and certify, and transmit sealed to the seat of the government of the United States, directed to the President of the Senate;—The President of the Senate shall, in the presence of the Senate and House of Representatives, open all the certificates and the votes shall then be counted;—The person having the greatest number of votes for President, shall be the President, if such number be a majority of the whole number of electors appointed; and if no person have such majority, then from the persons having the highest numbers not exceeding three on the list of those voted for as President, the House of Representatives shall choose immediately, by ballot, the President. But in choosing the President, the votes shall be taken by states, the representation from each state having one vote; a quorum for this purpose shall consist of a member or members from two-thirds of the states, and a majority of all the states shall be necessary to a choice. And if the House of Representatives shall not choose a President whenever the right of choice shall devolve upon them, before the fourth day of March next following, then the Vice President shall act as President, as in the case of the death or other constitutional disability of the President.—The person having the greatest number of votes as Vice President, shall be the Vice President, if such number be a majority of the whole number of electors appointed, and if no person have a majority, then from the two highest numbers on the list, the Senate shall choose the Vice President; a quorum for the purpose shall consist of two-thirds of the whole number of Senators, and a majority of the whole number shall be necessary to a choice. But no person constitutionally ineligible to the office of President shall be eligible to that of Vice President of the United States.

Article XIII

Section 1. Neither slavery nor involuntary servitude, except as a punishment for crime whereof the party shall have been duly convicted, shall exist within the United States, or any place subject to their jurisdiction.

Section 2. Congress shall have power to enforce this article by appropriate legislation.

Article XIV

Section 1. All persons born or naturalized in the United States, and subject to the jurisdiction thereof, are citizens of the United States and of the state wherein they reside. No state shall make or enforce any law which shall abridge the privileges or immunities of citizens of the United States; nor shall any state deprive any person of life, liberty, or property, without due process of law; nor deny to any person within its jurisdiction the equal protection of the laws.

Section 2. Representatives shall be apportioned among the several states according to their respective numbers, counting the whole number of persons in each state, excluding Indians not taxed. But when the right to vote at any election for the choice of electors for President and Vice President of the United States, Representatives in Congress, the executive and judicial officers of a state, or the members of the legislature thereof, is denied to any of the male inhabitants of such state, being twenty-one years of age, and citizens of the United States, or in any way abridged, except for participation in rebellion, or other crime, the basis of representation therein shall be reduced in the proportion which the number of such male citizens shall bear to the whole number of male citizens twenty-one years of age in such state.

Section 3. No person shall be a Senator or Representative in Congress, or elector of President and Vice President, or hold any office, civil or military, under the United States, or under any state, who, having previously taken an oath, as a member of Congress, or as an officer of the United States, or as a member of any state legislature, or as an executive or judicial officer of any state, to support the Constitution of the United States, shall have engaged in insurrection or rebellion against the same, or given aid or comfort to the enemies thereof. But Congress may by a vote of two-thirds of each house, remove such disability.

Section 4. The validity of the public debt of the United States, authorized by law, including debts incurred for payment of pensions and bounties for services in suppressing insurrection or rebellion, shall not be questioned. But neither the United States nor any state shall assume or pay any debt or obligation incurred in aid of insurrection or rebellion against the United States, or any claim for the loss or emancipation of any slave; but all such debts, obligations and claims shall be held illegal and void.

Section 5. The Congress shall have power to enforce, by appropriate legislation, the provisions of this article.

Article XV

Section 1. The right of citizens of the United States to vote shall not be denied or abridged by the United States or by any state on account of race, color, or previous condition of servitude.

Section 2. The Congress shall have power to enforce this article by appropriate legislation.

Article XVI

The Congress shall have power to lay and collect taxes on incomes, from whatever source derived, without apportionment among the several states, and without regard to any census or enumeration.

Article XVII

Section 1. The Senate of the United States shall be composed of two Senators from each state, elected by the people thereof, for six years; and each Senator shall have one vote. The electors in each state shall have the qualifications requisite for electors of the most numerous branch of the state legislature.

Section 2. When vacancies happen in the representation of any state in the Senate, the executive authority of such state shall issue writs of election to fill such vacancies: *Provided*, That the legislature of any state may empower the executive thereof to make temporary appointments until the people fill the vacancies by election as the legislature may direct.

Section 3. This amendment shall not be so construed as to affect the election or term of any Senator chosen before it becomes valid as part of the Constitution.

Article XVIII

Section 1. After one year from the ratification of this article the manufacture, sale, or transportation of intoxicating liquors within, the importation thereof into, or the exportation thereof from the United States and all territory subject to the jurisdiction thereof for beverage purposes is hereby prohibited.

Section 2. The Congress and the several states shall have concurrent power to enforce this article by appropriate legislation.

Section 3. This article shall be inoperative unless it shall have been ratified as an amendment to the Constitution by the legislatures of the several states, as provided in the Constitution, within seven years from the date of the submission hereof to the states by the Congress.

Article XIX

Section 1. The right of citizens of the United States to vote shall not be denied or abridged by the United States or by any state on account of sex.

Section 2. Congress shall have power to enforce this article by appropriate legislation.

Article XX

Section 1. The terms of the President and Vice President shall end at noon on the 20th day of January, and the terms of Senators and Representatives at noon on the 3d day of January, of the years in which such terms would have ended if this article had not been ratified; and the terms of their successors shall then begin.

Section 2. The Congress shall assemble at least once in every year, and such meeting shall begin at noon on the 3d day of January, unless they shall by law appoint a different day.

Section 3. If, at the time fixed for the beginning of the term of the President, the President elect shall have died, the Vice President elect shall become President. If a President shall not have been chosen before the time fixed for the beginning of his term, or if the President elect shall have failed to qualify, then the Vice President elect shall act as President until a President shall have qualified; and the Congress may by law provide for the case wherein neither a President elect nor a Vice President elect shall have qualified, declaring who shall then act as President, or the manner in which one who is to act shall be selected, and such person shall act accordingly until a President or Vice President shall have qualified.

Section 4. The Congress may by law provide for the case of the death of any of the persons from whom the House of Representatives may choose a President whenever the right of choice shall have devolved upon them, and for the case of the death of any of the persons from whom the Senate may choose a Vice President whenever the right of choice shall have devolved upon them.

Section 5. Sections 1 and 2 shall take effect on the 15th day of October following the ratification of this article.

Section 6. This article shall be inoperative unless it shall have been ratified as an amendment to the Constitution by the legislatures of three-fourths of the several states within seven years from the date of its submission.

Article XXI

Section 1. The eighteenth article of amendment to the Constitution of the United States is hereby repealed.

Section 2. The transportation or importation into any state, territory, or possession of the United States for delivery or use therein of intoxicating liquors, in violation of the laws thereof, is hereby prohibited.

Section 3. This article shall be inoperative unless it shall have been ratified as an amendment to the Constitution by conventions in the several states, as provided in the Constitution, within seven years from the date of the submission hereof to the states by the Congress.

Article XXII

Section 1. No person shall be elected to the office of the President more than twice, and no person who has held the office of President, or acted as President, for more than two years of a term to which some other person was elected President shall be elected to the office of the President more than once. But this Article shall not apply to any person holding the office of President when this Article was proposed by the Congress, and shall not prevent any person who may be holding the office of President, or acting as President, during the term within which this Article becomes operative from holding the office of President or acting as President during the remainder of such term.

Section 2. This Article shall be inoperative unless it shall have been ratified as an amendment to the Constitution by the legislatures of three-fourths of the several states within seven years from the date of its submission to the states by the Congress.

Article XXIII

Section 1. The District constituting the seat of government of the United States shall appoint in such manner as the Congress may direct:

A number of electors of President and Vice President equal to the whole number of Senators and Representatives in Congress to which the District would be entitled if it were a state, but in no event more than the least populous state; they shall be in addition to those appointed by the states, but they shall be considered, for the purposes of the election of President and Vice President, to be electors appointed by a state; and they shall meet in the District and perform such duties as provided by the twelfth article of amendment.

Section 2. The Congress shall have power to enforce this article by appropriate legislation.

Article XXIV

Section 1. The right of citizens of the United States to vote in any primary or other election for President or Vice President, for electors for President or Vice President, or for Senator or Representative in Congress, shall not be denied or abridged by the United States or any State by reason of failure to pay any poll tax or other tax.

Section 2. The Congress shall have power to enforce this article by appropriate legislation.

Article XXV

Section 1. In case of the removal of the President from office or of his death or resignation, the Vice President shall become President.

Section 2. Whenever there is a vacancy in the office of the Vice President, the President shall nominate a Vice President who shall take office upon confirmation by a majority vote of both Houses of Congress.

Section 3. Whenever the President transmits to the President pro tempore of the Senate and the Speaker of the House of Representatives his written declaration that he is unable to discharge the powers and duties of his office, and until he transmits to them a written declaration to the contrary, such powers and duties shall be discharged by the Vice President as Acting President.

Section 4. Whenever the Vice President and a majority of either the principal officers of the executive departments or of such other body as Congress may by law provide, transmit to the President pro tempore of the Senate and the Speaker of the House of Representatives their written declaration that the President is unable to discharge the powers and duties of his office, the Vice President shall immediately assume the powers and duties of the office as Acting President.

Thereafter, when the President transmits to the President pro tempore of the Senate and the Speaker of the House of Representatives his written declaration that no inability exists, he shall resume the powers and duties of his office unless the Vice President and a majority of either the principal officers of the executive department or of such other body as Congress may by law provide, transmit within four days to the President pro tempore of the Senate and the Speaker of the House of Representatives their written declaration that the President is unable to discharge the powers and duties of his office. Thereupon Congress shall decide the issue, assemblying within forty-eight hours for that purpose if not in session. If the Congress, within twenty-one days after receipt of the latter written declaration, or, if Congress is not in session, within twenty-one days after Congress is required to assemble, determines by two-thirds vote of both Houses that the President is unable to discharge the powers and duties of his office, the Vice President shall continue to discharge the same as Acting President; otherwise, the President shall resume the powers and duties of his office.

Article XXVI

Section 1. The right of citizens of the United States, who are eighteen years of age or older, to vote shall not be denied or abridged by the United States or by any State on account of age.

Section 2. The Congress shall have power to enforce this article by appropriate legislation.

Article 3.   The Size and Variety of the Union as a Check on Faction

In this Federalist paper, James Madison discusses the problem of factions and the dangers they pose to representative government. Madison feared the divisiveness of political parties and interest groups, which, in his view, could undermine democratic rule. A strong advocate of pluralism, Madison believed that a constitutional democracy, supported by a system of separation of powers, could prevent the excesses of factionalism. This is the best known of the Federalist Papers.

To the People of the State of New York:

AMONG the numerous advantages promised by a well-constructed Union, none deserves to be more accurately developed than its tendency to break and control the violence of faction. The friend of popular governments never finds himself so much alarmed for their character and fate, as when he contemplates their propensity to this dangerous vice. He will not fail, therefore, to set a due value on any plan which, without violating the principles to which he is attached, provides a proper cure for it. The instability, injustice, and confusion introduced into the public councils, have, in truth, been the mortal diseases under which popular governments have everywhere perished; as they continue to be the favorite and fruitful topics from which the adversaries to liberty derive their most specious declamations. The valuable improvements made by the American constitutions on the popular models, both ancient and modern, cannot certainly be too much admired; but it would be an unwarrantable partiality, to contend that they have as effectually obviated the danger on this side, as was wished and expected. Complaints are everywhere heard from our most considerate and virtuous citizens, equally the friends of public and private faith, and of public and personal liberty, that our governments are too unstable, that the public good is disregarded in the conflicts of rival parties, and that measures are too often decided, not according to the rules of justice and the rights of the minor party, but by the superior force of an interested and overbearing majority. However anxiously we may wish that these complaints had no foundation, the evidence of known facts will not permit us to deny that they are in some degree true. It will be found, indeed, on a candid review of our situation, that some of the distresses under which we labor have been erroneously charged on the operation of our governments; but it will be found, at the same time, that other causes will not alone account for many of our heaviest misfortunes; and, particularly, for that prevailing and increasing distrust of public engagements, and alarm for private rights, which are echoed from one end of the continent to the other. These must be chiefly, if not wholly, effects of the unsteadiness and injustice with which a factious spirit has tainted our public administrations.

By a faction, I understand a number of citizens, whether amounting to a majority or minority of the whole, who are united and actuated by some common impulse of passion, or of interest, adverse to the rights of other citizens, or to the permanent and aggregate interests of the community.

There are two methods of curing the mischiefs of faction: the one, by removing its causes; the other, by controlling its effects.

There are again two methods of removing the causes of faction: the one, by destroying the liberty which is essential to its existence; the other, by giving to every citizen the same opinions, the same passions, and the same interests.

It could never be more truly said than of the first remedy, that it was worse than the disease. Liberty is to faction what air is to fire, an aliment without which it instantly expires. But it could not be less folly to abolish liberty, which is essential to

James Madison, The Federalist Papers, No. 10

political life, because it nourishes faction, than it would be to wish the annihilation of air, which is essential to animal life, because it imparts to fire its destructive agency.

The second expedient is as impracticable as the first would be unwise. As long as the reason of man continues fallible, and he is at liberty to exercise it, different opinions will be formed. As long as the connection subsists between his reason and his self-love, his opinions and his passions will have a reciprocal influence on each other: and the former will be objects to which the latter will attach themselves. The diversity in the faculties of men, from which the rights of property originate, is not less an insuperable obstacle to a uniformity of interests. The protection of these faculties is the first object of government. From the protection of different and unequal faculties of acquiring property, the possession of different degrees and kinds of property immediately results; and from the influence of these on the sentiments and views of the respective proprietors, ensues a division of the society into different interests and parties.

The latent causes of faction are thus sown in the nature of man; and we see them everywhere brought into different degrees of activity, according to the different circumstances of civil society. A zeal for different opinions concerning religion, concerning government, and many other points, as well of speculation as of practice; an attachment to different leaders ambitiously contending for pre-eminence and power; or to persons of other descriptions whose fortunes have been interesting to the human passions, have, in turn, divided mankind into parties, inflamed them with mutual animosity, and rendered them much more disposed to vex and oppress each other than to co-operate for their common good. So strong is this propensity of mankind to fall into mutual animosities, that where no substantial occasion presents itself, the most frivolous and fanciful distinctions have been sufficient to kindle their unfriendly passions and excite their most violent conflicts. But the most common and durable source of factions has been the various and unequal distribution of property. Those who hold and those who are without property have ever formed distinct interests in society. Those who are creditors, and those who are debtors, fall under a like discrimination. A landed interest, a manufacturing interest, a mercantile interest, a moneyed interest, with many lesser interests, grow up of necessity in civilized nations, and divide them into different classes, actuated by different sentiments and views. The regulation of these various and interfering interests forms the principal task of modern legislation, and involves the spirit of party and faction in the necessary and ordinary operations of the government.

No man is allowed to be a judge in his own cause, because his interest would certainly bias his judgment, and, not improbably, corrupt his integrity. With equal, nay with greater reason, a body of men are unfit to be both judges and parties at the same time; yet what are many of the most important acts of legislation, but so many judicial determinations, not indeed concerning the rights of single persons, but concerning the rights of large bodies of citizens? And what are the different classes of legislators but advocates and parties to the causes which they determine? Is a law proposed concerning private debts? It is a question to which the creditors are parties on one side and the debtors on the other.

Justice ought to hold the balance between them. Yet the parties are, and must be, themselves the judges; and the most numerous party, or, in other words, the most powerful faction must be expected to prevail. Shall domestic manufactures be encouraged, and in what degree, by restrictions on foreign manufactures? are questions which would be differently decided by the landed and the manufacturing classes, and probably by neither with a sole regard to justice and the public good. The apportionment of taxes on the various descriptions of property is an act which seems to require the most exact impartiality; yet there is, perhaps, no legislative act in which greater opportunity and temptation are given to a predominant party to trample on the rules of justice. Every shilling with which they overburden the inferior number, is a shilling saved to their own pockets.

It is in vain to say that enlightened statesmen will be able to adjust these clashing interests, and render them all subservient to the public good. Enlightened statesmen will not always be at the helm. Nor, in many cases, can such an adjustment be made at all without taking into view indirect and remote considerations, which will rarely prevail over the immediate interest which one party may find in disregarding the rights of another or the good of the whole.

The inference to which we are brought is, that the *causes* of faction cannot be removed, and that relief is only to be sought in the means of controlling its *effects*.

If a faction consists of less than a majority, relief is supplied by the republican principle, which enables the majority to defeat its sinister views by regular vote. It may clog the administration, it may convulse the society; but it will be unable to execute and mask its violence under the forms of the Constitution. When a majority is included in a faction, the form of popular government, on the other hand, enables it to sacrifice to its ruling passion or interest both the public good and the rights of other citizens. To secure the public good and private rights against the danger of such a faction, and at the same time to preserve the spirit and the form of popular government, is then the great object to which our inquiries are directed. Let me add that it is the great desideratum by which this form of government can be rescued from the opprobrium under which it has so long labored, and be recommended to the esteem and adoption of mankind.

By what means is this object attainable? Evidently by one of two only. Either the existence of the same passion or interest in a majority at the same time must be prevented, or the majority, having such coexistent passion or interest, must be rendered, by their number and local situation, unable to concert and carry into effect schemes of oppression. If the impulse and the opportunity be suffered to coincide, we well know that neither moral nor religious motives can be relied on as an adequate control. They are not found to be such on the injustice and violence of individuals, and lose their efficacy in proportion to the number combined together, that is, in proportion as their efficacy becomes needful.

From this view of the subject it may be concluded that a pure democracy, by which I mean a society consisting of a small number of citizens, who assemble and administer the government in person, can admit of no cure for the mischiefs of faction. A common passion or interest will, in almost every case, be felt by a majority of the whole; a communication and concert result from the form of government itself; and there is nothing to check the inducements to sacrifice the weaker party or an obnoxious individual. Hence it is that such democracies have ever been spectacles of turbulence and contention; have ever been found incompatible with personal security or the rights of property; and have in general been as short in their lives as they have been violent in their deaths. Theoretic politicians, who have patronized this species of government, have erroneously supposed that by reducing mankind to a perfect equality in their political rights, they would, at the same time, be perfectly equalized and assimilated in their possessions, their opinions, and their passions.

A republic, by which I mean a government in which the scheme of representation takes place, opens a different prospect, and promises the cure for which we are seeking. Let us examine the points in which it varies from pure democracy, and we shall comprehend both the nature of the cure and the efficacy which it must derive from the Union.

The two great points of difference between a democracy and a republic are: first, the delegation of the government, in the latter, to a small number of citizens elected by the rest; secondly, the greater number of citizens, and greater sphere of country, over which the latter may be extended.

The effect of the first difference is, on the one hand, to refine and enlarge the public views, by passing them through the medium of a chosen body of citizens, whose wisdom may best discern the true interest of their country, and whose patriotism and love of justice will be least likely to sacrifice it to temporary or partial considerations. Under such a regulation, it may well happen that the public voice, pronounced by the representatives of the people, will be more consonant to the public good than if pronounced by the people themselves, convened for the purpose. On the other hand, the effect may be inverted. Men of factious tempers, of local prejudices, or of sinister designs, may, by intrigue, by corruption, or by other means, first obtain the suffrages, and then betray the interests, of the people. The question resulting is, whether small or extensive republics are more favorable to the election of proper guardians of the public weal; and it is clearly decided in favor of the latter by two obvious considerations:

In the first place, it is to be remarked that, however small the republic may be, the representatives must be raised to a certain number, in order to guard against the cabals of a few; and that, however large it may be, they must be limited to a certain number, in order to guard against the confusion of a multitude. Hence, the number of representatives in the two cases not being in proportion to that of the two constituents, and being proportionally greater in the small republic, it follows that, if the proportion of fit characters be not less in the large than in the small republic, the former will present a greater option, and consequently a greater probability of a fit choice.

In the next place, as each representative will be chosen by a greater number of citizens in the large than in the small republic, it will be more difficult for unworthy candidates to practise with success the vicious arts by which elections are too often carried; and the suffrages of the people being more free, will be more likely to centre in men who possess the most attractive merit and the most diffusive and established characters.

It must be confessed that in this, as in most other cases, there is a mean, on both sides of which inconveniences will be found to lie. By enlarging too much the number of electors, you render the representative too little acquainted with all their local circumstances and lesser interests; as by reducing it too much, you render him unduly attached to these, and too little fit to comprehend and pursue great and national objects. The federal Constitution forms a happy combination in this respect; the great and aggregate interests being referred to the national, the local and particular to the State legislatures.

The other point of difference is, the greater number of citizens and extent of territory which may be brought within the compass of republican than of democratic government; and it is this circumstance principally which renders factious combinations less to be dreaded in the former than in the latter. The smaller the society, the fewer probably will be the distinct parties and interests composing it; the fewer the distinct parties and interests, the more frequently will a majority be found of the same party; and the smaller the number of individuals composing a majority, and the smaller the compass within which they are placed, the most easily will they concert and execute their plans of oppression. Extend the sphere, and you take in a greater variety of parties and interests; you make it less probable that a majority of the whole will have a common motive to invade the rights of other citizens; or if such a common motive exists, it will be more difficult for all who feel it to discover their own strength, and to act in unison with each other. Besides other impediments, it may be remarked that, where there is a consciousness of unjust or dishonorable purposes, communication is always checked by distrust in proportion to the number whose concurrence is necessary.

Hence, it clearly appears, that the same advantage which a republic has over a democracy, in controlling the effects of faction, is enjoyed by a large over a small republic, — is enjoyed by the Union over the States composing it. Does the advantage consist in the substitution of representatives whose enlightened views and virtuous sentiments render them superior to local prejudices and to schemes of injustice? It will not be denied that the representation of the Union will be most likely to possess these requisite endowments. Does it consist in the greater security afforded by a greater variety of parties, against the event of any one party being able to outnumber and oppress the rest? In an equal degree does the increased variety of parties comprised within the Union, increase this security. Does it, in fine, consist in the greater obstacles opposed to the concert and accomplishment of the secret wishes of an unjust and interested majority? Here, again, the extent of the Union gives it the most palpable advantage.

The influence of factious leaders may kindle a flame within their particular States, but will be unable to spread a general conflagration through the other States. A religious sect may degenerate into a political faction in a part of the Confederacy; but the variety of sects dispersed over the entire face of it must secure the national councils against any danger from that source. A rage for paper money, for an abolition of debts, for an equal division of property, or for any other improper or wicked project, will be less apt to pervade the whole body of the Union than a particular member of it; in the same proportion as such a malady is more likely to taint a particular county or district, than an entire State.

In the extent and proper structure of the Union, therefore, we behold a republican remedy for the diseases most incident to republican government. And according to the degree of pleasure and pride we feel in being republicans, ought to be our zeal in cherishing the spirit and supporting the character of Federalists.

PUBLIUS

Article 4. Checks and Balances

In Federalist Paper No. 51, Madison offers the classic statement of the U.S. political system, which he wrote only months after discussing it at Philadelphia. He argues that the separation of powers between the three branches of government and the division of powers between the national government and the states are essential to the preservation of constitutional government. Like many of the other framers, Madison feared the concentration of power, which, in his view, necessitated a strong system of checks and balances.

To the People of the State of New York:

To WHAT expedient, then, shall we finally resort, for maintaining in practice the necessary partition of power among the several departments, as laid down in the Constitution? The only answer that can be given is, that as all these exterior provisions are found to be inadequate, the defect must be supplied, by so contriving the interior structure of the government as that its several constituent parts may, by their mutual relations, be the means of keeping each other in their proper places. Without presuming to undertake a full development of this important idea, I will hazard a few general observations, which may perhaps place it in a clearer light, and enable us to form a more correct judgment of the principles and structure of the government planned by the convention.

In order to lay a due foundation for that separate and distinct exercise of the different powers of government, which to a certain extent is admitted on all hands to be essential to the preservation of liberty, it is evident that each department should have a will of its own; and consequently should be so constituted that the members of each should have as little agency as possible in the appointment of the members of the others. Were this principle rigorously adhered to, it would require that all the appointments for the supreme executive, legislative, and judiciary magistracies should be drawn from the same fountain of authority, the people, through channels having no communication whatever with one another. Perhaps such a plan of constructing the several departments would be less difficult in practice than it may in contemplation appear. Some difficulties, however, and some additional expense would attend the execution of it. Some deviations, therefore, from the principle must be admitted. In the constitution of the judiciary department in particular, it might be inexpedient

James Madison, The Federalist Papers, No. 51

to insist rigorously on the principle: first, because peculiar qualifications being essential in the members, the primary consideration ought to be to select that mode of choice which best secures
these qualifications; secondly, because the permanent tenure by
which the appointments are held in that department, must soon
destroy all sense of dependence on the authority conferring them.

It is equally evident, that the members of each department
should be as little dependent as possible on those of the others,
for the emoluments annexed to their offices. Were the executive
magistrate, or the judges, not independent of the legislature in
this particular, their independence in every other would be merely
nominal.

But the great security against a gradual concentration of the
several powers in the same department, consists in giving to those
who administer each department the necessary constitutional
means and personal motives to resist encroachments of the others.
The provision for defence must in this, as in all other cases, be
made commensurate to the danger of attack. Ambition must be
made to counteract ambition. The interest of the man must be
connected with the constitutional rights of the place. It may be
a reflection on human nature, that such devices should be necessary to control the abuses of government. But what is government
itself, but the greatest of all reflections on human nature? If men
were angels, no government would be necessary. If angels were
to govern men, neither external nor internal controls on government would be necessary. In framing a government which is
to be administered by men over men, the great difficulty lies
in this: you must first enable the government to control the
governed; and in the next place oblige it to control itself. A
dependence on the people is, no doubt, the primary control on
the government; but experience has taught mankind the necessity
of auxiliary precautions.

This policy of supplying, by opposite and rival interests, the
defect of better motives, might be traced through the whole system of human affairs, private as well as public. We see it particularly displayed in all the subordinate distributions of power,
where the constant aim is to divide and arrange the several
offices in such a manner as that each may be a check on the
other — that the private interest of every individual may be a
sentinel over the public rights. These inventions of prudence cannot be less requisite in the distribution of the supreme powers
of the State.

But it is not possible to give to each department an equal
power of self-defence. In republican government, the legislative
authority necessarily predominates. The remedy for this in-
conveniency is to divide the legislature into different branches;
and to render them, by different modes of election and different
principles of action, as little connected with each other as the
nature of their common functions and their common dependence
on the society will admit. It may even be necessary to guard against
dangerous encroachments by still further precautions. As the weight
of the legislative authority requires that it should be thus divided,
the weakness of the executive may require, on the other hand,
that it should be fortified. An absolute negative on the legislature
appears, at first view, to be the natural defence with which the
executive magistrate should be armed. But perhaps it would

be neither altogether safe nor alone sufficient. On ordinary occasions it might not be exerted with the requisite firmness, and on extraordinary occasions it might be perfidiously abused. May not this defect of an absolute negative be supplied by some qualified connection between this weaker department and the weaker branch of the stronger department, by which the latter may be led to support the constitutional rights of the former, without being too much detached from the rights of its own department?

If the principles on which these observations are founded be just, as I persuade myself they are, and they be applied as a criterion to the several State constitutions, and to the federal Constitution, it will be found that if the latter does not perfectly correspond with them, the former are infinitely less able to bear such a test.

There are, moreover, two considerations particularly applicable to the federal system of America, which place that system in a very interesting point of view.

First. In a single republic, all the power surrendered by the people is submitted to the administration of a single government; and the usurpations are guarded against by a division of the government into distinct and separate departments. In the compound republic of America, the power surrendered by the people is first divided between two distinct governments, and then the portion allotted to each subdivided among distinct and separate departments. Hence a double security arises to the rights of the people. The different governments will control each other, at the same time that each will be controlled by itself.

Second. It is of great importance in a republic not only to guard the society against the oppression of its rulers, but to guard one part of the society against the injustice of the other part. Different interests necessarily exist in different classes of citizens. If a majority be united by a common interest, the rights of the minority will be insecure. There are but two methods of providing against this evil: the one by creating a will in the community independent of the majority — that is, of the society itself; the other, by comprehending in the society so many separate descriptions of citizens as will render an unjust combination of a majority of the whole very improbable, if not impracticable. The first method prevails in all governments possessing an hereditary or self-appointed authority. This, at best, is but a precarious security; because a power independent of the society may as well espouse the unjust views of the major, as the rightful interests of the minor party, and may possibly be turned against both parties. The second method will be exemplified in the federal republic of the United States. Whilst all authority in it will be derived from and dependent on the society, the society itself will be broken into so many parts, interests and classes of citizens, that the rights of individuals, or of the minority, will be in little danger from interested combinations of the majority. In a free government the security for civil rights must be the same as that for religious rights. It consists in the one case in the multiplicity of interests, and in the other in the multiplicity of sects. The degree of security in both cases will depend on the number of interests and sects; and this may be presumed to depend on the extent of country and number of people comprehended under the same government. This view of the subject must particularly recommend a proper federal system to all the sincere and considerate friends of republican government, since it shows that in exact proportion as the territory of the Union may be formed into more circumscribed Confederacies, or States, oppressive combinations of a majority will be facilitated; the best security, under the republican forms, for the rights of every class of citizens, will be diminished; and consequently the stability and independence of some member of the government, the only other security, must be proportionally increased. Justice is the end of government. It is the end of civil society. It ever has been and ever will be pursued until it be obtained, or until liberty be lost in the pursuit. In a society under the forms of which the stronger faction can readily unite and oppress the weaker, anarchy may as truly be said to reign as in a state of nature, where the weaker individual is not secured against the violence of the stronger; and as, in the latter state, even the stronger individuals are prompted, by the uncertainty of their condition, to submit to a government which may protect the weak as well as themselves; so, in the former state, will the more powerful factions or parties be gradually induced, by a like motive, to wish for a government which will protect all parties, the weaker as well as the more powerful. It can be little doubted that if the State of Rhode Island was separated from the Confederacy and left to itself, the insecurity of rights under the popular form of government within such narrow limits would be displayed by such reiterated oppressions of factious majorities that some power altogether independent of the people would soon be called for by the voice of the very factions whose misrule had proved the necessity of it. In the extended republic of the United States, and among the great variety of interests, parties, and sects which it embraces, a coalition of a majority of the whole society could seldom take place on any other principles than those of justice and the general good; whilst there being thus less danger to a minor from the will of a major party, there must be less pretext, also, to provide for the security of the former, by introducing into the government a will not dependent on the latter, or, in other words, a will independent of the society itself. It is no less certain than it is important, notwithstanding the contrary opinions which have been entertained, that the larger the society, provided it lie within a practical sphere, the more duly capable it will be of self-government. And happily for the *republican cause*, the practicable sphere may be carried to a very great extent, by a judicious modification and mixture of the *federal principle*.

PUBLIUS

Article 5. The Judges As Guardians of the Constitution

In this Federalist paper, Alexander Hamilton discusses the role of the federal judiciary under the new Constitution, emphasizing the importance of the courts in a system of limited government, protected by a written Constitution. Although the power of judicial review—the right of the Supreme Court to declare actions of the president, Congress, or other agencies of government at any level to be invalid or unconstitutional—was first expressed by the Supreme Court in *Marbury* v. *Madison* (1803), the theoretical basis of judicial review was initially espoused by Hamilton in Federalist Paper No. 78.

To the People of the State of New York:

WE PROCEED now to an examination of the judiciary department of the proposed government.

In unfolding the defects of the existing Confederation, the utility and necessity of a federal judicature have been clearly pointed out. It is the less necessary to recapitulate the considerations there urged, as the propriety of the institution in the abstract is not disputed; the only questions which have been raised being relative to the manner of constituting it, and to its extent. To these points, therefore, our observations shall be confined.

The manner of constituting it seems to embrace these several objects: 1st. The mode of appointing the judges. 2d. The tenure by which they are to hold their places. 3d. The partition of the judiciary authority between different courts, and their relations to each other.

First. As to the mode of appointing the judges; this is the same with that of appointing the officers of the Union in general, and has been so fully discussed in the two last numbers, that nothing can be said here which would not be useless repetition.

Second. As to the tenure by which the judges are to hold their places: this chiefly concerns their duration in office; the provisions for their support; the precautions for their responsibility.

According to the plan of the convention, all judges who may be appointed by the United States are to hold their offices *during good behavior*; which is conformable to the most approved of the State constitutions, and among the rest, to that of this State. Its propriety having been drawn into question by the adversaries of that plan, is no light symptom of the rage for objection, which disorders their imaginations and judgments. The standard of good behavior for the continuance in office of the judicial magistracy, is certainly one of the most valuable of the modern improvements in the practice of government. In a monarchy it is an excellent barrier to the despotism of the prince; in a republic it is a no less excellent barrier to the encroachments and oppressions of the representative body. And it is the best expedient which can be devised in any government, to secure a steady, upright, and impartial administration of the laws.

Whoever attentively considers the different departments of power must perceive, that, in a government in which they are separated from each other, the judiciary, from the nature of its functions, will always be the least dangerous to the political rights of the Constitution; because it will be least in a capacity to annoy or injure them. The Executive not only dispenses the

Alexander Hamilton, The Federalist Papers, No. 78

honors, but holds the sword of the community. The legislature not only commands the purse, but prescribes the rules by which the duties and rights of every citizen are to be regulated. The judiciary, on the contrary, has no influence over either the sword or the purse; no direction either of the strength or of the wealth of the society; and can take no active resolution whatever. It may truly be said to have neither FORCE nor WILL, but merely judgment; and must ultimately depend upon the aid of the executive arm even for the efficacy of its judgments.

This simple view of the matter suggests several important consequences. It proves incontestably, that the judiciary is beyond comparison the weakest of the three departments of power *; that it can never attack with success either of the other two; and that all possible care is requisite to enable it to defend itself against their attacks. It equally proves, that though individual oppression may now and then proceed from the courts of justice, the general liberty of the people can never be endangered from that quarter; I mean so long as the judiciary remains truly distinct from both the legislature and the Executive. For I agree, that "there is no liberty, if the power of judging be not separated from the legislative and executive powers." † And it proves, in the last place, that as liberty can have nothing to fear from the judiciary alone, but would have every thing to fear from its union with either of the other departments; that as all the effects of such a union must ensue from a dependence of the former on the latter, notwithstanding a nominal and apparent separation; that as, from the natural feebleness of the judiciary, it is in continual jeopardy of being overpowered, awed, or influenced by its coördinate branches; and that as nothing can contribute so much to its firmness and independence as permanency in office, this quality may therefore be justly regarded as an indispensable ingredient in its constitution, and, in a great measure, as the citadel of the public justice and the public security.

The complete independence of the courts of justice is peculiarly essential in a limited Constitution. By a limited Constitution, I understand one which contains certain specified exceptions to the legislative authority; such, for instance, as that it shall pass no bills of attainder, no *ex-post-facto* laws, and the like. Limitations of this kind can be preserved in practice no other way than through the medium of courts of justice, whose duty it must be to declare all acts contrary to the manifest tenor of the Constitution void. Without this, all the reservations of particular rights or privileges would amount to nothing.

Some perplexity respecting the rights of the courts to pronounce legislative acts void, because contrary to the constitution, has arisen from an imagination that the doctrine would imply a superiority of the judiciary to the legislative power. It is urged that the authority which can declare the acts of another void, must necessarily be superior to the one whose acts may be declared void. As this doctrine is of great importance in all the American constitutions, a brief discussion of the ground on which it rests cannot be unacceptable.

* The celebrated Montesquieu, speaking of them, says: "Of the three powers above mentioned, the judiciary is next to nothing." — "Spirit of Laws," vol. i., page 186. — PUBLIUS

† *Idem.* page 181. — PUBLIUS

There is no position which depends on clearer principles, than that every act of a delegated authority, contrary to the tenor of the commission under which it is exercised, is void. No legislative act, therefore, contrary to the Constitution, can be valid. To deny this, would be to affirm, that the deputy is greater than his principal; that the servant is above his master; that the representatives of the people are superior to the people themselves; that men acting by virtue of powers, may do not only what their powers do not authorize, but what they forbid.

If it be said that the legislative body are themselves the constitutional judges of their own powers, and that the construction they put upon them is conclusive upon the other departments, it may be answered, that this cannot be the natural presumption, where it is not to be collected from any particular provisions in the Constitution. It is not otherwise to be supposed, that the Constitution could intend to enable the representatives of the people to substitute their *will* to that of their constituents. It is far more rational to suppose, that the courts were designed to be an intermediate body between the people and the legislature, in order, among other things, to keep the latter within the limits assigned to their authority. The interpretation of the laws is the proper and peculiar province of the courts. A constitution is, in fact, and must be regarded by the judges, as a fundamental law. It therefore belongs to them to ascertain its meaning, as well as the meaning of any particular act proceeding from the legislative body. If there should happen to be an irreconcilable variance between the two, that which has the superior obligation and validity ought, of course, to be preferred; or, in other words, the Constitution ought to be preferred to the statute, the intention of the people to the intention of their agents.

Nor does this conclusion by any means suppose a superiority of the judicial to the legislative power. It only supposes that the power of the people is superior to both; and that where the will of the legislature, declared in its statutes, stands in opposition to that of the people, declared in the Constitution, the judges ought to be governed by the latter rather than the former. They ought to regulate their decisions by the fundamental laws, rather than by those which are not fundamental.

This exercise of judicial discretion, in determining between two contradictory laws, is exemplified in a familiar instance. It not uncommonly happens, that there are two statutes existing at one time, clashing in whole or in part with each other, and neither of them containing any repealing clause or expression. In such a case, it is the province of the courts to liquidate and fix their meaning and operation. So far as they can, by any fair construction, be reconciled to each other, reason and law conspire to dictate that this should be done; where this is impracticable, it becomes a matter of necessity to give effect to one, in exclusion of the other. The rule which has obtained in the courts for determining their relative validity is, that the last in order of time shall be preferred to the first. But this is a mere rule of construction, not derived from any positive law, but from the nature and reason of the thing. It is a rule not enjoined upon the courts by legislative provision, but adopted by themselves, as consonant to truth and propriety, for the direction of their conduct as interpreters of the law. They thought it reasonable, that between the interfering acts of an *equal* authority, that which was the last indication of its will should have the preference.

But in regard to the interfering acts of a superior and subordinate authority, of an original and derivative power, the nature and reason of the thing indicate the converse of that rule as proper to be followed. They teach us that the prior act of a superior ought to be preferred to the subsequent act of an inferior and subordinate authority; and that accordingly, whenever a particular statute contravenes the Constitution, it will be the duty of the judicial tribunals to adhere to the latter and disregard the former.

It can be of no weight to say that the courts, on the pretence of a repugnancy, may substitute their own pleasure to the constitutional intentions of the legislature. This might as well happen in the case of two contradictory statutes; or it might as well happen in every adjudication upon any single statute. The courts must declare the sense of the law; and if they should be disposed to exercise WILL instead of JUDGMENT, the consequence would equally be the substitution of their pleasure to that of the legislative body. The observation, if it prove any thing, would prove that there ought to be no judges distinct from that body.

If, then, the courts of justice are to be considered as the bulwarks of a limited Constitution against legislative encroachments, this consideration will afford a strong argument for the permanent tenure of judicial offices, since nothing will contribute so much as this to that independent spirit in the judges which must be essential to the faithful performance of so arduous a duty.

This independence of the judges is equally requisite to guard the Constitution and the rights of individuals from the effects of those ill humors, which the arts of designing men, or the influence of particular conjunctures, sometimes disseminate among the people themselves, and which, though they speedily give place to better information, and more deliberate reflection, have a tendency, in the meantime, to occasion dangerous innovations in the government, and serious oppressions of the minor party in the community. Though I trust the friends of the proposed Constitution will never concur with its enemies,* in questioning that fundamental principle of republican government, which admits the right of the people to alter or abolish the established Constitution, whenever they find it inconsistent with their happiness, yet it is not to be inferred from this principle, that the representatives of the people, whenever a momentary inclination happens to lay hold of a majority of their constituents, incompatible with the provisions in the existing Constitution, would, on that account, be justifiable in a violation of those provisions; or that the courts would be under a greater obligation to connive at infractions in this shape, than when they had proceeded wholly from the cabals of the representative body. Until the people have, by some solemn and authoritative act, annulled or changed the established form, it is binding upon themselves collectively, as well as individually; and no presumption, or even knowledge, of their sentiments, can warrant their representatives in a departure from it, prior to such an act. But it is easy to see, that it would require an uncommon portion of fortitude in the judges

* *Vide* "Protest of the Minority of the Convention of Pennsylvania," Martin's Speech, etc. — PUBLIUS

to do their duty as faithful guardians of the Constitution, where legislative invasions of it had been instigated by the major voice of the community.

But it is not with a view to infractions of the Constitution only, that the independence of the judges may be an essential safeguard against the effects of occasional ill humors in the society. These sometimes extend no farther than to the injury of the private rights of particular classes of citizens, by unjust and partial laws. Here also the firmness of the judicial magistracy is of vast importance in mitigating the severity and confining the operation of such laws. It not only serves to moderate the immediate mischiefs of those which may have been passed but it operates as a check upon the legislative body in passing them; who, perceiving that obstacles to the success of iniquitous intention are to be expected from the scruples of the courts, are in a manner compelled, by the very motives of the injustice they meditate, to qualify their attempts. This is a circumstance calculated to have more influence upon the character of our governments, than but few may be aware of. The benefits of the integrity and moderation of the judiciary have already been felt in more States than one; and though they may have displeased those whose sinister expectations they may have disappointed, they must have commanded the esteem and applause of all the virtuous and disinterested. Considerate men, of every description, ought to prize whatever will tend to beget or fortify that temper in the courts; as no man can be sure that he may not be to-morrow the victim of a spirit of injustice, by which he may be a gainer to-day. And every man must now feel, that the inevitable tendency of such a spirit is to sap the foundations of public and private confidence, and to introduce in its stead universal distrust and distress.

That inflexible and uniform adherence to the rights of the Constitution, and of individuals, which we perceive to be indispensable in the courts of justice, can certainly not be expected from judges who hold their offices by a temporary commission. Periodical appointments, however regulated, or by whomsoever made, would, in some way or other, be fatal to their necessary independence. If the power of making them was committed either to the Executive or legislature, there would be danger of an improper complaisance to the branch which possessed it; if to both, there would be an unwillingness to hazard the displeasure of either; if to the people, or to persons chosen by them for the special purpose, there would be too great a disposition to consult popularity, to justify a reliance that nothing would be consulted but the Constitution and the laws.

There is yet a further and a weightier reason for the permanency of the judicial offices, which is deducible from the nature of the qualifications they require. It has been frequently remarked, with great propriety, that a voluminous code of laws is one of the inconveniences necessarily connected with the advantages of a free government. To avoid an arbitrary discretion in the courts, it is indispensable that they should be bound down by strict rules and precedents, which serve to define and point out their duty in every particular case that comes before them; and it will readily be conceived from the variety of controversies which grow out of the folly and wickedness of mankind, that the records of those precedents must unavoidably swell to a very considerable bulk, and must demand long and laborious study to acquire a competent knowledge of them. Hence it is, that there can be but few men in the society who will have sufficient skill in the laws to qualify them for the stations of judges. And making the proper deductions for the ordinary depravity of human nature, the number must be still smaller of those who unite the requisite integrity with the requisite knowledge. These considerations apprise us, that the government can have no great option between fit character; and that a temporary duration in office, which would naturally discourage such characters from quitting a lucrative line of practice to accept a seat on the bench, would have a tendency to throw the administration of justice into hands less able, and less well qualified, to conduct it with utility and dignity. In the present circumstances of this country, and in those in which it is likely to be for a long time to come, the disadvantages on this score would be greater than they may at first sight appear; but it must be confessed, that they are far inferior to those which present themselves under the other aspects of the subject.

Upon the whole, there can be no room to doubt that the convention acted wisely in copying from the models of those constitutions which have established *good behavior* as the tenure of their judicial offices, in point of duration; and that so far from being blamable on this account, their plan would have been inexcusably defective, if it had wanted this important feature of good government. The experience of Great Britain affords an illustrious comment on the excellence of the institution.

PUBLIUS

Chapter **2**

Political Culture

Article 1. Back to Our Roots
by David Horowitz

David Horowitz assesses the agenda of the Fundamentalist Right, arguing that however well-motivated, conservatives must embrace the ideals of tolerance, understanding, and respect, as well as such classical liberal virtues as limited government, individual rights, democratic rule, private property, and the protection of minority rights.

I N HIS manifesto "Conservatism for the People" [Sept. 3, 1990], Paul Weyrich challenges the political Right to reformulate its agenda—until now largely an agenda of dis-

Mr. Horowitz is co-author with Peter Collier of Destructive Generation: Second Thoughts about the Sixties. *This article is one in an occasional series on the future of American conservatism.*

sent—as a governing philosophy, with a "populist" (i.e., majoritarian) appeal.

Weyrich lists several prescriptions for a new conservative agenda, dealing with such social problems as poverty, education, crime, and drugs. I found myself comfortable with most of the elements in Weyrich's proposal, but my optimism was shaken by one central inclusion and one pregnant omission.

Together these undermine any majoritarian aspirations the agenda might have and, in my view, serve as an emblem of conservatism's current impasse—the reason that many who finally become disgusted with liberalism still find themselves unable to cross the political battle lines to embrace a creed which otherwise, in their hearts, they know is right. I

From *National Review*, May 13, 1991, pp. 42–44. © 1991 by National Review, Inc., 150 East 35th Street, New York, NY 10016. Reprinted by permission.

am referring to Weyrich's inclusion of the "defense of the right to life" as a key element of his manifesto, and even more strikingly his omission of any mention of the subject of race.

Weyrich is himself aware of the obstacle that any agenda that includes "defense of the right to life" must pose to majoritarian political ambitions: "Our agenda must affirm the right to life. But we must understand that the vast majority of Americans are profoundly ambivalent on this issue." In fact, only 30 per cent are actually ambivalent. A critical minority—another 30 per cent—are more than "profoundly ambivalent"; they are as determinedly in favor of the right to abortion with *no* restrictions as the 30 per cent who are convinced that the right to life is absolute are against *any* form of abortion. As long as one remains on the terrain of these absolutes, the arithmetic adds up to an insuperable political barrier: 30 per cent ambivalent and 30 per cent in favor of unrestricted abortion make up a majority coalition that will defeat any political movement that mobilizes around the code words "right to life."

This points up a basic principle of majoritarian politics that is absent from Weyrich's discussion. A true philosophy of governance for Americans must recognize the irreducible pluralism of American society. This means, to begin with, that its political agenda must not be perceived as a threat to the existence of America's minority communities. Conceived as a battle over inalienable rights, the abortion issue poses such a threat. This means that barring a transformation of the American character itself, there is no way that a *political* movement with the "right to life" as a keystone of its agenda can become a governing philosophy for Americans.

But conservatives are not alone in attempting to force their particular morality on a recalcitrant majority. Liberals were the first to back themselves into a political corner over abortion. By claiming abortion as a constitutional right and ramming their preference through the Supreme Court, liberals created the political divisiveness of the "abortion issue" and in so doing confined themselves to a minority base among the electorate. Unfortunately, conservatives lockstepped along and thus squandered the opportunity that this liberal power grab presented. By meeting the radical demand for an abortion right with a counterdemand equally absolute, conservatives forfeited the natural majority that was already opposed to the liberals on the issue.

As an alternative, conservatives could have taken the approach outlined by Judge Bork (for which he was crucified by the liberal-left), that there is no basis in the Constitution for an abortion *right* and that the issue should be resolved through the legislative process. Once returned to the legislatures, the abortion question could be resolved by political compromise, reflecting the real divisions within America's plural communities.

Changing Places

UNTIL the Sixties, recognition of the pluralism of American society and commitment to the defense of threatened minorities was the primary strength of American liberalism. It is the subversion of this appeal in the last two decades by the radical agendas of "liberation," affirmative action, and other group-defined and government-enforced privileges—agendas that Balkanize America and threaten to turn its politics into a South African system of group entitlements—that has subverted liberal principles, and undermined the Democrats' majority coalition.

But not completely. Thus, the abortion issue was originally pressed by feminist ideologues under radical formulas like "reproductive rights," but the politicians of the pro-abortion movement shrewdly recognized that this would never command majority consent. Rhetorically, therefore, the pro-abortionists ran their campaign under the conservative banner of "choice" and "privacy," voicing the classic conservative concern of keeping government out of individuals' bedrooms and lives.

This liberal hypocrisy was indeed the homage that vice pays to virtue. But the radicals could never have stolen the conservative agenda in the first place if conservatives had not yielded it up.

There is no clearer example of the way in which the fundamentalist Right has detrimentally set the agenda of the conservative coalition than in its attitude toward homosexuality—a subject on which Weyrich is silent. Without exactly endorsing the proposition that AIDS is God's punishment for homosexuality, conservative spokesmen often seem to acquiesce in the conclusion. The notorious reluctance of the Reagan Administration to confront the AIDS issue head on is surely attributable to this fundamentalist disposition. In point of fact, if the AIDS epidemic demonstrates anything, it confirms the view that homosexuality is itself not a choice (for how many would choose to *join* a high-risk group where the risk is certain death?), but is a stroke of God or nature. This being the case, an appropriate conservative (or even religious) attitude toward homosexuality ought in the first instance to be one of tolerance and respect for difference.

Tolerance and respect for homosexuals does not mean endorsing the political agenda of the homosexual Left, however. This Left has laid siege to the very concept of the biological family, and hijacked America's public-health and health-care-delivery systems for its own political ends. If silence = death, as the homosexual radicals proclaim, promotion of promiscuity and the obstruction of proven public-health methods (testing, contact tracing, etc.) have been the most important factors ensuring the spread of the epidemic and therefore the needless deaths of tens of thousands of homosexuals and others (particularly Hispanic and black IV drug abusers) who were unknowingly in its path. The absolutist Left is a threat to its own constituencies (no surprise here). It is on this pragmatic ground that conservatives should join the political battle. For homosexuals as an American minority: tolerance and respect. For gay "liberation" as a radical agenda: no quarter.

Missing the Point

BUT Weyrich's most striking and significant omission is his failure even to mention the central social issue in America's history: race. Weyrich's omission is doubly odd because the issue of race provides the key to the transformation of

American liberalism since the 1960s. It has been observed that the battles of the Sixties were in fact a kind of second civil war. The Sixties were also, in a sense, the true end of the Civil War, its successful conclusion in a new social contract that repaired the faulty structure of the Founding, finally including black Americans (and by extension all minorities) in the constitutional covenant. It is this completed covenant on which a persuasive conservatism must be built.

And it is the rejection of this covenant by post-Sixties radicals that creates both the opportunity and the necessity for this conservative moment in America's political drama. For the radicals of the Sixties, the historic achievement of the civil-rights revolution was not an act of completion, but an occasion for a new offensive on the covenant itself—the "System" that radicals despised by nature. Thus in the wake of the historic achievement of equal opportunity for all Americans, a new agenda was advanced—black power, black liberation, affirmative action, racial entitlement.

When this radical agenda was sold to liberals, it changed the very nature of American liberalism, and not only in the area of civil rights. Charles Murray, in *Losing Ground*, identifies an epochal shift in the Sixties from efforts to achieve equal opportunity to demands for equal outcomes, from the concept of rights as *limits* to government to the agenda of entitlements as *claims* on government.

This radical agenda has subverted liberalism, leaving conservatives as the sole defenders of the liberal legacy. This is the real basis of the majoritarian opportunity. But to defend the liberal legacy, conservatives must defend it against the illiberal forces not only on the Left, but also on the Right. These forces, operating from the ground of a moral fundamentalism, share with left-wing radicals a coercive utopianism in the belief that America's civil society can be reconstructed according to virtuous ideas.

It has been said that with the collapse of Communism and the end of the cold war, the conservative coalition will lose its unity and disintegrate. Perhaps. But conservatives are united in an older battle than the one with the Marxist millenarians. The intellectual roots of modern conservatism reach back to Burke's quarrel with the French Revolution, which also marks the real birth of the modern Left. The animating spirit of conservatism lies in its opposition to the rationalist utopias of the radical Enlightenment—the totalitarian democracies of Rousseau and Marx. Its abiding purpose—and future opportunity—lies in its commitment to the classical liberalism that inspired America's own revolution: limited government, individual rights, democracy, property, and the protection of minorities against the tyranny of the majority.   □

Article 2. Waiting for Lefty
by Fred Siegel

The author maintains that current trends contradict the predicted revival of liberal politics—at least in the near future—and that given the social stratification of the Reagan Revolution and society's preoccupation with "self-aggrandizement," there is little likelihood of an emerging liberal consensus.

In *Waiting for Lefty*, the radical play of the 1930s, Clifford Odets's characters suffer not only from poverty but also from disintegrating families and a decline of individual honor. The audiences, caught up in a felt connection between their own plight and the play's version of the country's political failures, would often join the actors at the end in shouting "Strike! Strike!" American liberalism is these days experiencing its own "Waiting for Lefty"— waiting to forge a bond between political actors and the electorate. In the nearly ten years since the high-water mark of "The Reagan Revolution," Lefty's return has been predicted not only by Arthur Schlesinger, Jr., inheritor of his father's well-known theory that American history goes through alternating cycles of conservatism and liberalism, but repeatedly by others writing from a wide variety of perspectives.

In 1980 Schlesinger foresaw that "sometime in the 1980s" the "dam" holding back "commitment and uplift will break" and issue forth in a new burst of civic energy. In 1986 predictions of a liberal revival began in earnest with "Hands Across America," a celebrity-studded walk to dramatize poverty.

Despite a record low turnout, liberal victories in the 1986 congressional elections were hailed as proof that the pendulum was set to swing. The 1986 elections, wrote James Reichly, "have lifted the Democrats out of the morass of depression that has beset them since 1978." The strong liberal showing suggested to Reichly the beginnings of a post-Reagan politics. *Washington Post* reporter Paul Taylor argued that "the axis of resentment" was now shifting from "big government to big business." In the late 1980s corporate America, which had enjoyed a 70 percent approval rating a decade earlier, plummeted to a mere 35 percent, according to a Harris poll. Reagan, argued pollster William Schneider, had ironically "restored faith in government," setting the stage for a revival of activist liberalism.

In 1987 historian Robert MacElvaine caught the new spirit in his book *The End of Conservative America: Liberalism After Reagan* by quoting Governor Michael Dukakis on how "this second Reagan term reminds me so much of the second Eisenhower term that it's almost uncanny." "It was time," said Dukakis, "for something new, some energy, some vitality." Pointing to social decay in the cities and the loss of economic competitiveness, Arizona Governor Bruce Babbitt exclaimed that "it almost scares me to think how much the current period is like the late 1950s." Citing Yankelovich polls, *Time* wrote in March 1987 of a ground swell of support for shifting money "away from the military and toward the unsolved problems of health, housing, homelessness and education."

Dukakis and Babbitt weren't entirely off the mark. It's now been almost forgotten that 1987 and 1988 did seem like a reprise of Eisenhower's second term.

By 1987 Reagan no longer had a domestic agenda, while in the wake of the Iran-*contra* scandal, Speaker of the House Jim Wright seized control of American policy toward Nicaragua. And while Reagan was being humiliated by the rejection of Robert Bork as his nominee to the Supreme Court, even his very successes in foreign policy seemed to be working against him. With the collapse of communism, anticommunism, the one issue that had kept libertarian and communitarian conservatives in harness, was fading away—as was the probability of continuing big budgets for the military, the Republicans' chief source of patronage.

With Reagan facing the end of his effectiveness, conservatives seemed lost. While careerist conservative activists were bailing out of politics to cash in on their White House connections, true believers were dismayed to discover that after seven years of Reagan the culture had remained "resolutely liberal and permissive." Faced with the Iran-*contra* scandal, the closing of the cold war, and the bitter recriminations over Bork, conservatives, complained former White House staffer Aram Bakshian, were behaving "like Siamese fighting fish, colorful scrappy little creatures who reserve their best efforts for maiming each other rather than taking on enemy species."

Kevin Phillips, a student of political cycles, argued that periods of conservative ascendancy tend to produce "capitalist blowoffs" that accentuate inequality. He predicted that a populist push for "community minded reform" was not far off. The dynamics of social resentment set off in the sixties, said Phillips, were running out of steam. The conservative cycle that had been powered by a distaste for racial minorities was about to be replaced, argued both Phillips and *Time*, by a new cycle set in motion by disgust with growing disparities of wealth and privilege. The problem with the country, said Richard Gephardt on the 1987 presidential campaign trail, was that the fat cats "reward themselves with huge bonuses during the good times, but console themselves with layoffs as soon as times turn bad."

A new alignment seemed at hand. Yet Lefty hasn't arrived. What happened?

Initially the comparison with Eisenhower's second term seemed to hold. As in the late 1950s, the conservative collapse was matched with a liberal revival. The liberal resurgence of the late 1950s was largely labor driven, and the liberal victories of 1986 were similarly sustained by the unions, which, despite their loss of membership, had become more important than ever in a Democratic party largely without organizational muscle. Business, caught by surprise, seemed reconciled, after its sweeping antilabor victories in the Reagan years, to losing a few rounds. Referring to the big buildup of unmet needs, a General Electric (GE) vice president acknowledged, Schlesinger-like, that "there was a pent up need to legislate."

The legislation the GE veep was referring to was coming out of the Senate Labor and Human Resources Committee, where the new chair, Ted Kennedy, was, thanks to his collaboration with organized labor, ready to launch some new initiatives. The "new agenda for social progress in America," tagged as "workers' rights legislation," included plant-closing notification, job-hazard notification, minimum-wage increases, minimum health benefits for all employees, and mandatory unpaid parental leave when a child is born or adopted.

Kennedy and his aides approached each of these issues almost flawlessly. They avoided a call for new or enlarged bureaucracies. They insisted on the need not just to spend more but to set priorities. They didn't demand new spending and thus new taxes. Through what was described as "low-cost social justice," the use of targeted or dedicated spending, self-financing programs, off-budget expenditures, and mandated benefits, the Kennedy agenda managed to address a broad range of needs and constituencies without stirring up the standard fears about liberal activism.

Some of the new agenda, like self-financed catastrophic health insurance for the elderly, failed in part because of poor legislative craftsmanship and old-fashioned interest-group greed. But the rest, including such reasonable measures as giving workers advance notification of plant closings and requiring *unpaid* parental leave, were beaten back with presidential vetoes. Yet even those defeats seemed to contain the seeds of future victories. Plant-closing and parental-leave legislation, both broadly popular, promised to provide a platform for contesting the 1988 presidential elections.

If the 1988 contest had been carried out on the same playing field on which John Kennedy had won in 1960, the Democrats would have been able to gain enough public support to win the White House. Again, if the United States was still demographically and socially the country that had elected JFK, the 1988 elections could have been the start of something big.

Had the two strongest sources of liberal and Democratic electoral support—the trade unions and the cities—represented the same proportion of the population in 1988 as they had in 1960, Dukakis probably would have won narrowly. But the precipitous drop in American manufacturing employment—the United States lost two million manufacturing jobs in the 1980s—came largely in districts dominated by Democrats. Trade unions have lost roughly four million members since 1975. Union membership declined by nearly three-quarters of a million in 1984–85 alone. Membership may have now bottomed out at roughly 15 percent of the work force (only 12 percent in private industry), the lowest percentage among the major industrialized nations. The full extent of this decline has

been masked in part by the growth of unions among government employees, whose interests in redistribution are often at odds with the growth-oriented emphasis of unionists in the private sector. The net effect is that despite their clout in the low-turnout off-year congressional elections, the unions are a much diminished force when it comes to defining the national political agenda.

New York Mayor David Dinkins likes to speak of urban America as "the heart and soul of the nation." But compared to the suburbs, which saw employment jump by 25 percent in the 1980s while urban areas lost 30 percent of their jobs, the cities are a rapidly shrinking political force. In the eighties, as poverty became more firmly implanted in the big cities, ten of the eleven cities with large black communities experienced sharp population declines. Detroit lost nearly 20 percent of its people. In 1960 Chicago, crucial to JFK's election, represented more than 40 percent of the Illinois vote; today it is 25 percent. Baltimore, which once cast almost one out of every two presidential votes in Maryland, now accounts for little more than one in ten. But even that 10 percent figure overestimates Baltimore's clout, because its residents earn on average less than half of what their suburban counterparts make.

The mass political movements of this century, beginning with the rural revolt of the Populists and moving on to the New Deal insurgency of the industrial unions and the cities, were based on strong identities of interest created by a nexus of common work and communal concerns. But the new political center of the country is in the generally anti- or apolitical (but presidentially Republican) suburbs—settlements defined by secession from the common concerns of the cities. Between 1968 and 1988 millions fled the disorder of the cities; the suburban secession grew from 36 percent to 48 percent of the presidential vote.

And now, 1992 is likely to be the first election with a suburban majority. For at least a decade the suburban shift has had enough momentum to feed on itself. Ronald Reagan, elected with overwhelming suburban majorities, moved effectively to weaken the ties between city and federal government, central to American liberalism since FDR enraged the nation's governors in 1933 by directly funneling highway funds to the cities. Reagan's revenue-sharing program sent money once earmarked for the cities to the suburban-dominated state governments that have by and large proceeded to cut the cities' share of federal monies. In some cases, as in Philadelphia, those cuts plus a generous helping of local incompetence have sent cities into near bankruptcy.

When Philadelphia's African-American mayor, William Goode, turned to the state for relief from a crisis initiated in part in Washington and Harrisburg, he was rudely rebuffed. He found that a finger-waving state government dominated by suburban Democrats and rural Republicans and egged on by disaffected ethnic Democrats refused to help. Instead the anti-Philadelphia coalition—even more antiblack than anti-urban—has been only too happy to see Philadelphia's collapse as an example of liberal failure.

Separatism initiated by blacks is subject to censure; but many suburbanites are as separatist as any black nationalist, only more subtly so. When Governor Jim Florio of New Jersey tried to use a progressive income tax to rejuvenate inner-city education, he became the most unpopular governor in recent memory. In New Jersey middle- and upper-middle-class white separatism is expressed both in terms of partly legitimate distrust of government's effectiveness and an unwillingness to share tax revenues with "them," the poor from whom they fled in the first place.

Among the dependent individualists of the suburbs, community is defined not so much by close ties with one's neighbors and community organizations—those have eroded rapidly over the past quarter century—but by *who is kept out*. The suburbs are not so much Republican as anti-urban, and thus anti-Democratic.

The fastest growing form of government in the suburbs is the homeowners association presiding over covenanted communities—essentially private towns operating outside the purview of the Fourteenth Amendment. In return for erecting a bastion against the problems of the metropolis, "citizens" of the private towns agree to a "covenanted conformity" that dictates everything from the size of their mailboxes to the type and number of visitors permitted. Estimated to include as many as twenty million people, these covenanted communities generally establish "one dollar–one vote governments" that recreate the pre-industrial world of power to the property holders.

While the cities are pitted against the suburbs, city dwellers are increasingly divided against themselves. In Milwaukee, a city with a long liberal and even socialist tradition, black and white blue-collar workers devastated by the decline of heavy manufacturing seem to have moved into separate realities. The whites, decreasingly Democratic, support the Republican governor's Learnfare program, which penalizes parents on welfare whose children are truant. Blacks are reviving the separatist spirit of Malcolm X. Mike McGee, a born-again Black Panther complete with Castro-style beard and revolutionary regalia, has, to great media fanfare, threatened violence if "changes" aren't made.

It's some measure of the cynicism now surrounding race relations that the changes being made garner support from both the Republican governor pushing Learnfare and one of McGee's prominent supporters, Polly Williams, who is promoting a plan to dismantle the public schools. Governor Thompson sees the opportunity to interject market mechanisms into education by giving out vouchers redeemable at a school of choice, public or private. Williams, a black nationalist, wants to put public monies to parochial ends by creating Afrocentric academies funded by the vouchers. Williams argues, with some justice, that the white suburbs are already operating what in effect are white private schools with public money.

Milwaukee is by no means unique in seeming to have given up on both integration and public institutions. In the 1940s the CIO's "Operation Dixie" tried to unionize the textile mills of the South in order to liberalize southern politics. Something like the reverse has now occurred. The southern problem has come North and racial divisions that for so long held back southern progress now hold the entire country—and for that matter the political cycle—at bay. The ostentatious inequalities of the Reagan years haven't brought on a progressive politics, in part because the fight over racial issues in general and hiring quotas in particular has limited the possibilities for political renewal.

The disparity between personal prosperity and public poverty is driven home daily to residents of big cities who search and search to find a public phone that's working even as others cruise by in cars talking on their hand-held cellular phones. The privatization of public life has been attributed in part to the ability of the wealthy to simply buy their way out of public services, but the privatization extends far beyond the suburban and the wealthy. It's now common in the big cities for middle-class neighborhoods—whether black, white, or, as in my own, integrated—to rely on private police, private bus services, private schools, and private recreation. Perhaps even more important is that the residents of middle-class neighborhoods are also protected by private health and social insurance systems, benefits that come with their jobs, so that the collapse of public hospitals is another crisis from which they've largely insulated themselves.

Government itself is sometimes directly complicit in this growing privatization. In New York developers despairing of the city government's ability to provide that most basic of public services—safety on the streets—have built vast new developments like Battery Park City, which are in effect limited-access private cities, the urban counterparts of the covenanted suburbs. On a small scale, neighborhoods have turned to "special purpose taxes," for "special service districts"—in effect, limited private governments to provide services like street cleaning and police protection that the city itself is unable to supply. The net effect, writes John DiIulio, is that "we're moving away from a system that registers concern for general equity in the distribution of government services, toward a market system where citizens are treated very differently within the same jurisdiction based on their ability to pay."

The "special service districts" can be seen as a metaphor for the political system as a whole. Government and the public arena are not regarded by most Americans as vehicles to achieve worthwhile common goals; they are simply assumed to be public means to private ends. The notion that governments, and government employees, are "in business for themselves" is simply taken as a fact of life. In the New York City school system, for instance, it is widely understood that the schools are opened and closed not in accord with the needs of students and neighborhoods but at the pleasure of the custodians "union." The custodians are essentially public entrepreneurs who in the name of city services are in business for themselves.

When the superintendent of a New York school district was asked why in the midst of recent layoffs additional money had been appropriated for a school drop-out prevention program that had proved to be an abject failure, he replied anonymously: "This money is just to feed fat cows and let them get fatter."

The drop-out prevention patronage program of the New York schools was protected because of the political clout of its backers, but the nonaccountability now routinely associated with government spending is sometimes imposed for the best of reasons. Money for Special Education, that is, education for children deemed to be handicapped with severe learning, physical, or emotional problems, now covers 12 percent of all students and 23 percent of the school budget in New York City. Yet its benefits are at best uncertain. Part of the "Rights Revolution" of the 1960s and 1970s, Special Education became mandated in 1978 after a federal judge, citing the Education for All Handicapped Children Act of 1973, ordered a customized response to children with special problems. Protected from public scrutiny and democratic debate by having been juridically defined as an absolute right, the money mandated by the federal government for Special Education has become a swamp of nonaccountability.

Operating under court protection, Special Education has spawned a bureaucracy of psychologists, paraprofessionals, social workers, and teachers who need not account for their efforts. Jack Pollack, principal of Abraham Lincoln High School in Brooklyn, notes, "If the results justified the expense and the paper work it would be all right, but nobody has verified whether it does." These jobs, he explains, cannot be abolished unless the judge who ordered the program modifies his ruling. The net effect is that at a time when teachers in New York are being laid off, Special Education teachers are still being hired—as in a Brooklyn school where, despite overcrowded classes, a full-time teacher fluent in Cambodian is being hired for a single Cambodian student.

A politics purged of public purpose by self-serving government and court-ordered insulation has helped to sever the connection between the populace and the political process. "People don't feel any sense of ownership over the federal government," says Democratic pollster Geoffrey Garin. "It isn't them, and it isn't theirs." Voters, as repeated surveys suggest, believe, and with reason, that their choices count for less and less. The distance between the populace and its purported representatives is summed up by a San Franciscan who complained that government "seems like another world to me. It goes on, it functions, but I don't feel like it really directly affects us." It is these sorts of sentiments, what one recent survey described as "the astonishing indifference to politics and elections," that makes a full-scale liberal revival seem unlikely in the near future.

There is something inherently optimistic about the cyclical theory of American politics. It suggests, in effect, that no matter what changes take place, a turn in the wheel of fortune can be counted on. But, short of a revival of our cities and other institutions of social solidarity, there is little reason to assume that the next set of social shocks—whether they come from a severe recession or military setbacks—will produce Lefty's long-awaited return. Increasingly cut off as we are from one another not only by the sharpening social stratification of the Reagan years but also by the therapeutic "politics of personal identity," there is not much reason to assume that the near future will bring a return to a liberal politics based on common concerns. At least right now, the outlook for America seems best described not as a cycle of renewal but as a slow drift downward. This is not exactly good news, but it is, I fear, the truth. □

Article 3. The End Is Near for U.S. Conservatism
by David N. Dinkins

In this article, New York City mayor David Dinkins argues that while the conservative cause has scored several impressive victories in recent years, it can no longer dictate the social and political agenda of the nation—that the politics of apathy, alienation, and indifference have been replaced by a renewed commitment to tolerance, mutual respect, and government action.

"The conservative cause has become a spent volcano, still spitting and sputtering, but no longer capable of reshaping the political landscape."

THE CREST of the conservative flood has passed. The Republicans still occupy the White House, but the conservative coalition has lost its way. It no longer can dominate public and social policy. It has lost its ability to intimidate so many into silence and despair. A decade of reaction and retrenchment has begun to yield to a resurgence of progressive ideals.

The approach is not novel. The same process marked the 1920s in America, a time when cities and states were forced to design solutions of their own because of the withdrawal of the Federal government from the national stage. Many of them became the basis for Federal action in the 1930s.

As was true in the 1930s, we have a lot to overcome today. In the last decade, we saw the ethics and dreams of Martin Luther King, Jr., and John F. Kennedy traded in for selfishness and callousness. The national government once again withdrew from American cities, but the national problems did not fade away.

Mr. Dinkins is Mayor of New York City.

We watched as the Federal government washed away our national priorities with a wave of tax cuts that provided quick stimulation in exchange for a crushing burden of debt. It was cruelty masquerading as patriotism.

Each of the pillars upon which the conservative coalition was built—the Cold War, the politics of division and exclusion at home, the attack on a woman's right to make her own choices about reproduction, and regressive economics—has cracked and in some cases crumbled. For decades, the fear of communism abroad blocked the path to progress here at home. Ideas were tested not for their strength and effectiveness, but for the degree of their orientation to the right or left.

The progressive income tax, Social Security, labor laws, civil rights, national health insurance, gun control—all were suspect, all were sinister and socialistic, and all were fought bitterly by the right. The spectre of communism also dominated domestic politics, distorting our budgets and disrupting our pursuit of social and political fairness.

Military might became the sole measure of national security, leaving no room in our calculation of American strength for infant mortality, literacy, or economic opportunity.

Over the past decade, the Pentagon budget doubled while Federal housing assistance was cut more than 75%. Today, the conservatives cling to a war-time budget while the rest of the world celebrates the end of the Cold War.

In January, 1990, I joined my fellow mayors in Washington to call for a redirection of Federal spending from the Defense Department to American cities. Peace can bring us a tangible dividend, and we need that peace dividend to make our country stronger so that we can continue to assist those in Eastern Europe and elsewhere who will call on us again to lend a hand. The revolutions in Eastern Europe and the Soviet Union have created a dilemma for the conservatives. Without communism they have no enemy, and without an enemy they have no energy. Saddam Hussein is no substitute for the Russian bear.

One Administration official has declared that the end of the Cold War is the

Reprinted from *USA Today Magazine,* March, copyright 1991 by the Society for the Advancement of Education.

"end of history," and he may be correct, at least for the extreme right. There still must come a revolution in South Africa, and the students of Tiananmen Square must yet see their vision realized, but the Iron Curtain has been lifted.

To the conservatives, the end of the Cold War is just the first of many woes. There also is the end of the politics of racial antagonism. Since Richard Nixon, the Republicans' electoral dominance has been based on a southern strategy. The conservative crusade began in 1980 not by ringing the liberty bell in Philadelphia, Pa., but by winking at the enemies of liberty in Philadelphia, Miss.

Throughout the 1980s, those on the right resisted every effort to swing open the doors of opportunity more widely. They opposed the Equal Rights Amendment and equal pay for equal work. They struggled against the Voting Rights Act.

Their insensitivity to prejudice has been indefensible, but their attitude grows from ignorance and isolation. The Republicans sought not diversity, but uniformity. Of the more than 400 Federal judicial appointments made during the 1980s, only 26 were racial minorities and just 32 were women. The Bush Administration still has only one African-American, one Hispanic, and two women in the Cabinet.

When I declared my candidacy for Mayor of New York City, most thought that it would take a miracle for me to defeat first a popular three-term mayor, Ed Koch, and then a powerful prosecutor, Rudolph Giuliani. Nevertheless, African-Americans, Latinos, and Asians; Catholics and Jews; gays and lesbians; persons with disabilities and those who are able-bodied all came together in celebration of diversity. They voted their hopes, not their fears.

When the people of Virginia joined in, they threw the southern strategy and its politics of exclusion onto the ash heap of history. They redefined the realm of the possible for millions of Americans who now can dream again of holding public office.

The right won't be running against abortion, either. In November, 1989, voters in New York, New Jersey, and Virginia sent strong signals to those who would let government interfere with a woman's right to choose. Who would have thought a year ago that even the chairman of the Republican National Committee, Lee Atwater, would claim to be agnostic on abortion? The effort to make God a partisan political being has failed.

Finally, there was Reaganomics. More than anything else, the Reagan Revolution was predicated on the proposition that the government should lavish its largesse upon those with the most. No tax cut was too irresponsible, no special benefit too unfair, and no deregulation too extreme.

What a dowry it left us. The latest bill for the S&L bail-out is $300,000,000,000 and growing. The interest on just that portion of the debt, the amount needed to bail out the savings and loans, would go a long way toward rebuilding our urban housing stock to eliminate homelessness.

The Republican economic miracle turned out to be a mirage—all of it except for the national debt. That has proved to be painfully real, all three trillion dollars of it.

The conservative cause has become a spent volcano, still spitting and sputtering, but no longer capable of reshaping the political landscape. Sadly for Americans, though, the land the conservatives have left behind is scorched and scarred. The challenges they ignored—crack and crime, AIDS and education, homelessness and hunger, poverty and pollution—remain very much with us.

The conservatives regaled us with tales of resurgence while the rest of the world went whizzing by. So now we can remember the touching speeches and sentimental images of the 1980s while we travel across roads and bridges that are crumbling, to take our kids to schools that aren't teaching, to prepare them for life in a global economy that suddenly threatens to leave them behind.

Where are the solutions? Many of us outside of Washington are hard at work defining our goals, refining our methods, and preparing solutions for the 1990s. From the ground up, we're building a new foundation upon the rubble of the conservative decade. If progressive ideas were a stock, now would be the time to buy.

We must start with a fundamental commitment to democracy—a passion for participation that is opening our government to those who previously have not been invited or allowed in. It has to belong to no elite or narrow interest. We need an open forum that hears diverse views and voices before it decides, a democracy that appeals to what is best in us and strives to bring us together. This is not merely a matter of principle—it's practical politics.

Our society is a gorgeous mosaic of race and religious faith, of national origin and sexual orientation. No one person and no one group possibly can understand the ways and the worries of all. A government that includes all in the process will exclude fewer in the result. Representation—real representation—will reduce the alienation and frustration that too often characterize our society. Broad-based government is better government. That's the approach that will be required for this nation to realize its true potential.

Above all else, the problems and perils of American society today are matters of public safety. Crime and drugs—and the

fear and failures they cause—are tearing away at the fabric of our society.

Our cities are under siege. Entire neighborhoods across this nation have become free-fire zones. Children come to school wearing beepers that link them not to their teachers or their parents, but to the drug suppliers who command their highest loyalties. Some of our housing projects literally have become base camps for armies of drug dealers. High atop the gleaming skyscrapers that exemplify our economic predominance, young and not-so-young professionals—well-educated men and women with substantial monetary resources—foolishly remain drawn to the allure of cocaine and other illicit drugs.

We must take back our streets, by night as well as by day. We have to return law and order by making the police part of our communities and asking our communities to participate in policing.

However, respect for the law—and for each other—requires more than better policing; more than tougher statutes against group violence and bias crimes; more than a ban on assault weapons; more even than creating a penalty of life in prison without parole for those who commit the worst crimes—literally, to lock them up and throw away the key.

Assuming responsibility

What matters most is not our programs, as important as they are, but our values, especially individual responsibility. For too long, we have been hesitant to require from all who share this society that they carry their portion of the load. We must not allow barriers and obstacles to become an excuse. Life is not always fair and it's hard to get ahead, but each of us has an obligation to work hard, respect the law, be disciplined and strong, and take responsibility for our actions.

As Malcolm X said: "It is time to get together among our own kind and eliminate the evils that are destroying the moral fiber of our society," whether they be drug addiction or alcoholism, abuse or neglect, physical violence or economic inequality, giving in or just plain giving up. That's true for every community and every family, for people in power and for those who are powerless.

At the same time, we must recognize that we're all born into a world we did not make; that responsibility comes more easily with resources; and that individual effort must be tied to an ethic of social obligation.

That obligation is especially strong to the most vulnerable and the most precious of all our people—our youth. Who can defend the charge that the richest nation on Earth suffers the highest rate of children in poverty among Western industrial democracies? No matter how rich and powerful we become, we can not be satisfied when so many youngsters experience the sunset of opportunity at the very dawn of their existence.

More than anything else, the failure of governments on all levels in recent years has been their inability to conform public policy to public values. The result of the Reagan Revolution must not become an even deeper distrust and disillusion in the purpose of politics and the power of government. The conservatives failed not because they tried to remake the world, but because their vision and their values were so dangerously divorced from the reality of the society they temporarily dominated.

As we shed the weight of the past and seek a new consensus for the 1990s, let us recognize that new times require new approaches and new solutions. We need them from Washington and want to work with the Bush Administration, but if it continues to ignore our plea, our urban centers will take the lead. Then, when the next national government takes office, it will have to come to us to find out what works and what needs to be done.

Let us always remember that the politics of this nation must reflect the people of this nation—a diverse populace that demands democracy and participation; believes in individual responsibility *and* social obligation; works hard and wants government to work equally hard to meet *its* fiscal responsibilities; always comes forward when called on to contribute; and is prepared to move ahead. This nation is ready for its own democracy movement, an era when tolerance and mutual respect will mean greater freedom for each of us.

Chapter **3**

The Constitution

Article 1.   Is the Bill of Rights in Danger?
by D. Grier Stephenson, Jr.

The Bill of Rights, contends the author, is under attack from all sides, as special-interest groups seek to reinterpret its protections to serve their own political agendas. Its survival will depend, to a large extent, on the willingness of the majority to stand firm in its commitment to those fundamental protections that are essential to democratic government.

This keystone to American democracy is being battered from all sides, as special-interest groups strive to re-interpret it to suit their causes.

JUST over 200 years ago, Thomas Jefferson was in France on a diplomatic mission. When he received a copy of the proposed U.S. Constitution from his friend James Madison, he let him know as fast as the slow sailing-ship mails of the day allowed that the new plan of government suffered one major defect—it lacked a bill of rights. This, Jefferson argued, "is what the people are entitled to against every government on earth. . . ." Two centuries later, events in Europe have transformed Jefferson's words into a rallying cry. Old tyrannies have tumbled head over heels into the rudiments of constitutionalism. The idea of a bill of rights seems contagious. Yet, despite its embrace abroad, is the

American Bill of Rights in danger at home? Answering this question requires an examination of two preliminary ones: What is the Bill of Rights and why do we have it?

At the Constitutional Convention in 1787, John Dickinson of Delaware advised the delegates to let experience be their guide; theory might mislead them, he cautioned. Adopted in 1791 as the first 10 amendments to the Constitution, the Bill of Rights reflects the Founding Fathers' experience with, and understanding of, the dimensions of personal freedom. The First Amendment protects free expression—in speech, press, assembly, petition, and religion. The Second Amendment safeguards liberty against national tyranny by affirming the self-defense of the states. Members of local militia—citizens primarily, soldiers occasionally—retained a right to bear arms. The ban in the Third Amendment on forcibly quartering troops in

houses suggests the emphasis the framers placed on the integrity and sanctity of the home. Other provisions—the Fourth, Fifth, Sixth, Seventh, and Eighth Amendments— guard freedom by setting forth standards government must follow in administering the law, especially the criminal law. In addition, one clause in the Fifth Amendment forbids the taking of private property for public use without just compensation, and so limits the power of eminent domain. Along with taxation and conscription, this is one of the most comprehensive powers any government can possess. The Ninth Amendment mentions no specific rights, but reflects the dominant political thought of the 18th century. In the English tradition and in the spirit of the Declaration of Independence, a bill of rights did not itself confer rights, but merely recognized existing ones. The Ninth Amendment makes sure that the listing of some rights does not im-

---

Dr. Stephenson, Associate National Affairs Editor of USA Today, is Charles A. Dana Professor of Government, Franklin & Marshall College, Lancaster, Pa.

ply that others necessarily have been abandoned. If the Ninth offered reassurances to the people, the Tenth was designed to reassure the states that they or the people retained those powers not delegated to the national government. Today, the Tenth is mainly symbolic of the integral place of the states in the Federal system.

The protections found in the first 10 amendments do not exhaust the meaning Americans commonly give to the Bill of Rights. At the outset, it applied only to the national government, not to the states. Except for the few restrictions in the original text of the Constitution which explicitly limited state power, states were restrained only by their individual constitutions, not by the Federal Bill of Rights. So, Pennsylvania or any other state could shut down a newspaper or deny religious freedom without violating the First Amendment.

The first step in closing this gap came with the ratification of the Fourteenth Amendment in 1868. Section one contained majestic, but undefined, checks on the states that begged for interpretation: "*No State* shall make or enforce any law which shall abridge the privileges or immunities of citizens of the United States; nor shall any State deprive any person of life, liberty, or property, without due process of law; nor deny to any person within its jurisdiction the equal protection of the laws" (emphasis added). Acting for the most part in a series of cases after 1920, the Supreme Court has construed the Fourteenth Amendment to include almost every provision of the Bill of Rights. This was the second step in closing the gap. State and local governments became bound by the same restrictions that had applied all along to the national government. The consequences of this process scarcely can be exaggerated since so much government policy is that of state and local governments.

The Fourteenth Amendment also reinvigorated the debate over whether the Constitution protects rights not spelled out in the words of the document. As early as the 1790s, justices on the Supreme Court speculated that there were rights no government could infringe upon, even if they were not protected expressly by the Constitution. What are those other rights? Constitutionally protected liberty long has been viewed as open-ended. While including most of the liberties enshrined in the Bill of Rights, the Fourteenth Amendment does not stop there. The Supreme Court has said that other rights—those deemed fundamental—are protected.

Thus, in 1923, the Court struck down a Nebraska law banning the teaching of foreign languages to children below the ninth grade. In 1965, it set aside a Connecticut law that criminalized the use of birth control devices. In a 1973 decision that remains at the center of controversy, the Court invalidated the abortion laws of almost all the states. The reasoning was that laws forbidding abortions under all but the most extreme circumstances infringed on the fundamental right of the woman to decide whether to carry a pregnancy to full term. In cases such as these, the justices "discover" rights implied by the basic idea of liberty—even though the Constitution's words say nothing about learning a foreign language, preventing a pregnancy, or aborting a fetus.

In these situations, the question is not whether the framers of the Bill of Rights or the Fourteenth Amendment anticipated and therefore intended that their handiwork should apply to foreign language instruction, birth control pills, and terminated pregnancies. If that were the question, the answer to the question whether those subjects implicated the Constitution in a meaningful way almost always would be no. There is no requirement of omniscience to be a delegate to a constitutional convention or a member of Congress or a state legislature. Rather, in each of these instances, government had restricted personal liberty. Is the liberty at issue sufficiently important to be ranked as "fundamental"? If so, the Court requires that government adduce compelling justification for the infringement, a standard nearly impossible to meet. If the liberty is not fundamental, government only need have a reason—judges use the term "rational basis"—for the restriction. However, the important question remains: What makes a liberty fundamental? The answer is a function of the values of five justices of the Supreme Court.

This transformation leads to the second question: Why does the Constitution contain a Bill of Rights? The framers were united in their belief that government should rest on the authority of the people. That had been the premise of the American revolution. They were nearly as united in the belief that government should not be *too* responsive to the people. That had been the problem with other experiments in democratic government. Tyranny by the majority often had replaced tyranny by the few.

Diffusion of power

The framers preferred a different plan. They rejected the term "democratic" to describe their creation. Instead, they called it republican, or free, government. The system of checks and balances among the executive, legislative, and judicial branches plus a division of political authority between the national and state governments made sense because power thereby was diffused and dispersed. A majority of the people would have a difficult time seizing control of all parts of the political system and running roughshod over the rights of the minority. At least among those white males admitted to the political community in 1787, liberty would be secure because no group could easily become strong enough to deny liberty to others. Freedom would be assured through "political gridlock."

For some, this diffusion of power was sufficient. For constructive critics like Thomas Jefferson, however, the Constitution did not go far enough. Inherent in the idea of a written constitution are constraints on what government may do. In a government based on the consent of the governed, limits on authority mean limits on the majority. A declaration of rights would enrich the Constitution's design. A bill of rights would help political minorities get an untroubled night's sleep.

Opponents of the proposed Constitution, called Antifederalists, quickly seized on this defect. Ostensibly, they worried about the threat to individual liberty posed by the new government. Of greater concern were threats to the prerogatives of state governments. The standard response from supporters of the Constitution, called the Federalists, was that a bill of rights was unnecessary. If the national government was to be one of delegated powers, they reasoned, why bar the exercise of powers not delegated? Moreover, adding a bill of rights might be dangerous. Anything not expressly mentioned could be presumed to be omitted purposely by the framers.

The Federalist explanation backfired. As it left the hands of the framers, the Constitution contained several specific prohibitions on the power of the national government. Without a bill of rights, Antifederalists could make the valid point that all unspecified rights now stood in danger. The potential elasticity of the "necessary and proper" clause of Article One only strengthened their case. Moreover, existing bills of rights in state constitutions would be of little help because the new Constitution made it clear that national laws would pre-empt state laws and constitutions. The Federalists therefore promised a bill of rights to achieve ratification, and thus took the wind out of the Antifederalists' sails by removing the main cause around which popular opposition to the Constitution could gather. If it wasn't for the Constitution's sharpest critics, we might never have gotten the Bill of Rights.

The Federalists made good on their word. As one of the first orders of business in the new Congress, Madison introduced a series of amendments in the House of Representatives on May 26, 1789. House members added others. Seventeen proposed alterations then were sent to the Senate, which began debate on Sept. 2. Senators made editorial changes, fused some amendments, and forwarded a revised package of 12 amendments to the House on Sept. 19. By Sept. 25, both houses had approved the same list of 12. Of this number, the states ratified 10. Not ratified were two unrelated amendments—one dealing with the apportionment of the House and the other delaying any increase in Congressional salaries until after the next election. As the 11th state to act, Virginia's ratification on Dec. 15, 1791, made the Bill of Rights officially part of the Constitution. (Among the last to approve the Bill of Rights, Virginia had been first to adopt a declaration of rights in 1776, three weeks before the signing of the Declaration of Independence.) The remaining three states—Connecticut, Georgia, and Massachusetts—did not ratify until the 150th anniversary of the Bill of Rights in 1941.

Yet, the Antifederalists obtained little of what they wanted. States' rights weighed more heavily than their concern for personal rights. Instead of "substantial amendments," complained South Carolina's Pierce Butler, here were a "few milk-and-water amendments . . . such as liberty of conscience, a free press, and one or two general things already well secured." Georgia's Congressman James Jackson agreed, saying the amendments were not worth a "pinch of snuff."

The idea of a bill of rights was not original with the Antifederalists. Following the example of several English statutes, the Continental Congress had adopted a Declaration of Rights in 1774, and state constitutions since 1776 contained their own declarations of rights. The American contribution after 1791 lay in making liberty a juridical concept, devising a way to enforce constitutional guarantees. So, it became significant that the Supreme Court soon assumed the role of guardian of the Constitution. Through the development of judicial review—the authority of courts to set aside laws which in their view violate the Constitution—judges came to be protectors and even shapers of constitutional values. Without judicial protection, the words of the Bill of Rights might have remained little more than moral exhortations. Experience has taught that exhortation often may not be enough. In place of trust in the people, the Bill of Rights stands for mistrust. These amendments rest on the premise that the majority is likely to be neither correct nor tolerant all of the time.

Yet, is the Bill of Rights secure today? Ironically, the answer is that it is secure only if each generation of Americans believes its liberties are in danger. Consider, for example, the problems of interpretation, faithfulness, and reliance.

The Constitution ordinarily speaks in generalities, not particulars. It is a document of enumeration, not of definition. The First Amendment protects freedom of speech, among other values, but does not define the "speech" that is protected. Thus, one should not be surprised to find a cottage industry among scholars, judges, lawyers, and journalists grinding out competing interpretations.

Reasonable minds differ, for instance, over whether sexually explicit pictures and language merit constitutional protection. While the Supreme Court never has said that the First Amendment protects the sexually obscene, the definition of obscenity is so narrow that all but the hardest of hardcore pornography now is protected constitutionally. Some say that far too much explicit material is therefore available, contributing to abuse of women and children and to a general moral decay.

In similar fashion, people disagree over the constitutional protection to be accorded verbal attacks on other races and religions. Should a person be allowed to preach messages of hate? At a state university, which is founded on the utility of the free exchange of ideas, should students, faculty, and staff be disciplined for uttering remarks judged to be offensive to others? Moreover, recall the furor in 1989 and 1990 after the Supreme Court declared that the states and Congress were powerless to punish those who burn the American flag as a form of symbolic expression. For many, such speech contributes nothing either to the betterment of society or the advancement of knowledge. If such speech is worthless, no harm can be done by its suppression. Others reply that, if such words or acts are beyond constitutional protection, the net of criminality is bound to be cast too wide. Moreover, even if most could agree on a clear standard, it is risky to exempt speech from the First Amendment's protective shield. If one person's message is not safe, is anyone's? From this perspective, self-interest dictates tolerance of the thoughts and depictions we hate.

Which liberties should be protected?

Accordingly, one should expect debate when the Bill of Rights is applied to concrete situations. This debate is healthy because people learn about the purposes of liberty when they disagree over what those liberties should encompass. However, debate alone does not mean that the liberties in the Bill of Rights are beyond danger. Sometimes, the Bill of Rights has meant the least when its protections have been needed the most. Faithfulness to the document is essential to prevent its words from becoming empty promises.

The current war on drugs may test our faithfulness. Polls taken in the summer of 1989 indicate a willingness of a majority of the American people to give up some of their constitutional rights. They may get the chance. In war, there are few rules.

Consider the Fourth Amendment, for example: "The right of the people to be secure in their persons, houses, papers, and effects, against unreasonable searches and seizures, shall not be violated, and no Warrants shall issue, but upon probable cause, supported by Oath or Affirmation, and particularly describing the place to be searched, and the persons or things to be seized." For a long time, American courts construed the Fourth Amendment to mean that a person could not be detained or searched by the police without some evidence that he or she was violating the law. This is the standard of probable cause. Even when the police acted without a warrant—that is, without the prior approval of a judicial officer—a search would be deemed a violation of the Fourth Amendment unless the officer later could demonstrate to a judge's satisfaction that sufficient cause existed to justify the search or arrest. Judges have disagreed over how much "cause" is sufficient, but, until recently, all agreed that at least some particularized suspicion was necessary—that is, evidence which pointed to a single person as a possible lawbreaker.

In *Camara v. Municipal Court* (1967), the Supreme Court made an apparently harmless exception to this rule in a case involving building inspections. It held for the first time that inspection of a building for fire or safety hazards required a warrant. At a glance, the decision seemed to be an expansion of constitutional protections because now the Fourth Amendment applied to administrative searches, not just to those by police. However, the Court then added that the warrant did not need to be particularized. An official could conduct an inspection without showing evidence in advance that *this* house or *this* factory might be unsafe. All that was needed was a general showing that certain kinds of structures tended to have certain kinds of defects. No particularized suspicion was necessary because the purpose of the inspection was not to discover criminal violations, but to protect the public's health and safety.

Here was born the doctrine of special need. Where the government conducts a search for reasons other than punishing violators, the Fourth Amendment does not apply with its usual rigor. Instead, the Constitution is satisfied as long as officials act "reasonably"—a fuzzy standard that allows any behavior appropriate for the situation at hand.

This is the theory that allows searches of all persons in certain areas of airports. Officials conduct searches of passengers and their belongings not because they think they are lawbreakers, but because they want to prevent planes and passengers from being blown out of the sky.

When applied to drug testing, the results of this judicially crafted exception to the Fourth Amendment are plain. In 1989, the Supreme Court upheld the constitutionality of two different programs. *Skinner v. Railway Labor Executives Association* involved a policy of the Federal Railroad Administration requiring urinalysis of all crew members of a train involved in an accident, even when there was no evidence that any member of the crew had been using illegal drugs. *Treasury Employees v. Von Raab* contested a rule of the Customs Service mandating urinalysis for all employees seeking transfer to certain sensitive positions. No particularized suspicion was needed. In both situations, the Court found the testing compatible with the Fourth Amendment because the government's objective was something other than law enforcement—public safety in the railroad case and public confidence in a drug-free workforce in the customs case. Similar reasoning led the Court a year later, in *Michigan Department of State Police v. Sitz,* to approve brief stops by police of all motorists at sobriety checkpoints, even when they had no grounds to believe that any particular driver was intoxicated.

It remains to be seen whether the Court will extend this thinking to other testing situations. Nonetheless, the fact remains that the Court has upheld these policies. In each, the objective is laudable. Who can be in favor of buildings that are firetraps, airplanes that carry bombs, train engineers who use drugs, customs agents who are junkies, or drivers who are drunk? Would the same reasoning, however, excuse random searches of persons on the street in an effort to reduce the number of illegal handguns in circulation? If so, what is left of the Fourth Amendment? Does it hold out protection for a dimension of privacy Americans no longer prize?

These exceptions to the Fourth Amendment lead to a third consideration—reliance on the attitude of "leave it to the judges." When we expect judges to be the exclusive guardians of the Bill of Rights, our confidence may be misplaced. To say that courts are important protectors of liberties is not to say that they should be, or even can be, the only safeguard. In the first place, what courts say the Bill of Rights means sooner or later reflects the dominant opinion in the nation. It is unreasonable to expect an institution staffed by persons not exempt from the actuarial tables to hold out for very long against tides of change.

In the second place, undue reliance on the courts excuses the rest of us from taking responsibility for the preservation of our own liberties. Through expressions of citizenship ranging from the vote to government service, people have much to say about the scope of freedoms they enjoy. Actions and attitudes of school boards, city councils, legislatures, and administrative agencies help to determine the real freedoms of all Americans. Indeed, for most citizens, the police officer on the corner is the first interpreter of the Bill of Rights. Since so few arguable violations of liberty ever are actually adjudicated in court, the practical meaning of the Bill of Rights, by necessity, is a shared responsibility.

The current controversy over abortion is a good example. One may or may not agree with the Supreme Court in *Roe v. Wade* (1973) that the Constitution protects a woman's right to terminate her pregnancy in most instances. Still, from 1973 until 1989, the right to abortion was almost exclusively a judicially protected right. Then, in 1989, five members of the Supreme Court, in *Webster v. Reproductive Health Services,* cut back on *Roe,* making it clear that states could impose new restrictions on abortion. Now, restraints on abortion largely are matters for state legislators, not judges, to decide.

A cry of protest has gone up from pro-choice forces, lamenting the demise of a woman's freedom. They say the Constitution means less after the 1989 decision. However, what has happened? Long dependent on the courts, the pro-choice side has become more active politically, seeking support from the public at large. There has yet to be a stampede of states to impose significant restrictions on abortion. While the struggle is far from over, the practical meaning of a right to abortion will not be a question decided solely by the courts.

Yes, the Bill of Rights may be in danger. Its enemies, yesterday as well as today, are misguided intentions, insensitivity, and indifference. Designed to help democracy protect itself, the document ultimately needs the support of those—the majority—who endure its restraints. Without support among the people, its provisions rest on a weak foundation. As with religion, the risk in the democratic experiment is that the form may outlive the substance of the faith.

Article 2. Too Many Rights? Too Few Duties?
by Amitai Etzioni

While championing the importance of individual rights, many groups, such as the American Civil Liberties Union, pay scant attention to the other side of the equation—that is, the concomitant responsibilities that are essential to a democratic society. Clearly, such issues as AIDS, drugs, crime, and others demand an equal willingness to assume some "adjustments" in individual rights in exchange for greater order and safety.

Mr. Etzioni is professor of sociology at George Washington University. From "Too Many Rights, Too Few Responsibilities," by Amitai Etzioni, Society, *January/February 1991, pages 41–48:*

Sometimes a finding in a survey, while of limited significance by itself, illuminates the encompassing, even debilitating, deficiency of a broader issue. One such finding has it that young Americans expect to have the right to be tried before a jury of their peers, but are quite reluctant to participate in jury duty. This finding illustrates a more general societal imbalance of people who frequently oppose bigger government and higher taxes but are anxious to expand or add governmental programs in many areas, from child care to national health insurance. By the same token, there are the patriots who call upon the United States to show its flag, say, in the Persian Gulf, but who are simultaneously opposed to serving in the armed forces, or sending their sons and daughters to serve.

Some feel so strongly about the primacy of rights and are at the same time resentful of the implications of social or communitarian responsibilities that they are blind to the peculiarity of the positions they advance. Such contradiction seems to be at the core of thinking of organizations like the American Civil Liberties Union (ACLU). A telling example is the ACLU's opposition to searches at airports, i.e., the use of x-ray machines and metal detectors, measures which are minimally intrusive and which diminish only slightly the right to travel freely, but which have significantly enhanced public safety by curtailing high-jacking in the U.S. and reducing terrorism elsewhere. In a similar vein, Dr. Theresa Crenshaw, a member of the President's Commission on the HIV Epidemic, finds herself arguing against a common objection to AIDS testing, that "[t]here is no point in having yourself tested because there is no cure." This argument completely disregards the fatal effect on others who come into contact with the infected person. It is akin to saying that if a person exhales cyanide, there is no sense in telling him of his predicament as long as there is no cure. Other radical individualists oppose seat belts and motorcycle helmets, the war against drugs, and even such innocent measures as voluntary fingerprinting of children to help cope with kidnapping.

Most Americans, though, are more reasonable. They are willing to accept some limited adjustments in their individual rights and some enhancements of their moral and public commitments in exchange for improved public safety, less drug abuse, enough order in the schools to permit teaching to take place, and to advance other compelling shared needs. I choose the term "adjustments" to indicate first of all, that only limited changes are at issue and second, to emphasize that what some consider to be a diminution of rights, however small in the eyes of some, will be viewed by others as a threat to basic freedoms, and by still others as merely a reinterpretation of recent legal traditions. Thus, checkpoints on public roads to search for drugs may be a diminution of rights for some, while others view them as a new interpretation of what constitutes a "reasonable search." (The Constitution bars "unreasonable searches," but what is "unreasonable" is a matter of interpretation.) In either case, at issue is an adjustment in the interpretation of what is deemed legal and legitimate.

The public, it must be acknowledged, finds it difficult to deal in fine gradations, especially when the issues involved are highly emotional. Hence, there is always a danger that public concern may escalate and become overzealous, leading to support for measures that are excessive and unnecessary to serve the social goals at hand. While this essay focuses on the arguments advanced by radical individualists, specifically those of their most industrious proponent, the ACLU, I am even more troubled by the opposite extremists, radical communitarians who would quarantine AIDS patients, test every school kid for drugs, and hang criminals from lamp posts at random to curb violence

ADJUSTMENTS

and impose a new tight moral order. The quest for ways to adjust certain rights—and principles upon which such adjustments are to be based—seeks new ways to attend to urgent social needs and to prevent excessive reactions. While I am aware that the media and general public ask ever more for drama, I cannot state the need for moderation and careful action more strongly. We need to reset thermostats, not shatter windows, or tear down walls.

To proceed gingerly, I deal first with the main objections raised against making any adjustments in the balance between individual rights and social responsibilities, and follow with specific criteria for a guide of how far to proceed without endangering constitutional foundations. At issue are matters of privacy and recent interpretations of the Fourth Amendment—not modifications of fundamental rights of much longer and stronger standing, of the kind involved, say, if one were to curtail the First Amendment.

Rights and responsibilities are, of course, much more encompassing than constitutional and even legal issues; they embrace matters of public morality and personal agendas. Here, however, the focus is limited to issues inherent in the debate over whether or not some constitutional rights need to be adjusted, because these matters in particular get at the heart of the existing imbalance between excessive individual rights and insufficient social responsibility, and because they illuminate the deep connections between constitutional questions and other aspects of public morality, social values, and civic virtue. In other words, while the question of rights and responsibilities can be discussed abstractly or in grand philosophical terms, in reality the issues are fortunately played out in much lower keys. Should there be mandatory drug testing for train engineers? Can we expel a disruptive student from a public school without a full-blown hearing? Should we require AIDS patients to disclose their sexual partners? Should the Miranda rule, a suspected criminal's right to be informed of his or her rights, be curbed?

SUSPICION OF GOVERNMENT AUTHORITY

Beneath the opposition by radical individualists to all adjustments of individual rights lies a deep-seated suspicion of government authority. Gene Guerrero, an ACLU representative who opposes drug testing, cites Justice Louis Brandeis: "Experience should teach us to be most on guard to protect liberty when the Government's purposes are beneficent. Men born to freedom are naturally alert to repel invasions of their liberty by evil-minded rulers. The greatest dangers to liberty lurk in insidious encounters by men of zeal, well-meaning but without understanding."

However, if this viewpoint is applied to a functioning democratic government—if one plays on the fear that the nation might at any moment be overturned by a totalitarian movement—then one comes to quite untenable conclusions, including resistance to adjustments of constitutional rights, however compelling the social need. Constitutional rights end up being perceived not as a basis for sound government actions, but merely as protection against government.

This position is reflected in the ACLU opposition to mandatory contact-tracing for those infected with AIDS: "People fear that their confidentiality won't be protected because lists can be stolen and because, once the list exists, there can be no assurance that legislatures won't pass future laws permitting persons other than public health officials from having access to it. Once the government has a list of names, addresses, sexual preferences and other information about people who test positive for the AIDS virus and their partners . . . there is no way to guarantee that, whatever the confidentiality protections today, future laws won't be passed to allow insurers, school systems, or other state agencies to have access to such a list."

By that logic, one can never act because it is quite true that it is never possible to know with 100 percent accuracy what might occur at some point in the future. True, it is necessary at all times to bolster our freedoms, from providing civic education to imposing proper penalties on those who violate the law by unauthorized disclosure of information in government files, as has been done, with a high, although admittedly not a perfect, degree of success, with the Internal Revenue Service. The potential for leaks or other violations need not stop us from drawing on the government, when appropriate, only because at some unknown time, in some unknown way, somebody might abuse the information that is being collected. Despite some serious abuses of Internal Revenue Service files by the Nixon administration, the country is doubtlessly better off having such information on file. Without it, we could hardly finance our social services or defense.

Yet the lengths to which one can be driven by suspicion is highlighted by the ACLU's opposition to voluntary fingerprinting of children in the schools, so that kidnapped children when found—often years later—can be more readily identified. Fingerprinting also facilitates identification of bodies, sparing parents years of vain searching for a missing child. The ACLU devotes a policy position, "Children's Rights," to opposing the program. Why? Because the

45

government agencies might gain access to the fingerprints and disseminate records without the child's consent and without a warrant. Furthermore, the ACLU's institutionalized paranoia leads it to believe that "fingerprinting tends to condition children and society to accept without protest unnecessary personal data collection and other invasions of privacy." This is sociological rubbish, akin to saying that getting a driver's license or responding to the census will "condition" one to life in a police state.

This radical individualist position is a call for paralysis with human and moral consequences that may quickly exceed those of marginally modifying legal traditions, and one which directly invites grand disillusionment with the civic order. This, in turn, leads to calls to "suspend the Constitution." If we are not to act out of fear that somehow an innocent law may one day lead to tyranny, we may well set forth the conditions that cause the kind and level of social distress which serves those who call for "strong" government. What is needed is a lean, well-contained government, not to proceed at every step on the assumption that no government act can be sanitized.

The argument has been made that often dogmatic, if not extreme, positions taken by the ACLU and other radical individualists are useful because they keep the amalgam of politics, the result of numerous tugs and pulls among many forces, more closely allied with individual rights than it would be if they were more reasonable or accommodating. However, extremism in the defense of virtue is a vice. Arguments advanced by radical individualists do cause harm, as they are used by policymakers and by courts to block programs that respond to compelling social needs. These arguments are not part of a healthy give-and-take in which their extreme nature is mitigated by the equally extreme positions of others. Rather than doctrines of excess, what is needed is cautious crafting of middle-of-the-road policies that take into account ways of dealing with social needs while only minimally modifying individual rights—exactly the gentle mix the radicals undermine so effectively.

A SLIPPERY SLOPE

Probably the most commonly used argument against making adjustments in the balance between individual rights and social responsibilities is the one that draws on a bogus piece of sociological wisdom which says once one seeks to modify a tradition, it will crumble. This argument is often used by orthodox Jews to oppose any changes in Judaism (e.g. seating men and women together in synagogue), as well as by Catholic traditionalists

(e.g. conducting Mass in the vernacular). To use another analogy, it is widely held that moral order is like someone precariously perched on top of a hill; if one so much as sets a foot on the edge of the slope, one will end up on one's rear end at the bottom of the heap. Referring to the "dangers" of anti-smoking legislation, sociologist Barry Glasner takes the plunge: ". . . if this pattern continues, we'll have a homogenized population in which everybody will be within recommended weight ranges, and nobody will smoke anymore, and nobody will drink and everybody will work out."

Over the years, most people have become accustomed to having themselves and their luggage searched at airports without much inconvenience. Yet the ACLU opposed airport security not only because it violates, they said, the Fourth Amendment, but also because of what they feared it might lead to. Thus one of its policy statements reads: "Regrettably, we live in dangerous times. If the danger posed in one situation is thought to justify unconstitutional, emergency measures, where can the line be drawn? Today it is airports, tomorrow it may be banks or city streets." The argument is not wholly without merit. Once taboos are broken by a community and modification of its ethical code is tolerated, it is often not easy to find a stopping place. Those who challenge the traditional vows of fidelity in marriage often find it difficult to sustain their marital contracts and frequently end up with no stable relationships at all. And "reform" in Judaism was followed (although it may well have occurred anyhow) by a massive flight from religious commitment. At the same time, it is also equally evident that we do not end up at the bottom each time we collectively negotiate a step on the top of what are potentially slippery slopes. Not every young woman who allows herself to be kissed (let alone goes further) before marriage ends up a hooker, as some of our forefathers and mothers warned, and not everyone who experiments with marijuana ends up a crack addict. Similarly, sexual education in schools has not lead to new heights of promiscuity, orgies, and the destruction of American society as archconservatives had feared. This goes to show that societies can modify their moral codes without necessarily losing their grip.

PRINCIPLES FOR LIMITED ADJUSTMENTS

What is needed are principles that delineate how far one can travel in the new direction, what steps on the slope one is allowed to negotiate without free fall.

Clear and present danger. Adjustments should only be implemented if there is a clear and present danger—a real, readily verifiable, sizeable social problem or need. Unfortunately, in a "media-ized" society, prophets of alarm rapidly gain wide audiences. There are frequent calls on policymakers and citizens alike to tighten their belts and modify their lifestyles, as well as calls for laws and constitutional protection to combat some imagined or anticipated scourge. For example, in the mid-1970s Americans were told that they must be forced out of cars and into mass transit because the United States was running out of oil, and, more recently, that America must introduce central planning in order to compete with the Japanese, and so on.

If policymakers and citizens were to respond to all these cries of "wolf," society would periodically be run through the wringer, shaken and rearranged at great cost. Unfortunately, on most issues it is nearly impossible to discern well in advance which dangers are real and which are wildly exaggerated, if not outright false. Hence, one must, however reluctantly, reach the humble conclusion that the best way to respond is not to try to anticipate too far into the future and to embrace the humbler posture of not acting until there is a clear and present danger. Nuclear weapons, handguns, AIDS, and crack are clear and present. The evidence that they endanger large numbers of lives, if not the very existence of our society, are incontestable. Killer bees are not, and the heating of the climate may not justify the kind of draconian measures the alarmists advocate. Other measures are justified because of the direct link between the cause and effect; if someone points a machine gun at a person's head, one has a right to take away the others' "property," even wrestle the assailant to the ground. The danger is clear and present. At the same time, we would condemn, indeed penalize, the same conduct on the mere suspicion that a gun owner put a weapon to that use.

A good illustration of this issue is the case of transportation workers. After several train accidents, the United States Department of Transportation determined that there was enough of a problem to warrant random testing of train engineers (who drive the trains) for drug and alcohol use. Radical individualists opposed the policy on the usual grounds that only individualized case-by-case evidence of "probable cause" constitutes proper cause. Testing, according to their claim, is not even permissible if an engineer is seen stumbling away after a wreck unless there is evidence of drinking or drugs use, etc. In February of 1988, a Federal Appeals Court in California agreed with these individualists and ruled that it is unconstitutional to administer drug tests to those who drive trains.

The following evidence suggests which data may be considered sufficient to show a direct link. A 1979 study found that 23 percent of railroad operating employees were "problem drinkers," many of them having gotten drunk on the job. Of all the train accidents between 1975 and 1984, drugs or alcohol were "directly affecting" causes in forty-eight of them, accounting for thirty-seven fatalities and eighty injuries. Since then, the danger seems to have become only worse. Out of 179 railroad accidents in 1987, engineers in 39 of the cases tested positive for drugs, 34 percent more than in 1986. Following a January 1987 crash between an Amtrack and Conrail train, in which 16 people died and 174 were injured, the engineer and the brakemen were found to have been under the influence of marijuana.

While there are no simple mechanical numbers or criteria, it seems that when 23 percent, that is, nearly one out of four transportation workers is affected and when those involved deal directly with life and death (unlike the National Weather Bureau staff, which was also to be tested!), we hold that random testing of train engineers and other high-risk groups, such as airline pilots, for drugs and alcohol, is justified. Once it is established that there is a clear and present danger, the matter must then be examined against other criteria.

Modifying the constitutional balance. Assume we agree as a community that the human toll is such that we should discourage smoking (over 300,000 people in the United States die from smoking annually), especially among the young. Moreover, let us assume that we agree that the link between smoking and ill consequences is sufficiently tight for it to be considered a direct cause, hence, justifies an adjustment. Even if we accept the radical individualist notion that people ought to be free to choose their purchases, moral justification can be found in the fact that, as Robert Goodin points out, smoking seems to be harmful to others. Passive smoking has been attributed as the cause of approximately 2400 cases of lung cancer per year and in 1986 approximately 1600 people died in fires caused by smoking. In addition, the fact that smokers show that their real preference is to stop—90 percent of all smokers have tried to quit—is a signal for help.

Now assume that these findings, if they hold under further scrutiny (e.g., there are serious questions about the magnitude of secondary effects), indicate a clear and present danger; it does not yet follow that we need to make a constitutional adjustment. We first ought to look for ways that do not necessitate tampering with the Constitution. Armed with these criteria, we are likely to conclude that raising taxes on cigarettes is more justifiable than prohibiting cigarette ads. For one, the result is more efficient; a 10 percent increase in price is reported to correlate with a 12 percent decrease in demand. Other studies corroborate this by demonstrating that young people's taste for cigarettes is highly controlled by their price. Secondly, and more to the point, curbing ads raises constitutional issues of freedom of speech while raising taxes does not. Hence, even if curbing ads proved to be somewhat more efficent, raising taxes would still be preferable as long as one can show that cigarette advertisements are not significantly more influential than prices.

Ways of minimal intrusion. Once it is established that there is no effective alternative to adjusting the constitutional balance between individual rights and social responsibilities (e.g. that to prevent the harms of side-stream smoke and in order not to impose the health care costs on society caused by smoking), we must look for options that will make the most minimal intrusion possible, rather than proceeding with a sledge hammer.

MIRANDA RIGHTS

An examination of the debate over the issue of Miranda rights, the rule that a suspected criminal must be informed of his rights prior to being arrested, provides a good example of how ways may be found to trim rather than hack. In recent years, "Miranda" has come under criticism as being excessively favorable toward criminals. The extent to which these rules actually hobble the work of the police and prosecutors is a much-debated and scrutinized topic warranting long study just to sort out this question. It is difficult to tell whether recent court rulings have already sharply or only moderately affected the reach of Miranda, although most would agree that over the last ten years, the balance has tilted somewhat toward lesser rights for criminals and more toward public safety. Our concern here is to illustrate what a reasonable intermediary position looks like rather than settling many of the attending intricacies.

At one extreme is the radical individualist position that no changes are to be made whatsoever, as if a rather recent legal tradition, not in effect until 1966, has the standing of the Bill of Rights and the sanction of the Founding Fathers. On the other hand, radical communitarians argue that many rights accord criminals more constitutional protection than is afforded their victims. Former Attorney General Edwin Meese wanted to do away with Miranda Rights altogether because, he said, "it provides incentives for criminals not to talk" and "only helps guilty defendants." The Office of Legal Policy of the U.S. Attorney General under the

Reagan Administration issued a position paper that called for a wholesale overturning of the Miranda decision.

A reasonable intermediary position seems to be to let the evidence stand as it was collected despite possible technical errors as long as there is no indication of bad faith, and making sure to include an indication of the error in the relevant personnel file at the appropriate law enforcement agency to avoid repetition. In a 1985 Supreme Court case of a suspect who had confessed to a crime before he was read his rights, was later informed of his rights, and then confessed again, the Court unanimously agreed that the first confession could not be used as evidence even if given voluntarily and without coercion, but ruled, six to three, that the unsolicited admission of guilt did not taint the second confession. In 1987, the Supreme Court ruled that the police are not required to inform a suspect about each crime being investigated because the Miranda decision specifically requires that the police inform a suspect of his right to remain silent and that anything he says may be used against him.

Another example of a carefully honed adjustment is the introduction of some restrictions on the inadmissibility of evidence uncovered during discovery which was technically flawed. In United States v. Leon, the police thought they had obtained a search warrant for a house wherein they gathered incriminating evidence. Later it was discovered that the clerk had written the address incorrectly on the search warrant. In 1984 the Supreme Court ruled that the evidence gathered should not be excluded on the basis of the technical mistake. TECHNICAL FLAWS

The debate over the rights of students provides still another example of a reasonable intermediary position. Many observers agree that both substantive rights of students in public schools and their due process rights have reached a level that has made it difficult for public schools to function. Linda Bruin, legal counsel for the Michigan Association of School Boards writes, "Following the split decision in Goss v. Lopez, 419 US 565 (1975), which struck down an Ohio statute permitting student suspensions from school without a hearing, educators expressed fears that they no longer would be able to discipline students efficiently."

What is an intermediary position between according students full-fledged Fourth Amendment rights, in effect deterring teachers and principals from suspending them, and declaring students fair game for any capricious school authority? It seems reasonable that students who are subject to expulsion and suspension should be granted due process to the extent that they are notified of the nature of their misconduct and given an opportunity to respond; both actions must occur before the expulsion takes place. Expulsion need not guarantee students the right to counsel or cross examination and calling of witnesses. This would unduly encumber a school's ability to maintain an educational environment and their right to impose additional restrictions and simplified procedures for internal purposes. This is far from a novel approach, for several state courts have already modified school policies in the directions we suggest.

"NOTCHES" To reduce the danger of slipping down the slope, it is important to draw moral and legal "notches" along the way. While it may be appropriate for students charged with expulsion to insist on due process, they need not be granted the same opportunities when they want to protest a grade. Radical individualists are strongly opposed to any modification of due process with regard to searches, seizures, and tests without presentation, before the fact, of case-by-case compelling evidence to a third party, an independent judge. Radical communitarians would suspend such constitutional protections to "win the war on drugs." Others who, like the author, seek intermediate, principled "notches," find that one can make a strong case that random searches of automobiles on public highways are significantly different from random searches of homes. Automobiles are an optional means of transportation, convey passengers on public territory, and travel in places where behavior under the influence of drugs may affect others: homes are true castles, truly private, and what we do in them is much less likely to harm others.

Another reasonable measure is to require people who drive into open-air drug markets to show their driver's license and car registration. This situation arose in Inkster, Michigan, a small community just outside Detroit, where the drug trade was so furious local residents could rarely take to the streets and lived in constant fear of their lives and the corruption of their children. The county sheriff set up roadblocks from one to four each afternoon, checking drivers' licenses and registrations. The tactic broke up the open drug market but had to be stopped when the ACLU intervened and the court accepted its arguments.

Another option to abate open-air drug trafficking is the proposal by the Mayor of Alexandria, Virginia, to arrest those who are "loitering for purposes of engaging in unlawful drug transaction." Unlike old loitering laws which were used by the police to harass minorities, the new "loitering plus" statutes are designed to prevent such violations by defining eight conditions that must be met before an arrest can be made. The person must be on the street in a drug trafficking area for more than fifteen minutes during which he or she must have face-to-face contact with more than one person involving actions which indicate that they are concealing an object to be exchanged, and so on.

One may devise new measures designed to reduce the constitutional impact of the suggested adjustments. The Supreme Court, in June of 1990, approved of roadside sobriety checkpoints, which the ACLU had successfully opposed in several states. The searches at these checkpoints, the Supreme Court majority argued, are minimally intrusive and last less than thirty seconds. Going one step further, the "intrusion" of the checkpoints is diminished even more if the authorities systematically and repeatedly inform drivers that such checkpoints are being operated, without disclosing their precise locations. This hardly detracts from their efficiency but makes them less threatening to legal traditions, because once the potential of a search on a given road is posted, travel thereon can be construed as implied consent. Likewise, job requirements for all new train engineers, air traffic controllers, police persons, and other workers whose professions entail high risk to the public may include consent to be subject to drug and alcohol tests. (Workers who are already on the job may be given a year's time to relocate if they refuse to accept the new requirement.) Aside from legal considerations, there are matters concerning the practical burdens involved. For example, courts may correctly object to sobriety test points that create major traffic jams and insist that there will be safe places for drivers to pull off the road and that drivers have adequate warning that they must stop, etc. Indeed, the fact that these tests last less than half a minute is in their favor. So is the short delay airport searches impose. The objection that urine tests are highly intrusive, that, as one judge said, they "require employees to perform an excretory function traditionally shielded by great privacy," is quite compelling. While it is both useful and convenient to distinguish between legal and practical considerations, it should be noted that they are intertwined. To wit, practical burdens could rise to a point that they become a form of government harassment which is one of the main infractions from which the Bill of Rights is meant to protect us.

In short, far from yielding to demands to gun down any private, unidentified airplane or speed boat that approaches a United States border, break down doors of people's homes at midnight, quarantine all HIV positive persons, and so on, to combat drugs and AIDS, we see justification to introduce measures that are minimally intrusive, in either legal or practical

IMPLIED CONSENT

terms. Thus, sobriety checkpoints, searches of cars on public roads, testing of train engineers, pilots, air traffic controllers and other individuals whose jobs entail high risks to others, and requiring AIDS patients to disclose sexual partners if the precautions indicated are taken, are overdue, legitimate adjustments.

Minimize side effects. Aside from checking policies against the listed criteria, pains should be taken to reduce deleterious offshoots of a given policy. For example, AIDS testing and contact-tracing can lead to the loss of a job and health insurance if confidentiality is not maintained. Hence, any introduction of such a program should be accompanied by a thorough review of control of access to lists of names of those tested, procedures used in contacting sexual partners, professional education programs on the need for confidentiality, and penalties for unauthorized disclosure and especially for those who discriminate against AIDS patients or HIV carriers. All this may seem quite cumbersome, but in view of the great dangers AIDS poses for individuals and the high costs to society, these measures are clearly appropriate. A good example of a program that has kept negative side effects to a minimum and has enhanced its acceptability is the use of x-rays and metal detectors at airports to uncover weapons that may otherwise be brought on board and prevents high-jacking. The searches are deliberately not used to stop drug trafficking and other crimes.

MISUSE OF EFFICIENCY

An examination of numerous writings, court briefs, and congressional testimony of radical individualists reveals a common pattern. Much more attention is paid to the alleged inefficiencies of the suggested policy modifications than to the constitutional and moral legitimacy. This is surprising, because the opponents of the suggested adjustments are, as a rule, not particularly schooled or trained in technical evaluation of the policies involved and hardly care to find new or remodeled government "interventions" that work effectively. It seems that the underlying motivation is not a genuine quest for efficiency or cost-benefit assessment, an examination that definitely has its place next to, and in addition to, moral/constitutional evaluation. Obviously, if one can show that a planned step or program cannot work, or worse, that it is counterproductive, this is a more compelling way to lay it to rest than arguing that protecting, for example, some interpretation of the Fourth Amendment is more important than, say, preventing drunk and stoned train engineers from derailing trains, or removing guns from the schools.

The misuse, indeed disingenuousness, of the efficiency argument on the part of the ACLU and others is evident in several ways. First, when radical individualists evaluate any suggestions for government intervention, they predictably find them always to be unreasonable, unproductive, ineffectual, inefficient. Yet they reach these conclusions without making any scientific attempt to collect facts and interpret them systematically and fairly. Instead, facts are picked and interwoven to shape a "case" the way lawyers do while filing a brief, rather than as scholars or scientists would.

A typical example of this is an ACLU position *CONJECTURE* paper that evaluates "mandatory contact tracing" of AIDS patients in seven ways, finding no merits and only deficiencies. First, the ACLU claims that contact-tracing would drive people away from voluntary testing sites and hence have a counterproductive effect. No evidence is given, only conjecture. The question of whether the policy is efficient on the grounds that while some are driven away, many others are helped to stop infecting still others, is not examined.

Next, the ACLU argues that "contact tracing depends on the cooperation of the tested person." It is argued that "requiring" disclosure is meaningless, that it is "no more likely to achieve its ultimate goal of notification than a voluntary model." No evidence is given, and the total experience of sanctioning by law (the fact that the fear of sanction is a factor in one's decision-making), the expressive role of law (it captures and communicates our values), and the interactive effect between law and voluntary morality (we tend to do what is right in part so nobody will make us do it) are all ignored, and so on.

Evidence that mandatory testing will drive people away is taken from a highly speculative story in the *Chicago Tribune* which deals with the first days of the program, before people had a chance to discover the extent to which its confidentiality was maintained. In another case, the ACLU cites a statement by Senator Jesse Helms of North Carolina, advocating isolation of those who test positive, as evidence of potential government action. In still another ACLU position paper, the standards according to which tests are deemed acceptable, are set so high, nothing could qualify. According to their view testing for the HIV virus is worthless because "there is as yet no way to cure AIDS or to render it incommunicable."

Finally, it is evident that even if somehow these interventions could be made or would turn out to be beneficial, the radical individualists would continue to oppose them as vehemently as before. For example, a major argument against testing train engineers for drugs, even after a wreck, is that the presence of drugs is said not to be evidence of impairment. However, the same radical individualists also oppose sobriety tests, despite the fact that the presence of alcohol above a certain level certainly does impair performance and judgment. Similarly, the ACLU states: "Even if there was empirical evidence indicating that Miranda has impeded law enforcement, this would be an insufficient basis to overturn the decision . . . thus, even though the Office of Legal Policy's evidence of a negative impact on law enforcement is extraordinarily weak, its argument for overturning Miranda would have to be rejected even if the argument were based on stronger evidence."

So the underlying structure of many of these arguments is 'Let's argue for the inefficiency, but if it turns out to be efficient, let's oppose it anyhow.' In short, one surely would not favor even a small adjustment of the balance between individual rights and social responsibilities in favor of, say, public safety, if the policy is inefficient; nor does even a major gain in efficiency justify setting aside a major constitutional tenet. But when the policies can be shown to be effectual and the adjustment can be made to be limited, this is a direction in which we ought to go. The Constitution is a living creation; it has and will continue to be adjusted to new facts of life, although it needs to be tuned with great caution and care, never wantonly.

The world is not on fire, although those caught in the cross fire of gangs in some parts of Los Angeles or between drug dealers in the nation's capital, may think otherwise. Hence,

cries to set aside constitutional protections to "win the war" against drugs or any other enemy, are at this stage not justified. However, precisely because additional deterioration of the civic order may play into the hands of alarmists, and because the social needs they call to attention do constitute clear and present dangers, we need to act. Clearly, business as usual will not do. The purists, who wish to stick to their favorite interpretations of constitutional rights and not give an inch, do not allow us to adjust to the new societal realities.

Obviously much that needs to be done has to take place in other societal realms, from reforming schools to designing an economy that will provide better jobs for youngsters in ghettos. However, the moral climate is significant, as is its expression in the laws of the land. Unfortunately, there is a kernel of truth in the slogan that "me-ism" is rampant. To help shore up the civic order, Americans will need to give up some of their cherished rights to travel unencumbered, and those who work in high-risk jobs will need to be tested for drugs; some will have to disclose names of sexual contacts and take other such measures that are far from appealing to a free people in a free society, but which seem quite justified under the circumstances. The details of working out what needs to be done may seem complicated and cumbersome. They may well not be dramatic enough to play on the evening news. However, given the fragile nature of all freedoms, adjustments should be made gingerly rather than sweepingly, but adjustments should, nonetheless, be made.

Article 3.   Human Needs, Human Rights: Time for a Second Bill of Rights
by Paul Savoy

As the nation celebrates the 200th anniversary of the ratification of the Bill of Rights, it is time to seriously debate the pressing need for an economic Bill of Rights—one that guarantees every American such basic rights as a decent home, job, education, nutrition, and health care. In addition to the protection of civil rights, Americans must insist upon the expansion of the Constitution to include the equally important ideal of economic justice.

This year the nation will celebrate the 200th anniversary of the ratification of the Bill of Rights. The occasion provides a timely opportunity for liberals and progressives to consider constitutional reform as a means for achieving what the political process has so far failed to accomplish: closing the widening gap between the rich and the

poor, and assuring every person the means with which to secure a quality of life worthy of human dignity. It is time to seriously consider adopting an economic Bill of Rights.

The call to begin this debate has already issued from several sources. Former Senator George McGovern, in a commencement address at Lincoln

Law School on May 19, evoked the spirit of F.D.R.'s 1944 State of the Union Message, in which the President called upon Congress to explore means for implementing "a second Bill of Rights," which would make the right to economic and social security as important as the political ideals of freedom and self-government. "Although the Constitution has endured through the ages," McGovern said, "it is time to think about a Bill of Economic and Social Rights that secures the blessings of a decent home and a decent job, nutrition, education, public safety and public transportation, medical care and preservation of the earth's resources." The National Organization for Women's Commission for Responsive Democracy has been holding public hearings during the past six months to explore the possibility of a new political party that would include in its platform a "Bill of Rights for the 21st Century." That document, adopted by NOW at its 1989 annual conference, would expand equality rights and add to the Constitution reproductive rights, environmental rights, rights against violence and "a right to a decent standard of living, including adequate food, housing, health care and education."

In a nation endowed with such enormous private and public wealth, one out of every five infants is born into poverty, 30 million Americans are living below the poverty line, major cities in the United States are experiencing a 20 to 25 percent rise in hunger and homelessness, some 32 million Americans have no health coverage and more than 5 million children go to bed hungry every night. If Americans have become numb to these statistics, it is not because of the atrophy of the human heart but rather because of a radical failure of political will and moral vision.

Contrary to conventional wisdom, neither renewed consumer confidence nor increased productivity can remedy the growing economic insecurity of the American people. A 1989 Ford Foundation report, *The Common Good: Social Welfare and the American Future*, dispels the cruel illusion that the country can rely on economic growth alone to guarantee all Americans a decent standard of living: "A healthy economy, while essential, will not of itself generate the human investments and mutual caring that are necessary for a strong, just society. . . . While America has grown properly skeptical of programs that foster dependency, it has also learned that it is futile to ask people to take greater personal responsibility for their lives unless they have a real chance to escape from material conditions that foster insecurity and despair."

Before the clock strikes midnight, twenty-seven children in America will have died today from poverty, violence and social neglect. Although we like to think of ourselves as a generous people, there is in the very nature of our legal and political

Paul Savoy, an attorney specializing in constitutional law, is a former dean of John F. Kennedy University School of Law.

institutions a systematic indifference to human suffering. In a lawsuit brought in behalf of a 4-year-old who was brutally beaten by his father and suffered such severe brain damage that he will spend the rest of his life in an institution for the mentally retarded, the Supreme Court ruled in 1989 that county welfare officials could not be sued for failing to remove the child from his father's custody despite their knowledge of a long history of abuse. Although regretting the result as "undeniably tragic," Chief Justice William Rehnquist, in his opinion for the Court, declared that the Constitution "confer[s] no affirmative right to governmental aid, even when such aid may be necessary to secure life."

Our civil rights and civil liberties are rights in the negative sense. The provisions of the Bill of Rights guaranteeing freedom of speech and religion and due process of law are protections *from* government. They do not include affirmative obligations *on* government. We do not have a constitutional right to have the state provide us with health care, or give us shelter if we are homeless, or prevent a child from being beaten or from starving to death. This is what Columbia University law professor Louis Henkin describes as one of "the serious genetic defects" of our Bill of Rights. Professor Henkin, who is co-director of the Center for the Study of Human Rights at Columbia, points out that the "international human rights movement that developed after the Second World War gives equal place to economic and social rights, but these human rights have no constitutional status in the U.S." We have developed a broad range of legislative programs in America to provide aid to dependent children, health and nutrition services, housing allowances, unemployment and disability insurance, and other social protections for individuals. However, since they have not been put into the Constitution, these benefits are not fundamental entitlements but are subject to budgetary constraints, the shifting winds of the political process, and the competing demands of defense spending and other federal programs.

Moreover, the beneficiaries of most social welfare programs continue to be treated as charity recipients rather than rights-holders in the same sense that we regard *The New York Times* as the holder of a right to freedom of the press. Why, aside from a long history of social prejudice, should this be so? Why does a person have a constitutional right to free speech, or a right to a lawyer if charged with a crime, but no right to be fed if he or she is starving? By expanding the concept of constitutional rights to include the affirmative right to a decent standard of living, it is possible to create an entirely new form of politics out of what Vaclav Havel has called "the phenomenon of the human conscience."

The great challenge for men and women of conscience and vision in America is to build a politics that will elevate progressive causes to constitutional status. It is a politics that speaks to the fundamental right to live in a just and humane society, free not only from discrimination on the basis of race, sex, age, sexual orientation, health condition or physical disability but free from hunger, homelessness, unemployment, illiteracy, drug abuse, high infant mortality, inadequate health care and a toxic environment. It is a politics of institutional transformation that can begin with a call for a Bill of Human Rights and Services that would expand our existing constitutional rights to include:

§ the right to a quality of life worthy of human dignity, including adequate nutrition, clothing, housing, public transportation, health care and other social services necessary to satisfy basic human needs.

§ the right of families to special protection, guaranteeing prenatal care, child care, and a reasonable period of leave for family illness or the birth of a child, and family planning assistance, including the right to choose an abortion.

§ the right to an education sufficient to prepare individuals for suitable occupations or professions of their own choosing and to enable them to participate in the cultural life of their community.

§ the right to employment, with guaranteed public-sector jobs for those who cannot find work in the private sector, at fair and favorable wages, with equal pay for equal work.

§ the right to adequate income maintenance in the event of unemployment, illness, disability or other lack of livelihood in circumstances beyond the control of the individual.

§ the right to clean air, clean water and renewable sources of energy, with citizen-plaintiffs granted standing to represent the interests of an endangered planet.

§ the right to economic and social security for future generations of older Americans.

No constitutional plan can or should dictate a particular means for implementing economic and social rights. It would be up to Congress to decide, for example, how a constitutional guarantee of employment and job training should be apportioned between public-works programs and government contracts with private employers. Similarly, Congress would have latitude to decide whether the basic necessities of life should be provided by supplementing a full-employment plan with a guaranteed-income program or with an assistance program similar to the existing welfare system. Congress also would have discretion to determine whether a guarantee of universal health care should be implemented according to the Canadian model of public insurance, which uses tax dollars to provide essential medical care to everyone at no charge, or by allocating responsibility between government programs and publicly mandated employer contributions to private insurance plans. However, without a constitutional mandate for socializing economic opportunities and correcting the failures of the nation's system of health and social services, such proposals will be treated by Congress as so much pie-in-the-sky that can be ignored as too costly.

By requiring Congress to put human needs before military needs, a bill of economic and social rights would compel reductions in the defense budget and yield a substantial portion of the revenue needed to pay the bill. A 25 percent cut in defense spending would produce a quarter of a trillion dollars over a three-year period at current spending levels. The cost of launching two Patriot missiles would provide health care for 13,000 homeless children through a mobile medical outreach program. The cost of feeding U.S. troops in the Persian Gulf for one month would provide meals for a million children for a year through the National School Lunch Program. The cost of chemical protection suits ordered by the Pentagon would provide health, education and medical services for 4 million women a year through Planned Parenthood.

Adoption of an economic Bill of Rights can be accomplished by existing constitutional procedures. Article V of the Constitution provides two avenues for proposing amendments. The first would require the concurrence of two-thirds majorities in both houses of Congress. The second would permit a populist movement to circumvent Congress by calling for a constitutional convention to propose amendments. On the application of the legislatures of two-thirds of the states, Congress would be required to convene a constitutional convention for the purpose of proposing a Bill of Human Rights and Services. If adopted by the convention, those amendments would then be submitted to state legislatures or popularly elected state conventions to decide whether Washington would be required by a second Bill of Rights to invest at least as much in rebuilding Newark and New Orleans as it has spent in destroying Baghdad and Basra. Ratification of a Bill of Human Rights and Services by three-fourths of the state legislatures or conventions would finally make economic democracy the supreme law of the land.

Because it is on Main Street, not on Pennsylvania Avenue, that the impact of cuts in federal spending is felt, it is in state capitals, not on Capitol Hill, that a constitutional reform movement will most likely begin. America's greatest hope for real change in humanizing capitalism and redefining national priorities thus resides with grass-roots movements and leadership at the state and local level. As former Texas Agriculture Commissioner Jim Hightower has noted, "The truth makes sense in the places where we live."

The call for a constitutional convention may seem extreme, but the state of the Union is extreme. This is an economy in which our cities are in danger of becoming embattled citadels resembling scenes from *Escape From New York*. This is a nation in which a Democratic-controlled Congress lacks the political will to enact a strong civil rights bill or a comprehensive system of national health insurance. This is a democracy that, as a practical matter, is governed to a far greater extent by a one-party system than most countries in Eastern Europe; a democracy in which electoral politics has become so dominated by the power of money that civil rights and social programs are endangered as never before.

Some may see a call for constitutional reform by a populist movement as perilous to liberal and progressive causes. A constitutional convention summoned for the purpose of proposing a bill of economic and social rights could arguably propose other amendments that would repeal or restrict existing guarantees such as the separation of church and state, the rights of criminal suspects, and other civil rights and civil liberties. Although constitutional scholars remain deeply divided over the issue, fears of a runaway convention are exaggerated. In 1973 the American Bar Association, upon the recommendation of a Special Constitutional Convention Study Committee, approved a resolution stating that "Congress has the power to establish procedures limiting a convention to the subject matter which is stated in the applications received from the state legislatures." In 1984 the Senate Judiciary Committee, citing the opinions of a substantial number of constitutional scholars, approved a bill that would impose such limits on constitutional conventions and require selection of delegates by popular election. Stanford University law professor Gerald Gunther, expressing a minority view, cautions that "the final authority to determine the convention's agenda rests with the convention itself." As a practical matter, however, if Congress were to enact limiting legislation and later refuse to submit runaway amendments to the states for ratification, the Supreme Court, which is ideologically committed to judicial restraint, would most likely defer to Congress.

How a new Bill of Rights should be enacted—whether by constitutional amendment or, as some have suggested, by new civil rights legislation expanding the constitutional ideal of equality to include economic and social security, or by other means—is an issue that is likely to stir considerable controversy. What is essential is that a wide-ranging national debate begin and that we begin to chart the road toward establishing an adequate standard of living as an entitlement of all Americans.

The average citizen makes the mistake of leaving the Constitution to lawyers and matters of the common good to special interests. This is unfortunate because lawyers are not commonly advocates for constitutional reform and the public good is no gift of government lobbyists. As the country slides deeper into a recession of the economy and the human spirit, progressives confront a fateful choice: A broad coalition of civil rights groups, feminists, labor organizations, environmentalists, health activists, children's rights advocates and lower-income constituencies can either build a second civil rights movement—this one aimed at ending economic as well as racial apartheid in America—or we must learn to accept the consequences of politics as usual, with less blaming of our political representatives and fewer illusions.

The expansion and protection of civil rights and human services in America have been won only when grass-roots movements have held up a candle to the vision of the human spirit in the face of the indifference or opposition of the politicians. However difficult such a task may be, there are fair, progressive and dignified ways to share the burdens of our fundamental human vulnerability, and we should not shrink from finally declaring that this is one of the great purposes for which our Constitution should be reordained and rededicated.   □

Chapter **4**

Federalism

Article 1. The Backlash Against Government Threatens Those Least to Blame
by John Herbers

The author examines the status of "fend-for-yourself" federalism, which emerged in the 1980s as a result of the Reagan Administration's decision to return many previously funded federal programs to state and local governments. Although the policy produced some initial successes, it soon became clear that the federal system lacked the resources, responsibility, and leadership necessary to assist local and regional leaders to meet the increased challenges.

Back in the 1970s, not too long after he had left his job as secretary of the U.S. Department of Health, Education and Welfare, John Gardner observed that domestic problems are so difficult to solve that presidents had a way of escaping into foreign affairs in order to maintain some measure of popularity with the people.

He was right then and is right now. Gardner's remark comes back to mind at this time because the Persian Gulf crisis, like other foreign crises, whoever was to blame, has brought about the traditional rallying around the national government by friends and enemies alike. And that may well have sealed the fate of that unexpected and remarkable (though still partial) success known as "fend-for-yourself" federalism, which came into existence as the result of the federal government's withdrawal from domestic programs during the Reagan era. That left states and local governments to carry the burden.

Until recently, those who believe that government should act in behalf of the equality and well-being of its

From *Governing*, November 1990, p. 11. Reprinted by permission, *Governing* magazine, copyright 1990.

citizens could point to surprising dividends from the forced devolution of responsibility to the lower levels of government. It had the positive effect of setting off wave after wave of innovations and reforms at the state and local levels that promised to bring a governance far superior to the top-heavy, undifferentiated, sometimes ham-handed centralization that had evolved since the 1930s.

But for the fend-for-yourself system to succeed, there had to be a semblance of responsibility, leadership and resources at the national level. Step by step, the federal system failed to provide the minimum help needed. Congress and the administration heaped new Medicare and other costs on the states at the same time that it was denying them funds that had been earmarked for their benefit—the taxes collected for the Highway Trust Fund, for example.

As homelessness grew, federal housing programs were corrupted to enrich the wealthy. As the need for a well-educated work force became more urgently apparent, financial aid for college students was cut. At the same time, Washington ran up military outlays to a level long since proved to be excessive. The national debt soared out of control to the extent that the cost of servicing it exceeded grants to the states and localities.

Federal laws and policies increased the gap between the haves and have-nots. The administration, with congressional help (and, to be fair, some deplorable inattention at the state level) created a system that was virtually an open invitation to the savings and loan industry to squander billions—even steal outright—at public expense.

All of this put the states and localities in a bind: It became imperative that they either increase taxes to make up for the federal withdrawal or abandon all pretense of responsibility for the needs of the people. Most jurisdictions chose the former, and did so to the extent that the overall tax burden on citizens is now as great as or greater than before federal income tax rates were reduced under the serve-the-rich fraud of "supply-side" economics.

Now, an angry public backlash appears to be under way against those in public office who may be the least to blame for the mess we are in: elected officials at the state level, who were only trying to do their best in the face of an impossible situation.

The invasion of Kuwait and the American military response have simultaneously intensified both the discontent and the ill-directed backlash against the lower levels of government. As foreign crises always do, it wraps the president, and to some

extent the Congress, in a protective cocoon, a shield against criticism. The celebrated reforms and innovations of the past decade are threatened thereby.

Witness the debacle in Massachusetts, a state that only three years ago was at the forefront of education and welfare reforms as well as the remaking of tired old bureaucracies—that last an achievement now commonly forgotten, inside the state as well as out. Witness also the proposals to limit the terms of legislators. The invasion of the know-nothings and anti-government people appears to be at hand.

The danger in the dark days ahead, I believe, is that the progress of the past decade in fashioning a system that serves the diversity of the nation and challenges regional and local officials to live up to their increased responsibilities may be wiped out. If that happens, it could, in time, lead to the creation of another era of centralized national government, whatever its demonstrable flaws, such as grew out of the desperation of the 1930s Depression.

What is required is extraordinary patience, sacrifice and understanding of what is at stake by political leaders at all levels until the current wave of hysteria is spent. ☐

Article 2.   Now, Over to You, Fellas!
by Steven V. Roberts with Ted Gest, Dorian Friedman, and Gary Cohen

Saddled with a massive budget deficit, and widespread public opposition to increased taxes, Congress is searching for new ways to make businesses and state and local governments pay for those programs mandated by Washington. This decision has sparked cries of foul from many corporate leaders and municipalities as they struggle to cope with such difficult challenges as worker benefits, health care, bank regulation, and insurance reform.

As Congress staggers toward a much delayed adjournment, lawmakers are searching for ways to please the voting public that do not deplete the federal Treasury. Since there is no extra money to spend, a new era of buck-passing has begun: Congress is deciding to make others—businesses, state and local governments—spend *their* money on goals set by Washington. It's no-frills, off-the-rack government.

The impulse to impose federal mandates on others will grow in the future as voters demand cleaner water, quieter airports and broader health insurance. In addition, momentum is building on Capitol Hill to impose new regulations on industries as diverse as finance, fishing and cable television. Fees will go up on many government services, from flood insurance to grazing rights on federal land. "Pay as you go" will be a watch-

word, with lawmakers required to match new expenditures with revenues. "Nobody goes to Congress to do nothing," says Norman Ornstein, a congressional scholar at the American Enterprise Institute. "And when the two major weapons of government, the budget itself and the tax system, have effectively been disarmed, they will turn to the third weapon of government, which is regulation."

National politics in the '90s could be dominated by one question: Who pays for what benefits? The answer will dramatically reshape municipal and state finances and deeply affect the nation's competitive position as businesses try to cope with new expenses decreed by Washington. This trend has evoked cries of anguish from offices where the bill is landing. John Sloan, president of the National Federation of Independent Business, complains: "It is inappropriate for government to promote programs—often misguided programs—that it can't afford and to simply shift them onto the back of business."

That's an argument President Bush supports, and he has used threats of a veto to bolster his friends in the business community. On child-care legislation, for instance, he forced Congress to back away from proposals setting national standards for local facilities but accepted a provision directing the states to establish their own health-and-safety requirements. Congress and the White House have been unable to reach a compromise, however, on the 1990 Civil Rights Act, where 11th-hour fighting centers on how broad the antidiscrimination edicts will be and what kind of liability businesses will face. If Bush ends up vetoing the final measure, the veto will almost certainly be sustained by Congress. But the issue will come back.

Despite these arguments, the trend is gathering strength from a changing political environment. Ironically, the move to mandates has been pushed along, in part, by the fiscal policies Ronald Reagan said were designed to get government off people's backs. The public is also demanding more government services, from caring for their children to cleaning up toxic wastes. The savings and loan scandal has increased calls for greater government vigilance over business, and Representative Dan Glickman, a Kansas Democrat, says: "I sense the public is much more willing to have government set the rules than 10 years ago." Of course, Americans do not want to pay higher taxes for these services, and Democrats remain vulnerable to "tax and spend" charges by the Republicans. As a result, some younger Democrats, not wedded to New Deal and Great Society notions of centralized government, hope the private sector and local government can take up the slack. The Democrats' prospects, notes Representative Ron Wyden of Oregon, could

Where the push for new federal mandates will come

The battle over federal programs and regulations will intensify in the next Congress. Here are some of the broad areas of economic and governmental activity that legislators will be seeking to change:

■ **Worker benefits:** *Bush vetoed a parental-leave bill this year, but the issue will come back. The measure would require employers to grant workers three months' unpaid leave for a child's birth, serious illness or the illness of a family member. Estimated cost: $200 million a year. Another benefit that will cause a battle is the minimum wage; Congress wants to raise it from $4.25 an hour after 1992.*

■ **Health care:** *Senator Edward Kennedy's proposal for mandatory health insurance for all workers will be back. Congress says it could cost the business community $33 billion a year. And governors will fight federal ex-* *pansion of medicaid, for which states share substantial costs.*

■ **Bank regulation:** *To avert a taxpayer bailout of the federal deposit-insurance fund, Congress wants to impose higher insurance premiums and tougher capitalization standards on banks. The industry balks at further regulation by Congress.*

■ **Insurance reform:** *Life-insurance companies are regulated by states, but an increase in failed insurers is prompting some lawmakers to consider putting the industry under tougher federal standards. The insurance firms see nothing wrong with the present arrangement.*

turn on their ability "to create opportunities for people without just creating new agencies and new programs." That approach takes many forms:

■ **Mandated benefits.** After years of playing defense during the Reagan era, liberal Democrats, prompted by organized labor, took the offensive when Bush came into office, advancing a long series of social programs organized around the idea that business would pay. Their first measure, raising the minimum wage from $3.35 an hour to $4.55, produced Bush's first veto. Later, both sides agreed on a compromise raising the wage to $4.25, but the issue is likely to return in the next Congress.

So is family leave, a proposal requiring many businesses to grant up to 12 weeks of unpaid time off for employes with a family emergency, such as a new baby or a sick parent. Bush vetoed the measure last June, saying he approved of the policy but objected to a mandate that could cost business roughly $200 million a year. Congress upheld the veto, but Representative Marge Roukema, a New Jersey Republican, warned her colleagues that "you'll have to answer to your constituents on this." Business has fought so hard against mandated benefits because it fears passage of some worker benefits will open the door to legislation requiring group-health-insurance plans for the nation's 31.8 million uninsured workers—at a potential cost of $33 billion annually.

■ **Business behavior.** Congress is eager to control a wide range of business practices that impinge on public health, safety and economic security. The main event in this

field is the clean-air bill, now in its final stages of negotiation. Bush managed to tone down a number of provisions by threatening to veto any measure that was too harsh on industry, but the final version will still require much greater efforts by car manufacturers to reduce smog and impose costly cleanup standards on electric utilities that help cause acid rain. Private-sector expenses could reach between $51 billion and $91 billion a year.

Other mandates are designed to help the government cover its deficits. The budget bill contains a provision requiring pharmaceutical companies to give discounts to medicaid clients purchasing drugs. The cost: $2 billion a year.

A consensus farm bill contains a raft of new regulations, including the first national standard for "organically grown" produce not exposed to chemicals. To help monitor the impact of chemicals, farmers would be required to keep records of pesticide use. A provision banning the export of some farm chemicals was dropped under pressure from the industry, but it will be revived.

■ **Re-regulation.** Nowhere have Reagan's free-market theories taken a greater beating than in the banking world. With the government bailout of the S&L industry likely to cost as much as $500 billion and many commercial banks in deep trouble, sweeping changes are in the works. Congress favors sharp increases in premiums paid by banks to the Federal Deposit Insurance Corporation, whose reserves are dwindling sharply. A strong push will come next year to limit the amount of insurance available to any individual depositor, and to base insurance premiums paid by each bank on its performance. The aim: To discourage bankers from taking unsound risks with government-guaranteed deposits.

Another trend will expand the application of "user fees"—making those who use government facilities pay for them. A prime example is contained in the Senate version of the budget bill. It would impose $3 fees for each takeoff and landing at a major airport to pay for improvements. That same measure also requires the Department of Transportation to establish a national noise-abatement standard for airports; now, each community sets its own. While Bush remains committed to deregulation, he accepted a bill reducing the commercials shown on children's TV programs, and cable TV could also face tougher scrutiny.

■ **Individual rights.** With money scarce for new programs to help the disadvantaged, Congress is focusing on legal measures that would ease discrimination and enhance opportunity. But the fights will be as bitter as the one that surrounded the Civil Rights Act. Bush charged that Congress would require companies to employ hiring quotas to avoid litigation—a charge denied by supporters—but his hand was clearly strengthened by the Senate election in Louisiana, where David Duke, an outspoken foe of affirmative-action programs, tallied 44 percent of the vote. "The civil-rights bill caused a lot of liberals considerable heartburn," says one Southern Democrat. "This is the sort of thing that helped catapult David Duke into the limelight."

■ **State and local responsibilities.** Officials outside Washington have long complained that Congress keeps adding new clients to the medicaid program, while the states must keep picking up a large share of the cost. Last year, the nation's governors asked for a two-year ban on medicaid mandates, saying they were impairing the ability to finance education and other critical services. But some current proposals to cut medicare would saddle the states with an additional $2 billion in medicaid obligations.

Washington has long set standards for other governments, but federal funds to help fulfill those aims are now running out, leaving states and cities holding the bag. One costly example is the sewage-treatment program, started almost 20 years ago with 75 percent of the cost borne by the federal government. By next year, the federal share will drop to zero. But the mandate for clean water remains. That forces states and cities to pick up an estimated $69 billion tab.

■ **Creative financing.** In a little noticed vote last week, the House approved a plan that would more than quadruple fees paid by ranchers to feed their cattle on federal lands. Representative Mike Synar, an Oklahoma Democrat, says the government has been selling such assets at "fire sale" prices for far too long, and promises in future Congresses to press for increased fees paid by miners, loggers and commercial concessionaires in national parks.

The era of mandates clearly holds sizable risks. Local governments could be stifled by rigid rules and assaulted by rebellious taxpayers. Businesses fear the loss of competitiveness against foreign companies that do not have to clean up their wastes or pay minimum wages. But tight budgets could also liberate Congress to spend more time restructuring and supervising government—trying, in the words of Rutgers University political scientist Ross Baker, "to avert disaster, rather than simply perform post-mortems on catastrophes." If moderates in both parties can agree on a common goal—compassionate efficiency—Washington might find its way toward a new governing consensus. ■

Article 3.   How State Governments Are Looking Ahead
by Richard J. Gross

Faced with increasing gridlock—and declining resources—the federal bureaucracy is finding it less and less able to exert leadership, with the result that many states have demonstrated remarkable success in adapting to the changes. Seizing the opportunity, state governments are functioning as "laboratories of democracy," initiating programs and policies that are both innovative and farsighted.

With the federal bureaucracy nearing gridlock, America's state government leaders are leading the way in governmental innovation.

State government leaders are in the most strategic position of any group of U.S. government decision makers to grasp the opportunities presented by change.

Whether you read political commentators David Osborne or David Broder; whether you read the history of the eight years of the Reagan administration or the lips of his successor, George Bush; whether you read about the problems of former House Speaker Jim Wright or you read about the "smoke and mirrors" budget process that has failed to deal with huge U.S. budget deficits, you must agree that much of the federal government is in gridlock. There appears to be neither the wisdom nor the will to move ahead, to experiment, or to take risks. Leadership on the state level, on the other hand, has been passing through an unusual incubation period, and we are seeing many examples of remarkable adaptation in a period of real stress. We know that highly stressful or dramatic events can change one's character; that seems to be what is happening to the character of state governments.

From *The Futurist*, September/October 1990, pp. 16–18. Reprinted, with permission, from *The Futurist*, published by the World Future Society, 4916 Saint Elmo Avenue, Bethesda, Maryland 20814.

Three major trends have pressured states to take leadership: federalism, increased need, and fiscal austerity.

- **Federalism.** No single trend has had more impact on increasing the professionalism and improving the know-how and creativity of state government than federalism, the redistribution of authority over and responsibility for services and programs from the federal government to the states. Withdrawal of federal support for a broad range of programs and services has been extremely burdensome for states. So too have been congressional and court-ordered mandates, such as Medicaid mandates and court-ordered deinstitutionalization of mental patients. As often as not, these changes hit states before they have time to expand their own programs and services to make up for the lack of federal support.

- **Increased need.** The federalism of the Reagan years coincided with a time of great economic troubles in the states. Many have been weathering difficult economic transitions: rising energy prices, loss of industry, changes in the agricultural industry, and other adjustments. At the same time, the demand for government services has grown rapidly: We now have more homeless, a larger proportion of the population with inadequate health benefits or none at all, more families in need of family-care services, more elderly, more substance abusers — and the list goes on.

- **Fiscal austerity.** At the same time that the increased need for government services has risen independently of the states' ability to afford them, many states have experienced or are now entering a time of great fiscal austerity. Forty states are now having or are likely to soon have significant budget problems. For example, taxpayers in the state of North Dakota recently voted down three proposed tax increases, which resulted in general-funds cuts of 10%. This means that the size of the state's current budget is about equal to the state's 1981 budget, even though inflation has raised costs 42% in the interim and the demand for state government services has increased dramatically.

The Silver Lining

The last 10 years have been, for many states, a period of growing capabilities and growing awareness of the possible in the face of many roadblocks.

In the context of federalism, increased need, and fiscal austerity, states have moved into a period of concentrated experimentation and innovation. One example: In an effort to compete in a global economy, many states are instituting systems to help small and medium-sized firms identify and exploit export opportunities. And some states have been quite creative in improving their consumer support services; in California, for example, you can dial a "900" number, answer a series of questions about your car, your age, and the location of your home, and then receive in the mail a list of the five least-expensive car-insurance companies, with addresses and telephone numbers. These innovations get to the heart of citizen needs and concerns in concrete, accessible ways.

Having taken up the challenge and having seen what is possible, states will not let go of their new powers and responsibilities. They have developed, and will continue to develop, a set of muscles that they will continue to flex. They will continue to seek greater authority and will buck federal efforts to cramp their flexibility and their ability to institute meaningful change, both in how they govern and in the focus and objectives of their policies.

Unique Advantages

In rising to these challenges, state leaders have had advantages over their federal counterparts. Their policies take effect on a much more "human" scale. State officials can feel the local impact of the issues they deal with; they can get immediate feedback on the effect of their policies and programs. Less cumbersome and closer to the action than the federal government, state government also has the opportunity to replicate good experiences within a single state rather than trying to replicate them throughout an entire country.

State officials are more approachable as leaders. They are closer to their constituents than are their federal cousins. They live with the people who will be affected by their decisions, and they use the same banks, drive on the same roads, and have children in the same schools as their constituents do. They are more present, more real, than national leaders.

The messages sent to citizens by state governors — through their actions and their words — can seem more directly relevant than those from the federal government and can leave a more lasting, personal impression. However, of all state officials, the governor is seen by the public as the most-accountable party for all the things that go wrong in state government, in the courts — even in the federal government!

Foresight at Work in States

Thinking about the future has become a popular activity for state governments. I would count this, in itself, as a major accomplishment, because strong disincentives exist for state leaders to deal with the future. The political expediency of taking action and then taking credit for that action in the present tense is a simple fact of the American political system. Election and reelection are based more on what politicians do today than on how their actions will be borne out over time.

One of my primary responsibilities is to advise the governor of North Dakota on what the strategic direction and long-term goals should be for the state and to recommend strategies for accomplishing these goals. Others around him are charged with the primary responsibility of keeping him in office so that he can accomplish these goals. I understand this. Some of his advisers press for action *now*, before the next legislative session or next poll. This press for action is exacerbated, for every elected official, when the economic fortunes of states are at a low ebb.

The public is intolerant of actions by state officials to invest in the future if they feel they are not well served by their government today. They don't understand, of course, that the fact that they are not being well served today is, at least in part, due to the failure of the state officials in years past to invest in the future! Public intolerance of foresight efforts increases when citizens feel disconnected from the decision-making process for the allocation of government resources. And intolerance of spending money on foresight increases when people feel vulnerable to or are experiencing the consequences of economic dependency on the government.

Clearly, it takes special leadership skills to know how to respond to the pressures for immediate gratification in ways that won't be harmful in the long term. States are using and adapting tools of foresight to support and promote this kind of leadership — but it hasn't been easy. Foresight techniques that work in a business environment need an awful lot of retrofitting to make them useful in a governor's office. Yet, states are trying a variety of foresight techniques, from environmental scanning and policy forecasting to the establishment of statewide futures commissions.

Foresight programs have been initiated by governors, state agencies, legislators, party caucuses, judges, and state courts. The results have ranged from excellent to so-so, but each program or initiative adds to the body of knowledge from which state governments can draw.

Looking at State Foresight Efforts

Futures commissions and similar efforts can help state governments to determine the policy directions preferred by their citizens. A good example is the "Alternatives for Washington" study chaired by Washington state Governor Daniel Evans in the mid-1970s. The two main goals of the study were: (1) to find out what the people of Washington wanted their state to be like in 10 years, and (2) to identify the costs and trade-offs that would be necessary for those goals to be met. This second point helped

ground expectations in reality. It certainly made the results more useful for the state's elected officials and provided a positive framework for action.

"Alternatives for Washington" inspired many state and community programs and legislative actions. It remains a useful touchstone for decision makers.

A current foresight effort that bears watching is the Commission on Maine's Future. The state appointed a commission of 40 people to create a vision of the future that reflects the values, priorities, and expectations of the people of Maine. The Commission decided to take a unique approach and focus on the *process* of developing a vision, as well as creating the vision itself. The Commission completed the first ethnographic survey I know of for a state, as well as several other useful analyses of the state's economic history and demographics. The results have been combined into a set of recommended strategies for developing an "infrastructure" for planning and decision making, to help state government leaders act with foresight.

Maine's effort and other such initiatives are dealing with a critical fault of past foresight work in states. Most past government foresight efforts were not well integrated, in any meaningful way, with the policy development functions of government. This is what Albert Gore's Critical Trends Assessment Act, recently introduced in the U.S. Senate, is designed to improve. And a number of more-recent state foresight efforts have really improved in this regard. Policy making is a primary responsibility of government, and foresight techniques can and should help. [For more information on the Critical Trends Assessment Act, see THE FUTURIST, March-April 1990, page 22.]

In North Dakota, we've adopted an environmental-scanning process at the state government level to help us anticipate issues that will have serious implications for us, and the result has been that we are out in front on many issues. Our scanning network spotted solid-waste-management issues, health-

care-access questions, AIDS-related issues, concerns about biotechnology, and the new environmental emphasis long before they emerged as issues locally. Thus, the governor is seldom surprised by new trends. The future is known to us to the extent that it can be, and we hope this is reflected in the quality of our policy initiatives.

In Iowa, the governor's office has an issues-scanning team that sends out a report on emerging trends and issues to all the major state agencies. This prompts the agencies to deal with the future as a part of their own individual strategic-policy-development processes. Next, an interagency retreat helps the agencies to relate the implications of these trends and their impact on agency goals to one another. The result, called the Iowa Futures Agenda, has been a well-coordinated and visionary budgeting process. The fact that the agencies have incorporated information about the future into their own goal-setting processes makes their budget requests much easier to endorse.

Other states are developing similar processes. In each case, the idea is to tie the state's resources to realistic and responsible views of the future. No small feat.

Foresight can be a mechanism for finding neutral ground and, in some cases, rewriting relationships. On the international front, states are creating — sometimes by default — their own trade policies, as states' overseas trade offices are assuming the functions of state consular offices. As we think about how we want to be viewed in the international arena in the future, both as an economic force and as a culture, we should look for new ways for federal and state governments to collaborate.

In the area of foresight, states are truly functioning as laboratories of democracy. They have experimented, failed — and succeeded. The efforts undertaken and knowledge gained by some states have provided models others at all levels of government can learn from, modify, and emulate.

Chapter 5

Civil Rights and Civil Liberties

Article 1. A Crisis of Shattered Dreams
by Mark Whitaker with Mark Starr, John McCormick, Vern E. Smith, Marcus Mabry, Lynda Wright,
and Ginny Carroll

The authors explore the growing divisions between blacks and whites. In doing so, they study the roots of white resentment and black anger, concluding that future progress will depend upon increased self-help, affirmative action, education, and integration. The growing frustration in both communities has given rise to a wealth of interesting and, in some cases, controversial ideas about how to improve race relations in the country.

On a Wednesday evening in early April, more than 100 blacks and Jews gathered at the Union United Methodist Church in Boston for an unusual Passover celebration. With a moving mixture of Hebrew readings and black spirituals, they retold the story of the Jewish Exodus out of slavery in Egypt. It was a heartening example of racial togetherness—unless you listened closely to the words of the two featured speakers. The Rev. Charles Stith, a prominent black minister, called for a return to the civil-rights pressure tactics of the 1950s and '60s. But Lenny Zakim, a Jewish leader, clearly rejected that strategy, calling instead for a "new coalition cognizant of new realities." Privately, he was even more blunt. Whites have grown weary of black demands for "race-conscious remedies," Zakim said, and of endless accusations of racism. "White America," he said, "got tired of being called guilty."

That bittersweet scene in Boston reflects the kind of differences that divide even the most well-meaning of whites and blacks these days. All too often, the press distorts the race issue by focusing on ugly incidents of violence: the beating of Rodney King in Los Angeles, the rape of the Central Park jogger, the Charles Stuart murder case in Boston. For the most part, today's race crisis is not the stuff of bloody headlines and cities in flames—at least not yet. The riots of the '60s were a revolution of rising expectations; blacks had tasted power and wanted more, fast. The problem today is shattered dreams. After all the high hopes and genuine progress of the past 30 years, people on both sides of the color line feel they've reached an impasse, and that things are getting worse. In a NEWSWEEK Poll three years ago, 49 percent of whites and 33 percent of blacks thought blacks were better off than they had been five years before. In a new sounding last week, the optimists had dwindled to 38 percent of whites and only 21 percent of blacks.

Is there any way to keep from losing more ground? The question is so bewildering in part because the grievances on both sides have become so complex. There's no such thing as a "white view" and a "black view" on racial problems anymore. Among whites, attitudes range from the raw fear of a Miami private-car driver who locks all his windows when he goes through the black section of Coconut Grove to the gnawing resentment of Chicago cop Jim Cosgrove, who says affirmative action made him wait seven years for a promotion to sergeant. Sources of black anger range from the utter hopelessness felt by blacks in the projects of Detroit to the subtle prejudice that rankles Denise Martin Welch, a Duke-educated attorney in Atlanta who complains about the way her legal briefs were scrutinized when she was a clerk for a superior-court judge. At stake are interests and emotions that differ from income scale to income scale and region to region; yet at some level, the sore points all come down to skin color.

The deteriorating language of racial discourse hasn't helped matters. At the height of the civil-rights movement, blacks and whites spoke to each other in the lofty words of Martin Luther King Jr.'s "I Have a Dream" speech and Lyndon Johnson's promise of a Great Society. Today those appeals to constitutional principles and Biblical ideals have largely given way to the cheap and spiteful rhetoric of demagogues: the Louis Farrakhans and Al Sharptons, the David Dukes and Jesse Helmses. The ungainly word "quota" has become a sly way for politicians to play on white prejudices that run far deeper than opposition to the idea of setting aside jobs for blacks. Even the word underclass, the catchall term for the largely black populations of the inner cities, doesn't do justice to the depressing universe of crime, drugs and broken families it attempts to describe. It sounds more like an academic abstraction than America's gravest social problem—

one that while it persists may make reconciliation between the races impossible.

Does that mean there's no hope for more progress? Far from it. Growing frustration has given rise to some stimulating, controversial new ideas about how to improve race relations, ranging from black writer Shelby Steele's appeals to African-Americans to move beyond the politics of victimization, to white journalist Nicholas Lemann's re-examination of the poverty programs of the 1960s (and conclusion that they weren't the utter failures of popular myth). In places as different as the impoverished Dorchester section of Boston, where a group of Harvard-educated blacks have formed a religious community for street kids, and upscale black Atlanta, where a group of professionals called the Atlanta Exchange does fund raising and counseling for needy youngsters, blacks have begun to experiment with ways to help themselves without government assistance. The gulf war has held up the military as a model of an institution that can elicit loyalty and disciplined work from blacks in exchange for genuine opportunity. The problem isn't a lack of ideas; it's the absence of political will and public good will. The first step has to be better communication. In private and among their own kind, blacks and whites open up about racial issues in a way they almost never do when they're brought together. If the races are going to deal with the many problems that divide them, they first must learn to understand—or at least listen to—each other's views of today's realities:

WHAT WHITES RESENT: Many whites who think of themselves as liberal, or at least socially tolerant, are baffled about why blacks are still so angry about their condition. Many whites acknowledge that there is still room for improvement, but they think things have come a long way from the days of black restrooms, Jim Crow voting laws and police dogs in the doorways of all-white universities. In fact, the National Opinion Research Center in Chicago, which since the early 1970s has been tracking racial attitudes with its General Social Survey, shows that white support for integration and racial equality (in principle, at least) is at a record high. The wounded feelings are particularly strong among many liberals who have worked actively for black causes. Tom Donegan is an alderman and legal-services lawyer who lives in an integrated neighborhood in Milwaukee. Among his constituents, he laments finding "so many whites who were willing to make a personal commitment to integration [but] are now saying 'I did my part. I can't resolve this. I'm not going to keep bleeding.' They've had their bicycles stolen once too often, their cars broken into, they've been called names too many times."

For millions of more conservative, working-class whites, the issue isn't ingratitude; it's money and jobs. They resent quotas as unfair; but more to the point, they view them as coming at their own expense. Countless blue-collar whites, men in particular, share the frustration of Jim Cosgrove, the Chicago policeman. Cosgrove, 41, a 19-year veteran of the force, was made a sergeant last year. Based on his departmental-performance scores, he thinks he should have been promoted in 1983 or '84. During that time, he says, he was passed over for as many as 150 minority and women patrol officers with lower scores. Cosgrove says at first he supported affirmative action and greater diversity on the force, but that "now it's gone overboard. Historic discrimination wasn't imposed by the people being passed over for promotion today. What did I have to do with slavery? Why is the little guy paying this cost?"

Among working-class whites, that sense of being the little guy who can't afford "the cost" has grown steadily with the economic shocks of the past 20 years. At the height of the civil-rights movement the U.S. economy was still on its postwar roll. Then came the oil crises and inflation of the '70s, and the decline in the rust belt, which eliminated hundreds of thousands of jobs for blacks and whites alike. The recession of the past year has only deepened the worries about a shrinking pie. Many whites believe that they can't afford to be passed over or to pay more taxes for programs that mostly benefit blacks; besides, they suspect government will only squander that money. Keith Rush, a retired radio broadcaster from suburban New Orleans, says he's not a supporter of the Ku Klux Klan but that he planted a David Duke sign in his front yard when the former KKK leader ran for Congress in Louisiana. "I'm going to vote for David Duke," he said, "because it's the only way to let Washington know I'm pissed."

The past decade, many whites believe, has only given them more reason to be wary of blacks and their demands. The crime and drug epidemics in the inner cities have made people more afraid, even though those problems endanger far more blacks than whites. The seeming indifference of the Reagan administration sent a signal that whites didn't need to feel guilty about black concerns anymore. There are still whites who root for any form of black progress, but they are getting scarcer. Meanwhile, the number who believe the worst stereotypes of blacks is almost unwavering, even among people who have day-to-day contact with black co-workers and neighbors they like and trust. Despite the steady increase in overall white support for integration, Chicago's National Opinion Research Center has found that many whites continue to view blacks as violence-prone and lazy.

WHY BLACKS ARE STILL ANGRY: For the 31 percent of African-Americans who live in poverty, the roots of rage aren't hard to fathom. They are the sources of the grim and by now familiar litany of "black statistics": that one quarter of all African-American men are in jail or on probation or parole; that more than 60 percent of all

black children are born to mothers without husbands; that almost 40 percent of black males who drop out of high school can't find jobs. Much of this underclass lives all but penned up in projects and deteriorating ghettos—what the Reverend Stith of Boston calls "our brand of apartheid"—without any realistic prospect of escaping. All these blacks can look forward to is a life of inferior schools and menial jobs (if they can get them at all), where the only real prospect for enrichment lies in crime and dealing drugs. It's not hard to see how their plight feeds the alarmingly widespread view that whites are plotting "genocide" against blacks, or creates support for the demonizing anti-white messages of Farrakhan and Sharpton. When the Rev. Bruce Wall, a black minister in Boston, takes inner-city boys out for a meal, they don't talk about girls or sports; they discuss whether they'd prefer to get shot or stabbed.

Working-class and professional blacks view the ghetto poor with mixed emotions: anger that the government won't do more to help them; but also eagerness to steer clear of that dangerous and depressing world. Yet few blacks can completely escape white fears and prejudices fed by images of the underclass. When any black man watches the tape of the Rodney King beating in L.A., he has to wonder if that could happen to him. Chicago political-scientist Gary Orfield says numerous studies show that "whites don't differentiate among blacks very well ... If an upper-middle-class black man puts on old clothes and heads for the hardware store in a mostly white neighborhood, he's likely to be seen as a threat." Recently Johnnie Roberts, a Wall Street Journal reporter, was accused of shoplifting after he bought a $600 Hugo Boss suit at the elegant Barney's men's clothing store in New York City. After Roberts produced a receipt, store officials apologized—but insisted their suspicions were "understandable."

To white charges that affirmative action is unfair, middle-class blacks respond that it was unfair for them to be starved of opportunities by 300 years of slavery and discrimination. But at a deeper level they, like whites, see jobs and money at stake. Affirmative action, enforced with quotas or not, has helped give hundreds of thousands of blacks access to colleges, graduate schools, jobs and promotions they might not have achieved otherwise. Jobs and welfare programs have created a new class of black government employees. Some blacks may have squandered those opportunities, but most believe they have done their best to take advantage of them. "I'm sure that the last two jobs I had, I got because I was a black female," says Joceyln Roy, 27, now a Howard University law student. "I do think that I was a quota, positively. [But] it's a misconception that everyone who gets in on a quota isn't qualified." Besides, most blacks believe, affirmative action rarely gets them farther than just inside the door. As Janell Byrd, a lawyer for the NAACP Legal Defense Fund, puts it: "Corporate America certainly hasn't exercised any quotas in management."

Even blacks who do make it to the management level have to live with what Christopher Edley Jr., a black law professor at Harvard, calls "the exceptions theory." They have to cope with the fact that they are often the only blacks in a meeting or at a party, and that they have to work far harder at getting along with whites than most whites ever do at getting along with blacks. They have to deal with the worry that if they fail, it will be seen as a reflection on their race. And they feel the ambivalence that comes with knowing there are thousands of talented blacks who will never get the chance to go as far. As Eula Adams, 41, the first black partner in the Atlanta office of the national accounting firm of Deloitte & Touche, puts it: "I can't accept the fact that I'm so special, and that there are so few people like me who can be successful in an organization like ours."

WHAT CAN BE DONE? Publicly, many civil-rights leaders have denounced Shelby Steele and a handful of other black "neoconservatives" who argue that African-Americans should stop blaming whites for all their problems and do more to help themselves. But privately, an increasing number of blacks are embracing the self-help doctrine—and doing something about it. The efforts range from intensified efforts to elect black mayors and other public officials, to a return within the black mid-dle class to the tradition of fraternities, business groups and Masonic lodges. In one intriguing experiment, Eugene Rivers, a 41-year-old ordained minister who studied at Harvard, has moved into the poor section of Dorchester, Mass., with his Radcliffe-educated wife and two children and established a full-time home for street kids called the Azura Christian Community. Conceding that it's an uphill battle, Rivers is trying to spread the notion of a "liberation theology" for the ghetto that would bring middle-class blacks into the inner cities on a full- or part-time basis to act as role models and surrogate parents for the children of the underclass.

Yet the legacy of discrimination is still far too heavy for self-help alone to bridge the gap between the races. Ultimately most blacks still need to make it in the white world, and for that they require whites' help. Affirmative action is still needed, but it doesn't have to mean rigid quotas, which are a cheap way out for both whites and blacks. What's needed is a return to the notion that John F. Kennedy had when he first used the phrase affirmative action: the most aggressive possible attempt to find minorities who are qualified, or could become qualified, to do the job. To make that happen, companies and universities have to work harder not only at recruiting but at assisting blacks who may need help fitting in or catching up—what Atlanta accountant Eula Adams calls the "mentoring" process. In Denver, for example, the police and fire departments didn't just lower their standards when they found that blacks weren't scoring as well as whites on entry tests. They instituted a program to tutor blacks—and scores improved dramatically.

At all levels, education is a key to chiseling away at racial barriers. In the long run, it offers the best hope for getting blacks to the point where they don't need affirmative action and for tackling the problems of the inner city—provided whites are willing to meet blacks halfway. None of that will be easy—but it has to be tried. The military has put so much effort into training minorities and improving race relations as a matter not of altruism but necessity: blacks make up 22 percent of its recruits. In the next decade, more and more of corporate America will face the same reality as blacks, women and other minorities actually become the majority of new entrants into the workplace. NEWSWEEK's poll shows that the races now agree overwhelmingly on this one issue: 69 percent of whites and 68 percent of blacks say that African-Americans should focus most of their energy on improving education.

The other key is integration—a once "virtuous word" that has become "highly problematic," as Randall Kennedy, a black law professor at Harvard, puts it. At some level both races continue to resist it—whites with their rationales for not mixing more with blacks; blacks with the rhetoric of separatism and "community development." But ultimately prosperity in America has always resided in the mainstream, and the only way to dissolve racial differences is for more blacks to join it—and whites to welcome them in. The good news is that, despite all of their many grievances, Americans of both races still support that ideal. In NEWSWEEK's poll, 72 percent of blacks and 52 percent of whites said that they would prefer to live in a neighborhood that was racially "half and half"—more on both sides than felt that way three years ago. It's only by spending more time together that the races will learn that "workaday black people's aims and understandings aren't very different from white America's," says Kennedy. An African-American like Kennedy, who has spent his life moving between both worlds, understands that only too well; the challenge now is to get everyone else to see it.

MARK WHITAKER with MARK STARR in Boston, JOHN MCCORMICK in Chicago, VERN E. SMITH in Atlanta, MARCUS MABRY in Washington, LYNDA WRIGHT in Los Angeles and GINNY CARROLL in Houston

This editorial analyzes recent High Court rulings surrounding the Fourth, Fifth, and Sixth Amendments, which suggest that the constitutional balance has shifted decisively from the right of a defendant to a fair trial to the state's interest in prosecuting crime. This shift, warns the *Los Angeles Times,* poses a serious threat to the Constitution and serves to undermine the rights of all Americans.

High court ruling on criminal and police rights erode basic protections

March and April, 1991, may someday be regarded as a historic moment when the Fourth, Fifth and Sixth Amendments ceased to provide the protection they long have to individuals accused of a crime.

This term the new Reagan-Bush majority on the U.S. Supreme Court handed down several decisions that begin to dismantle the court's own traditions. Individually, these rulings are frightening and intellectually sloppy. Collectively, however, the court has tipped the historic constitutional balance between the state's interest in determining the guilt of defendants and the right of each defendant to a fair trial—and tipped it toward the state.

Consider what this conservative court has done so far in the name of "judicial restraint"—that rallying cry of political conservatives.

THE RULINGS: In late March, the court abandoned its "axiomatic proposition" that a criminal defendant is deprived of due process if his conviction is in any part founded on an involuntary confession. Chief Justice William H. Rehnquist stated that the court will now view some coerced confessions as "harmless error," not requiring an automatic reversal. Courts can declare forced confessions to be "harmless error" if they determine that other evidence introduced at trial, but obtained "independently" of the confession, would have sustained a guilty verdict, a difficult proposition indeed to prove.

Then the court slammed the door on Death Row inmates by artificially limiting the number of federal habeas corpus petitions they can bring. Henceforth, petitioners can bring more than one federal writ of habeas corpus only when they "can show that a fundamental miscarriage of justice would result from a failure to entertain the claim." In other words, when the petitioner can—in a way other than through the court system—prove his or her innocence, a standard that strains credulity.

Next, the court redefined the meaning of "search and seizure," bolstering the power of police to chase people, even when officers have no "reasonable suspicion" to believe a crime was committed.

And two weeks ago, the court declared it will no longer routinely accept all the appeals filed by those who are too poor to pay for an attorney. Instead, the court will now reject without consideration paupers' petitions that are "frivolous or malicious." However, such a determination implies a two-step process, possibly more time-consuming than its current one-step consideration of such petitions on their merits alone.

THE RATIONALES: In part the court coyly justifies its decisions as an effort to improve court efficiency. It argues that "perpetual disrespect for the finality of convictions disparages the entire criminal justice system" and that "the capacity of the system to resolve primary disputes" is threatened.

Listen closely to the language and one can almost hear the desperate cries for help of some court administrators and judges who feel themselves sinking into a quicksand of burgeoning caseloads, revolving-door justice and soaring crime rates. But while some federal and state court dockets are seriously delayed, others are not. Moreover, recent RAND Corp. research has found that, contrary to popular perception, the overwhelming majority of criminal defendants charged with certain serious crimes are convicted and imprisoned.

The causes of crime—and delayed criminal dockets—are complex; they arguably spring as much from economic hopelessness and despair as from prima facie "disrespect for the law." Moreover the deterrent effect of "swift and sure" punishment on the actions of would-be criminals has not been conclusively established.

These decisions are more than expressions of the Supreme Court's impatience with the substantive claims of criminal defendants. The cumulative weight of these technical changes alter the environment of expectations on the street, in the jailhouse, and in the courtroom. It signals that the court now regards establishment of factual guilt to be the primary objective of our criminal justice system. But the Founding Fathers did not write the Fourth and Fifth Amendments protecting the rights of suspects and defendants to make the work of police and prosecutors easier. They feared that police officers would sometimes act improperly and that prosecutors might withhold or tamper with important evidence; and they foresaw many criminal defendants getting inexperienced or inept representation, or no representation at all.

The Rehnquist Court's preoccupation with "abuses" of the criminal justice process—and the understandable but disingenuous argument on behalf of efficiency—serves to undermine the rights of all Americans. More worrisome still, other potentially explosive criminal decisions are yet to come this term.

Article 3. Campus Madness
by Walter E. Williams

In this article, Walter Williams, the noted economist and syndicated columnist, discusses the phenomenon of "political correctness" on college campuses, comparing this new vogue to neo-McCarthyism or neo-Nazism, and contending that such speech not only threatens individual freedom but serves to promote additional ill feeling among individuals and groups.

I don't try to keep up with the times. Holding one position long enough is a guarantee to be called a liberal in one era and a conservative, possibly a racist, in another. During the '40s and '50s, calling for the elimination of race designations on employment forms and hiring based on merit made you a progressive. Holding the same position, in the '80s and '90s, makes you a right-wing, racist Reaganite.

During the '60s, the progressive position was to support the emerging campus free-speech movement. That's changed. According to *Newsweek* (12/24/90), the new vogue on college campuses is neo-McCarthyism or neo-Nazi mandates for "politically correct" speech. At all costs, you must avoid "insensitive" speech that may offend homosexuals, women ("womyn," or in the case of girls—"pre-womyn"), blacks, Asians, and Hispanics.

The ban isn't just on racial, sexual, and sex-choice slurs, but anything smacking of criticism of a protected group. One Harvard professor faced an inquisition for assigning a text too critical of affirmative action. The University of Connecticut outlaws "inappropriately directed laughter" and "conspicuous exclusion of students from conversations." Thus, if a protected person says, "I be ready to axe a question," and you laugh, you're in a world of trouble. I know that laughter, especially among kids, is sometimes uncontrollable. Perhaps the University of Connecticut should provide students with soundproof laughing boxes to put over their heads in an emergency.

Last year, Mt. Holyoke students responded to the campus "Lesbian/Bisexual Awareness Week" by proclaiming their own "Heterosexual Awareness Week." President Elizabeth Kennan scolded the heterosexual gang for violating the "spirit of community." Campuses have prohibitions against other sins like: "Lookism," which sets certain standards for beauty; "ableism," which is defined as "oppression of the differently enabled, by the temporarily able." Being a college professor, I can make a contribution to the new speech: Whites ought to be called "pre-black," short people "pre-tall," alcoholics, "pre-sober," dumb students, who buy into all this "pre-smart," and administrators who let them get away with it "pre-brains."

The chief target for our neo-Nazi college brown-shirts is Western civilization. They see Plato, Shakespeare, Locke, and Hume as racists and sexists to be replaced with the enlightened teachings of Franz Fanon, Louis Farrakhan, Karl Marx, and Jane Fonda. Having little appreciation for Marx, our "enlightened" youth and their professors wouldn't know Marx said, of his one-eighth-black son-in-law, running for office in a section of Paris that housed the Paris Zoo, "Being in his quality as a nigger, a degree closer to the animal kingdom than the rest of us, he is undoubtedly the most appropriate representative of that district." Of Jews, Marx said the Exodus was "expulsion of leper people from Egypt." Marx referred to working-class people as "dolts" and "asses." Of Mexicans Marx asked, "Is it a misfortune that magnificent California was seized from lazy Mexicans who did not know what to do with it?"

Does anybody wonder now why college campuses, our vanguard of social engineering are rife with radical incidents and other forms of confrontation? When there's a blow-up, America's brightest call for additional measures of the kind of policy that creates ill feeling in the first place.

I teach at George Mason University, which is "pre-sensitive." Unlike the National Association of Scholars, which opposes campus neo-Nazism, I see value in allowing it to continue. That way we have a laboratory to test harebrained schemes, while Congress works to get a 1991 Civil Rights Bill passed for the rest of the nation.■

Walter Williams teaches economics at George Mason University in Virginia.

Distributed by Heritage Features Syndicate

SELECTED BIBLIOGRAPHY

Abraham, Henry J. *Freedom and the Court.* New York: Oxford University Press, 1982.

Almond, Gabriel A., and Sidney Verba. *The Civic Culture: Political Attitudes and Democracy in Five Nations.* Boston: Little, Brown, 1965.

Beard, Charles A. *An Economic Interpretation of the Constitution.* New York: Macmillan, 1913.

Dahl, Robert A. *Dilemmas of Pluralist Democracy.* New Haven, CT: Yale University Press, 1983.

Elazar, Daniel J. *American Federalism: A View from the States.* New York: Harper & Row, 1984.

Hamilton, Alexander, James Madison, and John Jay. *The Federalist Papers,* 1788.

Hartz, Louis. *The Liberal Tradition in America.* New York: Harcourt Brace, 1955.

Hentoff, Nat. *The First Freedom: The Tumultuous History of Free Speech in America.* New York: Delacorte, 1980.

Kluger, Richard. *Simple Justice: A History of Brown v. Board of Education and Black America's Struggle for Equality.* New York: Knopf, 1976.

Lewis, Anthony. *Gideon's Trumpet.* New York: Random House, 1964.

Mill, John Stuart. *On Liberty.* New York: Norton, 1975.

Peltason, J. W., and Edward S. Corwin. *Understanding the Constitution.* New York: Holt, Rinehart & Winston, 1985.

Reagan, Michael D., and John G. Sanzone. *The New Federalism.* New York: Oxford University Press, 1981.

Walker, David B. *Toward a Functioning Federalism.* Cambridge, MA: Winthrop, 1981.

Wills, Garry. *Explaining America: The Federalist.* Garden City, NY: Doubleday, 1981.

PEOPLE, POLITICS, AND POLICIES

After reading the selections that follow, you may wish to contact your congressman, volunteer for a political campaign, support an interest group, or express your views in the media. To do so, it is important that you follow those steps that are likely to bring you the greatest success. They are simple and direct and, if followed, will increase the likelihood of accomplishing your objective.

Most members of Congress are so busy that they cannot possibly read all of their mail—incoming or outgoing. However, you can take certain steps to make it more likely that the member of Congress to whom you write will see your letter. If your letter asks a question that cannot be answered by a form letter, someone will have to answer your letter personally. If you are an expert on a matter your letter discusses or have otherwise written a particularly persuasive letter with well-thought-out arguments, it is likely that the aide who opens the letter will set it aside for the member of Congress to read personally. But the best way to assure that the member will read your letter is to refer to any personal contact you might have had with his or her family, friends, or staff.

When writing to a member of Congress, be sure your letter is addressed properly to: Senator _____ or Representative _____, at the U.S. Senate or the U.S. House of Representatives, Washington, D.C. 20510 (Senate) or 20515 (House). In composing your letter, you should adhere to the following suggestions: if the subject of your letter is a bill or an issue, mention it in your first paragraph; write as soon as possible—do not wait until a bill has been passed; keep your letter as brief as possible; give your reasons for taking a stand; do not make threats or berate the member; and say "well done" when it is deserved.

If you wish, you can also contact the member by telephone, telegram, or personal visit. Telephone calls can be made simply by dialing (202) 224-3121 (the number for both the House and Senate) and then asking for the member's office. When the receptionist answers, identify yourself and ask for the member by name. If the member is not in or is busy, ask to speak with the "legislative assistant" who handles the subject you are concerned about. This person usually talks to the member every day and helps to develop his or her positions on issues, so your views are quite likely to be noted.

Communicating by telegram is more expensive than by letter, but also possibly more effective. You can send a "Personal Opinion Message" of fifteen words or less to a member of Congress or the president for only $2.00; it will be delivered within twenty-four hours. Or you can send a mailgram of up to 100 words, which looks like a telegram but is delivered within the next day's mail, for $2.75. Call Western Union at the number listed in your telephone book for more information on how to send your message.

If you are able to travel to Washington, you may be able to visit the member personally. Write or telephone for an appointment before you go. A better bet, however, would be to visit the member when he or she is in the district—most weekends, most holidays, and during congressional recesses. You will find a listing in the telephone book under "U.S. Government" for the member's local or district office. This office is always staffed by one or more assistants who will be pleased to hear your views, as well as to arrange appointments in the home district.

Positive contacts with your representative—whether by mail, telephone, or personal visit—will increase your access the next time an issue that concerns you arises. And if you find yourself in general agreement with the member, volunteering to assist in the local office or in the next campaign can be an excellent way to strengthen your access and even your influence. It is also a fascinating way to learn more about politics from the inside.

If you are interested in working for a political party, it is important to begin at the local level. Active involvement in a party will probably mean that you will have a greater role in choosing candidates for local offices and in defining the policies and issues discussed in a campaign. Your influence can be crucial. Numerous elections have been won or lost by less than one vote per precinct.

In this regard, register to vote. List yourself as a member of the political party of your choice (or as an independent) if you have not already done so. Although party leaders sometimes look askance at volunteers who do not back all of the candidates endorsed by the organization, you do not have to support anyone you dislike.

Secure the names and addresses of party leaders in your local area from the election commission, party, or newspapers. Contact your precinct leader or local political party leader, in person if possible. Volunteer your services. You can accept responsibilities and become involved in party activities immediately, even though you may have had little previous experience.

Find out when precinct or club meetings and state and local caucuses are held. Ask to be notified about them regularly so that you can plan to attend. Learn parliamentary procedure. This will enable you to follow what occurs in meetings and to find the best way to bring issues before the group. Become an expert on one or two issues so that you can express your views in meetings, in debates, and on resolutions committees. Others will soon come to depend on your expertise. Be willing to knock on doors. Your assignment may include going from door to door in your own neighborhood or another one. You may be asked to do canvassing, fundraising, identifying voters who will need absentee ballots or assistance in getting to the polls, and getting out the vote.

If lobbying interests you, you may discover that you already have been a lobbyist—a one-person lobby—if you have written or visited your state or federal representatives. Like other political activities, successful lobbying requires that you follow a set of rules. These include: be pleasant and nonoffensive; convince the official that it is important for him or her to listen—ideally by pointing out the relevance for his or her constituents of your concern; be well-prepared and well-informed, so that your presentation is helpful to the official; be personally convinced, but show that you understand the various sides of the issue; be succinct, well-organized, and direct; use the "soft sell," being careful not to push too hard and recognizing that compromise is an essential aspect of politics; leave a short written summary of the case you are presenting; and present your position, if possible, as a request for a favor.

Like many citizens, you may wish to express your views to your local television station or ask to present a rebuttal to an editorial. Commercial television stations are private businesses. They use the public airwaves for profit—and, sometimes, for news coverage and editorial statements that affect citizens' interests. Because they do so, the Federal Communications Commission and the courts are in the process of developing regulations and procedures for giving citizens access to the media. This is creating a new field within the law.

There are now many citizen action organizations seeking to improve broadcasting as they see it. You can form your own organization to influence local programming—or even to threaten to challenge a local station's license when it comes up for renewal every third year—if you believe it is not living up to its public service obligations as a free user of the public airwaves.

Such license challenges are sometimes based on programming (the percentage of time given to news and public affairs) and sometimes on hiring practices and the station's failure to put women and minorities on the air. To find out specifically what a local station does do, and how other citizens react to it, go to the station's headquarters and ask to see its "public file," which by law must be available free to the public during regular business hours.

Finally, if you wish to respond to a newspaper editorial, or comment on a specific story, you should write to the editor, whose name appears on the inside of the newspaper. Or you can call his or her office and ask for the name of the editor. In drafting your letter, you should adhere to the following rules: if possible, type your letter (double-spaced); express your thoughts as clearly and concisely as possible; deal with only one topic in a letter; carefully plan your first sentence; if you write to criticize, begin with a word of appreciation, agreement, or praise; avoid offensive language;

do not hesitate to cite a relevant personal experience; appeal to the reader's sense of decency, fairness, and justice; do not exaggerate or overstate your case; and always include your name, address, and telephone number.

Chapter 6, *Public Opinion and Political Participation,* begins with a discussion of congressional accountability, concluding that most voters do not hold individual members responsible for the failures of the institution. As a result, public policy-making has taken a back seat to individual constituent service. The second selection argues that voter alienation is due, in part, to the failure of the media to spark public debate, stimulate voter interest, and encourage citizen participation. In the final piece, the author contends that the "none of the above" voting option would discourage negative campaigning, reduce the advantages of incumbency, decrease the influence of money, and might even motivate some nonvoters to exercise the franchise.

Chapter 7, *Political Parties,* examines the consequences of divided government, arguing that the lack of congressional accountability is attributable, in large measure, to the inability of the voters to pass judgment at the polling booth on the Congress as a whole. The solution demands a return to responsible party government. The next article describes the disintegration of the Democratic Party, noting that intraparty squabbles threaten to do further damage to the party and reduce its chances of victory in 1992. This piece examines the party's present problems, pointing out that the fight is not primarily an ideological one, but a battle over strategy and direction. The final selection discusses the 1992 Bush reelection strategy, suggesting that the gulf war has given the president both an issue and a target, one that the president's key advisers plan to exploit in the upcoming election. Bush will underscore his commitment to traditional "values issues," show how presidential leadership made the vital difference in the gulf, and isolate those Democrats who raised early objections to the war.

Chapter 8, *Nominations, Campaigns, and Elections,* starts with a discussion of the recent savings and loan scandal and why meaningful campaign finance reform requires the total elimination of political action committees. As a result of the exploits of the Keating Five, the campaign reform movement has been given new impetus. If the Congress fails to act, there is every reason to believe that the voters may demand term limitations, which should certainly prompt congressional action. In the second article, the author describes the repackaging of Dan Quayle, concluding that in spite of the vice president's lack of intellectual acumen, speaking ability, and concrete accomplishments, he may well become a major contender in 1996. The final article examines the rise of negative campaign advertisements, focusing on the Bush campaign's 1988 television commercial featuring convicted murderer Willie Horton who, the author notes, was the vice president's most potent political weapon.

Chapter 9, *The Mass Media,* begins with an article on the changing nature of television journalism which, contends the author, has been blinded by high-tech wizardry, celebrity puff pieces, and sensational exposés. In the process, television journalists have sacrificed issues for personalities, depth for superficiality, and analysis for entertainment. It is essential, maintains the author, that the media, and especially television, be more vigilant in its watchdog role. It must challenge appointed and elected officials, raise tough questions, demand answers, and hold them accountable for their actions. The next piece describes news management in the gulf war, arguing that the Pentagon imposed restrictions on the press that made it impossible for the media to accurately report the war. The author attempts to show how government-controlled access to the battlefield influenced the public's perceptions of the conflict. In the final article, the author discusses the principle of journalistic neutrality, maintaining that even the appearance of "cheerleading" is sufficient to undermine citizen confidence in a free press. The argument is presented in the context of the gulf war, which underscored many of the failings of the media.

Chapter 10, *Interest Groups,* presents a case study of the automobile lobby, showing how the industry mounted a high-powered lobbying effort to defeat a bill that would have required increased quality and fuel-efficient cars. The article highlights the dangers of special-interest groups and how, in this case, as in others, the Congress caved in under the pressure. In the second selection, the author reveals how an amalgam of political action committees, including the automobile, steel, chemical, oil, natural gas, coal, and electric utility interests, were able to defeat a clean air bill by contributing nearly $612,000 to the campaigns of influential members of the House Energy and

Commerce Committee in 1989. The last article details the tactics of Common Cause, the nation's most respected and powerful public-interest group, and its recent failures in the area of campaign finance reform.

DISCUSSION QUESTIONS

1. Should voters hold their individual representatives accountable for the performance of Congress?
2. How does the electorate judge individual members of Congress?
3. What explains the decline in voter turnout at all levels?
4. To what extent, if any, is the media responsible for voter alienation?
5. Would a "no confidence" ballot option eventually force incumbents and challengers alike to address the issues seriously?
6. How has divided government undermined the responsiveness of Congress?
7. Would responsible party government promote increased accountability? Why, or why not?
8. Are term limitations the answer to what ails Congress? Why, or why not?
9. Is the Republican Party destined to retain control of the White House, at least in the short term?
10. Has the Democratic Party abandoned its traditional constituency?
11. In what ways, if any, has the gulf war contributed to President Bush's current popularity?
12. What, if anything, should be done to reduce the influence of big-money contributors?
13. How would the elimination of political action committees affect campaigns and elections?
14. Why has Congress acted so slowly on campaign finance reforms?
15. What dangers, if any, does image making pose to the democratic process?
16. Do the so-called negative or attack ads really work? Why, or why not?
17. How did the Willie Horton issue affect the outcome of the 1988 presidential election?
18. Has television journalism lost sight of its responsibility? If so, how?
19. Is television a reliable source of information? Why, or why not?
20. How has the Pentagon attempted to restrict and shape war coverage over the years?
21. Does national security justify suppression of the news? If so, why?
22. Did the press do a skillful job of covering the gulf war? Why, or why not?
23. Do special-interest groups wield disproportionate influence on Capitol Hill?
24. Has Common Cause lost its clout with Congress? If so, why?

KEY TERMS

ADVERSARIAL RELATIONSHIP   A relationship characterized by conflict between the press and the government.

COMMUNICATIONS REVOLUTION   Technical developments in the manner and speed with which information is disseminated around the world, which have social, political, and economic consequences.

ELECTRONIC MEDIA   The broadcasting media, including radio and television.

IMAGE BUILDING   The shaping of a candidate's style, as opposed to substance, in order to win an election.

INDEPENDENT VOTER   A person who disregards the party affiliation of candidates for office and casts a ballot for the "best person" or on the basis of issues.

INTEREST GROUP   An organized pressure group whose members share similar views and objectives and use their influence to affect government policies and officials.

INVESTIGATIVE REPORTING   An approach to journalism, in which reporters attempt to uncover facts that might reveal personal or official misconduct.

ITEM VETO   The power exercised by most governors to disapprove sections of an appropriations bill while signing the remainder of the bill into law.

MANAGED NEWS Information generated and disseminated by the government in such a way as to support official policy over complete disclosure.

MASS MEDIA The principal means of communication, such as radio, television, books, magazines, and newspapers, designed to reach large numbers of people.

MEDIA ACCESS The public's right to use the media to express its views and opinions.

PACK JOURNALISM A situation in which reporters depend on information prepared by one of their colleagues or press releases distributed by the source they are covering.

PARTY IDENTIFICATION Voters' feelings of attachment or loyalty to a political party.

POLITICAL CONSULTANT A paid professional hired to develop a candidate's campaign strategy and manage the campaign.

POLITICAL PARTY A group of people who seek to win elections, operate the government, and influence policy.

POLL A device to determine public opinion on issues or to forecast an election.

PUBLIC OPINION An aggregate of individual views, attitudes, or beliefs shared by a segment of a community.

STRAIGHT-TICKET VOTING Voting for all candidates of one party for all offices.

TICKET SPLITTING Voting for candidates of more than one party for different offices.

TWO-PARTY SYSTEM The division of voter loyalties between two major political parties, resulting in the virtual exclusion of minor parties from political competition or government power.

VOTER TURNOUT The actual number of voters who participate in an election, as opposed to the total number who are eligible to vote but fail to do so.

Chapter 6

Public Opinion and Political Participation

Article 1. Is the Public Really Angry?
by John Marini

Despite mounting criticism of Congress, the public appear unwilling to judge individual members by the performance of the institution, such that most representatives are able to win reelection in spite of huge pay raises, influence peddling, run-away spending, legislative gridlock, and partisan wrangling. According to John Marini, most voters draw a distinction between Congress, as a body, which is measured by its capacity to govern, and individual legislators, who are judged by their success in providing services to interested groups. In the author's view, congressional performance will not improve until the two are linked.

It is important, in a democracy, that vital issues be deliberated in a public forum by those charged to do so.

The American public has long scorned the U.S. Congress. In recent years, public indignation has intensified as a result of a series of widely publicized events concerning the legislature, which included backhanded attempts to raise legislators' salaries, various scandals concerning the leadership, members' involvement in influence peddling, the inability to control spending and balance the budget, and the widespread perception that Congress is unable to govern in the public interest.

Is the public angry at Congress? The recent elections results would not seem to indicate that this is the case. Yet public opinion polls taken just two days before the last election showed that 69 percent of the public disapproved of Congress' performance as an institution. Of telling importance, however, is that 51 percent of those surveyed in the same poll approved of their own congressman.

One of the paradoxes of contemporary American politics is that members of Congress are able to disassociate themselves from the fate of the institution to which they are elected. How does this happen? Why does the American public, on the one hand, scorn the institution that serves collectively as a representative body of the people and, on the other hand, often admire and vote for the individual member? Why do we observe, with increasing regularity, individual candidates for Congress—including incumbents—who run for national office by running against Congress as an institution? Perhaps the reason is, as Harvard professor Morris Fiorina has observed, that "the individual members can achieve their primary goals independently of (and even in opposition to) the ends for which the institution was created."

To put it simply, Americans no longer hold individual members accountable for the performance of the institution. Congress is not judged as a body; hence, those functions that contribute to collective goals, such as deliberation, policymaking, and lawmaking, have been overshadowed by those functions that are useful to individual members. The fate of the individual member depends upon the capacity of the legislator to represent the interests of electorally decisive minorities within the district.

Increasingly, this is possible through the member's ability to intervene in the administrative process. It is not accidental that the growth of congressional staff has coincided with the changing role of the legislator. As congressmen operate as individual entrepreneurs, staff serve to facilitate the function of ombudsmen. Furthermore, it has become difficult to distinguish the members' private interest from their public duty. When Congress is judged as a body, the standard by which it is measured is its capacity to promote the public good. When judged as individual members, voters often expect legislators to provide services for interested constituents.

The savings and loan (S&L) scandal has drawn public attention to this process, whereby individual members of the legislature attempt to intervene with the bureaucracy on behalf of selected clients, who are often large campaign contributors. What the public fails to note is the extent to which this has become the overriding concern of the typical legislator. Sen. Alan Cranston (D-California), one of the senators involved in the S&L scandal concerning Charles Keating, was not far wrong when he defended his action by noting, "if a senator cannot intervene on behalf of a constituent, he would have nothing to do."

Although Congress as a body created the bureaucracy, it is nourished and sustained by the actions of individual members operating on behalf of well-organized and well-financed constituents. The growth of a centralized bureaucracy has severed the connection between the performance of the institution and its accountability to the electorate.

An earlier view

Perhaps this change is made more intelligible by considering an older view of the role of the legislature. In an earlier debate in American history over salary raises for legislators, John C. Calhoun provided a classic argument in defense of the primacy of the legislature as an institution. Calhoun expressed an opinion about the role of Congress as the central political institution that would have commanded the assent of those who framed the institution. He noted:

This House [of Representatives] is the foundation of the fabric of our liberty. ... If ... understood correctly the structure of our Government, the prevailing principle is not so much a balance of power as a well-connected chain of responsibility. That responsibility commenced here, and this House is the centre of its operation. The members are elected for two years only; and at the end of that period are responsible to their constituents for the faithful discharge of their public duties. Besides the very structure of the House is admirably calculated to unite *interest* and *duty*. The members of Congress have in their individual capacity no power or prerogative. These attach to the entire body assembled here. ... We then as individuals are ... not less amenable to the laws which we enact, than the humblest citizen. Such is the responsibility, such the structure, such the sure foundation of our liberty. This, then is the essence of our liberty: Congress is responsible to the people immediately, and the other branches of Government are responsible to it.

Congress no longer operates primarily as a body, and individual members have considerable power and prerogative. Increasingly, the electorate judges not the institution, but the power of the individual member.

There is little doubt that the growth of a centralized bureaucracy has contributed to the difficulty of reconciling the conflicting demands and interests of members of Congress with those of the institution of Congress itself. What is good for the member is not necessarily good for the body as a whole, let alone the nation. Any attempt to explain this apparent paradox, however, must take into account the inherent tension that exists within a large or diverse liberal republic, between the public and private spheres, or the state and society. This tension provides a basis for the distinction between local and national interests, or the private as opposed to the public good.

In the past, the private and parochial interests of citizens were most often administered at the local and state level or, in society, in the economic marketplace. At that level, it was possible to resolve in a satisfactory manner the differences implicit in the distinction between the public and private, the general and particular, or the governing as opposed to the administrative elements of a regime. The nation was characteristically governed on the basis of general principles; it was both governed and administered at the state and local levels.

Decentralization

The secret to successful reconciliation of the differences involved in the public and private spheres lay in the decentralized character of the American regime. Prior to bureaucratization, Congress as an institution was held to the standard of governing in the national or general interest. After centralization, individual congressmen—not the institution—were judged by their ability to satisfy the private interests of their constituents. Political centralization thus undermined a crucial ingredient of liberal democracy, what Alexis de Tocqueville called "local institutions" or "provincial liberties." It also blurred the distinction, crucial to liberal societies, between the public and private, or the state and society.

The devitalization of local institutions, which made the distinction between the general and particular politically unintelligible, also made it practically impossible to achieve a reasonable reconciliation of those respective interests. As Tocqueville noted, "When the central administration claims completely to replace the free concurrence of those primarily concerned, it is deceiving itself, or trying to deceive you." This is so, he suggested, because, "a central power, however enlightened and wise one imagines it to be, can never alone see to all the details of the life of a great nation. It cannot do so because such a task exceeds human strength. When it attempts unaided to create and operate so much complicated machinery, it must be satisfied with very imperfect results or exhaust itself in futile efforts."

In the public mind, Congress as an institution is expected primarily to deliberate and legislate or make general laws in the national interest. Second, it is to represent and serve the particular or private interests and constituencies of the localities that make up the nation. When it is judged as a body or an institution, Congress is judged on its ability to make good public law in the national interest. On the other hand, individual members of Congress are more often judged on the basis of their ability to provide the kinds of goods and services that can satisfy the private interests of organized groups, or electorally decisive minorities, within a district.

The problem posed by this dilemma is that it is not possible to make good general laws in the public interest and, at the same time, provide the particular necessities sought by the private interests. At the national level, it seems to be impossible to govern and administer at the same time. This problem was solved in a satisfactory way for individual members—but not for the institution of Congress—by the creation of a bureaucracy whose public mandate was so large, its purposes so broad, that the impact of its rules and regulations touched upon nearly every interest and detail of life in society.

By delegating authority to the bureaucracy, Congress could avoid responsibility for the obtrusive regulations foisted upon society. The bureaucracy could be blamed for its meddlesome rules rather than congressional failure to provide proper guidelines in its delegation of authority, assuming national legislation was necessary in the first place.

Indeed, since 1975, the characteristic activity of the central government has become the regulation or the administration of the details of the social, political, and economic life of the nation. Such a development could not but strengthen the organized interests and their ties with the legislature.

Moreover, the expansion of federal governmental power in this period was not merely accomplished through creation of public agencies but through the proliferation of government-sponsored enterprises that are privately controlled, the so-called twilight zone bodies (such as the Communications Satellite Corporation, or COMSAT). The links between the public and private sector were forged and maintained through the growth of state budgets and increased control over economic and social relations. Nonetheless, public growth could not be calculated simply by looking at the size of state budgets. Public authority consisted of more than public expenditures or tax subsidies, not to mention regulatory power. Government could, and did, provide loan guarantees and other means by which certain public or even private enterprises were provided the opportunity to obligate the Treasury.

Such expenditures are not harmful merely because they have increased the scope and power of the central government or because they may constitute less efficient use of economic resources; they obscure responsibility and distort important distinctions in liberal governments. As Harold Seidman and Robert Gilmour have observed, "Distinctions between what is public and what is private are becoming increasingly blurred, but we cannot abandon these distinctions altogether without fundamental alterations in our constitutional system. The maintenance of this distinction has been considered essential both to protect private rights from intrusion by the government and to prevent usurpation of government power."

The administrators

For some time, many in Congress objected to the fact that the political function of Congress as a body was changed by its increased preoccupation with the administrative process. Rep. Gillis Long got to the heart of the matter when he noted, "We [Congress] were turning ours from an institution that was supposed to be a broad policy-making institution with respect to the problems of the country and its relationship to the world, into merely a city council that overlooks the running of the store everyday."

Objections such as those expressed by Long were ineffectual

and short-lived. After a few years of experience, members of Congress came to prefer administration and regulation to deliberation and legislation. Rep. Jamie Whitten (D-Mississippi) recently summed up the current view of many in Congress in an unusually clear way. He noted, "The smartest thing we ever did was to throw the weight of the federal government behind local problems."

It seems that the average member of Congress would prefer to remain in the shadows in regard to controversial issues, while at the same time exercising control through the oversight power. This kind of shadowing of the bureaucracy may have become the chief business of members of Congress. Through subcommittees and professional staff, the typical congressman is a kind of unseen coadministrator of a part of the executive branch bureaucracy.

The legislators are able to exercise this authority on a regular basis by subjecting administrators to the will, not of Congress as a body, but to that of the members who have jurisdiction over the agency. They are able to do so through control of agency budgets, personnel, and reporting requirements, as well as through the power of investigation. No president has a similar arsenal of administrative power at his disposal. Consequently, no president can compete with members of Congress when it comes to direct and ongoing control of those who, it can be said, only nominally can be considered part of the executive branch.

In short, Congress as an institution no longer deliberates or legislates in a meaningful manner, because members are more concerned with other, more direct, more profitable, less risky, and less open methods of rule. They prefer to participate in administration, rather than govern. They are assured of power without the necessity of being held accountable for the use of power.

Nonetheless, some members are uneasy in doing so. It is difficult to retain a Constitution with a genuine separation of powers when the principal branches no longer perform their constitutional functions. When Congress does not deliberate, no consensus on political or social issues can be created. And, it is not a question of whether controversial issues are decided in a manner suitable to Republicans or Democrats, or even that they be decided in a liberal or conservative way. Rather, it is important, in a democracy, that vital issues be deliberated in a public forum by those charged to do so. Only in this way can the institution be made accountable to the American people.

Furthermore, when individual members are judged by the performance of the body, it will become possible once again, as Calhoun suggested, to unite the interest and duty of members of the legislature.■

It seems that the average member of Congress would prefer to remain in the shadows in regard to controversial issues, while at the same time exercising control through the oversight power.

John Marini is associate professor of political science at the University of Nevada, Reno. He is coeditor of The Imperial Congress *(1989).*

Article 2.   Where Have All the People Gone?
by James Boylan

James Boylan argues that many nonvoters are not, in fact, apathetic, alienated, or uninformed. Rather, the media has failed to persuade them that there is a direct relationship between their vote and their political interests. Obviously, it would be unfair to blame the press alone for the increasing numbers of nonvoters. However, the media has failed, in many cases, to stimulate a political dialogue based on moral-ethical considerations and to involve the public in an active discussion of political issues.

Reflections on voter alienation and the challenge it poses to the press

Although it was forecast to be a veritable hurricane of voter anger and frustration, the 1990 midterm election neither breached sea walls nor blew down trees. In fact, it came and went much like its predecessors: it returned to Congress more than 95 percent of the incumbents who chose to run; it earned the participation of only a little more than one in three Americans of voting age, a proportion that has varied little since the post-Watergate election of 1974; and it revealed the further growth, to almost 120 million souls, of what has been called the "party of nonvoters," those of voting age who do not show up at a polling place on a national election day.

Political scientists continue to provide a standard set of explanations for the phenomenon of non-turnout: the declining ability of the major parties to stimulate political activity or create agendas; the failure of new campaign marketing techniques to mobilize support; the apparent voter weariness when the big business of officeholding demands attention to year-round campaigns; and, not least, the discouragement created by the legal and procedural obstacles still placed in the way of those who might otherwise vote. Blame is also apportioned to the nonvoters themselves, for ignorance, cynicism, and — the catchall term — apathy.

Less attention is given to the possibility that many members of the party of nonvoters are not irreversibly apathetic, cynical, ignorant, or self-indulgent. Many in fact may be making a political statement of their own — that they fail to see in current politics, as presented by the media, any connection between their vote and their political interests.

Historians have discerned an earlier party of nonvoters, persisting until the New Deal called it out of hiding. The new party-in-waiting, like its predecessor in the 1920s, is a reverse image of the present American electorate. American voters are drawn disproportionately from the better educated, better off, and elderly. In contrast with electoral democracies elsewhere, the United States has failed to gain in equal proportions the participation of the less wealthy, the less educated, the young, and, most recently and curiously, the male.

At this point, neither of the major parties appears to have a clue as to what the current party of nonvoters is waiting for; sometimes they do not appear eager to find out. Indeed, the mini-electorate has its apologists, who ask what is wrong with having those who are most interested and best informed do the voting.

One thing is certain: the causes of nonvoting are deeply embedded in our political culture and their alleviation will depend on the course of political change. This is not to imply that the problem is too vast and intractable to be addressed, but simply that it is too big for gimmicks. Specific measures can help. After all, federal legislation in the 1960s helped create the South's first black electorate since Reconstruction. Most of all, it appears, we need to rediscover what, if anything, politics is about or might be about.

Which brings us to journalism. Journalism fits into the problem somewhere, maybe not as obviously as many journalists (and their critics) would think. It is a given that mass communication provides most of the contact people have

CAMPAIGN '92

with candidates for major offices. And journalism supplies a good part of that contact but, what with the growth of candidate advertising on television, by no means all. Yet there is far from universal agreement that reading and viewing political news has an important relationship to voting. A recent book on nonvoters — *Why Americans Don't Vote*, by Frances Fox Piven and Richard A. Cloward — does not even mention journalism.

Still, it is probably more than a statistical curiosity that the three-decade decline in voting has coincided, almost to the year, with a similar proportionate lag in newspaper reading. Like voting, newspaper reading has become a more elite practice; in particular, the great cities are peopled with increasing numbers of nonvoters and nonreaders. This is far

Reprinted from the *Columbia Journalism Review*, May/June, © 1991.

from saying that there is a simple causal relationship — that people stopped voting because they stopped reading or vice versa. Nor is there necessarily support for the implication that the newer dominant medium, television, has smothered electoral politics.

Nonetheless, the two declines may share a common source — a lessening willingness by many Americans to consider themselves engaged in what, as recently as the 1960s, constituted a sense of common enterprise, that is, a national public life. In the years since, there have been many signs of a sea change in the content and manner of national politics. A *New Yorker* writer recently watched a recording of the first Kennedy-Nixon debate of 1960; so startling was the decorum, the attention to issues, the seriousness of the content, that the writer felt "as if this presidential debate were happening in some other culture."

Perhaps it was. As late as 1960 national politics could still be understood in terms defined by the Franklin Roosevelt years — domestically, the magnitude of economic entitlements; abroad, the American obligation to police the world. This rather constricted agenda held together an electorate through the middle years of the century, but even before the end of the 1960s it had lost its force. There was too much else crowding the docket — civil rights, racial upheaval, Vietnam, the environment, and more — to which elections may have seemed too tardy and too indirect a response.

There is no longer even agreement as to what to argue about. Some scholars — the worrying kind — have turned recently to inquire into the nature of public life in America, scrutinizing in particular the question of whether the press has carried out its historical function of offering the raw material for public debate.

James W. Carey, Daniel C. Hallin, and other media scholars have noted the long association between the press and public life. Newspapers, they point out, came into existence as an important auxiliary to political debate almost with the emergence of legislative and electoral politics. Carey, in a 1987 article in *The Center Magazine*, points to James Madison's conception of the First Amendment — that the rights of free assembly, free speech, and the free press were created less specifically to guarantee individual expression than to evoke the public debate that creates a vigorous society.

"The public," Carey writes, "is a group that gathers to discuss the news." Such a notion sounds a bit wistful in a time when we think of politics on a national scale as a struggle of clashing interests, causes, and elites for ninety seconds on the evening news. But it has a point: that news ought not to be grist merely for consumption, but for discussion as well.

How well does news serve that purpose today? Stated in its most positive light, today's journalism operates largely to supply information: journalists gather the raw materials from sources and process it into attractive news formats. Theoretically, the system opens the news to all subjects, to all the voices in a society, and the press should thus reflect the full range of society's concerns. But the reality is something else, for the simplest of reasons. Information, the raw material of news, usually turns out to be the peculiar property of those in power and their attendant experts and publicists.

The main link with the non powerful, non expert population is supposed to be the opinion poll. The problem with polls, as David L. Paletz and Robert M. Entman pointed out a decade ago in *Media Power Politics,* is that instead of finding out what is on people's minds, poll-takers usually — barring, say, a life-and-death question such as war or peace — find out what people think about questions of primary concern to the journalistic and political elites, issues on which public feelings may be "at best casual and tentative." Harry Boyte, director of the Hubert H. Humphrey Institute of Public Affairs at the University of Minnesota, warns that poll results should not be mistaken for debate: "We have public opinion now, which is people's private reflexes. But we don't have public judgment. So everything is broken down into market segments. You have no public process."

Journalism fits into the problem somewhere, maybe not as obviously as many journalists (and their critics) would think

Political journalism — that is, reporting on parties, candidates, campaigns — is a special case. Criticism of campaign reporting has chronically concentrated on the cliché that reporters focus on the "horse race" and disregard the "issues." But the difficulty may be not that politics is covered badly but that it is covered like other kinds of news and has the same constrictions. Political reporting, like other reporting, is defined largely by its sources. Political sources these days — candidates, consultants, free-floating quotesmiths — seem to be as addled about policy issues as the rest of us and prefer to deal in ethnic-cultural cant, marketing predictions, and tactical speculation.

Drastic measures have been proposed to bring substance to the fore. A feasibility study by Alvin H. Perlmutter, Inc., for the John and Mary Markle Foundation proposed the creation of a company, The Voters' Channel, to stimulate new political programming, primarily through public radio and public television. The study envisioned four main types of effort: (1) to present voters' feelings and concerns; (2) to scrutinize the truthfulness of political communications; (3) to present a state-of-the-nation agenda; and (4) to provide national candidates and parties air time for direct communication. Programming is now being planned.

Robert Entman goes farther: in his *Democracy Without Citizens,* he proposes the restoration of the politically underwritten press of 160 years ago — the creation of "national news organizations run by the major parties and subsidized by the government," to foster the dissemination of "more analytical information, more diversity, more readily accessible ideas." Entman does not make clear how the palsied hand of present-day party bureaucracy can be sufficiently reinvigorated to take on such a task. Nor is there much encouragement to be found in one predecessor effort, the *Democratic Digest* of the 1950s, a pocket-size organ of no great depth designed to rally the faithful while the party was out of power.

Such proposals, while valuable in charting new political channels outside mainstream journalism, do not directly address the issue of journalism itself. In the rhetoric of journalism, "the public" is frequently invoked; functionally, however, news organizations rarely go beyond treating the public as consumer. Journalism produces news; the public eats it — or not, as it chooses.

Even when the function of journalism is considered to be education, the public role is still likely to be conceived as passive. Not uncommonly, news media try to find out what their readers and viewers have learned. Always the students are revealed to be failing; every one of the polls designed to reveal Americans' grasp of what are called, in schoolroom terms, current affairs finds that most are ignorant of such facts as the date of Earth Day or the name of the Chairman of the Joint Chiefs of Staff. The implications of such polls are alarming, not because of what the subjects answer but because of what they show about the assumptions of the press: first, that people should look to the press for correct answers rather than raw material for argument; second and worse, that the press itself thinks of news as what it too often appears to be, just a jumble of unconnected facts.

In practice, American politics has come to be run by full-time insiders, and to a degree the press has aspired to be one of the insiders. It has taken on itself the task of scrutinizing and, on occasion, disqualifying candidates. It engages in as much speculation about campaign strategies as does any political consultant. And it has frequently made those consultants more central in the story of campaigns than the candidates themselves.

To change things around, to point the compass needle toward the public rather than the insider political networks, will be difficult, but it is a worthy challenge. Not because it implies vast upheavals in journalistic practice; it doesn't. But it proposes something more tortuous — a change in thinking.

Prescriptions from scholars of the public arena tend to be vague. What they have in common is their sense that journalism should be viewed as communication in which the recipient counts for something. Carey puts it: "The public will begin to reawaken when they are addressed as a conversational partner and are encouraged to join the talk rather than sit passively as spectators before a discussion conducted by journalists and experts." Indeed, the panel — a conversation conducted by journalists and experts — is one of the quintessential twentieth-century forms, and one of the most deadening; much of journalism is like a panel discussion in which those in the audience never get to ask a question.

The subject here, however, is not the public-access gim-micks that the news media adopted so widely in the 1970s, and often abandoned later. The question is whether political news as such can be written for a public instead of for participants, and in public language rather than codes.

It may be time, in the 1992 campaign, to try to break up familiar patterns. There are several ideas in the air that may point in the right direction.

In an essay in *Critical Theory and Public Life* (1985), Daniel Hallin urges that reporters become more "sensitive to the underlying message their reporting conveys about politics and the citizen's relation to it." That message, he contends, is that money and expertise count for everything and the citizen for little or nothing. For example, in an article in the January/February issue of CJR ("Whose Campaign Is It, Anyway?"), Hallin notes the virtual disappearance of voters from television campaign coverage in 1984 and 1988 and the influx of insiders and consultants.

The columnist David Broder suggests that one way to break the hold of insiders is to go first to the voters. In a speech last November, he proposed that journalists should "start each election cycle as reporters in the precincts with the voters, themselves, talking to them face to face, finding out what is on their minds…. Let their concerns set our agenda and influence the questions we take to the candidates … and help determine how we use the space in our newspaper and the air time on our broadcasts."

There may be another underlying message in political coverage — an implication that politics is either so esoteric or so dog-eat-dog that individual citizens should keep their distance. The political scientist Robert D. McClure has charged that journalism has taken on itself the task of becoming the chief interpreter of campaigns but has performed the task in a way that excludes "the reality of principle and moral purpose that forms the soul of a people's politics." Could there be a place in the political dialogue for those willing to discuss the moral-ethical dimension?

Another aspect of the problem may be journalistic specialists themselves, many of whom have long tenure and write with an air of magisterial entitlement. News organizations could vary their practice of consigning big-time politics to this aristocracy, not only by bringing in specialists from other fields but also, if such animals survive, generalists who write well, with a warning that they will be quarantined at the first sign of pontification.

It is, of course, not up to the media alone to reinvigorate American public life. But journalism remains the one non-official institution that is not, or at least should not be, itself a special interest. As such, it may in the long run be able to occupy a critical role in re-establishing a sense of common interests and common welfare. It can begin by seeking to emphasize its role of widening and deepening public discussion, of providing a record of its times, of doing no further harm to political life, if indeed it has done such harm.   ◆

> ## Much of journalism is like a panel discussion in which those in the audience never get to ask a question

Article 3. Give People a Choice: Let 'Em Vote for 'None of the Above'
by Micah L. Sifry

Increasingly, the public is turning off to politics as usual—so much so that, according to a Gallup poll one day after the 1988 presidential election, 30 percent said that they would have liked to vote "no confidence" in both candidates had there been a place on the ballot to do so. In this article, the author examines the pros and cons of the "none of the above" option, contending that such an option would function as a public veto. Other reforms are also discussed, as is the deeper problem plaguing the American political system—namely, the irrelevance of two-party politics.

Every day evidence mounts that the public is getting sick of politics as usual. Only 50.2 percent of eligible voters cast ballots in the 1988 presidential election and only one-third of the electorate is likely to vote in Congressional and statewide races this fall. Among those who doggedly fulfill their civic duty, there is growing distaste for the two major parties and their negative campaigns, entrenched incumbents and fealty to big funders. Indeed, the voters were so disgusted by the 1988 presidential campaign that the day after the election, according to a little-noted Gallup poll, fully 30 percent said they would have been likely to vote "no confidence" in both George Bush and Michael Dukakis had there been a place on the ballot to do so.

Well, maybe institutionalizing such a choice wouldn't be a bad idea. Consider, for example, last fall's gubernatorial race in New Jersey, a nasty mud-wrestle between Jim Florio, Democrat, and Jim Courter, Republican. So disenchanted were Jerseyans with this choice that a few weeks before the election only a minority of those polled had a positive view of *either* man. Florio won the election, but in all likelihood neither candidate would have emerged victorious had voters been able to pull a lever for "none of the above" (NOTA).

A serious NOTA ballot option covering all elective offices would function as a public veto. To make it work, state election laws would have to require a special election (held according to the existing rules for when an office becomes vacant) any time NOTA got more votes than any of the candidates. Political parties would then nominate candidates by whatever method they desire—provided that those who had lost to NOTA could not be renominated for that term. NOTA would of course be on the special-election ballot as well. By threatening incumbents and contenders alike, NOTA might well introduce a real choice into elections and eventually force candidates to address the issues seriously.

The proposal is not as alien as it may seem. In its essence, it should appeal to the American belief in freedom of choice. Why should we only be able to vote "yes" for someone or abstain? Many states already require an up-down referendum on sitting judges and, interestingly, more and more of them are being defeated. A nonbinding version of NOTA has been on the ballot in Nevada since 1976. In Vermont, State Senator John McClaughry, a Republican from Caledonia County, has introduced legislation that would give voters the option of choosing "none of the above" for all elective offices, save President and Vice President. By leaving out the presidency, McClaughry is trying to avoid entanglement in the byzantine procedures of the Electoral College. My reading of the Constitution, however, suggests that each state's electors could be directed to vote for "none"; if neither of the candidates achieved a majority, the election would be thrown into Congress. In any event, the Constitution leaves to the states the power to regulate elections to Congress and to state and local offices. Under McClaughry's proposal, statewide executive offices left vacant because voters chose "none of the above" would be filled by special vote of the legislature, though there's no reason why direct elections could not be held to fill these offices as well.

At a minimum, NOTA on the ballot for offices like mayor, governor, senator and representative might discourage a good deal of negative advertising. Contenders often promise not to "go negative," but, given the fact that smear attacks do work, that pledge is frequently abandoned as races heat up. If the people could vote their revulsion at such tactics, much gutter politics would be deterred by the prospect of mutually assured destruction.

Likewise, NOTA would reduce the advantages of incumbency and the dominance of money. One out of ten House incumbents ran unopposed in 1988, and the 402 incumbents who were returned to office averaged 74 percent of the vote. Incumbents are bolstered by their relatively high name recognition, by institutional perks like franking privileges and by a whopping disparity in campaign finances. According to the Federal Election Commission, as of June 30, senators bidding for re-election this year had $83.1 million in their campaign treasuries; challengers had $25.9 million. The gap was

From *The Nation*, September 10, 1990, pp. 1, 238–240. *The Nation* magazine/The Nation Company, Inc., © 1990.

even wider in the House, where incumbents had $112.8 million and challengers only $20.2 million. A big NOTA vote against an entrenched incumbent would at least increase the chances of recruiting serious challengers—from within the incumbent's party as well as without—the next time around. And moneyed interests might not invest so heavily in incumbents if their longevity was no longer guaranteed.

A NOTA choice might even draw some nonvoters back to the voting booth, though on this point experts like Frances Fox Piven, co-author of *Why Americans Don't Vote*, and Curtis Gans, of the Committee for the Study of the American Electorate, are skeptical. Piven doubts that people are sufficiently tuned in to the record of their local representatives to vote "no" in significant numbers but admits that in the intensity of a presidential election year, more might come out and upset the local status quo. Gans, who favors the NOTA idea, suggests that the purely advisory "none of these candidates" option extant in Nevada is a good test of whether NOTA would increase turnout. In 1976, when it was first tried, "none" received 47 percent of the vote in a Republican primary, topping two live contenders for the House of Representatives. (The "victorious" Republican nominee was trounced in the general election.) And in 1980, "none" narrowly lost to Jimmy Carter in the Democratic presidential primary, 34 percent to 38 percent. But overall turnout has declined in Nevada, albeit at a slightly slower rate than the national average. However, "none" in Nevada is only symbolic, and thus a true throwaway vote, which may be why it has drawn only in the single digits of late.

Recent elections in the Soviet Union show the power of being able to vote "no." Soviet voters cross off the names of candidates they reject rather than check the one they favor. They can thus reject all the contenders and even vote against an unopposed incumbent. Moreover, a winning candidate needs to receive an absolute majority of the vote, and the election is not valid if less than half the electorate votes. In the spring of 1989, when Soviet voters were given their first opportunity to nominate alternative candidates and vote in secret, an astounding number of local party and state officials were thrown out of office—even when they were the sole candidate. As a result nearly 200 out of 1,500 races for the Congress of People's Deputies had to be rerun.

How can we make NOTA a reality? Obviously, both parties are too comfortable with the current situation to enact anything so dramatic to enhance the democratic process. Letters to your representative are not in order. The best way to get things started is through the initiative and referendum process, which is available in twenty-three states. In the others, citizens will have to pressure their state legislators, perhaps by mounting widespread write-in campaigns or leaving their ballots blank. If a number of states independently enacted a NOTA provision, the others might follow or join in passing a constitutional amendment, in the same manner that direct election of senators was brought about at the turn of the century. Just possibly, NOTA may surface this fall in western Massachusetts, the birthplace of the nuclear freeze, where the Pioneer Valley Pro-Democracy Campaign is planning a NOTA write-in effort to protest the corruption of democracy by big money.

Pollsters could go a long way toward confirming public interest in having a real choice in elections by including a NOTA option in the battery of questions they ask about political races. Several say they would seriously consider trying it. Larry Hugick of The Gallup Organization says, "There's been so much continuing speculation about alienation, voter disaffection, et cetera, that it would probably be interesting to ask [this] more than once, especially to plot the effect of negative campaigning." Mike Kagay and Kathy Frankovic, the directors of polling at, respectively, *The New York Times* and CBS News, both noted that in the past three presidential races they asked likely voters if they wished there were other choices or if they were satisfied with the existing nominees. In October 1988, 64 percent expressed dissatisfaction.

*A*ll of these proposals, despite their good intentions, fail to address the deeper problem afflicting American democracy: the emptiness of two-party politics.

In recent months there has been no shortage of proposed ideas to deal with what *The New York Times* has called "the trouble with politics." Former Democratic and Republican party chairs Charles Manatt and Frank Fahrenkopf have offered to abbreviate their parties' conventions in exchange for free television time from the networks later in the fall. Similarly, a bipartisan commission of academic experts convened by the Senate leadership has called for providing free television time to major-party candidates to "strengthen" the two-party system and cut campaign costs. To reduce the use of thirty-second "attack ads," Senator John Danforth has proposed legislation that would force candidates to appear in all their commercials. The John and Mary Markle Foundation has proposed the creation of a "voters' channel" on public television that would try to focus on issues rather than personalities or the horse race. For their part, network news executives have made their ritual promises to do a better job next time.

Liberal hopes are currently riding on voter registration and campaign finance reform. A promising voter registration bill that would enlarge the rolls by mandating automatic registration when people apply for or renew driver's licenses and by prohibiting purges of nonvoters from registration lists passed the House by a veto-proof margin [see "Voting Block," February 12] and is now awaiting consideration in the Senate. Unfortunately, the current lack of Republican sponsors for the measure may spell its doom there. And while Senate Democrats have now passed a campaign finance reform bill that goes a long way toward driving big money out of Senate races [see David Corn, "Trapped Again," page 225], President Bush has already threatened to veto any bill limiting campaign spending.

These liberal reforms are undoubtedly needed, as are steps to allow same-day registration, to ease restrictions to getting on the ballot, to make free TV time available to candidates of all parties, to fully finance primary and general races from public funds and to limit the length of campaigns. But none of these measures stand much of a chance at present because one or both of the major parties see them as threats, and their technical nature makes it extremely difficult to build a movement that would force the system to respond.

Worse yet, all of these proposals, despite their good intentions, fail to address the deeper problem afflicting American democracy: the emptiness of two-party politics. It's no accident that Manatt and Fahrenkopf favor measures that would tighten their parties' hold on the political process, or that the Senate's academic advisers want free television time only for the two major parties. For all their partisan posturing on pseudo-issues like flag burning, nearly all members of the two parties actually share a variety of common assumptions on critical issues ranging from the S&L debacle to national health care. As Nelson Mandela joked at his meeting this summer with the members of the Congressional Black Caucus, "You would hardly know there was any difference between the Democratic and Republican parties. . . . In fact, we hope very soon to hear that they have merged."

Third-party campaigns are one way to break this logjam. But the state barriers to getting a third party on the ballot are high and the national ones are even higher. Ongoing efforts to transform the Democratic Party by electing progressive local officials may yet bear fruit, and the inside-outside strategy of Jesse Jackson is still worth watching.

But if we want to put real pressure on our white-bread politicians, NOTA seems to me the way to go. Who knows—a write-in/referendum campaign to put NOTA on the ballot could even galvanize a pro-democracy movement that would effectively push for the systemic reforms discussed above. One similar idea that has already got some attention is a proposal to limit Congressional and state terms to twelve years. Indeed, versions of this proposal will be on the ballot in California, Oklahoma and Colorado in November. Writing in *The New Republic* in support of a twelve-year limit, Hendrik Hertzberg marshals good arguments for breaking down the Congressional seniority system and shaking up the two parties' presidential-Congressional condominium. But he fails to explain how democracy is going to be enhanced if outgoing representatives can still use all the perks and powers at their disposal to anoint successors, or how the people's will is to be served if a genuinely popular and effective legislator is forced to step down. Hertzberg writes that "the term limit would mean that at least once every 12 years (and probably more frequently), every citizen would get a fighting chance to vote in a genuinely *political* congressional election."

Why not every two years? *The New York Times* has editorialized against a twelve-year term limit, arguing, "If voters think a member should be shown the gate, let them say so on Election Day." I agree. Let them vote NOTA. □

Chapter **7**

Political Parties

Article 1. A Victim of Divided Government
by James L. Sundquist

James L. Sundquist insists that the lack of congressional accountability is due, to a large extent, to the phenomenon of divided government—that is, a Republican president sharing power with a Democratic-controlled Congress. True reform, maintains the author, ultimately rests upon substituting an irresponsible divided government—which is typically gripped by paralysis—for a responsible party government.

Last November, Americans were told by journalists and pollsters alike that the people were in a mood to "throw the rascals out" of Washington. They saw the nation's capital as a city full of bumblers, unable to come to grips with the budget deficit, drugs and crime, the loss of American preeminence in the world economy, or any other problem that one might name. And they blamed Congress more than President Bush, whose public standing remained exceptionally high.

But there was little the people could do. In any congressional election, the individual voter has a crack at just one lone member of the House and only one of the 100 senators (and, in each election, one-third of the states have no Senate race at all). Incumbent legislators are ordinarily highly respected in their own communities and, if they have been in office long, will be friends, or at least acquaintances, to a high proportion of their constituents. So only one senator and only 4 percent of House members running for reelection in 1990 were defeated.

In a very real sense, Congress is unaccountable. The people cannot reform it by altering its makeup, for the country *as a whole* has no opportunity to pass judgment, with its votes, on the Congress *as a whole*. This, it should be noted, is a deficiency peculiar to the U.S. government; in parliamentary systems, when the people select a new parliament, they approve or reject the party or coalition that controls the government as a whole, since the legislative majority is responsible for both the executive and legislative branches.

The inherent problem of unaccountability in the United States has been compounded, in recent years, by the phenomenon of divided government—that is, a Republican president sharing power with a Congress controlled by his political adversaries, the Democrats. During the first century and a half of the Republic, divided government was a rarity. Most people identified with a political party and voted the straight party ticket (in the nineteenth century, the form of the ballot compelled straight-ticket voting), and, with rare exceptions, an incoming president could count on

the support of a Congress organized and led by his party colleagues. The government could then be truly held accountable—through the medium of the political party. Between the first inauguration of Grover Cleveland in 1885 and the second of Dwight Eisenhower in 1957—a span of nearly three-quarters of a century—not once did an incoming chief executive have to contend with a Congress controlled by the opposition party.

When the Republicans controlled both the executive and legislative branches, as it did throughout the 1920s, responsibility was clearly fixed, and the people could register approval by returning the GOP to office—as they did in each successive election in that decade—or disapproval by ousting it, as they finally did in 1932 during the Great Depression. For the next 20 years, the Democrats had total control (except for a Republican Congress in 1947-48), and the people in turn passed judgment on their behavior and accomplishments. They signaled approval in each election (except 1946) until finally, in 1952, they had had their fill of President Harry Truman and his party and gave the government—both the presidency and Congress—back to the GOP.

But then things changed. The very next election, in 1954, introduced the structure of divided government that has now become the norm. Republicans have occupied the White House more than two-thirds of the time since 1954, but every GOP president—Eisenhower in his last six years, Richard Nixon and Gerald Ford in all of their eight, Ronald Reagan in his eight, and Bush in his four (through 1992) has had to confront a Congress of which at least one house (most of the time, both houses) was under Democratic control.

Much of the animus directed toward the Congress these days is therefore misdirected. Insofar as the government has failed, the blame lies with both partners in the new system of coresponsibility (America's own version of coalition government) and with that system itself—which has been sought by neither party, is welcomed by neither party, but is forced upon them by the almost random outcome of the electoral process.

Consequently, reforming Congress is too narrow a definition of what is needed. Responsible and accountable government will be brought about only when unified party government is restored as the normal state of affairs. To make unified government a certainty would, of course, require fundamental change in the Constitution, and that fact is enough to put the objective beyond the bounds of practical consideration. The most direct approach would be simply to prohibit ticket splitting by requiring the voter to choose among party slates for president, vice president, senator, and representative. Such a change would find almost no support in Congress (although the Republicans really should advocate it; compulsory straight-ticket voting would surely have given them, over most of the past 36 years, the congressional majorities they so eagerly desired). But this or other devices to discourage ticket splitting and encourage unified party government need to be seriously debated by those who seek to make the government work better.

Possible Reforms

In the meantime, several approaches to the narrower task of reforming Congress have been advanced and can be examined in turn. (One of them, the item veto, is discussed in an accompanying article on p.23.)

Limiting terms. In last year's election, voters in three states approved measures to limit the number of terms that state legislators may serve. California, by a scant 52 percent margin, restricted state house members to 6 years of service and state senators to 8 years. Oklahoma, by a two-thirds vote, limited state legislators to 12 years. And Colorado, by 71 percent, placed caps of 8 years on its legislators and—alone among the three—also set a 12-year limit on U.S. senators and representatives. The latter provision is headed for a court test to determine whether a state has the power to set term limits for members of the national legislature.

If the answer is affirmative, the prospect is for a rash of similar proposals in those states that permit the voters to initiate changes in state constitutions. Future propositions may not fare as well as Colorado's, however. The argument against enacting term limits state by state is a powerful one, for all the benefits of seniority in the Congress would go to those states that did *not* limit their members' service.

Occasional polls over the years have indicated that a term limitation amendment to the U.S. Constitution applying to all states would easily win popular approval. But it finds no corresponding support within the Congress, where amendments must originate (except in the unlikely event that a new constitutional convention is proposed by two-thirds of the states). Proposals for term limits (usually 12 years) have been introduced in every recent Congress but have never been granted a hearing. Senior members are enjoying their lifetime careers in Congress, and junior members look forward to doing likewise.

Moreover, constitutional amendments require a two-thirds vote in each house, which gives senior members of both parties an unchallengeable veto.

Advocates of term limits contend, quite correctly, that replacing more old-timers with fresh new members at every election would make Congress more responsive to shifts in public opinion, including presumably the pro-Republican shift that has taken place in presidential voting. How much the Republicans would benefit is, however, questionable; more than half of the House membership and almost half of the Senate has turned over since the beginning of the Reagan-Bush era, but the Republican Party has made hardly noticeable inroads on the Democratic House majority and, after winning the Senate for six years, lost it again in 1986.

Opponents of term limits argue, also accurately, that a legislature stripped of its most experienced members would be disadvantaged in competing with long-tenured generals, admirals, and civil servants, and even in leading and controlling their own experienced staffs. Some congressional deadwood would be removed, but the members promoted would not necessarily be more able. And some of Congress' most distinguished leadership would be arbitrarily cast out. Would the present Congress perform better if such figures as Sam Nunn, Robert Dole, Edward Kennedy, Robert Michel, Thomas Foley, and Henry Hyde had been retired some years ago? Would the United States have fared better if in recent times such conservative stalwarts as Robert Taft and Everett Dirksen and such liberal pillars as Hubert Humphrey and Paul Douglass had been held to 12 years of service? And if the people of North Carolina want to be represented in the Senate by Jesse

> **Some congressional deadwood would be removed by term limitations, but the members promoted would not necessarily be more able.**

Helms, why should they not be allowed to work their democratic will?

Campaign finance. Contributing to the public disillusionment with Congress is the pervasive feeling that the institution is being bought. Senators and representatives are obsessed with the necessity to raise campaign funds, and the political action committees (PACs) that represent special interests are the obvious, most lucrative source. Next in line behind PACs are individuals seeking favors from the government, of whom Charles Keating of the Lincoln Savings and Loan empire is the current prize example.

The present system of campaign finance is also criticized, and properly so, for adding to the overwhelming advantage of incumbents over challengers. Sitting members get most of the PAC and other special interest money, for they hold the power and, statistics show, are certain to continue holding it after the election. Money is not the only reason; incumbents also have enormous advantages in generating publicity, in the privilege of franking mail to their constituents (the excesses of which Congress has now begun to curb), in the availability of government-

The Item Veto—Would It Help?

Many presidents—most recently, Ronald Reagan and George Bush—have asked Congress to grant them the power to veto items in appropriation bills. And every Congress has given them good reason. The pork-barrel projects added by committee members and other influential legislators to provide special benefits to individual states and districts are often outrageous instances of waste and favoritism. The item veto would enable presidents to kill these projects one by one because their vetoes would surely be sustained by the necessary one-third plus one of either the House or Senate.

Congress, of course, has routinely rejected these presidential requests. Always the jealous guardian of its power of the purse, it will continue to do so. Pork-barrel projects are far too valuable in getting members reelected to be laid open to presidential surgery. But in rejecting the item veto, Congress is plainly out of step with the American people who, the polls say, are heavily in favor of it. Who can be against a measure that, on its face, promises to cut spending and eliminate waste?

But will it? One thing that is clear is what the item veto will *not* do: It will not balance the budget. Every annual spending plan sent up by Presidents Reagan and Bush has been out of balance, with deficits generally in the $200-250 billion range. Congress has redistributed some spending, particularly from military to domestic purposes, but even if the president had vetoed every single item Congress added, that would have reduced the deficit by considerably less than 10 percent. Besides, the president would surely have accepted most of the additional items. Many of them Congress added to meet unforeseen circumstances, with the president's support. Others were sponsored by his political allies, inside and outside Congress, but even those initiated by political opponents he would be loath to reject. Presidents need friends in Congress, not enemies. Jimmy Carter began his presidency by striking from the budget a list of water projects he believed were wasteful; not only was he forced to yield on half of them, but he poisoned his relationship with Capitol Hill for months afterward. Pru-

dent presidents do not do that sort of thing.

While the direct fiscal effects of the item veto would be minuscule at best, its indirect effects could be profound. The president would be given a new bargaining chip of enormous value in dealing with Congress. He could use the threat of an item veto to win a member's vote for any unrelated purpose—for ratification of a treaty, confirmation of a controversial appointee, aid to the Nicaraguan Contras, or spending for the MX missile or some other high-cost military item. In recent years, presidents would probably have used the item veto bargaining power to win *increases*, not decreases, in the aggregate governmental budget.

David Stockman, President Reagan's first budget director, said the item veto had to do not with deficits but with power. He was right. The question is: Is a major shift in the balance of power from Congress to the president an idea whose time has come? Or is it an idea that happily faded away with the "imperial" presidencies of the Vietnam War era?

—*J.L.S.*

paid staff, and so on. But money, in close races, is often crucial in tipping the scales to the incumbent.

That, of course, is the central reason why the system is so difficult to reform. Any change has to be legislated by the very incumbents who benefit from the system as it stands. Any of the

changes that are widely advocated outside Congress—limits on total spending, further limits on PAC contributions or their elimination altogether, public financing of part or all of the cost of elections, free or cheaper access to television—would tend to equalize the competition and give challengers a better chance. But the

last thing incumbents want is a level playing field.

Yet all is not lost. Many members find the solicitation of campaign funds the most onerous, distasteful aspect of their jobs and want something done about it. Most are sensitive to the clamor for reform that comes from groups like Common Cause and to the charges by editorial writers and the public at large that the present system corrupts everybody, themselves included. The House and Senate both passed reform bills last year, but they were too divergent to be reconciled in the time available, given some foot-dragging in high places. Republicans find certain reforms to their liking, such as tax credits or deductions to encourage campaign contributions, and at least some Democrats endorse limits on total spending—both positions motivated by the general money-raising advantage of the GOP. The groundwork may have been laid, and public pressure may be sufficient now to force a genuine effort to achieve a compromise between partisan and Senate-House differences.

If investigation of the "Keating Five" senators arouses public indignation to the critical level, Keating will finally have made his contribution to the public weal.

Simplifying Congress' structure and strengthening leadership. The notion that there was once a golden age when leaders led, followers followed, and presidents could deal with a few powerful figures in Congress instead of 535 individuals is largely myth—at least since the dethroning of Speaker Joseph "Czar" Cannon in 1910. The strongest leaders since Cannon's time were probably Speaker Sam Rayburn and Senate Leader Lyndon Johnson in the 1950s. But they and the Democratic Party's program could be stymied, and often were, by any member of an oligarchy of Democratic committee chairmen entrenched in their positions by seniority. In the House, Rules Committee Chairman Howard Smith, who held his post by longevity, was on many occasions more powerful than Rayburn, who was elected by his peers. And Smith's loyalty was to conservative ideology, not to his party,

its leadership, or his colleagues.

Articles on "reforming Congress" a generation ago demanded that the legislative bodies be democratized to reflect the members' will. The seniority system had to be scrapped, committee chairmen stripped of autocratic power, and the Senate filibuster rule modified. These goals have now been accomplished, and the complaint today is just the opposite—of an excess of democracy. Now Congress is condemned as chaotic and anarchical, an institution that is victimized by the policy entrepreneurship of too many subcommittee chairmen and that forces presidents to deal with "535 secretaries of state."

Returning to a mythical golden age is both undesirable and impossible, given the democratic temper of the times. Today's legislators are too independent and assertive to submit to dictatorial leadership, even if it could be taken for granted that the dictators would be benign. Each member insists on his "piece of the action" and the number of subcommittees has grown accordingly, although their proliferation is also traceable in part to the sheer broadening of the legislative agenda arising from the ever-growing complexity of international and national affairs. And policy entrepreneurship is not all bad, for the entrepreneurs do recognize and begin to promote solutions to problems that would otherwise be neglected.

But democracy and decentralization need to be counterbalanced by a sufficiently strong central authority in each house, not to dictate but to coordinate. Overlapping of subcommittee jurisdictions is inevitable, but it has to be offset by responsibility in the House and Senate leadership to assign jurisdiction on particular matters to one or a very small number of committees in each body, with power to make the assignments stick. Party caucuses and policy committees, revived in

the past couple of decades, need to be further developed as makers and coordinators of policy. The new budget committees have contributed significantly to policy coordination, although their success is obscured by the annual turmoil of the process they go through. That ordeal would be reduced if the budget were written biennially instead of every year—a reform being actively advocated both outside and within Congress.

Both houses of Congress have been moving gradually toward improved coordination. But Congress, however organized internally, will always be too pluralistic and decentralized to substitute successfully for the president as the nation's policy leader and policy coordinator. Yet as long as it is controlled by the party opposed to the president, it is compelled to try and—much of the time—fail. The United States has no tradition of coalition govern-

> **Returning to the mythical golden age is both undesirable and impossible, given the democratic temper of the times.**

ment and, judging from experience, little aptitude for it. Those who are worried about reforming Congress should focus their attention on the fundamental weakness of the current American system—the substitution of an irresponsible divided government for the responsible party government the country knew throughout most of its existence.∎

James L. Sundquist is a senior fellow emeritus at the Brookings Institution. His most recent book is **Constitutional Reform and Effective Government** *(1986).*

Article 2. Family Feud
by Jacob Weisberg

This article describes the "blame game" that currently wracks the Democratic party—specifically, the much-publicized feud between the Democratic Leadership Council and the Coalition for Democratic Values, which the latter blames for forsaking its liberal base. Angered by their failure to capture the White House since 1984, conservative Southern Democrats—who call themselves "new Democrats"—have attempted to broaden their base and distinguish themselves from old guard "traditional Democrats," who they blame for recent election losses.

When Democrats lose, they not only blame the party "establishment," they also give way to a compulsion to form cliques with three-letter acronyms. In recent years, owing to the plenitude of booted presidential elections, the acronyms have multiplied. After a second crushing by Richard Nixon in 1972, an elite, Scoop Jackson-inspired schism called the Coalition for a Democratic Majority (CDM) organized a rebellion against the dovish McGovernite wing, which it claimed was too dominant in the Democratic National Committee (DNC). CDM had more or less petered out by the time of the second loss to Ronald Reagan in 1984 but was succeeded by the Democratic Leadership Council (DLC), which opposed what it saw as an interest group-beholden party leadership. The most recent contestant in the blame game is the Coalition for Democratic Values (CDV), which sees the 1988 disaster as the work of the DLC, for dragging the party too far from its liberal base. As of this writing, there are no DMZ, HIV, or MTV, but after 1992 look out.

There's nothing, of course, that these acronymic factions like more than a fractious, possibly insoluble quarrel about how their leaderless, rudderless party should position itself. The most significant reformist force within the party is now the DLC. The DLC's founding members were Southern Democrats like Sam Nunn and Chuck Robb; Jesse Jackson memorably dubbed it "the Southern White Boy Caucus." The DLC originally played down the party's liberal platform positions on issues like school prayer and abortion, and took a more conservative line on defense and fiscal issues. Though Richard Gephardt was an early member of the DLC, the candidates most strongly linked with it in 1988 were Al Gore and Bruce Babbitt. Since then the DLC has tried to shake its conservative label in order to attract broader support within the party. Its members call themselves "new Democrats" and contrast themselves with the "traditional Democrats" who keep losing elections.

This foggy image points to one of the DLC's inherent weaknesses. Thanks to its squishy rhetoric, the group has been able to expand its membership to include more than 400 elected officials nationally, and has recently opened affiliates in twenty states. But because it wants to be as inclusive as possible, it has failed to unite around a coherent set of positions. Though the ten Democrats who voted with President Bush on the Gulf war resolution were all DLC members, ten other DLC senators voted against him. The DLC faction is more hawkish than the party as a whole, but it lacks a clear stand on the war. On domestic issues the DLC emphasizes a pragmatic, what-works brand of neoliberalism. The group's idea shop, the Progressive Policy Institute, has developed an inventive neither-left-nor-right agenda for the party that includes the Moynihan Social Security tax cut, expansion of the earned income tax credit as an alternative to the minimum wage, and schemes for national service and youth apprenticeship. Unlike the congressional leadership, which is bound to organized labor, the DLC opposes protectionism, and will probably endorse the Mexican Free Trade Agreement at its annual meeting, which begins in Cleveland on May 5.

The conference will offer an early glimpse at possible Democratic candidates for 1992. Gore, Gephardt, Nunn, Bill Clinton, Doug Wilder, and Paul Tsongas are all scheduled to speak. Mario Cuomo turned down an invitation. George McGovern and Jesse Jackson weren't asked. The DLC has had a beef with Jackson since last year's conference in New Orleans, when he gave a speech titled "Delighted to be United," in which he congratulated the group for belatedly coming around to his point of view. Al From, the DLC's president, told the *Chicago Sun-Times* that Jesse and George weren't invited because ''we are trying to change the party, and Jackson and McGovern represent the ideological approach to government we are trying to change.'' The slight was swiftly returned. McGovern recently called the DLC ''part of the timidity and excessive caution that has kept the Democrats from defining an alternative to the Republican approach.'' Jackson took matters a step further, writing to Clinton, Nunn, and Robb to ask if From spoke for them too. Their responses have not been made public.

The slugfest coincides with an escalation in the ongoing war of words between the DLC and DNC. Last week Clinton was quoted in *USA Today* as saying, ''I'd like us to be what people think of when they think of the Democratic National Committee.'' This was a misquote; Clinton actually said ''the national Democratic Party.'' Nonetheless, Ron Brown took it as a jab. He and others at the DNC worry that in branching out nationally, the DLC is setting itself up as a rival to the official party. Some party officials also suspect that Clinton will try to use the DLC's state committees as a vehicle for a presidential run. In an interview with *The Atlanta Constitution* last week, Brown jousted that it was too bad Clinton couldn't be the DLC's presidential candidate, ''since he's already announced to the people of Arkansas that he will not be a candidate in 1992.'' DLC officials downplay the feud. ''They may get the wrong idea about what we're trying to do when we organize state chapters,'' says Bruce Reed, editor of the DLC magazine *The New Democrat.* ''We're not trying to take over the Democratic Party structure. We're trying to strengthen state parties with an infusion of ideas.''

The DLC-DNC fight is not, however, a primarily ideological one, like the From-Jackson scrap. The DLC has no objection to the DNC so long as it remains neutral in the party's ideological battles. For his part, Brown is not especially opinionated, and since his appointment as DNC chairman in 1989 has struggled, with considerable success, to transform the DNC into an effective fund-raising and campaign-support machine. Those who have worked with Brown say he will take the party wherever it needs to go politically in order to win elections. The real ideological counterpunch to the DLC comes from outside the official party organization, where a growing chorus is clamoring that Democrats must play to their old strengths by rebuilding the Kennedy-Johnson coalition: organized labor and blacks, with a few new additions like feminists and environmentalists.

The interest groups are part of this movement. Among the most significant are the AFL-CIO, its Committee on Political Education, the National Education Association, and Americans for Democratic Action, which gives congressional Democrats an oft-cited percentage rating based on litmus-test issues. They have been joined by a number of new groups as well. The most ambitious of them is the Coalition for Democratic Values, founded last year by Ohio Senator Howard Metzenbaum, who wants it to serve as a paleoliberal counterweight to the neoliberal DLC. ''We are what they are,'' says Heather Booth, the group's director, ''an attempt to move the party—in a more progressive direction.'' In a bid to steal the DLC's limelight, the CDV scheduled its own conference on economic issues in Des Moines on May 4, the day before the DLC convention begins in Cleveland. On hand will be many of those who spoke at the CDV's founding meeting in January: northern liberal senators like Ted Kennedy, Paul Simon, Chris Dodd, and Paul Wellstone, and populists Tom Harkin of Iowa, Jim Hightower of Texas, and Illinois Representative Lane Evans. The only potential candidate who plans to attend is Wilder, who stands, as usual, with a foot in every camp. Booth's mantra is: ''We do not need two Republican parties.'' DLC types respond that the CDV is redundant because it represents the tired ideas that already hold sway in the party.

Aligned with CDV are other Democratic traditionalists who have given themselves bright, futurish names in an effort to obscure their fusty agendas. Democrats 2000 is a labor-supported ''networking group for economically progressive elected officials,'' according to its executive director, Diana Peel. It shares most of CDV's membership and emphasizes the same issues: national health care, civil rights, and progressive taxation. A similar outfit is the Democratic Victory Group, an arm of pollster Vic Fingerhut, who works mostly for organized labor. Fingerhut's shtick is a simple one: ''Populist economic issues are still the Democrats' strong suit,'' he says.

The DNC doesn't particularly appreciate these squabbles, which its staffers often describe, in a current phrase, as factions ''pushing off'' against each other. Brown would like to lower the noise level, cool the temperature, and put on a show of unity. But the spats aren't likely to go away, since they indicate genuine ideological fault lines within the party. No crisp, partisan message can emerge until a candidate capable of delivering one steps forward. "The Democratic Party is now up for grabs," says Michael McCurry, a former DNC official. "Anybody who wants it can have it." ●

Article 3. Riding the Victory Train
by Matthew Cooper and Kenneth T. Walsh

This article examines the Bush reelection strategy for 1992, noting that the president's top advisers plan a three-pronged strategy: reinforce the administration's support of traditional American values; exploit Bush's leadership role in the gulf war; and isolate the president's critics for being outside the "mainstream." According to the Bush team, the war, more than any other issue, has accelerated cultural and political trends that proved successful in 1988 and will do so again.

Like war, peace is unpredictable. And the Persian Gulf conflict has already loosed a whirlwind of new social, economic and cultural forces upon America. The clearest results are new pride in the nation, a sharp increase in George Bush's political stature, fresh adulation for the military and heightened respect for America's high-tech prowess, at least on the battlefield.

Not surprisingly, the president and his strategists are making plans to take advantage of it all. So far, key advisers have identified three main approaches in the molding of postwar America:

■ Reinforce Bush's links to the values of patriotism, national self-esteem and a newfound can-do spirit. They plan to expand on the president's 1988 campaign strategy of using the Pledge of Allegiance and opposition to flag burning as "values issues." Already, Republicans are trying to make Democratic votes against war an antipatriotism issue.

■ Emphasize that the war proves what *leadership* can do for America, not what *government* can do. Bush and his surrogates will argue that initiative and teamwork made the difference in the gulf. They don't want Americans getting funny ideas that the nation's success in war somehow validates big social programs at home, as many Democrats contend.

■ Use the war to isolate strident critics. Even though many conservative Republicans opposed the war, Democrats who did so will be accused of being outside the "mainstream." So will liberal academics and liberal mainline church leaders who aggressively opposed the war. "It's a fundamental difference of values," says a Republican strategist. "The critics believe the world is a naturally passive place where aggressiveness needs to be nurtured to take root. We believe the world is naturally aggressive,

and that strength brings peace and weakness brings war."

Overall, White House strategists will try to filter all political discourse through the gulf war. For instance, the president introduced his warmed-over version of last year's crime bill with a burst of if-we-can-liberate-Kuwait-City-then-we-can-liberate-our-own-cities rhetoric. And Bob Dole, the Senate Republican leader, unveiled a GOP civil-rights bill last week, declaring: "Our military got the job done without quotas and without discrimination."

As usual, when it comes to national politics, Bush and his Republicans are thinking in terms of grand themes and overall strategy, while the Democrats, who control Congress, are thinking in terms of specific issues and legislative tactics. Democratic leaders are trying quickly to shift attention from vanquishing Saddam Hussein to their domestic agenda (see story on Page 26). Bush's response, in addition to regular trips to military bases to greet returning troops, will be simple: the veto. He has rejected 21 bills so far without a single congressional override — and the gulf war only strengthens his hand.

The basic presumption in the Bush camp is that the gulf war has accelerated cultural and political trends that were already underway — not that it has reconfigured the nation's political life in the manner of previous wars. Vietnam, for instance, spawned a debilitating syndrome of self-doubt and recriminations that scarred the nation's psyche for nearly a generation. World War II affected everything from birth rates to income distribution, made the United States a superpower and encouraged important advances for blacks and women. World War I ended in an immediate triumph for Democratic President Woodrow Wilson

but, over time, led to an era of Republican reign, shifting social mores. Without megachanges like that in store — at least so far — Bush confidants have no fears that they'll be swamped by the kind of postwar turbulence that nearly drove Harry Truman from office at the end of World War II. Bush can also be comforted by the fact that in this century it has always been Republicans who profited politically from the ferment caused by wars or their aftermath — usually because Democrats mishandled the conflict or the ensuing peace.

In the gulf war's aftermath, the biggest immediate fight will center on the invigorated claims that government programs for blacks and women should be expanded — in part because of the sacrifices they were being asked to make in the military during the war. In some quarters, Desert Storm has unleashed a faith in collective action similar to the commitment to civic involvement that followed the Civil War. Historian George Frederickson found that the War Between the States was paralleled by an "inner civil war" that energized many citizens to fight society's ills. Democrats already are picking up the theme, summoning martial rhetoric and arguing for wars at home to strengthen civil-rights laws, remedy economic inequities and correct other ills.

Bush will counter that the Democrats and other advocates of an activist federal government are missing the point. Above all, the president and his policymakers say, this war proved the enduring worth not of activist government but of basic American values such as the willingness to stand up for principle, to fight in a just cause for national interests and to support a weaker friend. It did not prove that government can and should be the instrument to tackle national ills.

In the words of conservative political scientist James Q. Wilson: "Americans know that if you brought [Gen. H.] Norman Schwarzkopf home and told him to tackle crime, he'd start looking like any other big-city police chief—harried and frustrated. The public understands that we just don't know how to solve a lot of problems at home." Princeton sociologist Paul Starr, a prominent war supporter, is like many liberals who hope that the victory will give Americans "greater confidence in the capacity of government," but he isn't banking on it.

No new programs. Bush and his surrogates will specifically take on the advocates of expansive civil-rights legislation by arguing that the war reinforces military values of discipline, teamwork, respect for authority and, most important, rewarding people on the basis of merit—not race, gender or other factors unrelated to job performance. Bush's aides think most voters are simply too cynical about Washington to believe new programs can work. "In the end, people will trust leaders, not government, to do what's right," says a Bush adviser.

The White House does hope Bush can find a way to connect the success of a half-million American troops to everyday triumphs back home. Administration officials do not want to repeat what one calls "the man-on-the-moon syndrome": The first lunar landing in 1969 was so thoroughly treated as a product of government-sponsored technology that many Americans, while proud of the achievement, felt it had no real relevance to their daily lives or values. To avoid that reaction, Bush talks about the performance of average Americans in uniform, doing their jobs, working as a team toward a clear objective. "The war contradicts some fundamental things we've been told over the last 25 years," says an administration official. "It contradicts the idea that things are more complicated than they seem, that things are not black and white, that technology doesn't work. It will increase the confidence of most people that their relatively simple attitudes and views are correct."

Bush also will use the gulf victory to isolate his more implacable critics, who opposed use of force. "If peace groups can't discriminate between just and unjust use of force, their arguments are totally vacuous," says Stuart Eizenstat, chief domestic adviser to President Jimmy Carter. "They took equally vociferous positions here as with Vietnam, Panama and Libya. It was a blanket rule."

The Bush effort to spin the war the administration's way may have its greatest effect on the generation of people who fought it. Those born between 1961 and 1981—authors Neil Howe and William Strauss call them the "13ers" because they're the 13th American generation and among the unluckiest—are already one of the most Republican generations in U.S. history. The war will probably make them more so. For one thing it will give them a much needed dose of self-confidence. In their new book, "Generations," Howe and Strauss note that the 13ers are the most incarcerated generation in history and among the most criticized for much discussed shortcomings in education ranging from spelling to math to geography.

No leap to liberalism. "The war may give this generation a greater sense of identity and pride that it can get things done," argues Howe. Even if the war is followed by a disappointing peace, economic doldrums or a continuation of policies that hurt their generation, like high Social Security taxes, the 13ers aren't likely to leap to liberalism or social protest. Howe, in words that could have been written at the White House, maintains: "They believe in working at a food bank, not in starting a big government food program. They believe in the individual sphere, not big government."

The political danger for Bush is that he could go overboard in exploiting his gulf triumph, possibly by lapsing into the mudslinging over patriotism that characterized his 1988 campaign—especially if his attempts to tar liberal churches become too strident. "It will cheapen and trivialize the war," says Eizenstat, "if they try to capitalize on it in tangential ways." Indeed, 71 percent of the respondents to a recent *Los Angeles Times* poll said they don't want the war to be treated as a political issue. How Bush resists that temptation will be a test of his own character, leadership and values. ■

Chapter 8

Nominations, Campaigns, and Elections

Article 1. The Keating 535
by Andrew Bates

Angered by the influence of big money, the author advocates the total elimination of political action committees—a recommendation proposed by President Bush in his 1991 State of the Union address. Exacerbated by the savings and loan scandal—and the antics of the Keating Five—the campaign reform movement has gained new favor among mainstream voters. Clearly, PAC contributions are corrupting the political process. Quick fixes, like spending ceilings or public financing, will not solve the problem. Nothing short of abolishing PACs will eliminate the pernicious influence of special-interest money.

"One of the reasons there is so much support for term limitations is that the American people are increasingly concerned about big-money influence in politics. So we must look beyond the next election to the next generation. And the time has come to put the national interest above the special interest—and to totally eliminate Political Action Committees."

Another Common Cause press release? The annual David Broder campaign reform op-ed? A stump speech by professor Paul Wellstone? No, this call for campaign reform came from President George Bush in his January 29 State of the Union address.

Thanks largely to the exploits of the Keating Five, the idea of campaign finance reform has quietly inched its way in from the fringes, claiming a plank on America's mainstream policy agenda for the first time since Watergate. And that's a damn fine thing. But as President Bush sets out to slay the PAC-men, he's making the same quick-fix mistake that turned Watergate campaign "reforms" into a nursery for folks like Charles Keating.

To understand this, all Bush had to do was take a hard look at the Keating Five scandal, which had nothing to do with PACs but everything to do with campaign finance's more subtle quid pro quo. Recognizing the broader relevance of their clients' actions, defense lawyers cynically turned the Senate Ethics Committee hearings into a sweeping indictment of 535 congressmen. It wasn't that the Keating Five "did nothing wrong" by intervening on behalf of a generous campaign donor; it was that "everybody else does it." Testifying on behalf of embattled colleague Dennis DeConcini, Senator Daniel Inouye admitted, "If [what DeConcini did] is improper, I think all of us at one time or another have done that."

As Jonathan Rowe of the *Christian Science Monitor* has argued, the Keating hearings presented a spectacle "worse than Watergate," since if Watergate "was about a few bad apples, the Keating Five is about the whole barrel." Still, there's been one healthy seed. By now, virtually every editorial page in the country has urged Congress to "get big money out of campaigns." And even though the only one nailed was the one not up for reelection, the Keating Five scandal has provided the impetus for reform that 20 years of Common Cause diatribes about "special interest money perverting the political process" never could.

Of course, it's easy to rant and rave that money is corrupting our political process—the most entrenched and PAC-financed congressmen do so every year. What's more difficult is to translate such apparent good intentions into meaningful reform. What we need aren't quick fixes like spending ceilings or public financing of campaigns. We need a treatment that goes to the root of today's gutter-pitched and skyscraper-priced congressional campaigns. Abolish the PACs, by all means. And then get to work at real reform.

Andrew Bates works for the Political Hotline, a daily political wire service.

From *The Washington Monthly,* April 1991, pp. 35–39. Reprinted with permission from *The Washington Monthly.* Copyright by The Washington Monthly Company, 1611 Connecticut Avenue, N.W., Washington, D.C. 20009. (202)462-0128.

Foley's follies

The best example of the folly of quick-fix reform comes, not surprisingly, from Congress itself, which last year turned a window of opportunity into the Potemkin Village of campaign reform.

Shamed into action by their Keating Five colleagues and prodded by a bipartisan advisory panel whose recommendations provided a reasonable blueprint for compromise, the Senate took the first wobbly step toward change. After years of filibustering or ignoring Democratic proposals, Senate Republicans realized that it would be political suicide not to back some sort of campaign reform. They emerged with a plan banning PACs and sharply restricting the flow of "soft money" generated by the political activities of unions and trade associations. The GOP proposal forced the Democrats' hand, helping produce a credible bipartisan bill that would have eliminated PAC contributions, prohibited the use of the frank for mass mailings during election years, limited out-of-state individual contributions to $250, and established voluntary, state-by-state spending limits.

It was a bill, amazingly, that addressed many of the inequities of the current system. But it didn't reach the president's desk last year. In fact, no campaign reform bill did, thanks, not to some PAC-engorged midwestern committee chair, but to Speaker of the House (and campaign reform "advocate") Tom Foley.

Unlike former Speaker Jim Wright, Foley has never been accused of any ethical wrongdoing. And unlike Majority Leader Richard Gephardt, the leading House recipient of PAC contributions ($650,000 during 1989-90), Foley does not loudly proclaim his commitment to reform and then quietly soak the PACs. Yet, despite his pristine image, Foley has become the greatest obstacle to campaign finance reform.

In 1989, after Wright's forced resignation, both Foley and House Minority Leader Robert Michel stated their intentions to make campaign reform a reality, Michel emotionally proclaiming that the stain of the Wright case would remain until the House passed a "dramatic reform of our campaign laws and practices." With staunch leadership, it appeared that this might be one of the House's rare bipartisan efforts, especially after Michel made overtures to the Democrats, saying that he was amenable to a spending limit. But House Democrats, with little scrutiny from the press, got away with a time-honored gimmick: proclaim your unswerving devotion to issue A, then pass a fluff bill that is so far from real reform that it can't help but derail conference negotiations. For, unlike the Senate, the House didn't have the ghost of the Keating Five hovering over it to spur an honest attempt at campaign reform.

In 1990, Foley and Michel deputized Reps. Al Swift and Guy Vander Jagt to lead negotiations on the issue. Under the agreement, if negotiations broke down over the most contentious questions (such as how high any spending limit should be set), Foley and Michel would then take charge themselves. Yet when the inevitable breakdown occurred in June, the leaders met only once. Foley made no attempt to construct a bipartisan bill of the sort that Senate Majority Leader George Mitchell skillfully put together, one that wouldn't automatically provoke a presidential veto. He refused Michel's invitation to meet to negotiate campaign spending limits as one element in a comprehensive package. He also didn't take the issue to the House Democratic Caucus or force Democrats to resolve their internal differences. As one congressional aide suggested, Foley's behavior made the real campaign agenda perfectly clear: "Stall 'til after the 1992 elections."

But, Congress being Congress, stalling had to look like working. So at the last minute, the House did pass a hastily written campaign finance bill (with Foley's approval)—a bill so bad that even moderate Republicans denounced it as a copout. (Iowa Rep. James Leach called it "a sham and a shame.") For proof, look at the "reform" the task force crafting the House legislation came up with.

First of all, Swift and his cohorts decided to limit spending in House races—to $550,000 per candidate, twice the current average. But that made some urban Democrats nervous. What if $550,000 proved too little after a tough primary fight? So the task force wrote in an additional $165,000 for those who get less than 67 percent of the primary vote. So much for a spending limit.

Next, they decided to limit a candidate's PAC contributions to 50 percent of that ceiling—$275,000, more than the average candidate now spends per campaign. By 1988 election standards, that provision wouldn't have affected the PAC receipts of three-fourths of the 435 members. Still, Congress didn't want to box itself in. At the last minute, a few more soft money loopholes were scribbled in, including exceptions to permit lobbyists to continue serving on members' fundraising committees and to exempt legal and accounting fees from the spending limit.

The net effect, intended or not, was to take a passable Senate bill, which had garnered the support of moderate Republicans and incorporated the GOP's plan to prohibit PAC contributions to federal candidates, and essentially sabotage it. Given the vast differences between the Senate and House versions and the lack of time before incumbent congressmen went home to campaign (and spend more PAC money), members of the Senate-House conference committee in charge of sending the president a bill never had a chance; recognizing this, they decided not to meet. (Even if the committee had met, little would have been accomplished: Foley, succumbing to pressure from both sides of the aisle, had appointed conferees such as John Dingell, chairman of the Energy and Commerce Committee, and William Ford, then chairman of the Post Office and Civil Service Committee, who had little desire for any serious campaign finance reform.)

The scenario the House incumbents were hoping for—let everyone vote for a campaign finance reform measure, and then let it die a quiet death in conference negotiations—came to pass.

Ad nauseum

During the debate on the House floor last year, Rep. Pat Roberts insisted that new campaign finance laws would be a sure bet from the 102nd Congress. "We will get a reform bill, a true reform bill next time, not this time." While we hold our breath, we have a moment to ponder the question: What is true reform?

Liberal congressmen and self-proclaimed public interest groups like Common Cause continually insist that the key to campaign finance reform lies in spending limits and public financing of campaigns. But as Congress so recently proved, spending limits can be set absurdly high or riddled with loopholes.

Public financing is necessary, the argument goes, because private money is inherently tainted and inevitably forces the type of tit for tat seen in the Keating case. But after the eighties' spate of noxious cam-

paigns, the public would rather pay for toxic waste dumps behind elementary schools. Right now only about 20 percent of taxpayers contribute to the presidential check-off fund; as a recent Federal Election Commission-sponsored focus group study suggests, the other 80 percent feel pretty strongly about leaving that box blank. "It was often difficult to keep the group focused on the subject at hand because of their anger at politicians and a perception of wasteful spending by the government," noted the report. "Their anger associated with those concerns contaminated their consideration of presidential campaign financing."

Imagine how furious the public would be at paying for congressional campaigns—and rightfully furious, considering the quality of most of those campaigns. What is necessary is a plan that doesn't merely say "let's hope the candidates don't spend too much" and offer them our tax dollars not to do so. Instead, we need to attack rising campaign costs at the source. So when the 102nd Congress gets together again to talk campaign finance, here's what they should do:

1) *Require free and truthful TV ads.* Real campaign reform must start with campaign spending. And one of the prime factors in accelerating campaign costs is the cost of TV ads. Thomas Mann of the Brookings Institution estimates that between 1976 and 1990, the cost of TV advertising in congressional campaigns rose 169 percent. That, of course, sharpened the imperative to raise money from folks like Charles Keating. The best way to stop this desperate money chase is to give candidates air time for free. Mandate that, in exchange for their broadcast licenses, the Federal Communications Commission require television stations to donate a few minutes every evening during the fortnight prior to the general election for ads from House and Senate candidates.

Still, Senate candidates, who now spend 60 percent of their overall budgets on broadcast ads, don't just blow it filming commercials and buying time on the local network. The real money goes to high-paid political consultants like David Garth and Roger Ailes, whose thinking helps shape those trenchant and sophisticated ads. A corollary reform could dramatically cut their receipts. In exchange for free air time, restrict all TV ads to having the candidate speak directly to viewers or be seen debating his opponent. Not only does this dramatically cut production costs, it also improves the substance of commercials. Anyone who's ever read the transcript of a fabulous TV news segment knows how this works. Without the blue skies and swaying cornfields in the background, the words sound a little different than you remembered. During campaigns, of course, that's a good thing—you'll get a far better look at what you're voting for. For instance, instead of an MTV-style edit showing the candidate orating a crowd into a frenzy, all you get is the candidate orating—letting his *words* stimulate frenzy, if they can.

Talking-head commercials won't just improve the content of innocuous meet-the-candidate spots; they'll also reduce the likelihood of the sleaziest sort of negative ads. Suddenly it's Candidate Kane accusing his opponent of cuddling up inappropriately to zoo creatures —not the faceless Independent Committee to Protect Zebras and Elect Candidate Kane. Making the candidate take responsibility for every word that airs won't make ads all sweetness and light— and shouldn't. (What would campaigns be if candidates couldn't criticize each other's decisions and character?) But it will make candidates more concerned that what they say about their opponents is true. Apply the same rules to radio.

> **Forget public financing: What with congressmen spending $78 million a year on franked mail, we've already got it—but only for incumbents.**

Had these provisions been in effect last year, New Hampshire Republican Bill Zeliff probably wouldn't have used 30-second TV spots to label his leading primary opponent, who had done consulting for foreign corporations, a "paid foreign agent." Texas voters probably would've learned more about their gubernatorial choices than that some of them smoked pot in the seventies. And Rep. Denny Smith of Oregon would've had to scrap that informative ad featuring a backdrop of Adolf Hitler addressing a delirious crowd—the one that accused Democratic challenger Mike Kopetski of siding with Saddam Hussein. "Mike, appeasement is wrong," the announcer intoned. Kopetski's crime? Urging the UN, rather than the U.S., to take the lead in responding to Iraq's invasion of Kuwait. Do such commercials really enhance politicians' stature or improve public discourse?

The chief critics of these proposals would be TV ad departments and the David Garths of this world. However, in 1988, TV stations earned roughly $27 billion in advertising; a few minutes here and there every other year is not going to destroy their revenues. (Clearly, the specifics have to be more precisely worked out for primary elections with larger fields of candidates.) And putting Garth, Ailes, and their cronies out of work is in itself a reason to adopt these changes.

2) *Set out-of-state contribution limits.* There is nothing wrong with a congressional candidate raising, say, $10 from every constituent in his district. There is something seriously wrong with a candidate having 40 percent or more of his campaign spending financed by out-of-state PACs and individual donors. More than a dozen of the 31 senators running for reelection in 1990 received more than half of their campaign funds from outside their home states. Jesse Helms and Harvey Gantt counted on non-constituents to raise 69 and 67 percent, respectively, of their campaign funds—a major reason why the North Carolina Senate race was the most expensive in the nation, with a total of $24.7 million spent. Any comprehensive campaign finance reform must therefore stipulate that 75 percent of the money a candidate raises must come from within the state. For obvious reasons, candidates should be required to raise virtually all their money from the constituents they intend to serve.

3. *Ban all PAC contributions.* It's long been obvious that PACs give money for a single purpose: to influence legislation. And PACs realize that the worst way to do that is to support candidates who don't have a prayer of winning. The easiest way, of course, is to fill the coffers of incumbents, especially those who serve on or chair committees that have jurisdiction over a particular PAC's interests. That's why oil, gas, utility, and other energy industry PACs contributed $236,500 to Senator J. Bennett Johnston, chairman of the Senate Energy Committee, during 1989 and the first quarter of 1990. That's why the powerful trial lawyers' lobby bankrolled the campaign of Senator Ernest Hollings, chairman of the Senate Commerce Committee, who has used his po-

sition to thwart tort reform. If one needed any more proof of what the PACs were up to, last year they gave nearly $80 million to incumbents and a mere $5 million to their opponents. Former Senator William Proxmire puts it succinctly: "The [PAC] contributions, in effect, are bribes."

Critics say that eliminating PACs would only make candidates more dependent on wealthy contributors. But the $1,000 limits on personal and corporate contributions, holdovers from the post-Watergate reforms, would still be in place. Moreover, the out-of-state spending limits would make a lot of those well-to-do contributors irrelevant.

4) *Virtually abolish the franking privilege*, except when a congressman is responding directly to a constituent's query. The frank, which allows members to sign their names to mail in lieu of postage, has long allowed congressmen to flood their districts in election years with what is essentially paid political advertising. Paid for by the taxpayers, that is. Up for re-election in 1990, Senator James McClure had his office send out 608,170 pieces of mail at a cost of $90,300 during the first three months of 1989—more than had been spent on his behalf throughout the previous year. From April to September 1990, Senator Dan Coats of Indiana, who had been appointed to fill Vice President Quayle's seat and faced a special election in November, mailed out a whopping 13.1 million pieces of franked mail—$1.8 million worth.

Members, of course, insist that the frank is used for official business, which begs the question: Why do these mailing costs surge during election years ($78 million in 1988, as compared to $44 million in 1987) and nearly double between the first and last required quarterly reporting periods as an election draws near? Forget public financing: At $34 million a year, we've already got it—but only for incumbents.

5) *Put some bite into the Federal Election Commission (FEC)*. Banning PACs, franking, and slick TV campaigns will do a lot to lower costs and lessen sleaze. But what purpose is there in enacting reforms without a tough, independent regulatory agency to enforce them? By itself, the FEC's structure is a guarantee for gridlock, being made up of six members (three from each party) who are appointed specifically for their partisanship. The result, former FEC Assistant General Counsel Daniel Swillinger explains, is that candidates know "the commission is never going to get four votes, so they can do anything they want. . . . It is undercutting what was anyway a rather weak enforcement system and making it even more toothless."

During the 1988 Senate elections, for instance, the National Republican Senatorial Committee was charged with failing to report nearly $3 million in contributions earmarked for 12 campaigns. The FEC's general counsel found that the committee was in violation of the campaign act; the commission, however, voted along party lines. With a three-to-three tie, no action was taken. The answer here is either to add an odd member or remove the presumption of partisanship in selecting commissioners.

The other major problem with the FEC is a procedural one: The commission is notoriously slow in resolving cases. By the time the FEC figures things out, Mr. Smith is already well into his term. Take one 1982 North Carolina campaign, in which Rep. Charlie Rose charged that his opponent accepted illegal services from a direct mail operation associated with Senator Jesse Helms. Two years later, with the 1984 campaign well under way, the FEC was still investigating those old charges.

FECless

To make comprehensive reform work, the FEC will have to be aggressive, making sure that complaints filed during a particular general election period can be resolved before the campaign is over. To that end, Congress should give the FEC the power to conduct field investigations and random audits, to seek injunctions in enforcement cases so that it can act promptly when a violation is about to occur, and to impose stiff fines on transgressors.

These FEC reforms aren't radical: In fact, they're made every year by the commission itself in its annual report to Congress. The real difficulty, as David Magleby and Candice Nelson point out in *The Money Chase*, is that the FEC is currently "just the kind of agency Congress wants to regulate campaign finance laws; it provides disclosure but rarely acts in a way that could influence an election outcome."

The same bluff applies in all aspects of congressional campaign reform. And members of the House, many of whom raise twice as much from out-of-state PACs as their challengers raise overall, are sure to balk at these five proposals, as they have done through the years at even the most tepid legislative reform.

That fact shouldn't surprise us: Who expects morality from Congress? What we *do* expect, however, is self-interest. And that may be what ultimately pushes Congress toward real campaign reform. A few more Keating Five-type episodes may do more than erode the institution's sagging credibility. It may prompt voters to start slapping term limits on their members. And that should do the trick. For the one thing incumbents hate more than campaign reform is not getting the chance to campaign at all.

Article 2.   The Repackaging of Dan Quayle
by Christopher Hitchens

The author describes the packaging—and repackaging—of Vice President Dan Quayle—and the steps taken by Bush campaign strategists to "sell" him to the American public. Despite the media's attempt to portray the vice president as a "clown," the real Dan Quayle is far brighter than his critics acknowledge. Assuming that the Bush-Quayle team is reelected in 1992—and that GOP handlers continue to polish the Quayle image—the vice president could well be a formidable presidential candidate by 1996.

A freezing January morning at Logan Airport caused the alighting passengers on Air Force Two to wince —as well they might do anyway, in anticipation of a visit to Democratic Boston in the company of J. Danforth Quayle, Deputy Leader of the Free World. The Vice President was spending one of his increasingly adventurous "days out," and with little to keep me in Washington—Congress recessed, the President and his OMB director huddling to scheme how *not* to cut the defense budget— I'd requested permission (granted late and with reluctance) to accompany the man who wants to be—and, more important, could be—the next president of the United States.

As Quayle was borne away from the tarmac on a tide of handlers and Secret Service men, I noticed how his pointless good looks and uncheckable grin already seemed familiar to me— and this after only a short flight in his company. A Coast Guard launch swept him across the snowy estuary (1), and then a cavalcade set out for Mission Hill, stopping on St. Alphonsus Street—where Carol Stuart and her son-to-be, Christopher, were found with the gut-shot Charles, whose lies and suicide had just reminded Boston about itself, again.

I never quite know what conservatives think when they come to neighborhoods like this one, in the heart of deprived Roxbury. Do they see poten-

Christopher Hitchens is the Washington editor of Harper's Magazine.

tial enterprise zones? Do they think they'll meet blue-collar Democrats to lure? Do they ever ask what we need an underclass for? Anyway, in this case the location of St. Alphonsus Street was coincidental, set up by an advance team well before the Stuart case became a complex, rather than a simple, race problem. Quayle was here to visit Mission Grammar School: Catholic, devoted to traditional values, and celebrating its centennial.

Quayle entered a classroom of first-graders and sat, without affectation or embarrassment, on a tiny chair. He talked easily to the children and to their teacher. He secured a press photograph of himself embracing, in delightful miniature, the united colors of Benetton.

He moved on to a specially called assembly, to which he spoke, without special passion, about "just saying no" and the possibility that the young may live to see the Stars and Stripes hoisted on Mars. The school pastor had made mention, in his opening prayer, of the unborn, but the Vice President made no such mention. The pledge to the flag was made stirringly by all (2). The children said that they would enter the Vice President's name on their "prayer list," and he seemed to like that (3).

Then it was off to a GOP fundraiser at the Copley Plaza Hotel. No united colors of Benetton here. Quayle got two standing ovations from the $100-a-plate capacity

crowd, many of whom had paid $500 extra to be photographed with him. Quayle blasted *Time* magazine for making Gorbachev its man of the decade; Reagan and Bush, he declared, should have shared that honor. And he invoked the Stuart case—to remind the Republicans that they are the party of Lincoln; that they miscued on civil rights in the Sixties and must not do so again (4).

After this exhortation, greeted with no better than tepid applause, he dashed off to the Union Oyster House to chat with the Boston Police Patrolman's Association. They presented him with a golfing jacket and pounded him on the back—more tenderly, I couldn't help but think, than their brethren had pounded for weeks on the doors (and skulls) of Mission Hill in their "stop and search" hunt for Carol Stuart's killer. This was the second "payback" visit to the patrolmen from Messrs. Bush and Quayle, who have not forgotten the blow that the cops' highly visible Republican endorsement dealt to Michael Dukakis on his home turf. The air was clotted with "making nice" and boisterous male bonhomie.

Finally to Faneuil Hall, cradle of American liberties, for the swearing-in of GOP moneybags Peter Senopoulos as a new member of the American Battle Monuments Commission. Flags and drums were provided by the Ancient and Honorable Artillery Company, once described by James M. Curley, Democratic boss here for half a century, as "invincible in peace, invisible in war." Quayle spoke throatily of those who made the supreme sacrifice and of his own recent visit to an American war memorial in the Philippines (5). It could hardly have subtracted from his joy or his pride that the outgoing—that is to say, shoved out—commissioner was one Joseph Canzeri, the very same Joseph Canzeri who told Jack Germond and Jules Witcover, for their book on the '88 campaign, that Quayle was "like a kid. Ask him to turn off a light, and by the time he gets to the switch, he's forgotten what he went for." (6)

Yet to recall that campaign, and to carefully review my notes 1–6, is to see that Quayle successfully touched the following bases on his day trip to Boston. He was (1) ferried in style across Boston Harbor. He took part (2) in a genuine flag salute and Pledge of Allegiance. He heard himself put on a "prayer list" (3) without any embarrassing reminiscence about his debate with Lloyd Bentsen, a debate in which he said that were he to become president suddenly (the heartbeat-away scenario), the first thing he would do would be to pray. He dealt cleverly (4) with the shade of Willie Horton and race and class justice. He managed a sentimental address to veterans (5) without any awkward bringing-up of his notorious reluctance to shoulder a rifle and pack for Indochina. (Who now remembers the campaign gag about crossing a hawk and a chicken to get a Quayle?) He saw off a minor but irritating political critic (6) and saw him replaced by a right-wing Massachusetts Greek.

I should add that Quayle made no gaffes that day and very few slips in delivery; that he managed to insert a compassionate reference to Kitty Dukakis's recent difficulties; and that he returned to Andrews Air Force Base looking pretty pleased with himself. He had, in effect, pressed all the Democrats' bells and run away. The next day's *Boston Globe* carried a long, positive, respectful report on the visit, complete with a large front-page picture of the Benetton moment.

This experiment in the political exorcism of past crimes and blunders was not the last I witnessed. Later that week, the United States Conference of Mayors convened in the capital (in the regrettable absence of Marion Barry, whose character and associations were set out in my Letter of last October). I happened to be on the telephone with David Beckwith, Quayle's genial, obstructive press officer, when he dropped the receiver. As he struggled back onto the line, he was gurgling and panting. "Guess who I've got for you?" he said. "Art Agnos just dropped by to make up."

I didn't quite believe it, until he actually put the mayor of San Francisco on the line. After all, Quayle's post-earthquake visit to S. F. had generally been accounted one of the worst disasters of his infant vice presidency, with Agnos ridiculing Quayle's photo-op tactics on *Nightline* and accusing him of getting in the way, and the press snickering as Quayle discovered that the suffering in the Bay Area was "heart-rendering" and that "the loss of life is irreplaceable." Yet here was Agnos, making a courtesy call and saying that he'd dropped by, among other things, to make amends for a duel with Beckwith on Larry King's TV show. "We wanted to make sure we weren't the assholes we seemed on TV," Agnos explained to me. (I later was told by witnesses that he'd actually *kissed* Beckwith.) It was the work of an instant to whisk the Democratic chameleon into the vice presidential office for a manly hand-

clasp and to start making triumphant telephone calls to the West Coast.

Is it possible that, after all, Roger Ailes and the boys were onto something when they pressed the idea of J. Danforth Quayle on George Herbert Walker Bush? The liberal press, which has learned less than nothing from its consistent underestimation of first Reagan and then his vice president, continues to miss the point. Reporters and editorialists alike prefer to concentrate only on the Quayle *style*, the gaffes and embarrassments. As if there weren't enough real flubs, the papers have taken to manufacturing some—e.g., the one about Quayle saying he wished he'd learned Latin in order to get on better with Latin Americans.

The difficulty with this shallow journalism is twofold: It gets boring and repetitive after a bit, and it puts Quayle in a position where he has nowhere to go but upward. As both Reagan and Bush have good cause to know, the latter is not such a bad position to be starting from. And Quayle's admittedly impressive tomfooleries and fatuities are a bagatelle compared to the lying and boasting of Ronald Reagan or the train-wreck sentences and syntactical miasma of the present incumbent.

Which brings us to a third point—namely, that all may be forgiven of those who make it in the end. A tendency to gaffe and an inability to get on good terms with the language can become part of your likable, human persona if you are in power. The authors of the current *Dan Quayle Quiz Book* may not yet appreciate the catchpenny favor they are doing their target. A day may come when Middle America makes Quayle's vulnerability an occasion for sympathy and affection. It's been done before.

This is not to say that Quayle is any less of an empty vessel than he has been represented as being. Watching and listening up close, I saw nothing to suggest that if his brains were made of TNT they would generate enough explosive power to disarrange his hair. And he has the most nervous and protective media staff I have ever encountered. At our first discussion, press boss Beckwith, a *Time* magazine hack of nearly two decades' standing, leveled with me. "I've got to tell you, Mr. Hitchens," he said hurriedly, "we're all a bit gun-shy around here." The relief that members of the staff displayed when the trip to Boston was over and we were heading for home was touching in its intensity.

Quayle's staff is, in many ways, the most interesting thing about him. To visit the vice presidential floor of the old Executive Office Building is to visit the last ark of the Reagan Revolution, with choice youngish specimens of all the species of 1980s conservative somewhere on board. As chief of staff we discover William Kristol, son of neo-con Irving and a veteran of that lost and mysterious time spent by William Bennett at the Department of Education. Kristol's secretary, Kathleen Connolly, is the sister of raver Pat Buchanan. Robert Novak's daughter Zelda is on the research staff. Joseph Shattan, formerly an aide to Jeane Kirkpatrick, is a speechwriter. In charge of foreign policy is Carnes Lord, a shell-back conservative and probable disciple of Chicago savant Leo Strauss. If the now dispirited and ambivalent movement calling itself American conservatism has any focus for its teleology in the age of Gorbachev, that hope is located somewhere among the Quayle bestiary as now accoutred and assembled.

Note, however, that this right-wing galère represents a qualitative step up for young Danforth. Around the house he has been nurtured not by conservative thought but by barking, irrational, thoughtless quackery. Mom and Dad are faithful Birchers; Dad has endorsed *The National Educator*, a magazine in which one can read that while the Democratic party is

"firmly committed to the Moscow wing of the Communist Party," the Republicans are "firmly committed to the Trotskyite wing of the Communist Party, headquartered in Tel Aviv." And at home, in the domestic bliss of D.C., we find the tempestuous Marilyn Quayle, wife, mother, and devotee of the Reverend Colonel Robert Thieme Jr., a drool-flecked pulpit banger and paranoid separator of fools from money. It's a wonder Quayle is as calm and reflective as he is.

On arriving at the Senate in the great Reagan levee of 1980, the young Quayle got off to a rough start by granting a lavish interview to *Spotlight*, published by the Liberty Lobby, which likes to keep an eye on Semitic activity around town (and internationally). He shepherded the nomination of Indiana fruitcake Daniel Manion to a widely ridiculed federal judgeship. Then he hired Robert Owen as a staffer and allowed this lachrymose acolyte to employ his office for crazoid meetings between Oliver North's private army and various drifters from Central America. It was in the Quayle sanctum that Owen introduced North to John Hull, now under multiple indictment in Costa Rica.

This is no longer Quayle's scene. The handlers and imagemakers have gotten him away from the clerical kooks and out of the frazzled *Soldier of Fortune* milieu. Stuart K. Spencer, the marketing and packaging genius whose consulting firm ran the Quayle vice presidential campaign (and, more recently, was paid $350,000 to help General Noriega with *his* intractable image problems), was very blunt in a 1988 interview. "Dan Quayle doesn't know about cities," he said. "He doesn't know who lives there, ghettos, traffic, race, crime, housing, all of that stuff, but we'll teach him." Spencer also said, "First, we had to shut that John Birch father of his up." It seems to me that in Boston I was shown some evidence of the Spencer effect, and all of us will be seeing more of it.

Dan Quayle was no doubt willing to be repackaged. He shied away from the Judiciary Committee not long

after his election to the Senate, complaining that "they are going to be dealing with all those issues like abortion, busing, voting rights, prayers. I'm not interested in those issues, and I want to stay as far away from them as I can." Though he made the obligatory attacks on Senator Edward Kennedy while addressing Boston Republicans, Quayle's first imprint on the nation's greatest deliberative body was as cosponsor, with the senior senator from Massachusetts, of the Job Training Partnership Act. He may be no Ted Kennedy, but the subliminal association probably did him no damage in the eyes of the professional pols.

"He is a conservative Republican who always wanted to be part of the governing majority." Thus the highly polished William Kristol, in a brief and exquisitely careful interview with me. "He was often more liberal than Reagan—he voted to override the veto on South African sanctions and he favored the Martin Luther King holiday. But most conservatives regard him as one of them."

That's not especially bad strategy if you think about it: Quayle is distancing himself from the Right in consensus terms while retaining his option as their only plausible champion for the next round. Kristol went on to surmise—cleverly, I thought—that "at the generational level" there is a point where old distinctions within the conservative movement don't matter anymore, or as much as they did. "[Quayle] doesn't have the baggage that Ronald Reagan was carrying," Kristol said, on matters like states' rights and the Vietnam War. The younger conservatives for whom Quayle is being groomed are not going to ask—are not going to care about—where Quayle stood "back then." This is postmodernism, and this makes the repackaging a good deal easier.

I wonder, though, if any handler can train the Vice President to accept the passing of the Cold War. Within the administration and within the Republican party, Quayle hangs as tough as he dares on any question affecting "national security." And, difference of "tone" or not, he has made it plain that he is nostalgic for the Russia bashing and all that goes with it.

Kristol seemed defensive on this point. "The Vice President has been reading William Manchester's second volume on Winston Churchill," I was told, "and has also been talking to Stephen Sestanovich at the Center for Strategic and International Studies. He was very struck by Steve's phrase 'Weimar Russia.'" Of course I'm familiar with the idea that all Republicans in a tight corner will reach for their Churchill, and of course CSIS has been indispensable for the Cold War head-bangers of both parties, but I don't think that Quayle had heard of either Manchester or Sestanovich when he recommended that Tom Clancy be made an adviser to the National Space Council, and I have a journalistic instinct about whose prose has been the more influential.

Let us not forget that Quayle's major stand in the Senate, aside from his "bipartisan" moment with Kennedy, was with the arms lobby in favor of the grandiose AWACS sale, wherein he acted as point man. Or that his first real tooth-cutting as Vice President involved a fight for Senator John Tower, the defense lobby's faithful executant, in his now forgotten nomination for secretary of defense.

These days Quayle's relationship with the defense establishment is both more intimate and more discreet. As he demonstrated by his uplifting clichés about Martian exploration to the trusting children of Mission Hill, he can cloak this relationship in concern for "space." As head of the National Space Council, he is free to pursue a fantasy—the fantasy of the Star Wars shield—that is too embarrassing to be avowed publicly by an administration as timid and surreptitious as this one. His two senior appointments to the council have been Lieutenant Colonel Pete Warden, an underling of Lieutenant General James Abrahamson when the latter ran the Strategic Defense Initiative for Reagan, and Mark Albrecht, a former chief defense aide to SDI fanatic Senator Pete Wilson. With Wilson, then-Senator Quayle helped preserve the idea of interceptors in the outer atmosphere and the even

wilder idea of testing antisatellite weapons. On one occasion, he spoke movingly of the latter on the Senate floor, paying another debt to Tom Clancy (rather than to Winston Churchill) by saying that the United States prevailed in *Red Storm Rising* only because of its antisatellite capacity. On another, he gratified his father by making the working assumption that the earth was flat, saying, "Eventually we will probably see agreements to establish self-defense zones in space that will actually divide up space between the Soviet Union, the United States, and other nations. If others come within our zones, then in fact they would be infringing on our territory."

"Come within our zones..." Yet it is not these ludicrous and sinister gaffes that get Quayle his reputation as a clown. Every tired caption- or headline-writer drags out a stale allusion to the Veep's fondness for golf, but how many stories have you read about Quayle's role in the "Brilliant Pebbles" proposal? This little scheme, which involves the seeding of space with thousands of tiny orbiting interceptors, has also been termed "Smart Rocks." Research and development of "Smart Rocks" is now official administration policy, which makes it less funny; and the SDI cabal credits Quayle as much as Defense Secretary Dick Cheney with the decision to proceed. The Cold War, in other words, *can* continue to be fought by contractors and pseudo-scientists even if there is no longer a believable adversary. (In Bush's "trimmed" defense budget for 1991, one finds a proposed 22 percent increase for Star Wars, with almost all the new money—about $800 million—pegged for "Smart Rocks.")

All of which is to say that if the more fierce and senseless bits of the Reagan–Bush legacy are to be carried through the 1990s, it is likely that Dan Quayle, rather than, for example, Jack Kemp, will be doing the bearing. (Quayle is *not* at a loss in space; Kemp is as earthbound as possible, mired in the sludge of post-Reagan HUD.) You object, perhaps, that Quayle has no weight, no authority, no power to dispense reassurance

or inspiration. No, he does not. But these things can be simulated, as they were for Reagan and for Bush, each rightly considered a joke candidate in his day.

Six of the last eight vice presidents have received their party's nomination for the presidency. Quayle himself is qualm-free about the prospect, telling the *New York Times,* "When you get into public life and particularly when you run for the Senate, there are only two offices left: president and vice president." One has to credit the presumption and sheer gall of someone who can say this when the only smart thing ever associated with his name is a rock (and that a pebble). But by 1996, if the schedule goes smoothly, Quayle may have been remade and may come before the country as someone no longer an *enfant,* if still unquestionably *terrible.* ∎

Article 3. Most Valuable Player
by Roger Simon

This article examines the Willie Horton phenomenon—specifically, how the Bush campaign succeeded in turning a convicted murderer and rapist into an explosive campaign issue—so much so that the now-infamous television commercial, which ran for twenty-eight days and imputed that Democratic presidential candidate Mike Dukakis was "soft on crime," did more to elect the vice president than any other single issue.

HE WAS BIG. He was black. He was ugly. He was every guy you ever crossed a street to avoid, every pair of smoldering eyes you ever looked away from on the bus or subway.

He was every person you moved out of the city to escape, every sound in the night that made you get up and check the locks on the windows and grab the door handles and give them an extra tug.

Whether you were white or black or red or yellow, Willie Horton was your worst nightmare. "I thought of all the late nights I had ridden in terror on the F and A trains while living in New York City," Anthony Walton, a black writer and filmmaker, would write in *The New York Times Magazine*. "I thought Willie Horton must be what the wolf packs I had often heard about, but never seen, must look like. I said to myself, 'Something has got to be done about these niggers.' "

Horton defied common sense, which dictated that criminals committed crimes for some reason, for some gain. Give them what they wanted and they would leave you alone.

But Willie Horton did not care if you gave it to him or not. As he would demonstrate at least twice, giving him what he asked for would not make any difference. Horton liked crime. He did it for pleasure, for power, for control.

Decent people had no defense against him. That was the most terrifying thing of all. Capture him and take away his knife and sentence him and put him behind bars—we pay taxes for these things!—and what would happen?

He would be given a weekend furlough. Ten times, Michael Dukakis opened up the prison doors in Massachusetts and said to Willie Horton: "Go and sin no more."

Nine times Horton followed instructions. But the tenth time, he went to Maryland and broke into a home and tied a man to a joist in the basement, slashed his chest and stomach with a knife, then beat and raped his fiancée while she screamed and screamed and screamed.

Willie Horton was a killer, a rapist, a torturer, a kidnapper, a brute.

In other words, he was perfect.

BY 1988, the average television viewer had the set on for 6 hours and 59 minutes per day. There was entertainment, sports, drama, adventure, comedy, sex, documentaries, anything. And it was free. All you had to do was put up with the commercials that paid for it all. Every week, the average viewer saw about 1,000 commercials. They became part of our lives. We could recognize the jingles, the catchphrases, the music. We could date ourselves by the time stamp that commercials placed on our memories: "You'll wonder where the yellow went, when you brush your teeth with Pepsodent." The Marlboro Man. "I can't believe I ate the whole thing!" The Gardol shield. "See the USA in your Chevrolet!" L.S.M.F.T.

We didn't "watch" commercials. They were just there. They entered into our subconscious. Which made them a very potent force in American politics.

"The [political] commercials make the American public captive in two respects," Curtis Gans, director of the Committee for the Study of the American Electorate, wrote. "Since they occur in the midst of regular programming, they cannot be readily shut off. And since their primary appeal is not to reason but rather to emotions, they are virtually unanswerable."

The first political video commercial preceded television. In 1934, Upton Sinclair, the great muckraker, ran for governor of California as a Democrat. His big issue was hardly surprising considering the country was in the depths of the Great Depression: he wanted to eliminate poverty.

To combat him, the Republicans hired an ad agency and the first political consulting firm in the country, Whitaker & Baxter, to paint Sinclair as a crazed Bolshevik.

"Whitaker & Baxter produced phony newsreels of staged events," wrote Edwin Diamond and Stephen Bates in *The Spot: The Rise of Political Advertising on Television*. "In one, dozens of bedraggled hoboes leap off a freight train. . . . Explains one bum: 'Sinclair says he'll take the property of the working people and give it to us.' In another commercial, a bearded man with a Russian accent explains why he'll vote for Sinclair: 'His system vorked vell in Russia, so vy can't it vork here?' "

The phony newsreels were shown in movie theaters all over California thanks to Louis B. Mayer, head of M-G-M and a power in the Republican Party. Though more than a half century has passed, the fundamentals of that first negative video commercial are the same that are used in negative TV ads today: fear, danger and stereotyping the enemy.

Thomas Rosser Reeves, Jr., the son of a Methodist minister, became a millionaire in the advertising business by inventing something he called the USP: unique selling proposition. If you had a candy-coated piece of chocolate, you didn't say it was "delicious" or the "best" candy in the world. You said it "melts in your mouth—not in your hand."

"We discovered that this was no tame kitten; we had a ferocious man-eating tiger," Reeves said. "We could take the same advertising campaign from print or radio and put it on TV, and, even when there were very few sets, sales would go through the roof."

Harry Truman saw the possibilities of the infant medium. At the 1948 Democratic convention in Philadelphia, Truman delivered his acceptance speech in a white suit and dark tie, which *The New York Times* noted was "the best masculine garb for the video cameras." When another speaker at the convention announced plans to dramatize high food prices by waving a piece of meat at the cameras, the publicity director of the convention insisted the speech be scheduled for something called "prime time." People were learning.

But it was Reeves who saw the real possibilities of political ads. If TV ads could sell M&Ms, they could also sell a President. So he went to Thomas E. Dewey, Truman's Republican opponent. "This could be a very close election," Reeves told him. "I can pretty much tell which states are going to be close. If you would start two or three weeks before election day and saturate those critical states with spots, it could swing the election."

Dewey wouldn't even consider it. "I don't think it would be dignified," he said.

Dewey lost. In 1948, there were fewer than 500,000 TV sets in America. Four years later, there were nearly 19 million.

And nobody ever said no to television again.

☆

WILLIE HORTON was already famous in Massachusetts by the time Michael Dukakis began his campaign for President. But in July 1988, *Reader's Digest* gave America its first in-depth look at Horton in an article the Bush campaign would reprint by the tens of thousands. The article was titled "Getting Away With Murder" and free-lance writer Robert James Bidinotto began by recounting Horton's first big-time crime.

It was October 26, 1974, and Joey Fournier, seventeen, was working alone at a gas station in Lawrence, Massachusetts. William Robert Horton, Jr., Alvin Wideman and Roosevelt Pickett entered the station, brandished knives and demanded money. Fournier gave them $276.37 and pleaded for his life.

They killed him anyway.

Minutes later one of Fournier's friends dropped by and found Fournier's lifeless body stuffed in a trash barrel. He had been stabbed nineteen times.

Horton and the two others were arrested and all confessed to the robbery, but none confessed to the murder. Horton had previously served three years in South Carolina for assault with intent to commit murder and prosecutors believed he had done the stabbing.

In May 1975, all three men were convicted of armed robbery and first-degree murder. (Just which of the three actually stabbed Fournier—or whether it was done by one or two or all three—was not established in court. Under the law, it was irrelevant who actually delivered the killing blow. Under the law, all three were guilty of murder.)

A few weeks before they were sentenced, Michael Dukakis had vetoed a bill that would have instituted the death penalty in Massachusetts. But the state had a very severe first-degree murder law, which mandated life without parole.

Under a furlough program begun by Republican Governor Francis Sargent in 1972, however, Horton and the others would be eligible for unguarded forty-eight-hour weekend furloughs. Horton was granted ten such furloughs. On the last one, from the Northeastern Correctional Center in Concord on June 7, 1986, Horton went to a movie, a church, a few stores in Lawrence, and then disappeared.

"I didn't plan to do that," he later said. "It was spontaneous. I was out of bounds in my conduct."

OVER THE DECADES, we have learned not to demand absolute, technical truth from TV commercials. The negative TV ads directed against Michael Dukakis and his furlough program never told the complete, absolute, technical truth. They were TV commercials; they didn't have to. Ads are not about facts anyway. They are about emotions. They are very often about fear. Psychoanalyst Erich Fromm was the first to note that fear was the basis for much of American advertising. The famous and long-running "ring around the collar" ads featured people embarrassed in front of their bosses or co-workers or friends by having dirty shirt collars. But they could be rescued from the future fear of humiliation by a laundry detergent.

"This general fear operates primarily on an unconscious level," wrote Hal Himmelstein in *Television Myth and the American Mind*. "The solution to our rejection comes in the form of miracles." In political ads, the miracle that will cure our problems, save our nation, reduce the deficit and eliminate our fears is a person who represents a particular way of life. Ronald Reagan understood it well. He continually promised miracles: he would build a great nation, lower taxes, spend more for defense and balance the budget all at the same time.

Eight years later, the fear was of crime and any atavistic terror that lay deep within the souls of the voters. George Bush was the miracle. He was the cure. He would keep us safe. Safe from crime, safe from harm, safe from Willie.

WILLIE HORTON left Massachusetts and went to Maryland by car. On April 3, 1987, he broke into a home in Oxon Hill, a working-class suburb of Washington, D.C. The home was owned by two people who came to be known to America as "the Maryland couple." They were Clifford Barnes and Angela Miller and they were engaged to be married.

Cliff was twenty-eight and a sales manager for a car dealership in Washington. Angi was twenty-seven and did accounting work for a development company in Virginia. They were both registered as independent voters.

At 7:20 p.m., Cliff came home from work. His wedding to Angi was two months off. She was spending the evening at a birthday party with friends.

Cliff started unbuttoning his shirt as he walked up the stairs. He stripped off his tie and went into the bathroom. While there, he heard noises from downstairs and figured Angi might have come home early.

"Angi?" he called out. There was no answer.

Willie Horton kicked in the bathroom door. He was wearing a stocking mask. Earlier in the day, he had broken into the house through the basement and had searched the place. He had found Cliff's handgun. Now he hit Cliff across the head with it, while screaming obscenities at him at the top of his lungs.

Horton pushed Cliff to the floor, tied his hands behind his back and went through his pockets. Then he led him to the basement and tied him to a two-by-four support, using telephone cord and Cliff's shirt and necktie. He blindfolded and gagged him.

Then the torture began. Horton told Cliff he was going to hang him by his neck in the basement and watch him strangle. Then he jammed the gun barrel into Cliff's eyes hard enough to blacken them. Then he rammed the gun into Cliff's mouth. Then he began slashing Cliff with a knife. He slashed him across the stomach in all directions.

"Do you know how scary it is to have somebody drag a knife across your body and never know when they're going to push it in?" Cliff said later.

Cliff told Horton where his credit cards and bank cards were. He told Horton everything Horton asked. But the torture did not stop.

About 2:30 a.m., Angi came home. She walked up to the bedroom, where she noticed a broken beer bottle and Cliff's eyeglasses. As she walked back out into the hall, Horton jumped her.

He rammed the gun into her face, grabbed her by the throat and dragged her into the bedroom. He tied her hands behind her back and blindfolded her. Then he tore open her shirt and camisole. He cut her jeans open with his knife, dragged the knife over her body and raped her.

"Total disbelief," Angi said later, describing her emotions during the rape. "Then fear. Constant fear. Constant survival mixed with fear. Do anything you can to just get out of it alive. And then if you get a chance to kill them, that's what you want. You just want to get a chance to get ahold of that gun."

After he was done, Angi tried to distract him. She asked him to get her a beer, which he did. She asked him to watch TV, which they did. All the while, Horton held the gun to the back of her neck.

Then Horton raped her again, in the living room this time with the stereo turned on. Angi tried to grab the gun, but failed. "He got really violent with me," Angi said.

She did not know if Cliff was dead or alive, but Cliff could hear her screams while she was being raped and beaten. When he heard the second attack starting, Cliff knew he might be able to escape.

"This is really terrible, but if he hadn't attacked her, raped her a second time, I wouldn't have tried to escape because the way he had me blindfolded, I couldn't really tell where he was at," Cliff said.

Cliff managed to get free. Bleeding from his many knife wounds, his clothes hanging from him in shreds, he fled the house and ran for help. He pounded on the doors of four neighbors before one let him in to call the police.

When Horton had finished with Angi, he discovered Cliff had escaped from the basement. Knowing the police would soon be there, he began loading up Cliff's Camaro with booty from the house. While he was doing this, Angi escaped through a bathroom window.

Horton took off in the car and led police on a chase northbound down the southbound lane of a nearby highway. After a shoot-out with officers in which he was wounded, Horton was captured. It was now about 7 a.m.

Horton was tried and convicted of multiple counts including rape, kidnapping and attempted murder. Prince George's County circuit judge Vincent J. Femia sentenced Horton to two consecutive life terms plus eighty-five years and refused to allow Horton to return to prison in Massachusetts until he was done serving his time in Maryland.

"I'm not going to take the chance you'll be on the streets again, because you're dangerous," Judge Femia told Horton. "You should never breathe a breath of fresh air again. You should be locked up until you die."

("I never did the rape," Horton indignantly told me. Horton was not the only person feeling sorry for Horton. The Bush campaign's use of Horton would make him into the one thing he was not: a victim. There would be stories sympathetic to him. "During this whole ordeal, nobody has cared about *me*," Horton said. "I was used. Nobody knows the truth of my innocence. Someday they will." Horton had no shortage of people wishing to tell his story. While he was in prison, he had an aide to help him screen media interview requests.)

Later, Cliff found out that while in prison in Massachusetts, Horton had been cited for eleven disciplinary violations, including possession of drugs and drug paraphernalia. Yet during that period, Massachusetts prison officials had given Horton evaluations of "excellent" and said "he projects a quiet sense of responsibility."

Dukakis eventually would call Horton's furlough a "terrible mistake." But he would never apologize to the Barneses. The Dukakis campaign said there was no need for Dukakis to apologize for something that was not his fault. The Barneses never forgave Dukakis for that.

Cliff and Angi did not return to their home (though they had to continue the mortgage payments on it). They rented a house for a while—and got five large guard dogs—before buying a new home. Cliff checks all the doors and windows each day. Angi doesn't like to go out after dark anymore and doesn't like to be anywhere alone. She is withdrawn. Cliff is angry. They don't mind admitting that their sex life suffered.

Cliff, Angi and Horton were all tested for AIDS. All tested negative, but the Barneses worry that it might show up later. They worry about that because Horton was using drugs in prison. "How many clean needles can you get in prison?" Cliff asks.

Cliff doesn't sleep well and Angi wants to sleep all the time. When she does, she keeps a knife on the nightstand. Sometimes she keeps one by the bathtub.

Every time Cliff and Angi saw Willie Horton's face on TV during the election campaign, they remembered how lucky they were to be alive.

"The last guy who met Horton wasn't so lucky," Cliff said.

WHEN ROGER AILES heard the story of Willie Horton, he immediately saw its potential as an ad campaign for George Bush.

"The only question," Ailes said, "is whether we depict Willie Horton with a knife in his hand or without it."

THE FURLOUGH of Willie Horton was a supremely rational decision. Prisons are expensive ($15,000 to keep a person in prison for a year; up to $75,000 for each new cell built) and crowded. Over the decades, many governors of Massachusetts had commuted the sentences of men sentenced to life without parole.

Some of these men were old. Some were sick. Some were of no further harm (the governors hoped) to the community. So a furlough was a way of helping a man adjust to the outside world, a world he might eventually enter even though sentenced to life without parole.

Besides, furloughs were a way of maintaining discipline. A man with no chance of getting out of prison had no reason to behave himself while in prison. He was a danger to the guards and other inmates. But the possibility of a weekend pass was an incentive for good behavior.

Nationally, first-degree murderers serve only eight years on average before they are paroled or have their sentences commuted. So Massachusetts was hardly out of step with the rest of the nation. Under Michael Dukakis, Massachusetts had one of the lowest crime and incarceration rates of any industrialized state in the country. Furloughs were cost-effective and progressive. They were sensible. Michael Dukakis understood that kind of thing. His life revolved around that kind of thing. Government was based on sense. And furloughs made sense. As do a lot of things. Until they go wrong.

LEE ATWATER always insisted he first learned about the furlough issue from the Democrats. It was one of the few things he ever gave the Democrats credit for. Al Gore had raised the furlough issue on April 12, 1988, in New York during a primary debate, though he did not name Willie Horton.

The Republicans already were looking for dirt, however. Atwater had already formed what he called his "Nerd Patrol."

"The only group that I was very interested in having report to me directly," Atwater said after the election, "was opposition research." Opposition research was headed by Jim Pinkerton, thirty, who had worked in the 1980 Reagan campaign, at the White House and at the Republican National Committee. "He had about thirty-five excellent nerds who were in the research division," Atwater said. "They came back with enough data to fill up this room."

The Nerd Patrol researched the Democratic candidates, every controversial thing they had ever said, every controversial position they had ever taken or policy they had carried out. Dukakis, as the likely nominee, soon became their chief target. In the end, the thirty-five excellent nerds produced 125,000 quotes from 436 different sources and put them all on a computer disk for instant recall.

But Jim Pinkerton, too, claimed he first heard about the furlough issue from the Democratic debate in New York. A light went off in his head. And he called one of his best Massachusetts sources, Andy Card, a former Republican legislator now working at the White House. Pinkerton asked Card about furloughs. Card filled him in on Willie Horton and more. "If you think that's bad, let me tell you about the Pledge," Card said to Pinkerton. Dukakis had vetoed a bill that would have required teachers to lead schoolchildren in the Pledge of Allegiance because the state supreme court and the attorney general had said it was unconstitutional and unenforceable. Now Pinkerton had two issues.

"It was sort of like looking for penicillin and discovering nylon instead," Pinkerton said.

So Pinkerton told Atwater about Willie Horton and a light went off in Atwater's head, too. "It's the single biggest negative Dukakis has got," Atwater said.

And that's the way the Bush campaign insisted it happened: the Democrats raised furloughs first. So go blame Al Gore for injecting Willie Horton into the campaign. Don't blame us.

But if Pinkerton really did first hear about the furlough issue from Al Gore, he should have been fired for incompetence. (Instead, Pinkerton was sworn in as deputy assistant to the President for policy planning on January 23, 1989.)

Because Pinkerton didn't need a Nerd Patrol poring over news clippings and transcripts of Democratic debates to learn about furloughs and Willie Horton. All he had to do was read some national magazines or watch TV.

Newsweek not only wrote about furloughs three months before Al Gore mentioned them during the New York primary but also provided details about Horton. On January 25, 1988, *Newsweek*'s Boston bureau chief, Mark Starr, wrote a half-page story about a voter registration drive in Massachusetts prisons. (Massachusetts is one of the very few states where inmates can vote.) The prisoners were organizing into a voting bloc because they were worried that the furlough program would be curtailed because of the "William Horton, Jr." scandal.

"The Massachusetts program has been under attack since last April, when William Horton Jr., a convicted killer who fled while on furlough, was arrested in Maryland after raping a woman and stabbing her companion," Starr wrote.

The article did not mention Dukakis' name and was not treated as a political story. But Pinkerton could have been expected to know who the governor of Massachusetts was even without the Nerd Patrol.

And if nobody in the Bush campaign was reading *Newsweek*, that still left *Business Week*. In the March 28, 1988, issue at the end of an opinion column attacking Dukakis, there was this: "One escapee from a 'Dukakis furlough' dropped in on a Maryland couple last year, stabbing the man and raping the woman. Maryland Judge Vincent Femia locked the prisoner away for several lifetimes after refusing to return him to Massachusetts. The Boston *Herald* quoted Judge Femia: 'I am not going to take the chance that he will be furloughed or released there again.'"

Which brings up another point. The Massachusetts press had been writing about Willie Horton for months and months before Al Gore ever opened his mouth. The Lawrence *Eagle-Tribune* had done more than two hundred stories about the furlough program in 1987 and had won a Pulitzer Prize for them in March 1988. There had been public meetings, stormy debates, legislative maneuverings and a petition with 70,000 signatures to place the furlough issue on the ballot.

And even if nobody at the Bush campaign was reading any printed matter, all they had to do was watch the *CBS Evening News* on December 2, 1987, to hear all about Willie Horton and furloughs.

But Bush officials always insisted they first heard about furloughs from Al Gore. Once they heard, though, they knew what they had. "The Horton case is one of those gut issues that are value issues, particularly in the South," Atwater said. "And if we hammer at these over and over, we are going to win."

Nobody had to ask what Atwater meant by "particularly in the South." Everybody knew how the Bubba vote would react to a black man raping a white woman.

Dukakis was not especially worried about furloughs. It was a local issue. It was an old issue. He had handled it. Besides, he had all sorts of facts and figures in his defense. And on May 17, 1988, a *New York Times* / CBS poll showed Dukakis leading Bush by 10 points. On May 25, the furlough policy came up once more in the last Democratic debate in San Francisco, raised by one of the panelists. Dukakis brushed it off, and many papers, including the San Francisco *Chronicle* and *The New York Times*, didn't even mention it in their coverage. The furlough issue was not a big deal.

The next day, a Washington *Post* / ABC poll gave Dukakis a 13-point lead over Bush.

But on that same day, Bush's top handlers got together behind a two-way mirror in Paramus, New Jersey.

BY THE MEMORIAL DAY weekend the Bush campaign was in low gear. Bush had spent almost all the funds he legally could on the primaries and now, except for a few events, he had to coast until the Republican National Convention in August. It was not a good period for the campaign. Bush's negatives were high, up around 40 percent, and he was doing especially poorly with women, his so-called gender gap.

At the same time, the Democrats seemed to be sending out signals as to what kind of campaign they were planning for the general election. On May 20, Paul Kirk, chairman of the Democratic Party, had called Bush "a quintessential establishment elitist Republican" who had "neither the toughness to govern nor the compassion to care."

Bush had seethed when he heard it. This was "wimp" under a different label! But conventional campaign wisdom dictated that Bush would have to establish a strong positive image of himself before he could strike back at the Democrats.

Lee Atwater didn't care about the conventional wisdom. He believed in attack. Attack early, attack late, attack often. Attack was always good. Driving up the opponent's negatives had been his strategy in every campaign he had ever run. "I knew we had to go on the attack," he said. "If we waited until our convention to go on the attack, we would have been hopelessly behind. And I knew if we could pick the right three or four issues for a frontal attack we could shave off ten points from the polls."

Bush had retreated to his home in Kennebunkport, Maine, to powwow with his top advisers over the Memorial Day weekend. But few of his top advisers seemed to be around. Bush was around (he greeted reporters on Memorial Day with a cheery "Happy Veterans Day!" and nobody bothered to correct him), but where were the important people? "Where's Teeter?" David Hoffman, a ferociously tenacious reporter for the Washington *Post*, kept asking people. "Where's Lee? Where *is* everybody?"

EVERYBODY WAS HUDDLED at a modernistic white-sided, black-windowed office building off a shopping strip in Paramus, New Jersey, about a dozen miles from Manhattan. A marketing company hired by the Bush campaign had assembled two groups of people in a conference room. The people were being paid thirty dollars apiece to sit in comfortable blue-backed chairs around a round wooden conference table for ninety minutes. They had been carefully selected.

"They all had voted for Reagan last time," Roger Ailes explained later, "but they said they were going to vote for Dukakis this time. They were lower-white-collar, upper-blue-collar types. And they were not going to vote for George Bush. We were trying to determine why." The people were white, largely Catholic, over twenty-five years of age and making more than $40,000 per year.

They were swing voters, those people who swung back and forth between one party and another and determined the outcome of elections. (Some campaign strategists feel that each party has a base of 41 percent of the vote and the real election is a battle for the remaining 18 percent.) These particular swing voters were, in campaign terminology, "Joe Six-Pack" voters: white, urban and ethnic.

Republican consultant Stuart Spencer had identified a "Mediterranean tilt" among swing voters in general. Many swing voters were Catholic, many were Italians, and while they had supported Ronald Reagan in the past, they could be expected to feel a certain affinity for the "ethnic" Dukakis. So the Bush campaign wanted to know what it would take to swing these swing voters away from Dukakis and toward George Bush.

On one wall of the focus-group room was a huge two-way mirror. The participants were told they were being watched, but they could hardly have missed it anyway: the mirror was the size of a small movie screen. Behind it were Atwater and Ailes; Robert Teeter,

Bush's pollster; Craig Fuller, Bush's chief of staff; and Nicholas Brady, Bush's senior adviser. They sat in upholstered white-backed chairs and watched through the mirror as the moderator began to tell the story of Willie Horton to the group. And then he told them about Dukakis and his veto of the Pledge of Allegiance bill. And then about his opposition to prayer in the schools and to capital punishment.

Some of the people reacted with outrage; almost all reacted with surprise. They had not known these things about Dukakis. They hadn't realized, until the moderator told them, how liberal Dukakis really was. And they sure hadn't heard about furloughs and how he let that guy out of jail.

At the beginning of the focus groups, all had been Dukakis supporters. By the end of the evening, about half had switched to Bush.

"Basically, their mouths fell open," Debra Vandenbussche, in charge of interactive group research for Market Opinion Research, said. "They were appalled that he would let first-degree murderers out on furlough. There was some real strong reaction. In that hour and a half we ended up switching as many as half the voters from Dukakis voters to Bush voters."

Behind the mirror, just about all the Bush aides were impressed. The reactions of the Paramus focus groups were taped and brought back to Kennebunkport for Bush.

ROGER AILES was pretty much alone in his opposition to focus groups. A focus group, he said, "is five professionals in a room who say: 'We don't know what to do, so let's get twenty amateurs to tell us what to do.'" Even so, the Bush campaign used focus groups for everything, including testing Ailes's commercials.

But these focus groups were different from the one in Paramus. For these later groups, citizens were gathered in Birmingham, Alabama; Orange County, California; Livonia, Michigan; Toledo, Ohio; Cleveland; and Chicago. These groups included Bush voters, Dukakis voters and undecided voters and represented a broader cross section of the public.

And no longer did the focus-group members just talk. Instead, they were wired to a computer. Each had a device called a "perception analyzer" that was about the size of transistor radio and had a dial on it. You sat in a chair and watched, say, the first debate between Bush and Dukakis. If something you saw on the screen made you likely to vote for Dukakis, you turned the dial to the left. If it made you more likely to vote for Bush, you turned it to the right. The more you turned the knob in either direction, the stronger you felt. You could turn the knob for any reason. It could be a statement, but it could also be the way the candidate looked or sounded or gestured.

The focus groups were shown the primary debates, the convention acceptance speeches by each candidate and their TV commercials. Prospective one-liners for Bush to use in his first debate against Dukakis were also tested. But the Bush campaign didn't stop there. It also aired fake news broadcasts for focus groups. In these broadcasts a handsome (though somewhat beefy) actor, with dark curly hair and wearing a gray suit, white shirt and red tie, plays anchorman. As he speaks, a smiling picture of George Bush appears over his shoulder, just as it would in a real news show. "Bush said if his Democratic opponent, Mike Dukakis, was elected, Americans could expect more of the failed economic policies of the Carter-liberal Democrats," the anchorman says.

As the forty people in the focus group watched this "news" broadcast, they turned the dials on their perception analyzers. A computer instantly translated the information into a graph with three lines marching across it. The top line was the reaction of likely Bush voters, the middle line was the reaction of undecided voters and the bottom line was the reaction of likely Dukakis voters.

The graphs were then superimposed over the actual footage. Thus when Bush and his handlers wanted to see reaction to his convention speech, for instance, they could watch Bush deliver the actual speech and, while Bush is talking, see the graph lines travel up and down in reaction to his every word, glance and facial expression.

There on the screen was Bush delivering his line: "Read my lips— no new taxes!" and all three lines rose toward the top of the graph. But when Bush mentioned crime and furloughs, that's when he got real results.

"The graph could hardly cope," said Michael Crick, the Washington correspondent of Britain's Independent Television News, who obtained the focus-group tapes. "It convinced the Bush staff that crime was the major issue on which to attack Dukakis." And when Bush's furlough ad attacking Michael Dukakis later was screened for the focus groups, not only did the graph line of Bush voters head for the stratosphere, but so did the graph line of the undecided voters.

This was not the first time perception analyzers had been used. Comparable devices—sometimes called "people meters"—were used in 1984 by Republican pollster Richard Wirthlin, who tested reaction to the Reagan-Mondale debates. Wirthlin then used them during Reagan's second term to test reaction to his televised speeches and news conferences.

In July 1987, in a West Des Moines Holiday Inn, eighty-five Iowa Democrats, gathered by a Democratic polling firm, also had used such devices to measure reaction to the first Democratic debate in Houston. This was done mainly to show off the potential of the new technology. But not everybody was pleased.

"So you put people in a room and wire them and watch the needles go up and down," Joe Trippi, political director of the Gephardt campaign, had complained afterward. "It cost $25,000. Pretty soon, two weeks before a debate, we'll all put eighty people in a room and pay the $25,000 and find out what makes the needles go up and then we'll have the candidate say that."

Trippi talked about this with mild outrage. But the Bush campaign saw it as the next logical step in campaigning. Orwell's *1984* had come to 1988.

One of the things that made the perception analyzer groups so popular with the Bush team is that everybody loves data that confirm what they already believe. And the data from the focus groups told the Bush handlers that the furlough issue was especially potent with women. Home invasion and rape were subjects that could be expected to outrage women. And women were exactly the voters Bush needed; this could wipe out his gender gap.

Atwater could barely believe his good luck. If the Bush campaign needed Bubba and Joe Six-Pack and women, the furlough issue was one good way to get them all. Willie Horton was going to be 191 pounds of rompin', stompin' dynamite.

The Bush campaign had found its poster boy.

ON JUNE 9, at the Texas Republican state convention in Houston, Bush officially launched his negative campaign against Michael Dukakis. Though there were to be pauses in it, it would continue to election day.

Bush did not have to lead the attack himself. It could have been left to surrogates, so he could keep his own hands clean in order to lead the nation unsullied after being elected. But this idea was rejected. "We knew that if we left it to surrogates, it wouldn't have the impact," Atwater said. "Plus, Bush didn't have an image of personal meanness, so we knew he would be credible."

And George Bush did a very credible job.

"Declaring that 'today, it's a whole new ball game—spring training is over,' Vice President Bush ripped into Massachusetts Gov. Michael S. Dukakis . . . as a tax-raising liberal who let murderers out of jail and whose foreign policy views were 'born in Harvard Yard's boutique,'" David Hoffman wrote of Bush's June 9 speech. Attacking how Dukakis had given "unsupervised weekend furloughs to first-degree murderers," Bush said: "The question is: Is this who we want to put in charge of our drug program? Is this who's going to get tough with the kingpins and break the cartels?"

(Jack Katz, associate professor of sociology at the University of California, Los Angeles, would later identify an intriguing parallel between Willie Horton and George Bush: ". . . the politicians seem to be seduced by the symbolism of crime in much the same way as are street criminals, as a resource for showing themselves to be 'tough' when others might doubt it.")

"What it all comes down to," Bush said, "is two different visions."

Dukakis was not worried by Bush's speech when he read it the next day. He was even a little contemptuous of it. The presidential race, he knew, was not about "visions." It was about programs. Policies. Getting things done. It was about competency. Because, deep down, which was more important? Letting Willie Horton out of jail or creating 400,000 new jobs?

Dukakis' communications director Leslie Dach made the official response to Bush's speech: "The American people aren't interested in mudslinging and tearing down."

Yeah. Right. That would never work.

"WHO WAS THE WILLIE HORTON AD made for?" Murray Fishel, a political science professor at Kent State University, asked after the election. "It was made for the sixty-eight-year-old lifelong Democrat in Parma, Ohio, who saw it and said: 'If I vote for Mike Dukakis, Willie Horton will be my next-door neighbor.'"

ON JUNE 22, Bush used Willie Horton's name in a speech for the first time. He was speaking in Louisville to the National Sheriffs Association. "Horton applied for a furlough," Bush said. "He was given the furlough. He was released. And he fled—only to terrorize a family and repeatedly rape a woman!"

The Bush campaign knew what it was doing. Mention furloughs in a speech and that got reported. Keep mentioning it, give the press a name, and you set the press in motion. You started reporters looking into the Horton case on their own. And that would produce more stories in print and on TV. And both media liked pictures. Mention Willie Horton and you got Willie Horton's picture on TV. You never had to mention Willie Horton's race. The pictures would do it for you.

On June 27 *Time* magazine published an article about Willie Horton titled "The One That Got Away" and subtitled "Why an escaped murderer haunts Michael Dukakis." More importantly, however, *Time* did what *Newsweek* had not: it ran Horton's picture.

Menacing, evil, brooding, Willie Horton stared out from the page and into the homes of millions of Americans.

ON THE WALL above his desk at Bush campaign headquarters, Mark Goodin, deputy press secretary, pasted a mug shot of Horton. He was now a member of the team.

"I felt if we could keep the Democrats tied up until our convention," Atwater said, "we could open wounds and build their negatives up."

Building up their negatives was critical? "Some voters will go for you because of your positive message," he said. "But most of the swing voters are 'aginners'—they tend to vote according to who's on their side against the common enemy."

And everybody knew just who the "common enemy" was. Big guys who break into your home, tie you up, slash you and rape you are, generally speaking, the common enemy. And George Bush was "on your side" against those kinds of people.

Willie Horton was what the Bush people called a "wedge" issue. It was an issue that separated people. It was a "hot button" issue, one that drives people to instant anger.

"We can't worry about being too negative," GOP analyst Ed Mahe said. "If we don't get the anti-Dukakis message out, we can't win—period."

After the election, E. J. Dionne of *The New York Times* heard rumors of a Massachusetts furlough case similar to Willie Horton's, where the facts "were more devastating to Governor Dukakis, where somebody was pardoned and then murdered someone."

Dionne confronted Atwater with his suspicions at a seminar. "You never used that case, and it appears the guy is white," Dionne said.

"E.J., about what you just said, I learned about that case after the election," Atwater replied. "Frankly, had I known about it, we would have been smart to go with that and never mentioned Willie Horton. If the guy was white, there would have been zero question about our intent."

But Atwater didn't learn about that white guy until after the election. He had sources in Massachusetts, he had Pinkerton, he had the Nerd Patrol—thirty-five excellent guys tapping away at those computer keyboards!—but he didn't learn about a white example until *after* the election.

Gosh. Darn.

MICHAEL DUKAKIS was still not worried. He felt he had already handled the issue. After Horton's arrest in Maryland in April 1987, Dukakis had halted further furloughs until the policy could be studied. And after outrage from both the public and the state legislature convinced him he could not really veto a bill ending furloughs, he signed it into law in April 1988. And that, he thought, was that.

Besides, the polls after the Democratic convention were very good. Oddly, the same polls that pleased Dukakis also pleased Atwater.

"I was pleased when we came out of the Democratic convention seventeen points down," Atwater said. "Being seventeen points down was a victory. Without the attacks we would have been twenty-seven points down. And I was pleased with their convention for being so ungracious and unwise in their personal attacks. It gave us all the room we wanted to be personal back."

The Democrats had been in high spirits at their convention in Atlanta. The keynote speaker said Bush had been "born with a silver foot in his mouth." And Jim Hightower, the Texas agriculture commissioner, had called him a "toothache of a man." Hightower was a genuinely funny man, in the Will Rogers mold. Humor to Hightower was the means of getting attention, of making a point.

"Mah friends," he would tell people during the campaign, "ah'll tell you, if ignorance ever goes to forty dollars a barrel, I want drilling rights on George Bush's head. Here comes George Bush, strapping on those Gucci boots he wears, got himself a little tweed farmer suit. His idea of a good farm program is *Hee Haw*. And check out his running mate, Dandy Dan Quayle. He thinks Cheerios are doughnut seeds. And as for George Herbert Walker Bush the second, he's just another Kennebunkport millionaire with four names, three home addresses, five presidential appointments and five weeks to go in his political career!"

Yep, that Hightower was one funny hombre. He believed in busting guts.

The Republicans believed in busting kneecaps.

AFTER the Republican convention in August, the polls were no longer so good for Dukakis. The negative campaign was hurting him. So Dukakis struck back. Speaking in Massachusetts on August 30, he said: "Here's a man who supported the sale of arms to a terrorist nation, one of the worst foreign policy disasters of this decade; was part of an administration that was doing business with drug-running Panamanian dictators, funneled aid to the contras through convicted drug dealers; went to the Philippines in the early '80s and commended Marcos and his commitment to democracy—and he's talking about judgment?"

Afterward, Dukakis explained why he was now giving as good as he had gotten. "I came to a reluctant conclusion that if it continues, you have to respond," he said. "I think that's unfortunate, but I think it's very clear what kind of campaign the Republicans are running, and I think we're going to have to deal with it."

By Labor Day, the polls showed Dukakis and Bush running even. Now it was time for the Republicans to go nuclear.

Just after Labor Day, the National Security Political Action Committee (also known as "Americans for Bush") called a news conference to launch a thirty-second commercial featuring the face of Willie Horton.

Titled "Weekend Passes," it went like this:

VISUAL: Side-by-side photographs of Bush and Dukakis.
SOUND: "Bush and Dukakis on crime."

VISUAL: Picture of Bush.
SOUND: "Bush supports the death penalty for first-degree murderers."

VISUAL: Picture of Dukakis.
SOUND: "Dukakis not only opposes the death penalty, he allowed first-degree murderers to have weekend passes from prison."

VISUAL: Police photograph of a glowering Willie Horton.
SOUND: "One was Willie Horton, who murdered a boy in a robbery, stabbing him fourteen times."

VISUAL: Picture of Willie Horton towering over a police officer who has him in custody.
SOUND: "Despite a life sentence, Horton received ten weekend passes from prison. Horton fled, kidnapped a young couple, stabbing the man and repeatedly raping his girlfriend."
VISUAL: The words "Kidnapping," "Stabbing" and "Raping" appear on the screen.

VISUAL: Photo of Dukakis.
SOUND: "Weekend prison passes. Dukakis on crime."

"When we're through, people are going to think that Willie Horton is Michael Dukakis' *nephew*," Floyd Brown, a political consultant for the group, told reporters.

The group notified James Baker, the Bush campaign chairman, that the commercial would run for twenty-eight days. It ran only on cable TV, but that didn't matter. The network news shows picked it up and used it as an example of how negative the campaign had become.

On the twenty-fifth day of the ad's run, and after considerable public criticism over the use of Horton's picture, Baker announced his official disapproval of the ad and sent a letter asking that the commercial be stopped.

Floyd Brown responded: "If they were really interested in stopping this, do you think they would have waited that long to send us a letter?"

The Bush campaign disavowed the ad and said it was made by an independent group and the campaign had nothing to do with it. But as *The New York Times* would point out in a front-page story, the ad was filmed by a former employee of Roger Ailes and the group claimed to have the tacit support of Bush officials. "Officially the [Bush] campaign has to disavow themselves from me," Elizabeth I. Fediay, the group's founder, said. "Unofficially, I hear that they're thrilled about what we're doing."

The Dukakis staff was pleased with the *New York Times* story, of course. But it couldn't help noticing that on the front page the *Times* had run a freeze frame from the commercial. It was the picture of Horton towering over his guard, with the words: "Horton Received 10 Weekend Passes From Prison."

So even when Dukakis won, he lost.

PRISONER NO. 189182 at the Maryland State Penitentiary was allowed a television set. "I had borrowed a set to keep up on the ads," Willie Horton told a reporter. "I had it in my cell. The first time I saw it was on the eleven, eleven-thirty news. With Mary Hartman. What's the name of that news? *E.T.* That's right. *Entertainment Tonight*. They had me on that.

"When I woke up in the morning, I saw the ad again. When I went to bed at night it was on again. On again the next morning. They even had it on at midnight. One night I watched a midnight show and they was making a joke of me."

Mark Gearan, Dukakis' deputy press secretary, now was beginning to see signs of Horton mania. "I knew the election was over," he said, "when I returned a phone call to a newspaper and I was told the reporter couldn't take my call because she was talking to Willie Horton."

DUKAKIS UNLEASHED his own negative ads. ("I have the video-tapes of *nineteen* Dukakis negative ads," Ailes would fume after the election. "People just don't remember his because they weren't very good.") One ad showed black-and-white photos of padlocked factory gates. The announcer said: "Should there be a law to give you and your company sixty days' notice? George Bush says no."

Six days later, the Bush campaign responded with "Crime Quiz," the ad that asked: "Which candidate for President gave weekend passes to first-degree murderers who are not even eligible for parole?"

There were two pictures: Bush, brightly lit, looking handsome and clean and American. Dukakis, shrouded by a dark background, looking swarthy and foreign. Not quite as menacing as Willie Horton, but close.

Once again, the news media gave a huge boost to the Bush ad. Though "Crime Quiz" ran only in Texas and California, newspapers, newsmagazines and network TV picked it up and ran it everywhere. The three network newscasts were reaching into more than 25 million homes every night. A one-minute commercial on the nightly news cost about $90,000 and to get on all three network newscasts would cost more than a quarter of a million dollars. But the networks were running Willie Horton's picture for free.

The value to the Bush campaign was incalculable. By election day, there were few people in America who could not have picked Willie Horton out of a lineup.

THE DUKAKIS CAMPAIGN floundered for a fresh response. On September 21, it had released a five-page document titled "George Bush Distorts Mike Dukakis' Record." Within twenty-four hours, the Bush campaign responded with a 127-page refutation.

So on September 30, the Dukakis campaign aired "The Packaging of George Bush." The commercial featured actors playing the Bush handlers (one looked a little like Roger Ailes) sitting around a table and saying wry, cynical things:

"I think we need another TV commercial on this furlough thing."

"No way. They're beginning to write about Dukakis' real crime record."

"Nobody reads anymore."

"Let's hope not. First of all, Dukakis changed that furlough program. Look at this: more cops on the street, more drug offenders behind bars, crime down thirteen percent in Massachusetts."

"Just what I mean—how long do you expect to get away with this furlough thing?"

"How many more weeks to the election, Bernie?"

They laugh.

Then the announcer says: "They'd like to sell you a package. Wouldn't you rather choose a President?"

The Bush campaign conducted a focus group to test the effectiveness of the Dukakis ad. They found that people were confused. They didn't know if it was a Dukakis ad or a Bush ad.

"We didn't worry about it from then on," Ailes said.

Some Dukakis staff members were equally confused. They knew it was their commercial all right, but they couldn't figure out why

Michael Dukakis was spending millions of dollars on a commercial that brought up the furlough issue.

In Texas, where the campaign was being especially hard fought, Ed Martin, executive director of the Texas Democratic Party, was near despair at how the Dukakis campaign was being run. And he didn't believe the "Packaging of George Bush" ad was the answer.

"Maybe if you tied Bubba in a chair and tortured him with cattle prods, you'd get him to pay attention through the whole thing," he said.

AILES UNVEILED the kind of ad Bubba would watch without a cattle prod. It was called "The Revolving Door." It was made by the Milwaukee ad agency of Dennis Frankenberry & Associates and it was a beaut.

It was in black and white. Grainy. Documentary style. (Marvin Baiman, a pollster who conducted a survey for *Adweek*, found that viewers frequently couldn't distinguish between ads and news. "People are confused as to what is advertising and what is not advertising," he said. This was no accident, of course. Some commercials were meant to look like news.)

Ailes might not know Erich Fromm from Erik Estrada, but he knew all about fear. In an interview with the *Gannett Center Journal*, Ailes said the Bush campaign's most effective commercials against Dukakis were "thematic" ones like "The Revolving Door." How did the commercials make people feel about Dukakis? "They're afraid of him," Ailes said.

"The Revolving Door" was a brilliant play to fear. It began with throbbing, ominous music in the background.

VISUAL: A security guard walking up the steps of a tower.
SOUND: "Governor Michael Dukakis vetoed mandatory sentences for drug dealers. He vetoed the death penalty."

VISUAL: A long line of prisoners walks slowly through a revolving door made of iron bars.
SOUND: "His revolving door prison policy gave weekend furloughs to first-degree murderers not eligible for parole."

VISUAL (on screen): "268 escaped. Many are still at large."
SOUND: "While out, many committed other crimes like kidnapping and rape and many are still at large. Now Michael Dukakis says he wants do for America what he has done for Massachusetts. America can't afford that risk."

Only a few of the men who streamed through the revolving door in the ad were black. Ailes said that he and Atwater had made sure that only "one or two" were black. But as *The New York Times* noted, the ad's "dull gray tones make it hard to identify the men by race."

Numerous stories were done about how "The Revolving Door" ranged from misleading to untruthful. The 268 escapes from Massachusetts prisons were over a ten-year period, and only four of them involved convicted murderers. And at least 72 of the 268 were not really escapees, but had returned from their furloughs more than two hours late. Only three were still at large, not "many," and none of them was a convicted murderer.

There were also long detailed stories about furlough policies across the country. On an average day around 800,000 people are in prison or jail in America and temporary releases from custody are granted to almost 10 percent of them.

But the absolute "truth" about furloughs was not the point of "The Revolving Door." Ailes wanted to create a feeling and he had. People were scared to death.

ON OCTOBER 18 Willie Horton was asked by the Gannett News Service whom he supported for President. "Obviously, I am for Dukakis," Horton said.

The next day, Dukakis was on a campaign bus, waving to supporters through an open window. Sam Donaldson came up the aisle with a camera crew and asked: "Did you know Willie Horton said he would vote for you?"

Dukakis didn't even turn around. "He can't vote, Sam," Dukakis said in a tired voice. "He can't vote."

CLIFFORD AND ANGELA BARNES went on a tour of seven California and Texas cities to speak against the furlough program. Cliff said part of his motivation was that Dukakis had never apologized to them or shown the least bit of concern.

When he heard this, Roger Ailes went to see a psychiatrist. Not for himself. But to check out Dukakis.

"I talked to a psychiatrist about him, because I was worried Dukakis was going to turn around and start apologizing for the furloughs and everything and we'd be in trouble," Ailes said. "The psychiatrist said: 'Forget it. This is a classic narcissistic personality; he's right and everybody's wrong and he's smarter than everybody else. He'll never apologize.' "

GINGERLY AT FIRST and then more openly, the press began questioning whether the use of Willie Horton was racist. It was an obvious question and there seemed to be an obvious answer. But the Dukakis campaign didn't want any part of it. The Dukakis campaign didn't want to accuse Bush of racism. Only after the campaign did Susan Estrich, the campaign manager, explain why.

" 'We can't afford to alienate white voters,' I was told by many in my party and my campaign; whites might be put off if we 'whine' about racism," Estrich wrote. "I am not proud of our silence."

The Dukakis campaign needed Bubba and the Six-Pack vote as much as Bush did. So it kept silent about the racial aspect of the Horton attack. Which left it to Jesse Jackson to say that the Bush campaign's use of Willie Horton and "the furlough ad with black and brown faces rotating in and out of jail" was "designed to create the most horrible psychosexual fears."

Finally, when Dukakis' silence on the subject threatened to alienate his black supporters, Lloyd Bentsen, his running mate, was allowed to speak. In an October 23 appearance on *This Week with David Brinkley*, Bentsen was asked whether the Bush campaign's use of the furlough issue contained racial elements.

Bentsen paused and then said: "When you add it up, I think there is, and that's unfortunate."

After the campaign, Estrich, speaking as a white woman who had herself been raped by a black man, said: "There is no stronger metaphor for racial hatred in our country than the black man raping the white woman. If you were going to run a campaign of fear and smear and appeal to racial hatred you could not have picked a better case to use than this one."

THERE WERE MANY ATTACKS on Dukakis besides the furlough issue. He was attacked for his membership in the ACLU, his veto of the Pledge of Allegiance bill, phony reports that he had seen a psychiatrist, phony accusations that his wife, Kitty, had burned a flag while in college and even rumors that he supported bestiality.

But no issue was as potent as Willie Horton. In October pollster Lou Harris said the furlough ad and attacks on Dukakis' opposition to the death penalty had influenced voters more than anything else in the 1988 campaign. "Really more than the debates, more than anything else, they have determined the set of the election until now," he said. Some 63 percent of the voters now saw Dukakis as soft on crime as compared with 52 percent before the Bush attacks were aired. And 49 percent now termed Dukakis out of the political mainstream as compared with 34 percent before.

Time magazine declared in a headline that Willie Horton had become "Bush's Most Valuable Player."

So in the end, everybody wanted to know the same thing: why did Dukakis wait so long to respond to Bush's attacks?

But the real problem in responding to the Willie Horton ad and the furlough ad was that Dukakis had nothing to say. This was best demonstrated by a senior Dukakis aide who disgustedly pushed a piece of paper across a table at me and said: "O.K., *you* write our response to Willie Horton. You write the catchy phrase. You come up with the thirty-second spot. You come up with the jingle. What are we supposed to say? That Horton *wasn't* let out of prison and that he *didn't* rape that woman? What the hell are we supposed to say?"

The Willie Horton attack did not succeed against Dukakis because Dukakis responded to it too late. It succeeded because race and fear worked in America in 1988. And every time Dukakis responded by mentioning furloughs or Willie Horton, it only reminded people of how Dukakis had let this terrible man out of prison.

In desperation, Dukakis took another route. There is an old saying that you should never get down in the mud with a pig because you will get dirty and the pig will like it. But with his ad about Angel Medrano, Michael Dukakis got down in the mud with George Bush.

"George Bush talks a lot about prison furloughs," the Dukakis ad said. "But he won't tell you that the Massachusetts program was started by a Republican governor and stopped by Michael Dukakis. And Bush won't talk about the thousands of drug kingpins furloughed from federal prisons while he led the war on drugs."

Then the photo of Angel Medrano, a convicted heroin dealer, appeared on the screen.

"Bush won't talk about this drug pusher—one of his furloughed heroin dealers—who raped and murdered Patsy Pedrin, pregnant mother of two." Then the picture of Patsy Pedrin being carried away in a bodybag flashed on the screen.

"The real story about furloughs," the ad concluded, "is that George Bush has taken a furlough from the truth."

The Bush campaign felt that Dukakis had given up any moral superiority by running that ad. After all, the Bush campaign had never "officially" used a picture of a black man, while the Dukakis campaign had "officially" used the picture of a Hispanic.

"What about their ad about the halfway house?" George Bush asked reporters whenever they brought up his furlough ad. "Is that racism against Hispanics? That's what I think."

Michael Dukakis was sure that the voters would see through Bush's ads. "The American people can smell the garbage," Dukakis said.

But by the end of the campaign, neither side was exactly smelling like a rose.

THE BUSH HANDLERS recognized that Willie Horton had set off a hue and cry in the press. They read the analytical pieces saying they were making Dukakis look like a victim and gaining him sympathy. They read predictions that the public would become disgusted with their tactics and reward Dukakis with a victory.

They read these pieces and they shrugged them off. They were not going to change course now. By October 18, the Bush campaign had earmarked half of its remaining $30 million advertising budget for negative commercials. "We decided against changing our ad flow," a Bush aide said. "It would be foolish."

And they prepared a doomsday device just in case Dukakis turned things around in the final days of the campaign. They prepared a new negative commercial and they sent it to TV stations for safe-keeping so it could be released onto the air immediately if they needed it. It was a "Greatest Hits" commercial, one that contained snippets from all the previous attacks: furloughs, the Pledge, etc. There was no clearer sign of the Bush handlers' faith in negative ads. Let others question the ethics of negative ads. They never questioned how well they worked.

Not that the Horton campaign had no downside. It was dirty. It was vicious. It was racial. Many people were upset by it. But little of that rubbed off on George Bush.

That was no accident. The Bush campaign team knew the enormous value of compartmentalizing blame. The handlers had seen it work in the Reagan White House. The Iran-contra scandal? The Ed Meese scandal? The arms procurement scandal? All the other scandals? They all had happened on Ronald Reagan's watch, but the public did not blame Reagan for them.

Reagan was off to one side in his safe, attack-proof compartment while others took the fall. Nobody seemed to blame Reagan. The worst people said about him was that his "management style" was "detached."

The Bush campaign protected Bush in exactly the same way. It was rarely called the *Bush* furlough ad or the *Bush* attack, even if Bush was speaking the words. It was almost always the Ailes ad or the Atwater attack. Others, voters were assured, were making Bush do what he was doing. He was too nice a guy to *want* to do it.

(To make compartmentalizing work, the candidate had to yield power. The aides around him had to be credible as Svengalis. This is why the strategy worked so well for Reagan and Bush and could not work for Dukakis. Dukakis wouldn't yield power. He could barely delegate it. Which is why, both during and after the campaign, most of the criticism was directed at him.)

Bush's aides took pains to point out how Bush had to be dragged— kicking and screaming!—into going negative. Atwater told me he needed the data from Paramus not because he believed so much in focus groups—Atwater would have gone negative without focus groups—but in order to persuade Bush.

"I needed that [Paramus] to convince everyone on the staff so we could all go to the candidate united and convince him," Atwater said. "That was the purpose. When we went to Kennebunkport and explained it to him, he understood. If you have a valid point, you can make it to him."

So what was your valid point to Bush about going negative? I asked.

Atwater said: "I said to Bush: 'We're seventeen points back and they'll pick up ten more points at their convention and we won't win. Even with a good campaign we won't win. You can get so far behind that even a good campaign won't win it for you. That's what happened with Jerry Ford.' And that's what I told him."

And?

"And after that," Atwater said, "it was an easy sell."

As revealing as that anecdote is about Bush's character, it still covers up as much as it reveals. The fact is that Bush began attacking Dukakis *before* the Paramus focus groups and before the Memorial Day meeting at Kennebunkport. Weeks before Paramus, Bush had attacked Dukakis about his lack of foreign policy experience and his decision not to support the death penalty for drug dealers. And on May 25, the day before the Paramus focus groups were conducted, Bush attacked Dukakis for vetoing the Pledge of Allegiance bill.

Still, anecdotes his aides recounted always had the same point: you had to twist Bush's arm to get him to attack.

You had to twist his arm in Houston. You had to twist his arm with Dan Rather. You had to twist his arm with the Straddle ad in New Hampshire. And you had to twist his arm with the Paramus data on Willie Horton.

But viewed another way, George Bush appeared to be a man who went around with his arm stuck out saying: "Twist it! Twist it! Somebody twist it quick!"

George Bush saw early how going negative worked. A silly little put-down of Pete du Pont at the first Republican debate in Houston had won him huge accolades. And for each attack after that—against Rather, against Dole—the rewards seemed to be greater and greater. He looked more like a winner and less like a wimp each time.

George Bush wanted to win. That was his bottom line. The press would start writing about Good George and Bad George. How in the mornings Good George would tell crowds that he wanted to become the education President and how in the afternoons Bad George would attack Dukakis for being soft on crime.

But it was not a matter of Good George vs. Bad George, each struggling for the soul of the candidate. From virtually the first day of the campaign to the last, there was only Flexible George. Pliable George. Expedient George.

To him, the question was not whether it was the right thing. The question was whether it was the winning thing.

"I have no regrets," Bush told reporters shortly before election day. And he didn't.

Earlier in the campaign, on the same day Bush had first used Willie Horton's name in a speech—thus assuring Horton's picture would be on television that night—reporters had gathered around him shouting questions on the negative slant of the campaign and his use of Horton.

Bush said it wasn't a matter of being negative; it was a matter of his opponent's real record.

Then Bush raised both his arms to the sky and said: "God strike me down if I'm not telling the truth!"

All eyes followed his arms upward.

But the heavens did not open. No lightning bolt rent the sky. George Bush lowered his arms.

Some thought he looked relieved.

Chapter **9**

The Mass Media

Article 1.   Can Democracy Survive the Media in the 1990s?
by Judy Woodruff

Judy Woodruff assesses the state of television journalism, arguing that as the quantity of news has increased, the quality has decreased. Too many industry executives view television as a battle for numbers and profits, where ten-second sound bites, eye-catching graphics, fast-paced delivery, and blood-and-guts reporting take precedence over detailed explanation and hard analysis. In the process, many television journalists have lost sight of their mission, which is to serve the public—that is, to bring them the information they need to make intelligent judgments about important issues facing their families, community, nation, and the world. Although Americans have access to myriad sources of information, the reality is that fewer and fewer people are reading newspapers or books, which underscores the vital role that television must play in a free society.

LET'S examine the media from two perspectives—international and domestic—the latter being more complicated, naturally. If we step back and look at the rest of the world, I think we would agree that democracy generally has flourished where a free press has existed. Examples readily come to mind, including England, France, West Germany, and Japan. When the press has been restricted, for whatever reason, it has come hand in hand with a move away from democracy, whether in Panama, South Africa, China, or wherever.

Most of the movement recently has been in the other direction. Thanks in part to Mikhail Gorbachev, communism is on its deathbed and *glasnost* is changing the way the press operates in the Soviet Union and gradually in the rest of the Eastern Bloc. Who would have dreamed even a year ago that we would see this? It is truly an exciting time to be a journalist watching and reporting these ongoing changes.

The argument used to be that, with a free press, democratic nations engaged in

---
Ms. Woodruff is chief Washington correspondent for the "MacNeil/Lehrer News-Hour."

---

too much harmful self-criticism and generally were less tidy than totalitarian regimes that were not saddled with an inquisitive media. When Libya's Muammar al-Qaddafi wants something done, he doesn't have to answer questions from a bunch of nosy reporters. You can bet that China's Deng Xiaoping and his cronies were not bothered by a pushy press after their bloody crackdown at Tiananmen Square. South Africa has similar muzzles on the press.

Nevertheless, the notion that a controlled press brings stability has been all but disproven by what has transpired in Eastern Europe and Nicaragua. What a controlled press does is suppress temporarily a population's opinions and people's hopes and aspirations. All that is stifled does not disappear, however, and what is forced into hiding is almost sure to bubble up later in clandestine ways that hardly produce stability. So, on an international level, a free press goes hand in hand with a democratic form of government.

Focusing on the U.S., the question is: Can the world's best democracy survive, given the way our free press sometimes functions? I will take the liberty of mostly discussing television, since that is where

my experience has been. When I think back to the time when I entered journalism and began covering government and political campaigns, it is as if everything back then moved in slow motion. Politicians gave speeches, made statements, and/or answered questions and they usually could expect a reasonable facsimile of what they said to be reported in the newspaper and on television. Entire thoughts were transmitted in a condensed form, to be sure, but it felt as if there were substantive airings of views that took place. When I covered the Democratic primary in the Georgia gubernatorial race in 1970, Carl Sanders and Jimmy Carter had a real disagreement over how to improve the state's education system. There was some criticism of the other candidate by each side—Carter said Sanders was too wealthy to understand the problems of the little guy, while Sanders claimed Carter was inexperienced—but it did not seem to dominate the campaign the way it does today.

In the early 1970's, when I covered the Georgia legislature and there was a big debate under way about the budget, or taxes, or even whether wide-load trucks should be able to travel state roads, my news director gave me three, four, or sometimes five minutes to tell the story on the six o'clock news. I used 45-second or one-minute-long excerpts of various state senators and representatives engaging in floor debate or speaking in an interview or at a news conference. The politicians were not all handsome, well-coiffed fellows, articulate to a fault, and many of them spoke in a kind of shorthand that I and everyone else had to decipher.

Nowadays, a campaign run the way those were in 1970 or a politician who does not know how to speak in sound bites would not last 10 minutes in a competitive situation. In the 1988 presidential campaign, the average network news sound bite lasted seven seconds, down from 13 seconds in 1984. Television advertising in the late 1980's became so mean-spirited and personal in its attacks on other candidates that, as long-time Republican consultant Doug Bailey put it, "If you don't go negative—even heavy negative—you are considered a wimp!" George Bush's campaign commercials helped erase any lingering "wimpy" impressions of him; indeed, they had the effect of making Michael Dukakis seem weak. Just recall the prison furlough and Boston harbor pollution ads and the unforgettable scene of Dukakis riding in an army tank, wearing that wonderful helmet!

Negative advertising

In 1989, the predictions that negative advertising is here to stay came true. During the gubernatorial race in Virginia, the Republican ran ads accusing the Democrat of being soft on rapists. In the New York mayoral campaign, there was an unrelenting barrage of negative ads from both sides. Meanwhile, in the New Jersey governor's race, the Democrat accused his Republican opponent of having toxic dumps in his back yard. All of these things are misleading or at least exaggerated and, in some cases, right on the edge of what is factual.

What also has changed about the negative ads is that they are assumed to be true! Unless the other side runs a denial right away, the ads are taken at face value. How does most of television news cover these campaigns and commercials? We usually play it as it lays. We don't bother with much perspective or analysis—we don't have time.

As for covering government, there is not a chance in the world that I would be given three, four, or five minutes on a legislative debate if I were working today for a commercial station. It would be more like a minute and a half to two minutes, with average 10-second sound bites. The legislators or members of Congress who get interviewed nowadays are the most articulate ones, the ones who have learned how to look good and talk short for television. Issues that used to be explored in depth now are dealt with in abbreviated form with lots of helpful visuals and as little detail as possible to save time.

If I were to ask you if TV news—local, network, weekend, or weekday—is contributing to a more informed electorate, what would your answer be? Certainly, more people are hearing and seeing more about government and political developments than ever before. There are more television channels reaching into more communities: weekend network news shows; early morning, late night, and middle of the night news; and public affairs talk shows on over-the-air and cable television channels. There are more shows with groups of pundits sitting around telling us what to think. When "The MacNeil/Lehrer Report" went on the air in 1975, it was an unusual format. Now, everywhere you look, there is another interview or talk show or, more recently, a quasi-information-entertainment show, trying to win an even bigger audience.

Second, the local and network news broadcasts are far better illustrated (with eye-catching graphics), sometimes better written, and often reported by a more experienced professional, who even may be a specialist in his or her area. When we watch Bob Bazell reporting on science or medicine news for NBC, or Carl Stern on the Supreme Court, we know we are hearing from someone who makes it his business to know the issues and the people involved in the story.

So, much is improved, and nowhere is it clearer than when there's a breaking story such as a hostage crisis in Lebanon, an earthquake, or an election night. The big networks cover these exhaustively. The technological advances are mind-boggling, including satellites that produce a picture in an instant wherever a microwave truck can get a signal out. The world has shrunk dramatically and we can witness starvation in sub-Saharan Africa, terrorism in the Middle East or by Colombia's drug cartels, or the brutal repression of college students in Tiananmen Square. The sounds, even without the picture, are powerful. Who can forget CBS reporter Richard Ross describing the approach of the Chinese soldiers and their assault on him and his camera crew as transmitted by Ross' portable telephone in contact with his office in New York?

The trade-off

So, we are bombarded by events, newsmakers, and fast-breaking developments. However, there has been a trade-off in exchange for all this technology and fast-paced, eye-catching delivery of the news. The trade-off has been an explanation of what it all means for the rest of the world, the nation, our community, our culture, and our families.

It seems to me that, as the quantity of news has increased, the quality has diminished. Political campaigns play themselves out in the willingness of too many news organizations to take candidates and their campaign statements and commercials at face value. There is too little questioning of facts, challenging of assertions, and offering of background information that might put today's attack on an opponent into perspective. Political consultant Doug Bailey claims there is too little "truth-telling" going on. Lies sit out there unchallenged till they become political lore. When a candidate airs a new commercial, Bailey says, the media immediately should dissect it to discern if it is truth or fiction, exaggeration or innuendo, or just plain misleading.

When candidates, as they did skillfully in the presidential campaigns of 1980, 1984, and 1988, stand day after day carrying American flags in front of cheering high school students, but don't say anything new of any substance—other than more attacks on the opponent and a recitation of familiar positions—that ought to be reported exactly as it happened. If there is no news, as on most nights of the 1988 presidential campaign, then Tom Brokaw, Dan Rather, and Peter Jennings ought to do what the former president of CBS News, Richard Salant, said several years ago. When the candidates aren't addressing the issues, he advised, the networks should go on the air and say, "George Bush or Michael Dukakis didn't say a damn thing today. So, instead, we are going to report on his record in public office or his past statements on the budget deficit." The news media are far too timid about looking into the past records of candidates and searching out the contradictions, the inconsistencies, as well as the accomplishments. We are just plain lazy sometimes. It's easier to cover the mudslinging.

There's little doubt that one factor that exacerbates all this is the increasing emphasis on profits at the network news headquarters. When the Loews Corporation bought CBS, General Electric bought NBC, and Capital Cities Broadcasting bought ABC, a much greater concern about the bottom line was introduced. I think we have to ask if the corporate chieftains calling the shots at the networks care more about their quarterly profit and loss statements than they do about journalism. Not that there is anything wrong with the good old American free market system—that is what made us great, after all. I just think that the question has to be raised simultaneously.

The networks have faced the double whammy of competition from cable, independent stations, video tapes, and all the other visual offerings that the public can choose instead of ABC, CBS, or NBC. The networks' share of the audience has dropped and, as that has taken place, the commitment to long-form news gradually has eroded. How often do you see documentaries on the networks anymore? What we see instead are the new prime-time ''news and entertainment'' shows, which are cheaper to produce than pure entertainment. In some instances, they have raised questions among critics and journalists about the validity of what they present. In a lengthy front-page report, *The Wall Street Journal* took the networks to task for their policy of using dramatic re-enactments, rather than real news footage, to tell a story. Maybe I am an old fuddy-duddy, but I agree with the *Journal* when it says that these re-enactments, which have been used on all three networks, are further blurring the distinction between fiction and reality in television news. *The New York Times* made the same point in an editorial, stating that journalists have a duty to the truth and to their audiences. How will the public know what is real and what is not after watching these shows?

Closely akin to the re-enactments, which are coming out of network news divisions, are programs like the docudrama aired on ABC based on the book *The Final Days* by Watergate reporters Bob Woodward and Carl Bernstein. ABC admitted the program was not wholly factual, and attorney Leonard Garment, who was counsel to former Pres. Nixon, said it was a lot worse than that. In an op-ed piece in *The New York Times*, he condemned it as ''littered with false pictures, false sequences, and words that were not spoken by the people who spoke them.'' Garment asserted that the last scene of the program, which shows Nixon collapsing in front of Henry Kissinger, is pure fiction. Garment predicted that the show will be defended as a piece of journalism and protected by the First Amendment. He also forecast that, if the courts diminish First Amendment protection over the next decade, it will come in the area of docudramas. He obviously had an axe to grind in a show about the Nixon Administration, but I think he had a point when he said it will be difficult to invoke the First Amendment—one of the cornerstones of our Constitution—as a protection for shows like ''Cops,'' ''Most Wanted,'' and ''A Current Affair,'' all of which employ docudrama techniques, which, he claimed, are far removed from any respectable definition of journalism. If someone sues a network, what jury will believe a dramatic re-enactment over the testimony of people who actually participated in the event? He raised a point for all of us in television journalism to think about. Once the erosion of the press' freedoms begins, how easy will it be to stop?

As we look to the future, will we find more robust news media in this country, ever more vigilant in their watchdog role, overseeing how elected and appointed officials are handling the public trust, raising tough questions, demanding answers, looking after the public interest, and holding politicians accountable? Or will we find, in the year 2000, in the words of ethicist Michael Josephson, that ''the operative definition of newsworthiness will favor virtually unrestricted use of personal, sensitive, and intimate facts.'' In other words, will we find the worst of today's journalistic ethics and practices magnified a dozen times over? I would like to say that it will not happen, but the trend over the past few years has not augured well for a turnaround in the 1990's.

Some of us in the media, especially television, have gotten caught up in the size of our audience, the profits to be made, catering to short attention spans, and seeking the sensational. Consequently, we seem to have forgotten something basic—that we are here to serve the public, to bring them the information they need to make informed judgments about their community, the nation, and the planet. What could be more important at a time when the world has grown smaller and the problems seem more complicated, if not more difficult, than ever before? If the media don't feel that responsibility, if television news, which reaches more people than any other medium, does not feel some responsibility, then who will? Will Americans read more? The trend does not seem to be moving in that direction.

When my colleagues argue, as I have in the past, that television is only one of the sources of information to which Americans have access, I repeat a statistic that I heard recently—the average number of books people in Great Britain read last year was eight. That is not very impressive, until you hear that the average in the U.S. is one-quarter of a book!

We are in for some pretty exciting, uncertain times. If communism is not dead, it is dying, and democracy is on the ascendancy. Will journalism, especially television journalism, operate in these other countries as it has in the U.S.? Or is there something uniquely flawed and simultaneously strong about our system that will let democracy succeed in spite of the new journalism we practice? It is something to think about. I am usually an optimist, but I still am undecided about this question.

Article 2. War Stories
by Vicki Kemper and Deborah Baldwin

The authors discuss Pentagon-media relations and the quality of war coverage, concluding that in recent years—and in the gulf war in particular—the Pentagon imposed a virtual news black-out until it became clear that the news was positive. In this conflict, as in others, the public was denied access to the full story, such that the Pentagon—and the White House—were able to manage the news with enormous skill. In addition to censoring the news, the Bush Administration provided the moral and political framework for war coverage, as well as daily interpretations of developments in the gulf.

This winter Americans were on the receiving end of information equivalent of saturation bombing: suspenseful, day-to-day predictions of the coming "showdown," dramatic coverage of Day One, round-the-clock coverage of the ensuing attacks and counter-attacks, daily gulf-crisis supplements in the major newspapers, back-to-back cover stories in the news weeklies and countless hours of talking heads on late-night TV. How did the soldiers on the frontlines *feel?* Would the war end soon? And why were all those reporters shooting nasty questions at nice Gen. Schwarzkopf?

Rarely has so much been written and said about the role of reporters during a war. The issue isn't new; books have been written about media-military relations during World War II and Vietnam. But this war has been different.

The biggest change has been an extraordinary effort by the Pentagon to restrict and shape coverage. When the ground war started the Pentagon went so far as to impose a virtual news blackout — until it became clear that the news was favorable. By imposing "onerous, unnecessary" restrictions on the media, the military was "trampling on the American people's right to know," former CBS anchor Walter Cronkite testified at a February 20 Senate subcommittee hearing. "Americans are not being permitted to see and hear the full story of what their military forces are doing in an action that will reverberate long into the nation's future." If public opinion polls indicated strong support for such restrictions, Cronkite added, that could "only be because the press [had] failed to make clear the public's stake in the matter."

The other change, ironically, stems from today's sophisticated electronic communications, which create the kind of instant ringside reporting that never before existed during a war. "Immediacy does not necessarily mean better, more thoughtful reporting," Pulitzer Prize-winning author David Halberstam observed in one of the countless "op-ed" articles that appeared on the media's handling of the war. As *Los*

Angeles Times television critic Howard Rosenberg said of CNN's live, non-stop war coverage, "It's almost as if it goes in the ear and comes out the mouth without hitting the brain."

It will be years before scholars finish analyzing how government-controlled access to the battlefield affected the public's perceptions of the war. But interviews with media critics suggest that the Pentagon — and the White House — managed the war news with skill. After watching endless days of live, instantaneous television war coverage, journalist Bill Moyers wondered aloud, "Doesn't that make journalists an extension of the vast [U.S.] government propaganda machine?"

GET ME REWRITE

Generals and their commanders-in-chief have long recognized the importance of favorable publicity to their war efforts, and military "spin control" can be traced at least as far back as the Crimean War. In that mid-19th century multinational conflict for the right to dominate southeastern Europe, the British commander-in-chief was advised to "court" war correspondents in a way that would create a journalistic "bias in favor of authority."

Military officials, knowing that good news about a war was necessary to maintain popular and financial support for it back home, began to view the media as an important weapon in their arsenals. "War made news a strategic commodity," according to military historian William Hammond, and during World War I the media operated under strict censorship. Specializing in human-interest stories that romanticized the war, journalists were effective soldiers in the battle for civilian morale.

This pattern prevailed throughout the second world war. Military censors delayed — or suppressed altogether — information that might tarnish the image of "our boys in uniform" or raise doubts about the human costs of the war. Items subject to censorship ranged from photographs of dead American soldiers — which newspapers were not allowed to publish until 1943, more than a year after the Japanese attacked Pearl Harbor — to accounts of Lt. Gen. George Patton's slapping of a battle-weary soldier.

Journalists learned that glorified accounts of allied battles and heroic depictions of American soldiers could win them official praise and professional renown. In effect, they censored themselves. Many journalists were little more than "cheerleaders," functioning as "a propaganda arm of [their] governments," one Reuters reporter later confessed.

The Korean War began only five years after World War II ended. There are conflicting reports about the nature of censorship during this bloody three-year conflict. British journalist Phillip Knightley, in a book about military-media relations called *The First Casualty*, describes heavy-handed efforts to censor material that was deemed embarrassing to the military. But former newspaper reporter Peter Braestrup, who covered the Korean war and the war in Vietnam, says the military adopted a World War II-style review system only after the press requested it. Some reporters were tired of being beaten by their rivals and wanted the military to deliver them from competition by policing everyone's copy.

Despite some censorship in Korea, the military generally "did not inhibit 'news analysis,' even of the gloomiest sort, or criticism of the military, which was routine," according to *Battle Lines: Report of the Twentieth Century Fund Task Force on the Military and the Media*, written by Braestrup.

Vietnam was the first — and, so far, the last — "uncensored" war. The military established basic ground rules designed to safeguard national security but otherwise allowed reporters to travel freely and report without restriction on American casualties, military tactics and views of soldiers in the field.

Early in the war, the press was generally sympathetic and supportive of U.S. goals, according to an exhaustive analysis of *New York Times* and network news coverage by journalism professor Daniel Hallin. But as the fighting ground on, a profound confusion of purpose on the part of the White House, coupled with efforts to mislead the public, drove a sharp wedge between the military and the media.

The greatest obstacle to media efforts to present a full and accurate accounting of the war was the succession of official lies and mistruths propagated by military spokespersons at daily news briefings, known to reporters as the "five o'clock follies." Military officials used the briefings to "sell" the war to the American public. But when reporters in the field uncovered the United States' use of napalm, its bombing of civilian targets in North Vietnam, the likelihood of a protracted and indecisive conflict and other information that contradicted military statements, the damage inflicted on the military's credibility was as crippling to the U.S. war effort as defeat on the battlefield.

In the early stages of the war "the media basically replicated the official point of view," says Hammond, a historian with the U.S. Army's Center of Military History. Only when public and official criticism of the war increased, particularly after the Tet Offensive in 1968, did coverage become more independent, widening the military's credibility gap and fueling antiwar sentiment back home.

"The military saw the media as the representative of civilian opposition," Hammond says, "and focused all its frustration on them."

In fact, the military *blamed* the media for its defeat in Vietnam. The perception of powerful evening news footage as an agent of change, however,

"doesn't stand up to intense scrutiny," Hammond says. "It's a gut-level judgment that's just wrong."

Wrong or not, an embittered generation of military commanders believed that televised and unrestricted news coverage — rather than the gradual buildup, mounting casualties or Vietnamese nationalism — were responsible for their humiliating defeat. "And that generation of officers trained the next generation and that attitude is still there," Hammond says.

For these commanders the best example of a well-covered war was probably the 1982 assault in the Falklands. A handful of photographers, technicians and reporters accompanied the British fleet when it sailed to this British colony to dislodge an occupying force from Argentina. Back in Buenos Aires a frustrated press corps of about 500 awaited news from the front. British censors reviewed the correspondents' copy, telling them to remove or rewrite certain passages. Because there were no satellite hookups, film had to be shipped back to London. The invasion practically ended before the public had a chance to see it begin.

THE EVOLUTION OF SPIN

The development of skilled "spin control" was one of the more notorious achievements of the Reagan administration. The White House mastered management of the news, taking formal steps to restrict access to information and staging events designed for network consumption that bypassed an adversarial press already disarmed by Reagan's immense popularity and ability to strike emotional chords.

Meanwhile Pentagon officials, determined never again to lose the public relations battle as they had in Vietnam, were developing ways to regulate coverage of military operations.

In October 1983, only 16 months after the Falklands war, the Reagan administration devised secret plans to invade Grenada, a small, politically unstable Caribbean island where the administration said Cuba was helping to build a runway able to accommodate Soviet aircraft. The administration shrouded its plans in so much secrecy even Larry Speakes, the principal White House spokesman, did not learn of the invasion until after it began. For the first 48 hours of combat, journalists were not allowed onto the island.

When a few reporters tried to approach the island by private boat, the military stopped them.

During Day One of the operation the "simple fact that the government was now censoring the news was barely reported at all," Mark Hertsgaard reported in his book, *On Bended Knee: The Press and the Reagan Presidency*. "It was almost as if the very fact that censorship had been imposed had itself been censored. None of the five leading national news organizations pointed out in its Day One coverage of Grenada that the Reagan administration was preemptively censoring news about the invasion and that everything it said should be evaluated with that fact foremost in mind." It wasn't until October 28, three days later, that CBS flashed the words "Cleared by Defense Department Censors" over pictures of the invasion released by the Pentagon.

Meanwhile 369 journalists had descended on Barbados, and many of them, as *Battle Lines* points out, had no experience covering the military. Some, armed with the latest TV equipment, were under extraordinary pressure to deliver instant footage to the networks. Later, the administration released sanitized videotapes of the operation, which the major networks broadcast. Between the media's shortcomings and the Pentagon's suppression of information, the news out of Grenada was misleading and incomplete.

"High estimates of the Cuban presence got the benefit of the doubt in official statements," Braestrup notes, "and the fact that Grenadian troops suffered by far the larger number of

Like soldiers, pool reporters were ordered to be ready for "duty" at a moment's notice.

official recorded enemy casualties was not emphasized. . . . Exactly why [some Cubans] were fighting and what they intended to do remains unclear. The U.S. government did not extend itself to provide information concerning this and other matters to reporters in Grenada, even after the operation's first few days."

Michael Deaver, Reagan's public relations adviser at the time, later told Hertsgaard he thought "the country was so hungry for a victory" there was little chance of backlash when the world's biggest power attacked a tiny Caribbean island. "But to *ensure* that the public applauded the invasion, Deaver believed the government had to control to the maximum extent what Americans were told and especially what they were shown about it."

POOL POLITICS

Incensed by their exclusion from Grenada, media organizations immediately demanded some way to cover the next military operation. The Pentagon appointed a panel of eight officers and six journalists who recommended that "pools," or representative groups of reporters and technicians, cover such operations on behalf of all the media.

In laying the groundwork for a system of pools, Pentagon officials made it clear that they would control how and to what extent the media could cover military operations. The concept called for the Pentagon, working with major news organizations, to designate a group of reporters to be on "standby" for military duty. In the event of action, the Pentagon would activate the pool, transport its members and provide them with the logistical support necessary to witness the action, gather information and report the news. Much like soldiers, pool reporters were ordered to be ready for "duty" at a moment's notice; when they got the call, they would not be told where they were going. They would be dependent upon their Pentagon handlers for everything.

The Pentagon conducted several "dry run" pools to acquaint reporters with the system, and when it activated the first pool to cover the Navy's patrolling of the Persian Gulf in July 1987, journalists had few complaints.

But the pool system met — and failed — its first major test in December 1989, when U.S. forces invaded Panama. Because of Pentagon secrecy, political decisions at the White House, logistical problems and poor planning, pool reporters — and the public — never learned what really happened in "Operation Just Cause." Pentagon-engineered coverage produced an image

of an invasion that was quick, clean, successful and relatively painless, and without information to the contrary, the media served to sanction it (see box).

Former AP reporter and Pentagon spokesman Fred Hoffmann helped devise the pool system but now says, "Panama wasn't the place to use it." According to Hoffman, pools were "never meant to be the only means of covering" a war, but rather the "minimum American news presence" in the earliest stages of an operation in a remote area where no American journalists were based. This was not the case in Panama, where there was already a large contingent of American journalists with extensive knowledge of the area and experience in covering the Bush administration's squabbles with dictator Manuel Noriega.

In his Pentagon-commissioned review of the Panama pool deployment, Hoffman says that the Pentagon assembled a Washington-based pool that was called out too late and arrived in Panama four hours after U.S. forces launched their attack. Defense Secretary Dick Cheney told Hoffman he made his decision "with full knowledge" that it would stymie coverage.

The Pentagon failed — at times refused — to transport pool members to areas of fighting, failed to provide regular briefings and caused substantial delays in the transmission of articles and photographs from Panama, Hoffman concluded. Pentagon control was so effective that pool reporters had to rely for most of their information on CNN broadcasts or briefings from Washington. "The result of all this was that the 16-member pool produced stories and pictures of essentially secondary value," Hoffman added.

Panama was "a stark example of how the American public has been misled by [government] control" of news coverage, says Ben Bagdikian, a Pulitzer Prize-winning journalist and author of *The Media Monopoly*. It was the Pentagon's success in Panama — in controlling information and shaping public perception through the media even more than on the battlefield — that "emboldened" the military to impose even greater restrictions on reporters in the Persian Gulf, he says.

Pools were an integral part of the military's thinking from the moment the gulf situation began heating up.

And if pools weren't designed for lengthy operations, they proved to be a handy means of crowd — and copy — control. "The military has learned a helluva lot since Vietnam and has found a way to control TV very well and the press as well," says Edward Fouhy, a former executive producer at NBC News who served on the *Battle Lines* task force. "The fact that they can control access to the battlefield has made all the difference."

Estimates of the number of reporters and media technicians in the gulf in mid-February ranged as high as 1,400. But only about 115 of them ever got out of Riyadh before the four-day ground war began. Assigned to one of 15 or so pools, representatives of organizations as varied as CBS News and fashion magazine *Mirabella* were escorted to various locations, where in some cases they were allowed to interview, photograph or videotape only certain people and events.

"Every word of the pool copy went through military censors in the field," Reuters reporter Deborah Zabarenko says of her experience filing reports from Dhahran, Saudi Arabia, during January. "Then the copy went through censors in Dhahran, which got more juice sucked out of it." While many news organizations were paying dearly for the opportunity to carry a Saudi dateline, Zabarenko says a big source for many stories was CNN, which was broadcast in the hotels where most of the press hangs out. "I can watch CNN at home," she says.

There were also the daily military briefings, which sometimes conflicted with the pool reports and subsumed them, says Robert Kearns, a Reuters reporter at the Pentagon who served in

> "The American public has been misled by government control of news coverage."

a pool in Panama and one in the Persian Gulf two years ago. He says news organizations are inclined to give greater authority to the Pentagon's version of events than the pools'. Pool reports also came from "all over the place and were pretty fragmented," while the Pentagon attempted to deliver a coherent story line.

In a recent article James LeMoyne, who reported for the *New York Times* from September to December in the gulf, described censorship as a significant obstacle even before the war began. Three Pentagon press officials told him they had spent significant time analyzing reporters' stories to make recommendations on how to sway coverage. After LeMoyne wrote an article quoting enlisted men critical of the war effort, his longstanding request for an interview with U.S. commander Gen. Norman Schwarzkopf was rejected. (Schwarzkopf later denied this was the result of the negative story.) LeMoyne learned that the soldiers he had quoted were cross-examined by their senior commanders. For the next six weeks the military rejected almost all print reporters' requests for visits to Army units. When LeMoyne and a fellow reporter drove into the desert on their own, they were warmly welcomed by an Army officer who said his troops would be delighted to share their lives. "Two hours later," LeMoyne recalled, "the officer, in acute embarrassment, said he had been ordered to throw the reporters out of his camp."

Censors were known to have held up time-valued copy. Many apparently had a hard time drawing a line between protecting America's strategic interests and trying to make their bosses look good. When Frank Bruni of the *Detroit Free Press* described returning pilots as "giddy," for example, a censor changed the word to "proud." The presence of a military "minder" reading his copy "has kind of a chilling effect," Bruni said later. "When you have a situation where access is everything, and people in the same channels are looking at your stories, it's impossible not to·be a little afraid that how much access you get will be affected by what you write."

"The press sounded like it was whining because Schwarzkopf was on all three networks and on the talk shows, and Cheney and [Joint Chiefs of Staff Chair Colin] Powell have been available," says Fouhy. "But it's easier to control the news when it's coming out of so few mouths." Fouhy says that Schwarzkopf and other commanders had professional "charm school" training in how to deal with the media.

Defenders of the pool system said it was the only way to protect the media from the fate of CBS correspondent Bob Simon and his three crew members, who were captured by the Iraqis after they broke ranks and drove toward the front January 21. Yet the treatment of other journalists who tried to strike out on their own suggests a military concern other than safety. In the early weeks of the war, U.S. and Saudi officials detained more than two dozen non-pool reporters and photographers, sometimes revoking their press credentials or even threatening to shoot them. Members of the Alabama National Guard held a *Time* magazine photographer for 30 hours, at times blindfolding and interrogating him.

Ironically, in an interview taped for ABC's *Nightline* just days before Simon's disappearance, he complained that restrictions prevented journalists from getting and reporting a full picture of the war. "No crowd of seven journalists is going to be taken to a village which is being torched," he said, referring to an incident recorded by television cameras in Vietnam.

Today's instant electronic coverage necessitates censorship and pool control, defenders of the system say, because on-the-spot information could have been valuable to Iraqi strategists. Finally, they contend, there was the sheer number of journalists in the region.

THE BIGGER PICTURE

While problems with pool coverage get lots of attention, they don't account for a larger problem facing the media. "There is a rally-round-the-flag" pattern once fighting has begun, Hallin says. "Ever since Vietnam we have had this desire to have back this image of [America] as invincible and unambiguously the good guys in the world," and the media, he says, "especially TV, are afraid of being out of step with public opinion." The result was some coverage that he describes as "gung-ho."

Critics also accuse the media of covering U.S. activities overseas in a superficial manner that belies the complex political and economic factors involved. For example, during the Panama invasion journalists provided little information about U.S. policy aside from the fact that the United States was anxious to remove former ally Noriega. Critics say the media

failed to examine the administration's political motives or long-term strategic goals and underplayed Noriega's links to the CIA and President Bush.

The surprise element of the Panama invasion was cited as one reason for the superficial reporting. But the media had more than four months to do their homework on the Middle East and still coverage of "the political and economic context [of the Persian Gulf situation] has been extremely shallow," Bagdikian says.

Part of the problem is the particular style of television news reporting. "TV likes to personalize the news," Hallin says, so it ends up doing "up close and personal coverage."

In the months leading up to the gulf war the three major television networks virtually ignored opposition to Bush administration policy. A survey conducted by the New York-based media watchdog group Fairness and Accuracy in Reporting found that out of a total of 2,855 minutes — almost two full days — of pre-war coverage by ABC, CBS and NBC only 29 minutes were devoted to popular opposition.

In addition to its censorship, the Bush administration constructed not only the political and moral framework for war coverage but provided daily interpretations of events in the gulf. Almost overnight Saddam Hussein evolved from an ally into a madman who was bent, like Hitler, on regional domination. The U.S. had "no choice" but war. The air strikes proved that battle would be quick and painless — "the impression from the footage, which was selected and controlled, created such euphoria that the president had to go on TV and say it won't be that easy," Bagdikian points out.

"The PR model is a political campaign," *Newsweek* reported February 11. "Every morning the administration settles on a 'message of the day.' . . . White House spokesman Marlin Fitzwater tests the message at his late-morning briefings. By refusing to allow in cameras, Fitzwater can experiment with his rhetoric. . . . The message is then fine-tuned for the later State Department and Pentagon briefings, which are on camera and thus more likely to make the evening news."

One of the most renowned practitioners of the art of spin control, Michael Deaver, told the *New York Times*, "The Department of Defense has done an excellent job of managing the news in an almost classic way." He added, "If you were going to hire a public relations firm to do the media relations for an international event, it couldn't be done any better than this."

As a result, a number of issues remained largely unexamined by the media both before and after the war. Former *Washington Post* reporter Scott Armstrong recently asked why no one followed up his 1981 probe of a U.S.-supported $50 billion project to prepare for a war by creating a NATO-like air defense system in the gulf. Most media organizations also failed to ask why, when the CIA was predicting Iraq's invasion of Kuwait, the U.S. took "no position" on the Kuwaiti-Iraqi oil-pricing dispute that touched off the attack; why the Commerce Department approved $1.5 billion in exports to Iraq of high-tech equipment with potential military applications; and how many billions of dollars in foreign aid and loan forgiveness the Bush administration has promised its anti-Iraq allies.

The openness of the media to dissenting voices "depends enormously on whether the political elites are divided," Hallin says. While some members of Congress spoke out against war, gradually its "inevitability" and the Bush administration's seemingly pre-determined march into it overwhelmed much of the debate. Even when former Chair of the Joint Chiefs of Staff William Crowe argued against the use of military force in the gulf, "he got eight seconds on the evening news," said David Halberstam, who covered Vietnam for the *New York Times*. "That's a disgrace."

Once the war was under way and the public's appetite for news seemingly insatiable, "You'd think the media would turn to America's past relationship with Hussein, with Iraq . . . to the dynamics of the Mideast," Bagdikian says. "But that's not the thing television likes. They like footage, not talking heads. . . . It complicates the neat picture and the flag-waving. It's more complex and disturbing. It forces consideration of things that can't be solved with military action."

Hallin says it's "very important not to forget that war is a political policy, not just a matter of winning and losing." Even after a war begins the media should "continue to discuss the politics of the war. It's important not to fall into the trap of glorifying war."

That's been a difficult assignment for news organizations, which want to make clear their support for U.S. troops, and individual war correspondents, who must work within the Pentagon's restrictions to meet the competing demands of breaking news deadlines and the need for more thoughtful, analytical coverage.

The week before allied forces started bombing Baghdad, *Newsday* reporter Knut Royce, who had been covering the crisis since August 2, wrote a story revealing that the Bush administration had "exaggerated or distorted U.S. intelligence analyses in its campaign to cast [Iraq] as an evil and outlaw state." Despite the article's significance, it wasn't a breaking news story, so the paper delayed its publication, first because of events in Soviet Lithuania and then because of the gulf war itself, Royce says. When the article did run, it was overshadowed by the daily tally of bombing raids, military briefings and "smart bomb" videos.

Royce expressed hope that his article — and the questions it raises — would get more attention now that the war is over. ◆

Article 3. TV News & The Neutrality Principle
by John Corry

The author maintains that television news must be governed by the principle of neutrality. This requires that the networks studiously avoid even the appearance of impropriety. For example, television coverage of the gulf war raised serious questions about the role of the media—most notably that of CNN, which was accused of acting as a broadcasting service for Saddam Hussein. In the end, all journalists report selectively. In doing so, they must strive to be even-handed, or face the wrath of the public, which harbors a huge dislike of the press.

ALMOST unremarked, we have passed a turning point in journalism, particularly as journalism is practiced on television. Exactly when this happened is unclear—although by the 1980's there were hints—but American broadcasts from Baghdad while American warplanes flew overhead finally made it certain. The old journalistic ideal of objectivity—the sense that reporting involves the gathering and presentation of relevant facts after appropriate critical analysis—has given way to a more porous standard. According to this new standard, reporters may—indeed should—stand midway between two opposing sides, even when one of the two sides is their own.

This is no academic matter. Neutrality is now a principle of American journalism, explicitly stated and solemnly embraced. After Dan Rather of CBS reported from Saudi Arabia last August that "our tanks are arriving," the Washington *Post* gave him a call: wasn't it jingoistic, perhaps

JOHN CORRY, formerly a television critic for the New York *Times*, now teaches at the College of Communications at Boston University, and is at work on a book about the media.

xenophobic, to say "our tanks"? Rather apologized and promised he would never say such a thing again. He should have known better in the first place. After all, Mike Wallace, Rather's CBS colleague, made the new standard clear well before the Gulf crisis started. At a conference on the military and the press at Columbia University on October 31, 1987, Wallace announced that it would be appropriate for him as a journalist to accompany enemy troops into battle, even if they ambushed American soliders.* And during the war itself, Bernard Shaw of CNN, explaining why he had refused to be debriefed by American officials after he left Baghdad, declared that reporters must be "neutral."

As it happens, Shaw once said that the late Edward R. Murrow of CBS was his great hero. Indeed, a whole generation of television newsmen regard Murrow as their hero, invoking his name every time they give one another an award. They ought to go back now and listen to his broadcasts. In the Battle of Britain and other engagements, Murrow was outspoken about which side he was on, and he was never a neutral reporter. It would have been unthinkable for him in 1944, say, to make his way to Berlin, check into the Adlon Hotel, and pass on pronouncements by Hitler.

Still, this is the New World Order, and rules everywhere are changing. The great place to be for television journalists this winter was the Al Rashid Hotel in Baghdad, in the basement of which, according to the Pentagon, was a command-and-control center, although the journalists holed up there were (neutrally) unable to find it.

Colleagues did complain when Peter Arnett of CNN stayed on in Baghdad after other journalists had been expelled; the complaints, however, were not so much about whether CNN (which has outlets in 104 countries) was acting as a broadcasting service for Saddam Hussein as about whether it was taking advantage of its competitors. When CBS, ABC, and NBC got their own correspondents into Baghdad, the complaints ended.

"You must avoid the appearance of cheerleading," Ed Turner, the vice president of CNN, said during the war. "We are, after all, at CNN, a global network." Turner, no relation to his boss

Ted Turner, although obviously they think alike, went on to stress that CNN wanted to be fair to *all* nations. But the truth was that CNN had a mission. Speaking from Baghdad, Arnett told us what it was:

I know it's Ted Turner's vision to get CNN around the world, and we can prevent events like this from occurring in the future. I know that is my wish after covering wars all over and conflicts all over the world. I mean, I am sick of wars, and I am here because maybe my contribution will somehow lessen the hostilities, if not this time, maybe next time.

Old-style journalists grew sick of wars, too, although few thought their presence would prevent them. New-style neutral journalists, however, have their conceits, and the constraints that bind fellow citizens are not necessarily binding on them. At the Columbia conference, Mike Wallace was asked if a "higher duty as an American citizen" did not take precedence over the duty of a journalist. "No," Wallace replied, "you don't have that higher duty—no, no." But if a neutral journalist does not owe a higher duty to citizenship, where does his higher duty lie? Old-style journalists seldom thought about that. A story was a story, and a reporter went out and reported it. Our age is self-consciously moral, though, and higher duties now weigh on us all. Arnett was clear about his higher duty, even without being asked. "I don't work for the national interest," he asserted in another broadcast from Baghdad. "I work for the public interest."

A ND it may be here that neutral journalism flies apart and breaks up into shards. What is this public interest, and who determines it, anyway? The national interest is determined by consensus and people are elected to serve it. The recent consensus was that the U.S. national interest lay in driving Iraq out of Kuwait and decimating its war machine. But the public interest is amorphous, and usually it turns out to be closer to the interest of its advocates than to that of the public.

Consider the performances in Baghdad. The correspondents there could not gather relevant facts, and if they had tried, they would have been expelled, or worse, from Iraq. What the correspondents did was listen to government-controlled Baghdad Radio (with a translator, presumably; none of the correspondents seemed to speak Arabic), tour Baghdad neighborhoods (with government guides and monitors), and, in the fashion of journalists everywhere, pick up what they could from other correspondents they met.

There is not much chance to do real reporting in a situation like that, and most of the time, one suspects, the correspondents knew it. Anchormen pressed them on questions they could not possibly answer. Tell me, Peter (or Bill, or Tom, or Betsy),

---

* A Marine colonel at the conference, George M. Connell, had a different perspective. "I feel utter contempt," he said when responding to Wallace, who had been supported in his declaration of neutrality, even if hesitantly, by Peter Jennings of ABC. "Two days later they're both [Wallace and Jennings] walking off my hilltop; they're 200 yards away, and they get ambushed, and they're lying there wounded—and they're going to expect that I send Marines up there to get them. . . . But I'll do it, and that's what makes me so contemptuous of them. And Marines will die going to get a couple of journalists." Colonel Connell was not being fanciful. When the correspondent Bob Simon vanished with his crew near the Kuwaiti border, CBS called the Pentagon for help.

an anchor would ask, how do Iraqis feel about this statement from President Bush? And Peter (or Bill, or Tom, or Betsy), from a cubicle in a hotel, an eight-hour time difference away, in a country whose language he did not understand, would reply as best he could.

The most accurate reply would have been, "I don't know," but you cannot say that very often and keep your job in television. So the reporting from Baghdad inevitably turned into an exercise by the correspondent in appearing to know something when he probably did not know much, while bearing in mind that he could not offend the host government.

Obvious questions arise: what if a correspondent in Baghdad had discovered something the host government did not want revealed? What if a correspondent had uncovered news about a party purge, or an outbreak of civil disorder, or the whereabouts of Saddam Hussein? Or—and this is not far-fetched—what if a correspondent, being bused from Baghdad to Basra, had come across an artillery battery with shells loaded with nerve gas and pointed toward U.S. Marines? The profession was uncomfortable with questions like that. Nonetheless, they could not be entirely ignored, and obliquely the correspondents in Baghdad addressed them. Were they, for example, holding back information?

"There are lots of things that you can't report," Betsy Aaron of CBS acknowledged. "If you do, you are asked to leave the country, and I don't think we want to do that. I think you do a very valuable service reporting, no matter what you are allowed to report."

No matter what you are allowed to report? Imagine Ed Murrow saying that. Neutral journalism assumes that what the reporter reports is not nearly as important as the fact that the reporter is there to report it. Journalism becomes a symbolic act, distinguished by form and not content. Operate under that standard, and censorship will not be a problem. Here is Bill Blakemore, speaking over ABC from Baghdad:

The script process is very normal for wartime, I would say. We write our scripts. We find one of the censors who's down in the hotel lobby, and we show it to the censor who reads it, and sometimes there's a slight change of a word here or there. Very often you may say something you didn't realize would touch a sensitivity, but there's not been any kind of heavy censorship in my experience here so far. It's a fairly easy understanding we have.

Clearly, the "fairly easy understanding" between correspondents and one of the world's most repressive governments meant that the correspondents simply censored themselves. If they were uncertain how to do this, they could always get help. Here is Blakemore again, in an exchange with his anchorman, Peter Jennings:

"Bill, are you operating on a completely uncensored basis?" Jennings whimsically asked.

No, Blakemore responded, "we got organized just now and managed to get somebody over here to listen and make sure we don't have any military or strategic information."

NEUTRAL status means that a journalist does not report objectively; he reports selectively. Arnett, visiting what had been Baghdad's two main power plants, now destroyed by bombs and missiles, spoke of "relentless attacks on civilian installations." He did not mention that those installations had been covered in camouflage paint. When he reported on the famous target that the Pentagon said was a biological-weapons factory and the Iraqis claimed was a "baby-milk plant"—"innocent enough from what we could see," observed Arnett—he did not notice the camouflage there, either. (Visiting German peace activists, of all people, did notice it and talked about it when they got back to Europe.) After being taken to another bombed-out site, Arnett reported that "while we were there, a distraught woman shouted insults at the press and vented anger at the West." Then we saw and heard the woman, who was standing next to a crater. "All of you are responsible, all of you, bombing the people for the sake of oil," she screamed in perfect English. She also turned up on French television speaking perfect French. Several days later, a CNN anchor in Atlanta identified her as an employee of the Iraqi Foreign Ministry.

Arnett, an old hand at covering wars and seeing through propaganda, presumably knew that when the "distraught woman" was shouting. Surely he at least noticed that her jogging suit had "United Nations" printed down one leg. A neutral journalist must narrow his vision and report with one eye closed.

The Baghdad correspondents, as individuals or as a group, most likely will sweep this year's television-journalism prizes. A claque formed almost immediately for Arnett, heaping encomiums on his head (especially after his patriotism was questioned by Senator Alan Simpson). He was a "dukes-up guy," "brave" and "independent," and an ornament to his profession. In the true spirit of neutral journalism, government-controlled Iraqi newsmen joined the claque, too. "The Iraqi press wrote favorably about me," Arnett told Larry King, the CNN talk-show host, who interviewed him when the war was over. Arnett also said he had become a "third-world hero."

Certainly Arnett and the other Baghdad correspondents displayed physical bravery in placing themselves in a war zone; and they did report, loosely speaking, to the best of their abilities. On the other hand, the correspondents as individuals were incidental. If there had not been Peter, Bill, Tom, or Betsy, there would have been John,

Morton, Arthur, or Susan, and the "reporting" would have been much the same. For them, the great thing was that anyone was in Baghdad at all, and it did not matter that a great many other Americans were disturbed. When a Washington *Post*-ABC News poll asked if we should bomb a communications center in the Baghdad hotel where the reporters were staying, 62 percent of the respondents said we should issue a warning and then bomb even if the reporters were still there; 5 percent said we should forget the warning and just go ahead with the bombing.

In fact, the press as a whole did not come off well in the war. Television tarred more reliable print, and polls showed a huge dislike of the media. The essential reason was captured by the headline over a story in *Time* about disenchantment with the press: "Just Whose Side Are They On?" The "they," of course, were journalists, and simply by raising the question *Time* went a long way toward providing the answer, even though the story itself predictably took a different position: "The attacks from both sides probably mean that the press is situated just about where it usually is: in the even-handed middle ground."

Well, perhaps, but the even-handed middle ground becomes an increasingly elusive place in the television age. There were no American reporters in Kuwait when Iraq salted and pillaged that country; it was not in Iraq's interest to have them there. It was in Iraq's interest, however, to have reporters in Baghdad; when the war was over, Iraq kicked them out. Could the press have found a more even-handed middle ground here? Why, yes. It could have insisted that if it was going to be in Baghdad it must also be in Kuwait. Obviously, no network did insist on that.

THE principal signs of television's search for a middle ground were "cleared by censor" titles; they were even-handedly applied to film approved by either American or Iraqi censors, showing skepticism of both sides. But the new neutral journalism also went a long way toward suggesting which side it was the more skeptical of. As long ago as last August, Michael Gartner, the president of NBC News, in a piece for the op-ed page of the *Wall Street Journal*, had alerted us to danger: "Here's something you should know about the war that's going on in the Gulf: much of the news that you read or hear or see is being censored."

Actually, the American part of the war had not begun yet, but that did not deter Gartner. He went on to quote, disdainfully, from a list of things the Pentagon did not want us to know. They included:

(1) Number of troops.
(2) Number of aircraft.
(3) Number of other equipment (e.g., artillery, tanks, radars, trucks, water "buffaloes," etc.).

(4) Names of military installations/geographic locations of U.S. military units in Saudi Arabia.
(5) Information regarding future operations.
(6) Information concerning security precautions at military installations in Saudi Arabia.

And so on, ending with "(9) Photography that would show level of security at military installations in Saudi Arabia" and "(10) Photography that would reveal the name of specific locations of military forces or installations."

While it would be easy to dismiss Gartner as merely frivolous, it may be assumed that his peculiar ideas about censorship and war and the military and the press got passed on to his reporters. Surely they were reflected in an NBC special, "America: The Realities of War," when Arthur Kent, the NBC correspondent in Saudi Arabia, took on Pete Williams, the Pentagon spokesman in Washington.

"Why are you trying to put your hands so far into our business?" Kent asked peevishly. "We're not trying to tell you how to run the war. We're just trying to cover it. Why do you want to control us so completely?"

Williams did not mention Gartner's laundry list of complaints, although if he had he would have made a reasonable argument not just for controlling the press but for banning it altogether. Williams did not say either that some of the television coverage was so goofy the Pentagon might have thought its higher duty was to straighten it out. In an interview when the war was over, General H. Norman Schwarzkopf remarked that he had "basically turned the television off in the headquarters very early on because the reporting was so inaccurate I did not want my people to get confused."

On the same program in which he attacked Williams, Kent also offered a choice specimen of the reporting General Schwarzkopf probably had in mind:

"Saddam Hussein is a cunning man and nowhere does he show that more clearly than on a battlefield when he's under attack," Kent told Faith Daniels, who was anchoring the special.

"And that, Arthur, really seems to be this administration's greatest miscalculation," Daniels replied.

"That's right, Faith," Kent continued. "He is ruthless, but more than ruthless. In the past eleven days, he's surprised us. He's shown us a capable military mind, and he still seems to know exactly what he's doing."

With "reporting" like that, is it any wonder that 57 percent of the respondents in one poll said the military should exercise more, not less, control over the press, and that 88 percent in another poll supported censorship? For, in addition to the other problems—moral, political, and professional—it has created, the neutrality principle has evidently turned many otherwise intelligent people into fools.

Chapter 10

Interest Groups

Article 1. King of the Road
by Jeffrey Denny

This article discusses the efforts of the automobile lobby to kill a Senate bill that would have required U.S. and foreign car makers to increase the fuel efficiency of their new automobiles. Armed for battle, the auto industry opposed the bill, insisting that customer demand, not government regulation, should determine additional auto improvements. The bill, sponsored by Senators Richard Bryan (D-Nev.) and Slade Gorton (R-Wash.) and thirty-three other Democrats and Republicans, countered by organizing a coalition of environmental and consumer groups. Supported by the White House, the automobile lobby narrowly defeated the legislation, which its supporters contend is needed to curb America's thirst for gasoline and to prevent future energy shortages. The article reveals the behind-the-scenes actions of both sides.

Ola and John Coalson will never forget the oil crisis of 1979, when revolution in faraway Iran touched off a bit of strife at their Citgo service station in suburban Springfield, Va.

"It started on a Saturday afternoon," Ola Coalson recalls. "All of a sudden I looked out on the front and there were lines up to the gas pumps. I called for help and said, 'What in the world is going on?' I had no idea we even had a gas shortage. It happened just like snapping your finger."

The cars stretched from the Coalsons' pumps to the intersection two blocks away. Things got so bad that before opening for business each day the Coalsons had to sneak into the station and do their paperwork in a back room so that anxious customers wouldn't see them and start banging on the windows. "It was a real hairy situation," Coalson says.

It wasn't the first hairy situation for gas stations and their customers. Only five years earlier, the United States had gotten an even harsher lesson about energy profligacy and dependence on foreign petroleum. The Mideast oil producers squeezed exports to raise prices and for weeks motorists idled in gas lines.

Jeffrey Denny is senior editor. Intern Ian Fisk assisted with research.

Today, after yet another sudden, painful lesson about dependence on Mideast oil, the United States is still addicted to the stuff and still paying the price. But when it comes to curbing oil consumption to ward off the next crisis, nobody wants to bite the bullet.

Particularly when it involves the "right" to drive. After three Mideast oil crises, the automobile continues to be a guarded American icon of power, mobility and individualism. Mass transit has never been a high priority in Washington and many American communities were designed around the auto. Most people can't even fetch a gallon of milk and a newspaper without jumping into the car.

The Bush administration is not about to challenge America's auto addiction; its new "national energy strategy" urges more carpooling, alternative fuels, use of mass transit — and increased oil production. And if the ongoing battle over fuel efficiency standards is any measure, the automobile also reigns in Congress.

Last fall the auto industry mounted a high-pressure lobbying effort, advanced by a "grassroots" campaign and White House clout, and narrowly killed a Senate bill that would have required U.S. and foreign automakers to increase the fuel efficiency of their new cars.

The bill, sponsored by Sens. Richard Bryan (D-Nev.), Slade Gorton (R-Wash.) and 33 other Democrats and Republicans, sought to expand the 1975 law that established the Corporate Average Fuel Economy (CAFE) standards. The CAFE rates haven't risen in six years; the Bryan bill would have raised them 20 percent within four years and 40 percent by 2001.

This year, in the wake of the Persian Gulf war, the drive to make automobiles more fuel efficient by law is more alive than ever. A coalition of environmental and consumer groups have made a revived Bryan bill a litmus test for sound energy policy and started their own lobbying barrage. While improved CAFE rates may not be the whole solution to America's fuelish ways, they're considered a crucial step in the right direction, proponents say (see box, page 20).

"The fuel economy law passed in 1975 has been one of the most effective conservation measures ever undertaken," Bryan says. But "larger, gas-guzzling cars are again being built, and the United States has increased its reliance on imported oil. We are moving backward, not forward."

Proponents say that hiking average auto mileage by 40 percent would save 2.8 million barrels of oil a day — four times the amount imported each day from Kuwait and Iraq before the Persian Gulf war. It also would significantly reduce emissions of carbon dioxide, a major "greenhouse" gas contributing

From *Common Cause Magazine*, May/June 1991, pp. 18–24. © 1991 *Common Cause Magazine*, 2030 M St. NW, Washington, DC 20036.

to global warming. Though his bill might increase the cost of each new car by $500, Bryan argues it also would save about $2,000 in gas costs over the car's lifetime.

The auto industry has shifted its drive against stringent CAFE standards into high gear. "This is the most important issue for the auto industry in this Congress," says John Guiniven, Chrysler's public relations director in Washington. "We consider it an extreme threat."

The industry maintains that customer demand, not government regulation, should dictate improvements to the auto. The industry also has battled federal exhaust emissions and safety standards such as crash-protection air bags. "If it's not needed, particularly when it jeopardizes large segments of workers, we're going to be opposed to it," says William Noack, director of General Motors' Washington office.

Noack estimates that the industry spent several hundreds of thousands of dollars last year fighting Sen. Bryan's legislation. This year, the auto lobby has raised the ante. Lobbyists are tight-lipped, but a congressional aide with industry contacts told Common Cause Magazine that Detroit has budgeted some $8 million to block stringent CAFE rules in 1991.

The auto industry's all-out fight against higher CAFE standards illustrates the hazard-strewn road Congress faces as it strives to curb America's thirst for gasoline and prevent future energy crises.

FUEL FOR LOVE

It's a thirst unrivaled in the rest of the industrialized world, as statistics show:

■ Americans make up only 5 percent of the world's population but use 26 percent of the world's oil.

■ The United States is more dependent on foreign oil today than during the last two Mideast crises. Almost half the oil consumed here last year was imported.

■ About half the U.S. trade deficit is due to oil imports.

■ The United States uses some 17 million barrels of oil a day, 43 percent of it in its cars.

■ Americans use twice as much gas per capita as the world's second-largest consumer, Sweden.

■ More than 188 million passenger vehicles were registered last year, more than one per licensed driver.

■ Eighty-two percent of all travel was by private vehicle; public transportation was used for only 2.5 percent of all trips taken.

■ Americans drive about 1.4 trillion miles each year — the equivalent of 7,256 round-trips to the sun.

"Automobiles are the root cause of U.S. oil dependence," says Christopher Flavin, an energy specialist at the Worldwatch Institute, a Washington-based environmental think tank.

All of this — not to mention traffic-snarled highways and the smog they produce — makes the automobile a natural target for any national energy strategy that tries to curb oil consumption.

The 1973 oil crisis was so disturbing that Congress managed to overcome the auto industry's objections and adopt the initial CAFE law. It required each domestic car maker — at the time, Ford, General Motors, and Chrysler and American Motors (which later merged) — to increase the average mileage of the new cars it sold each year until attaining 27.5 miles per gallon by 1985.

Under CAFE rules, auto companies can still sell gas guzzlers, but to meet the *average* fuel efficiency rates they also have to sell even more gas sippers. Companies that fail to meet each year's CAFE rates must pay a fine, while those that do better than required earn credits they can use in years when they fall below the mark.

The 1975 CAFE law has saved an estimated 1.8 million barrels of oil per day. Annual gas consumption per car plummeted from 785 gallons in 1972 to 507 gallons in 1988. While saving gas, cars stayed relatively roomy thanks to innovations such as front-wheel drive and electronic fuel injection. Ford's stately Lincoln Town Car got better mileage in 1985 than the company's far smaller Pinto did ten years earlier.

But auto mileage standards have stalled out. They were actually rolled back by the Reagan administration in 1986 and then restored by the Bush administration to the 1985 level. Still, "the levels of fuel economy established by that [1975] law have not increased since 1985, and the fuel economy of some manufacturers' fleets is actually

decreasing," says Sen. Ernest Hollings (D-S.C.), an architect of the 1975 CAFE law.

With gasoline prices currently about half what they were 30 years ago when adjusted for inflation, motorists are putting power and luxury ahead of fuel economy. Automakers are happy to oblige, particularly since it's more profitable this way. Ford, for example, makes an estimated $10,000 profit on each $30,000 Lincoln luxury car it sells but only $1,000 on the $10,000 Escort economy car, an industry analyst told the New York Times.

"As the 1990 model year begins, the automakers are wheeling out some of the biggest and brawniest cars in years," the Wall Street Journal reported. Buick's massive 1991 Roadmaster station wagon, for example, drinks a gallon of gas every 16 city miles.

THE PETROLEUM PRESIDENT

President Bush once called for a "national energy strategy" that includes "energy conservation and efficiency." But the administration's energy plan is short on both. Its centerpiece is a call to open the coastal section of Alaska's vast, ruggedly stunning Arctic National Wildlife Refuge to oil drilling, a proposal that died in Congress last year following the Exxon Valdez oil spill. This endeavor would produce about a tenth of the oil that would be saved by raising auto mileage to an average of 40 mpg, environmentalists argue.

The closest the energy plan gets to an endorsement of auto mileage standards is a lukewarm request for a federal study of the price and technology required to meet increased CAFE standards and the impact on auto safety. "We must avoid unwise and extreme measures such as excessive CAFE standards that would seriously hurt America's jobs and American industries," Bush said just before unveiling his energy plan.

Not everyone in the administration agreed. "The majority opinion within the administration is that CAFE is the wrong approach," one government analyst says, but "there's a minority who think it's the right approach."

Leading this pro-CAFE minority was the man who now is chiefly responsible for selling the Bush energy package to a skeptical Congress, Energy

Secretary James Watkins. The respected former chief of naval operations who won praise as chairman of a government AIDS commission, Adm. Watkins had suggested strong energy conservation measures early on, including increases in fuel efficiency standards and a "golden carrot" plan to give federal rebates to car-buyers who chose gas-saving models.

Senior White House staff reportedly excised stepped-up CAFE standards from the energy plan at the last minute and left Watkins to defend a plan he disagreed with. Senior Energy Department officials reportedly are dismayed with the final package; the White House has denied reports that Watkins was planning to resign over the issue.

The White House claims its fuel efficiency measures would reduce gasoline consumption by 13 percent "without the harmful effects of higher taxes, oil import fees or unjustifiable CAFE levels." But Roger Dower, one of the outside environmentalists whom the administration consulted prior to issuing its plan, disagrees. "Without CAFE, it's hard to say it's an energy efficiency bill," says the World Resources Institute energy analyst.

Members of the president's own party also remain unconvinced.

Sen. Nancy Kassebaum (R-Kan.), who has been lobbied by the auto industry and constituents of hers who work at a General Motors plant, was "very disappointed" with the Bush energy package because it failed to include improved mileage standards, an aide says. The senator had withdrawn

> **Automakers say they've been forced to defend themselves against an onslaught by environmentalists who've organized their massive grassroots memberships.**

her support of the Bryan bill last year expecting the president to come through with improved CAFE measures.

OVERDRIVE

The automakers say they've been forced to defend themselves against a well-oiled onslaught from environmental groups who've organized their massive grassroots memberships to press for higher mileage standards. But the auto interests certainly know how to put up a defense.

"It is a fairly formidable group to go up against — they are incredibly affluent, and they have the administration on their side," says Jim Mulhall, Sen. Bryan's spokesperson. The auto lobby's fight last year, he says, "in its sheer size and scope was pretty impressive."

It's impossible to determine exactly what the domestic and foreign auto industry — or the environmental lobby, for that matter — spent fighting the CAFE legislation last year. Ford, General Motors and Chrysler (known as the "Big Three") have scores of lobbyists and hire outside firms as well. But the Motor Vehicle Manufacturers Association (MVMA), the auto industry's chief trade association, alone spent more than $1.3 million in 1990 on lobbying costs, according to its federal disclosure forms. The association is bankrolled by the Big Three, Honda of America, Volvo of North America and two truck makers.

Auto industry PACs also have helped out friendly lawmakers. Democrat Don Riegle of Michigan, who carried Detroit's banner against the CAFE bill last year, received $38,350 in industry PAC contributions from 1983 to 1990. Sen. Don Nickles (R-Okla.), ranking minority member of the Senate energy conservation subcommittee and Sen. Riegle's battle partner, received $37,050. In contrast, Bryan received $8,250 in auto PAC money.

"Obviously we support people who support us," says Chrysler's Guiniven.

Auto industry executives also helped out. For example, a December 1990 fundraiser held by Chrysler in Detroit and hosted by company Chairman Lee Iacocca reportedly yielded 16 checks of $500 each for Michigan Sen. Carl Levin (D) from corporate big-wigs.

Auto lobbyists fanned out on Capitol Hill and at such executive branch agencies as the Treasury Department, EPA and the Department of Energy. Environmental lobbyists also made the rounds, but the auto industry had more resources — financial and human — to make its case.

"When you talk to environmental groups, they don't have a big staff so they tend to give you broad, somewhat nebulous arguments," says one administration policy analyst involved in drafting the Bush energy plan. "When you talk to the car people, they give you hundreds of pages of printouts and test results. Anything you could possibly ask for that you've ever thought of, they'll have their specialist in Dearborn call you up to tell you the results."

The auto industry also has a priceless Washington commodity called access. On the first day of spring this year, two days after the Senate Commerce Committee approved the Bryan CAFE bill by a vote of 14 to 5, the chief executive officers of General Motors, Ford and Chrysler lobbied against stiff CAFE rules at a rare face-to-face meeting with President Bush at the White House. The Big Three offered to fly 40 members of Congress to the Motor City in late April for an overnight, whirlwind tour of the industry aimed at educating lawmakers on CAFE and other issues.

Throughout its anti-CAFE campaign, the auto industry also has done a masterful job of organizing just about everybody who makes, sells or uses automobiles — in other words, just about everybody.

"They're clearly very powerful in certain states where producers are," says Sen. Joseph Lieberman (D-Conn.), a staunch supporter of the Bryan CAFE bill. "They also expand that power, insofar as they cleverly make coalitions with other groups [such as] auto dealers." Lieberman adds, "Not all of us have an automobile plant in our states or districts. But all of us have automobile dealers. And they tend to be the kind of people who we know and like, who are active in community affairs, our neighbors."

Auto manufacturers distributed form letters last year for their employees to fill out and send to Washington. Trade associations mobilized auto dealers. The United Auto Workers shared the industry's argument that the Bryan bill would mean a loss of jobs and tapped its members to pressure Congress.

In an effort to spread support, the auto manufacturers' chief trade association spent $500,000 to retain the Washington, D.C., public relations firm E. Bruce Harrison Co., which established the Coalition for Vehicle Choice. Operated from the firm's Washington office and headed by its executive vice president, Jeffrey Conley, the coalition gathered scores of national and local vehicle users' groups as diverse as the Livestock Marketing Association, the National Roofing Contractors Association, the International Professional Rodeo Association, the Motorcycle Industry Council and a boat owners' group.

The Bryan bill wouldn't require horses, motorcycles or watercraft to use less fuel. But cowpokes, bikers and boaters apparently fear the loss of brawny vehicles to haul their stuff around. "There are 18 million boat owners," explains Ron Defore, an E. Bruce Harrison executive who speaks for the vehicle users' coalition. "Most would resent the social architects who think that for whatever reason . . . [they] have to suffer. Boat owners resent that attitude."

BACKFIRE

The trouble began when the Big Three domestic automakers hired FMR, a Washington political consulting firm, to create "grassroots" groups in Nevada (Bryan's home state) and West Virginia, home of Democratic Sen. John Rockefeller, a member of the Energy and Natural Resources Committee and cosponsor of the Bryan bill last year.

The grassroots groups, called Nevadans or West Virginians for Fair Fuel Economy, organized activities such as letter-writing campaigns. But FMR apparently didn't make clear to the people it tapped to lead the campaign that the auto industry was bankrolling the effort, and when the truth came out in the press some leaders of the grassroots groups rebelled.

"I can guarantee you that the guy who talked to me did not tell me that the auto industry was involved," Desert Cab Co. owner George Balaban, who quit the Nevada grassroots group, told the *Detroit Free Press*.

Sen. Bryan was steamed.

"Your corporate efforts, executed through this Washington-based firm, were not aboveboard," Bryan wrote to the Big Three's chief executives. "Nowhere in this mailing did you identify that this mailing was paid for by the automakers. Nowhere did you say that

you hired political operatives to influence Nevada public opinion. Nowhere did you say that this purported Nevada-based organization was, in truth, organized by and for the automobile manufacturers. Nowhere did you honestly disclose your firm's participation. In effect, your firm came into my community under a false flag."

This was not the grassroots campaign's goal, but Chrysler's Guiniven says, "I don't think it backfired at all. I know it rankled some senators but we felt a real need to tell the world what this bill meant for them. Everyone knew the auto industry was behind this. It was totally aboveboard." FMR principal Glenn Cowan also denies there was anything underhanded about his firm's job for the auto industry.

Another case of unintended consequences occurred when the auto interests hired Bonner & Associates, a Washington firm that "specializes in organizing and conducting grassroots campaigns at the federal and state levels" and whose clients have included Exxon, Chase Manhattan Bank and Philip Morris (the cigarette and beer people), according to a trade association directory.

In March last year Bonner rounded up leaders of local groups for an anti-CAFE press conference in the Dirksen Senate Office Building organized by E. Bruce Harrison Co. and led by Sens. Riegle and Nickles. Bonner had contacted farm, religious, minority, business, youth and other local groups, telling them CAFE would be a disaster for their constituencies.

In contrast to FMR, Jack Bonner, president of Bonner & Associates, says his firm was "very up-front" about the fact that it was working for the auto industry. Bonner flew in the heads of the Florida Silver-Haired Legislature (a seniors' group), the Nebraska Farm Bureau, a Big Brothers/Big Sisters chapter and an official of the National Sheriff's Association. Bonner also persuaded Linda Werkmeister, then head of client services at South Dakota's Easter Seals, to explain how the Bryan bill would harm her organization's efforts to help disabled people.

But the South Dakota Easter Seals had taken no official position on CAFE, and Werkmeister, warned in advance not to participate in the press conference, was fired over the incident.

Getting dragged into the CAFE debate was an embarrassment for Easter Seals, says Joe Romer, director of its national office. The organization takes care not to get involved in political causes not directly related to its work, Romer says, adding that he resents the fact that "corporate interests try to manipulate and use small nonprofits like ours . . . as a pawn in a political battle not related to people with disabilities."

SHIFT TO REVERSE

The auto industry's main offensive against the CAFE bill came down to a two-week stretch last September when CAFE opponents launched a lobbying ground war that turned defeat into victory.

Bryan's bill was scheduled to come to the Senate floor for action in early September. Such a step usually begins with an informal, untallied voice vote. But friends of the auto industry, led by Sen. Riegle, moved to prevent the senators from bringing the issue to the floor for consideration by filibustering, which stops action.

Filibusters are a rare, last-ditch parliamentary maneuver and in this case reflected the industry's fear that the Bryan bill would pass because of the Persian Gulf crisis. The tactic failed at first; Bryan bill supporters mustered more than the 60 votes needed to reach "cloture" to break the filibuster on bringing up the bill, and debate began. But when the bill was temporarily set aside to allow the Senate to vote on the federal budget, the industry got a crucial opening.

Its lobbyists and supporters began putting the squeeze on undecided senators. On another front, car dealers and auto plants prompted their employees to swamp congressional offices with letters and phone calls opposing the Bryan bill. Sen. Claiborne Pell (D-R.I.) got some 250 letters that week, an "amazing" amount for a small state like Rhode Island, an aide says.

The auto industry also owes a lot to the Bush administration. "The administration really turned up the heat," says one Capitol Hill staffer who was there for the blitz.

When the Senate took up the Bryan bill again on September 25, opponents filibustered again. This time 11 senators — three Democrats and eight Republicans — switched sides and the filibuster held. "The minority won a small and shortsighted victory," Sen. Bryan

Detroit says it can't improve fuel economy without shrinking cars. But the stately 1985 Lincoln Town Car got better mileage than the 1975 Pinto.

said as he pulled the bill. "We will be back next year."

Senators who responded to queries denied they "switched" votes—Sen. Sam Nunn (D-Ga.), for example, voted to sustain the second filibuster because he wanted more time for debate than was allotted, his office says. At the same time, it's worth noting that most of the 11 were among the auto industry's favored PAC recipients, with an average take of $30,940 between 1983 and 1990.

As auto lobbyists descended on Senate offices between the two CAFE votes, a controversial PAC financed by foreign car dealers and run by Tom Nemet from his Queens, N.Y., showroom distributed $35,000 in PAC contributions around the Senate. Nemet's network, the Auto Dealers and Drivers for Free Trade PAC, or AUTOPAC, traditionally has thrown its financial support behind lawmakers who opposed barriers to foreign car imports. But foreign car makers oppose the Bryan bill because it would hike domestic and foreign mileage standards by the same percentage, in effect punishing imports for past performance. Foreign auto dealers oppose any law they think might hurt sales.

Fred Glacken, spokesperson for AUTOPAC, says the timing of the contributions was coincidental — they were just part of the PAC's home-stretch giving for the 1990 elections. Besides, the money was doled out according to candidates' stances on a number of issues, not specific votes, he says, adding, "We don't give out money legislatively, but politically."

MPG EQUALS DOA

U.S. automakers have argued that higher CAFE standards would fail to curb air pollution or save much gas, but

would force massive layoffs of American workers and rob Americans of their right to drive big cars. This year, however, the industry is banking on an argument with perhaps greater emotional impact: The Bryan bill would force families into unsafe cars, they say.

The industry says it's technologically impossible to meet the tough CAFE standards in the Bryan bill without making cars much smaller and lighter — and unsafe. The safety argument is a risky one for the domestic auto industry to make, since even the Big Three now build and sell hundreds of thousands of economy cars each year. Four of the ten best-selling cars in the United States last year were compacts; three others were subcompacts.

But the Bush administration has been happy to help out. Transportation Secretary Samuel Skinner dubbed the Bryan bill "the Highway Death Act of 1991." The Transportation Department's National Highway Traffic Safety Administration (NHTSA) backed the original 1975 CAFE law, but under Bush appointee Jerry Ralph Curry it has been outspoken in its opposition to the Bryan bill. "The declared motor vehicle fuel economy savings in this bill cannot be met without causing death and injury," Curry says.

NHTSA is the same agency that recently came under fire for its *lack* of concern for auto safety. The Institute for Injury Reduction, a nonprofit group formed by trial lawyers, charged that NHTSA, by failing to address known problems with auto child restraints, has "increased child exposure to injury in car crashes." The institute also characterized the agency's reluctance to require air bags in all new cars as a "tragedy."

Clarence Ditlow, Washington's auto-safety guru and the industry's *bête noire*, rejects NHTSA's stance on fuel efficiency as nonsense. CAFE doesn't legislate small cars, he says, citing a study by the Energy Department's Lawrence Berkeley Laboratories that concludes existing technology could increase average car mileage to 40 miles per gallon within four years without any reduction in auto size or performance. But even if automakers choose to shrink cars to meet higher mileage standards, Ditlow argues, "we can make small cars safer."

Ditlow, whose Center for Auto Safety fought strenuously for federally mandated air bags, says auto fatalities actually have *fallen* by 40 percent since the first CAFE law was enacted. Part of that can be attributed to get-tough drunk-driving laws, federal auto-safety measures mandated during that period and reduced highway speed limits, but most of it resulted from better engineering, he says.

"As fuel economy doubled over the past decade, cars became safer because they were better designed," says Deborah Gordon, a former environmental engineer for Chevron and policymaker at the Lawrence Berkeley lab, who testified in support of Bryan's bill for the Union of Concerned Scientists.

In theory, large cars do fare better than small ones in a collision. But in reality, many small cars on the road today are safer than many big cars, as a

"Obviously we support people who support us," says an executive at one of the Big Three automakers, which together made $3.3 million in PAC contributions from 1983-90.

glimpse in the April 1991 *Consumer Reports* illustrates.

The 1991 Ford Escort, for example, a small car that averages 34 mpg, rated "superb" in federal crash tests, the magazine says. The Escort scored the magazine's highest possible rating on driver and passenger protection and structural integrity even without air bags.

Meanwhile, crash tests show that "severe or fatal injury is virtually certain" for passengers in the barge-like 1990 Chrysler Imperial, which gets only 20 mpg, the magazine reported. Similarly, passengers in the 18-mpg 1991 Chevrolet Caprice, so massive that "the extremities of the car are hard to gauge," face a "high likelihood of a severe or fatal injury," the magazine says.

Benjamin Kelley, president of the Institute for Injury Reduction, says automakers could make cars that are both safe and fuel efficient if they wanted to.

"It may be true that if the companies comply with tighter fuel economy standards without using modern crash-worthiness technologies, they could end up merely building greater volumes of downsized, less-safe cars," Kelley says. "But that would mean a tragically missed opportunity to introduce advanced materials and design approaches able to increase the crash protection levels of all cars."

As proponents of higher CAFE rates point out, the automakers' plaints about mileage and auto size have a too-familiar ring. Ford predicted in 1974 that the CAFE standards proposed then "would require a Ford product line consisting of either all sub-Pinto-sized vehicles or some mix of vehicles ranging from a sub-sub-compact to perhaps a Maverick."

Chrysler's Guiniven concedes that this point has given automakers "a lack of credibility" in the CAFE debate. "It's our own doing," he says.

ON THE ROAD AGAIN

As the heat shimmers off the Capitol dome this summer, Congress will be wrangling over how to save the nation's energy.

When a vote in the Senate on the CAFE issue appeared imminent in mid-spring, Transportation Secretary Skinner threatened to recommend a Bush veto if Congress adopted a strong CAFE bill. Meanwhile, an effort was afoot in the Senate to amend the current federal CAFE law to permit states to set their own, higher rates.

But before any strong CAFE legislation gets to the president's desk, it also must overcome its chief obstacle in Congress, Democratic Rep. John Dingell of Michigan, who as chair of the House Energy and Commerce Committee has kept CAFE legislation bottled up. "Fuel efficiency is about as high as you can get it now," he once growled. But given the number of pro-environment lawmakers on the House

energy panel, "he's gonna have to deal with [the CAFE issue], but he's not happy about it," a House aide says.

Sen. Lieberman, who as Connecticut's attorney general was the state's consumer advocate, believes the CAFE debate is a classic example of powerful special interests opposing the nation's best interest.

"It's a choice we have to make," he says. "Sometimes the general public interest — in this case, energy efficiency and environmental protection — must come before private and corporate interests."

The auto industry "is a potent lobby," Lieberman adds. "But I do think this is one case where we have to listen to the voice of the majority, not to mention our own sense of what's good for the country. And I think the majority is ready for change and for leadership here."   ◆

Article 2. As Clean Air Bill Took Off, So Did PAC Donations
by Chuck Alston

Chuck Alston describes the industry-led fight to defeat clean air legislation, which saw the seventeen biggest political action committees mount a massive campaign to influence the nation's top lawmakers. Indeed, in 1989 the oil, gas, and automobile PACs contributed nearly $612,000 to influential members of the House Energy and Commerce Committee, which voted down the legislation. This article discusses the role of PAC contributions, raising the question of whether PAC money does, in fact, determine the outcome of legislation.

Industries fighting over clean-air legislation contributed nearly $612,000 to the campaigns of House Energy and Commerce Committee members in 1989 — the year barriers that had blocked committee action on air pollution for 12 years began to fall.

Auto, steel, chemical, oil, natural gas, coal and electric utility interests gave Rep. Philip R. Sharp, D-Ind., who chairs the Energy and Power Subcommittee, 21 cents of ev-

ery dollar he raised last year — $36,025 in all. These same interests supplied Rep. Joe L. Barton, a junior Republican from Texas and former oil company engineer, with $28,000, or 33 cents of every dollar he took in from political action committees (PACs).

By contrast, Rep. Henry A. Waxman, D-Calif., who tried to push strong environmental amendments through his Health and the Environment Subcommittee, got stiffed. He took in just $4,000, most of it from hometown interests.

In all, nearly a nickel of every dollar that committee members raised in 1989 — an average of about $15,000 each — came from one of 154 PACs

Congressional Quarterly identified as having a significant stake in the outcome of the clean-air bill. The tally is based on Federal Election Commission (FEC) reports filed by the candidates and the PACs. (Committee markup begins, p. 828; CQ methodology, p. 813)

The biggest PACs — the 17 whose spending topped $10,000 — clearly stepped up their efforts in 1989. Their donations increased 55 percent to $223,125 in 1989, compared with 1987, the last non-election year. "There is more money available to an industry when they have something hot," says Rep. Al Swift, D-Wash.

From *Congressional Quarterly Weekly Report,* March 17, 1990, pp. 811–817. Copyright © 1990 Congressional Quarterly Inc. Reprinted by permission.

The Energy and Commerce panel began marking up the clean-air bill March 14.

Clean-air legislation is by no means the sole concern of an electric utility, a natural-gas distributor, an oil refiner or an automaker, particularly in a committee given wide berth to regulate the nation's commerce. Just last year, for instance, the committee handled legislation eliminating natural-gas price controls. These PACs' 1989 contributions, moreover, represent only a fraction of the tens of millions of dollars their industries have spent for political donations to members of Congress over the past decade. The campaign for re-election money has escalated to the point where lobbyists and members alike can dismiss tens of thousands of dollars as insignificant.

"It's not a lot of money in the overall scheme of things," says Thomas Dennis, a Washington-based regional vice president of Southern California Edison Co., an electric utility. Kansas Republican Bob Whittaker, a committee member who plans to leave Congress after this year, says: "$15,000 doesn't sound like that much, although it was a non-election year. The average [committee] member can raise $250,000 from PACs."

Even so, the industry contributions to Energy and Commerce members shed light on the political economy of legislation in the House's "money committees." And what is unmistakable is the financial embrace of the regulators and the regulated, a relationship under increasing scrutiny as Congress grapples with campaign-finance issues. *(Campaign finance, Weekly Report p. 725)*

Contributions to Panel Members

How much each member of the House Energy and Commerce Committee received in 1989 campaign contributions from political action committees with a major interest in clean-air legislation.

$50,800	Tom Tauke, R-Iowa		$12,350	Jim Slattery, D-Kan.
$38,550	W. J. "Billy" Tauzin, D-La.		$12,250	Thomas J. Manton, D-N.Y.
$36,025	Philip R. Sharp, D-Ind.		$11,600	Dan Schaefer, R-Colo.
$31,750	John D. Dingell, D-Mich.		$11,500	Thomas A. Luken, D-Ohio
$28,000	Joe L. Barton, R-Texas		$11,450	William E. Dannemeyer, R-Calif.
$26,750	Ralph M. Hall, D-Texas			
$24,800	Jack Fields, R-Texas		$10,650	John Bryant, D-Texas
$22,100	Carlos J. Moorhead, R-Calif.		$10,525	Michael Bilirakis, R-Fla.
			$10,000	Doug Walgren, D-Pa.
$20,150	Rick Boucher, D-Va.		$7,650	Bob Whittaker, R-Kan.
$20,070	Edward Madigan, R-Ill.		$6,500	Matthew J. Rinaldo, R-N.J.
$19,500	Michael G. Oxley, R-Ohio		$4,000	Cardiss Collins, D-Ill.
$19,300	Terry L. Bruce, D-Ill.		$4,000	Henry A. Waxman, D-Calif.
$19,125	Al Swift, D-Wash.		$2,500	Jim Bates, D-Calif.
$18,750	Norman F. Lent, R-N.Y.		$1,500	Gerry Sikorski, D-Minn.
$17,900	Thomas J. Bliley Jr., R-Va.		$1,350	Ed Towns, D-N.Y.
$16,350	Alex McMillan, R-N.C.		$1,300	Jim Cooper, D-Tenn.
$15,500	Ron Wyden, D-Ore.		$500	Howard C. Nielson, R-Utah
$14,825	Don Ritter, R-Pa.		$0	Edward J. Markey, D-Mass.
$13,650	Bill Richardson, D-N.M.		$0	James H. Scheuer, D-N.Y.
$13,525	J. Roy Rowland, D-Ga.		$0	Mike Synar, D-Okla.
$13,500	Dennis E. Eckart, D-Ohio			
$12,400	Sonny Callahan, R-Ala.		**TOTAL: $611,945**	

The Energy and Commerce Committee tends to the nation's rails, trucks and airwaves, its environment, health and telephones. It oversees Hollywood, Wall Street and the Oil Patch. A seat on the committee makes raising campaign money as easy as licking the stamps for invitations to fund-raisers.

Few inside the process contend that PACs try to buy votes outright. Rather, the spending reflects the cost of doing business in Washington. Companies, unions and trade associations want to make sure their voices are heard clearly in a committee where decisions worth millions in profits are frequently decided by one or two votes. Donations also ensure that like-thinking candidates enjoy a well-stocked war chest to face re-election.

"There is so damn much money out there that anybody who gives anybody anything for it is an idiot," Swift says. "If you can't get it from the oil guys, you can get it from the natural-gas guys. If you can't get it from the communication guys, you can get it from the rail guys."

Columbia Gas Gets Competitive

Business and labor PACs gave $136 million to congressional candidates for the 1988 elections, one-third of all the money candidates raised, according to FEC records. About $11.9 million of this came from industries interested in clean-air legislation, according to the Center for Responsive Politics, a Washington-based organization that studies Congress.

> **"There is so damn much money out there that anybody who gives anybody anything for it is an idiot."**
>
> **—Rep. Al Swift**

The recent history of The Columbia Gas System, a Wilmington, Del.-based natural gas producer, transmitter and distributor, illustrates the extent to which PACs have become an essential adjunct to a Washington lobbying operation.

The $3 billion company sells natural gas primarily in Northeast and mid-Atlantic states. Add in its pipelines and wells, and Columbia's operations sprawl across 20 states and 90 congressional districts. Rick Casali, vice president in charge of the Washington office, says that while the company is one of the industry's largest,

136

its PAC operation was among the smallest — until 1989.

"We had some adverse decisions that came out of federal regulatory agencies," Casali says. "That caused us to have to make some very serious decisions, cutting our dividend, things that employees really felt. We pointed out that Columbia's PAC was smaller than it should be. So we got major increases in the number of dollars and members in our PAC. That gave us a larger resource base to stay competitive with other industries."

Columbia's PACs spent $89,360 on contributions to federal candidates last year, close to the $116,325 they spent during the entire 1987-88 election cycle.

Energy and Commerce members were among the chief beneficiaries. The Columbia Gas Employees Fund, the largest of the company's three federal PACs, increased contributions to committee members nearly fivefold to $12,275 in 1989, compared with 1987. Two smaller Columbia PACs chipped in another $10,325, for a total of $22,600. In all, one-fourth of its donations to federal candidates went to Energy and Commerce members.

"That's really our bread-and-butter committee in the House," Casali says, "because it handles so many issues that have an impact on our operations and our future business: natural-gas decontrol, legislation impacting the Public Utilities Holding Company Act, the Clean Air Act."

All of this sounds familiar to Joe Hillings, vice president for federal government affairs for Enron Corp. Like Casali, he makes the rounds of members' Capitol Hill cocktail parties where the entry fee is $250 and up and has been rising. Subcommittee chairmen charge as much as $650 a ticket.

Houston-based Enron, which operates more miles of pipeline than any other natural-gas company, uses typical criteria to decide which parties Hillings will attend. The PAC supports members representing its areas of service or operation, members on committees with relevant jurisdiction, pro-energy members and pro-business members. Of late it also has considered their stand on natural-gas decontrol.

Enron's contributions to committee members increased 43 percent to $12,000 in 1989, compared with 1987. A new arrival at Energy and Commerce in the 101st Congress, Alex McMillan, R-N.C., the former president of a grocery store chain, was a first-time recipient of Enron money.

"He is now very much involved in our issues," Hillings says. "We want to have somewhat of a relationship."

Enron was not unique. After McMillan moved from the Banking Committee, the money he raised from PACs interested in clean-air legislation rose to $16,350 in 1989, compared with $5,700 in 1987. PACs sponsored by Alabama Power Co., Baltimore Gas & Electric Co., Atlantic Richfield Co., the Edison Electric Institute, the National Coal Association, Philadelphia Electric Co., Southern California Edison Co., Texas Utilities Co. and Virginia Electric & Power Co. took note of his arrival by giving to him for the first time.

"Because I had been in business 20 years, there seems to be a natural affinity," McMillan says. "My own impression is that support tends to follow interest, and not vice versa."

Like McMillan, Democrat Thomas J. Manton of New York moved to Energy and Commerce from Banking as the 101st Congress began. His contributions from industries interested in clean-air legislation surged 231 percent to $12,250 in 1989, compared with 1987. He collected more contributions from these industries, 26 compared with 12, and their average size increased to $471 from $308. *(Box, p. 817)*

The Southern Co.: $7.5 Billion

The contributions pale in comparison with the money at risk in clean-air legislation itself. The cost to industry is expected to reach $20 billion or more annually. Much of it will be passed along to consumers through higher prices for gasoline, cars and electricity.

Consider The Southern Co., an Atlanta-based holding company that sells electricity to most of Georgia and Alabama and large sections of Florida and Mississippi. Coal-fired plants generate 80 percent of its electricity. Most of them burn high-sulfur coal, a leading cause of acid rain. Southern tells lawmakers that installing what are known as scrubbers and bag houses at its plants to meet new emission standards for air toxics and acid rain would cost $7.5 billion in today's dollars and could force rate increases of 25 percent.

One way Southern's management has responded is to increase PAC contributions to committee members. At one of its subsidiaries, Alabama Power Co., the Employees Federal PAC doubled contributions to $12,450 in 1989, compared with 1987. Sister PACs at Georgia Power Co., Southern Co., Mississippi Power Co. and Gulf States Power Co. kicked in another $15,950, bringing the total to $28,400.

"Utilities are heavily regulated, and what Congress does can have a major impact on the company," Southern spokesman John Hutchinson says. "Our employees realize that."

Southern and Columbia are not alone in their multiple-PAC arrangement. Texas Utilities Co., the parent company of Dallas Power & Light and Texas Power & Light,

---

Methodology

To study the money and politics of clean-air legislation at the committee level, CQ examined Federal Election Commission reports for 1989, cross-checking contributions from political action committees (PACs) with reports from members of the House Energy and Commerce Committee. Panel membership was studied as of Feb. 15, when there were 42 committee members and one vacancy (since filled by Tom McMillen, D-Md.). 1987 data is based on the committee's membership at that time.

PACs affiliated with industry, including business, labor and trade groups, were studied. To be selected, the PAC's sponsor was one for which clean-air legislation was a significant economic issue and among its principal concerns with the committee in 1989. Within the chemical industry, for instance, companies that primarily manufacture pharmaceuticals were left out. Similarly, although several unions are involved peripherally in lobbying efforts, only one, the United Mine Workers, was included.

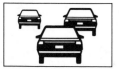

110 PACs Gave at Least $1,000...

One hundred and ten political action committees with an interest in clean-air legislation gave more than $1,000 to members of the House Energy and Commerce Committee in 1989. The first name on a line in each listing is the official sponsor of the PAC, generally a corporation or trade association. Where the name of the parent company is signficant — as when a parent company is affiliated with more than one PAC through its subsidiaries or the parent is better known — the parent company's name is in parentheses. Abbreviations:

TA — Trade association
Auto — Automobile manufacturing, retailing
EUtil — Electric utility
Oil — Oil exploration, refining or distribution
Oil-Ret — Gasoline and oil products retailing
Gas — Natural gas exploration, transmission, distribution
GasEUtil — Gas and electric utility
HEQ — Maker of heavy off-road vehicles
Chem — Chemical makers
Energy — Diversified producer of oil, gas and coal
Steel — Steel making
Coal — Coal mining

$19,150	Auto-TA	National Automobile Dealers Assn/Dealers Election Cmte of the National Automobile Dealers Assn
$18,600	Auto	Ford Motor Co./Ford Motor Co. Civic Action Fund
$18,000	Auto	General Motors Corp./Civic Involvement Program, General Motors Corp.
$13,350	Oil	BP America Inc. (British Petroleum Co.)/ BPA-PAC
$12,950	EUtil	Southern California Edison Co./Federal Citizenship Responsibility Group
$12,850	EUtil	Virginia Electric & Power Co./Cmte for Responsible Gov't-Dominion Resources Inc.
$12,700	Oil	Atlantic Richfield Co./Atlantic Richfield Co., ARCO PAC
$12,450	EUtil	Alabama Power Co. (The Southern Co.)/Alabama Power Co. Employees Fed PAC
$12,400	EUtil-TA	Nat'l Rural Electric Cooperative Assn./Action Cmte. for Rural Electrification
$12,275	Gas	Columbia Hydrocarbon Corp. (Columbia Gas System Inc.)/Columbia Gas Employees Political Action Fund
$12,000	Gas	Enron Corp./Enron PAC
$11,900	Oil	Amoco Corp./Amoco PAC
$11,900	Oil-Ret	Petroleum Marketers Assn of America/Petroleum Marketers Assn of America Small Businessmen's Cmte
$11,050	Gas	Pacific Enterprises/Pacific Enterprises Political Assistance Cmte
$10,950	Energy	American Natural Resources Inc. (The Coastal Corp.)/The Coastal Corp. Employee Action Fund
$10,900	Oil	Ashland Oil Inc./Ashland PAC for Employees
$10,150	Oil-Ret	Scty. of Independent Gasoline Marketers of America/Scty. of Independent Gasoline Marketers of America
$9,750	EUtil	American Electric Power Co. Inc./American Electric Power Committee for Responsible Gov't
$9,700	Oil	Texaco Inc./Texaco Political Involvement Cmte
$9,550	EUtil	The Southern Co./The Southern Co. Services PAC
$9,250	Oil	Chevron Corp./Chevron Employees PAC
$8,950	Coal-TA	National Coal Assn/COALPAC
$8,800	Gas	Columbia Natural Resources Inc. (Columbia Gas System Inc.)/Columbia Employees Pol Action Fund
$8,600	Auto	Chrysler Corp./Chrysler Corp. Pol Support Cmte
$8,600	Chem	CIBA-GEIGY Corp. (CIBA-GEIGY Ltd.)/CIBA-GEIGY Employee Good Govt' Fund
$8,550	EUtil	Texas Utilities Electric Co./Texas Power & Light Div Employees PAC
$8,500	EUtil	Houston Industries Inc./Houston Industries Inc. PAC
$8,500	Steel-TA	Institute of Scrap Recycling Industries/ISRI PAC
$8,250	Oil	Mobil Corp./Mobil Oil Corp. PAC
$7,750	Chem	W. R. Grace & Co./ W. R. Grace & Co. PAC
$7,700	GasEUtil	Pacific Gas & Electric Co./PG&E Employees Federal Good Gov't Fund
$7,050	Coal	Peabody Coal Co./Peabody PAC
$6,600	EUtil-TA	Edison Electric Institute/Power PAC of Edison Electric Institute
$6,450	EUtil	Texas Utilities Co./Texas Utilities Co. PAC
$6,350	Coal	International Union United Mine Workers of America/Coal Miners Political Action Cmte
$6,300	Oil	Union Oil Co. of California/Union Oil Political Awareness Fund
$6,100	Oil	Exxon Corp./Exxon Corp. PAC
$6,100	Coal	The Pittston Co./The Pittston Co. PAC
$5,750	Oil	Shell Oil Co./Shell Oil Co. Employees Political Awareness Cmte
$5,400	EUtil	Georgia Power Co. (The Southern Co.)/Georgia Power Co. Federal PAC
$5,150	EUtil	General Public Utilities Corp./General Public Utilities Political Participation Assoc
$5,000	HEQ	Deere & Co./Deere & Co. Civic Action Fund
$5,000	HEQ	Navistar International Corp. (formerly International Harvester)/Navistar Int'l Corp. Good Gov't Cmte
$5,000	Oil	Phillips Petroleum Co./Phillips Petroleum PAC
$4,950	EUtil	Entergy Corp. (formerly Middle South Utilities)/Entergy Services Inc. Good Gov't Action Cmte
$4,850	Chem	Freeport-McMoRan Inc./Freeport-McMoRan Inc. Citizenship Cmte
$4,800	EUtil	Duke Power Co./Employees Federal PAC-Duke Power Co.
$4,750	Energy	Burlington Resources Inc./Burlington Resources Inc. PAC
$4,550	Chem	Allied-Signal Inc./Allied Signal PAC
$4,500	EUtil	Carolina Power & Light Co./Employees Federal PAC-Carolina Power & Light Co.

...To House Panel's Members

$4,400	GasEUtil	Northern States Power Co./Northern States Power Political Interest Cmte
$4,400	Gas	The Williams Cos./The Williams Cos. PAC
$4,350	Gas	Arkla Inc./ArklaPAC
$4,250	EUtil	Texas Utilities Elec. Co. (Texas Utilities Co.)/Texas Elec. Service Co. Div of Texas Utilities Electric Co. PAC
$4,050	Gas-TA	American Gas Assn/Gas Employers PAC
$4,050	Gas-TA	Interstate Natural Gas Assn of America/Interstate Natural Gas Assn of America PAC
$3,850	Chem	Air Products and Chemicals Inc./Air Products and Chemicals Inc. Political Alliance
$3,650	Chem	Hoescht Celanese Corp./Hoescht Celanese Corp. PAC
$3,500	GasEUtl	Baltimore Gas & Electric Co./BG&E PAC
$3,500	EUtil	Florida Power & Light Co. (FPL Group)/Good Gov't Management Assn of FP&l Co. Employees' PAC
$3,500	Gas	Transco Energy Co./Transco Energy Co. PAC
$3,300	Gas	Panhandle Eastern Corp./Panhandle Eastern Corp. PAC
$3,220	GasEUtil	Illinois Power Co./Illinois Power Employees' Federal PAC
$3,000	Gas	Valero Energy Corp./Valero Energy Corp. PAC
$2,950	Oil	Enserch Corp./Enserch Corp. Employees Political Support Assn
$2,900	EUtil	Detroit Edison Co./Detroit Edison PAC
$2,900	Gas	El Paso Natural Gas Co. Div of El Paso Co. (Burlington Resources)/El Paso Co. PAC
$2,850	EUtil	Philadelphia Electric Co./Philadelphia Electric Co. Federal PAC
$2,800	Oil	Marathon Oil Co. (USX Corp.)/Marathon Oil Co. Employees PAC
$2,625	EUtil	Florida Power Corp. (Florida Progress Corp.)/PAC of Florida Power Corp. Employees
$2,600	EUtil	New Orleans Public Service Inc. (Entergy Corp.)/New Orleans Pub. Svc. Inc. Cmte for Responsible Gov't
$2,550	Gas	National Fuel Gas Co./National Fuel Gas Co. Federal PAC
$2,450	SteelOil	USX Corp./USX Corp. PAC
$2,350	Steel	Bethlehem Steel Corp./Bethlehem Steel Good Govt' Cmte
$2,350	GasEUtil	Public Service Electric & Gas Co. (Public Service Enterprise Group Inc.)/Public Service Electric & Gas PAC
$2,300	Oil	Pennzoil Co./Pennzoil PAC
$2,300	Oil/Gas	Tenneco Inc./Tenneco Employees Good Gov't Fund
$2,250	GasEUtil	Arizona Public Service Co./Arizona Public Service Co. PAC
$2,250	EUtil	Texas Utilities Electric Co./Dallas Power & Light Div, Texas Utilities Electric Co. Active Citizenship Cmte
$2,200	Chem	American Cyanamid Co./American Cyanamid Good Gov't Fund
$2,200	HEQ	Caterpillar Inc./Caterpillar Inc. Cmte For Effective Gov't
$2,200	Gas	Sonat Inc./Sonat Inc. PAC
$2,000	GasEUtil	Central Illinois Public Service Co./Central Illinois Public Service Co. PAC
$2,000	GasEUtil	Midwest Energy Co./Midwest Energy Co. Employees Gov't Cmte
$1,850	EUtil	Commonwealth Edison Co./Commonwealth Edison PAC
$1,850	GasUtil	Commonwealth Energy System/Com-Energy Services Co. Employees for a Responsible Congress
$1,825	EUtil	Louisiana Power & Light Co. (Entergy Corp.)/La. Cmte on Political Action of Louisiana Power & Light Co.
$1,800	Coal	Mapco Inc./Mapco Employees PAC
$1,800	Chem	Union Carbide Corp./Union Carbide Corp. PAC
$1,700	EUtil-TA	American Public Power Assn/American Public Power Assn Public Ownership of Electric Resources PAC
$1,700	MISC	Combustion Engineering Inc./Combustion Engineering Inc. PAC
$1,650	GasEUtil	Consumers Power Co./Consumers Power Co. Employees for Better Gov't-Federal
$1,600	Steel	Armco Inc./Armco Employees' PAC
$1,600	Auto	BDM International Inc. (Ford Motor Co.)/BDM Int'l Inc. PAC
$1,600	EUtil	Centerior Energy Corp./Centerior Fund
$1,550	EUtil	Duquesne Light Co./Duquesne Light Co. Federal PAC
$1,550	Gas-TA	National LP-Gas Assn/National Propane Gas Assn PAC, PROPANE PAC
$1,525	Gas	Commonwealth Propane Inc. (Columbia Gas System Inc.)/Columbia Gas Distribution Employees PAC
$1,500	EUtil	Puget Sound Power & Light Co./Puget Power Good Gov't Cmte
$1,500	GasEUtil	San Diego Gas & Electric Co./San Diego Gas & Electric Co. Citizens for Good Gov't Cmte
$1,300	EUtil	Public Service Co. of Indiana Inc./Public Service Co. of Indiana Inc. PAC
$1,275	EUtil	Pennsylvania Power & Light Co./Pennsylvania Power & Light Co. People for Good Gov't
$1,250	Gas	Texas Gas Transmission Corp./Texas Gas Transmission Corp. PAC
$1,200	Coal	Cyprus Minerals Co./Cyprus PAC
$1,150	Gas	Atlanta Gas Light Co./ Atlanta Gas Light Co. for Good Gov't Cmte Inc.
$1,150	GasEUtil	Orange & Rockland Utilities Inc./Orange & Rockland Utilities Inc. Employees PAC
$1,000	Oil	American Petrofina Inc. (Petrofina Societe Anonyme)/American Petrofina Inc. & Fina Oil and Chemical PAC
$1,000	EUtil	Iowa Electric Light & Power Co./Iowa Electric Light & Power Co. PAC
$1,000	Gas	LaSalle Energy Corp./LaSalle Energy Corp. PAC
$1,000	Oil/Coal	Sun Co. Inc./Sun Co. Inc. PAC

maintains four PACs that together gave $21,500 to committee members.

It is no surprise that Sharp, the chief ally on the committee for coal-burning utilities, has been one of the prime recipients of electric utility and coal money. The Midwestern utilities he speaks for would bear the brunt of acid-rain provisions. Sharp is one of the few Energy members who continually faces tough re-election battles. *(Box, p. 816)*

Three times in the 1980s voters returned Sharp with less than 55 percent of the vote. He raised about two-thirds of the $444,422 he spent on his 1988 campaign from PACs, and his Republican opponent made an issue of it.

In 1989, $36,025, or 21 percent, of the money Sharp raised came from industries with a stake in clean-air legislation. Of this, $16,750 came from coal and electric utility interests.

Another Midwesterner, Republican Tom Tauke of Iowa, led the committee tee in clean-air fund raising, garnering $50,800. Tauke is running for the Senate, increasing his need for money. He expects to spend at least $5 million for his Senate race. *(Box, p. 812)*

More than one-fifth of what Tauke raised came from makers of off-road construction and farm equipment. Caterpillar Tractor Co., Deere and Co. and Navistar International Corp. together contributed $11,000. Deere is a major employer in Iowa. A member of the Environment Subcommittee, Tauke was instrumental in negotiating a deal for a study of the air pollution caused by off-road vehicles before the government takes any action.

Choosing Among Members

Committee Chairman John D. Dingell's Michigan district is a microcosm of the nation's industrial heartland. It is home to Ford Motor Co. and a sprawling collection of auto factories, steel mills, foundries and chemical plants.

For years, he has been the chief defender of industry interests in the clean-air debate and a key reason legislation hasn't moved. One reason committee members do so well with these interests is that Dingell has used his clout to make sure recent Democratic appointments reflect his views.

Nonetheless, the chairman ranked fourth among committee members in this fund raising, with $31,750. Because his seat is safe and his war chest well-armed ($268,707 at year's end), most Washington lobbyists consider his

Two Key Members

The chairman of the Energy and Commerce Subcommittee on Energy and Power, Philip R. Sharp, D-Ind., is the champion of coal-burning Midwestern utilities. He faces a tough re-election challenger who in 1988 criticized his dependence on PACs.

A member of his subcommittee, Al Swift, D-Wash., emerged as the leader of the so-called Group of Nine, moderate Democrats who joined together in the 100th Congress to try to find a compromise on the main issues of the clean-air bill.

	Sharp					Swift				
	All PACs	Clean-Air PACs	%	No. of Gifts	Total Donations	All PACs	Clean-Air PACs	%	No. of Gifts	Total Donations
1989	$133,325	$36,025	27	57	$173,939	$ 81,245	$19,125	24	31	$154,789
1987	62,008	23,000	37	54	86,143	108,813	10,375	9.5	23	144,639

fund-raising demands modest. He holds but one Washington fund-raiser a year.

Three relatively junior committee members ranked just behind Dingell in fund raising even though they do not hold leadership positions, a fact best explained by geography. Democrat Ralph M. Hall and Republicans Barton and Jack Fields represent the Lone Star State, and their toughest moments come when they must make a Texan's choice between mom and

---

Members of Congress who backed oil and auto interests on one big amendment got twice as much from the industry PACs as those who didn't.

---

apple pie — oil and natural gas.

Fields and Hall were the chief sponsors of an amendment adopted 12-10 in the Health and the Environment Subcommittee in October 1989 that stirred a controversy when its adoption was portrayed as gutting a key portion of the Bush administration's clean-air legislation (HR 3030). The amendment weakened a provision that would have forced greater use in automobiles of alternative fuels such as natural gas.

Oil companies and automakers — and, after considerable pressure from members and other lobbies to fall in line, even natural-gas interests — backed the Hall-Fields amendment. *(1989 Weekly Report p. 2700)*

Texas' natural-gas interests carried no grudges. "We consider everyone in the Texas delegation pro-energy and extremely important," natural-gas lobbyist Hillings says.

Such sentiment helped Barton, Hall and Fields each surpass the $24,000 mark. A fourth Texan, Democrat John Bryant, raised $10,650, a figure that does not reflect his entire fund-raising effort in 1989. He spent most of the year raising money for a state campaign for attorney general, a race he abandoned late in the year.

Republicans fared better than Democrats. The 17 Republican members raised $17,278 each. The 25 Democrats on the committee as of Feb. 15 raised $12,729 each.

The bottom end of the fund-raising totem pole was filled mostly with liberals, lame ducks and members who for various reasons avoid PACs. Consistent environmental votes such as Democrats James H. Scheuer of New York, Gerry Sikorski of Minnesota, Cardiss Collins of Illinois and Jim Bates of California fared poorly.

Jim Cooper, who raised $1,300, falls in the category of those who eschew PACs, a relatively new stance for the moderate Tennessee Democrat made possible in part by a peaceful district and inherited wealth. In years past,

Two New Members

1989 was the first year on the Energy and Commerce Committee for Thomas J. Manton, D-N.Y., and Alex McMillan, R-N.C. Each came from the Banking, Finance and Urban Affairs Committee and had tried to move to Energy and Commerce in the previous Congress. McMillan's Charlotte-based district leans more to banking and insurance than to heavy industry, but it also includes trucking and construction firms. Manton's district in Queens has seen much of its manufacturing facilities turned into trendy lofts.

	McMillan					Manton				
	All PACs	Clean-Air PACs	%	No. of Gifts	Total Donations	All PACs	Clean-Air PACs	%	No. of Gifts	Total Donations
1989	$91,335	$16,350	18	36	$97,550	$194,329	$12,250	6.3	26	$250,144
1987	51,950	5,700	11	13	132,186	105,546	3,700	3.5	12	137,956

Cooper turned almost exclusively to PACs to retire the large debt he piled up in winning his seat in 1982. In the 1987-88 election cycle, for example, he raised $292,770 from PACs of all stripes.

"I feel uncomfortable with how few PACs give you money for good-government reasons, with how many give you money when there is a hot issue before the committee," he says now. "I raised a lot of money from PACs in the past, and if I had to rely on good-government contributions ...." He completes the thought with a wan chuckle.

A ban on PAC contributions, though, does not translate into freedom from special-interest fund raising. Democrats Edward J. Markey of Massachusetts and Mike Synar of Oklahoma shun PAC money but not money from the executives who run them.

Synar, for example, comes from a district with substantial oil and gas interests. He received at least $16,375 from officials of companies, mostly in the energy industry, with a stake in clean-air legislation, according to FEC reports.

'Not Just a Single Vote'

The vote on the Hall/Fields amendment in October 1989 raised once more the chicken-and-egg question of political fund raising: Does money determine a lawmaker's position? Or does it merely reflect it?

Once natural-gas interests signed off on the critical amendment, and the Bush administration turned neutral, the battle became a test of strength between the oil and auto lobbies and Waxman. Detroit faced the prospect of building cars it feared it couldn't sell. Oil companies faced the loss of gasoline sales to alternative fuels.

With Dingell at the fore, the subcommittee sided 12-10 with the auto industry. And whether the chicken or egg came first, the vote broke down largely along money lines.

The 12 members who voted yes raised $72,250 in 1989 from auto and oil interests, an average of $6,021 each.

The 10 who voted no raised $27,550 from the same interests, an average of $2,755 each. Three who voted no — Tauke and Democrats Bill Richardson

of New Mexico and Ron Wyden of Oregon — accounted for all but $1,250 of that. Five of the no votes raised nothing.

Detroit's biggest spenders, General Motors Corp. and Ford, taken together raised their contributions to the committee by 55 percent to $36,600 in 1989, compared with 1987.

"We do look closely at the people who have our future in their hands," GM spokesman Grey Terry says. But he added that the company "doesn't try to PAC the committee" and couldn't buy votes if it wanted to.

Dennis, the Southern California Edison lobbyist, says: "A contribution doesn't sway a member's vote. It just does not work that way. Anyone who draws that black-or-white inference is not an effective student of the way the Congress works."

So what does a PAC tell members?

"They tell me they are interested only in good government," Swift says. "You don't look them in the face and call them a liar."

What, then, do PACs want?

"There are a lot of fish to fry with members," says Dennis, whose PAC gave Swift $1,000 in 1989. "It's not just a single vote. They are in it for the long term, and so are political action committees."

Republican Whittaker of Kansas, who cast a yes vote on the crucial Hall/Fields amendment, represents an oil- and gas-producing district. "I think in my case the chicken follows the egg," he says. "I have always been convinced my support follows a very conservative philosophy."

Whittaker says he has never studied his list of contributors, a luxury he attributes to a safe seat and service on lucrative Energy and Commerce. After six terms he has decided not to seek re-election, and he will leave with an embarrassment of riches.

At the end of 1989, with no election contest in sight, his campaign account had a cash surplus of $524,099. ■

Article 3. Common Cause: A Watchdog That Barks at Its Friends
by Chuck Alston

Unlike the spate of PACs and special-interest groups that haunt the corridors of Congress in search of tax breaks or industry subsidies, Common Cause has labored long and hard in support of bills synonymous with "good government." In recent years, it has used its influence in support of campaign-finance legislation. Protective of its reputation, Common Cause is known for its aggressive and, at times, combative style, as well as its extensive grassroots network and professional research and public relations machine. Although its tactics rankle many members, including some of its friends, Common Cause remains the most effective public-interest lobby in the nation.

It was February 1988 when Common Cause, a 275,000-member public interest lobby, sought to break a Republican-led filibuster blocking campaign-finance legislation. Lobbyists identified suspected swing-vote senators, then launched a strategy that would make Dale Carnegie cringe.

The group bought full-page advertisements featuring Common Cause's chairman, Archibald Cox, the former Watergate prosecutor, in senators' home-state newspapers. Looking stern and wearing his trademark bow tie, Cox assailed the senators for "protecting the current corrupt campaign financing system." Yet, a spokesman said, these senators were among those "we think we have the best chance with on this issue."

One of the targets, Sen. Arlen Specter, R-Pa., dryly concluded: "That selection system hardly encourages senators' interest in reform."

Nor did it. Positions hardened as Republicans railed at Common Cause in floor speeches. Cloture failed by seven votes.

This was vintage Common Cause: passionate, persistent, strident, the very characteristics that at once energize and imperil its role in the widening debate over ethics. The lobby has labored for years to whip up public outrage at the role special-interest money plays in Congress, and now its hour is at hand.

President Bush is set to send Congress his campaign-finance legislation shortly after the August recess. House task forces on ethics and elections are to report this fall. And while Senate leaders remain far apart on the election-money issues, they have at least indicated a willingness to tackle them.

Common Cause can take a large share of the credit for this movement. Years before the savings and loan, defense procurement and housing scandals refocused attention on influence peddling, its activists were pointing fingers all over Washington.

But the finger-pointing watchdog can make trouble for its alter ego, the lobbyist. Consider the words and phrases Common Cause President Fred Wertheimer uses when he talks about Congress. *An ethics swamp. Corrupt. The money chase. Scandalous. Legalized bribery.* This is curious language for a lobbyist — the tactical equivalent of throwing rocks at a door and then knocking on it, expecting to be welcomed inside.

Welcome or not, Common Cause keeps knocking. And after 19 years, its name is nearly synonymous with "good government" issues.

"They have a great deal of credibility on the Hill," former House Democratic Whip Tony Coelho of California says. "But I think they rub some people wrong with some of their issues. Many members don't like people who try to tell them what to do."

While other lobbies pursue tax breaks or cleaner air, Common Cause seeks something far more precious and elusive on Capitol Hill: a say in the allocation of power. It exerts pressure through an extensive grass-roots network and an impressive research and public relations machine.

Sen. Dave Durenberger, R-Minn., tells a story about two Common Cause members who turned out in a blizzard and then waited through an hour and a half of hearings on groundwater pollution to speak with him for a few minutes. Durenberger was impressed with their perseverance,

but not with their arguments about election laws. Back in Washington, Common Cause lobbyists working this issue have grown used to leaving the Capitol empty-handed.

Still, the self-appointed sheriff of Capitol Hill isn't about to become a backslapper. "We are not going to be successful if we play it like Washington insiders," Ann McBride, Common Cause senior vice president, insists.

A well-publicized boot to the backside is more the Common Cause style. In the past 18 months it has not only miffed several senators with its ads, it also helped drive Speaker Jim Wright from office, alienating some Democrats, and then attacked a House Democrat who is a key player on electoral issues, Al Swift of Washington.

"Aggressiveness is their calling card," says Rep. Mike Synar, D-Okla., who has worked with Common Cause on campaign finance and arms control issues. Sometimes they are too tough, he adds. "Fred is unique in that he looks at every battle as the last battle of the war. He doesn't care how many bridges are burned, or how many men are lost."

While these scorched-earth tactics can make enemies on Capitol Hill, they can also enhance Common Cause's credibility. Pressing for the Wright investigation, for instance, established bona fides with Republicans who have long considered it a liberal lobby masquerading in nonpartisan clothing.

Conflict is inevitable, Wertheimer says. "We are trying to convince elected officials to make changes that affect their own lives. There is simply a built-in tension that's always there."

Wayne Hays: 'Common Curse'

The bare facts about Common Cause: an $11 million annual budget; 275,000 dues-paying members ($30 per year for families); accepts no corporate or union contributions of more than $100; relies heavily on direct-

From *Congressional Quarterly Weekly Report,* August 26, 1989, pp. 2204–2207. Copyright © 1989 Congressional Quarterly Inc. Reprinted by permission.

mail appeals to make up its budget; pays 66 full-time and 4 part-time staffers in Washington, 40 full-time and 35 part-time staffers in 46 state offices; most members are at least 50; most are upper-middle class.

Common Cause founder John Gardner envisioned a "people's lobby" with a professional edge. After 19 years of operation, though, there is still no satisfactory label for Common Cause. Government watchdog, self-styled citizens' lobby, citizens' lobbying organization, public affairs lobby, public interest group — the descriptions it attracts reflect the difficulty of locating it within the political universe. (History, p. 2206)

Wayne L. Hays, the Ohio Democrat (1949-76) who chaired the House Administration Committee, which had jurisdiction over many of Common Cause's issues, settled for calling it "Common Curse."

The fight over the congressional pay raise earlier this year drew a sharp distinction between Common Cause and the group it is often compared with, Congress Watch, an arm of Ralph Nader's Public Citizen. Nader was a vigorous and vocal opponent of the raise. Common Cause argued for it. The position is one that members no doubt will remember.

Rep. Jim Leach, R-Iowa, often sees "implications of class division" in Nader's approach. By contrast, he says, "Common Cause is a quintessentially upper-middle-class movement."

David Cohen, a former Common Cause president who is now co-director of the Advocacy Institute, a Washington-based organization that trains public interest advocates, distinguishes between representing *a* public interest and *the* public interest. Common Cause, says Cohen, does the former. "It meets the test of the marketplace, but it doesn't speak for the whole world."

The interest it represents is its membership. The members are routinely polled on issues and they annually elect one-third of the 60-member board that charts broad policy.

Mobilizing Volunteers

Wertheimer and Cox, two Harvard-educated lawyers, are the public faces of Common Cause. But its heart and soul are members like Sue Freeman, 75, in Princeton, N.J.; Dorothy Wylie, 74, in New Port Richey, Fla.; and Helen Sheingorn, 70, in Washington, D.C.

Tuesdays and Thursdays find Sheingorn at Common Cause's downtown Washington headquarters. It is a cluttered office with the look of a shoestring political campaign, decorated with coffee cups, pamphlets and mass-produced letters. Some of the chairs in the conference room match. Homemade signs stenciled in Magic Marker denote the occupants of individual offices.

A 10-year veteran volunteer, Sheingorn works in a section known as "The Connection," the link between headquarters and the field. She has never been to North or South Dakota, the two states she tends. There, as elsewhere, Common Cause has tried during this August recess to blitz members of Congress with information and queries about campaign finance. Sheingorn gets Common Cause volunteers to supply her with the schedules of members. In turn, she directs other volunteers to the meetings.

Enthusiastic, she nonetheless understands when issues like drought and the farm bill override ethics in the heartland. "Some of these people are wondering where their next mortgage payment is coming from," she acknowledges.

Florida Common Cause state chair Wylie leads 18,000 members. Her husband, Bud, a former editor for the Associated Press, edits the Common Cause state newsletter. The two regularly write their congressman, Republican Michael Bilirakis, and she activates the Common Cause network when headquarters sends out an "alert" to pressure members.

What do her friends think of Common Cause? "Those on the right think we are too far left," she says. "Those on the left think we are too far right."

Freeman, the former New Jersey chairman, considers corruption an inherent evil of government. Cleaning it up, she says, is protracted war, and if a cynic can be an optimist, that is she.

"The interest in campaign finance reform — Fred Wertheimer's baby, has been for years — is partly a result of what Common Cause has done," she says. "I must confess there was a time when I wished he'd had another horse to ride, but I've come to believe that's the way you get things done: You have to push hard, and everything takes a lot longer than you think."

Consequences of 1974

Wertheimer revels in the story of how Common Cause tweaked nemesis Hays, the House Administration chairman, against the backdrop of Watergate. Hays in 1972 had called for a General Accounting Office investigation of Common Cause. In 1974, he also chaired the Democratic National Congressional Committee, and on the eve of an important committee fund-raising dinner, Hays opened his *Washington Post* to read this:

"There's another scandal in town, and this one belongs to the Democrats."

The ad pressed House Democrats to move campaign-finance legislation, and they did. But Hays didn't go as far as Common Cause wanted. Led by Hays, the House stripped the Common Cause-backed, Senate-passed public financing provisions for congressional campaigns from landmark 1974 campaign-finance legislation. Corporations and unions won important fights that led to the subsequent explosion of political action committees (PACs). The courts later tossed out spending limits on congressional campaigns.

Critics see the 1974 "reforms" as proof of the law of unintended consequences: The law opened new avenues for special-interest money. Common Cause pressed for these reforms. Ergo, it must share the blame for the very swamp it seeks to once again drain.

Wertheimer calls this the "1974 mythology." He argues that the real problem is not that Common Cause got what it wanted, but that it got only half. "PACs were there at the insistence of unions and corporations, not Common Cause," he says. Moreover, he contends that it is foolish not to expect continual tinkering. "You run into incremental problems and you correct them."

So it was that 14 years later the familiar strains of this debate echoed through the Senate as it moved in February 1988 toward its eighth cloture vote, a record for a single issue, on a campaign-finance measure (S 2). The measure, sponsored by then-Majority Leader Robert C. Byrd of West Virginia and Oklahoma Democrat David L. Boren, carried Common Cause's backing. S 2 would have capped PAC contributions and introduced spending limits into congressional campaigns. And it relied on an incentive: Any candidate who violated the spending prohibitions would watch his opponent receive public funds.

So it was, too, that Common Cause returned to a tried, if not true, tactic: embarrassment by newspaper ad. Sen. William S. Cohen, R-Maine, received a "Dear Bill" ad from Common Cause chairman Cox. Seeking redress on the Senate floor in a Feb. 23 speech, Cohen summarized the ad as, "You do not support S 2, therefore you are corrupt."

Cohen had encountered a Common Cause credo — no permanent friends, no permanent enemies — and he was livid.

"I have enjoyed the support of Common Cause," he said. "But if they

John Gardner's War Baby

The meat and potatoes of the Common Cause agenda is the structure and process of government. It wasn't always that way; the group grew out of the Vietnam War.

"August 1970 turned out to be a particularly propitious time to launch such an effort," political scientist Andrew S. McFarland wrote in "Common Cause," his 1984 book. "As we know now, the constituency for a general-purpose citizens' lobby would be predominately upper-middle-class professionals, generally holding to liberal social beliefs. At that time ... the potential constituency for Common Cause was extremely disaffected from the federal government. Many were looking for new ways of expressing their dissatisfaction, but were not attracted to demonstrations or more radical protest."

The man who harnessed these feelings was John Gardner, former head of the Carnegie Foundation, secretary of Health, Education and Welfare in the Johnson administration and chairman of the Urban Coalition. He used newspaper ads and mass mailings to tap this audience and within six months attracted 100,000 members. Membership peaked, at about 340,000, in August 1974, the month Richard M. Nixon resigned as president.

Common Cause's first crusade set its tone, for it attacked the war effort by pressing for a change in the structure of government. Senior House chairmen had been blocking the House from voting on war policy, so Common Cause lobbied against the seniority system of selecting chairmen. The system was changed by 1975.

In 1977 it pressured both chambers to adopt codes of conduct, and the next year it supported the Ethics in Government Act (PL 95-521), which established financial-disclosure requirements for officials of all three branches.

The group has delved into other issues along the way. It played a key role, for instance, in opposition to the MX missile and funding for the strategic defense initiative.

Gardner served as chairman until 1977. He was succeeded by Nan Waterman, a Common Cause activist. In 1980, Archibald Cox took over. He was then a Harvard law professor who gained fame as the Watergate scandal prosecutor fired by Nixon.

President Fred Wertheimer worked as a legislative counsel to Rep. Silvio O. Conte, R-Mass., before joining Common Cause as a lobbyist in 1971. He was elected president and chief executive officer in 1981.

—*Chuck Alston*

---

think that I am somehow corrupt, then obviously I do not deserve their support. But the corollary is also true: To the extent that they continue to support tactics like this, frankly, I do not think they are worthy of our support."

T. Scott Bunton, former staff director of the Senate Democratic Policy Committee, worked closely with Common Cause during the Senate battle, although he was not consulted about the ad campaign. With hindsight, he says, it appears as a mistake. "It may have hardened them," he says of its targets. On the other hand, he continues, a succession of less-pressured tactics such as constituent letters and phone calls had failed. "This step was not first or second, or even sixth, on your list of preferences, but we'd already been through those."

For his part, Wertheimer refuses to concede any tactical error. "We had reached the point where we thought it was important that these issues be dealt with locally by members."

In May 1988, Common Cause made enemies among House Democrats by sending a letter to the House ethics committee seeking an investigation of Speaker Wright. California Democrat Leon E. Panetta, for one, said that Common Cause should "decide whether issues are more important or personalities."

Before the year was out, Common Cause went after another potential ally, Swift, chairman of House Administration's Election Subcommittee. Common Cause mailed an "Action-gram" to members in Washington state criticizing Swift for not moving comprehensive election-finance legislation.

Swift wrote constituents back: "I can understand Fred's irritation with the lack of progress on campaign finance reform legislation (I share it), but he knows full well that I have been

working diligently on this issue, and he should be able to deal with his frustration without turning on his allies instead of his adversaries."

Synar says these tactics don't make sponsoring legislation with Common Cause's imprimatur easy. Wertheimer "goes out and bangs on people that will help him, if he'll just give him room."

But Wertheimer, like his organization, is irrepressible. Asked about Swift, he says: "We're working with him. We're talking to him. We're meeting with him."

McBride, who serves as Common Cause's chief lobbyist, measures the pressure tactics with an unusual barometer. "As we become more unpopular, it's an indication that we are making progress," she says. "It's true, because on the issues we're pressing, a lot of members don't want to deal with us."

Media Credibility

If Common Cause has a reliable ally in its Capitol Hill battles, it is the nation's press.

More than 300 newspapers, for example, wrote editorials in favor of the Common Cause-backed Senate bill in the 100th Congress. Dozens of the pieces were identical; critics suspected they had been written by the group. Not so, according to Randy Huwa, the Common Cause vice president who handles the press. Common Cause supplied background papers. The newspapers, many owned by the same chain, copied one another's editorials, he says.

"You don't read an article on this subject in which Fred Wertheimer isn't quoted," Steven F. Stockmeyer, a lobbyist for the National Association of Business PACs, a PAC advocate, says with envy. Common Cause is "seen as

---

> ## "As we become more unpopular, it's an indication that we are making progress."
>
> —Common Cause lobbyist Ann McBride

---

expert in this area and one reason is that they do their homework."

Countless publications, including this one, publish information about election finances and honoraria supplied by Common Cause. Its staffers and volunteers descend on the Federal

Election Commission as reports are filed. They assemble and disseminate the information faster than the FEC.

Frank Sorauf, a University of Minnesota political scientist who has written extensively about campaign-finance matters, sees in Common Cause the nation's most important broker of campaign-finance information. Being first, he notes, carries the added benefit of getting the first crack at an interpretation. "It influences and colors a lot of reporting," he says.

The extent to which journalists draw on Common Cause's expertise was made clear June 29 by *The New York Times*. In response to a Times request, Common Cause compiled figures for a chart entitled: "How PAC money flows to party leaders." Philip Taubman, deputy Washington bureau chief for the Times, says although it was an uncommon request, it was a reasonable one for a newspaper to make of a lobby. Of Common Cause, he says, "When they stick strictly to the facts, the numbers, they provide a useful function."

Long Dry Spell

Common Cause can count only a few clear-cut victories since it helped win public financing for presidential campaigns in 1974. "It's easier to tell Congress that the president is dishonest than to tell Congress that Congress is dishonest," Sorauf says.

The House has not voted on a major election-finance issue since 1979. Senate Republicans still claim enough votes to block the latest version of the Boren-Byrd bill. A majority of the House earlier this year "took the pledge" requested by Common Cause not to accept honoraria payments. But an honoraria ban hasn't been put to a vote.

What does Common Cause want? It applies four tests to campaign-finance measures: 1) reducing the role of PACs; 2) fixing limits on campaign spending; 3) providing "alternative resources" for congressional campaigns (such as low-cost mail, television, public financing); 4) eliminating soft money, money raised by parties outside the federal campaign reporting system.

President Bush's June 29 proposal failed Common Cause's test, although Wertheimer widely praised the president for advancing the issue. Common Cause has backed two bills in the 101st Congress, HR 14 and S 137. Nearly all of the cosponsors are Democrats. Senate Republicans, like Bush, remain adamantly opposed to spending limits or public financing.

"For a nonpartisan, public service good-government group, they sure spend a lot of time being used by Democrats, at least on campaign-finance reform, for Democratic gain," argues Bill Canfield, legal counsel to the National Republican Senatorial Campaign Committee.

Nonetheless, Common Cause representatives have made several trips to the White House and entered talks with the House Republican leader, Robert H. Michel, and Guy Vander Jagt of Michigan, the top Republican on a House task force named to study this issue. Some observers detect new flexibility in Common Cause's decision to abandon its flat-out call for public financing.

Not Canfield. "There'll never be enough reform for Common Cause," he predicts. ∎

SELECTED BIBLIOGRAPHY

Abramson, Paul R., John H. Aldrich, and David W. Rohde. *Change and Continuity in the 1988 Elections.* Washington, D.C.: Congressional Quarterly Press, 1990.

Asher, Herbert. *Polling and the Public: What Every Citizen Should Know.* Washington, D.C.: Congressional Quarterly Press, 1988.

Bagdikian, Ben H. *The Media Monopoly.* Boston: Little, Brown, 1987.

Berkman, Ronald, and Laura W. Kitch. *Politics in the Media Age.* New York: McGraw-Hill, 1986.

Berry, Jeffrey M. *The Interest Group Society.* Glenview, IL: Scott, Foresman, 1989.

Cigler, Allen J., and Burdette A. Loomis. *Interest Group Politics.* Washington, D.C.: Congressional Quarterly Press, 1986.

Crespi, Irving. *Public Opinion, Polls, and Democracy.* Boulder, CO: Westview Press, 1989.

Crotty, William. *American Parties in Decline.* Boston: Little, Brown, 1984.

Crouse, Timothy. *The Boys on the Bus.* New York: Random House, 1973.

Eldersveld, Samuel J. *Political Parties in American Society.* New York: Basic Books, 1982.

Erikson, Robert S., Norman G. Luttbeg, and Kent L. Tedin. *American Public Opinion: Its Origins, Content, and Impact.* New York: Wiley, 1980.

Graber, Doris A. *Mass Media and American Politics.* Washington, D.C.: Congressional Quarterly Press, 1989.

Halberstam, David. *The Powers That Be.* New York: Knopf, 1979.

Hertsgaard, Mark. *On Bended Knee: The Press and the Reagan Presidency.* New York: Random House, 1989.

Holloway, Harry, and John George. *Public Opinion: Coalitions, Elites, and Masses.* New York: St. Martin's, 1986.

Key, V. O., Jr. *The Responsible Electorate.* Cambridge, MA: Harvard University Press, 1966.

Kolbe, Richard L. *American Political Parties: An Uncertain Future.* New York: Harper & Row, 1985.

Ladd, Everett Carll, Jr. *Where Have All the Voters Gone?* New York: Norton, 1978.

Lowi, Theodore J. *The End of Liberalism: Ideology, Policy, and the Crisis of Public Authority.* New York: Norton, 1979.

Maisel, L. Sandy. *Parties and Elections in America: The Electoral Process.* New York: Random House, 1987.

Parenti, Michael. *Inventing Reality: The Politics of the Mass Media.* New York: St. Martin's, 1986.

Sabato, Larry J. *The Party's Just Begun: Shaping Political Parties for America's Future.* Glenview, IL: Scott, Foresman, 1988.

Salmore, Stephen A., and Barbara G. Salmore. *Candidates, Parties, and Campaigns: Electoral Politics in America.* Washington, D.C.: Congressional Quarterly Press, 1989.

Sorauf, Frank J. *Money in American Elections.* Glenview, IL: Scott, Foresman, 1988.

——, and Paul Allen Beck. *Party Politics in America.* Boston: Little, Brown, 1988.

Truman, David B. *The Governmental Process.* New York: Knopf, 1971.

Wolfinger, Raymond E., and Steven R. Rosenstone. *Who Votes?* New Haven, CT: Yale University Press, 1980.

POLITICAL INSTITUTIONS

In any society, there are two systems of government: the myth system and the operational system. The myth system consists of the stories we like to tell one another. These are often romantic tales that have been handed down from generation to generation to glorify our own history. The myth system is also influenced by political theory, idealism, and even by a healthy fear of such persistent human vices as corruption and nepotism.

The operational system describes the way the system actually works. The myth system and the operational system cannot be the same for two important reasons. First, some people wish to take bribes, assist their relatives, further their own economic interests, gratify their vanity, and not work very hard. Second, the myth system always reaches for the ideal which, by its very nature, is impossible to achieve. Yet, the myth system affects the operational system in a constructive way. The myth system provides a standard by which the operational system can be judged and deviations from the myth's ideals arouse guilt among those in the operational system for their misbehavior.

The divergence between the myth system and operational system is important to bear in mind when studying American government, as there is an ongoing tension between what political theory tells us ought to happen in our political affairs and what actually occurs in the day-to-day operation of our real government. For example, Americans love democracy, but hate the politicians who make it work. Ever since the early days of the American Republic, we have searched persistently for schemes to liberate democratic government from the democratically elected politicians who are required to administer it.

During George Washington's second term as president, he warned his fellow citizens of the dangers of political parties, which he argued were organized to promote their members' special interests. Washington's observations are, of course, true today. Throughout the political system, there is a tendency for politicians to cultivate the support of narrow, special interests on the understanding that if elected, they will advance the interests of their supporters at the expense of those who did not vote for them.

The primary challenge of any real government is not to design an ideal system based on unrealistic theoretical assumptions, but rather to accept political institutions and human nature with all their vices and imperfections and make them work more or less acceptably. American government is characterized everywhere by a measured straining in opposite directions. For example, the national government strains toward centralization, while the state, county, and city governments strain toward local authority. Ideological politicians like former president Ronald Reagan strain to achieve radical reform, while the permanent civil service strain to preserve the status quo. Elected officials strain to consign controversial political issues like abortion or the regulation of interest rates to the federal courts or independent agencies, while the voters strain to have these subjects addressed by their elected officials so that they can be affected in elections. The president strains to consolidate his power over the foreign policy process, while Congress strains to set limits on the president's power.

The most challenging aspect of this measured straining in opposite directions is that nothing remains static. A balance that is thought to be acceptable today will become wholly unacceptable tomorrow. For example, the consensus that allowed President Franklin Roosevelt to prosecute World War II without constraints did not survive into the presidency of Lyndon Johnson, when he attempted to win the war in Vietnam. In all social systems, the solution to any specific problem then changes the problem. An "imperial presidency" will be tolerated when the very survival of the nation appears to be at stake, but it will not be tolerated in circumstances when different constituencies disagree over what proper national policy should be.

As you will see in this section, one of the major reasons that the myth system is seldom congruent with the operational system is that in the real world there is little consensus on what constitutes the "public interest." Obviously, all politicians attempt to justify their actions in the name of the "public interest," but aside from endeavors such as fighting crime or finding a cure for cancer, most government undertakings involve a conflict of differing private interests. For example, in the 1987 federal highway appropriations bill, we can see a clash of differing views on the "public interest." The president believed that the bill would add to the national deficit, help fuel inflation, and destroy the longstanding tradition in highway legislation of avoiding ad hoc pork barrel projects. Senators and congressmen, however, believed that the billions of dollars of federal funds, even if they were borrowed, would put hundreds of thousands of people to work.

Chapter 11, *The Congress,* begins with an analysis of congressional performance, focusing on the problem of incumbency. Although many voters are dissatisfied with Congress's overall performance, those same voters are generally satisfied with the performance of their own representative. This apparent contradiction has led to the disappearance of competitiveness in House elections, which has in turn reinforced the status quo. The second article chronicles the demise of Senator David Durenberger (R-Minn.), who entered the Senate with a reputation for high integrity, but who, like others before him, succumbed to the temptations of power. In the third selection, the author examines the compromise budget accord and the factors that drove rank-and-file members of both parties to repudiate the package worked out by the leadership of both parties. The article also describes the conflicting pressures that affect the voting decisions of members of Congress.

Chapter 12, *The Presidency,* recounts an "average" day in the life of a president, revealing the sundry people, meetings, activities, and decisions that consume a president and his staff. The article affords the reader a glimpse into the fast-paced world of presidential politics, replete with thumbnail sketches of key players. Like its predecessors, the Bush team prides itself on effective organization and planning, which is clearly evident in the day-to-day operations of the White House. In the second selection, the author asks the question why great men are not chosen president, concluding that the nominating process is not necessarily structured to produce great presidents. The final article discusses the Bush management style, noting that the president's approval ratings reflect his success in the foreign policy arena—not the domestic sphere. This piece takes an in-depth look at the president's approach to problem solving, his interaction with top aides, his dealings with the bureaucracy, his relationship with Congress, and the way in which he makes decisions.

Chapter 13, *The Bureaucracy,* starts with a critique of bureaucratic behavior, explaining why the term *bureaucrat* has come to have such a negative connotation. In the author's view, the bureaucracy's reputation is well-deserved. In too many cases, it is indifferent, inefficient, and unresponsive. The next article profiles the political exploits of Rockwell Schnabel, the embattled head of the U.S. Travel and Tourism Administration, who has, at least up to this point, managed to outwit his critics and expand the role of his agency. In the final article, the author explores the typical problems faced by an AIDS victim in battling Los Angeles County's public health system, concluding that it is a bitter saga of tears, prejudice, and hurt.

Chapter 14, *The Judiciary,* describes the powers and prerogatives of the courts, beginning with a behind-the-scenes look at Yonkers, New York's decade-long war with the federal courts, which have charged the city with intentional discrimination in schools and housing. The second piece examines the personality and style of Supreme Court Justice Antonin Scalia—an unabashed conservative—who is determined to remake the High Court into his own image. A persistent thorn in the side of liberals, Scalia continues to march to the tune of his own drummer, preaching the traditional virtues of judicial restraint. The last article discusses the rise of state-court radicalism, showing how these are using state constitutions to expand the rights of citizens in such areas as privacy and discrimination.

DISCUSSION QUESTIONS

1. Why, in spite of widespread dissatisfaction with Congress, do the voters routinely reelect House incumbents from both parties, often by substantial margins?
2. What are the chief advantages of incumbency?
3. Do the ethical standards of Congress need to be strengthened? If so, how?
4. What, if anything, should be done to curb the power of political action committees and special-interest groups?
5. What are the major factors that affect the voting decisions of members of Congress?
6. How does the mass media affect the outcome of legislation?
7. What are the essential attributes that a president should possess?
8. Why is it so difficult to nominate and elect topflight presidential candidates?
9. Does the political process encourage the election of great presidents?

10. Do professional politicians make the best presidents?
11. What are the primary characteristics of President Bush's management style?
12. Does Bush's style serve him well? Why, or why not?
13. Why is the bureaucracy viewed so negatively?
14. How can the bureaucracy be made more accountable?
15. What constitutes success and failure within a government agency?
16. Do judges have too much power? Why, or why not?
17. Has the judicial selection process become too politicized?
18. What are the main differences between judicial activism and judicial restraint?
19. Should judges be required to stand for election? Why, or why not?
20. What accounts for the rise in state-court activism?

KEY TERMS

BALANCED BUDGET AMENDMENT   A proposed constitutional change that would prohibit the government from spending more than it collects in taxes and fees, except in war.

BICAMERAL LEGISLATURE   A law-making body composed of two houses or chambers.

CASEWORK   Personal work performed by legislators on behalf of constituents, as opposed to groups of constituents.

CHIEF EXECUTIVE   The role of the president as head of the executive branch of the government.

CIVIL SERVICE   Those persons employed by government, with the exception of the military, who are appointed or promoted under the merit system without regard to political affiliation.

CONFLICT OF INTEREST   A situation in which an official's conduct may be influenced by personal gain.

CONSTITUENTS   Voters in a political district, to whom the member is responsible.

FEDERAL ELECTION COMMISSION   A body set up to enforce the laws created by the Federal Election Campaign Act.

FIRST BUDGET RESOLUTION   A resolution approved by Congress in May to set overall revenue and spending goals and, hence, by definition, the size of the federal deficit for the following fiscal year.

INCUMBENT'S ADVANTAGE   The political benefits enjoyed by a person currently in office.

JUDICIAL ACTIVISM   A philosophy that holds that judges should refrain from exercising the power of judicial review or otherwise intervene in the political process.

JUDICIAL RESTRAINT   A doctrine that requires judges to avoid constitutional questions when possible and uphold acts of Congress except where they violate the Constitution or are obviously unreasonable.

LOBBYIST   A representative of an interest group who seeks to influence public policy through direct contact with lawmakers.

MAJORITY LEADER   The head of the majority party in the Senate and the second ranking member of the majority party in the House.

MINORITY LEADER   The chief spokesman of the minority party in the House and Senate.

NATIONAL DEBT   The sum total of the federal budget deficits over the years.

POLITICAL ACTION COMMITTEE   Independent organizations, but more often the political arms of corporations, labor unions, or interest groups that contribute to candidates or work for general political goals.

SECOND BUDGET RESOLUTION   A resolution passed by Congress in September that sets "binding" limits on taxes and spending for the next fiscal year beginning October 1.

SPEAKER OF THE HOUSE   The presiding officer of the House and its most powerful and influential member.

VICE PRESIDENT   The second highest executive officer of the nation, who is designated the presiding officer of the Senate by the Constitution.

WHITE HOUSE CHIEF OF STAFF   The principal aide to the president.

WHITE HOUSE STAFF   A group of top officials who give the president advice in carrying out official duties.

Chapter 11

The Congress

Article 1.   Congress and Its Reputation: The Issue of Congressional Performance
by Everett Carll Ladd

The author focuses on the issue of congressional reform, insisting that the incumbency problem lies
at the heart of Congress's poor institutional performance. Despite public criticism of Congress, little
evidence exists that the nation is particularly concerned about the problem, even though many people
are dissatisfied with Congress's overall performance. Still, the voters routinely reelect incumbents of
both parties by wide majorities. According to the author, this is explained by the fact that public
dissatisfaction is largely unfocused—and thus far politically inconsequential. To date, the issue of
incumbency lacks immediacy. It simply cannot compete with such issues as taxes, abortion, and drugs.

*Mr. Ladd is
president of the
Roper Center for
Public Opinion
Research. From
"Public Opinion
and the 'Congress
Problem,'" by
Everett Carll
Ladd,* The Public
Interest, *Summer
1990, pages 57–67:*

*T*he current debate over whether America's federal government needs institutional reform focuses on the Congress. It, and
not the presidency or the federal courts, is the
branch seen by a large and growing corps of
critics to be working poorly.

At the heart of the problem are the advantages that incumbents have over their opponents in contests for the House of Representatives. Over the last quarter-century, these advantages have become so great that popular
control has been lost in practice, though it remains guaranteed in law. The electoral sanction is central to democratic governance.
When present and functioning satisfactorily, it
enables the public to control its officials by removing them from office—whenever their performance is deemed inadequate, to be sure,
and sometimes just to shake things up. This
electoral sanction is alive and well in contests
for a great many offices in the U.S.—including
president, senators, governors, and mayors.
But in the case of congressmen, a conspiracy
of circumstances has, *de facto*, robbed the
electorate of a meaningful say in who does and
does not belong in office.

The incumbent congressional establishment
has powerful incentives for maintaining the
status quo. As a result, action to end prohibitive incumbency advantages, and thus to restore the virtues of real competition to the
House, is unlikely unless and until substantial
segments of the public signal that they want action. Where does the public stand?

As we will see from the survey data below,
Americans are clearly unhappy with congressional performance. But at present they can't
put their fingers on the source of their unease,
and so they are not prepared to act coherently.
What's more, the public is not at all unhappy
with one prime by-product of House incumbents' ascendancy—the divided institutional
control that, for the first time in U.S. history,
has become the norm, as Republicans win the
presidency regularly and compete fairly evenly
in Senate contests but are unable to break the
Democrats' incumbency-sustained lock on the
House. The problem of entrenched incumbency can't be addressed successfully by appeals to let one party have a chance to govern
at both ends of Pennsylvania Avenue.

THE INCUMBENCY PROBLEM

American voters now routinely reelect
House incumbents from both political parties,
returning them by overwhelming margins.
They do so even though they are dissatisfied
with Congress's performance as an institution—in part because their House vote decisions are largely divorced from substantive
judgments about parties and policies. While I
won't discuss it here, much the same thing
seems to be happening in state legislatures, for
the same basic reasons.

It was more than a decade and a half ago
that political scientist David Mayhew called attention to the "vanishing marginals"—House
seats where the winner's margin is small
enough that the contest can be seen as competitive. In 1960, when most observers thought
both parties had too many safe seats, 203 of
the 435 contests (47 percent) were at least marginally competitive, with the winner held to
less than 60 percent of the vote. Two decades

later, the low competitiveness of 1960 seemed robust. In 1980 the winner had less than 60 percent of the vote in only 140 House elections (32 percent). And by 1988 the number had plunged further to 65 elections, 15 percent of the total.

Over 98 percent of House incumbents seeking reelection in 1988 won, and most of them won by margins that can't be explained by the mix of party loyalties and policy preferences in their districts. The 1988 House elections were the least competitive in U.S. history. The winner either was unopposed or beat his opponent by at least forty percentage points in 242 of the 435 districts; the margin was twenty to forty points in 128 districts, and ten to twenty points in another 36. In only 29 districts—7 percent of the total—did the loser come within what might properly be considered striking distance, trailing by ten points or less. Open seats, where no incumbent is running, are often quite competitive, but in 1988 there were just twenty-six of them. Only six incumbents seeking reelection lost, and five of them had been tinged by personal scandal.

INHERENT ADVANTAGES   This virtual disappearance of competitiveness in House elections results from a mix of factors. Incumbents typically have many more resources than their rivals for promoting their candidacies. Over the course of the 1960s and 1970s, Congress tripled the staff provided to House members, and members have put many of their new assistants to work back home in their districts. Staff expansion was justified on the grounds that it would make Congress better able to do battle with the expert-laden executive branch, and that individual members would be better equipped for their legislative business. The former argument is certainly true, though whether the effect is salutary is debatable. The latter may not be true at all. But in any case, the augmented staffs are a potent year-round electoral resource—serving constituents and in general keeping members' names before district voters in a way that virtually no challengers can rival.

Incumbents also enjoy big leads in campaign contributions. Knowing that current officeholders are likely to be reelected and will have to be dealt with in future legislative struggles, the formidable array of organized interests that now envelops the national government backs them heavily through its political action committees (PACs). The $94 million that PACs contributed to House campaigns in 1987–1988, in contests in which an incumbent was running for reelection, went to incumbents over challengers by slightly more than eight to one. Preliminary data on spending in the 1989–1990 election cycle suggest that the share of interest-group contributions received by incumbents continues to be very high. A *Washington Post* analysis of contributions data submitted to the Federal Elections Commission found that in 1989 PACs contributed $57 million to congressional candidates; more than 90 percent of this sum went to incumbents. "Not surprisingly," the *Post* noted, "much of the money went to members of committees with jurisdiction over the PACs' industries and unions." Even challengers in House races targeted by their parties for special effort usually have less financial support than the members whom they seek to unseat.

In races for governor and U.S. senator—as well, of course, as that for president—many voters know something substantial about the candidates' records. In these contests, even well-funded incumbents who are better known than their opponents may readily be defeated when the electorate wants policy changes. But House members simply don't have the visibility of governors and senators. Their stands and performances are largely unknown to most of the electorate. And voters are more likely to have a vaguely favorable image of the member than of his resource-poor challenger.

Political-party ties are the one thing that could upset this dynamic. That is, a voter might not know anything consequential about a member's record but still vote for a less well-known challenger, because the voter preferred the challenger's party. That is in fact exactly what happened historically. But over the last quarter-century, as incumbents have accumulated election resources far greater than before, the proportion of the electorate bound by strong party ties has declined precipitously. Better educated and drawing their political information largely from the media, American voters feel that they need parties less than did their counterparts of times past. In many ways they may be right in this inclination to dispense with parties and to focus on the candidates alone. But the inclination is misguided in the case of House candidates, since voters typically won't exert themselves to learn enough to form a coherent independent judgment.

In highly visible races such as those for president, senator, and governor, voters often do acquire enough information to make up for the decline of the guidance that party ties long provided. At the other end of the spectrum, in elections for school-board members, aldermen, and other local officials, voters often have enough close-up, personal knowledge to reach reasonably informed judgments. House races and some other "intermediate" contests are where we now have our problem. Here, party voting is no longer decisive, but substantive knowledge of the candidates' records is insufficient to furnish a substitute base. Enjoying huge advantages in resources for self-promotion, incumbents can't readily be challenged so long as they avoid public scandal.

PUBLIC UNEASE

Survey research provides no indication that any significant segment of the general public is very aware of, much less worried about, its loss of control over House members. But, to begin our review of the data, it is clear that many people are unhappy about Congress's overall performance, though not about the performance of their own representative. In fact, the proportion of Americans who are dissatisfied with Congress has grown dramatically over the past two decades.

A number of poll questions tap the present unease. Various survey organizations—including those of ABC News and the *Washington Post*, CBS News and the *New York Times*, as well as Gallup—now ask respondents whether they "approve or disapprove of the way Congress is doing its job." The "approve" and "disapprove" shares bounce around a good bit, depending in part on the overall national mood and the latest headlines. In 1986, when the public was especially optimistic, virtually all national institutions—Congress included—got higher marks than they had been receiving. In the spring of 1989, when the tribulations of House Speaker Jim Wright got headlines, the share of those who disapproved

of Congress's performance grew. Despite this short-term movement, however, one can see a clear pattern from the early or mid-1970s on to the present. Throughout this span, disapproval has generally been high. Of the thirty-five national surveys I've located that asked the simple approve/disapprove question between January 1975 and March 1990, only five found more people positive about Congress than negative. The approval share averaged just 36 percent.

Even in our age of pop cynicism, 36-percent approval is low. Presidents' approval scores rise and fall too, of course, but with few exceptions over the past fifteen years they have been higher than Congress's. In early 1990 the gap between approval of President Bush and approval of Congress was over thirty percentage points. For the last fifteen years the gap has averaged about twenty points.

When Congress's standing is compared with that of a variety of other institutions besides the presidency, the same picture is evident. For example, Gallup asks its respondents whether they have "a great deal, quite a lot, some, or very little" confidence in the military, banks, the Supreme Court, and other institutions. Congress is consistently back in the pack. It always lags well behind churches, the military,

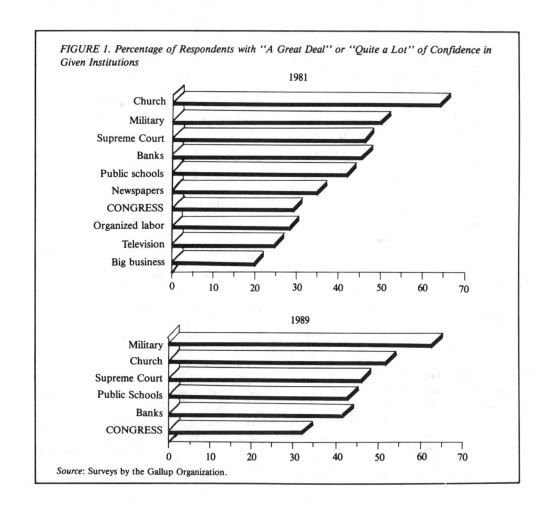

FIGURE 1. *Percentage of Respondents with "A Great Deal" or "Quite a Lot" of Confidence in Given Institutions*

Source: Surveys by the Gallup Organization.

public schools, and the Supreme Court. Its peers are such relatively low-rated institutions as organized labor, television, and big business. In September 1989, when 63 percent said that they had a great deal or quite a lot of confidence in the military, only 32 percent held Congress in such esteem.

A battery of questions about Congress included in a May 1989 ABC News/*Washington Post* survey illustrates the general tone of public assessment of Congress in recent years—though the level of criticism is probably a little higher in this case than the norm, given the attention that the Jim Wright affair was then receiving. Seventy-one percent agreed that most congressional candidates will make promises that they have no intention of fulfilling in order to win elections, 76 percent agreed that most members will lie if they think it expedient, and 75 percent agreed that most members "care more about special interests than they care about people like you." Such testimony should not be read literally. The public often takes advantage of specific poll questions to convey a general message—here, that it's somehow dissatisfied with the performance of its national legislature.

Dissatisfaction wasn't nearly so high in the past. No single question has been repeated over the entire span covered by polling—the late 1930s to the present—but a great many questions similar to those of recent years were asked in the earlier periods. For example, a Gallup poll of August 20–25, 1958, asked whether Congress was doing a "good job" or a "poor job." It found only 12 percent saying poor. In September 1964, another Gallup study asked how much "trust and confidence you have" in Congress. "The top of the ladder in this case means the greatest possible confidence, the bottom no confidence at all." There were eleven rungs, numbered zero through ten. Only 2 percent placed themselves on one of the lowest three; 46 percent chose the highest three. The median was between rungs six and seven.

As late as 1970, Americans were still rating Congress quite positively. In June 1970 Gallup showed its respondents a card on which there were ten boxes, numbered from +5 (for institutions "you like very much") down to -5 (for those "you dislike very much"). Only 3 percent assigned Congress to the -4 or -5 boxes, while 36 percent put it either in +4 or +5. Only 10 percent gave Congress a negative score of any sort. It was during Watergate that Congress's standing took its big plunge. Despite some short-term movement over the past fifteen years, public confidence in the national legislature has remained low.

UNFOCUSED DISSATISFACTION

But while unease with Congress is substantial, the criticism lacks focus. Some observers claim that the response to a CBS News/*New York Times* poll of March 30–April 2, 1990, indicates that the diffuse dissatisfaction is now taking shape in support of a constitutional amendment to limit congressional tenure. Sixty-one percent of the respondents favored a limit on the number of times a House member can be elected, with Republicans, Democrats, and independents all endorsing a limit by about the same margin. But earlier polls, conducted when Congress's standing was much higher than it is now, recorded high across-the-board support for limiting terms. Americans are wedded to separation of powers and limited government. As the . . . table suggests [see Table 2], support for term limits isn't a new response to the current unease with Congress; its roots run deep into the nation's historic commitments to limited government.

TABLE 1. *Percentage of Respondents Who Agree or Disagree That "Most Members of Congress . . ."*

Question	Percentage	
	Agree	Disagree
Will tell lies if they feel the truth will hurt them politically.	76	
Care more about special interests than they care about people like you.	75	
Make campaign promises they have no intention of fulfilling.[a]	71	
Care more about keeping power than they do about the best interests of the nation.	66	
Make a lot of money using public office improperly.	57	
Care deeply about the problems of ordinary citizens		52
Have a high personal moral code.		47

Source: Survey by ABC News/*Washington Post*, May 19–23, 1989. Respondents were told: "I'm going to read a few statements. For each, can you please tell me if you tend to agree or disagree with it, or if, perhaps, you have no opinion about that statement?"

[a]This question began: "To win elections, most candidates for Congress. . . ."

TABLE 2. *The Enduring Appeal of Term Limitation*

	1952[a]			1990[b]	
It has been suggested that no United States senator or representative should serve more than a total of twelve years in office. Do you think this is a good idea or a poor idea?			Do you think there should be a limit to the number of times a member of the House of Representatives can be elected to a two-year term, or not?		
	Good (%)	Poor (%)		Favor (%)	Oppose (%)
Everyone	63	24	Everyone	61	31
Republicans	64	26	Republicans	64	28
Democrats	62	23	Democrats	60	30
Independents	65	23	Independents	58	33

[a]*Source*: Survey by the Gallup Organization, March 27–April 1, 1952.
[b]*Source*: Survey by the *New York Times*/CBS News, March 30–April 2, 1990.

Despite being unhappy with Congress, Americans return House incumbents of both parties by huge majorities. Some observers explain this phenomenon by saying that voters like their own representatives, even though they don't like the institution's performance. It's true that polls asking people about their local members get a positive assessment every time, but this doesn't tell us anything new. After all, voters overwhelmingly reelect their representatives every time, so in some sense they must be positive about them. The important question is, in what sense?

Polls provide the answer: in contrast to what is often the case with regard to presidents, senators, and governors, the public knows next to nothing about individual congressmen. An ABC News/*Washington Post* poll of May 1989 is typical; it found that only 28 percent could *name* their congressman. People "like" their representatives only in the sense that they have heard something about them more often and for a longer span than they have heard about the challengers. And usually the public—save for the dwindling minority who vote along party lines and who back the party out of power in the district—has not absorbed anything negative about the incumbent. Members sail through elections virtually unchallenged because they are better known, and most voters don't see any connection between their general dissatisfaction with the institution and the dynamic of their congressional voting.

COGNITIVE MADISONIANISM

Part of the reason that voters' dissatisfaction is almost wholly unfocused—and hence thus far politically inconsequential—is in the nature of the issue: institutional performance lacks the concrete immediacy of matters like taxes. Unless government officials commit such obvious sins as taking bribes, the public is not readily engaged. But something more must be involved here. Otherwise, the tension between the public's general unease with Congress's performance and its persistently massive endorsement of House incumbents would have intruded more than it has into the public's consciousness.

The claim that the House has an "incumbency problem" appears to most voters as an argument that something is wrong with regularly electing Republicans to the presidency while returning an entrenched Democratic majority to the House. And most voters simply don't think that divided control is in fact a problem. They see it as a natural extension of the historic U.S. commitment to the separation of powers, and they rather like it. For example, in a survey taken in Connecticut from November 29 through December 6, 1988, the University of Connecticut's Institute for Social Inquiry asked: "The way the election came out, the Republicans control the White House but the Democrats control both Houses of Congress. Do you think this is good for the country, or would it be better if one party had both the presidency and the Congress?" Sixty-seven percent favored divided results. By 55 percent to 36 percent, those who had voted for George Bush on November 8 and who declared themselves very pleased with his victory endorsed as "good for the country" a Democratic congressional majority! A survey taken in January of this year for NBC News and the *Wall Street Journal* asked whether "it is better for the same political party to control both the Congress and the presidency, so they can work together more closely, or . . . better to have different political parties controlling [them] to prevent either one from going too far. . . ." Sixty-three percent backed divided control; only 24 percent favored having one party responsible for both branches.

I have seen a number of polls in which people are asked about the desirability of limiting governmental institutions—either by extending the branches' independent authority to check one another (e.g., by giving the president the line-item veto) or by dividing control of the branches between the parties. A majority of respondents invariably supports the proposed limitations in such polls. Early public-opinion surveys got much the same response that we see today. For example, in a study that he did for *Fortune* in April 1944, Elmo Roper asked his respondents whether it would be a bad thing "if a president from one party is elected next time, and the majority in Congress belongs to the other party." Only 31 percent thought that it would be.

But a new wrinkle has been added to this old American endorsement of sharply limited government. I have often noted that contemporary public-opinion research in the United States shows a public highly ambivalent on many major questions of public policy. For example, Americans endorse high levels of governmental protections and services, but at the same time they consider government too big, too expensive, and too intrusive. They want somewhat contradictory things from the modern state, and they understand that the two parties differ significantly over the proper scope of government. Is it surprising, then,

that a kind of cognitive Madisonianism in modern guise has emerged? The public wants to set the two parties' views of government's role in creative tension, with a Republican executive pushing one way and a Democratic legislature pushing the other way.

In theory, of course, Americans could reject the advice of many scholars that unified party control is better than divided control, and turn a deaf ear to the Republicans' plea that they merit a House majority, yet still turn out individual incumbents regularly so as to restore "responsibility." But they haven't found their way to this fairly abstract and complex conclusion. And Democratic leaders have compelling reasons of partisan self-interest for trying to prevent them from ever doing so.

The public probably won't again be content with the operation of Congress until it finds a way to reassert the control that it has lost over the last three decades. But the case that the massive advantages that House incumbents now enjoy precludes the competition on which effective democracy depends has not been made in the court of public opinion. Americans think that Congress is a problem, but they don't know why, or where to turn for answers.

Article 2. Washington Gets to Mr. Smith
by Tom Hamburger

Tom Hamburger chronicles the political odyssey of Senator David Durenberger (R-Minn.), a decent man who came to the Senate with a high ethical reputation and a desire to "restore trust in government." The article describes Durenberger's fall from grace, which culminated in a unanimous Senate decision to denounce him for violating the institution's expense and income rules through a series of questionable business practices. The author describes the perquisites of power and how an honest man like Durenberger fell victim to its lure. A behind-the-scenes account of what occurred, the article examines the money-mad environment of Washington politics.

"What happened to you?"

Curt Johnson, president of the Minnesota Citizens League, put the question bluntly to Senator David Durenberger on a public affairs television show early this summer. The question lingers with his constituents.

Durenberger came to Washington 12 years ago, an intellectual moderate with bipartisan support and a reputation for high integrity. He was a founding member of his state's ethics board; in his campaign he pledged to "restore trust in government." But something went wrong. The TV appearance came

just weeks before the Senate voted unanimously to denounce Durenberger for breaking its expense and income rules through a series of unsavory business deals.

The answer to Johnson's question can't be found in the trial transcript, the 106-page Ethics Committee report, or in campaign and personal financial disclosures required by Watergate-era reforms. Nor can it be found in the explanations ultimately offered by Durenberger—and informally accepted by the Senate—that his moral compass was off because of a period of emotional, family, and financial crisis.

Durenberger did experience wrenching family turmoil in the mid-1980s. But his financial misdeeds

Tom Hamburger is a Washington correspondent for the Minneapolis Star Tribune.

and disclosure violations came before and after the crisis period. Given the rash of ethics cases recently, it seems there is something more at work here. Durenberger arrived in Washington in the middle of the astonishing parallel transformations that have swept through the capital city and national politics: Over the past 20 years, the cost of living well in D.C. and the cost of winning elections have risen drastically. By the late seventies, representatives were discovering they couldn't afford elegant homes or fancy meals out on a government salary; they were also learning that getting reelected might have less to do with constituent service than with fundraiser service. Durenberger was not the only one to lose his way in this strange new world.

Durenberger's ethical lapses bear striking resemblance to those of former House Speaker Jim Wright. Like Durenberger, Wright came to Washington a strong advocate of financial disclosure. Long before disclosure was required, Wright released copies of his tax forms to reporters.

By the end of the 1980s, however, both men were in trouble over condominiums provided or subsidized by well-heeled friends. Both had unorthodox book deals that earned them tens of thousands of dollars from special interests. And both had ceased extolling the virtues of disclosure.

In Wright's case the Ethics Committee's special counsel suggested that, in addition to the other charges, the speaker improperly intervened with regulators on behalf of S&L executives who were also campaign contributors. The committee declined to charge Wright with that violation.

In Durenberger's case there was no suggestion of legislative conflict of interest from the special counsel. Not because those conflicts didn't exist. They did. But the conflicts involved legal campaign contributions and honoraria similar to those received by most other members. The Durenberger case is replete with reminders of the familiar adage that what's most shocking is not what's illegal, but what's legal.

Durenberger's most serious offense, according to the Ethics Committee, involved a pair of real estate deals he cooked up to justify billing the Senate for staying in a condo in which he held hidden ownership. The next most troubling was a book publishing scheme that earned the senator $100,000 above the Senate's honoraria limit, not from selling the books but from making speeches promoting the books to medical associations and other special interest lobbies.

Nearly all of the 113 lobbies that paid to hear the senator thought they were paying honoraria for speeches—not "book promotion." Only a few of the groups bought copies of the book in bulk. One admitted that it did so only because the senator's office required it.

The Senate found that Durenberger had pursued these ventures even though he knew they were unethical and against the rules. And his colleagues came

down hard, denouncing him on the floor and requiring, among other things, that he pay at least $95,000 in restitution for improperly receiving honoraria.

But the Ethics Committee never questioned whether it was right to receive all that money from groups interested in Senate business, or how the money might have affected the senator's votes on key legislation.

Those questions hit too close to home.

Civic slide

A close look at this case and the conflicts of interest that weren't pursued yields some insights into the peculiar, money-mad environment of Washington, D.C. To focus on the environment is not to excuse Wright or Durenberger. Both men, it appears, were not well-moored ethically. Both developed a need for a more lavish lifestyle than they could afford. That craving clouded their judgment.

Perhaps the most disturbing element in this morality play is that if any politician ever seemed ethically well-moored, it was David Durenberger. Minnesota, after all, is the land of 10,000 civic organizations. Public affairs shows even get good ratings there. The state's political tradition includes a generous view of the role of government and an antiseptic code of political conduct. Along with Hubert Humphrey and Gene McCarthy, Walter Mondale probably best reflects the state's personality, with his midwestern style and suicidal attachment to honesty ("I will raise taxes").

When Humphrey died in 1978, Durenberger was hustled onto the Republican ticket. He seemed tailor-made for the high-minded Minnesota electorate. He grew up on the grounds of a Benedictine abbey in central Minnesota, in a tiny cluster of homes called Flynntown. His father was the adored football coach of the abbey's St. John's College, where Dave studied as an undergraduate. Durenberger's senior yearbook pegged him as the graduate "most likely to translate St. John's Work and Pray Ethic into public service."

In his 1978 campaign Durenberger said he wanted "to address the decline of public confidence in American institutions." He won handily and swept ebulliently into Washington. It was no accident that shortly after he arrived in D.C. Durenberger was asked to serve on the Senate Ethics Committee, where he sat in judgment of his peers. He rose swiftly in the Senate. Within two years of his election, he was chairman of his own Finance subcommittee, Health, where he took to the arcana of health policy with gusto.

Durenberger's most outspoken defender in the Senate, Minnesota's millionaire senator Rudy Boschwitz, said, "I think it's a matter of fact that if he had had a very large and secure financial base that he might not have made the book arrangement or he might not have done the housing arrangement. All of us are subject to pressures, and if you don't have money, that's an additional pressure."

Not having money is, of course, a matter of perspective. To Boschwitz, Durenberger is a pauper. To Durenberger's constituents, who make an average of $17,746 a year, he's loaded.

By common reckoning Durenberger came to Washington with real money. He sold his house in Minneapolis for a sizable profit. His first year's financial disclosure form revealed that he had about $80,000 in savings, after purchasing a comfortable house in McLean, Virginia. And Durenberger has a congressional salary with perks that include a generous pension, medical benefits, free postage, telephone, and travel, as well as per diem expense reimbursement.

The problem wasn't that Durenberger had too little money but that his peers had too much. Washington is the country's premier city of affluence. The 1990 Census shows that the beltway that rings the city slices through five of the nation's 10 highest income communities. And if the District of Columbia were a state, it would rank third in per capita income. It wasn't always so. Even in the late sixties, Washington was still a quiet southern town. Upper-level civil servants and congressmen could afford nice homes in Georgetown and Chevy Chase; dinner at even the best restaurants was within reach. Then came the rapid proliferation of trade associations and other special interest groups, increasing business, fees, and expense accounts for Washington's lawyers. The D.C. economy ceased to be geared to civil-servant pay. Real estate prices in the best neighborhoods shot up. At cocktail parties, congressmen discovered they were wearing the cheapest suits in the room. At dinner, senators and their wives began eyeing the right side of the menu.

On Capitol Hill, where lobbyists and hot-shot journalists can now pull in over $200,000 a year, an income of $125,000 (the maximum including honoraria a senator may earn in a year) might seem inadequate. But to many of today's senators, that salary is play money. Last fall, Senators Warren Rudman and Robert Dole told *The New Republic* that up to two-thirds of their colleagues were millionaires (the elliptical disclosure forms show that only one-third are). Class warfare has erupted a couple of times in the Senate recently, once last November, when many of the Senate's millionaires voted against a proposed pay raise, infuriating members who felt they needed the money.

This August, after Chris Dodd proposed legislation to limit earned income of senators, Daniel Moynihan, who makes money from writing and teaching on the side, countered with a proposal to limit *unearned* income. The Moynihan proposal quickly took the wind out of the sails of all the senators who could (literally) afford to be reformers. As Lloyd Bentsen put it, "If Moynihan becomes law, I couldn't stay in the Senate." Others might also have to rethink their careers—like Herb Kohl, who spent $6.1 million of his own money to win his seat, and Jay Rockefeller, whose monthly mortgage payment on his Washington mansion reportedly equals the amount senators may legally earn in a year, and John Heinz III, whom *Forbes* has listed as one of the richest 400 people in America. No wonder Durenberger continually poor-mouthed to friends. While his peers—the Heinzes, the Boschwitzes, the Danforths—could spend with abandon, Durenberger had to watch it.

But Durenberger drew the wrong conclusion from all this. During the spat over the pay raise, which he favored, Durenberger observed, "There are just more millionaires than us average folks than ever before" pursuing Senate seats. Only after being insulated from his constituents could he possibly consider himself "average." He was well off. But his friends say Durenberger, like successful people everywhere, was intensely competitive. He was driven to keep up with the Boschwitzes.

To his pleasant surprise, Durenberger learned early that he could significantly supplement his Senate income simply by speaking, something he enjoyed doing. In 1980, he took in $21,000 in honoraria from hospital and securities firms, homebuilders, bankers, and others interested in getting to know a member of the Finance Committee.

As Durenberger came into money, he spent it. That year, his third in Washington, Durenberger built an addition to his modern, commodious home in McLean. He also put in a swimming pool and a tennis court. These amenities helped cut capital gains taxes on the sale of his Minneapolis home, but they still ate substantially into the senator's budget.

Even as Durenberger cranked up his speaking schedule, his relative lack of resources vexed him. He complained to his staff about the expense of keeping tuxedos, noting that if he were CEO of a major company, he would not have to worry about such costs. Even with the house, the tennis court, the pool, and the perks of office, Durenberger complained. In explaining why he got into the book and condo deals last winter, he lamented his life on a congressional salary.

"It's difficult to take vacations and other things that normal people get to do," he said. "You can't buy a home at the lake, you can't have a boat in the backyard and some of those things."

Brooks Jackson, a Washington reporter who writes frequently on money and politics, noted in a recent book that "the longer congressmen served, the

Durenberger's reaction to questions about the propriety of taking trips from firms seeking tax breaks? "I think it's wonderful that they do that. I don't see the conflict."

more vulnerable they seemed to be to the temptations of honest graft"—that is, of accepting money and other benefits from groups with an interest in legislation.

This pattern helps explain Jim Wright's change of heart, according to Jackson. Through 1975 Wright was an advocate of financial disclosure by politicians. That advocacy ended in 1976, when a lobbyist friend arranged a dinner fundraiser for Wright so the congressman could retire nearly $100,000 in personal debts.

Not all members worry as much as Durenberger and Wright did about personal finances. But they all worry about campaign finances.

Since Durenberger was elected to fill an unexpired term, he faced reelection in four years. To wage even an average senate race in 1982 would take millions, Durenberger was told. He at first resisted the pressure to chase after campaign funds, but when he realized his opponent would be Mark Dayton, heir to a department store fortune, Durenberger attacked fundraising with the same intensity he brought to his committee work. Faced by a challenger with bottomless pockets, what incumbent wouldn't throw himself into the arms of the PAC men? Still, the incumbent at least has a chance. A poorer challenger without the credential of incumbency is likely to be intimidated right out of the race; if he does run, he's going to have trouble finding anyone who'll give him money. Thanks to wealthy candidates, PACs, and special interests, a Senate seat on average now costs just under $4 million, and we've returned to a Senate full of millionaires—the same kind of group we had before 1913, when the institution of direct election of senators was supposed to put an end to this problem.

Even if Dayton hadn't provided the incentive to raise funds, the environment of the Senate would have done it. At his ethics trial this summer, Durenberger was denied the opportunity to make an opening day statement because the committee needed to finish work by 6 p.m. The nightly cocktail fundraising receptions had already begun.

Pocket envy

So the midwestern reformer who came to town skeptical of the campaign finance system ended up joining in. Some say the turning point was the February recess of 1982. Instead of flying to Minnesota as usual, Durenberger flew to the West Coast to meet with a handful of Californians, who helped funnel thousands into his campaign.

Durenberger found that raising money wasn't so difficult. In fact, he found he was good at it. Durenberger is the senator from central casting. He has classic good looks and a deep, rich voice, and he's appropriately gray at the temples. More important, he had membership on the Finance Committee.

Members of the Finance Committee have a leg up on other senators because that committee, after all, writes the nation's tax laws. In 1982, Durenberger

was able to raise $3.1 million for his race against Dayton. He raised more that year from political action committees than did any other senator. Most of it came from industry groups with a stake in legislation before the Finance Committee.

"Boy, I'd have taken money from anybody in that campaign," Durenberger later told *The Wall Street Journal*. What about his objection in years past to the campaign finance system?

"Maybe in the first couple of years I would have said that, maybe even through the campaign." But now, he added, "There's probably a sense of realism that comes with one reelection that says, 'That's the way it is.' Bad though it may seem, it's still better than second place." This from the Minnesotan who, a St. John's annual once noted, "intends to put Flynntown on the map by reforming national politics."

Durenberger went on to explain: "I don't feel sleazy having to ask the same people that are lobbying out here and all that sort of thing for money, that doesn't bother me."

And ask he did. Durenberger championed an ill-fated tax proposal that allowed rust-belt industries to sell their tax credits to more profitable firms. The industries that benefited—steel, railroads, and airlines—all contributed substantially to his campaign. To a questioning reporter, he quipped, "PACs are the United Way of politics."

Durenberger worked hand-in-hand on the Finance Committee with Senator Robert Dole to secure a tax break for gasohol, the alternative fuel made partly from grain. Their efforts to "promote production through tax cuts" earned them appreciation from farmers and especially from Archer Daniels Midland, the agribusiness giant that manufactures more than half the gasohol produced in the U.S. The firm, chaired by Dwayne Andreas, has profited from gasohol thanks to the reduced tax rate, which costs the U.S. Treasury $95 million a year. The company's PAC gave $9,000 in 1982 to Durenberger. Andreas family members gave an additional $10,600.

The year after his victory over Dayton—1983— Durenberger's personal earnings from speeches soared to $93,000, nearly one and a half times his Senate salary. The extra money came in handy. His eldest son was reaching college age. And his improved house cost more to maintain.

But the next year, disaster struck. Congress, under pressure to reform, passed legislation limiting honoraria to 30 percent of a senator's salary. Durenberger voted against the limit, with good reason: The rule slashed his income in 1984 by nearly $70,000.

To cope with higher bills—some related to his family's counseling needs—Durenberger began borrowing more and more money from Commercial State Bank in St. Paul, run by a college friend.

Over the years, the bank loaned Durenberger nearly a million dollars, some of it at very low interest rates—and he was seldom asked to provide collateral. Durenberger repaid the loans, but he failed to record some of the low rates and some of the larger loans on his financial disclosure statement, as required by law.

Even with low rates and no requirement for collateral, Durenberger seemed to have money on the brain. At a party for visiting Minnesota Republicans at Boschwitz's spacious home in McLean, Durenberger complained about his lack of resources. "I'm the senior senator, I came out here first," some in attendance recall him saying. "Rudy and I each have four boys. I looked at this house. But I couldn't afford it. So Rudy bought it."

Durenberger groused that ethics questions were driving all but the wealthy from office. "If the ethics frenzy keeps going, most of us are going to bail out of the place and let Jay Rockefeller and those folks run it," he said.

Durenberger's staff members were well aware of their increasingly difficult boss's desire to make money.

The growing size of Senate staffs has increased the isolation of senators from their constituents. A senator is courted by staff and lobbyists from the time he leaves home to the time he returns. To be sure, he will pose for pictures with school children and find time for a brief talk with visiting farmers, but he spends most of his time with lobbyists representing monied interests and staff members eager to please.

"He became a different guy," recalled his old friend and former press secretary, Lois West, after leaving Durenburger's employment. "You stride down these impressive hallways and six people are running after you to do your bidding. It has an effect. You get to be one of the most powerful people in the world. And then you forget why you wanted to be that."

West recalls driving with Durenberger a couple of years ago when the senator ran a red light. Durenberger shrugged it off, noting that Senate privilege protected him from traffic tickets and prosecution.

In the mid-1980s, Durenberger's marriage fell apart. He had an affair with a Senate employee, then moved out of his home to a Christian retreat house in Arlington, where he contemplated divorce, the serious drug problems of two of his sons, and his financial burdens. Durenberger recalled this period during his ethics trial to explain his behavior. While it's easy to have sympathy for his predicament, one needn't sympathize with his solutions.

Piranha politics

As Durenberger's appetite for campaign and personal cash expanded, his aides say he looked around and saw senators with lucrative book and television contracts. He saw some of them going on luxurious free vacations (sometimes picking up honoraria, too), getting good deals on real estate, and getting travel expenses and free media coverage through foundations they set up.

His defender on the Senate floor, Robert Dole, was certainly an instructive model. Dole had found myriad ways—all of them apparently legal—to enhance his income, stature, and national visibility.

Dwayne Andreas, his family, and his company sent a total of about $130,000 to Dole in the eight years before his 1988 presidential run. According to *The Wall Street Journal,* about $45,000 went to Dole's personal campaign fund and the PAC (Campaign America) he started to give money to others. In addition, an Andreas foundation gave $85,000 to a charity Dole established in his name to assist the disabled. And the Doles found a bargain-priced condominium at the Sea View Hotel in Bal Harbour, Florida, previously owned by Andreas.

Of those contributions, only the campaign donations were easily accessible through disclosure laws. (Individuals are permitted to give only $2,000 per election cycle to a candidate's campaign ($10,000 for PACs). In addition, they can provide up to $2,000 a year in honoraria.) The others were uncovered only when news organizations looked into Dole's financial background during the 1988 presidential race.

In the mid-1980s, Durenberger let his staff know that he wanted a piece of this action. He leaped at an offer made in 1984 by a little-known Minneapolis magazine publisher, Piranha Press, to put his defense policy papers together in book form. Documents show he and his top staff saw early that he could use the deal as a way to collect speaking fees from special interests.

Durenberger also grabbed at a chance to save rent and taxes by putting his condo into the "Durenberger-Scherer Partnership." His wealthy friend Roger Scherer agreed to the 50-50 condo partnership, which required him to pay a share of Durenberger's mortgage. (Scherer's apartment was clear of any mortgage, so it wasn't a clean split.) When the partnership deal went bust after a few years, Durenberger's former campaign manager agreed to buy the condo and return it to the senator whenever he wanted. The ex-manager never recorded the sale, but paid the mortgage, the condo fees, and other bills.

When Durenberger began submitting requests to the Senate for reimbursement for staying in the condo, he changed the name of the partnership to "603-703 Partnership" and never disclosed his ownership. Around the same time, Durenberger's staff began to look to private companies and lobbies to pay for Durenberger's vacations and other personal trips.

Durenberger also started two foundations. Like Dole's, both had legitimate public purposes, so they were not investigated closely by the Ethics Committee. In addition, they served to boost the senator's name recognition and occasionally to pay for his travel.

Many of the financial benefits Durenberger received via these machinations were legal and didn't need to be reported. Most also came from people and organizations with an interest in matters before the Finance Committee. Until the Senate returned to Democratic hands in 1985, Durenberger was one of the committee's most powerful members, particularly since he chaired the Health subcommittee.

Health lobbies dominate his list of contributors. The American Medical Association independently purchased more than $100,000 of television advertising for Durenberger during his 1988 reelection race. And consider the money that flowed from the Massachusetts Mutual Insurance Co., which, like the insurance industry generally, received favorable treatment from the Finance Committee in the 1986 Tax Reform Act. Through its PAC, the company gave Durenberger $9,946. In 1985, Massachusetts Mutual provided Durenberger with airfare and lodging for a conference in Fort Myers, Florida. And in 1986, the company also gave him $2,000 in honoraria.

After Durenberger reached the maximum honoraria limit in 1985 and 1986, groups requesting a speech would be told to write their honoraria checks to Piranha Press. In 1986, Massachusetts Mutual did so to the tune of $4,000, twice the honoraria maximum. The company then took the unusual step of ordering copies of Durenberger's books in bulk, providing an additional $1,500 to the senator's unorthodox honoraria dodge.

At the same time this was going on, the insurance lobby fought successfully to preserve reduced tax rates on the cash value of life insurance. According to the Campaign Research Center, Massachusetts Mutual alone gave more than $200,000 in campaign contributions to members of Congress. Several insurance companies ultimately received exclusive tax breaks, including Massachusetts Mutual, which saved $11 million in 1986.

Massachusetts Mutual and other insurance companies took a keen interest in Durenberger's Americans for Generational Equity Foundation (AGE). Massachusetts Mutual contributed to AGE during this period, but the exact amount is not available because AGE recently shut its doors. (Similarly, the $2,000 Massachusetts Mutual gave to Durenburger in 1986 went to his Foundation for Future Choices.) AGE had done some pioneering work challenging conventional wisdom about social security and other benefits for the elderly. But the executive director quit in 1987, claiming that he had been pressed by Durenberger's staff to direct the organization's funds to a new Minnesota chapter during the senator's reelection campaign. Durenberger denied the charge. Other insurance companies that received tax breaks contributed to AGE. Prudential gave $10,000 to AGE in 1989. Archer Daniels Midland gave $5,000.

Taxes for sale

In 1985 and 1986 Durenberger arranged a series of four-hour therapy sessions with a psychologist whose offices were located about 35 miles outside of Boston. To help defray the cost of traveling to these sessions, the senator's staff would call lobbyists in the Boston area to arrange trips.

Since Massachusetts Mutual had offices near Boston, Durenberger accepted a company offer to provide air tickets, hotel, and limo service. After the counseling session, the limo took Durenberger to lunch with company executives. Of all the money

and favors provided by Massachusetts Mutual, only the limo rides were considered troublesome by the Ethics Committee.

Durenberger didn't accept free travel only from Massachusetts Mutual. He also got it from other companies that got breaks under the tax bill.

For example, the Puerto Rico-U.S.A. Foundation provided a one-week vacation for Durenberger and two of his sons after the senator spoke to members in San Juan. The members, by the way, were officials of about a dozen U.S. companies with factories in Puerto Rico. They wanted continued tax breaks for doing business there. They contributed $31,200 to Durenberger's campaign. They got the tax breaks.

Durenberger's reaction to questions about the propriety of taking trips from firms seeking tax breaks?

"I think it's wonderful that they do that. I don't see the conflict. Those people are creating jobs and participating in the political process."

If you want to know who is really influencing a member of Congress, the Durenberger case proves you have to dig beyond campaign finance and financial disclosure reports. You have to go home with him. In Durenberger's case, wealthy friends who might have been interested in legislation picked up personal bills and supplemented the lawmaker's income—like his bank president buddy who offered the senator sweet rates on unsecured loans.

Several of the senator's friends said Durenberger adopted a rationalization for his questionable deals: Since he was doing great work for the public and suffering financially as a consequence, he felt entitled to take a few perks, maybe even cut a few corners. Some friends and one long-time staffer warned Durenberger against making these moves. A trusted aide, Jimmie Powell, quit the senator's personal staff in protest over the book deal. The senator ignored the warnings and pushed ahead with the deals that would eventually lead to his formal denunciation on the floor of the Senate.

Is it any wonder that Durenberger couldn't answer the question posed to him by the Minnesota Citizens League president? Clearly, Durenberger's attitude for years had been, "Why not?"

You can't really blame Durenberger for being surprised at how hard his fellow senators came down on him. After all, a dozen members have book deals. Most are rolling in dough. And, as their reluctance to examine Durenberger's legislative conflicts of interest demonstrates, most senators are too busy picking up tens of thousands from wealthy contributors to discuss ethical questions.

In his final plea to the Ethics Committee, Durenberger asked the panel to "look at your own lives when making a judgment about mine." This plea apparently moved many senators, a dozen of whom rose to praise Durenberger before voting to denounce him. But one member was clearly unmoved: Warren Rudman, the vice-chairman of the Ethics Committee, a former prosecutor with little income outside his salary who lives modestly. Rudman had heard this plea from

Durenberger before. In 1987, Durenberger was mildly reprimanded by the Ethics Committee for discussing classified information at a fundraiser sponsored by a pro-Israel committee. Rudman was frustrated that Durenberger got off lightly. The Durenberger defense was that his breach was unintentional. Now, two years later, Durenberger was before the panel again.

Just prior to Durenberger's Senate hearings, Rudman was asked about the temptations to violate Senate rules in a city consumed by money and power. Rudman answered simply, "It's not difficult to be ethical." □

Article 3.   A Failure of Leadership
by William W. Pascoe

This article analyzes the October 6, 1990 compromise budget accord, which called for tax increases and alleged spending cuts. Despite President Bush's often-repeated promise not to raise taxes, the president, with the support of top Democratic and Republican leaders, shifted positions and supported the agreement. The author examines those factors that led rank-and-file members of both parties to spurn their leaders and oppose the package. The article also profiles top House and Senate leaders, both in terms of style and philosophy, and explains the conflicting pressures brought to bear on members of Congress.

Early on October 6, 1990, months of confusion, intrigue, back-room deal-cutting, intra-party squabbling, and partisan and ideological warfare came to a conclusion: In a stunning rejection of both the president and the congressional leadership of both parties—who together had spent the previous five months behind closed doors, fashioning a "hold your nose and vote for it" compromise budget accord combining tax increases with alleged spending cuts—an overwhelming majority of the House of Representatives rejected the deal and forced the budget summiteers back to the drawing board.

Only in retrospect can the enormity of that vote be understood. The House's No. 2 Republican, Rep. Newt Gingrich (R-Georgia), led the insurrection from the right wing of his party. Republicans were furious that the president had abandoned his "no new taxes" pledge and refused to renege on their own pledges—especially so close to an election. By the time of the vote, only three of the GOP caucus' seven elected leaders supported the deal; the rest were leading the opposition to it. And the huge majority of GOP House members voted against the package.

Democratic leaders fared no better: On the final vote, more than half the committee chairmen spurned the package. Even a majority of the subcommittee chairmen of the powerful Appropriations Committee—men dubbed the "College of Cardinals" due to their extraordinary influence over the course of legislation—voted against the package. Rank-and-file Democrats revolted against the higher charges to Medicare recipients. The leaders had not even been able to keep their own colleagues in line. As with the Republicans, a majority of the Democrats rejected the budget deal.

Better than any other vote in recent memory, that vote is a microcosm reflecting all the myriad pressures that come to bear on congressional decision making. The stew contained equal parts of the conflicts pitting Congress against the president, ideology against pragmatism, bare-knuckled partisanship against harmonious bipartisanship, grass-roots pressure (such as electoral imperatives) against inside-the-Beltway pulls, and special interest groups against taxpayers in general. Each of these conflicts played a role in determining the outcome, which stands as the best example in a generation of a revolt against the congressional leadership.

What drove rank-and-file members of Congress from both parties to repudiate their leaders? What role do the conflicts named above—pragmatism versus ideology, self-sacrifice versus the electoral imperative, partisanship versus bipartisanship—play in the legislative process? How do political action committees (PACs), special interest groups, and the mass media affect the outcome?

To understand the impulses affecting legislation, one must first grasp their effect on the congressional leadership. And to do that, it is necessary to understand who they are—and who they will be in the coming decade.

Though incumbent members of Congress have been reelected in recent years at record-shattering rates, this has not translated into stability at the leadership level. Since 1984, for example, three different men have served as speaker of the House of Representatives; three others have swapped the post of House majority leader; and two have served as House minority whip, the No. 2 position for House Republicans. And the Senate, contrary perhaps to what the Founding Fathers intended, has not been any more stable: Over the same period, there have been four Senate majority leaders.

At the present, the Senate Democrats are led by George Mitchell of Maine, and the Republican leader is Robert Dole of Kansas. On the House side, the Democrats are led by Speaker Thomas Foley of Washington; the Republicans follow Minority Leader Robert Michel of Illinois.

Both Mitchell and Foley are relatively new to their leadership roles: Mitchell took over from Robert Byrd of West Virginia at the start of the last Congress, and Foley ascended to the speaker's post only after Jim Wright of Texas—who had himself been in the job only a little over two years—was forced to resign for ethical improprieties in May 1989.

Both men are noted for their low-key, compromising, bipartisan styles, which puts them in direct opposition to their predecessors' penchants for high-visibility partisan attacks; both come from the more liberal wing of their party, again putting them in direct opposition to their predecessors, who had come from the conservative side; and both are masters of the media in comparison to their predecessors. (In fact, Byrd resigned his position as Senate majority leader before he could be voted out of the position by the Democratic caucus for precisely this reason.)

There are some differences, however: Mitchell, as the senior senator, is the nation's highest-ranking Democrat—which makes him, by default, the Democratic Party's leading spokesman. It is a role he clearly relishes, as he makes the rounds of television talk shows and holds press conferences to offer the Democratic spin on the issue of the day. Though slightly less partisan than Byrd, Mitchell is clearly more partisan than Foley, and he appears to enjoy playing the bad cop to Foley's good cop.

Republican leaders, by contrast, have served in their positions much longer. Dole took over leadership of the GOP Senate caucus following the resignation of Howard Baker of Tennessee in 1985; Michel has led the House Republicans since the start of the Reagan era in 1981. While Dole is known as more of a fighter than Michel, neither comes from the conservative wing of the party, and both are held in suspicion by more conservative members.

Most importantly, these two men represent the interests of the old-line Washington Establishment. They are much closer to one another—and to the Democratic leadership—in world outlook, temperament, ideology, and style than they are to other younger, more aggressive members of their own party. For Dole and Michel, partisanship and ideology count for only so much; they are viewed with disdain, as something to engage in only when absolutely necessary—as when the other members of the party caucus make it clear that *not* to engage in partisanship is to risk losing one's position.

In large part, Dole and Michel are responsible for the Republicans' continuing status as the minority party in Congress. Their aversion to open partisan and ideological warfare with their Democratic counterparts has robbed the congressional GOP of

the issues that GOP presidential candidates have used successfully to polarize the country in their favor.

The next generation

The next generation of leadership in both the House and Senate, however, is not nearly as averse to partisan and ideological warfare. Comers for the next decade in the Senate are Al Gore, Jr. (D-Tennessee) and Phil Gramm (R-Texas), both of whom harbor presidential aspirations. In the House, the ones to watch are Democratic Majority Leader Richard Gephardt and GOP Conference Secretary Vin Weber, the "Mr. Inside" to Newt Gingrich's "Mr. Outside."

Gore will come into his own in the next four years. A candidate for the Democratic presidential nomination in 1988, he is the favorite of many party members who recognize the need to return to the center when offering presidential candidates to the American electorate. Gore's 1988 candidacy was designed specifically to appeal to the general electorate: He was a moderately conservative senator who scored well in the Super Tuesday southern primaries but whose message got lost amid the other news stories of the day and whose candidacy folded shortly thereafter. Nevertheless, he finished third in the Democratic field and is well positioned for a future run for president.

Gramm, too, has presidential aspirations. He is considered a strong contender for the GOP nomination in 1996 and is said to be building a national organization. His assumption of the chairmanship of the National Republican Senatorial Committee (the Senate GOP's campaign wing) will allow him to spend the next two years raising money for, and providing other support to, GOP senators all across the country, including (coincidentally?) candidates in the mega-states of California, Florida, and New York. Gramm, historically a conservative's conservative, has disillusioned leading members of the party's right wing, however, by his support for the ill-fated budget package and its tax increases. It remains to be seen how well he manages to get back into the conservatives' good graces.

Gephardt also has presidential ambitions. Another 1988 Democratic candidate, his message scored well—he won the Iowa caucuses, traditionally the jumping-off point for Democrats—but he failed to raise enough money to clinch the victory in later contests. Upon his election to the position of majority leader, he promised his colleagues that he would not be a candidate for president in 1992; President Bush's sagging approval ratings, however, appear to have whetted Gephardt's appetite for a run, and the promise appears now to be good only to the extent that Gephardt may want to use it as an excuse in the event he decides to pass up a candidacy next year. In the meantime, Gephardt is staking out a leadership role for himself, doing what he can to speak out against the president whenever and wherever he can.

The final comer for the 1990s is Minnesota's Vin Weber, a strong conservative who nevertheless comes across moderately. Widely viewed inside the GOP House Conference as a brilliant strategist, he combines sure political instincts with a vision for the future and an understanding of the electoral uses of partisan and ideological warfare. It is precisely his willingness to do battle with his opponents (both inside his own party and outside)—but more importantly, his understanding of how to do it and win while not seeming offensive—that has endeared him to his GOP colleagues and won him respect on the other side of the aisle as well.

Conflicting pressures

Into this mix must be thrown the conflicting pressures brought to bear on all members of Congress as they work through their own decision-making process. Generally speaking, the influences on individual legislators can be ranked as follows:

1. The electoral imperative. For all members, at all times, there is no factor more salient to the decision-making process than a given decision's effect on the legislator's reelection efforts. What good does it do a member to vote the "right" way on a given bill, they think, if the cost is his seat in Congress—which means he can never again have the opportunity to vote "right"?

This calculation also brings into play the influence of special interests; in today's congressional scheme, special interests and PACs provide the lion's share of the funds needed to wage a successful reelection campaign. Good politicians can always find a way of balancing their district's stand on a given issue with the special interests' stand on the issue; that way, they can kill two birds with one stone.

The mass media, too, play an important role at this stage of the decision-making process: The particular spin that the media give to an issue affects the way it is viewed by the constituents back home and, therefore, affects the issue's impact on a member's reelection effort.

For instance, when Congress was voting on catastrophic health care legislation two years ago, the media portrayed the issue as a social security-type issue, swaying members to vote in favor of it. Less than a year later, when the tax implications of the new legisla-tion became clear, the media switched sides and portrayed the issue as a tax increase on older voters, leading scores of members to reverse themselves. The legislation itself had not changed; but the media's portrayal of the legislation had changed, leading Congress to turn itself around in its attempt to stay on the "right"— that is, the vote-winning—side of the issue.

On very few occasions do members willingly vote against the perceived will of their electorate; usually, the only way to get a member to do so is through …

2. The "leadership vote." So-called leadership votes occur when the party leadership of one or both parties decides to make the issue a litmus test of loyalty to the party. At stake are the highest-priority perks that go along with membership in the party caucus—office space, committee assignments, leadership positions, party funds for reelection campaigns, among others. If a member of Congress votes against the will of the leaders on a leadership vote, he or she risks retribution. Because the Democrats have been the majority party in both houses for the vast majority of the last half-century, their perks—and hence, their leaders' ability to threaten perks realistically—have been much better than the Republicans'. As a result, Democratic leaders resort to leadership votes far more frequently than do GOP leaders.

Next in line of priority when deciding how to vote is …

3. Ideology. Contrary to the way most of the public sees most of Congress, it is *not* divided into neo-Marxists on one side of the aisle against Birchers on the other. Only a relatively small percentage of either party—perhaps one-third—actually worry at all about ideology. That is, on any given issue, the position of roughly 100-

120 liberal Democrats can be adduced in advance according to the ideological impact of a vote, while on the Republican side there will be perhaps 70-80 hard-core conservative votes. For these ideologues in both parties, ideology is a key determinant in their votes, and in many cases actually can compete with leadership votes as a cross-pressure pushing them in one direction or the other. But for the overwhelming majority of the Congress, ideology plays only a small role in the decision-making process.

The emerging second-tier leadership in both houses of Congress is more ideologically oriented and less interested in bipartisanship than the current leadership is. But not to worry: Partisanship and ideology are what the

The emerging second-tier leadership in both houses of Congress is more ideologically oriented and less interested in bipartisanship than the current leadership is.

two-party system is all about. Congress over the last 50 years has suffered greatly from one-party dominance, and the American

electorate has suffered for it as well. A return to a more partisan frame of debate, in which real differences are clearly laid out and real alternatives offered for debate, would be good for the system. It would allow voters to make better-informed choices on who they want their representatives to be and what they want those legislators to do once in office. And at a time when public confidence in Congress is nearing record lows, clearer frames of reference for the public policy debates to come would be welcomed by all involved.∎

William W. Pascoe is chairman of Pascoe, Norquist, Jones & Jones, a Washington government affairs and political consulting firm.

Chapter **12**

The Presidency

Article 1.   A Day in the Life
by Burt Solomon

The author describes a "typical" presidential workday, focusing not only on the president, but on his top staff as well. What emerges is a fascinating, behind-the-scenes portrait of the Bush White House. In reproducing this log, the author provides the reader with a ringside view of the people, processes, and institutions that are so pivotal to the success of any president. It gives lie to the popular view that White House staff lead glamorous lives, arriving late, leaving early, and taking long lunch breaks. It also reveals the daily pressures that tend to age any occupant of the Oval Office and make the job so incredibly demanding.

White House staff members, everyone knows, work ungodly hours. But even their spouses and children wonder what they do within the maze of corridors from dark to dark. One day last spring, the veiled curtain was drawn back . . .

5:30 A.M. Barbara Bush's eyes popped open. It was a rainy morning that seemed too chilly for spring, and she'd had a

heavy schedule the day before in Dallas, where she attended two Republican functions and a literacy event. But once she was up, she was up. As her husband stirred, she took Millie, their English springer spaniel, for a walk on the South Lawn. A tinge of daylight set birds singing from trees that still couldn't be distinguished from one another. No one cleaned up after Millie.

5:45 A.M. At the Southwest gate, a Secret Service agent cursorily checked the trunk of Edward M. Rogers Jr.'s 1988 Mercury Cougar and then waved it through. Rogers, executive assistant to White House chief of staff John H. Sununu, glided up West Executive Avenue and found Timothy J. McBride's car taking up his parking space. "He's out running," Rogers presumed aloud about President Bush's personal aide (soon to be named to a Commerce Department post). Rogers also likes to run but hasn't had much time to, what with a schedule that got him home the previous midnight and up this morning (as usual) at 4:50.

He slipped into an extra parking space by the door. Then he entered the White House basement and threaded through narrow corridors to a barrier posed by a plain wooden door, labeled:

SITUATION ROOM
RESTRICTED AREA

He went in and moments later emerged, carrying a thin leather folder containing the Overnight Summary of world events for Sununu's perusal. He passed through a cinder-block corridor and up the stairs until he arrived at Sununu's door. He unlocked it. Security already knows we're here, he said, though he wouldn't say how.

Rogers, a genial Alabaman, chauffeured Bush around his native Birmingham in 1977 and then had a family friend pass along his résumé to a golfing buddy—Brent Scowcroft, now Bush's national security adviser—as he scouted for a job after the 1980 elections. While in law school, he volunteered as an advance man for President Reagan and Vice President Bush, literally carrying bags for Richard G. Darman (now Bush's budget director) and Chase G. Untermeyer (the President's suzerain of personnel). At a crucial point, James A. Baker III confidante Margaret D. Tutwiler—from one of Birmingham's first families—vouched for him with Lee Atwater. Rogers became Atwater's deputy campaign manager in 1988, sharing office space with a campaign moonlighter, then-New Hampshire Gov. Sununu.

Here, the digs aren't so cramped. Sununu's corner office has clean, elegant lines, with an elaborate chandelier rendered superfluous by indirect lighting. Small portraits of Lincoln and Jefferson share the peach walls with an oversized New Hampshire state seal and a large watercolor of birches near Sununu's computer and immaculate desk.

Rogers, at the conference table, set off a *thunk, thunk* of pages being ripped from a stapled news summary, circling items and jotting notes to fashion an agenda for the daily 7:30 A.M. meeting of Bush's senior staff. Soon Andrew H. Card Jr. strode in. Card, Sununu's deputy, is a sleek former Massachusetts politician who labors to soothe feelings ruffled by Sununu. (In 1988, he and Sununu dug up dirt about Michael S. Dukakis, and last year, Card considered trying to succeed Dukakis as Massachusetts governor.) He sat opposite Rogers and scanned the classified summary and then the morning's newspapers that covered the table.

They chatted intermittently about how T. Timothy Ryan Jr., Bush's nominee to regulate savings and loans, was "getting beat on" and about cold fusion's latest travail and about Card's 20-minute wait the previous night—"even at 10"—at Red Hot and Blue, the Arlington (Va.) barbecue place part-owned by Atwater, now the chairman of the Republican National Committee.

A man dressed in green lit a blaze in Sununu's fireplace, using a *Washington Post* and some hardwood. A butler brought coffee on a silver tray. The telephone started to jingle. The first call was from scheduling chief Joseph W. Hagin II, who was in Florida, advancing Bush's planned parley with French President François Mitterrand. Then Sununu once, twice, phoned from his car. Then Rep. Newt Gingrich, R-Ga., looking for Sununu.

Hours would pass before the *brrinng, brrinng, brrinng* would subside.

6-7 A.M. The Bushes, lounging in their bedroom, riffled through the morning papers (both Washington newspapers, three New York City dailies, *The Wall Street Journal* and *USA Today*). Mrs. Bush had coffee and juice, the President abstained. At 7, they flicked on the morning shows on their three-screen television set.

6:15 A.M. For Roger B. Porter, just arriving, the day seemed auspicious. His wife was just home from the hospital with their fourth child, Rachel Elizabeth, and *The New York Times* had published its profile of Bush's "amiable, meticulous and tenacious" economic and domestic policy adviser—"an acknowledged black belt in white paper."

Today promised more than the usual frenzy, what with a crucial Senate vote at 3 P.M. on the clean air bill (which Porter had worked on for hundreds and hundreds of hours) followed by a House vote on child care. He'd surely have to scramble his schedule and perhaps extend his long hours. He ordinarily got in about now and stayed until 8 P.M., typically putting in 85-hour workweeks.

Bush's White House works less-crazy hours than Jimmy Carter's, with its visceral activism, or Ronald Reagan's, which sought to remake the world in a trice. But it's still the White House, hardly hospitable to slouches. The place values "input measurement," an aide said, as well as output.

6:52 A.M. Sununu arrived, seven minutes late, with the pussycat demeanor reporters always see. Today, a lot was on tap. The clean air vote (on an amendment by Sen. Robert C. Byrd, D-W.Va., to help coal miners who'd be thrown out of work)

was closely contested—and important. A Byrd victory—a White House loss— might cost big bucks and force a veto, threatening Bush's grip on an issue that's kept Democrats off balance and fostered the President's stratospheric public favor. The House's child care vote expected late in the day looked worse, though Bush's AIDS speech in Arlington (Va.)'s Crystal City this morning would bring a kinder, gentler mien to the evening news.

Closeted with Card and Rogers, Sununu set about planning his day, knowing that the urgency from events on Capitol Hill plus the usual throng of courtesy calls, conferring with the staff and huddling in the Oval Office would see much of his planned day sidetracked.

7 A.M. A flower truck pulled into the driveway, delivering its daily profusion of flora to the White House flower shop, which does the arranging.

7:15 A.M. Bush, arriving with Millie "in the Oval"—as White House slang has it—ventured into his adjacent study and breakfasted on mixed fruit and tea. Soon, he started lobbying Senators by phone on the Byrd amendment, from a list of nine that Frederick D. McClure, his chief congressional lobbyist, had supplied the day before. (Bush hadn't returned from a dinner for the U.S. Olympic Committee until the Senate had adjourned.) McClure would add three more names in the course of the day. Bush, by nature diligent to duty and to details, eagerly obliged, aware that his deftness at friendship was his best weapon against a Congress he doesn't scare.

7:19 A.M. Darman, his suitcoat over his forearm, crossed from the corridor into Sununu's office, a few minutes later than usual. Every morning, he stops by for coffee and the morning papers and to kick around strategy and tactics. Card and Rogers stayed behind, and soon communications director David F. Demarest Jr. wandered by, then William Kristol, Vice President Dan Quayle's chief of staff. Then Porter stopped in, followed by staff secretary James W. Cicconi, just back from his grandmother's funeral.

As 7:30 drew near, their talk rolled from clean air to child care to the supplemental budget to a tax cut for capital gains. Kristol provided a back channel for a State Department suggestion that Bush make a statement on the 15th anniversary of the United Nations's Zionism-is-racism decree.

In Sununu's anteroom, it was hushed, as if the carpets were even thicker than they are. Once, Sununu stuck his head out and asked Katherine Winklejohn, his special assistant, to get Sen. Bob Packwood,

R-Ore., on the phone. "He's probably still at home," Sununu said. Minutes later, she reported that Packwood was "out of pocket," evidently headed to work.

7:30 A.M. After the White House's household staff (which totals 98) had swept the grounds around the outdoor heated pool, Barbara Bush started her daily mile swim. With her Yankee pluck, she had rarely missed a morning all winter.

7:30 A.M. The doughnuts weren't great, and only Kristol was helping himself to coffee at the sideboard. But the senior staff meeting in the Roosevelt Room was the place to be at this hour. Aides who weren't were ipso facto second-rank.

Sununu sat at the head of the long table in the dark, formal room. Elbow-to-elbow around it sat the 13 assistants to the President plus Council of Economic Advisers chairman Michael J. Boskin, Darman, Rogers, Kristol and Susan Porter Rose, Mrs. Bush's chief of staff.

This morning, Sununu called first on Marlin Fitzwater, Bush's press secretary, who said he thought the main White House story today would be Bush's AIDS speech. Demarest outlined its theme. Then McClure capsulized prospects on the clean air and child care legislation and on long-stalled aid for Nicaragua and Panama. That touched off a lively tactical debate on child care that concluded it would be harder to coax Democrats to vote against the procedural rule than in favor of the plan the White House wants. Aides at the end of the table opposite Sununu cracked jokes that had a half-life of seconds.

7:35 A.M. Alixe R. Glen had finished doing the MIPOD—the Most Important Paper of the Day, gleaned from newspapers for Fitzwater to present at the 7:30 meeting—and found time at last to retreat to the ladies' room and use her curling iron. A childhood friend of Treasury Secretary Nicholas F. Brady's kids, she'd worked for Bush since college—on his vice presidential press staff and then in the 1988 campaign. As one of three deputy press secretaries, she does MIPODs one week out of three, which entails rushing from her house—hair still wet—by 6:15. During her leisurely weeks, she's in by 7:15.

8 A.M. In the Oval Office, Bush received his morning CIA briefing, then one from Scowcroft on the state of the world. Darman was on hand for a while, and Scowcroft and Robert M. Gates, his deputy, until 9. Sununu stayed 45 minutes more, getting action from Bush on items

in his three-ring binder, such as publicizing Bush's filling out his census form to encourage others to.

Sununu would stick his head into the Oval Office from time to time during the rest of the day. Scowcroft, Gates and Fitzwater also would, keeping Bush abreast of what was doing beyond the White House fence.

8:10 A.M. Card, Kristol and Pentagon policy chief Paul D. Wolfowitz broke bread in the White House mess and conversed about defense.

8:30 A.M. McClure met in his second-story office with his three deputies, then canceled his appointments for the rest of the day to spend it on Capitol Hill, roaming between phones and collaring Members about clean air and child care.

8:32 A.M. Eighteen members of Fitzwater's staff crowded into his office, spilling onto the floor or standing, for their morning meeting. (An afternoon meeting is at 5.) Fitzwater, behind his curved desk, went through the schedule: a Bush meeting with Education Secretary Lauro Cavazos at 10, with no press coverage, and then the AIDS speech at 11:15, which was open.

"Do we have anything on the commission?" Fitzwater asked, referring to the AIDS commission whose leaders Bush would meet just before his speech. "How often they've met?"

"I can get that," Glen said.

"I frankly lost track of them after their big report," Fitzwater said.

He asked about an advance text and was told they'd have to check with Cicconi's office. "Can we shoot for 10?" he said. "Well, let's do it right after the briefing. I'll brief at 10." That way, the White House press would be ready to leave for the AIDS speech at 10:45.

Fitzwater, resuming his rundown, mentioned speeches at an awards ceremony at Bolling Air Force Base for White House military communications specialists and at a broadcast journalists' black-tie dinner at the Washington Hilton, and a *New York Times* interview for a magazine cover story on Bush's friendship with Secretary of State Baker. Other topics might come up during the interview, he was told. "In other words, getting in under false pretenses," he said. "Well, we will hold our breath."

Then press aides summarized—newspaper by newspaper—stories they'd all need to know. A woman reporting on *The Washington Post* had highlighted its front page in yellow. Sean Walsh presented the *Times* profile of Porter, which he judged "nice or not so nice, depending on where

you're sitting," noting the remark by Senate Majority Leader George J. Mitchell, D-Maine, that Bush's domestic policy "is notable primarily for its absence."

Lynn McKenzie cited "a nice article" in *USA Today* on Carter's visiting the White House and how he'd felt welcome after eight years in exile—though he'd frowned on Bush's recent broadside against broccoli. Somebody mentioned peanuts, and Fitzwater said, "We gotta go through all the basic food groups here?"

Afterward, back in her office, Glen lit a cigarette and called agencies to assemble two sentences about what the AIDS commission had been up to. "It's going to be a crazy morning," she said.

9 A.M. Sununu assembled a phalanx of Bush aides (including Darman, Kristol, McClure and top House lobbyist Nicholas E. Calio) to jawbone four moderate House Republicans who were thought to be leaning against them on child care. Sununu also made 20 phone calls during the day on the Byrd amendment.

9 A.M. Card, whose job (as he puts it) is to "tweak the system" to make sure that what Sununu wants done gets done, followed up on the senior staff meeting by phoning Health and Human Services Secretary Louis W. Sullivan on some final details for the AIDS speech and then a Treasury Department official to confer on Ryan's prospects in a Senate committee confirmation vote the following day. Then he arranged for a photo of Bush the next day filling out his census form.

9:26 A.M. Demarest was beeped as he was heading from the press room to a meeting upstairs with his staff. He was rerouted into the Oval Office along with Cicconi, whom Patty Presock, Bush's executive assistant, had summoned from the basement. The President had three small changes in mind for his AIDS speech on the balance between cancer and AIDS research that required budget breakdowns that weren't included in the paper on hand. Demarest worried about cutting it too close with the teleprompter, for a speech planned six weeks before as the White House's only newsworthy event of the day.

Demarest and Cicconi divvied up the factual and rhetorical questions. Cicconi returned to his office downstairs, phoned the Office of Management and Budget (OMB) to collect the budget numbers and typed a quick memo himself. Then he conferred with Demarest and speechwriter Edward E. McNally and returned to the Oval Office for a two-minute chat. Bush decided the comparison was too complicated to make; only one minor change was made.

So Demarest reconvened his staff for a meeting at 9:45, while Cicconi returned downstairs to meet with the health director at the University of Texas, Cicconi's alma mater, whom he'd kept waiting for a half-hour.

9:30 A.M. Porter, in his second-floor office, started the latest of scores of strategy sessions on clean air with officials from the Environmental Protection Agency (EPA), OMB and the White House counsel's office. From time to time, they escaped into Porter's anteroom to use the fax machine. "These people spend so much time here, they just make themselves at home," said Nancy M. Jones, Porter's confidential assistant.

9:35 A.M. "Yes, yes, no, yes, no, no, no, yes, no, no." Rogers, in his office, riffled through Bush events that Sununu would or wouldn't go to. Mia G. Kelly, a special assistant, took notes. Rogers asked her to contact Bush's voluntarism office about one request and to find out whether Sununu planned lunch with Bush today and to move his session with newsmagazines to noon if he didn't.

9:53 A.M. Bush met for five minutes with speechwriter Dan McGroarty and Demarest deputy Chriss Winston about that evening's speech to radio and TV correspondents.

9:59 A.M. "First of all, the President's schedule for today is, he met at 10 A.M.—right now, a meeting with Secretary Cavazos on the Secretary's recent trip to . . ."

Fitzwater, peering down from his podium on an uncharacteristically uncrammed White House briefing room, ran through Bush's schedule. For the White House Communications Agency ceremony, "we'll have a travel pool to accompany, but I guess there's no coverage."

"Will there be a mult?" a reporter said, inquiring after the broadcasting equipment.

"Not that works," Fitzwater laughed.

Fitzwater's light touch has diffused the hostility that characterized the briefing room during Reagan's tenure, when reporters loathed Larry Speakes, and he them. But Fitzwater doesn't say more than he intends to, a mix of geniality and guardedness. In that respect, he's like Bush, who invites journalists to lunch or the movies and then gets riled at their criticism.

When reporters pressed Fitzwater today on British Prime Minister Margaret Thatcher's phone call to Soviet President Mikhail S. Gorbachev on Lithuania, Pascal Taillandier of Agence France Presse wanted to know why Bush wasn't also calling Gorbachev.

"Because we believe the appropriate posture is to consider this matter with our allies and in the context of our own interests and policies in that area," Fitzwater replied, drawing from his years in the bowels of the bureaucracy. "And again, I can't get into why he doesn't call everybody around the world—why didn't he call this person or that person—but suffice to say we don't think it's appropriate at this point."

Was it because Bush feared butting into an internal matter, ABC News's Brit Hume wondered, or because he felt that it just wasn't worth it?

"Well, I think it's fair to say that when we say this is a complex and delicate diplomatic matter, the corollary is that we would not want to take moves that disrupted that diplomatic effort," Fitzwater responded. "And the President simply feels that this is not the time to make a direct contact to Chairman Gorbachev for those reasons."

At 10:36, the briefing ended, in time for the travel pool to assemble for Arlington. The stenographer's tape went to typists in the Old Executive Office Building next door so that a transcript could be ready by noon. No one had asked about the AIDS commission.

10 A.M. With Quayle on vacation in Hawaii and calling in at the beginning and end of each day, Kristol used his uncustomarily free morning to catch up on paperwork and return phone calls. Press secretary David C. Beckwith took the day off, as he'd tried to two days before, until Quayle said something on his way west (defending Soviet commanders for disciplining Lithuanian deserters) that put him back on the front pages.

10:01 A.M. Porter stopped into Sununu's office to report on his phone conversation with Senate Leader Mitchell on clean air. Two minutes later he left and Pierre S. (Pete) du Pont IV, the former Delaware governor, was ushered in. He had a notion he wanted to peddle on educational "choice."

"So what's cooking?" Sununu said, pleasantries over. Du Pont inquired about the child care vote, wondering when it was and how it would go. Sununu, drumming his fingers against the air at the side of his armchair, asked again, "Anything we can do to help?"

10:03 A.M. Bush, joined by Porter, listened to Cavazos on his recent Mexican trip. Bush is interested in Mexico—a daughter-in-law's homeland—and in nurturing relations with its new president.

He's also interested in stroking Cavazos, who's been criticized by the press as a Cabinet dud. Bush asked for ideas for a commencement address he'll give at Texas A&I, which is heavily Hispanic. (Cavazos, the first Hispanic Cabinet officer, had headed another Texas school.) Porter stayed behind a minute and spoke with Bush about clean air, then returned to his office and asked Jones to arrange a car so he could go to the Hill.

10:30 A.M. White House counsel C. Boyden Gray, back a day early from visiting Disney World with his daughter, met for an hour and a half in his second-floor office with EPA and Energy Department lawyers on a recent court decision subjecting some power plants to stiffer pollution standards. John P. Schmitz, his deputy, talked next door with officials from California and the natural gas industry about an approach to alternative fuels that both could stomach.

10:40 A.M. In the Oval Office, Secretary Sullivan and Card "prebriefed" Bush before his conversation with AIDS commission leaders, who entered shortly after. After Sununu and White House physician Burton Lee arrived, they all left at 10:55 for the 10-minute motorcade to the Crystal Gateway Marriott near National Airport. A gaggle of aides went along, including Cicconi, whose morning labors on the speech left him curious about how many demonstrators might show up.

Bush, addressing 400 business executives, called movingly for compassion for AIDS victims. "We don't reject the cancer patient who didn't quit smoking cigarettes," he said, recalling—as he rarely does publicly—his young daughter's death from leukemia. He drew demonstrators, but not very many. To hecklers in the hall, he flashed a goofy grin that suggested discomfort.

11:50 A.M. In the blessed calm the President's party left behind, Card met in his office (next to Sununu's) with Demarest and Deborah A. Amend, Demarest's new aide, to hatch a communications plan for the White House's global warming conference three weeks hence.

12:18 P.M. Bush, back in the Oval Office from Arlington, lunched on chicken salad on croissants, mixed fruit cup, milk and frozen vanilla yogurt with Reps. John Paul Hammerschmidt, R-Ark., and G.V. (Sonny) Montgomery, D-Miss., his cronies from Congress. He'd invited them just this morning, what with Quayle—his usual Thursday lunch partner—away. Down the hall, Sununu finished his backgrounder with *Time*, *Newsweek* and *U.S.*

News & World Report reporters, who were mostly interested in Lithuania and clean air.

Upstairs in the residence, Barbara Bush lunched with Sally Atwater, wife of the ailing party chief. In the White House mess, several advisers ate at the senior staff table, considered the best place in the White House to do business.

1 P.M. The National Security Council assembled in the Cabinet Room for an hour's discussion of Soviet trade. Bush arrived a few minutes late.

1-3 P.M. Three busloads of investment managers from Mitchell Hutchins Asset Management Inc. bounced into the Old Executive Office Building to get a briefing on the economy from three Administration policy officials.

1:57 P.M. In Porter's outer office, a woman emptied the trash into a waist-high paper bag, as she had two or three hours before. Jones and staff assistant Ann Haines discussed where Porter might rent a white tie and tails for the Gridiron Club dinner on Saturday night. (Getting a $10 deposit to a tuxedo rental shop near his home wouldn't be easy.) Porter rushed in at 2:09, having spent the morning testifying to a congressional appropriations panel about his staff's fiscal 1991 budget and conferring with Senate leaders Mitchell and Robert Dole, R-Kan., on clean air.

In his office, Porter started phoning Republican Senators who were still thought to be swayable on the Byrd amendment. "You've probably been besieged," he started. "I want you to know how strongly the President feels about it, with respect to the precedent this would set. . . ." Porter had already canceled his 3 P.M. meeting with the president of United Way, who couldn't reschedule for at least a month, though his 3:45 meeting on food safety was still on.

When does he get time to think? "Either very late at night," he said with a laugh, "or very early in the morning."

2 P.M. Sununu met with Rep. Dean A. Gallo, R-N.J., who had three or four people he was trying to find Administration jobs for.

2 P.M. Demarest conferred separately with Rogers and Amend about publicizing the White House's objections to legislation that would raise EPA to Cabinet status. (Democrats had written in a statistics agency deemed too independent.)

Then *The Wall Street Journal*'s Gerald F. Seib interviewed Demarest on a range of matters. He talks often with reporters but doesn't return calls about breaking stories. "I don't want to get in that role because I'll never get out of that role," he explained. Instead, he deals with op-ed pieces and editorial boards and with Bush's appearances and speeches. Four impending speeches were sitting on his desk to be reviewed. He would get to only three.

3 P.M. Gray met with F. Lee Bailey about a reformulated, presumably cleaner gasoline the famed defense lawyer had taken an interest in.

3:09 P.M. As the Senate clerk called the roll on Byrd's amendment, Sen. Joseph R. Biden Jr., D-Del., a swing vote, left the floor to take a phone call from Sununu. Biden asked whether a victory for Byrd would bring on a veto and was told it would. Biden's vote gave the White House its 49-50 victory.

3:12 P.M. A helicopter lifted Bush from the South Lawn for the 10-minute trip to Bolling to give awards to the military communications specialists.

4 P.M. Shiree Sanchez, an associate director for public liaison, met with four Cuban-Americans to ponder how to mark Cuban Independence Day seven weeks hence.

4:09 P.M. On Bush's return, he and Scowcroft met for 27 minutes with Sen. Edward M. Kennedy, D-Mass., just back from Moscow. Kennedy reported that Gorbachev had felt undermined by American knocks at his Lithuania moves. That night, despite Fitzwater's demurral, Bush would dispatch Gorbachev a soothing note.

4:30 P.M. Demarest convened his weekly events meeting in the Roosevelt Room, squiring 15 aides from around the White House through the details of 20 presidential appearances in the week to come. An official from the White House political office pointed out that the planned Cincinnati fund-raiser for Ohio Republican gubernatorial candidate George V. Voinovich wasn't a reception followed by a dinner—as the event sheet had it—but a reception followed by another reception; 700 people would stand and eat hot dogs, requiring a less formal speech. There were hundreds of details, Demarest remarked later, that determine whether an event goes right.

4:45 P.M. Their usual 4:30 conclave delayed by the Kennedy meeting, Sununu took 5 minutes now with Bush and 19 minutes at 5:20 to go over the day, mainly the clean air and child care bills. In between, Bush hosted Joseph Zappala, his ambassador to Spain and an old friend and fund raiser. At 5:39, White House social secretary Laurie Firestone arrived for 17 minutes of presidential guidance on coming guest lists.

5:40 P.M. Sununu returned phone calls and engaged in informal, late-afternoon staff time. Untermeyer stopped in, along with Card and Rogers.

6:03 P.M. Deputy press secretary Stephen T. Hart's TV was turned to C-SPAN, showing the House defeating the child care proposal the White House had backed. The four moderate Republicans Sununu had lobbied split their votes.

6:10 P.M. Natalie Wozniak, Fitzwater's executive assistant, helped White House photographer David Valdez with the studs of his tuxedo. Wozniak had brought a black flapper dress to wear to the radio-TV correspondents' dinner.

6:20 P.M. Bush, on his way to the residence, toted his briefcase into Fitzwater's office and chatted for five minutes about a day that had gone fairly well.

7:35 P.M. Bush left by motorcade for the radio-TV correspondents' dinner. His wife met him there, coming from a 7:15 speech to book publishers at the Library of Congress. Bush's speech was filled with one-liners. " . . . At this juncture. Wouldn't be prudent," he ended, mimicking *Saturday Night Live*'s Dana Carvey mimicking him.

8:30 P.M. Congressional lobbyist McClure returned to the White House from Capitol Hill, changed into his tuxedo and left for the broadcast correspondents' dinner.

10:10 P.M. The Bushes, home at last, soon went to sleep. Cicconi had made sure the President's overnight reading was light—the Cincinnati speech only. Bush would return it—read—early the next morning. ■

Article 2. Why Great Men Are Not Chosen Presidents
by Stephen Hess

Stephen Hess analyzes the presidential selection process, concluding that while the process may test some presidential attributes, it will neither predict nor determine whether the winner will be a great president. Indeed, the desire to lead does not necessarily equate with presidential leadership. Obviously, not all great men make great presidents. The best predictor of presidential greatness, maintains Hess, is the nominee's choice for vice president, which, argues the author, is the best place to fine-tune future presidents.

On October 22, 1888, as voters were getting ready to decide whether Grover Cleveland should continue to reside in the White House or should be evicted in favor of Benjamin Harrison, the future Lord Bryce (he was made a viscount in 1913) signed off on what was to be the first edition of *The American Commonwealth.* This massive description of late-nineteenth-century democracy in the United States would have a profound influence on a generation of political scientists, but today it is recalled largely because of the name of its eighth chapter: "Why Great Men Are Not Chosen Presidents."

Although James Bryce was Regius Professor of Civil Law at Oxford when he wrote *The American Commonwealth,* his approach was journalistic, a reporting of data gathered largely by talking to politicians and others. As a conventional British gentleman, albeit one who loved America, he might have been offended by this classification: journalists were not gentlemen. But in a sense Bryce was the Theodore H. White of his day, and the impact of his book was not unlike that of the first *Making of the President* when it was published in 1961.

Bryce was fascinated by the presidential selection process, which he considered largely controlled by party organizations that determined nominations and preferred mediocre candidates. While he had high praise for presidents "down till the election of Andrew Jackson," he considered subsequent executives, with several exceptions, to be "personally insignificant." It was apparently the most recent presidencies that loomed largest in his vision. (Even Oxford dons cannot repeal the laws of perspective.) When he first visited the United States in 1870, the White House was occupied by Ulysses S. Grant; the presidents on his next visits were Rutherford B. Hayes (in 1880) and Chester A. Arthur (in 1883). His low opinion of American chief executives, Bryce might have claimed, was based on personal observation. Yet to have made his case for the debasing influence of parties, he would have had to prove that the parties pushed aside more distinguished figures. This was not necessarily what happened. Should the Republicans have preferred John Sherman to Hayes? Should

the Democrats have chosen Thomas Bayard over Cleveland? There are times that seem to lack great men. Perhaps Bryce was merely observing one of history's troughs, regardless of how the candidates were chosen.

Bryce never felt the need to define greatness. He apparently thought that any intelligent person would recognize its presence or absence. This tends to turn the hunt for great men into something of a parlor game. Why, for instance, did he not pay more attention to early twentieth century nominees? (The book was extensively revised in 1910 and 1914, with editions coming out until 1922, the year of his death.) During this period the Republicans and Democrats nominated what a British gentleman should have concluded were some of the finest candidates since the nation's founding generation. For sheer brilliance it would be hard to surpass Theodore Roosevelt, William Howard Taft, Woodrow Wilson, and Charles Evans Hughes. While the populist William Jennings Bryan would not have appealed to Lord Bryce, the Great Commoner was a person of extraordinary qualities as well. All but one of Bryce's revised editions contain a footnote stating that "of Presidents since 1900 it is not yet time to speak"; still, he did change the 1910 text to read, "Great men have not *often* been chosen Presidents." By leaving himself wiggle room to elevate his friend Roosevelt to the pantheon of greatness, Bryce also aided the cause of Anglo-American friendship, for which he had assumed some responsibility upon appointment as British ambassador to Washington in 1907.

Necessarily, Bryce recognized that some great men would prove to be not-great presidents (Grant), and that others of more modest prepresidential achievement (Lincoln) would become great presidents. There are bound to be surprises galore once a person enters the White House.

The title of Bryce's essay still reflects historical fact in that no major party has nominated a woman for president, which suggests the obvious: whenever an excluded group is allowed into the pool of presidential contenders there will be more possibilities, some of whom might be great. When a religious barrier came down with the 1928

From *Society,* July/August 1988, pp. 46–52. Reprinted by permission of Transaction Publishers. Article drawn from Stephen Hess, *The Presidential Campaign,* 3rd edition, pp. 96–118. © 1988 The Brookings Institution.

nomination of Alfred E. Smith, a Roman Catholic, and with John F. Kennedy's election in 1960, the pool expanded, but not the type of contenders. Smith and Kennedy were professional politicians, differing from the other contenders in their generation primarily in religious affiliation. The first woman presidential nominee most likely will have been vice president, as the first woman vice presidential nominee of a major party was a member of Congress.

If Bryce's evaluation of the American system is tinged by a parliamentarian's preference for the way prime ministers are selected, however, his critique cannot be dismissed as mere chauvinism. He argued that in the America he had observed, great men were less drawn to politics than to "the business of developing the material resources of the country"; that compared with European countries, American political life offered "fewer opportunities for personal distinction"; that "eminent men make more enemies"; and that the American voter did "not object to mediocrity." But the heart of his argument was that great men were not chosen president because of the party system. Political bosses, he observed, gauged the strength of local organizations and the loyalty of voters and then calculated which candidate would add the right demographics to ensure victory. The objective was winning, not governing. He illustrated:

> On a railway journey in the Far West in 1883, I fell in with two newspaper men from the State of Indiana, who were taking their holiday. The conversation turned on the next presidential election. They spoke hopefully of the chances for nomination by their party of an Indiana man, a comparatively obscure person, whose name I had never heard. I expressed some surprise that he should be thought of. They observed that he had done well in State politics, that there was nothing against him, that Indiana would work for him. "But," I rejoined, "ought you not to have a man of more commanding character. There is Senator A. Everybody tells me that he is the shrewdest and most experienced man in your party, and that he has a perfectly clean record. Why not run him?" "Why, yes," they answered, "that is all true. But you see he comes from a small State, and we have got that State already. Besides, he wasn't in the war. Our man was. Indiana's vote is worth having, and if our man is run, we can carry Indiana."

The paradox of revisiting Lord Bryce one hundred years after he said great men were not chosen presidents because of political parties is that political parties are in decline, and there is still no certainty that great men will be chosen president.

"The media in the United States are the new political parties," James David Barber contends. "The old political parties are gone." Former Democratic House Speaker Thomas P. O'Neill has said that members who entered Congress since the upheavals of Watergate and the Vietnam War "had no loyalty to the party whatsoever. They looked down on it. They said, 'The party didn't elect me, and I'm not beholden to the party.'" Campaign consultant David Garth even notes that "the [political] boss is a plus to have against you."

Although some experts see new life in the old parties, the way presidential candidates get nominated has irrevocably changed since Bryce's day. In 1901 Florida enacted the first presidential primary law, an invention designed to take nominations out of the hands of the party regulars. By 1980, primaries selected 71 percent of the delegates to the Democratic national convention. The number of primaries dropped in 1984, but by then the news media had turned important party caucuses, such as Iowa's, into quasi-primaries. Accompanied by much greater voter independence and major technological changes, notably the coming of television, the new system was expected to produce a different type of presidential nominee. As one careful student of presidential politics, Byron E. Shafer, wrote in 1981, in *Public Interest*, "Neither Jimmy Carter nor Ronald Reagan were unlikely nominees for the system under which we now choose our presidents, as Harry Truman and Thomas E. Dewey were not unlikely nominees for the system under which we once chose them."

A tenet of political science and political journalism is that as the process changes so too do the outcomes. This notion is laudable and essentially optimistic. We are capable of changing the way we nominate presidential candidates, ergo we can improve the quality of presidents. Then if improvement schemes turn out otherwise, we can rail against the shortsightedness of reformers or the ignorance of those who fail to foresee unanticipated consequences—or both. The rules have affected some contenders' prospects in the past. Neither James K. Polk nor Woodrow Wilson would have been nominated had not Democratic conventions operated under a two-thirds rule, which was repealed in 1936. Jimmy Carter's treasurer claims that his candidate could not have won the 1976 nomination had not the law been changed to limit the amount that "fat cats" could give to campaigns. The rules will continue to affect contenders' prospects unevenly. Indeed, there are those who suggest that candidates who best figure out how to use the rules to their own advantage deserve to win, although others argue that the skills needed to win a nomination are not presidential skills.

Do changes in process really result in different kinds of persons seeking the presidency? Following the 1968 and 1972 Democratic conventions, party commissions imposed major changes on the demographic mix and selection of delegates. To abide by the new rules many states established primary elections. Moving from a caucus to a primary system meant that the media would play a much more important role in candidates' strategies. Changes in finance rules also changed candidates' strategies; but analyses suggesting that the nominees chosen under the new rules were different in kind because of these changes may simply be placing too much emphasis on too few cases. After all, there have been only eight nominations since 1972, and four of them were already sitting presidents. For every obscure senator from a small state who has been nominated in recent times (George McGovern of South Dakota), one can find an earlier obscure senator from a small state (Franklin Pierce of New Hampshire, for example). An obscure governor (Jimmy Carter of Georgia) can be juxtaposed against an earlier obscure governor (Alfred M. Landon of Kansas). History is wondrously full of contrary examples to confound theories.

One consequence of the new system, some say, is that successful candidates are more extreme in their views, in part because activists on specific issues are overrepresented among primary voters. Observing the 1952 Democratic presidential convention, Richard Rovere, in the *New Yorker*, compared contenders' activities with a game of musical chairs in which each chair represents an ideological position (liberal through conservative); if a chair is occupied when the music stops, the player is forced to seek a different chair. (Averell Harriman unexpectedly found himself in the liberal seat, Alben W. Barkley was suddenly thrust into the conservative seat.) In terms of Rovere's formulation, when Hubert Humphrey, a lifelong liberal, entered the race in 1968, he discovered Robert Kennedy already sitting in the liberal chair and had to find another place to sit. This does not mean that Humphrey or Kennedy (or Walter Mondale or Gary Hart, George Bush or Robert Dole) as president would respond to similar pressures in dissimilar ways. Quite the contrary: professional politicians are likely to have similar responses. They are not clones, but they tend to weigh opportunities and constraints on the same scale. Hence some of the claims that today's candidates are markedly more ideological than those in the past may be simply taking too literally the images that contestants have drawn of themselves, and of their opponents, during recent intraparty disputes. The new system's winners to date have been Reagan and Carter, one of the most ideological candidates and one of the least. The jury is still out on this question.

Following his defeat in 1984, Walter Mondale publicly worried that because of the voters' growing reliance on television, future presidential candidates would have to be masters of the "twenty-second snip, the angle, the shtick, whatever it is." Having just been run over by a former actor, who also happened to be one of the great politicians of this century, Mondale commanded sympathy. One could imagine Alf Landon making the same statement in 1936 after his landslide loss to Franklin D. Roosevelt, although Landon's concern would have been directed against the impact of radio. Politicians will adapt the technology at hand to their needs. What is most surprising about the television age is that besides Reagan and John Kennedy, the others who have won presidential nominations—Nixon, Johnson, Goldwater, Humphrey, McGovern, Carter, Ford, and Mondale—are no more telegenic than any cross section of middle-aged white males. Nor do the politicians who are at the starting gate for 1988 appear to have come from Central Casting. All of which suggests how little things change as the nation moves from party democracy to media democracy.

Throughout American history those picked to be major party presidential candidates, above all else, have been professional politicians. This is even more true today than it was in the nineteenth century. The reason is that "just wars" generate viable amateur candidates. Between 1824, when Andrew Jackson first ran for president, and 1892, when Benjamin Harrison last ran, persons who had been generals were nominated in all but three elections (1844,

Who gets the nod for vice president is the single most important predictor of future nominees for president.

1860, 1884). In this century just World War II yielded a nominee, Dwight Eisenhower. The twenty-nine men nominated by the major parties since 1900 have a collective record of officeholding that includes service as governors (thirteen), senators (nine), members of the House of Representatives (nine), vice presidents (eight), judges (three), and cabinet members (two). These men have moved through a maze of political jobs in order to reach the ultimate goal, and in eighty-four years only two members of that charmed circle—business executive Wendell L. Willkie and General Eisenhower—had never held civil public office before running for president.

To draw career histories of presidential nominees, thus illustrating the extent to which they have come from the ranks of professional politicians, is not to imply that the only way to reach the White House is to climb a political ladder, step by step, starting perhaps in the state legislature and gradually rising to a governorship or a seat in the Senate before attempting the final ascent. While the ladder metaphor reflects the most common pattern, lateral entry into a governor's chair or Congress is not uncommon. Ronald Reagan was not the first person to transfer fame or wealth earned outside politics into success as an officeseeker.

With the decline of parties, it would be expected that more persons could reach elected office without serving an apprenticeship—and this has happened. However, Americans always have had what Robert Dahl, in the foreword to Joseph A. Schlesinger's *How They Became Governor,* called "our belief in the supposed superiority of the amateur," a belief, he contends, that "we hold to only in politics and in the athletic activities of a small number of private colleges and universities whose alumni permit them the luxury of bad football teams." Twentieth-century Americans may attribute special leadership qualities to astronauts, but nineteenth-century Americans attributed similar qualities to explorers. Recall that John C. Frémont, the Pathfinder of the Rockies, was the first Republican presidential nominee in 1856. A journalist-celebrity, Horace Greeley, was the Democratic choice for president in 1872. Those advantaged by birth, whether an Adams, a Harrison, or a Roosevelt, have had a leg up since colonial times. Nor did the cleric-turned-politician begin with Pat Robertson and Jesse Jackson. The Muhlenberg family of Pennsylvania, for example, sent three ordained ministers to Congress. In contrast, the businessman-celebrity has fared poorly in politics, despite Calvin Coolidge's axiom that the business of America is business.

With the passage of time, what changes is which groups of celebrities turn to politics. The sports celebrity, such as Jack Kemp, is a recent political phenomenon. At least the only nineteenth-century athlete-politico that comes to mind, also an upstate New York congressman, was John Morrissey, who had been world heavyweight champion.

Contenders for presidential nominations may have to appeal to different selectors as the selection process changes, but the winners in the television-and-primaries era are not unprecedented in what they offer the voters. Whether today's nominees get there by climbing a political ladder or by lateral entry, they still would be recognizable to Lord Bryce. The system in Bryce's time promoted those experienced in coalition building; today's system promotes expert persuaders. Both are qualities considered presidentially important. The finite differences between politicians running for president under the old system and politicians chosen by newer rules are mainly of interest to those who make a living sniffing such fine distinctions.

The idea of a political career ladder based on ambition was masterfully presented by Joseph A. Schlesinger. "Ambition lies at the heart of politics," he wrote in 1966 in *Ambition and Politics*: "Politics thrive on the hope of preferment and the drive for office." Others then used Schlesinger's theory to show how elimination occurs as politicians attempt to move up the rungs. The final ambition is the presidency, which rises so high above the other steps as to constitute a separate ladder. The dramatic distance between the presidency and lower levels of public employment has consequences for what Schlesinger calls progressive ambition ("The politician aspires to attain an office more important than the one he now seeks or is holding"). While no person becomes vice president without being willing to become president, what of the others whose jobs make them eligible to be mentioned as prospective presidential candidates? Ordinary ambition can carry a supplicant to the level of United States senator or governor, but then, because of the wide gap that must be bridged, another dynamic takes over. President Eisenhower once mused that the only thing successful politicians have in common is that they all married above themselves. The only common denominator I have observed for those politicians who would be president is the depth of their ambition. What distinguishes the candidates seeking their parties' 1988 presidential nominations from other high officeholders of their generation? It is not their intelligence, accomplishments, style, or the reality of their prospects. What distinguishes them is presidential ambition, the ultimate in progressive ambition.

In applying the concept of progressive ambition to the presidency, scholars assume almost all United States senators would accept the highest office if it were offered to them without cost or risk. It cannot be. Costs of running for president can be very great. In some cases the candidate must give up a Senate seat, as Barry Goldwater did in 1964. In all cases there are physical costs. When Senator Dale Bumpers declined to become a candidate for the 1988 Democratic nomination, he publicly questioned whether he had the stamina for the "18 months of 18-hour days" that presidential campaigns can require. There are financial costs. Donald Rumsfeld and Paul Laxalt said they were not prepared to go deeply into debt in order to seek the 1988 Republican nomination. Potential candidates must also consider the almost total loss of privacy. What are the effects that running for president can have on a candidate's family? Whether to expose spouse, children, even parents and siblings to this ordeal could be considered the test of what divides those with presidential ambition from others who are simply eligible to be contenders. Meg Greenfield wrote in the *Washington Post,* "People who have made a serious run for the office or been around those that do will tell you that until you have experienced a presidential candidacy close up, nothing prepares you for the total onslaught on your life and that of your family that comes with the campaign." Mario Cuomo seemed to have all the political attributes necessary to run for president in 1988. He was reelected governor of New York in 1986 by the biggest gubernatorial landslide in his state's history and had more than $3 million left over from that campaign. But he was not prepared to subject his family to "the total onslaught" and announced in 1987 that he would not seek the Democratic nomination.

In their imaginative attempt to factor risk-taking potential into the equation, in the *Journal of Politics* in 1984, Paul R. Abramson, John H. Aldrich, and David W. Rohde show that Democratic senators who are proven risk takers have been "a good deal more likely to run for

> Three unsuccessful runs for the nomination turn a candidate into a laugh line for late-night television comedians.

president [since 1972] than those who were not." Yet as is shown in *Change and Continuity in the 1984 Elections,* seventeen Democratic senators were "well situated" to run for president and thirteen of them chose not to make the race.

This finding is in keeping with my survey of Senate news coverage, *The Ultimate Insiders:* ten senators received 50 percent and thirty-five senators received 5 percent of the national media attention in 1983. Some of the underexposed senators were too old or too young to be of interest to the national press corps: their time had passed or will come. Most of the senators who are rarely, if ever, on network television do not wish to be president. Quentin Burdick, one of seventeen senators never seen on the networks' 1,095 evening news programs during 1983, told a Washington reporter, "I'm very conscious about what they're saying in North Dakota, but not outside the state. I'm not running for president." His press secretary added, "To him if it doesn't happen in North Dakota, it doesn't happen." In any event, Burdick's age, eighty in 1988, barred him from a run for the presidency. Yet many younger senators will never offer themselves as candidates for the top office. The Senate is their ceiling of progressive ambition. Some of them may have judged that they are not qualified; but mainly their reasons are deeply personal, beyond scholars' tools of measurement. Strangely, a Senate leadership position (given the ego and attributes that it implies) fails to correlate with presidential ambition, which strikes some leaders (Lyndon Johnson, Robert Dole) and not others (Mike Mansfield, Hugh Scott).

How best can we describe presidential ambition (apparently so much more intense than senatorial ambition)? William Howard Taft, in *Our Chief Magistrate and His Powers,* may have come close in a story he told about a friend's "little daughter Mary":

> As he came walking home after a business day, she ran out from the house to greet him, all aglow with the importance of what she wished to tell him. She said, "Papa, I am the best scholar in the class." The father's heart throbbed with pleasure as he inquired, "Why, Mary, you surprise me. When did the teacher tell you? This afternoon?" "Oh, no," Mary's reply

was, "the teacher didn't tell me—I just noticed it myself."

Taft's gentle tale was his way of chiding Teddy Roosevelt for placing him in a presidential class with James Buchanan, while placing himself in a class with Lincoln. But it was Roosevelt's concept of the presidency as a stewardship that separates the modern era from the nineteenth century. "My view," he wrote, "was that every executive officer [read president] . . . was a steward of the people bound actively and affirmatively to do all he could for the people, and not to content himself with the negative merit of keeping his talents undamaged in a napkin." Indeed, given the Rooseveltian way of doing the president's business, Bryce's 1910 edition deleted a paragraph designed to remind Britons that the United States president "ought not to address meetings, except on ornamental and (usually) non-political occasions, that he cannot submit bills nor otherwise infuence the action of the legislature."

It may well be that in the days when presidents "ought not to address meetings," presidential ambition was less the motor force that governed the number and kind of contenders. After all, William Howard Taft did not have presidential ambition in 1908 (Teddy Roosevelt had it for him). Deeply deadlocked nineteenth-century conventions sometimes produced surprised winners, notably Horatio Seymour, the Democrats' choice in 1868, who was so opposed to becoming the nominee that the convention quickly adjourned before he could refuse the honor. Today, before submitting oneself to the obligations of being "the leader of the free world," one might apply the litmus test of ambition stated by John F. Kennedy, who told 1960 audiences:

> I want to be a President who acts as well as reacts—who originates programs as well as study groups—who masters complex problems as well as one-page memorandums. I want to be a President who is Chief Executive in every sense of the word—who responds to a problem, not by hoping his subordinates will act, but by directing them to act—a President who is willing to take the responsibility for getting things done, and take the blame if they are not done right.

One recognizes the hyperbole of the moment. Still, something more distinguishes Kennedy's statement from the garden-variety ambition of most politicians (perhaps *chutzpa*, the Yiddish word that Leo Rosten, in *The Joys of Yiddish,* translates as "presumption-plus-arrogance such as no other word, and no other language, can do justice to"). Or as Alexander Haig urged the voters of New Hampshire on the day in 1987 that he announced his candidacy, "Inside this exterior, militant, turf-conscious, excessively ambitious demeanor is a heart as big as all

Some great men prove to be not-great presidents.

outdoors." If this looks like a strictly contemporary phenomenon, consider William Jennings Bryan, thirty-six years old in 1896, a former two-term member of the House of Representatives from Nebraska, most recently defeated for the United States Senate, who won the Democratic presidential nomination. Or Thomas E. Dewey, thirty-eight, New York City district attorney, defeated Republican candidate for governor of New York, who almost captured his party's presidential nomination in 1940. Yes, the serious candidates are a self-anointed breed whose ambition sets the contours of presidential selection.

Not all presidential contenders really expect to get the nod. Some are in the race primarily to further policy goals or to focus attention on the needs of certain groups or to advance themselves in other pursuits. Archconservative Patrick Buchanan, for example, thought about running for the 1988 Republican nomination because "there is no better forum to advance the ideas you believe in and to give them elevation." It is only the serious candidate to whom must be attributed the italicized form of presidential ambition.

William Herndon, in *Herndon's Life of Lincoln,* said of his law partner, Abraham Lincoln, "His ambition was a little engine that knew no rest," and Alexander and Juliette George, in *Woodrow Wilson and Colonel House,* wrote of the "insatiable" and "compulsive" ambition that governed Woodrow Wilson's career. Yet psychological insights cannot predict when an ambition will turn presidential. Franklin Roosevelt was said to view the presidency as "his birthright." Jimmy Carter claims that he did not see himself as belonging in the White House until 1971 and 1972, when he met "other presidential hopefuls, and I lost my feeling of awe about presidents." Nor does presidential ambition describe a set of personality traits, given candidates as diverse as Eugene McCarthy and Lyndon Johnson.

Presidential ambition sets off a sort of biological clock. The Constitution requires that a president must be at least thirty-five years of age. Realistically, candidates do not run much before their mid-forties or after their mid-sixties. With elections coming at four-year intervals, this allows five shots at the office. At least one chance must be deducted, though, because incumbents are almost always renominated. A Republican who reached the age of presidential ascent after the 1952 election, for example, would have had to stand aside in 1956 and 1972 while Presidents Eisenhower and Nixon ran for second terms. Thus presidential opportunity is more like a four-per-lifetime proposition. Yet the odds are even longer in that three unsuccessful races for the nomination turns a candidate into a laugh line for late-night television comedians. Reagan escaped this fate by winning the nomination on his third try. Indeed, the fact that sitting presidents were seriously challenged for renomination in 1968, 1976, and 1980 can be partly explained by how narrow is the window of opportunity for those with presidential ambition.

In short, contenders have remarkably little maneuvering room, and much of their strategic planning is held hostage to fortuity. Take the case of Richard Nixon who reached the White House in 1969 via this Rube Goldberg "stratagem": (1) run for president in 1960 against John Kennedy and lose by a hair; (2) seek a way to sit out the 1964 race so you can run in 1968 when Kennedy's second term ends; (3) decide to run for governor of California in 1962 so you can promise you will serve a four-year term; (4) lose the gubernatorial race, move to New York, and retire from seeking office; (5) watch the Republican party self-destruct in the 1964 election and the Democratic party self-destruct over the Vietnam War; (6) return from exile to be elected president in 1968. Unlike the lower rungs on the political ladder, where aspirants for an office have more time to wait for their most opportune moment (and may even be rewarded for being the good soldier, putting party above self), a person on the presidential track has little incentive to wait. To do so means that professional staff, volunteers, financial backers, and sympathetic political leaders will drift into other camps. A rule of thumb might be that each serious contender gets three chances and one bye. Robert Taft, for instance, sought the Republican nomination in 1940, 1948, and 1952, but passed in 1944. William Jennings Bryan was the Democratic nominee in 1896, 1900, and 1908, passed in 1904, and became increasingly implausible after his third defeat. Nor are there Damon-and-Pythias relationships in this hardball world. If a bunch of greats happen along in the same era, some will be pushed out of the way on the road to the White House. Thus are all persons with presidential ambition generationally trapped. Years from now we will be able to identify the politicians for whom 1988 was the year of the bye.

This formulation does not assume that all persons with presidential ambition will run for president, merely that persons without presidential ambition will not run for president and all persons who run for president have presidential ambition. Likewise, all professional politicians do not run for president, but all serious candidates for president are professional politicians—at least until the nation produces Ike-like heroes again. It is this combination of ambition and political professionalism that limits the field in any given election year. For example, Lowell Weicker, a liberal Republican senator, said in 1987 that he had presidential ambition but would not run for president in 1988. As a professional politician he knew that when his party was in a very conservative mood he "would stand no chance whatsoever . . . for getting the nomination."

In our eternal search for the structural fix—Charles Krauthammer's felicitous phrase—there are modest ways to expand the pool of presidential contenders in a particular presidential generation, such as by repealing the Twenty-second Amendment, revising gubernatorial election schedules, and revoking the constitutional ban against naturalized citizens serving as president. But under the Twenty-second Amendment, added to the Constitution in 1951, only three persons have been prevented from running for president—Dwight Eisenhower in 1960, Richard Nixon in 1976, and Ronald Reagan in 1988—and none of them would have sought the office again anyway. An additional governor or two might be encouraged to seek the presidency if they did not have to give up their state job to make the race, but there are now only twelve states in which presidential and gubernatorial elections fall in the same year. While naturalized citizens (discriminated against under Article II, Section 4) deserve to be treated equally with the native-born, removal of this impediment would not result in a massive incursion of presidential hopefuls. Another means of encouraging more candidacies, some contend, would be to lower the cost of running for president. Contemplating the 1988 nomination fight, Edward J. Rollins, who headed President Reagan's 1984 campaign, said, "Anyone who isn't able to raise between $6 million and $8 million in 1987 is not going to be a player." This is a great deal of money in terms of personal wealth, but in commercial terms it means that the race for a presidential nomination has about the same price tag as a small fleet of New York City taxicabs (at $100,000 per medallion) or a midwestern newspaper of 10,000 to 12,000 circulation.

If fine-tuners wish to alter the type of persons who seek the presidency, the best place to tinker is the vice presidential selection process. For who gets the nod for vice president is the single most important predictor of future nominees for president. Thirty percent of the men who have been major-party candidates for president since 1900 previously had been vice presidents or vice presidential candidates, 50 percent since 1960. The presidential nominee's choice for vice president is usually a governor, senator, or House member—that is, another professional politician. The conventional wisdom is that a running mate can add electoral weight to the ticket; but, in fact, John Kennedy may be the only president who owes his election to his choice for vice president, since Lyndon Johnson was the reason the Democrats carried Texas in 1960. When voters decide who will be the next president, the attributes, or lack thereof, of the vice presidential candidates are a very modest influence, suggesting that presidential conventions can afford to be a lot more daring if they desire to bring new blood into the political system,

that is, if Americans prefer to have their leaders come from outside the ranks of professional politicians.

The fascination with process that has governed the energies of political science and political journalism has made academics increasingly useful to politicians and other practitioners. A the same time, journalists such as David S. Broder have added a new richness to the public understanding of politics. The matter of process has consequences for the presidential selection system, and the rapidity of change since 1968 has seemingly created a series of near-laboratory experiments. By changing the composition of the national convention can a party increase its chances of electoral success? In what proportions should parties use delegate slots to reward the faithful or encourage converts? Will an altered convention produce a different sort of platform? Which changes fuel ideology and which changes tamp it? Will presidents differently chosen become beholden to different groups and individuals? What changes increase voter participation? Has a decade of changes invigorated the parties or made them even less important in our society? These are all questions worth asking—and answering.

Yet, in the paramount purpose of the parties' process—choosing the nominees to be president of the United States—which narrows the voters' choice from any native-born American of thirty-five years or older to two finalists, changes in the system since Lord Bryce's time do not limit the field of serious candidates or alter the character of the winners. While there are a few contenders who would not have previously emerged, such as Jesse Jackson and Pat Robertson, they have not yet been successful. There may also have been marginal or regional contenders of the past, such as Richard Russell of Georgia in 1952, who would not enter the race today. But in broad outline then and now, and with rare exceptions, these contenders for the nomination are professional politicians, people of extraordinary ambition who cannot be discouraged by changes in the rules of the game. This ambition determines the number who seek the presidency at any one time, taking into account the modest room for strategic maneuver. No doubt a particular contender will be more advantaged by one change in the process than will another, just as different contenders will be differently affected by the rate of employment and the rate of inflation. Those possessed by presidential ambition will participate regardless of whether selection occurs through a national primary, a series of regional primaries, a combination of state primaries and caucuses, or any permutation of these.

Any democratic system is likely to produce the same range of contenders; in this regard, process does not determine outcome. A change in process may have some effect on which contender wins a specific nomination, and some presidential attributes are tested by the process. Regrettably for voters, journalists, social scientists, and students, the process will neither predict nor determine the chances of the winners' turning out to be great presidents. □

READINGS SUGGESTED BY THE AUTHOR:
Brauer, Carl M. *Presidential Transitions*. New York and Oxford: Oxford University Press, 1986.
Orren, Gary R. and Polsby, Nelson W., eds. *Media and Momentum*. Chatham, N.J.: Chatham House, 1987.

Polsby, Nelson W. *Consequences of Party Reform*. New York and Oxford: Oxford University Press, 1983.
Pomper, Gerald et al. *The Election of 1980*. Chatham, N.J.: Chatham House, 1981.

Stephen Hess, a senior fellow at the Brookings Institution, is the author of The Presidential Campaign, *now in its third edition, copyright 1988 by the Brookings Institution, from which this article is drawn. A new edition of his* Organizing the Presidency *is forthcoming.*

Article 3.   How Bush Manages the Presidency
by Ann Reilly Dowd

The author analyzes the Bush presidential style, which is a hands-on, high-energy approach driven by a zeal for problem solving. Her study reveals that Bush understands the mechanics of government, which he exploits with success. Although he respects the bureaucracy, the president does not hesitate to bypass it when it does not suit his objectives. Although Bush relishes the art of policy making, he is equally adept at deal making and arm twisting. Unlike some ex-presidents, Bush detests controversy, values secrecy, and enjoys surprise. Although he is cautious by nature, he will take calculated risks. While the president solicits a broad range of opinion, he will, in most cases, rely on the recommendations of a few top aides. Bush demands loyalty and team play, but loves calling the shots.

NOTHING tests a President like a world crisis. The one Saddam Hussein handed George Bush in early August had just about everything: blatant aggression, horrendous economic ramifications, and no easy way for the U.S. to exercise its power. To make the testing even more severe, the Iraqi tanks rolled into Kuwait just as a few other things were unraveling for the President.

Bush had wafted into his second summer on a cushion of good will. The Cold War was over. The economy was still growing, although sluggishly. Despite 13 successful vetoes, Bush's relations with Congress remained chummy. And his approval ratings topped the charts.

Then his charmed life abruptly ended. Bush broke his no-tax pledge. The price of the S&L bailout exploded to $100 billion-plus, and the President was dramatically linked to the scandal through his son Neil's directorship of a bankrupt S&L. His deficit reduction talks with Congress collapsed, and it looked as if he had given away the defining Republican issue for nothing. His approval ratings dropped sharply. When the Iraqi invasion sent oil prices soaring and the Dow plummeting, murmurs began around Washington demanding stronger action. One Washington disc jockey taunted: "Kick ass, George. Kick ass."

Sorry, boys. In calm or crisis, manager Bush is much the same: energetic, engaged, consultative, and ever cautious. While Ronald Reagan governed with bold ideas expressed passionately and often, Bush prefers behind-the-scenes dealmaking with friends. Not only does he feel uncomfortable in the bully pulpit, he believes public sabre-rattling—whether aimed at recalcitrant Democrats in Congress or an Arab dictator running amok—is counterproductive. Instead he goes out of his way to build consensus one-on-one, behind closed doors. Yet, if

Americans begin demanding bolder leadership, and Bush seems stymied in the Middle East, he could stumble on vision as Reagan did on details.

George Bush's is a high-energy, do-it-yourself presidency driven by a zest for problem solving—or as he put it in his acceptance speech at the Republican National Convention, "missions defined, missions completed." He understands the mechanics of government, and he loves to pull the levers. While he respects the bureaucracy, he often circumvents it, going out of channels for information. He dives into the nitty-gritty of policymaking. And yes, he likes to check who's playing on the White House tennis court and horseshoe pit, who's flying on Air Force One, and who's sitting next to whom at White House dinners.

Bush hates controversy, values secrecy, and delights in surprise. He is cautious but will take a calculated risk. Though he reaches out for a broad range of opinion, in the end he turns to a very few close aides, mostly in the White House, where power within the Administration has become increasingly concentrated. He delegates, but like a CEO who's held every job in the company, he sometimes can't resist penciling himself in. He insists on loyalty and team play, but make no mistake, he loves being captain of the team.

WHILE MOSTLY a plus, Bush's hands-on management style has its minuses. During the abortive coup against Panamanian strongman Manuel Noriega that preceded the successful U.S. invasion, the President's attention to detail proved paralyzing. Taking calls directly from the field, he turned the Oval Office into a military operations center replete with maps and raw intelligence data that he personally ordered from the CIA. Buried in unfiltered and often contradictory information, the President hesitated and the coup fizzled.

Since then, procedures for crisis management have emphasized more thorough staffing. The invasion itself was a model of delegation. After Bush made the basic decision, he let Defense Secretary Richard Cheney and his generals manage the operation. Between phone briefings by Cheney every 20 minutes or so, Bush called world leaders to inform them of the U.S. action.

Bush's handling of the Iraqi crisis followed the same pattern. After he learned of the attack around 9 P.M., he instructed U.N. Ambassador Thomas Pickering to call a meeting of the Security Council. While National Security Adviser Brent Scowcroft worked through the night in the White House situation room, Bush slept. Scowcroft awakened Bush at 5, and the President signed orders freezing Iraqi assets and blocking most imports, including oil. The President was in his office by 5:45, watching the news, reading reports, and talking to aides.

Though it turned out to be a very long day, it included most of what Bush had on his original calendar. He flew off to Colorado for a scheduled meeting with Britain's Margaret Thatcher, who joined Bush in strongly denouncing the invasion. In between meetings, speeches, and a press conference, Bush squeezed in detailed discussions by phone with the leaders of Egypt, Jordan, Yemen, and Saudi Arabia. Though the Pentagon got three carrier battle groups moving toward the region, the President understood that his military options were difficult at best. He worked for consensus among Arabs, whom he recognized would be key to any move against the Iraqis.

Bush did not have to phone Soviet President Mikhail Gorbachev, because Secretary James Baker was already meeting with Soviet Foreign Minister Eduard Shevardnadze in Siberia. After flying to Moscow, they made a joint statement demanding Iraqi withdrawal and an end to arms shipments to Iraq by all countries. Throughout the early hours of the crisis, Bush characteristically revealed little in public.

The President's emphasis on teamwork has its occasional downside. Says one aide: "Sometimes controversial ideas and issues get swept under the rug." Adds former Bush chief of staff Craig Fuller: "People tend to watch where Baker and [Budget Director Richard] Darman are coming down on an issue, then fall into line." Sometimes the President may put too much faith in individuals. After the Tiananmen Square massacre, Chinese leader Deng Xiaoping, who once called Bush "old friend," would not even return his phone call.

His near obsession with secrecy can backfire too. Had he talked with conservatives before breaking his no-tax pledge, Bush might have avoided an embarrassing vote in the House Republican conference against any tax increases. His misinformation campaigns have from time to time undercut his otherwise warm relationship with the press.

The presidential management style took shape during Bush's struggling days as a Texas oilman. Recalls younger brother William "Bucky" Bush, who worked on his rigs as a roughneck: "He knew all his people by their first names. He studied geological charts and logs to figure out what properties to buy. Then he'd assemble rights, raise money to drill, and get a chunk of the common stock for his sweat equity." He was a risk taker, but within limits: Unlike many wildcatters, he didn't personally guarantee anything. His deals always had more upside than downside.

Most important, the young Bush placed a high priority on people and trust. "In those days deals were done on a handshake," says Bucky Bush. "On closing day you'd whip up a two-page contract, then you were off and running. The key was personal trust and knowledge of character—and boy, were there some characters in Midland in those days! If you didn't know the good ones from the bad, you were history."

Such personal skills helped George Bush boost morale at the Republican National Committee during Watergate, and at the CIA after congressional revelations of wrongdoing. At the CIA's Langley, Virginia, headquarters, he often rode the employee elevator instead of the personal one reserved for the director, and he asked that staffers call him George. (When he left a year later, he received a standing ovation in a crowded CIA auditorium.) His first day as President Nixon's Ambassador to the United Nations, he shook every employee's hand at the 12-story U.S. mission in New York. Says White House Chief of Staff John Sununu: "He is a master of the small gesture."

With the exception of four years as a Texas Congressman, Bush's management experience has always been in executive jobs where business was conducted mostly in private. Loose lips don't work for oilmen, party chairmen, diplomats, spy masters, or Vice Presidents. A member of the secret Skull and Bones Society at Yale, Bush reveled in the cloak-and-dagger privacy of the CIA: He once stunned aides by coming to a meeting in a CIA disguise—a red wig, a big nose, and thick glasses. As Vice President he steadfastly refused to tell even his closest aides what he was saying to Reagan. His Chief of Staff Admiral Dan Murphy told prospective employees: "If you leak, you will be fired." Not surprisingly, his office was known as a tight ship.

AT THE WHITE HOUSE, Bush's past is prologue. Outraged by the internal warfare that characterized the Reagan Administration, Bush put a high priority on team play. While Reagan turned to a headhunter to fill most Cabinet and White House posts, Bush personally chose loyal and seasoned friends. Sitting around the pool at Camp David, First Lady Barbara Bush told Environmental Protection Agency Administrator William Reilly, the only newcomer to Bush's inner circle, "I said to George: 'You know, almost your entire Cabinet are our friends.' He said: 'Well, what would you expect?' "

Beyond the Cabinet, Bush chose personal friends for most top White House positions as well as some judgeships, ambassadorships, and a surprising number of key agency positions. Among them: the Peace Corps, the Federal Trade Commission, the Federal Energy Regulatory Commission, and the Overseas Private Investment Corp.

To drama seekers' dismay, the bickering has stopped. It's not that Bush's team lacks ego or differences of opinion. No one has ever called Baker, Darman, or Sununu fainting flowers. But in sharp contrast to the Reagan years, Cabinet members and senior White House aides have direct and frequent access to the President. He invites strongly argued points of view and takes his time deciding. But once he's spoken, he expects his troops to fall in line. Bush told a packed Republican fund-raiser on his 66th birthday in June: "I thank my lucky stars that we can fight like cats and dogs in Cabinet meetings but once I make a decision, move on as a team." He also likes to point out: "Loyalty is not a character flaw."

Bush shares credit, often allowing his Cabinet Secretaries to announce new initiatives. He also shares blame. After his devastating defeat in the Iowa caucuses, his Iowa campaign manager Richard Bond said, "It's my fault." Replied Bush: "No, it's mine." Similarly, in policy battles the loser is rarely punished. More often he's built up. Shortly after Transportation Secretary Sam Skinner lost to Darman in a bid for more money for roads, bridges, and other items of infrastructure, Bush invited him to Kennebunkport for a weekend of golf, boating, and family fun. At 6 A.M. on Saturday, Skinner heard a knock on his cottage door. When he opened it, he found the President in his robe, carrying a tray with a pot of steaming coffee. "It's your wake-up call," said Bush.

While Reagan inspired his staff with a few big ideas articulated often and with feeling, Bush keeps his team of problem solvers on their toes with rifle-shot questions. Bred on sports and socializing, he prefers people and action to theory. He was raised in preppy Connecticut, where grand notions passionately expressed were considered freakish. While Reagan focused on a single issue of the day, Bush handles dozens at a time, often blurring his message in a whir of activity. When he talks off the cuff, sentences disappear in a tumble of words and clipped phrases. Even when he's listening, he's apt to be fiddling with something.

TYPICALLY Bush begins his day at 5:30 to strains of country music, after about 6½ hours' sleep. As he sips coffee and watches CNN, he skims the New York *Times*, the Washington *Post*, the Washington *Times*, the *Wall Street Journal*, *USA Today*—for the baseball scores—and the Houston *Chronicle*. By 6:30 he's eating a breakfast of grapefruit, coffee, and sometimes bran cereal in his private study behind the Oval Office, usually alone. Then there's an hour for reading, note writing on his electronic typewriter, and phoning unsuspecting aides before his regular national security briefing at 8:15. When Treasury Secretary Nicholas Brady caught a glimpse of Bush walking from the residence to the Oval Office for that briefing, his old friend and campaign chairman pointed to his watch in mock disapproval. Minutes later a note arrived in the Cabinet Room: "Brady, I've been at work since 7:10. I just got back from a meeting at the residence."

After his national security briefing, Bush meets with Sununu for up to an hour, working through a briefing book of "action items" that could range from a California poll to a speech draft to a legislative update. Afterward his day is scheduled minute by minute with meetings and events until 4:30 or so, when Sununu returns with the "P.M. agenda," a second notebook filled with items for the President's approval.

Even with his tight schedule, Bush often squeezes in spontaneous events—an unannounced appearance at a meeting, an impromptu news briefing, a quick lunch on the Hill—before leaving the office around 6:45. Says Deputy Chief of Staff Andy Card, a former Reagan aide: "Reagan was comfortable with structured events. Bush invites spontaneity. He manages by walking around."

Most evenings the President has either a formal event or dinner with friends. It's not unusual for him to phone Cabinet members, staffers, or old friends on the spur of the moment to "come over for a beer and a movie." Or he may go out to one of his favorite local restaurants. He never dines with four if he can find 40, and he loves house guests. Says one aide: "In the past the White House family quarters were as accessible as the Dalai Lama's palace. But with Bush, it seems the mattress in the Lincoln Bedroom is never cold." He also may fit in some exercise—maybe tennis, horseshoes, racquetball at the House gym, jogging at Fort McNair, or a fast game of golf. (He rushes through the course, rarely finishes, and never reveals his score.)

Still, Bush manages most nights to spend some time in his study on the second floor of the White House, where he writes more notes, reads up to 30 briefing papers, and signs decision memos. Friends say he does not agonize over choices. When he needs a break, he might fiddle with a favorite fishing rod or box of lures he keeps in the closet. As he told his brother Bucky: "I like to play with them. I put the orange ones with the orange ones. The green with the green. I check the lines. And I think about fishing off Islamorada," the area in the Florida Keys where Bush has fished for 20 years.

Says Bucky: "He relaxes with friends, family, and exercise. It's part of his ecosystem. It's the way we grew up. There were always games." When the Trinity River flooded in Texas last May, Bush choppered into the area and tromped around in the steamy heat. Then he flew on to Houston, landing at the Deerwood Country Club, where pro golfer Doug Sanders, an old friend, was playing host at a charity golf tournament. Bush played 18 holes on foot—relishing every minute, save a few short putts. Said a weary cameraman at the sixth hole: "Hey, this is nothing. A few weeks ago he played 18 holes, three sets of tennis, and then went jogging. He never stops." One staffer calls such marathons "weekends from hell."

Bush's warmth, energy, and accessibility have saved him from the isolation that plagues the presidency. While Reagan was Olympian with staff, Bush treats them like family. By now most have been invited to some homey event at the residence, Camp David, or Kennebunkport. Many have jogged, fished, motorboated, or played tennis, walleyball, golf, or horseshoes with the boss. Most feel they get a fair hearing. At his first Cabinet meeting, he encouraged calls and memos. When he gets them, he promptly responds by phone, note, or comments scribbled in the margin. When Sununu asked Cabinet members to keep him informed of such communications, Bush cut in: "When you think of it." Nor has Sununu been a bottleneck. Says EPA Administrator Reilly, "During the Reagan years EPA administrators had problems getting access not just to the President but to Don Regan, the Chief of Staff. Such a thing is unthinkable in the Bush White House."

In general Bush prefers getting information from people rather than from memos. So did Reagan. But while Reagan was usually a passive participant, Bush is an active questioner. In preparation for Reagan's Soviet summits, the CIA produced movies and staged lectures. Bush's pre-summit briefings, by contrast, were interactive events involving heads of state and experts in and out of government. Before meeting Soviet President Mikhail Gorbachev at the Malta Summit last year, Bush got in touch with Prince Sadruddin Aga Khan, a U.N. official involved in aid to Afghanistan whom Bush had known since his own U.N. days. Bush invited his old friend to Camp David for a discussion of how Afghan factions were faring after the Soviet pullout. Before this year's summit he spoke with West German Chancellor Helmut Kohl, French President François Mitterrand, and British Prime Minister Margaret Thatcher, as well as several well-known Soviet experts.

In such meetings Bush is moved by information, not ideology. Says Brady: "He believes if you do the pick-and-shovel work, the solution will jump out. He likes a discussion framed by facts." If he can't get the answers he wants, he'll pick up the phone and call experts four and five levels down in the bureaucracy. Nor does he suffer unprepared pleaders gladly. When one Congressman questioned Bush's timid response to the Soviet embargo of Lithuania, the President shot back: "What do you have in mind? What should I say when Soviet tanks roll in? We'll be right there? We couldn't protect the Lithuanians under any circumstances. They're not even in our orbit." Or as he often asks recalcitrant aides: "If you're so smart, why weren't you elected President?"

Bush's independent style was evident in his nomination of Federal Appeals Court Judge David Souter of New Hampshire for the Supreme Court. With his top aides divided, the President retired to his small study behind the Oval Office, where, as is his habit, he jotted down on a legal pad in order of importance short phrases outlining the pros and cons of each candidate. He decided on Souter, a solid conservative jurist without a paper trail on controversial issues like abortion, then called his staff to tell them.

IN FOREIGN POLICY Bush often circumvents the bureaucracy. When a lengthy government-wide foreign policy review failed to produce the bold arms control plan he wanted for his first NATO summit, Bush turned to Baker, Sununu, Cheney, National Security Adviser Brent Scowcroft, and William Crowe, then chairman of the Joint Chiefs, to come up with an alternative. Scowcroft proposed deep cuts in U.S. and Soviet manpower and planes in Europe. Bush liked the idea but wanted it studied more thoroughly by his military advisers. Days later Crowe told Bush the Pentagon could live with a 20% cut in manpower and a 15% cut in aircraft. Baker argued for a more dramatic 25% reduction. After checking with Cheney, Bush settled on 20%. "OK, that's consensus," said the President. "Let's go."

He generally feels more confident on foreign than domestic policy issues. Aides say Bush phones four or five heads of state a week for a total that exceeds that of the last six Presidents combined. It's a habit that helped mightily in the Iraqi crisis. His wooing of Gorbachev, Kohl, and Mitterrand also paid dividends in European affairs. Says former U.S. diplomat Robert Hormats, now vice chairman of Goldman Sachs International, who recently dined with Kohl: "Bush's personal diplomacy enabled him to discuss a new European security arrangement with Gorbachev in Washington without the Germans feeling he was going behind their backs. It's all about trust."

In the domestic arena Bush is more likely to rely on the bureaucracy as a way of sorting out different points of view. But even then he often pulls the management of policymaking into the White House. The Administration's education, crime, child care, and clean air proposals were developed in small meetings with Cabinet members around an antique table in the West Wing office of Roger Porter, the President's domestic policy chief.

To whatever is done by staff, Bush adds his own layer of personal intelligence gathering for what national security types call "sanity checks." After the Senate sustained his 11th veto (Amtrak) and before it took up his 12th (the Hatch Act revision), the President slipped up to the Hill for a friendly, pulse-taking lunch with Senate Minority Leader Bob Dole, who was his GOP primary rival but is now a staunch ally, and longtime friend and hunting buddy Alan Simpson, the Wyoming Senator who is minority whip. A quick visit to the kitchen staff topped off the lunch.

Before deciding to convene a budget summit, the President met separately in the family quarters with Dole, Senate Majority Leader George Mitchell, House Speaker Thomas Foley, and Minority Leader Robert Michel. Says Porter, who taught Harvard's course on the presidency before joining the Bush Administration: "Every President does some of this. But Bush does a great deal more."

WHILE the President casts his net wide for information, he turns to a few key aides when it's time to decide. Says one aide: "At the top it's very small, very clubby. There's lots of camaraderie, humor, and male bonding. That's how the boys defuse tension and avoid burnout." The President's inner circle is filled with heavyweights, though of surprisingly different temperaments. There are three hard-nosed competitors—Baker, Sununu, and Darman—and two soft-spoken ones—Brady and Scowcroft. A step removed from the inner sanctum are two brainy but mild-mannered professors: Porter, the domestic policy chief, and Michael Boskin, chairman of the Council of Economic Advisers. Chief White House counsel Boyden Gray, an old Bush friend and tennis partner, is also a trusted adviser.

Bush is clever about using different personalities for different tasks. Sununu, the brusque but brainy engineer and former New Hampshire governor, plays bad cop to Bush's good cop. When Democratic Senator Daniel Patrick Moynihan proposed cutting Social Security payroll taxes, some conservatives appeared to be circling favorably around the idea. The White House thought for a while that the U.S. Chamber of Commerce might back Moynihan. Sununu reportedly phoned Chamber President Richard Lesher and threatened to "cut your b---- off with a chainsaw." The Chamber did not lobby for the proposal, which went nowhere.

Darman, who has built a powerful alliance with Sununu, is the President's chief economic strategist. Baker drives foreign policy. Scowcroft and Brady are trusted counselors who mainly stick to their respective areas of expertise—defense and finance. But the President knows neither has ambitions beyond making the Bush presidency work, so they are often the last guys in the room before the President decides.

Still, Bush has no single guru. He enhances his personal power by sharing information only on a "need to know" basis. When Bush sent Scowcroft and Deputy Secretary of State Lawrence Eagleburger on a secret mission to China after the Tiananmen Square massacre, he didn't tell Sununu. When he met with congressional leaders before calling a budget summit, he didn't tell his own congressional aides what he was going to talk about. Though the President drops FYIs to aides, his White House staff has long ago stopped trying to keep track of all his private conversations. Says one aide: "If the President is making the decisions, the only important thing is that *he* keeps track."

At times it seems no decision is too small or innocuous for Bush. During the development of his 1991 budget, he made about 70 relatively micro decisions, most of which would have been settled by staff in the Reagan years. He's often his own foreign desk officer, political strategist, even his own office manager. When Bush discovered that his correspondence unit was 70,000 letters behind, he trotted down to the letter-writing shop to see what the problem was. The pace quickened and the backlog is down to a few thousand.

ON MORE substantive issues his peripatetic presence makes for a very personal and unpredictable pattern of decisions. When there is controversy, Bush typically splits the difference. When the steel quotas were about to expire last year, Labor Secretary Elizabeth Dole argued for a five-year extension. Commerce Secretary Robert Mosbacher and U.S. Trade Representative Carla Hills pushed for four with a reassessment after two. Boskin wanted only one, limited to certain product lines. The President asked Porter to propose an alternative. The final compromise was a 2½-year extension for all product lines.

When there is consensus, Bush usually goes with it—but not always. After the Tiananmen Square massacre he bucked his staff and vetoed a popular bill allowing Chinese students to remain in the U.S. Even when he goes with the broad consensus, he often fiddles with the final details at the last minute. He picked the exact dollar-and-cents increase for his minimum wage and federal employee raise proposals. After three discussions with Porter over what constitutes an assault rifle, he decided to propose a ban on all automatic weapons with magazines that hold more than 15 rounds.

Accessibility and unpredictability are clever strategies for keeping the opposition off guard. In only 18 months Bush held 57 press conferences, more than Reagan did in eight years, and many on less than an hour's notice. "How's the temperature out there?" Bush often asks Press Secretary Marlin Fitzwater. If it's rising, Fitzwater quickly briefs Bush on likely questions.

Then he's off to meet reporters. Though wooden in formal speeches, Bush's grasp of detail and zest for competition let him shine when jousting with the press, despite his occasional woolly syntax. Fitzwater has never had to issue a correction, a frequent occurrence with Reagan. Congress has also found it difficult to categorize this President. While Reagan took bold stands but then compromised, Bush focuses quickly on what's possible. Faced with hopeless odds, as in aid to the Nicaraguan contras, he caves artfully and proclaims victory. When he agrees with Congress on the objective—such as the Clean Air Act—he works closely with the opposition. When he thinks he can win, as in the case of his successful vetoes, he doesn't budge. Says Brookings Institution scholar Thomas Mann: "He's a very adept tactician."

But what about a strategic plan? When reporters bring up the "vision thing," Bush's stock answer is: "Don't put me on the couch. Don't analyze me." Insiders say dealmaker Bush doesn't want to invite criticism or limit his options by defining goals. Outsiders wonder whether he knows what he wants. Brother Bucky's explanation is pure Bush pragmatism: "I think George would agree with investor Warren Buffett, who says that long-range planning has extreme limitations, especially when it comes to macroeconomic policy. What really counts are the day-to-day things. If you do well in the short run, the long run will take care of itself." So far in this Administration, vision is what works today. ∎

Chapter 13

The Bureaucracy

Article 1. How to Cut the Bureaucracy in Half
by Scott Shuger

The author maintains that bureaucratic fat is due to five **main problems**: slot syndrome, grade creep, headless nails, meeting and memo mania, and sleep and creep. Driven by these influences, good people become indifferent and indifferent people become bad. Government becomes worse. Apart from the moral gains that would derive from eliminating them, there would be substantial economic benefits as well. The bureaucratic system is, concludes the author, fat, lazy, and indifferent. Despite these criticisms—which are widely shared—reform remains stalled, owing, in large part, to complacency, sabotage, and turf building.

In the summer of 1940, in order to accommodate the many new military agencies then cropping up in Washington, Franklin Roosevelt authorized the construction of office buildings all along the city's Mall. Roosevelt had wanted the buildings, which quickly became known as "tempos," to be so poorly made that they couldn't last more than 10 years. But the tempos became a perfect symbol of self-sustaining government bloat: Many of them were still standing and full of government workers 20 years after much of the need for them had vanished.

As FDR developed one alphabet-soup agency after another in response to first the Depression and then World War II, the federal government grew from its 1932 level of about 500,000 civilian employees to 1.1 million in 1940 and 3.5 million by V-J Day. Today, with no catastrophes of equivalent dimension confronting us, it's still nearly as large—3.1 million employees. Ronald Reagan won office by running against Washington; his promises to cut back the federal government included plans to eliminate whole cabinet departments. But the spirit of the tempos reigned instead: During his two terms, the number of government workers increased 7.5 percent.

Analysts of corporate performance know that the companies that came through the eighties best had learned to be leaner. For instance, over the past 14 years, Conrail has cut its workforce by 61 percent—and has gained market share in the process. Here are some other examples from a recent book by Rosabeth Moss Kanter, the editor of the *Harvard Business Review*:

➤Beaten by Xerox in copiers and suddenly threatened by Japanese camera and film companies, Eastman Kodak eliminated 24,000 jobs between 1983 and 1986—a reduction of 17.5 percent—and closed its central film-processing facility. This allowed the company to reorganize, giving managers much more direct responsibility, which in turn promoted diversification and the farming out of marginally profitable work.

➤In leading Apple Computer back from the failure of its much ballyhooed Lisa computer and its first quarterly loss as a public company, CEO John Sculley consolidated the company's operating divisions, closed plants, and laid off one-fifth of its employees.

➤Before Shenandoah Life Insurance combined the operations of several divisions, a particular form was being routed to 32 people, across nine sections and three departments. Afterwards, the task was handled by a team of six people who did 13 percent more work, with greater speed, fewer errors, and 80 percent less supervision.

Why can't government learn these lessons too?

And you don't need to appoint yet another Hoover Commission or Grace Commission or Volcker Commission to learn them. Instead, behold the GS-13s and GS-14s, the federal common man. In a graded pay structure that begins with GS-1 and ends with the Senior Executive Service, these 200,000 workers are the middle of the government's middle. (There are additional middle-level employees not included in this figure, such as those at the Postal Service and the intelligence agencies.) A GS-13 makes up to $55,000 a year and a GS-14 up to $65,000. GS-13 is the last stage of federal employment for those who don't have supervisory responsibilities; GS-14 is the first stage for those who do. These are the highest levels most government workers attain. Their military counterparts are the 0-4s and 0-5s, the majors (in the Navy and Coast Guard, lieutenant commanders) and lieutenant colonels (commanders). These in-the-trench bureaucrats already know what the symptoms of government's fatal overstaffings are—and most of those symptoms suggest their own cures.

"The civil service is a unique and talented mix of people with diverse skills and abilities that can't be found anywhere else in the world," George Bush said recently. "And their hard work is not only seen in Washington, but in communities across the country." That's certainly true of many federal employees, but some of those well below Bush in his overstaffed government put it differently. A former GSA employee tells me how her bureau chief made a habit of taking most of the hour before lunch every day to read aloud to his staff from the *National Enquirer*. And a young Department of Justice attorney complains that the most intense interest in his office seems to be directed towards something called the Porky Preakness, a weight-losing contest. "Half my employment in the past year—no, probably 90 percent— has been useless," admits Sid Finn*, a 10-year veteran of Health and Human Services, who was also at the agency's predecessor, HEW, before that. Finn describes the office he works in as a good example of the idea that "the more inspectors you have, the more mistakes you have. . . . The office says to Congress that we could do better if you give us more people. But ever since I've been there, I've been aware that we're understaffed in the regions and incredibly overstaffed in Washington." A GS-14 auditor with 23 years experience at the General Accounting Office sums up this different view for me: "If you're results-oriented, the government's not the place to be."

*All the people are real. None of the names are.

Such bureaucratic self-criticism is rare, however. Bush's view prevails—and with it, bureaucratic bloat—in part because of a simple fact of human nature: People don't like to admit that they're wasting their lives. The GS-14s know what the problems are, but you have to ask the right questions to hear about them. If a government employee has the remotest chance of presenting his job to the wider world as meaningful, even inspirational, that's what he'll do.

For instance, if you met me at a party I probably wouldn't be terribly reticent about my past service as a naval intelligence officer. And it wouldn't take too much additional cajoling to get me to embark on a story or two about some of the important and exciting things I did in that capacity. But as long as you were unarmed, I would never tell you about The World's Greatest Code Book.

Military Scrabble

Once during a seagoing exercise I participated in, our admiral expressed displeasure about what he correctly viewed as his aviators' poor radio security. It's really not that difficult to make improvements in this area: a few additional radio-code procedures will do the trick. But when the airwing commander heard the admiral's comments, he took the whole thing as a personal affront. *He*'d show that deskbound two-star a thing or two! So instead of merely doing the tactically correct thing, he decided to put together a dictionary of code words so immense, so exhaustive, that it would cover any possible radio message that the admiral or anyone on his staff would ever want to have pilots encode. And not only did this guy want the dictionary assembled immediately, he wanted it assembled in complete *secrecy*. He was planning for the delicious moment when his boss would ask him why his fighter pilots on station couldn't say X in a tactically safe manner, and he'd be able to produce this mammoth document and coolly reply, "Ah yes, admiral, that would be on page 1,007. The pilots already have them."

Now once such a brilliant scheme is conceived there is the little matter of execution. Who would actually assemble the WGCB? From the first rumor of the plan, every junior intelligence officer onboard the carrier knew the answer to that one. "I'll do it," said my boss. Which all the junior intelligence officers knew freely translated as "*We*'ll do it."

So it was that the 10 or so of us were called together to "get cracking." As my boss explained it, the job broke down into two manageable tasks: a) identifying everything that you could ever want to say from an airplane, and b) making up a code word for it. Then he left, saying that he expected the results in two days. There we were—captive participants in the world's first Military Scrabble tournament. The perfect chord for the program was struck when one of my coworkers suggested that the first message we needed to encode was "My radio is broken."

For the next few days, in between our normal duties, we worked feverishly on the project. Just before the deadline, we produced a huge list. At this point it was clear that what we'd done was tactically useless, if for no other reason than if this dictionary were ever put on the actual "kneeboard cards" that pilots use, it would weigh 30 pounds. No doubt the Russians would have approved. In a matter of days, on just a few typewriters, we had developed a weapon that could herniate every aviator in the Seventh Fleet.

Nevertheless, my boss was beaming when he handed the list in. No junior intelligence officer was surprised that it was never heard of again.

Spills and floods

This debacle has a number of important morals. When my airwing was confronted by a legitimate worry, its irrelevant response used up as much effort and morale as the right one would have (probably more). So it's not accidental that cockpit radio procedures didn't improve for several more months. And if there had been only, say, two or three junior intelligence officers attached to the airwing instead of 10, this nuthatch project couldn't have been mounted instantly on such a grand scale; it would have been small and slow and hence probably would have passed out of existence before it ended up consuming anywhere near as much effort as it actually did. Here's the punchline: When a bureaucracy is screwed up, it does not automatically mean that all or most of the bureaucrats are lazy or stupid—we worked like dogs and with considerable ingenuity on that code book—and a modern organization can usually do more real work quicker with fewer people and fewer tasks.

I say *usually* because a big enemy of efficiency is the blanket generalization. The Department of Commerce does not need more people (although it probably needs some *different* people). But the Coast Guard could use some more—at least in the field. According to a PBS "Frontline" documentary, the *Exxon Valdez* proceeded unnoticed towards its fateful grounding on Bligh Reef because the responsible Coast Guard station had, in a manpower crunch, eliminated round-the-clock radar supervision and manual plotting of ships' courses. And the government is falling behind in its attempt to make cases and recover funds in billions of dollars worth of S&L frauds because of a dearth of FBI agents. *Time* reports that the FBI recent-

ly sought funds for 425 additional agents to investigate bank scams but received only enough for fewer than half that many. Of the 3,500 major criminal S&L cases pending, 1,500 are inactive, due to such manpower shortages. It's a similar story at the IRS. With delinquent taxes now estimated to be approaching $100 billion, it would certainly make sense to hire more examiners and auditors.

This failure to get specific about jobs is what's wrong with the IRS's and the Defense Department's current hiring freezes. With a hiring freeze, jobs are eliminated by attrition. But attrition is a random process—people do not quit or retire according to some intelligent overall plan. Freezes do not distinguish between Jones with his feet up on his desk and Smith with his finger in the dike. If Smith quits or retires before Jones does, you don't get improved efficiency—you get a flood. Reductions in force (RIFs) are no better, because they operate by the principle of seniority; if Smith doesn't have enough time in service to make the cut, there's still going to be a disaster. Freezes and RIFs assume from on high that every office has similar manning needs and that within each office, each job is equally needed and equally well performed. But to find dead wood, you can't rely on satellite photos; you have to walk through the forest.

Gang of five

When I recently took that walk—when I asked bureaucrats about the causes and effects of the fat in their offices—I learned that there are five main problems.

The Slot Syndrome. FDR's tempos are the paradigm of this one. If an organization is confronted with a need, it must respond by creating jobs that meet that need. But if the need goes away, whether because the jobs are performed well or because of other factors, it's just as important that those jobs go away too. But in government this hardly ever happens—bureaucratic slots, once created, tend to take on lives of their own. If the world ebbs and flows while bureaucracies stay put, the slot syndrome is the reason why.

Derek Rodgers, a GS-14 at the Commerce Department with 24 years' government service, gives me a clear example: "The payroll in my office is about $600,000," he says. "It had some things to do years ago—there were special projects all over the world. But there's no big money to fuel those anymore and yet the bureaucratic entity that was to promote this still exists."

According to Jane Gustafson, an attorney who

worked in one of HUD's regional offices for over 10 years, HUD's inefficiency is certainly not confined to the scandal at headquarters. Gustafson says that from 1976 to 1982, she was pretty busy with legal work, reviewing contracts, doing closings, and the like. But even then, she recalls urban renewal specialists being added to the office when there was virtually no urban renewal going on. Later, when the big Reagan housing cuts began to take effect, Gustafson's office still didn't scale back. "After that, there was less and less work to do and I had more time on my hands," she remembers. "There was very little professional challenge for me."

That leads to one of the most damaging effects of the slot syndrome—goldbricking. Much of the inner office life of today's bureaucrats could come from the pages of the late-forties play *Two Blind Mice*, which is set in the "Office of Seeds and Standards," a department with so little to do that it had been abolished five years before—but persisted because it had never been notified.

The official HUD description of Gustafson's job states that her duties were "to handle litigation for which the office of regional counsel has lead responsibility as well as litigation for which the general counsel's office claims lead responsibility." That meant that she was supposed to "prepare all necessary legal documentation and do all things necessary to competently and professionally represent the department and/or support the general counsel's office." Gustafson is a very bright person who would have eagerly undertaken such a formidable assignment had it been offered to her. But what did she actually wind up doing?

"By the end, I was really fudging my time." Suddenly Gustafson breaks into laughter as she blows a professional secret: "In the bottom drawer of one of the file cabinets, the secretaries had a lot of trash novels; in the last two years, I got a lot of reading done in the office. A *lot*."

"We have enormous numbers of people who don't do anything," says Sid Finn of HHS. "And I mean *anything*. One sells real estate. I spend an enormous amount of time on my volunteer work. There's a tremendous amount of socializing. People fall into

each other's arms every day as though they had not seen each other for a year, catching up on what they had for dinner the night before. It's very social."

"In every major defense plant you have three, four, five officers, usually colonels," explains George Tracy, who worked as a Defense Department auditor for 26 years. "They give them that assignment three to six years before they retire and that's when they make the contacts with these people they end up going to work for. They receive the reports of the technical people who work for them, but they're not expert in any of the areas. And they 'liaison' with the contractors by going to lunch with them. There's very little they do that's productive. I'd say they contribute virtually nothing to the performance of the procurement function. They screw off. They've got their Wednesday afternoon golf and their long weekends."

Derek Rodgers tells me about coworkers selling real estate or computer software from their office desks. "There was one guy who finally got his income in real estate up to the point where he said, 'I don't need this anymore.'" So he decided to retire. "And to do that he ran another scam: He used to dress like an absolute slob in the office. He walked around the office without his shoes. He looked terrible. He carried this charade on for two years just to get what they call a discontinued service retirement." As a result, at age 50, the man got out with 90 percent of a full pension. "The day he retired he had on a neatly pressed suit, his hair was all slicked back. He looked great.

"Today most people in the international trade administration don't have a full day's work," Rodgers continues, readily counting himself in that category. (Nevertheless, his official job description runs five single-spaced typed pages.) He says that out of 1,500 workers, only 100 are "notable exceptions" to that characterization. "We have GS-14s and GS-15s running around without jobs. We're talking about people that make $60,000 and $70,000 a year."

Supervisors who have slots added to their domain find themselves with additional subordinates and a weightier payroll. And since supervisors are conditioned to feel a greater glory anytime such augmentation occurs, they aren't going to take any steps to

> **Although Daniel Stein was convicted of attempted extortion two years ago, he's still employed at the State Department. As a convicted felon, he can't vote, but he can pull down a GS-14's salary and, someday, a GS-14's pension too.**

undo it. "Your pay and your position all depend on the number of people that you supervise and the size of your budget," explains Rodgers. "That's the battle in Washington."

The assignment of intelligence officers to *every* squadron in a carrier airwing is a perfect example of the slot syndrome. Every squadron skipper enjoys having his own intelligence officer, even though only a handful of the wing's squadrons really need them or, indeed, ever find anything productive for them to do. In other words, the slot syndrome was the reason I found myself sitting around a table with nine other earnest young intelligence officers trying to think of a cryptic way to say, "My foot's asleep"—instead of oh, say, collecting intelligence.

The solution to the syndrome isn't all that complicated. The problem exists only if the number of people you command and the amount of money you control are allowed to be more important than *what you accomplish.* If organizations are forced to articulate clear goals with a reward/punishment structure to match, there won't be much prestige or advancement in diddling around, no matter how many people are doing your diddling for you. (Sure enough, the Navy's fondness for the slot syndrome is borne out by its confused reward structure. The captain of the *Vincennes* and his weapons officer were recently awarded medals for the period of service that included their shoot-down of a civilian airliner.)

Grade Creep. In 1955, 8.2 percent of those in the federal civilian workforce were in grades GS-12 through GS-15, the middle levels of government. In 1975, that figure was 23.2 percent. The latest available figures indicate that it is now 28.9 percent. In 1955, 2.9 percent of all military personnel were officers at the O-4 and O-5 level. In 1975, that figure was 4 percent, and it remains 4 percent today. This progression toward the middle is grade creep; it's primarily caused by an advancement scheme that's too generous until you hit the top of the middle ranks, and it's behind a lot of the trouble. When I ask Derek Rodgers of Commerce if government is getting more cumbersome, he grabs the legal pad out of my hand and starts drawing charts. In no time, he's drawn me a couple of interesting pictures of his agency—a series of boxes and arrows that get more and more baroque. "In the early Carter years, international trade administration"—where Rodgers works—"was headed up by one assistant secretary. He reported to the undersecretary. At the time, the undersecretary was the number two man in the department. That assistant secretary had in the next line under him, four deputy assistant secretaries. And under those four deputy assistant secretaries there were the various office directors. That's not the case today," continues

Rodgers, now on page two. "Under Carter, we got 13 deputy assistant secretaries in international trade administration. And under Reagan, we got 26. That's quite an expansion." The pad in front of us now looks like hell.

The chief consequence of this gross expansion at the middle is that there are too many layers to traverse to get anything done. Dividing up into more empires doesn't produce more trade; it just produces more emperors. Rodgers recalls that under the old scheme, office directors supervised hundreds of employees and controlled millions in resources. By contrast, Rodgers's office director today has only 15 employees. However, there is one thing that has gotten much larger—the office director's salary.

Grade creep is a sign of, as well as a cause of, the slot syndrome: most vestigial slots are filled by employees in the middle grades, and an increase in the number of such employees fuels a need to find fancier-seeming slots to put them in, a need not tied to real-world demands.

Not only that, but grade creep actually pushes government away from the problems it should be solving. The higher end of the middle job grades is dominated by policy-making and policy-evaluating slots while the lower end bears the burden of most of the policy-*implementing* and policy-*enforcing* jobs. It's in these line positions that you'll find most of the overworked government employees, and their plight is considerably aggravated because they serve so many underworked people in staff positions. "As a street agent you don't have as much autonomy as people think," Len Cartwright, an FBI agent for 19 years, explains. "Say you're working a major criminal case, and they give you a background investigation"—a routine check into a federal job applicant's history—"the case gets put off until you get that done. That happens constantly. There's just tons of paperwork. For example, they need surveys, they need this, they need that. You have to stop everything you're doing in the field to furnish survey data about how much time you're spending on this particular case."

At HUD, Jane Gustafson's boss became obsessed with developing work plans—individual work plans, the regional counsel's work plan, and the regional office's work plan. The only problem was that none of this was coordinated with Washington's plans, which were the only ones that mattered. But that didn't stop the planning from becoming a major project. Gustafson estimates that although in the seventies, the office spent only 5 percent of its time on such internal matters, by the end of her tenure there, it spent 40 percent. While she was sitting in an office slaving away at her boss's nonsensical work plans, nobody was in the field to catch Marilyn Harrell skimming millions.

Again, if government organizations would get clear on what they are supposed to be doing—catching crooks, providing low-cost housing—and adopt a reward structure that reflects that, this trend could be reversed. Most of the government jobs that should be eliminated are top-of-the-middle staff slots; most of the jobs that should be added are middle-of-the-middle line slots. Under grade creep, government has become a football team with too many quarterbacks and not enough interior linemen. Teams like that don't win.

Headless Nails.

One retired military officer I spoke with gave a succinct answer when I asked him why businesses don't seem to have as much goldbricking as the government: "Simple. Businesses can fire people." As the saying goes, government workers are like headless nails—you can get them in, but you can't get them out. Many government offices are saddled with employees in their seventies who can't really cut the mustard anymore but who possess the virtual lifetime tenure that came in 1978 with the abolition of mandatory federal retirement. The old mandatory rule came about because most supervisors were uncomfortable with going up to old Joe and telling him he was no longer doing adequate work. But now, without that rule, courage to say that kind of thing is even more important. The absence of it has fostered the belief that government employees have an inherent "right" to their jobs.

Government workers who are totally incompetent or worse seem to have these "rights" too. A senior official at one agency told me that he had $300,000 in salary—10 percent of his office budget—tied up in nonproductive employees he can't fire. To get fired from a government job, says Derek Rodgers, "you have to be a drunk and refuse treatment or curse at your supervisor or hit somebody. Short of that, you can get away with about anything."

Scandalous, but true. While serving as the head of the civil rights office of HHS, Betty Lou Dotson took 126 trips to 38 U.S. cities and nine foreign countries at a cost to taxpayers of nearly $94,000. In the face of a congressional investigation, HHS removed Dotson from her job, but did not fire her. Instead, she was appointed to the Bicentennial Commission on the Constitution long enough for her to become eligible for her pension.

Daniel Stein got the same kind of ridiculous protection. Although he was convicted of attempted extortion almost two years ago, he's still employed at the State Department. As a convicted felon, he can't vote, but somehow he can pull down a GS-14's salary and, someday, a GS-14's pension too.

The way things stand now, to fire somebody from the civil service you have to compile a well-documented three-year record of the person's unsatisfactory performance. Most supervisors aren't likely to put in that kind of time. What they do instead the first chance they get is transfer nonperformers—just inflict them on another part of the government. (Sometimes the transfer even gives the headless nail a chance to drive in a little deeper: the first thing one malingerer did upon being transferred was to file a grievance against his new supervisor, so he could claim any subsequent adverse evaluation was merely retaliation.) The same logic that keeps no-loads and criminals employed also leads to promoting the undeserving, thus striking another blow for the slot syndrome and grade creep.

Business has begun to show that there is a way out of all this. Rosabeth Moss Kanter notes that a key step in Kodak's recovery was tying financial rewards more closely to individual performance and getting rid of unproductive managers while making it easier to bring in new, more promising ones from outside the company. She also points out that General Foods is having success with a "pay-for-skill" program, in which bonuses are earned by workers for each new job they learn. Government should aggressively open up its offices this way and get away from the three-year firing process and a hiring process that can sometimes last six to nine months. You can have promotion and retention rules that protect employee rights without punishing the organization for having common sense about job performance. Doing so will require government offices to identify their real goals, a good thing in any case.

As for the elderly, the alternative to age-based mandatory retirement—which is unfair to capable older employees—is not lifetime tenure. It's merit-based continuance. There is a place in government for an 80-year-old man who can do the job. There is no place in government for a 30-year-old man who cannot.

Meeting and Memo Mania.

When I ask a GAO auditor what he did during the previous workweek, here's what he tells me: "I went to three briefs on Capitol Hill, I attended three meetings with the Army materiel command. I got four briefs at the Army budget office. I went to a couple of internal staff meetings. And I played golf once." Actually, I don't begrudge the guy the round of golf; after a dozen meetings in five days, my head would explode. Part of the problem is that make-work *feels* just like real work.

But the question is, "How many of those get-togethers were really necessary?" It's the same with memos. You can get as bad a headache from reading 400 memos as you can from reading 400 pages of an important report. What's more, you can spend a huge amount of time crafting those memos—picking just the right phrasing or addressee list so that your boss replies to it, or endorses and forwards it, or just files it, depending on what you want to happen. And living on in the files as they do, memos are the perfect proof that you are busy. But how many of those memos are important for what the office is really supposed to accomplish and how many are, for example, explanations of when to use sex-specific job titles in official correspondence, notices of an upcoming review of all the different types of envelopes in the office, or evidence that a shaving waiver is being processed separately (all actual examples)?

"Memos are a very important thing," remarks Bob Michaels, who put in nine years as a foreign service officer, "in terms of covering your ass. You want to have the proof that so-and-so agreed or that you sought so-and-so's advice, so that if something goes wrong, you're covered."

But memos (and meetings) aren't just for coalition-building. They are also mechanisms by which the government worker can convince himself that he's not wasting his life and our taxes. "You start doing memos for everything," says Michaels. "It becomes a way of life. Memos for who you're going to have lunch with. Memos for where you're going to be at 3 o'clock in the afternoon." Perhaps the ultimate example of memos for everything is what the State Department calls a "memcon," a "memorandum of conversation." For almost any conversation with a non-American, says Michaels, "you were supposed to put down what you said, how that person replied, etc. A lot of people get into the habit of doing them because they enhance the apparent importance of their contacts. They make it look like you're out doing your job.

"You want to get your name on as many pieces of paper as possible," says Michaels. "It's like running

for office. There's a vast incentive to turn out repetitious documents, replications of reports that were done six months or a year earlier. It's the 'heft test.' Repeatedly, my colleagues and I were criticized for not turning out enough material. Even though the general consensus was that it was never read."

"My office did nothing but churn out policies very slowly, which no one heeded," recalls Elizabeth Carlson, formerly at EPA. "I was in charge of working on a memo outlining how the Clean Air Act should be implemented on certain federal lands. The people living on the land submitted a plan, and this came to us out of the regional office." After going several years without getting a definitive response from headquarters, someone in the regional office wrote a legal opinion. "She probably spent a year or two on that. Then somebody else at headquarters got the project. She probably spent a year revising the memo. Then it was given to me to revise." Why did this take so long? "Nobody cared. . . . Nothing was propelling it—what moves the agency mostly is litigation and congressional pressure." Eventually Carlson got the memo through all the hoops in Washington—all but one. "On the last day of one general counsel's tenure, we brought the memo for him to sign. And he said, 'I'm going to leave this to my successor even though everything looks fine.'" By the time the new man signed the memo, it had been sitting in *his* in-box for another year and a half.

Carlson says that much of her job was reviewing things, like letters going out in response to congressmen's inquiries. "You review the draft that somebody

Civil Servants Who Serve

Despite the federal workplace's general ineffectiveness, there are still good bureaucrats who know how to make their work count. Here are just two examples that readers have brought to the *Monthly*'s attention:

➤Terry Kincaid works for the Department of Interior's Bureau of Land Management in Idaho. He often works overtime without pay before, during, and after busy holiday weekends to clean up recreation sites. During a period of scarce funding, he has recruited a volunteer force including job trainees, Boy Scouts, juvenile offenders, and adult inmates; together they've built a boat dock, a picnic facility, and numerous new campsites. Without Kincaid's creative use of unpaid help, not only would none of these additions have been made, but in his supervisor's opinion, some of the recreation sites in the area would have been forced to close.

➤As an employee of the National Institute of Mental Health (NIMH), Paul Curtis implemented a checklist system to ascertain whether the nation's

Community Mental Health Centers were providing the patient services required by law in return for the federal funding they receive. With virtually no administrative help or secretarial support, Curtis discovered that many programs were flagrantly noncompliant and that therefore they owed the government money. After NIMH decided not to give Curtis legal support to recover this money, he took it upon himself to secure the help of attorneys at the Public Health Service. With their assistance, Curtis was able to recover $3.8 million.

So pervasive are the problems of the government workplace that it's nearly impossible to hear uplifting stories like these without also thinking of the downside. While Kincaid is pressed to the limit in the field, in Washington the Department of the Interior is thick with excess administrators. And since Curtis retired in 1986, NIMH hasn't recovered a single additional dollar.

—*S.S.*

in the program office has written, and that has to go up your chain of command too, and everybody has to circulate it. There's an office that's specifically responsible for circulating congressional inquiries. A lot of the responses were just EPA being evasive. Depending on the complexity of the answer—uh, evasion—responding would take anywhere from a month to four or five months.

"Everything took on a bureaucratic tone. We would have lunches and letters and memos about how people were going to choose offices. This went on for years. We were still working on a formula for who had priority—it was a very convoluted formula based on years of government service, and how long you had been at the agency, and what grade you were—when I left."

One major hidden cost of all these memos and meetings is that even the ambitious and talented (especially the ambitious and talented) have to read them and go to them. An office director at EPA tells me, "I'm probably a bad example because I actually have an exciting job," and that his condition for staying has been that "most of my personal time has been addressed towards current real issues." But when he begins accounting for his time, it becomes clear that there are lots of obstacles between him and real issues. "A typical day would include meetings with people at other government agencies, on a large committee that plans cooperative research strategies so that we can address issues together without balkanizing it, . . . internal staff meetings with our own staff here, and then a staff meeting twice a week with my boss and my peers."

In addition, "If you are ambitious and you want to get promoted," he explains, "you have to devote a lot of time to internal agency committees and task forces and personnel review boards and all sorts of other things like that, that allow you to become more broadly known around the agency." As examples of these "developmental assignments," he mentions a committee on the Earth Day celebrations, and task forces on personnel or compensation changes, on reorganization, and on improved budgeting. "You name it, and it's out there."

Here's the reverse logic of bad bureaucracy in all its glory. Too many people doing the same thing requires extra committees to coordinate their activities and extra assignments designed not to produce real output, but only to provide a chance to break out of a too-large employee pool.

Do these task forces ever accomplish anything? "People go off for hours at a time and for weeks at a time," says the EPA man, "and some document gets written, and whether or not it actually gets implemented, I don't know." However, there is at least one measurable consequence of all these meetings and committees. "The time for actually studying things and reading is just abysmally short."

"I would think that at certain periods we spent as much as half our time in meetings," a recently retired Marine lieutenant colonel says of his two tours of duty at the Pentagon. "With 20 or 30 people sitting around a table, going over a document line by line: 'Is everybody happy with 'cat'? Oh, you want 'feline'? Well, let's think about that."

"We had 58 offices that we had to report to that controlled our program," says a retired Air Force colonel who managed an aircraft project. "Let's say we decide to change the canopy on the aircraft. Probably we'd have 20 meetings on it and several hundred drawing packages and, oh, within 18 months there would be some kind of decision about whether to do it or not. . . . In the meantime, of course, you're still building the planes the way they were. If the reason you changed the canopy was that it was bad, you're building at least 18 months worth of planes with the old canopy that you will someday have to replace. And it was all paperwork, because you and me and an engineer could sort all this out in a week."

According to Paul Quentin, a civilian who has worked for the Pentagon since 1966 both full-time and as a consultant, "The amount of time spent on actual technical thought on what makes weapons good, as opposed to having meetings, writing memos, and writing propaganda for more money, is only about one-tenth." So why all the memos and meetings? "To increase the budget."

Janet Kostas, a GS-13, tells what happens to a letter when it comes into the Department of Commerce, where she works. "It tends to get held up right there at the secretary's level, but when it comes down through the undersecretary to our group we're only given three days to write [a response] and it usually gets done and then frequently it will sit for three or four weeks." Why the delay? "Once it gets back up to the undersecretary's office, it has to go around for clearance, it has to go around to all the assistant secretaries. It gets cleared by the division director, the office director, the deputy assistant secretary, the assistant secretary, laterally to three more assistant secretaries, then the undersecretary. About nine clearances before it gets to the secretary's level. And there's the general counsel, and congressional affairs."

Clearance delay is very hard to contain because some messages are important and no deputy assistant secretary is going to let the other 25 deputy assistant secretaries get a leg up on *those*. That's why no one I asked could remember any bureaucrat ever requesting to be dropped from a clearance list. Still, the key is not to get a lot of deputy assistant secretary's assistant's deputies off the list. It's to get them off the payroll.

Meetings and memos are a vital clue in the search for ways to make government leaner. If there are people in government office A who aren't busy all day, should we fire them all? No—because most of them do *something* worthwhile. If there are needs that are not currently being met by government office B, should we automatically hire new people in response? No—that way lies the slot syndrome. A better idea is to find the people in office A who can go over to help in office B. And one excellent way to find them is to determine who in A and B spend a lot of time at the same meetings, trading memos with each other, and talking together on the phone regularly. Once these people are identified, two wonderful things can happen: 1) Offices A and B can spend less time communicating about X and more time *doing* something about it; 2) The time saved by thus solving the problem with X can be applied in a similarly effective fashion to doing something about Y.

While there are undoubtedly personnel cuts to be made in most government offices—and the workers I talked to tended to estimate the number of useless personnel in their offices at between 25 and 50 percent—too much talk about bureaucratic reform emphasizes body counts: Department X announces (or is urged to announce) a hiring freeze to hold its staff to n employees; Department Y announces (or is urged to announce) that it will be laying off n employees. But going by body counts is just as much a fallacy in this war as it was in Vietnam. The issue is not how many bodies are served up, but what they did and what the ones still out there are doing. You don't achieve 1) and 2) above just by eliminating people—you do it by *consolidating functions.* In effect, most communications channels are like friction points in an engine. Paying attention to the wasted energy they throw off helps you improve the design.

Of course, the key to pulling off this kind of redesign of government is flexibility—especially since it must be achieved without switching the engine off. The experiences of the bureaucrats I talked to confirmed the need for government to avail itself of two of the most effective tools corporations have been using to become more competitive: decentralizing and contracting out. These measures are crucial for consolidating functions. Cutting down on checkpoints puts more responsibility in the hands of on-the-line managers, and temps make much more sense than tempos.

Although the government employs some part-time and temporary workers, federal regulations discourage the practice. The *Federal Personnel Manual* states that no agency can abolish a full-time position

> **A GS-13 tells what happens to a letter when it comes into her office at the Department of Commerce: "It gets cleared by the division director, the office director, the deputy assistant secretary, the assistant secretary, laterally to three more assistant secretaries, then the undersecretary. And there's the general counsel, and congressional affairs."**

in order to create a part-time one, and that no person employed full-time can be required to accept part-time employment instead. This sounds fair for jobs where the work is really there all the time—but there are a lot of government jobs where that is not true. Why should taxpayers support the difference in *those* jobs? Good candidates for a changeover to career part-time (workers in these jobs would have some health and pension benefits) are park rangers, whose work is seasonal, and air traffic controllers, whose workloads vary drastically during the day. Part-time positions can be especially good for workers. They provide income for many, such as students and parents of young children, who would otherwise have none. And part-time workers are by design task-oriented; you don't bring them in to go to pointless meetings.

Sleep and Creep Creep.
Perhaps the most pernicious feature of the slot syndrome, grade creep, headless nails, and meeting and memo mania is that they are silent killers of the spirit. Under these influences, good people become indifferent and indifferent people become bad. Government becomes worse.

"I get paid too much for what I do, which is checking off things and following procedures," confesses Sid Finn. "I've gotten so lethargic." "I have preached to my children," says a GSA employee, "that I would never want to see them make a career in government."

"You don't take on too many things that might put you in a grey area," confesses FBI agent Cartwright, who was once investigated by the U.S. attorney for the procedural violation he committed by giving $5 to a prisoner so he could make a long distance call to his dying mother. "So after a while, what you see is a lot of guys who are totally mediocre who gravitate to the top."

Bob Michaels, the former foreign service officer, points out that the competition for FSO slots is incredibly stiff—last year only 205 out of 13,903 applicants were accepted. As a result, many junior foreign service officers are quite skilled and eager to do great things. "And then," he explains, "they find they are not doing great things. . . . And yet they fought so hard to get in that they don't feel they can quit. After 10 years of this stuff, the work ethic gets sapped away. . . . You know you're probably not going to make ambassador, so then it's how are you going to get through the day as easy as possible? . . . People start looking through the want ads for real estate deals, start calling their stockbroker five or six times a day . . . some guys have televisions in their offices."

Janet Kostas paints a similar picture: "There are people that I work with today who are every bit as competent and intelligent and hard-working as the people I worked with at [she names a large corporation], but the average person isn't. I can't think of anybody at [that company] who was sitting around not busy. Here they periodically write a briefing paper for the undersecretary if someone is coming in to meet him"—a two- or three-page outline giving the background on a problem a visitor is coming to talk about. "If you're knowledgeable in your field, it shouldn't take more than several hours," explains Kostas. "But they feel overworked if they get one a week because they're not used to it anymore.

"You can't see why it would benefit you to work harder for the rest of the day. . . . Most people won't take the extra initiative. Most people will just grab the extra time and do their checkbook or write a letter. Ten years ago, I would have gone looking for something to do with the extra two hours at the end of the day." It's especially significant to hear this from a woman who will tell you in an instant why she came into government—"It was Kennedy: 'Ask not what your country can do for you. . . .' Now, I would take that time to get something else done for myself, or just unwind a bit."

Besides the moral uplift that would come from doing away with the slot syndrome and all that goes with it through personnel cuts, job consolidation, and the aggressive use of part-time employees, there would be a great economic benefit as well. Last year, civilian government salaries totaled $85 billion. And under typical life expectancies, all those GS-14s and O-5s out there will eventually draw around $1 million apiece in total pension income. In addition, the government sets requirements for the office space and equipment and travel per diem and geographical pay adjustments, etc., proportionally due these service grades—requirements that are just as ironclad as salaries and pensions. That's why, for instance, the amount of office space per civilian government employee has gone up 66 percent since 1965. So, undertaking the above reforms could save billions.

Despite these spiritual and material advantages, the cause of government personnel reform has remained completely stalled. Why? Well, first, there's the Washington "it's too hard" syndrome—a tendency that is aggravated by a long history of no change and by the growing complacency of even the good people inside the system. Second, there's the active resistance of all those not-so-good people inside the system. The formidable job protections in the civil service were adopted to shield against the possible excesses of the spoils system, but they have also encouraged many government employees to think they have "rights" to a job that take precedence over the public interest. One of the biggest obstacles to streamlining government is this wrongheaded belief that the civil service is not a tool for doing what needs to be done, but a jobs program.

The politicians who could bring about the needed changes are only too aware that the headless nails can still draw blood. An interesting local example of this came recently in the D.C. mayor's primary race. One candidate kicked off his campaign by pledging to reduce what he criticized as a bloated local government, but retreated after receiving numerous complaints from city workers, saying he was "not going to get into this numbers game." Of the five announced Democratic candidates in the race, only one has flatly proposed a substantial job cut. She is lagging behind the rest of the candidates, who appear less concerned with overstaffing than with the potential endorsements of the 15 unions representing city workers. This is just a microcosm of the problem facing congressmen and senators, who worry about how hard it would be to run against the various federal employees' unions. There is a solution, though: political courage. If even just a few key elected officials would show some, the federal government could be made to work again.

Up against D. Wall

It's a shame that "bureaucrat" has a negative connotation (my dictionary *defines* a bureaucrat as "a government official who follows a narrow rigid formal routine . . . ") because government will never improve without good ones. But almost all the bureaucrats I spoke with were frustrated by their office's tendency to drift away from real problems into make-believe. Paul Quentin summed up the problem when he told me that the workaday world of the GS-15s and 0-6s at the Pentagon isn't about winning in combat: "It's about managing technology, it's managing systems, it's managing personnel, it's managing computers," he explains. "You use the words 'victory' and 'defeat' in the Pentagon, and people look at you a little funny."

For the people Quentin is talking about—people who change the subject from what they ought to think about to what's easier to think about and who in the process lose sight of their real purpose—'bureaucrat' is way too good a word. You want the strongest possible expletive for that kind of person.

If you think that an interest in government bureaucracy is slightly quaint, just remember that Danny Wall is that kind of person. Michael Binstein reported in *Regardie's* magazine that when Wall took over the job of overseeing the rapidly deteriorating S&Ls, "he decided that the bank board's headquarters needed a face-lift. So instead of putting out financial fires, he did housekeeping. He replaced and rearranged furniture. He ordered a new desk phone because the color of his didn't match the shoulder rest. He loved to redraw organizational charts. . . . One of Wall's first requests was to call for a thorough inspection of the building. With engineers in tow, he noted the changes he wanted made. 'I proceeded with the building supervision people just to try to get things going in sprucing up things so that it was a more businesslike environment,' [Wall] explains. 'There were letters missing from the sign downstairs. Nobody paid any attention to that.'" And Wall recently told Joseph Nocera of *Esquire* that "I never lost any sleep. I knew I had done my best."

Danny Wall is a very expensive variant of the make-believing bureaucrat. But there's lots more where he came from. Let's get them before they get us, and leave government in the hands of those who know what it means to have done their best. □

Article 2. The Education of Rockwell Schnabel
by Deborah Baldwin

This article profiles the career of Rockwell Schnabel, head of the U.S. Travel and Tourism Administration, a small but savvy opponent of wasteful government spending. Although three presidents have sought to close its doors, all three have failed. Headquartered within the U.S. Department of Commerce, the agency operates on a shoestring budget, while waging open warfare against its critics. Its future will depend on an unlikely ally, George Bush, who, like his predecessor, might be expected to view the agency as politically expendable. However, USTTA has won a strong advocate in its newest chief, Rockwell Schnabel, who admits that he has been won over to the cause. One of the founders of Citizens for America—a lobby group that challenges "wasteful" government spending—Schnabel finds himself in the hot seat as he leads the charge for his embattled agency.

Rockwell A. Schnabel folds his lanky body into a government-issue chair and gazes across a desk the approximate size of a small landing strip. Actually, he doesn't sit in his chair so much as perch on the edge of it, as if ready to take off.

"There are certain people who like to sit on the beach," he says when asked what inspired him to accept his hectic new job as U.S. travel czar. "I was happy to keep running."

Fate and political connections have put Schnabel in charge of a federal fiefdom called the U.S. Travel and Tourism Administration (USTTA), by all accounts one of the tiniest and toughest agencies ever to outwit opponents of government spending. Three presidents have tried to shut it down; all three failed. Ensconced within the U.S. Department of Commerce, a sprawling empire that straddles an entire block of downtown Washington, the USTTA is not so much the mouse that roared as the mouse that prevailed, subsisting on crumbs from the federal groaning board while running a guerrilla war against its foes.

Now President George Bush must help decide its fu-

Washington Ways and Means

ture, and as heir to the Reagan administration's budget-balancing mandate he might be expected to propose USTTA's elimination too. But the travel agency has found an advocate in its newest chief, who confesses that he has become something of a convert to the cause. "It is true that if you don't know the workings of a particular department it's easier to say it does not have a function," says Schnabel, by vocation an investment banker and by avocation a conservative political activist. "Once you learn about its functions you change your perspective."

An unlikely point man in the battle to ensure government support for anything — he was one of 150 founders of Citizens for America, which lobbies against "wasteful" government spending — Schnabel now finds himself in the throes of an agency's continuing struggle for survival. Interviewed several months before the administration's budget requests were put on paper, he was reluctant to say where the White House would come down on the USTTA matter. But he hinted that he might have helped open the president's eyes. "I have a sense he thinks it's important," Schnabel says, adding with a smile, "He

From *Common Cause Magazine,* January/February 1990, p. 24. © 1990 Common Cause Magazine, 2030 M St. NW, Washington DC 20036.

knows we're out there hustling."

There's something for everybody in this classic tale of Washington seduction, in which our hero, the starry-eyed ideologue, is wooed by powerful congressmen, zealous lobbyists and bureaucratic survival artists. Together they manage to fend off a key opponent, the deficit-conscious White House Office of Management and Budget (OMB), and save the life of an agency.

Tiny USTTA's roots go back to the early 1960s, when federal programs started blossoming along the Potomac River like so many perennials. Congress created the U.S. Travel Service to encourage foreigners to come to the United States, an effort that mainly involved publishing brochures and distributing them overseas. Before long, however, the program developed a political constituency, which in turn led to an interest on Capitol Hill. During the 1970s congressional travel subcommittees were created to help look after the Travel Service, as was a wildly popular congressional Travel and Tourism Caucus, which took funds from the travel industry. (Widespread criticism compelled the House of Representatives to bar direct outside funding for all caucuses in 1983; they are now taxpayer-supported.)

But storm clouds were already gathering at OMB. Things looked bad for the Travel Service when President Gerald Ford's budget meisters couldn't come up with a rationale for spending federal dollars promoting an industry that could easily afford to promote itself. OMB tried to cut the service's budget; under President Jimmy Carter, it tried to ax it altogether. But such threats only seemed to strengthen the will of the service and its small army of supporters in the industry and on Capitol Hill. And so the Travel Service lived on.

In an article in January 1981 *The Washington Post* predicted — correctly, as it turned out — that even President Reagan would have a hard time standing up to this particular iron triangle. In a direct challenge to Reagan's tight-fisted OMB director, David Stockman, the Senate generated legislation elevating the service to the status of an independent agency, to be governed by an industry-dominated advisory board and empowered to sidestep OMB by submitting its budget requests and legislative recommendations directly to Capitol Hill. Stockman went ballistic, but when Congress came up with a weaker bill, giving OMB control (although barring it from reducing the size of the service's overseas staff), he soon caved in.

Thus was the U.S. Travel and Tourism Administration born and placed under the protective wing of the Commerce Department.

Not that USTTA will ever be rich by government standards. Taking up only two modest corridors on the ground floor of Commerce, a long walk and elevator ride away from the boulevard-like hallway that leads up to the secretary's office on the fifth floor, USTTA consumes a mere $14 million out of a total department budget of $2.8 billion — the Washington equivalent of "a rounding error," sniffs one government budget analyst. A quick trip through the warren of crowded USTTA offices where civil servants actually perform the agency's work does not exactly call to mind the word "waste." And with a worldwide staff of only 90, USTTA barely qualifies as a bureaucracy. In contrast, Commerce as a whole employs nearly 39,000.

But if USTTA is a mere speck on the federal landscape, it has evolved into a symbol for critics and supporters alike. An apt example of the kinds of programs Citizens for America set out to eliminate in a 1986 nationwide campaign, it was also a target of the Heritage Foundation in its massive annual work, *Mandate for Leadership*. A spokesman for the foundation calls USTTA's very existence "absurd," arguing that the airline, hotel and other affected industries ought to cough up their own money to promote U.S. tourist attractions overseas.

As Rep. John Dingell (D-Mich.) once put it, "[W]hen you're cutting programs involving health, welfare, research . . . we could no longer justify the expenditures of public funds for this purpose." For these and other reasons Congress hasn't passed legislation actually authorizing the agency since

1981, a mainly symbolic gesture that nevertheless pains its supporters.

USTTA survives because whenever the pressures of the Gramm-Rudman-Hollings budget measure persuade the House of Representatives to zero out the little agency, the Senate comes to the rescue, led by a number of former state governors who are passionate on the subject of tourism's role in providing jobs back home. Among them is the very same budget-cutting Sen. Ernest Hollings (D-S.C.), chairman of the Commerce Committee (and former South Carolina governor). Hollings personally sees to it that funding is restored when USTTA comes before the Senate subcommittee on Commerce appropriations — which he also chairs.

The multibillion-dollar travel industry throws its support behind USTTA, too, partly because it is alarmed by periodic OMB proposals to fund USTTA out of fees levied on the industry — a concept Hollings calls a "a cockamamie tax scheme" — but also because it's hard for an industry to object to a taxpayer-funded effort to bring in more customers. The agency "does the Lord's work," according to American Express spokesman Matthew Stover. Warming to the subject during congressional testimony in October, AmEx's Jonathan Linen, who serves on USTTA's advisory board, made this plea: "Let us now not let sincerity, even sincerity rooted in genuine concern for the federal budget deficit and the many hard choices that must be made — let us not have sincerity make us losers."

If USTTA is small, it nonetheless has the trappings of a duchy. Congress installed an under secretary at the helm and created a post for an assistant secretary to run its marketing programs, mighty titles for so minute an enterprise. Unlike the average government-program director, Under Secretary Schnabel is only two rungs down

from the secretary, himself only one down from the president. Government regulations further allow the under secretary to roost in a nicely carpeted 500-square-foot office outfitted with a full complement of heavy furniture. On the walls are large, smiling portraits of Secretary of Commerce Robert Mosbacher and President George Bush.

The White House doesn't just give away such jobs: They are awarded to party loyalists and major campaign contributors, and Schnabel is no exception.

Born in Holland 52 years ago, he came to the United States in the 1950s. By the mid-'80s he was deputy chairman of the board of Morgan, Olmstead, Kennedy & Gardner, an investment banking firm in Los Angeles, and had served as an honorary consul for the government of South Africa, which presented him with its prestigious Commander of Hope award at a banquet in Los Angeles in 1981.

He had also become active in politics, and with his wife Marna (and in one case their three children) contributed generously to conservative candidates and causes, ranging from supply-side economist Arthur Laffer's quixotic run for the Senate in 1986 to the primary campaigns of several Republican presidential candidates in 1988.

In 1983 the Schnabels signed up as founders of Citizens for America, a group that called itself "President Reagan's Grassroots Citizens Lobby." Chaired by conservative Republican Lew Lehrman, the drug-store entrepreneur who poured $7 million of his own money into a campaign against New York Gov. Mario Cuomo, CFA was designed to build constituent pressure in congressional districts to further Reagan's agenda, including its goal of slashing government funding for just about everything outside the Pentagon. Members of Congress who failed to go along were awarded "Congressional Excess Cards."

But Schnabel wasn't one to let ideological distaste for government stand in the way of a desirable political appointment. Made ambassador to Finland in 1985, he promptly sold his interest in Morgan, Olmstead and moved his family to Helsinki, leaving behind a Frank Gehry-designed luxury home then under construction in Brentwood, Calif. "I had been in the business world for 25 years and had done pretty much what I'd wanted to do," Schnabel explains. "I was very much interested in doing something with the United States government, particularly in the field of international diplomacy." To mark the occasion, Citizens for America threw a reception for him at the State Department.

The Schnabels remained enthusiastic campaign contributors, ultimately advancing more than $126,000 toward the election of George Bush. Ambassador Schnabel was a member of Team 100, an elite corps of $100,000 donors to the Bush election effort, and thus gained preferred status as a candidate for a political appointment. He was rumored to be seeking the number one position at the Export-Import Bank, but when he got the call during inauguration week, it was for the job at USTTA. According to news reports, Schnabel ("Rock" to his friends, "Mr. Ambassador" to the rest of us) had beat out at least two other important travel czar wannabes when his friend Mosbacher, finance chairman for Bush's presidential campaign, made him his personal pick.

He's not the only well-connected appointee. Bush and Mosbacher — who once publicly complained that not enough desirable positions in the administration were being made available to key party donors — filled more than 150 political slots at the Commerce Department. While many appointees bring years of experience to their jobs, others obviously are being thanked for helping out during the campaign. Tiny USTTA alone had openings for four political appointees, including one former American Express official who had served as a fulltime volunteer in the Business Coalition Division of the Bush-Quayle campaign.

"The appointees like these jobs because they're sexy sounding and you don't have to have [unique] skills," says one knowledgeable insider who is critical of the disproportionate number of top jobs at Commerce filled by appointees. "The administration turns these slots into 'policy' jobs because theoretically it's appropriate for political appointees to have them, but it would make more sense to have them be 'nuts and bolts' jobs filled by civil servants. That was proposed last year but the White House objected. They

like it the way it is because they can dump 40 people into [Commerce's International Trade Administration] alone."

Once on the inside, political appointees tend to get caught up in the spirit of the place. "We like to say there are no conservatives in government," deadpans one civil servant at Commerce. "They all become wild-eyed spenders."

Surrounded by a program's boosters and armed with arguments that have been carefully honed and handed down, a political appointee may wake up one day an articulate advocate for expansion. Schnabel, for one, no sooner had taken off his coat and made himself at home before internally requesting a 58-percent budget hike for his $14 million agency, sources say; he's also been talking up the idea of opening a USTTA office in Korea. Mosbacher apparently persuaded him to cut his proposal from $24 million to $17 million before sending it to OMB, where analysts shook their green eye shades in dismay. In its fiscal 1990 proposals, OMB had gone on record in favor of collecting fees from industry and doing away with USTTA's government appropriation altogether.

Today the main way Schnabel gets to use his diplomatic skills is not overseas but on Capitol Hill, where he must simultaneously lead his agency into battle for more funds and pull back when OMB issues the order to retreat. Such pressures, rampant when money is tight, lead to ritualized mini-dramas during congressional hearings on an agency's activities: The loyal administration official shares his modest OMB-sanctioned vision of what his agency's requirements might be, then members of the oversight committee rail about the important job that remains to be done. The script calls for the official to sit there politely, looking needy, while the members hector him to be more forceful.

That's what happened when Schna-

bel was asked to testify at hearings in October before the Senate tourism subcommittee. Asked to say something enthusiastic about the subcommittee's pet "tourism policy" bill, which would enlarge USTTA's mission, he looked stymied, apparently unable to decide whether to stick to his wishy-washy OMB-censored testimony or toss it aside. "He's new to this war," one sympathetic Senate aide said later.

But he must be a quick study. In early December OMB finally signaled defeat, dropping its fee scheme and okaying a fiscal 1991 USTTA budget request of $14 million.

As even USTTA's biggest defenders will admit, the single greatest factor in boosting the influx of foreign travelers isn't advertising and brochures but the state of the U.S. dollar. As it weakens, foreign currency grows stronger, drawing foreigners inexorably toward America's single greatest cultural contribution: the shopping mall.

The current boom — more than 40 million foreign tourists are expected to cross U.S. borders in 1990, bearing nearly $50 billion — cuts both ways. On one hand it makes USTTA look like a huge success; on the other, critics wonder how $14 million can have had much influence on a promotional effort that was wallowing (well, wading) in money to begin with. Companies like Pan Am and Hilton Hotels spend heavily to promote tourism, and even AT&T is helping the cause, presumably because travelers make lots of long-distance calls. Because tourism is a top-three industry in 35 states, state lawmakers set aside money for promotion too: South Carolina spends $8.5 million annually and maintains a tourism office in Frankfurt, West Germany, and Arkansas — not widely known as a travel hot spot — will spend about $6.5 million next year. Las Vegas has an annual promotion budget of $10 million — and it isn't even a state.

"The problem with USTTA is you never know when it's reached its goal," according to one government budget analyst who spoke off the record. "When the dollar is strong and it's expensive for people to come here, the argument is to spend more and promote harder. When the dollar is weak and lots of people come, the argument is to spend more because now's the time when we have the opportunity."

An agency in constant search of self-justification, USTTA has its small research staff working overtime to churn out the kinds of statistics that have made number-crunching, Washington-style, famous. One typical USTTA bar graph documents a 180-percent upswing in visits by foreigners to Alabama between 1985 and 1987 (raw figures not included). Chart after chart prove tourism is not only promotion-worthy but that USTTA efforts help improve the economy. "There are 38 million people coming from abroad," declares Schnabel, "and they're spending in excess of $44 billion. That is the biggest number we've ever seen and USTTA plays a very definite role in that effort." Not long ago the agency devised a new formula for computing the impact of tourism that suggests every dollar invested in promotion yields even more than previously thought.

In what has virtually become a mantra around its headquarters, USTTA says it aims "to increase U.S. export earnings through trade in tourism." Put another way — which the agency does repeatedly — the U.S. earns more in exports by hosting foreign tourists than it does through agriculture. ("And look how big the Agriculture Department is. . . . ")

In USTTA's trendy economic development scenario, the globe is swarming with well-to-do Japanese, Germans and (apparently) Koreans as well, all in search of fresh vistas. Fondly referring to the Germans as "great wanderers," Aubrey King, executive director of a 33-member travel-industry lobbying coalition, argues that attracting them "pays off" because Germans pour money into areas adjacent to our national parks. Unfortunately, other nations are eager to have the Germans too. As a popular refrain among USTTA advocates has it, Pakistan and Thailand spend more per capita on tourism promotion than the United States. Or, to turn once more to AmEx's quotable Jonathan Linen, "There are 10 million Japanese who are traveling internationally every year

and we are not getting our fair share."

Loaded down with strong foreign currency that travels further in America than it does in Tokyo or Munich, foreigners suggest images of mobile gold mines, particularly in areas of the country where heavy industry has died out. What we lose to the Japanese by buying Mitsubishis and VCRs we can make up in sales of souvenirs and pancake breakfasts — or so the thinking goes.

Which brings us to another USTTA obsession — rural tourism. This cause célèbre arose, no doubt coincidentally, around the same time non-rural areas started carrying out so much promotion on their own that USTTA almost seemed superfluous. Now enthusiasts burble about the pull of America's hinterlands, where they say foreigners seek exposure to authentic American subcultures.

Naturally, the first step is to introduce foreigners to the idea, and that's where USTTA's 10 overseas offices come in. For years they've stocked brochures advertising the obvious watering holes like New York and San Francisco. Now the message is "Catch the Spirit," and the targeted hotspots are regional areas of "the Heartland."

All roads, of course, lead from Capitol Hill, which deserves the credit for the rural tourism concept. In 1988 tourism subcommittee chair Rep. Ike Skelton (D-Mo.) pushed for a $250,000 USTTA study of rural tourism and small business, which (again, no doubt coincidentally) USTTA produced with the help of the University of Missouri. Reading much like a term paper written by a college student who isn't at all sure why he was given this assignment, the resulting analysis comes down — surprise, surprise — resoundingly in favor of developing a "federal policy on rural tourism."

Parochialism isn't peculiar to the House; senators from the Heartland

are also vying for attention. As tourism subcommittee Chair Jay Rockefeller (D-W.Va.) pointedly remarked to Schnabel during the October hearing on the proposed tourism policy bill, "Sens. Bryan, Burns and I all represent states that are not on an ocean." That's Richard Bryan, of tourist-rich Nevada, a moving force behind a proposed federal "rural tourism foundation"; Conrad Burns, of tourist-lusting Montana; and former Gov. Rockefeller, of economically wracked West Virginia, who helped line up $100,000 in federal funds to do a feasibility study of converting his state's coalmine territory into a nine-town tourist attraction.

As one USTTA official privately concedes, the notion that Japanese tourists will respond to brochures by jumping on buses bound for homespun Missouri "is a bit of a stretch." But that hasn't stopped Schnabel from gamely doing his best to fulfill his agency's latest marching orders. The tall, energetic travel czar, who has the appearance of someone about to take flight partly because he almost always is, zooms about the globe to drum up interest, recently hitting Mexico City and Tokyo in the space of a month. He says USTTA's efforts are paying off: On a visit to remote northern Montana, he found evidence that Japanese couples — an astounding 85 percent of whom are said to honeymoon abroad — and German tourists like nothing more than to vacation on an authentic American dude ranch. He also points to two projects aimed at promoting travel along old frontier trails in states like Montana and the Dakotas. "The Japanese have taken to it," he insists. "They like to come to the Heartland."

A man who is clearly caught up in the game, Schnabel seems to be settling in to Washington and quickly learning its ways. While maintaining his family home in California, he paid $835,000 this year for a house in fashionable Georgetown. "I'm basically a skeptical businessman and I had to be shown," he says of his government mission. But these days, "I feel like a very strong believer and I'm happy about it, my heart is in it."

Fondly referring to his new place of business, he adds, "I can clearly say — and it may be self-serving — there is without any doubt a function for it." ◆

Article 3. To Live and Die in L.A.
by David Ferrell

No doubt, AIDS is a tragic disease—a physical and psychological nightmare for those unfortunate enough to fall victim to its ravages. But the privation does not stop there. Indeed, many AIDS patients, in such urban communities as Los Angeles, California, are forced to deal with a confusing and sometimes unfeeling public health system, which makes it difficult if not impossible to receive prompt attention. In Los Angeles, for example, the waiting list for outpatient care may be as long as four months. The delay is particularly serious, since the average AIDS patient lives twenty-two months after diagnosis. In addition, AIDS victims are caught in the vice of insensitive doctors, uncaring insurance companies, inadequate counseling, insufficient facilities, and cumbersome rules and regulations.

KIMON BEAZLIE MANAGED to reach his mid-40s retaining a free spirit and unflagging energy. He was a Hollywood costume designer with stocky good looks, almond brown eyes and a penchant for six-day workweeks—a habit that earned him, in good times, as much as $80,000 a year. In off hours, he was an amateur rock climber and a breeder of exotic birds. He wore his hair in a style befitting his Hawaiian descent: a thick, dark mane hanging to his waist.

But one night last summer, Beazlie's life took a sharp turn. He was brushing his teeth when pain stabbed the roof of his mouth—a canker sore, he thought, craning to look. What he found, instead, was something startling: Behind a front tooth hung a bulbous mass. A second one, nearly identical, hung at the rear of his mouth. Beazlie tilted closer to the mirror, wondering, "Oh, my God, what is *that?*"

The discovery—it would turn out to be Kaposi's sarcoma, a rare skin cancer—thrust Beazlie into the world of AIDS. It would turn his life completely around, shutting off his past as if a steel curtain had clanged down behind him. In failing health, Kimon Beazlie surrendered his job, lost his health insurance and fell out of touch with many friends in the movie and television industries.

In a series of jolting events, he found out what it is like to live as an AIDS patient in Los Angeles County. The experience, he learned, just as so many others learn, is a relentless nightmare; it is a bitter story of government snafus and family prejudices, tears and T cells, compassion and profound hurt. While one faces death and grasps desperately for time, fighting the medical bureaucracy can be almost as difficult and debilitating as the disease. Beazlie is one of thousands who, as the moments of his life slip away, has grown angry and cynical about the under-funded, conservatively administered county system, which is ranked among the worst in the nation at dealing with the AIDS epidemic.

"In Los Angeles, where the numbers [of infected persons] are increasing daily—by enormous leaps—it is startling to see the level of denial or detachment [that the county has shown]," says Dr. June Osborn, chairwoman of the National Commission on AIDS. During special hearings held in Los Angeles earlier this year, Osborn and other commission members castigated the Board of Supervisors for what they considered chronic shortfalls in funding and commitment to AIDS programs. "There was a sense that local government was trying to distance itself from the epidemic as if it was somebody else's problem," she says.

Already, the countywide death toll from AIDS has reached 7,000. And the future looks worse. According to the county's estimates, 2,800 patients are now fighting the disease, and that number is expected to climb to 24,000 in three years. A total of 112,000 people in Los Angeles are believed to be infected with the deadly virus; they, too, are living on borrowed time.

Each faces daunting hurdles. The disease is one thing: Acquired immune deficiency syndrome is particularly pitiless—a dark, ever-deepening tunnel of physical and psychological horrors. The average AIDS patient lives 22 months after diagnosis, but that, like nearly every other aspect of the disease, is unpredictable. The eroded immune system tends to break down under stress, or in reaction to powerful, toxic medications designed to control the virus. AIDS allows any number of infections to hit where the patient is weakest, often creating a grim cycle of illness, recovery and deeper illness.

Moreover, at this time of extreme frailty, the person with AIDS must master the tricky and sometimes cruel ropes of the public health system. The waiting list for outpatient care at Los Angeles County-USC Medical Center—the hub of the county's AIDS treatment program—can be as long as four months, long enough for some patients to seriously weaken or even die. The clinic, which treats people who cannot afford private care, was handling 400 patients a month just a few years ago; now the number exceeds 2,000, rendering personalized care all but impossible. A new three-story clinic, with four times the medical examining rooms and a capacity for 3,500 patients, was expected to open this year. But faulty initial designs have delayed the target date to next spring.

Beazlie, who sought health care at County-USC after losing his private insurance, is one of five patients who agreed to share a chronicle of what it is like to deal with life as an AIDS patient in Los Angeles. Each of the five faced different problems and responded with different attitudes, emotions and fears. A maverick among them, who dropped out of treatment against his doctor's advice, Beazlie is the most disillusioned.

"The county is a very unfeeling group," he says matter-of-factly. "You get the impression, after a while, that you're just delivering a slab of meat for them to do their little thing on."

As he talks, Beazlie strolls through County-USC's crowded, windowless outpatient clinic, known as 5P21. The clinic is unique in Los Angeles—the only full-time public clinic for AIDS treatment as well as the county's center for experimental drug research into the disease. In jeans, a turtleneck shirt and three-day growth of beard, Beazlie moves familiarly through the pale-yellow hallways.

The halls are as long as 70 yards, lined with wood benches crowded with men awaiting treatment. In their 30s mostly, they form an eerie sight: Hollow-faced, many of them move with the trembling slowness of the elderly. Beazlie strides past them, past an overhead television, and enters a section of hallway blocked by two metal chairs lashed together with a sign: "Restricted area: Only those patients receiving treatment allowed beyond this point."

Here, on Thursdays, Kaposi's sarcoma patients like Beazlie line up, a dozen or so at a time in the hallway, for intravenous blood transfusions and chemotherapy. "You have people just starting out, trying to be optimistic, sitting next to people who are a breath away from being dead," Beazlie says, gesturing to the metal IV racks, now idle. "It's like, 'This is where you're going . . . . You're going to die.'"

Moments later, a patient trying to sit in a wheelchair collapses to the floor. "Loss of motor control," Beazlie explains calmly, seemingly inured to such scenes. He sees a nurse he knows and lavishes praise ("She can find veins that don't exist!") and later talks enthusiastically about a doctor, just one of many unsung heroes here, who shows promise "as a healer."

Beazlie has learned to talk dispassionately about his own eventual death. He forecasts it by year's end because his sarcoma is eating at his insides: "There are days when I can't get out of bed. If I get a coughing spasm, I faint. I hyperventilate. You just learn to deal. That's what life is all about, anyway. We're just getting a concentrated crash course on dealing."

Then, a new wheelchair rolls in. In it is an angular young man with sandy brown hair so delicate it might belong to a child. His legs are stick-thin. In his expressionless face are wide, staring eyes—the eyes of someone who sees but does not understand. It is a young man whom Beazlie recognizes, someone he knows from long-ago visits here. Beazlie's eyes fill with tears.

"I just haven't seen him in a while," he says, his voice breaking. "He's only 24. He's a street kid, has no family. And he's really gotten bad." And for a long moment, Kimon Beazlie cannot speak.

SILVIO R. HERNANDEZ, 59, is known to friends as Rudy —notwithstanding a mix-up on his birth records, he was named after Rudolph Valentino. He fled Cuba as a young man, studied briefly at Louisiana State University and came west in the early 1970s, drawn by the excitement that California offers. Charming and affable, he took an apartment in the burgeoning gay community near the Sunset Strip and surrounded himself with artwork and film posters. He managed a storage company, and his health was good except for bouts of asthma.

Then one evening four years ago, as he watched television, Hernandez was seized by a galvanizing sensation "like a positive and negative cable coming together" in his head. The jolt lasted several seconds, followed moments later by another one. Screaming, he summoned help by telephone and was rushed to a hospital emergency room.

The diagnosis was vertigo—an unexplained dizziness. For several days, Hernandez was confined to a hospital room, his equilibrium so poor he had difficulty reaching the bathroom. Aware that he belonged to a high-risk group because he was gay, he asked to be tested for the human immunodeficiency virus.

The results were positive. For a year, Hernandez stayed home on disability because of the vertigo. Doctors could never link the HIV virus with the strange episode of dizziness, but soon Hernandez experienced other health problems: His asthma worsened; he couldn't walk three blocks without gasping for breath. Bursitis set in. He could not raise his arm over his head. He became so fatigued he sometimes could not pick up light objects from the floor.

> Hernandez's claim for Social Security benefits was answered in four months: *Denied.*

He fretted incessantly that the virus, once dormant in his blood, was now attacking. Months passed, and a particularly severe asthma attack nearly suffocated him. He was taken again to an emergency room. Psychologically, the torment grew, day and night, an unshakable curse that left him crying, unable to sleep.

"Already, I was getting a lot of emotion," Hernandez says in a voice that still sings with a Cuban accent. "I was dealing with the fact I was going to die. You wake up at 1 or 2 in the morning and you start *thinking, thinking, thinking.* You cannot go back to sleep for three or four hours. You wake up in the morning and you are so tired because you spent four hours at night thinking."

As his year of state disability neared an end, Hernandez ran head-on into the first of the insurance problems that would plague him for years. His private health-care provider, which had been charging $600 a month for coverage, raised his premiums to $1,000. A $50-a-month supplemental policy from another company was canceled because he lived in a "high-risk" neighborhood.

Hernandez suspects that the insurance companies learned of his HIV diagnosis through his medical records. The huge increase in premiums forced him to drop his private coverage, and in early 1987, a year after his attack of vertigo, Hernandez boarded a bus for East Los Angeles. The trip to County-USC Medical Center, including a transfer downtown, took 90 minutes, and the wait inside 5P21, even with an appointment, was often three hours. But Hernandez had heard that the medical care, once you got it, was excellent.

One of his first experiences was a laboratory blood test of his T-4 helper cells, the agents of the immune system that are attacked by the HIV virus. Once in the cell, the virus replicates, destroying the cell in the process. Measuring the T-cell counts gives doctors a rough—and sometimes suspect—barometer of the health of the immune system. Healthy human blood contains 800 to 1,200 or more T-4 cells per cubic millimeter. In AIDS patients, the counts are often dramatically lower, and can fluctuate widely even in a single patient. Under current guidelines, patients can begin receiving AZT—the relatively effective, but potentially toxic drug for slowing the replication of the virus—when T-cell counts drop below 500, or when full-blown AIDS is diagnosed.

At the time of Hernandez's test, however, AZT was not prescribed until T-cell levels fell below 200. Hernandez's reading was 219. "I was not too familiar with the T-cell situation," he recalls. "I say, 'What does that mean?' [The doctors] say, 'You are OK.'"

The pronouncement was something Hernandez had difficulty believing. His T cells, monitored every three months, showed an improvement to more than 400 in a subsequent test, but his health was getting worse. He had difficulty walking because of pain, and at night he woke up sweating and feverish. He had diarrhea continually, and again he was rushed to the emergency room with an asthma attack.

A records clerk at County-USC Medical Center signed a letter for Hernandez in September, 1988, declaring him medically disabled. Armed with that, Silvio Hernandez took the first step in his long dealings with the government bureaucracy: He applied for Social Security benefits, a process that usually takes four months.

TIM WALSH TOOK STOCK of his fast-paced life in the summer of 1987 and told himself: *You've got to slow down.* He was 25, a lanky kid from Westlake Village with thin, brown hair and large, serious eyes. He worked as a computer specialist at a law firm and kept a social calendar packed with events—gourmet meals that he cooked at home, traveling, parties. He and his lover, a transplanted Northern Californian named Ron Satora, shared a West Hollywood apartment near the night life.

Like Hernandez, Walsh was aware that he belonged to a high-risk group in a city that was being hit harder by the epidemic than anywhere in Southern California. Walsh also was feeling ill—anemic, feverish. His bones ached. A burning sensation developed in his throat and spread down his esophagus, making it difficult to swallow even water. He started losing weight. Like many gay men, he paid enormous attention to each real or imagined change in his physiology, and yet he argued with himself: He felt he was just running himself ragged.

A vacation would help, he decided. He had blood drawn for an HIV test and left for Waikiki with the sandy-haired Satora, a bank operations specialist and prize-winning amateur bowler, for the relaxation that might heal him. But increasingly, he knew: Something was drastically wrong. He barely made it through the 10-day trip. While Satora sought out the Hawaiian night life, Walsh returned early to their room on the beach. The test results were awaiting him on the mainland, but he knew in his gut what they would show.

At the testing center, Walsh listened, lit a cigarette and cried.

Then he became sicker—rapidly. Just three weeks after getting the test results, he was admitted to Queen of Angels Hospital with bleeding ulcers, tuberculosis, anemia and herpes of the esophagus. "The consensus among doctors not versed in AIDS was that he was going to die," Walsh's private physician, Dr. Peter Kennedy, says. Walsh's hospital stay lasted all of October; his T-cell count hovered ominously near zero.

Rallying some strength, Walsh finally went home, but his struggles were only beginning. In a condition so fragile that he cries when he remembers it, Walsh was forced to confront the realities of his life: He needed help. He began visiting his doctor regularly under a private health-care plan, often undergoing transfusions, often becoming demanding and loud. "It was very clear he was just scared to death," Kennedy says.

Meanwhile, Satora was wondering: *Me, too?*

Keeping the relationship together was to be one of the tender and stormy challenges of Walsh's life. One bone-chilling autumn night, Walsh began reaching out for help, for himself and Satora. Escorted by his mother, Bonnie, and Satora, he joined a crowd of nearly 300 assembled by activist Louise Hay in a West Hollywood park—a regular meeting of meditation, chanting and encouragement for AIDS patients. As individual members of the crowd were invited to speak, Walsh asked for the microphone. He grasped it and, looking around at the crowd, could not utter a word before he began crying.

Members of the crowd soon engulfed him, offering cards, telephone numbers. It was an omen of good fortune. Walsh would get help.

Walsh's employer kept him on its payroll and essentially ordered him to stay home. ("They didn't think I was going to last," he says.) He also left his apartment, where Satora was awaiting results of an HIV test of his own, and returned temporarily to his mother's house in Culver City. Bonnie Walsh took charge of her son's daily regimen of drugs. She put the multitude of pills, about 10 in all, in plastic bags, and Walsh took a bag's worth every four hours, day and night. Meanwhile, Walsh was on the phone to local nonprofit help groups, including Being Alive, Aid for AIDS and Aids Project Los Angeles. From them, he learned of the state's year-old Health Insurance Premium Program (HIPP), through which the government pays insurance premiums for AIDS patients to help them maintain their private insurance plans and keep them out of the public health-care system. It would enable him to retain his private physician and possibly, because of that doctor's great interest in Walsh's welfare, play an important role in keeping him alive.

"He's taken hold of his illness," Bonnie says.

Satora, meanwhile, tested positive for the virus, a result he expected. He and Walsh talked about it. Facing death was one thing; but now, what Satora dreaded was facing his family.

The eldest of six children, Satora had grown up in conservative surroundings in the town of Livermore, near Oakland. His father had been the type to tell homosexual jokes. His mother, a strict Roman Catholic, had become alarmed when Satora first started living with a male roommate years earlier. She would

> # K
> eeping the relationship with Satora was to be one of the tender and stormy challenges of Walsh's life.

call at 4 and 5 in the morning, waking her son and demanding: "Are you gay? I can't accept you that way!"

"No, I'm not gay," Satora would say, lying to appease her.

Now he would give his parents a double whammy, the same double whammy that so many parents have received throughout the epidemic: He was not only gay, he was also HIV infected. He planned to break the news on a trip home for Thanksgiving. He flew north and re-entered the household of his youth, where his father and younger brothers made flip remarks about gays and AIDS. His mother gave him that same old accusing look.

"It just made me sicker inside," he recalls.

So Satora stayed for the holiday, told no one in his family about his diagnosis and came home.

UNDER THE TOWERING main building of the County-USC medical center is a cavernous basement the size of a football field, packed with color-coded folders containing the vital charts, laboratory reports and other medical records of more than 1 million patients. The files fill row upon row of high shelves seemingly into infinity. Sometimes, partly because of the sheer volume, files become lost; patients' claims for Medi-Cal or Social Security reimbursements—the only income that keeps some AIDS patients off the streets—are inexplicably denied or tied up in months of red tape.

Silvio Hernandez's claim was answered in four months: *Denied.* His file, the agency said, contained insufficient information.

The news was followed, a month later, by a change in his medical condition. The silver-haired movie fan developed a herpes rash covering much of his body. As the rash disappeared with medication, something worse appeared: herpes-related shingles affecting nearly all of his right leg. The nerve condition was so excruciating that Hernandez was referred to County-USC's Cancer Pain clinic.

"He was in pain severe enough to keep him from sleeping," remembers Dr. David Cundiff, who prescribed a drug similar to morphine. "He was virtually immobilized."

Hernandez was not without help: He was sharing his apartment with a longtime companion who was not infected—a man who could cook and attend to chores. Many other friends were there for moral support. But not one of them could stop the agony.

"I was screaming, yelling, in my home at 2 [and] 3 o'clock in the morning, putting on ice, things like that," Hernandez says. During the same month he visited the Cancer Pain clinic, he submitted a new application for Social Security benefits.

TIM WALSH WAS BACK in the hospital at St. Vincent Medical Center only three months after his near-death. Admitted this time with a fever of 105, he recuperated for three weeks, and left with the same dismal T-cell level.

The stay marked a turning point, however. He and his lover had reached a decision: Walsh would return home to their apartment. Somehow, against almost insurmountable despair, they would try to sustain a relationship.

And occasionally, there were times worth savoring—day trips, dinners out. Walsh spent many idyllic afternoons poolside at the Los Angeles Center for Living, a now-defunct gathering place in a quiet neighborhood where people with life-threatening illnesses were able to sit and chat. Surrounding the pool was a yard with ferns and brick, and usually there was music and an afternoon meal of salad, cheese and rice.

Satora, however, who was still without symptoms, shied away from such groups. He bowled, continued working and tended to Walsh in the evenings. At times, when the pressure built to more than he could handle, he shouted, threw things, slammed his fist into the wall.

On a day in April, nearly five months after his trip home for Thanksgiving, the mounting fears about his own health and the possibility that he could begin an experimental drug treatment even before developing symptoms prompted Satora to act. He telephoned his family and finally broke the news: He was gay, he was HIV positive and he was seeing a private doctor.

The reaction was much as he feared. His father, the more understanding of his parents, has not told a gay joke since. But his mother came apart with fury. She sent him a letter saying he was no longer her son—she disowned him. His lifestyle, she ranted, was disgusting.

In the two years since Satora opened the letter, he and his mother have hardly spoken, and even their one or two exchanges have been angry. "My mother died April 28, 1988," Satora says. "That's the day I got the letter."

BY EARLY 1989, the county's death toll was 4,484 and the number of reported new AIDS cases averaged 214 a month, more than double the rate of just three years earlier. The numbers were so routinely horrifying that they had begun to lose their shock value. It was in July that Kimon Beazlie became one of those statistics, discovering the fleshy masses on the roof of his mouth that represented full-blown AIDS.

Beazlie, who had known he was HIV-infected and quit his job as a costume designer, found himself without insurance and needing urgent medical care. The solution was obvious: 5P21. But the wait was nearly two months.

He stopped at the clinic every week during that time, trying to see a doctor because he "kept freaking out," Beazlie says. Patiently, a nurse practitioner explained each time that he would have to wait. The clinic was booked. He was not bleeding. He was not so desperately ill that he had to be admitted to an AIDS ward or an emergency room. His lesions would be examined when the time came for his appointment.

Having no money for private care, Beazlie passed the time at home as the two sarcoma lesions ate sores into his tongue. "They were like very potent battery acid," he recalls. "The pain was too excruciating." To sleep, he taped a four-inch wood dowel in his mouth to keep his tongue from touching the boils. The lesions "finally erupted and drained down my throat before I ever got to see a doctor."

After seven weeks, Beazlie kept his appointment at 5P21. Doctors prescribed chemotherapy, which, he was told, would put the Kaposi's sarcoma into remission and give him some months of relatively good health.

RIC ABEYTIA ALSO BECAME another of the growing number of statistics last year. A banker who resides in South Pasadena,

Abeytia was hospitalized three times before doctors diagnosed his condition as an AIDS-related infection.

Abeytia had just changed jobs and, like Beazlie, was without health insurance. At 37, he is a thoughtful, disarmingly witty man with the look of a young college professor, sporting wire-frame glasses and a thick shock of black hair.

Abeytia entered County-USC Medical Center via the emergency room. A week after developing flulike symptoms, he began vomiting blood. Emergency room attendants pumped his stomach and talked about him, as he lay on the gurney, as if he were an ulcer-plagued alcoholic ("Wait a minute," Abeytia recalls saying, "Why are you treating me as an alcoholic? I don't drink!"). He was fed intravenously for several days and sent home, undiagnosed. Probably a bleeding ulcer, he was told.

The next month it flared up again—the same problem, the same trip to the E.R., the same weeklong stay on a gurney.

Abeytia was becoming exasperated. A month later, *deja vu.* More vomiting, more blood. Back into the E.R. for a third time, for another stomach pump, for more IVs. Assertive by nature, Abeytia pressed for answers. *Something* was wrong. *Something* was causing this. What *was* it?

Months earlier, fearful because several friends had developed AIDS, Abeytia had submitted to an HIV test. The result was negative, a finding he doubted then and which now had become more suspect. He lay for several days on a gurney in a unit called the Red Blanket Room—for patients with internal bleeding—until he at last got lucky: He saw a friend, a one-time musician named Francisco Garcia, who happened to be a research nurse at the medical center. Garcia's specialty was upper-gastrointestinal hemorrhages, and he was screening patients in the Red Blanket Room to find candidates for internal scoping—a procedure, technically called an endoscopy, in which a fiber-optic tube is inserted into the stomach to look for problems.

Garcia, who hardly recognized his sickly friend, scheduled Abeytia for an endoscopy, which identified the problem as *Candidal esophagitis,* a fungal infection associated with AIDS.

Abeytia was indignant that it took three hospital visits—a total of about 12 days—before the endoscopy was performed, but Garcia noted that at a county hospital, where funding is chronically short, not every test can be performed on every patient. "We see masses of people here," Garcia says. "It's not like going to a private hospital where you have the total attention of the doctors and nurses and you can run as many tests as you want."

Regardless, Abeytia was now at the right place: 5P21. Like several hundred patients there, he chose to take advantage of one of the clinic's most important services—experimental drug trials. At any given time, about 70 different AIDS drugs are being tested on county patients who volunteer to take them. In Abeytia's case, the drug was one formulated to stop the *Candidal esophagitis* infection.

It seemed to work, but his T cells—monitored frequently during drug trials—declined during the next few months. Abeytia became a scholar of the illness, learning about drugs and his own body as if he were trying to master the programs and hardware of a home computer. Only in this case, the hardware was failing. He soon developed tuberculosis, which required a drug incompatible with the stomach medication. He gave up the stomach drug only to have a relapse of internal bleeding, which landed him once again—for the fourth time—in the hospital.

A new T-cell report was back from the lab soon after he was released: He was down to 120, a drop of nearly 400 T cells in three months. Abeytia was alarmed. The numbers just kept dropping. What would they be in the next three months? Or even in three weeks? He would have no T cells left—he was dying. He left the clinic and took the freeway home, crying.

The T-cell counts finally stabilized. He was now taking the drug AZT, which caused nausea and vomiting, but in late summer, Abeytia enjoyed a short span of relatively good health. The next problem that developed was by now, at least, familiar: the rather hollow feeling in his gut that invariably preceded the bouts of internal bleeding. This time he was ready for it. All he needed was the stomach drug.

Could he get it?

He was talking with the physician's assistant who handled most of his appointments at 5P21. The medical staffer was skeptical. He was reluctant to prescribe the drug because Abeytia was showing no obvious symptoms. Drugs frequently have side effects, and it was quite possible that Abeytia was reacting to only fear and paranoia. An argument ensued, and Abeytia left without the medication. He was persuaded, instead, to schedule an appointment with a county psychiatrist.

Life is learning how to deal, Beazlie says. 'We're just getting a concentrated crash course.'

SILVIO HERNANDEZ'S second claim for Social Security, following the paralyzing nerve problem in his leg, went unanswered for three months. He was now a familiar sight in the AIDS clinic; it had been 3½ years since his attack of vertigo and 18 months since he had become a regular at 5P21. It was also eight months since he had first applied for monthly Social Security payments.

Hernandez, still suffering intensely and walking with a cane, was becoming obsessed with his quest for the long-term disability benefits, which would total nearly $650 a month. The urgency was fueled by the recent death, of AIDS, of a close friend from Puerto Rico, a man who had responded to his declining health by going on a rampage of drugs and alcohol; Hernandez had just attended his memorial service.

His sense of mortality inflamed, he called the Social Security office and demanded to know the status of his case. His file, someone explained, was not there—it was lost.

"How can that be?" Hernandez shouted.

Sorry. It wasn't there.

He cried during the night. He could not sleep. "I think that damaged my situation more than the disease," he says. Hernandez—who keeps thick files documenting his case—reports that the missing file was discovered a month later. It had not been reviewed, however, so he was asked to wait three additional weeks while a decision was made. He was given a date and time, he says, and assured that a call would come.

Hernandez waited by the phone. It never rang.

Even angrier, Hernandez again badgered the office, only to be told—once again—that his file was incomplete. A Social Security official offered to send him, free, to a doctor in the San Fernando Valley, where the necessary reports could be obtained.

Hernandez indignantly refused. Had he not been seeing county doctors for 18 months? Why was that not good enough for Social Security? Why were they doing this to a man who was sick? A man who was dying?

Although Social Security officials cannot comment on individual cases, hang-ups in processing a claim occur for any number of reasons, says Joe Carlin, Los Angeles/West branch chief for the state's Disability Evaluation Division, which contracts with Social Security to decide on patient eligibility. Typically, analysts request necessary medical records from county hospitals—a process that is at best hit-and-miss, he says.

"Generally, on cases where we're dealing with county medical facilities, it is a problem getting records," Carlin says.

So disorganized are the records that two years ago the Disability Evaluation Division stationed a full-time employee named David Stewart at County-USC just to track down missing medical reports needed by Social Security officials. Stewart says the million or so files stored in the hospital basement are in constant motion, trundled to various clinics as needed by doctors, with laboratory reports and doctors' notations being added all the time. "It's amazing . . . the amount of papers that flow from one place to another."

In any single case, Carlin says, it is difficult knowing where to pin blame. "It's either, A, we didn't get the records, or, B, we got the records and there wasn't enough detail," he says. "The final possibility is, we did not do the case properly."

The benefits claim became a crusade for Hernandez; the sleeplessness, the anger swallowed him up. *Why? Why? Why?* How could they deny him? At one point, he says, he entered the records room himself, determined to see what his file contained. There was nothing about his nerve-damaged leg. But there was a medical report concerning a different Hernandez altogether, somebody who was perhaps also trying in vain to get his benefits.

Tired, bitterly frustrated, Silvio Hernandez took a T-cell test in the fall of 1989. The count, previously in the 400s, was now down to 95.

KIMON BEAZLIE SHAVED off his long hair. Like many chemotherapy patients, he found it disturbing to see the long locks fall out whenever he showered. He was receiving treatments on alternate Thursdays and getting to know members of his own treatment group, those who joined him for intravenous therapy in the pale-yellow hallway.

One, in particular, became a favorite of Beazlie: a young man named Brian, only 23, who attended each session with his mother. "You just don't see parents here," Beazlie says. The three would pass the time chatting.

Brian began missing days—he was sometimes too ill to keep his appointments—and eventually, the youngster dropped out of the group. A nurse told him that Brian had switched weeks, coming in on the Thursdays when Beazlie was not there.

Beazlie visited the clinic the following Thursday to look for him, but Brian was nowhere to be found. "Finally, I confronted [a nurse], and I said, 'Brian's not here, is he?' " Beazlie remembers. "And she said, 'No, he passed away.' "

Soon after Brian's death, Beazlie temporarily dropped out of treatment. He packed for a trip to Hungary, where he planned to visit his lover, who was working overseas. He also hoped to buy drugs on the European underground.

One question that nearly all AIDS patients ask themselves sooner or later is whether they should try medications—and there are hundreds—that have not yet been approved by the federal Food and Drug Administration. In recent years, liberalized policies have made many of those medications available in experimental trials at clinics such as 5P21; and yet the underground remains vitally active. Rumors percolate through all levels of the gay community about interferon treatments developed in Africa or purported wonder drugs manufactured only in Japan. Such drugs are imported to the United States, but many patients find them dismally disappointing.

"It's like the '20s speak-easies," Beazlie says of the medication underground. "Someone might say to you, 'Get in touch with so-and-so, he's involved in it.' And you go to someone's house and say, 'Joe sent me.' "

In the States, Beazlie had not found anything on the underground. On the trip to Hungary, all he managed to pick up was a German-made drug called Balachek, an elixir fortified with minerals that cost $1 a bottle.

RIC ABEYTIA WAS BACK in the hospital with internal bleeding. Well before his scheduled psychiatric appointment last fall, the *Candidal esophagitis* had returned. And now here he was, sick again, hooked up to IVs, receiving stomach medication that he had pleaded for earlier. With bitter solace, he told himself: *You were right! They didn't listen!*

However, according to Dr. Fred Sattler, the clinic's head physician, the drugs for *Candidal esophagitis* are never prescribed at the onset of the infection because the fungus can mutate and become more resistant.

Abeytia's attention soon turned to the health of his best friend, a once burly, 250-pound college pal who was admitted to the County-USC AIDS ward the same month. The 20-bed ward, separate from the crowded out-patient clinic, provided his friend with terrific care, Abeytia says. But his friend was down to 140 pounds and dying. When he returned home, Abeytia and the patient's mother took turns at his bedside.

"We discussed very common-sense things," Abeytia says, recalling those conversations with his friend. " 'What do we do about the funeral?' 'What do we do about your house?' 'How about your car?' 'Is the will taken care of?' And at the same time I was trying to be as comforting to him as possible because he was very scared. I'd crawl into bed with him and just hold him, just to try to make him feel a little better."

The friend returned to the hospital the first week of December. He slipped into a coma and died five days before Christmas.

"I CANNOT WALK, I cannot sleep, I'm having diarrhea at night in bed. I cannot control my bowels. I have to start using diapers like a baby."

That is how Silvio Hernandez describes his medical condition as of late last year. He had developed mixed emotions about the health care at 5P21. He appreciated the apparently sincere efforts of his doctor to help him, and yet he was rushed in and out so fast—five or 10 minutes, on most visits—that he did not really understand what was being done for him or why.

And he wondered whether his doctor even understood what

Because of staffing problems, the waiting list at the clinic grew to four months.

treatments he needed most. "There are just so many people," he says ruefully. "The system is just so overworked."

Hernandez stopped taking the bus from West Hollywood to 5P21, relying instead on volunteers from AIDS-assistance organizations to drive him. It was the Los Angeles-based Minority AIDS Project that now intervened in his nearly year-old battle for Social Security benefits.

That organization put Hernandez in touch with the office of State Sen. David A. Roberti (D-Los Angeles), where an administrative assistant named Lynn Shepodd took charge. She saw Hernandez's case as "an abomination."

"They were asking him to jump through all these hoops and I just couldn't figure out why," Shepodd recalls. "Every time he would go to a doctor, they would either misplace his records or they'd tell him he had to go see someone else. He was just so tired and worn out. He just called [our office] in desperation."

Sheppod's telephone calls were effective. Four days after Christmas, 1989, Hernandez was asked to visit the Social Security office on Hollywood Boulevard. He grins as he remembers the office manager meeting him at the door. "They apologized 15 times," Hernandez says. "They say, 'This is not the way [we] operate.' They wanted to know who I was that they received three calls from Sacramento. I say, 'I am nobody. I am just a poor man that works very hard, and I have a disease that I don't know how long I'm going to live. And I need my money *now*.'"

He got it—a check for $630. Two weeks later, he got a second check for $7,755.53, representing retroactive Social Security payments for more than a year.

Hernandez sent Shepodd a dozen roses in a gold box.

AT DR. PETER KENNEDY'S Wilshire District office, the physician and his patient, Tim Walsh, had a confrontation. If he didn't go back into the hospital, the doctor told him in December, he was going to die.

Walsh had picked up a bacterial pneumonia and had been eluding the doctor during office visits, obtaining prescriptions from a nurse and skipping out, even though he was rapidly losing weight, Kennedy says. Walsh was now persuaded to enter the hospital. Soon, he was hovering near death. For two days during the holidays, he went home, a sojourn that required 24-hour nursing care; once, as he tried to walk, he fell while connected to an intravenous needle, spilling blood in the apartment.

By the time the hospital stay was over, Walsh was connected with a subclavian catheter—a tube under the collarbone that enabled him to administer his own intravenous medications. Through that tube, he took antibiotics, a hormone to boost red blood cells, and a high-calorie mixture of protein, carbohydrates and vitamins—home therapies generally difficult to get through the public health system. "I'm sure [the nutritive mixture] kept him alive at times," Kennedy says.

All of this—the drugs, the coughing, the IV tubes that Walsh wore to bed—was taking a toll on Ron Satora. Still asymptomatic, Walsh's lover carried the burden of nearly all the work at home, from feeding the two cats to fetching cold towels for Walsh.

It was Satora's nature to keep his frustrations in him, bottled up. His doctors were now prescribing larger and larger doses of anti-depressants. Occasional temper tantrums—the venting of those clamped emotions—were punctuated this spring by an attack in which his blood pressure shot up and his heart rate leaped to 250. He temporarily lost his eyesight and he was rushed to the hospital.

Nerves. Just nerves. "It's all on my shoulders," Satora says.

AS THE SUMMER ARRIVED, anger and frustration mounted. Furious activists shouted down the federal health and human services secretary at yet another international AIDS conference where medical progress seemed dim.

Los Angeles County, early in the year, had authorized the hiring of additional medical personnel to reduce the waiting list at 5P21 to only two or three weeks, Sattler says. But for several months the positions were not advertised, he says, and have remained unfilled, largely because county salaries are far below those in private health-care. So the waiting list grew from three months to four.

The personal battles, too, wore on:

• Silvio Hernandez adds to his videotape collection, fretting over his health. He has lost 40 pounds—down to 125. Lately, letters have been arriving from Social Security saying the agency has overpaid him, one demanding a refund of $27, another a refund of $98.

"It is confusing. What is going on, I don't know," Hernandez says. "They make so many mistakes. I don't know what I'm supposed to receive every month any more."

• Tim Walsh was back in the hospital for much of June with bacterial pneumonia. He looks very thin, coughing heavily. His speech is slurred and he complains of tiredness; his doctor talks pessimistically about the chances of real improvement. Satora, meanwhile, took an 11-day vacation in Hawaii alone, at the insistence of his own doctor. "I worry too much," he said as he packed for the airport. "There have been times I felt like I don't know how much longer I can deal with this. But I don't think I could ever leave him."

• Kimon Beazlie, the one-time rock climber and Hollywood costume designer, is very ill at home. Doctors at 5P21 wanted to insert a tube in his chest, similar to Walsh's, and to place Beazlie on an alternating schedule of blood transfusions and chemotherapy. Instead, Beazlie withdrew himself entirely from treatment. In his renegade outlook he asks himself: Why get a transfusion one week when chemotherapy would destroy your new blood the next?

The German drug Balachek had done nothing for him, Beazlie says, talking painfully, as if he had just come from the dentist. The sarcoma lesions have returned and now fill his whole mouth. He coughs violently.

Two months after taking a visitor through the county clinic, Beazlie now keeps to his apartment except to settle last-minute affairs. He is trying to find a home for one of his dogs. Two other dogs are so old they probably will be put to sleep, he says.

On a sunny Monday in late July, Beazlie arranged to be cremated. He talks of going on a morphine drip—the way out for many AIDS patients.

Dying, he says, will be an end to pain.

• Ric Abeytia is a healthy man—or so he feels. Eighteen months after the vomiting and internal bleeding that marked his introduction to AIDS, the former banker works full time at the offices of Being Alive, a Los Angeles-based help group. Abeytia is now on a clinical trial for the experimental drug DDI because AZT was causing him too much discomfort. He takes stomach medication when necessary and follows the medical bulletins for possible breakthroughs, for hope. He was preparing to enter the county AIDS ward for 10 days of treatment for a lingering bacterial infection, but he planned to take his briefcase and file folders with him.

"I'll make it an office," he says. The work for Being Alive pays a quarter what he made as a banker, but, he says, helping others makes it easier to deal with his own illness.

"I'm sure he has his bad days when he's down and depressed and cries like the rest of us," says Abeytia's friend, Ian Barrington, who also has AIDS. "We talk on days when he can't work, when he's really ill. But I can always count on him calling me three or four days later, back on his feet and dancing again. A lot of courage." ▬

Chapter 14

The Judiciary

Article 1.   The Siege of Yonkers
by Lorrin Anderson

In this article, Lorrin Anderson details the five-year battle of Yonkers, New York, to overturn a judge's decision that found the city guilty of intentional discrimination in schools and housing and imposed sentence. In this decade-long fight, the city has steadfastly resisted the power of the federal courts, insisting that it is the victim of "social engineering." The article reviews the facts of the case, the closed-door negotiations, the issues surrounding the debate, and the prospects for a resolution.

Our Story So Far

Medium-sized Eastern city, mired in racial sin, rescued by the redemptive power of the federal courts. Or so we think. But Yonkers resists. And resists. And resists. Yielding under pressure, then reneging, giving ground, coming back to fight again, getting a painful education, along the way, in the peculiar workings of the legal system. It has been ten years since the filing of the lawsuit charging Yonkers with intentional discrimination in housing and schools, five years since the judge found it guilty and imposed his scatter-site sentence. Still, not one of the prescribed low-income projects has appeared in the city's middle-class neighborhoods. They may be about to: ground was finally broken at one of the sites in mid April. But that could be less than the victory some housing proponents are claiming. It's high noon now: the last legal shootout has begun, and a long-shot possibility remains that Yonkers might still be able to head off what many of its citizens see as the blueprint for yet another urban disaster.

The Cast

Federal Judge Leonard B. Sand, social engineer *par excellence*, dreamer of utopian dreams at other people's expense, understandably a tad frustrated, but determined as ever to impose his version of communal morality on the recalcitrant bourgeoisie.

Oscar Newman, theorist and expediter of race-conscious housing reform, appointed by Judge Sand to guide Yonkers through its travail to the promised land of class-integrated harmony.

Michael Sussman, former hotspur in the U.S. Civil Rights Division and, since 1982, legal counsel and general gadfly for the Yonkers NAACP, which joined the action against the city soon after the Justice Department filed the original lawsuit in the waning days of the Carter Administration. (The Reagan Administration's later embrace of the suit is a long, richly paradoxical story.)

The Mayor of Yonkers, Henry Spallone (Republican), consistent and highly vocal opponent of Judge Sand's remedial prescriptions but now suspected, by some of his erstwhile allies, of diminished zeal if not a *sub rosa* sellout—of wanting to see Yonkers accommodate the court enough to get Judge Sand off its back.

Jack O'Toole (Democrat) and *Bernadette McLaughlin* (Republican), spearheads of the opposition to Judge Sand, leaders of the Save Yonkers Federation, a coalition of neighborhood organizations intermittently allied with Spallone but now rife with the aforementioned suspicion that the mayor has caved in to the forces of compliance, which remain strong in the city's political and commercial establishment. Henry Spallone is not fond of Jack O'Toole.

Raymond Fitzpatrick, architect of a famous Supreme Court victory allowing white firemen to challenge racial quotas in Birmingham, Alabama, now signed on by Yonkers—under civic pressure orchestrated by O'Toole and Mrs. McLaughlin—as legal general in its war against Judge Sand.

From *National Review,* May 13, 1991, pp. 28–33. © 1991 by National Review, Inc., 150 East 35th Street, New York, NY 10016. Reprinted by permission.

Supporting Players

Former mayors unhorsed by the housing imbroglio.

Assorted councilmen and deposed councilmen—pro-compliance, anti-compliance, or, in most cases, both at different times.

Black voices, some strongly in favor of the housing edict, others ambivalent, a few opposed.

Mario Cuomo.

John Cardinal O'Connor.

The Supreme Court.

The progressive press.

Al Sharpton.

Chorus

Citizens of Yonkers (fortissimo).

Backs against the Wall

THE SLIM possibility that Yonkers's resistance might ultimately succeed glimmered a little more brightly, late in December, with the City Council's designation of Ray Fitzpatrick as chief counsel for the housing battle. Fitzpatrick replaces Thomas DeRosa, the latest in a string of lawyers who eventually came to be seen by Save Yonkers as inept at best or, in a darker view, secret saboteurs.

Fitzpatrick mobilized in January, but there wasn't much time to block the first housing contract, and it was signed in the middle of the month. An offensive on several fronts is now before the courts, however, attacking not only the legally dubious maneuvers and irregularities that have marked the case, but Judge Sand himself.

Sand has made no attempt to hide his personal views, making them known in press interviews and other public statements over the years. (In 1988, after the Yonkers City Council agreed, under fierce court pressure, to accept the housing plan, the judge commended the plaintiffs—the NAACP and the Justice Department—for "a long and hard effort, but a productive one.") Fitzpatrick has now moved to have Sand taken off the case, charging that he has travestied all appearance of impartiality and, specifically, that he violated judicial ethics by holding improper *ex parte* discussions with the plaintiffs and other involved parties in the absence of city attorneys—both on his own and through his intermediary, the housing consultant Oscar Newman.

At the heart of the case, Fitzpatrick is attacking the 1988 consent decree in which the City Council finally voted to accept the housing plan, on the grounds that the councilmen were acting under duress, and that like any other contract signed under duress the whole agreement is tainted. Other lawsuits have been filed by Save Yonkers and private citizens, charging violation of HUD regulations, federal environmental laws, and the legal rules covering site acquisition, building codes, and zoning changes.

The latest challenges now have to wind their way through the system, starting with Sand himself—no chance there, of course—and then the 2nd Circuit Court of Appeals, which in the past has been unreceptive to the city's arguments. Probably the only prospect of success lies with the Supreme Court—if it agrees to look at the case one more time.

Setting the Scene

YONKERS lies directly north of New York City, in Westchester County. Its population of 188,000 is down about 3 per cent from 1980, but it's still the fourth largest city in the state, partly a bedroom suburb but at the same time an urban center in its own right. It's a blue-collar town, in many ways, but with its moneyed neighborhoods too, and a rich ethnic mix: Italians, Irish, Jews, Arabs, Scots, Sassenachs, Slavs, Orientals, blacks, and, increasingly, Hispanics, who now make up almost 17 per cent of the population. (The city's Democratic leader, Ralph Arred, is Cuban.) About 14 per cent of the city's people are black.

Yonkers is bisected by the Saw Mill River Parkway, a four-lane thoroughfare that wasn't such a symbolic demarcation line until the court case made everybody think in terms of East and West. Both the West, along the Hudson River, and the then-less-developed East were almost all white before World War II, but since the 1960s the old downtown and surrounding areas in the Southwest have gradually become heavily black and Hispanic, some of the other sections on the West Side more or less integrated. The neighborhoods of East Yonkers, which range from lower-middle-class to very affluent, have remained largely white.

Judge Sand's 1985 ruling broke legal ground by linking "segregation" in housing and schools: Yonkers, he said, had officially and deliberately fostered racial separation by siting almost all its public housing in the Southwest, thereby producing not only a residential ghetto but segregated schools as well. The semi-autonomous Yonkers Board of Education accepted an extensive (and costly) school-integration plan with hardly a whimper. Housing was something else again. Sand decreed his "remedy" in 1986, but it wasn't until January of 1988 that the City Council finally capitulated. Then, in the face of popular revolt, a couple of councilmen reversed field. A 4 to 3 Council majority defied the judge: Yonkers would *not* acquiesce. It was not until Sand imposed crushing contempt fines, on the city and on the councilmen personally, that Yonkers gave in, in the summer of 1988. Subsequent appeals by the city and private suits by homeowners have so far resulted in only one minor victory: a Supreme Court decision that voided personal fines against the offending councilmen.

The plan Judge Sand finally imposed is ambitious, involving two phases. The first provides for two hundred low-income apartments, to be paid for by the federal Department of Housing and Urban Development, on seven scattered sites in East Yonkers. Construction was supposed to begin in 1987, but problems with sites and financing—and foot-dragging by the city—held it up again and again until the contract for the first 142 units was finally signed this January. For reasons that have not been publicly explained, the developer—a Pennsylvania-based outfit called DeLuxe Homes—has backed out of a commitment to build the other 58 units, and finding another company willing to take on the job is likely to be a long process.

With a nod to the reality of public-housing disasters in the recent American past, the plan for the first two hundred units calls not for high-rises but for three-story townhouses, with a minimum of public space for the convenience of drug merchants and other criminals. Bernadette McLaughlin of Save Yonkers is, to understate her views, unconvinced. Like many people in Yonkers, she grew up in the Bronx, and she has vivid memories of what happened when the projects moved into her old neighborhood. The townhouses? "Crack heavens," she predicts.

The second phase of the judge's plan, still in limbo, envisions eight hundred additional units of subsidized low-to-moderate-income housing in East and mostly white Northwest Yonkers, in buildings that would also include free-market apartments—a total of four thousand government-assisted and market-rate units in addition to the first two hundred units of public housing. The city has been ordered to provide tax breaks and other incentives (which of course would shift a tax burden to private homeowners), but no developers have climbed aboard for the second phase, partly because of the legal uncertainties and partly because a lot of them think the whole concept is unrealistic—not many people able to pay the going rate would want to share buildings with assisted-housing tenants. The problem is compounded by the sagging real-estate market in the New York area and especially in Yonkers, where the prospect of scatter-site housing projects has made it all but impossible for some people to sell their houses, unless, as they say, "you want to give them away."

The school situation—especially busing—is hardly an inducement for young families to buy homes in Yonkers. Judge Sand's desegregation edict requires the closing of six schools, some of them still serviceable, and the construction of two new ones, at a cost to the city of $30 million. The plan puts heavy emphasis on "magnet" schools and involves the busing—some voluntary, some not—of more than half the district's 18,000 students. The Board of Ed and Superintendent Donald Batista are trying with some success to make the whole thing work, enlisting enthusiastic cooperation from the local press in painting a somewhat rosier picture than the facts warrant. It's possible to report enrollment and racial-ratio statistics in various ways, and critics suspect that school administrators are doctoring the numbers. But even the official figures show a big drop in the proportion of whites, from 53 per cent in 1985 to 40.6 per cent this year. (The 59.4 per cent "minority" total comprises only blacks and Hispanics; by Judge Sand's decree, everybody else—East Asians, American Indians, Indian Indians, any stray Aleuts or Pacific Island-

ers—are included in the "white" number.) In short, it looks like the same pattern that has become so familiar in other cities, like Boston, where, after all the agonies of "desegregation" under Federal Judge Arthur Garrity, racial rejuggling has become pointless because the public schools are now 80 per cent "minority": the system runs short of white balancing fodder.

Race or Class?

IN HIS pioneering decision of 1985, Judge Sand documents ad infinitum what nobody really disputes: that Yonkers officials, from the 1950s on, repeatedly retreated from plans to build public housing in middle-class areas. Sand's reasoning went something like this: 1) the tenants were likely to be predominantly black, and 2) neighborhood residents loudly and vehemently opposed the projects, so 3) race was a significant factor in the official rejection. He threw in all the supporting testimony he could find, but whatever prejudices Yonkers may or may not secretly harbor, one thing that has been notably absent is overt racism. About the strongest example the judge could find was a 1958 statement from a citizens' group that expressed concern about school costs and about "having to absorb the overflow from Puerto Rico or Harlem."

Judge Sand grudgingly conceded the city's point that nobody has a "right" to public housing. But then he went on to find a constitutional violation of the Fourteenth Amendment's equal-protection clause, on the grounds that as long as the government was in the subsidized-housing business at all, it had to proceed in a race-neutral manner. Well, fair enough. But conspicuously absent from his ruling is any real acknowledgment that the reason people don't want to live next door to the underclass might not be vulgar skin-color prejudice but well-founded class perceptions, an all too realistic fear of the crime, the drugs, the noise, the graffiti, the welfare dependency—all the social disintegration that might well seem just as threatening in an identifiable underclass that was mostly white. In effect, he decided that *class* was beside the point—perhaps a more glaring distortion of reality than any claim that race is completely irrelevant.

In convicting Yonkers of deliberate racial discrimination Judge Sand ignored one curious fact: at the time most of the housing projects were built in West Yonkers, in the three decades following World War II, *the area was mostly white—and so were most of the tenants in the projects.* And there are reasons for "tipping" to an almost all-black tenancy that have nothing to do with official siting discrimination: some of the whites in the projects may have left because of racial prejudice, but it seems likely that many more fled because of the simple realities of life in buildings increasingly populated by a destructive and demoralized underclass. It was not only working-class whites who left, after all, but also working-class blacks, for many of the same reasons—because they could afford something better, away from the residential turmoil, or because their rising incomes, in the postwar boom, made them ineligible for public housing. The deterioration of the projects was accelerated, in the Sixties and Seventies, by civil-liberties advances that, combined with lax government administration, made it more and more difficult to screen tenants and evict criminals or otherwise destructive people.

More questionable even than Judge Sand's reasoning is his drastic "remedy." It is difficult to avoid reading his ruling—its tone as well as its substance—as anything but a long polemic on behalf of the idea that the way to fix things is to use all the coercive power of the state to spread the underclass around, though of course he declines to put it in those terms. And since the court's correctives have been clearly punitive as well as "remedial," they raise disturbing questions about collective guilt.

The Case of the Well-Connected Judge

LEONARD SAND was elevated to the federal bench in 1978, by Jimmy Carter. (The judge's brother-in-law, the entrepreneur R. Peter Straus, was a big Carter fundraiser in the 1976 campaign.) A former real-estate lawyer, Sand is a rich man and very well connected: his wife, Ann, springs from a cadet branch of the Sulzberger family and is a cousin of the publisher of the New York Times.

Sand has a reputation, in the judge business, for settling cases before trial, and the Yonkers initiative is by no means his only venture into social activism. In the mid Eighties, to correct a dearth of black captains in the New York City Fire Department, he gave his blessing to an intricate plan in which black fire lieutenants were leapfrogged to promotion over whites with higher test scores. Early last year Sand overturned a ban on begging in New York City's transit system, deciding that the panhandlers there were merely exercising a right of free speech guaranteed by the Constitution. That was too much even for the Times, which noted the presence of "wild-eyed vagrants who just might be loony enough to push someone in front of a train" and suggested editorially that the judge was out of touch with reality. Sand was finally overruled, by an appeals court that fired some sharp words in his direction: When such social problems are viewed "from the imaginary heights of Mount Olympus," the court said, "a rigid, mechanistic application of some legal doctrine" can redound "to the great detriment of the common good."

In Yonkers, the judge has found a convenient way around various obstacles: he "deems" them out of existence. Is there trouble finding sites because condemnation would violate local ordinances? Judge Sand "deems" the ordinances superseded. Would some of the sites encroach on irreplaceable parkland? Judge Sand "deems" the parkland available, ignoring a New York

law that says conversion of parks to other uses requires the approval of the state legislature.

Since the first two hundred units are to be in multi-family dwellings, they would ordinarily have to meet stiffer fire and other safety standards than single-family homes. DeLuxe Homes balked at that because it's more expensive. So Judge Sand ordered the city to waive the building codes.

Getting sites for the new public housing has been a burden, both for Judge Sand and for the consultant Oscar Newman, but for Newman, at least, a rewarding one: his bills to the city, including many creative expense vouchers, are now approaching a million dollars. Newman picked the locations, churning the suburban skies in a helicopter, and one of his choices, on land owned by St. Joseph's Seminary, touched off a disagreeable contretemps with the Archdiocese of New York—Cardinal O'Connor indicating, after considerable hell-raising by Yonkers parishioners, that he had agreed to turn over the seminary land only because he was led to believe it would be condemned if he didn't.

The seminary site was ultimately de-selected, constitutional freedom of religion having become an issue, and replaced by another that had originally been rejected as too expensive. The alternative site, off Gramercy Avenue, will require the building of an access road and, probably, base-rock blasting—extras that are likely to boost the cost to $235,000 per apartment unit: more than you'd have to pay for a typical single-family house in Yonkers, if you wanted to buy one these days. And the environmental objections to the over-all housing plan are more than mere obstructionism. Questions about the effect on traffic, residential congestion, and Yonkers's overburdened sewage system have been routinely ignored, prior legalities be damned.

The total cost overrun for the two hundred units is likely to be substantial, with much of the indirect expense borne by the city. But HUD Secretary Jack Kemp has promised as much federal money as it takes for basic construction. His own view, reportedly, is that he'd like to "get Yonkers out of my head—as soon as possible." Like a lot of other people, including Governor Cuomo. The governor suggested at one point that the roots of the conflict might lie more in class than in race, but in general his tactic has been to keep as much distance as possible between himself and this political nettle. It hasn't always been easy. At the height of the city's confrontation with Judge Sand, in 1988, Cuomo attracted considerable press criticism for declining to remove the defiant councilmen from office. ("Must Judge Sand Stand Alone?" the Times wondered.)

Mousetrapped

AS OTHERS have noted, the Yonkers story drips with irony. The city has a little over a fifth of the population of Westchester County, but more than two-fifths of its public housing, and many of its citizens feel by now that Yonkers has been mousetrapped by its own good intentions. Rich neighboring towns like

Scarsdale and Bronxville have avoided the problem because they never accepted public housing in the first place. Or take Pound Ridge, in the picturesque reaches of northern Westchester. It's the fourth richest community in one of the nation's richest counties, with a population of 4,500 that includes about a dozen black families, most of them upper-middle-class. Not only does Pound Ridge have zero public housing, the mere mention of downzoning to permit more "affordable" residences is enough to send the villagers off to the barricades.

Yonkers residents are particularly interested in Pound Ridge because Judge Sand lives there, on a 32-acre estate. (He and his wife also have an apartment in Manhattan.) People from Yonkers have picketed his home, suggesting that perhaps he might like to have a project or two in Pound Ridge. The judge told a television reporter he wouldn't mind, but unfortunately Pound Ridge doesn't have the infrastructure—bus lines, things like that. (In Yonkers, Sand has ordered the city to provide new transportation and other services if present facilities are inadequate.)

References to Judge Sand's personal residential arrangements are of course ad hominem. But it is hardly irrelevant, underscoring as it does the way fashionable leveling nostrums have been imposed on the middle and working classes by judges, bureaucrats, and civil-rights lawyers who themselves remain insulated, to a large degree, by wealth, position, and geography.

In the Yonkers case, the phenomenon is not limited to Judge Sand. Michael Sussman, the energetic NAACP lawyer, lives even further upstate in the exurban town of Chester (3 per cent black, zero public housing), where he ran successfully for the town council on a platform that included opposition to a 950-unit housing development (which apparently had nothing to do with race). Oscar Newman, the idealistic scatter-site specialist, lives in affluent Great Neck, Long Island. Donald Batista, the positive-thinking school superintendent, pulled his own daughter out of the public system there and sent her to a nice Catholic school in New Rochelle. Et cetera, et cetera.

Even the key word in the Yonkers debate—desegregation—is a loaded one. Yonkers is not "segregated": what the avenging courts are talking about is racial imbalance, which is quite a different thing. A sociological survey in the mid Seventies found that Yonkers, in the period 1940–1970, when it was supposedly engaging in all that deliberate segregation, was the ninth most integrated of 109 large and medium-sized cities across the nation. Blacks, in short, are not barred from East Yonkers. There's not a single Census tract in the city that doesn't have at least a few black residents, and the 1990 Census shows that the black percentage, while still small in most cases, has doubled or even tripled in

many East Side sections since 1980. And no, you don't have to be Lena Horne or Sidney Poitier.

But the controversy has been made to order for the prejudices of the progressive press, and the sanctimony of Times editorials has been outdone by the Gannett press in Westchester. Gannett's local paper, the Herald Statesman, approvingly cites the judge's "insistence that the U.S. Constitution applies in Yonkers"—the Constitution as exegized by Leonard Sand, that is. And in promoting the school-integration plan the Statesman sometimes carries its zeal to the point of carelessness with the truth: one glowing editorial, in January, noted happily (and falsely) that "the district's racial makeup over the past two years has remained 50 per cent minority and 50 per cent white." Would editor Milton Hoffman run a correction, since the actual 60–40 ratio of minorities to whites told a rather different story? Well . . . don't hang by your thumbs.

Such editorial views tend to be reflected, somewhat more circumspectly, in the news columns. The problem, we are encouraged to believe, is all those benighted Northern rednecks unleashing their bigotry in an unruly attempt to thwart the forces of enlightenment— a superior tone polished to perfection by Gannett columnist Nancy Q. Keefe, who, after the Supreme Court threw out Sand-imposed personal fines against the defiant councilmen, noted that the celebration at Yonkers City Hall featured *pink* champagne. "Egad," Miss Keefe sniffed, "these people have no class and no taste." (Nancy Keefe lives in Larchmont, a pleasant, leafy Westchester suburb with zero public housing and a black population of 1.4 per cent.)

It is certainly true that the Yonkers protest has often been short on tastefulness. The City Council chamber has rung with catcalls and epithets, as hundreds of people turn out for sessions that concern the housing battle. One of the most bizarre episodes began in January of 1988, when a 34-year-old Yonkers woman named Laurie Recht took the floor to urge compliance with Judge Sand's orders. The heckling by the audience was merciless, and Miss Recht became an instant heroine to the press—all the more sympathetic when she reported getting telephoned death threats, and when menacing graffiti, including a swastika, started appearing on the wall outside her apartment. Michael Winerip of the Times devoted a long column to her under the headline "As a Mob Howls, One in Yonkers Pleads for Sanity." In May, the "lone voice" got an honorary doctorate from a Catholic college in New Rochelle. Unhappily for the cause of sanity, however, monitoring equipment revealed that the telephoned death threats were nonexistent, and a camera set up in the hall discovered that the person spray-painting the menacing graffiti was—Laurie Recht. She pleaded guilty to fraud and is now on five years' probation, sentenced to perform three hundred hours of community service and participate in a mental-health program. (The *Times* sort of lost interest in Miss Recht and, to the best of Constant Reader's knowledge, neglected to report the sentence.)

That whiff of seeming anti-Semitism in the Recht episode—the spurious swastika—is, by the way, another irony, since the resistance to Judge Sand has considerable support in Yonkers's sizable Jewish community. The first president of Save Yonkers was Jewish, and Save Yonkers still holds most of its meetings at the Jewish Center in the heavily Jewish (and racially integrated) Lincoln Park neighborhood.

The feeling in the black community is a little hard to gauge. At the outset, there were a number of black voices saying that the housing money should be spent to improve the Southwest rather than to scatter low-income projects in East Yonkers. And in January 1988, when eight hundred people from Yonkers went to Washington to protest the housing plan, the caravan included several busloads of blacks, about 150 all told. Early in 1990, fissures in the black community were apparent when the Reverend Al Sharpton came to Yonkers and mounted one of his celebrated marches. He was joined by some local militants, but the NAACP dissociated itself from the demonstrations and there was considerable acrimony, Sharpton calling one NAACP leader an "Aunt Jemima." But Al Sharpton has many battles to fight in the war against racism, and he has apparently put Yonkers on the back burner.

It is not difficult to find black homeowners in Yonkers whose private views on living next door to low-income housing projects differ little if at all from those of their white counterparts. But it's not easy for them to speak out publicly. And the local NAACP has a new chairman—28-year-old Kenneth Jenkins—who has been pushing the housing issue into the forefront.

Predominantly white community organizations have sprung up from time to time to counter Save Yonkers, with carefully crafted acronymic names like COMPLY, CANOPY, and YIELD—the latter an interfaith group powered mainly by the clergy, which by and large supports accommodation. (One Save Yonkers leader, Jack Treacy, says he hasn't gone to church for a year, not because he's lost his religion, but because he can't take the endless social sermonizing any more.) Some people appalled at the crime, blight, and decay in the projects of Southwest Yonkers focus on America's historical injustices, with a probably genuine sympathy for the decent black people trapped among the sociopaths, and sincerely believe that Judge Sand's approach offers some prospect of amelioration. "It's a start," to quote one idealistic real-estate agent (oxymoron alert!). Other accommodationists live in neighborhoods not targeted as housing sites and would like to cut a deal that would leave them relatively unscathed.

In the meantime, life in Yonkers is ever more politicized. Henry Spallone is running hard for re-election, and the vote in November will be crucial because Yonkers is dispensing with its city manager and giving its mayor full executive power. But in the Byzantine byways of Yonkers politics, "unity" among the defiant has never been more than a matter of contentious expediency, and Spallone has enthusiastic detractors as well as avid partisans. City Manager Neil DeLuca describes him as "an utter fool" who has "no idea what's going on." Jack O'Toole says the only thing worse than the housing projects would be "Hank Spallone becoming a strong mayor." A pro-Spallone group called Concerned Citizens says O'Toole's real aim is to lose the housing case so he can blame Spallone and further his own putative political ambitions. You get the flavor.

The politicization extends even to the rechristening of schools as part of the court-imposed reorganization. There was some talk of a Martin Luther King magnet school, but Judge Sand thought that might discourage white students from enrolling. A proposal to honor the black poet Countee Cullen likewise fell by the wayside, as did suggestions that at least one school might be named for Yonkers. The ultimate winners were two recently deceased local educators, one black and one white; the Puerto Rican patriot Eugenio María de Hostos; the Polish general Casimir Pulaski; and, in a breathtaking, come-from-behind finish, the late Lebanese thinker of stimulating thoughts Kahlil (*The Prophet*) Gibran. The new names still require the approval of Judge Sand and the NAACP, but that is expected to be forthcoming.

Why Not Give In?

THE ARGUMENT for compliance can't be easily dismissed. There are those who argue that the city could have gotten off with a far less stringent "remedy" if it had knuckled under at the outset: "You can't beat a federal judge." Worked over by the courts, financially buffeted—wouldn't it be better if the city made the best of a raw deal and moved on? Maybe. Jack O'Toole and his friends don't see it that way. And even if Yonkers loses in the end, its long, dogged resistance may have had an effect on the way the nation looks at what does or doesn't make sense in dealing with the plight of the underclass.

Yonkers has its intellectual defenders, and there are others, like Professor Peter Salins at Hunter College, who, while not necessarily defenders, have skewered the hypocrisy of putting such an onerous burden on Yonkers while the Scarsdales and Bronxvilles escape. But Salins also says the issue is not "whether the location of publicly subsidized housing in middle-class white neighborhoods is an effective means" of "ending residential racial segregation." And here he's mistaken. That is *precisely* the issue, in Boston and Detroit and Los Angeles, in Yonkers and Scarsdale and even Pound Ridge: the coerced commingling of classes, under the guise of racial reparations, is a strategy that has left a trail of wreckage across the social landscape, sapping the vitality of American cities. To surrender to the premises, the philosophical mindset, is to join the latter-day Bourbons of the bench who have forgotten nothing and learned nothing. □

Article 2. Bulldog Justice
by Ethan Bronner

A political profile, this article focuses on Supreme Court Justice Antonin Scalia, who the author describes as "a wise guy, a street fighter, and a scholar." A talented pianist, a biblical authority, and a literary pundit, Scalia is a pugnacious brawler who is likely to torment his liberal critics, who fear that he will turn the clock back on civil rights, sex discrimination, and reproductive freedom. Conservatives, on the other hand, applaud Scalia's appointment, hopeful that he will stand fast against expanding the role of the High Court into uncharted areas and resist efforts to litigate every social problem brought before the justices. For now, Scalia seems content to preach the sermon of judicial restraint and hope that he will win sufficient converts to prevail.

James Lynn carries a permanent image of Antonin Scalia—that of a wavy-haired, furrow-browed boy from Queens, just out of law school, unabashedly lecturing eight Cleveland attorneys on the validity of Sunday "blue laws."

All of 23 years old that winter night in 1960, Scalia had been wooed to Ohio by Lynn, then with the law firm Jones, Day, Cockley, & Reavis, now chairman of Aetna Life & Casualty Co. The two had first met at Harvard, where Lynn was recruiting for the firm and Scalia was a law-review editor. Lynn approached Scalia, who was buried at the time in a manuscript, late in the

> He's a Wise Guy, a Street Fighter, and a Scholar. He Plays a Mean Piano; He's an Old Testament Prophet. And Make No Mistake About It: Justice Antonin Scalia Intends to Make the Supreme Court See Things His Way.
> By Ethan Bronner

evening in the top-floor library of the law review's Gannett House. It took a lot of talk—two hours in the library and then a 1 AM snack of bacon and eggs in Harvard Square—to persuade the ambitious Scalia that Cleveland might be in his destiny.

Now, two months later, here stood the young prospect, drink in hand, leaning on the Wedgwood-blue mantle in front of a fire in Lynn's Shaker Heights colonial home. But instead of seeking to ingratiate, Scalia, a startling mix of wise-guy street fighter and meticulous scholar, took on his hosts with brazenness, breadth, and machete-like wit in a session that lasted till 3 AM.

Reprinted with permission from *The Washingtonian*, December 1990, p. 136.

"He already had that habit of getting intensely serious with those heavy black eyebrows of his scrunching up and his jaw setting so that he spoke without moving his mouth much," Lynn said. "We were shouting at each other, saying things like, 'How did you ever make law review?' It didn't seem to bother him that everyone was on the other side."

"It was one against eight," adds partner Richard Pogue with fondness. "He was so intense and enthusiastic. I tell you, it was the best recruiting session I have ever been to."

Scalia's hair has thinned, but little else has changed about him in the 30 years since he took up lawyering in Cleveland and then made his way through law teaching jobs, including seven years at the University of Virginia, legal posts in the Nixon and Ford administrations, and an appellate judgeship in Washington before gaining a seat on the Supreme Court in 1986. He still engages in debate with raffish, right-wing enthusiasm. His style of questioning lawyers remains as it was during his years on the DC Circuit Court, when someone once described him as "a knife-fighter—but a friendly knife-fighter."

A rather lonely Goldwater and William Buckley follower in the early 1960s, he has gained ideological company in the past fifteen years, but the companionship hasn't made him complacent. Scalia still fiercely defends tradition against the onslaught of the modern, be it the encroachment of the vernacular on his beloved Latin Mass or the discovery of a right to privacy in the Constitution. And he still goes one-on-eight with boyish zeal—but now with the other justices of the Supreme Court.

Alone, he has lectured the rest of the bench on the futility of the Court's deliberations on the right to abortion and the right to refuse life-saving medical treatment, saying the Constitution does not address these issues. The justices are no more qualified to settle the life-saving question, he argued last summer, than "nine people picked at random from the Kansas City telephone directory."

Alone, too, he dissented from a landmark ruling upholding the constitutionality of the independent counsel, charging that the Court had succumbed to the temptation of an "all-things-considered" approach that offered practical solutions with little or no textual basis in the national charter. And, alone, he has taken the position that states and cities may not, under any but the most egregious circumstances, use affirmative action to overcome past effects of racial discrimination.

But if Scalia still writes often in dissent and if he seeks to draw brighter lines in constitutional doctrine than do his colleagues, his deeply conservative positions are far less marginal today than they were at one time. With the federal bench now consisting of some two-thirds Reagan and Bush appointees and with the liberal wing of the Supreme Court in tatters after the July retirement of Justice William J. Brennan Jr., many Court watchers think Scalia is emerging as the most important and influential force of American law in the 1990s.

Vigorous and driven at age 54, Scalia may have to wait for the older generation on the Court to retire or die before fully exerting his leadership. And the arrival of the newest justice, David Souter, complicates an assessment of Scalia's future. Souter has given the impression of being more moderate and more practical than Scalia, although his record as a state judge in New Hampshire suggests an attraction to the kind of conservatism Scalia advocates. Many believe that what Scalia is doing is sowing the seeds for a key leadership position on the Court if the Republicans retain the White House.

"He plants his flag often and well," observes liberal Harvard constitutional law professor Laurence Tribe, no fan of Scalia's interpretations. "The position he stakes out has special coherence and appeal. It's a sad trend, but . . . on many issues, this is the dawn of Scalia's day."

For liberal critics such as Tribe, a Scalia-dominated Court would turn back the clock to a time when the justices did not see it as their special obligation to protect politically underrepresented groups, such as blacks and women, from suffering the tyranny of the majority. It would be a Court that would not object to politicians regulating sex and reproduction the way they regulate commerce. It would be a Court generally unwilling to expand the protection of the Constitution into unforeseen areas, believing such questions best left to representative democracy.

The result, liberal critics say, would be a less uniform—and less uniformly tolerant—society, at least at the official level. Prayer, properly packaged as a voluntary moment of silence, could well return to many public schools. Affirmative action, stripped of constitutional protection, would likely wither in places where it is most needed. Abortion, remanded to the political sphere, would probably be closely regulated or banned in some states, leaving the middle and upper classes largely unaffected but burdening the poor.

Conservatives believe such a Court is precisely the tonic needed for this ailing society where, they say, every social problem is litigated and nearly everyone—children included—whines about his rights without the least idea of the responsibilities inherent in self-government. Scalia, they hope, is the kind of justice to set things right again and reverse the sad Court trends of the 1960s and '70s.

To some analysts, such as New York University School of Law's Burt Neuborne, a former legal director of the American Civil Liberties Union, Scalia might be to the legal right what Brennan was, for three decades, to the legal left—the intellectual guiding light.

Like Brennan, Scalia is a writer of power and style who is not afraid of big arguments or bold judicial steps. Like Brennan, Scalia also is charming, difficult to dislike even for his opponents. But unlike the avuncular Brennan, Scalia is not universally loved. He is gruffer and tougher, and at least so far he has declined to engage in a practice that helped give Brennan's work its ultimate impact—subtly negotiating with other justices to gain agreement. As Brennan frequently reminded his clerks, "Five votes can do anything around here." Without a majority on your side, legal principles run the risk of having little force.

For the moment, Scalia sees his role differently. Like an Old Testament prophet, he is preaching a return to fundamentals and true faith, apparently hoping that the sheer power of his argument will one day prevail.

"For Scalia, to abandon the ideal is a most serious matter; it happens because of original sin," says Lee Liberman, a former Scalia clerk and now an associate counsel in the White House Counsel's office. "Men aren't angels, but you don't give up easily."

Scalia indirectly addressed his current role on the Court two years ago at the University of Cincinnati in a talk devoted partly to William Howard Taft, the former president who was Chief Justice throughout the 1920s.

Scalia referred to a Taft biographer who argued that because Taft had not helped move the Court where it ultimately went—a more liberal direction—he lacked "a large vision of things to come." Then Scalia added: "This is presumably the school of history that assesses the greatness of a leader by his success in predicting where the men he is leading want to go."

It's not a school to which Scalia aspires.

When Scalia was put up for a seat on the Court in 1986, he was a sleeper nominee—a Robert Bork without the paper trail.

He was named for confirmation at the same time that William Rehnquist was nominated by President Reagan to move from associate justice to Chief Justice. Elevating Rehnquist, a known and despised commodity to liberals, acted as a lightning rod for frustration on the left. Scalia waltzed in unopposed.

It was not that Scalia was thought to be anything other than he was—a profoundly conservative legal analyst. But there was something so appealing about him, this first Italian-American nominee with his robust smile and weakness for music, his zesty Boston Irish wife, and nine handsome children. Better still, he was funny. Despite the upcoming confirmation hearings by the Senate Judiciary

---

Scalia is preaching a return to fundamentals and true faith, hoping that the sheer power of his argument will one day prevail.

Committee, Scalia pounded liberal committee member Howard Metzenbaum on the St. Albans tennis court and then, chided about it in front of the entire committee, replied without missing a beat: "It was a case of my integrity overcoming my judgment, Senator."

Several women's and abortion-rights groups did oppose Scalia, knowing he would vote to overturn *Roe* v. *Wade* in an instant. But *Roe* seemed far enough away from danger in those days that their concerns had no political reverberations. And Scalia had friends and colleagues testify to his fairness toward women.

Sally Katzen, a partner at Wilmer, Cutler & Pickering, who first came to know Scalia through their mutual interest in administrative law, testified for him because she genuinely likes and respects him despite their ideological differences and because he had, during his leadership of the administrative law section of the American Bar Association, brought women into positions of leadership there.

"I remember being told that a number of women's groups were going to oppose him and my first thought was, 'Oh Christ, how many of them do I belong to?' " Katzen recalls.

One of the reasons liberals had so little to go on in deciding whether to oppose Scalia was that, through dumb luck, he had been passed over in 1981 for the job of solicitor general, the government's advocate before the Supreme Court.

Ernest Gellhorn, managing partner of the Jones, Day Los Angeles office and a friend since the early 1960s, recalls well Scalia's chagrin after being flown to Washington from the University of Chicago for the solicitor-general interview with Attorney General William French

Smith and then failing to get an offer. Scalia was one of two finalists—the winner was Rex Lee—and his loss of such a coveted appointment in that first Reagan administration was hard for him to take.

Over lunch at the Hay-Adams, Gellhorn tried to comfort his friend by suggesting that the turn of events might prove a blessing in disguise. If Scalia should ever get a Supreme Court nomination, he would arrive without the dangerous baggage that solicitors general carry from all the briefs they sign in controversial cases. Five years later, his nomination in hand and the solicitor general's office an ideological battleground, Scalia took Gellhorn out to lunch and reminded him of his prescience.

No cameras or recording devices are allowed into the Supreme Court, the marble temple of our shared constitutional faith. Its workings are on view only to the few who attend the 150 hours of oral argument each year and the small community of Court watchers that reads the final opinions.

Unelected and essentially unaccountable, the justices carry out their unusual task of defending and interpreting our sacred texts in surroundings that evoke the inner sanctum of a priesthood. The Court has its own seamstress and cabinetmaker, its own laundry and police. Its writings employ the upper case for any term remotely related to its work—Court, Term, Nation, and so on. Its marshals maintain a decorum rare in contemporary government, urging compliance to rules with warnings to visitors such as, "Keep all body parts off the brass rail."

The justices sit on custom-made leather chairs at a mahogany bench with brass spittoons at their feet. Before entering the marble-filled courtroom itself, they don their black robes behind a velvet curtain and engage in a ritualistic handshake with one another.

When members of the public file into the columned courtroom, they often slide into the benches as into church pews, taking on stiff, Sunday-morning gestures. Jewish men have been seen unconsciously trying to cover their heads in an instinctive reach for a yarmulke.

The work of the justices is to determine whether the words and structure of our constitutional and legal texts, some written long ago, are being applied correctly to new situations. Brennan and his liberal colleagues of recent decades—men such as Earl Warren, William O. Douglas, and Hugo Black—argued that the grand, ample constitutional guarantees of liberty and equality were crafted to be vessels that, if not empty, certainly contained plenty of room. The justices were to fill out the meaning in an effort to make America a more just society. Such justices always spoke of a "living charter" and of the special role of the judiciary to prevent political majorities from running roughshod over the unorthodox, the unrepresented, the weak.

Since World War II, that prevailing wisdom has played a vital role in opening the nation's institutions to those who are not white, male, and materially comfortable. But to analysts such as Scalia, Bork, and Rehnquist, such judicial approaches distort the political process. By injecting the liberal values of the intellectual class into the Constitution and imposing them throughout the country, judges deprive the states of their vital and traditional role of communal self-definition. Too much emphasis on individual liberty and federal power sucks dry the practice of self-government, they argue.

Scalia is in awe of the Constitution but less for its added-on Bill of Rights and inspiring talk of individual liberty than for the governmental structure it establishes in its main sections. He has written, for example, that a constitutional guarantee is "like a commercial loan; you can only get it if, at the time, you don't really need it."

In his view, general notions of free speech and religious freedom are so deeply embedded in the nation's psyche that they would survive with or without a written Constitution. What is more fragile for him—and therefore more needy of preservation—is the separation of powers, the independence of the branches, the formal system of checks and balances that the Constitution set up.

Scalia believes that liberals have effectively oversold the Constitution to the nation: Americans, he complains, seem to think that all of their values—all that is good, wise, and just—can be found within the document's text if only they look hard enough; if only, like some Renaissance sculptor, they labor to free the exquisite form within.

Scalia agrees that the Constitution stakes out certain areas of individual liberty as off-limits to government. Nor is he averse to a little modernism in interpretation. When the Constitution speaks in value-laden terms—"cruel and unusual punishment," for example—contemporary values may be applied since what is unusual today differs from what was unusual then. But most of the rest

of the big questions of the day—sexual mores, the prolongation of life through technology, and much that is still unforeseen—must be worked out through the legislative process.

One of Scalia's main thrusts is to get some of the most interesting and divisive societal questions out of the courts entirely, thereby reducing the tendency to litigate national disputes. As he noted in a 1987 speech to the American Bar Association, the number of civil filings in federal district courts has increased from 58,000 in 1960 to more than a quarter of a million. Gone, he lamented, is any meaning to the phrase, "Don't make a federal case out of it."

A year and a half ago, Scalia angrily protested when the high court decided the *Webster* abortion case by upholding several state-imposed restrictions on abortion without addressing the funda-

---

Americans, Scalia complains, think that all of their values can be found within the Constitution if only they look hard enough.

---

mental question of whether the 1973 *Roe v. Wade* ruling was correct. Scalia favored overturning *Roe* outright, thereby sending the question of whether abortion is legal and under what circumstances back to state legislatures.

"The outcome of today's case will doubtless be heralded as a triumph of judicial statesmanship," he wrote. "It is not that, unless it is statesmanlike needlessly to prolong this Court's self-awarded sovereignty over a field where it has little proper business since the answers to most of the cruel questions posed are political and not juridical."

He went on to complain that the Court's retention of control of the issue "distorts the public perception of the role of this Court. We can now look forward to at least another Term with carts full of mail from the public, and streets full of demonstrators, urging us—their unelected and life-tenured judges who have been awarded those extraordinary, undemocratic characteristics precisely in order that we might follow the law despite popular will—to follow the popular will."

Scalia considers himself an "originalist," meaning that he looks to the origi-

nal meaning of the Constitution's words and then to the traditions of the nation in trying to decide whether and how the words apply to a situation today.

"Originalism is a moderating force because its opposite, non-originalism, caters to the major vice of all life-tenured judges, and that is the tendency to pour your own prejudices into a case," Scalia told George Washington University law students during a recent seminar.

For Scalia, who reveres precision in language and also sports something of a libertarian streak, when a right is made explicit by the text or when generations of rulings build up an unassailable interpretation of a textually asserted right, then that right must be defended fully against incursions he might support as a citizen or politician.

Thus, Scalia had no trouble joining the two rulings that protected flag-burning as political expression under the First Amendment although he is a deeply patriotic man with nothing but contempt for flag-burners. He dissented from a mandatory drug-testing ruling, and he opposed efforts to make it easier for alleged victims of child abuse to testify against their accused abusers without having to confront them directly in court, because the Sixth Amendment requires "confrontation."

Last year, Justice Sandra Day O'Connor wrote for a majority of the Court that testimony by closed-circuit television in such circumstances—a growing practice in states trying to shield such children from emotional trauma—was constitutional. She said the Constitution did not give an *absolute* right to face-to-face confrontation. Scalia lashed out in dissent: "Seldom has this Court failed so conspicuously to sustain a categorical guarantee of the Constitution against the tide of prevailing current opinion."

But on questions of personal habit or family practice, where the Constitution is to him silent, Scalia's social conservatism can be seen plainly.

The most famous—or notorious—example came in a 1989 case concerning whether a man who fathered the child of a married woman could make, under the Constitution, paternity claims on the child, which he had been denied by California law. In his much-discussed Footnote 6, Scalia sought to announce a new and quite narrow approach to discerning tradition. He said that the only way to determine whether a claimed right had constitutional validity was to "refer to the most specific level at which a relevant tradition protecting, or denying protection to, the asserted right can be identified."

In other words, if there is no specific history of giving such paternity rights to lovers when the disputed child is living in a closed family unit, then their constitutional claims are dead. Scalia referred half a dozen times to the union that produced the child as adulterous.

For strong conservatives, it was a fine decision. Robert Bork, in inscribing a copy of his book, *The Tempting of America,* for Scalia, wrote, "Tighten up Footnote 6." But Scalia's approach was so narrow that while he had a majority for the result, three of the concurring four justices—all, except Rehnquist—specifically distanced themselves from Footnote 6.

To liberals it was a frightening effort. Brennan, writing in astonished dissent, said that if such specificity had been the rule until then, many landmark decisions would have turned out differently. He said the use of contraceptives by single and married people, the freedom from corporal punishment in schools, the freedom from an arbitrary transfer from a prison to a psychiatric institution, and even the right to raise one's natural but illegitimate children were not, as Scalia sought to limit them, " 'interests traditionally protected by our society' at the time of their consideration by this Court."

Brennan went on: "The document that the plurality construes today is unfamiliar to me. It is not the living charter that I have taken to be our Constitution; it is instead a stagnant, archaic, hidebound document steeped in the prejudices and superstitions of a time long past."

The only child of Sicilian immigrants—a professor of Romance languages at Brooklyn College and a schoolteacher—Antonin Scalia was born in Trenton, New Jersey, and grew up in Queens. A star pupil and whiz kid on radio contests, he attended a Catholic military academy in Brooklyn and graduated as valedictorian at Georgetown University before beginning at Harvard Law.

At Harvard, Scalia became engaged to Maureen McCarthy, a doctor's daughter. A smart and funny Radcliffe student, she launched the college's Young Democrats as John Kennedy sought his party's nomination, but she embraced the Republican party soon after. Married to Scalia, she turned into a model mid-century mother and homemaker, running a large, happy home with a successful husband. The mother of nine, she has never worked professionally but has been an active community volunteer, notably at an abortion-alternative center and in programs aiding the handicapped.

In McLean, the Scalias' current home, she has volunteered in the schools.

The family—the children range in age from 10 years old to 29—is deeply and conservatively Catholic. They attend weekly Mass and, in the old tradition, avoid meat on Fridays. Ann, the eldest, works for a Chicago-area advertising company; Eugene, 27, the second child, was editor-in-chief of the University of Chicago Law Review last year and now is an associate in a Los Angeles firm; John, 25, is in his third year at Northwestern School of Law. Two of the children are married; there are, as yet, no grandchildren.

Scalia tries to spend time with his family and has invested in a series of large-capacity vans over the years, packing in up to seven children at a time and driving cross-country for vacations, appearing to all the world like the head of some kind of commune on holiday. Someone once observed that Antonin Scalia had the shortest hair of any VW van owner in America in the late 1960s.

Nino, as his friends have always called him, has been religious, conservative, and self-confident from his youth. A compulsive debater, he dominates oral arguments at the high court through his mix of jugular attack and leavening wit.

Patricia Wald, chief judge on the DC

> ## "In the immortal words of one of his high school classmates, 'The kid was a conservative when he was seventeen.' "

Circuit and a firm liberal who had a stormy professional but friendly personal relationship with Scalia during their four years as colleagues, introduced him to the DC Circuit judicial conference two years ago with sly references to the justice's habits.

Saying she was pleased that Scalia had consented to speak, she added: "I am especially grateful—in light of what goes on up there at oral argument—to get a word in edgewise before he begins."

Running quickly over Scalia's professional ascent to the Court, she said, "Through the breathtaking climb, Nino was always exploring, learning, growing, changing. In the immortal words of one of his high school classmates, reported in the press: 'The kid was a conservative when he was seventeen.' "

Scalia is not a man to wake up in the middle of the night, wondering if he is doing the right thing. "This is no Hamlet," says Henry Goldberg, a Washington communications lawyer who served with him in the Nixon administration.

Despite his sometimes harsh judicial and political conservatism, Scalia has a number of moderate and liberal friends, even if they disagree vehemently with him. Ruth Bader Ginsburg, a Carter appointee to the DC Circuit, is a very close friend. Alan Morrison, director of Ralph Nader's Public Citizen Litigation Group, and his wife see the Scalias socially and have for a number of years. Scalia often hires at least one clerk out of four who is politically liberal; he seems to like making sure there is at least some mix of views in his chambers, although the one liberal has been known to feel timid at times.

Paul Verkuil, president of the College of William and Mary, an old friend of Scalia's but no fellow traveler, says: "I feel very strongly about his character and integrity and quality of mind but wouldn't always vote with him."

One of the reasons Verkuil likes Scalia is the justice's lack of pretension or undue deference to institutional grandness. Verkuil remembers coming to visit Washington and sitting with his wife in the VIP section of the Court listening to oral argument. Suddenly a clerk handed him a scrawled note from Scalia: "Who let you guys in here?"

If Scalia socializes with those less rigidly conservative, it may be from force of habit as well as inclination. In the worlds Scalia inhabited as a young man—prestige law firms, university faculties—there simply were not very many ideological soul mates available. He jutted his chin, advocating Goldwater for president and the dismantling of much of the regulatory state, but he was so much fun that few held it against him. In fact, many admired it, looking upon his views as exotic. Despite his arrival at dizzying heights, Scalia still stays in touch with many old friends.

"I always smile when I think of Nino," says Sally Katzen, the administrative-law practitioner. "He's a very warm, engaging, embracing man. He has that wonderful Italian heritage and intellectual curiosity driven by wit and humor. He likes to tease but he doesn't take advantage of people."

She recalls an incident at the American Bar Association convention in New Orleans in 1987. Both had attended a late party, and Scalia challenged her to join him for a jog early the next morning. She

215

went but felt awful and kept falling behind. Scalia poked fun at her inability to keep up until he realized that she really couldn't face the run. "Once he realized that, he stopped immediately and we walked off and had beignets and coffee."

Beginning in the mid-1970s, Scalia found more people who shared his ideas moving into positions of power.

Rosalie "Ricky" Silberman, now vice chairman of the Equal Employment Opportunity Commission, and her husband, Laurence Silberman, now a federal appeals judge in Washington, became among the Scalias' closest friends. They got to know one another when Scalia worked under Larry Silberman in Gerald Ford's Justice Department, and their paths continued to cross through their shared tenure on the DC Circuit. Some of the Silbermans' fondest memories of their days at Justice are captured in photographs of them standing around the piano with Nino playing and all singing.

Scalia is a fine storyteller and speaker. In a 1988 speech to the DC Circuit, he told the assembled bar:

"I think it is generally agreed among all the justices of the Supreme Court that the most unadmirable characteristic of appellate counsel is mispronouncing the word 'Sca-LEE-ah.' Better you should say simply, 'Justice,' or 'Mr. Justice,' or 'Sir,' or even 'Madam,' than that you should say, 'Justice SCAL-ya.' Several regrettably important cases have been lost because of that. . . .

"Of course, I have always been confronted with this problem. . . . Sometimes my colleagues on the bench would come to my assistance. I recall one of those days, in what were known as the golden years of the DC Circuit, when I was sitting on an appellate case and Judge Bork was one of the other members of the panel. Counsel consistently kept pronouncing my name wrong, 'Judge SCAL-ya,' and finally Judge Bork just couldn't take it anymore. He said, 'Counsel, that is 'Sca-LEE-ah.' And I looked over at Judge Bork and said, 'Thank you, Judge Burke.' I was a very young judge then. I've been working a lot on my judicial demeanor."

The Silbermans and Scalias got closest when, after Carter was elected, both men found themselves out of a job and went to the American Enterprise Institute, along with Bork—who lost his job as solicitor general at the same time—and Irving Kristol.

"It was a glorious intellectual feast," Ricky Silberman says. "We were engaged in defining our conservatism at the time.

Many of us were neoconservatives, which, as Larry defines them, are conservatives who used to be wrong for the right reasons. Nino was deeply involved in those conversations and, I think, testing his ideas along with the rest of us. Much of what was being said then has been proved right, and I think, in fact, that he is mellower today than he was then."

Mellower, perhaps, but hardly mellow. One has only to see him at oral argument, hear of his missives to fellow judges, read his opinions in majority or dissent to grasp that this is not a relaxed man. Or see him on the tennis court.

Ask his clerks.

"He and I used to play tennis together, and he would demolish me through sheer competitiveness," recalls former clerk Paul Cappuccio, now a Washington lawyer. Cappuccio said the hardest part was that after the tennis, "There was no four-o'clock tea party, only a fifteen-rounder discussion of cases."

Another former clerk says that what he most remembers about his year at the high court was his boss's intensity:

"When Scalia's hard at work on an opinion, he has a glowering quality. He leaves his door open and proclaims an open-door policy. But one of the first times I had to interrupt him while he was working at the word processor, he was so concentrated I had a feeling of stopping a train."

Scalia's dealings with his colleagues have been equally intense. He has a reputation for sending what have been dubbed "Ninograms," sharply laying out his concerns regarding a case. Once a justice has begun to circulate a draft of an opinion, Scalia has been known to respond in the smallest

---

Harry Blackmun does not hide his contempt for Scalia and has complained of his tendency to dominate oral argument.

---

detail, annotating line by line and suggesting changes. Scalia once offended soft-spoken Justice Lewis Powell by correcting his grammar in such a draft months before Powell's 1987 retirement. And in a widely noted barb at Sandra Day O'Connor in the *Webster* ruling, he said her opinion "cannot be taken seriously," calling one of her main points "irrational."

Scalia, who is devoted to nothing if not the ruthless exposure of what he thinks of as bad ideas, has lamented a lack of vigorous debate among the justices. It is clear that he occasionally uses oral argument as a means of sending a message to another justice down the bench.

Justice Harry Blackmun, a kindly, almost grandmotherly figure who has pegged his place in history on his authorship of the *Roe* decision, does not hide his contempt for his young colleague and has complained of Scalia's tendency to dominate oral argument. And Chief Justice Rehnquist once watched Scalia pound a lawyer before the Court so fiercely with procedural questions that he abruptly stepped in, saying to the attorney, "I hope when you're given an opportunity to do so, you'll address some of your remarks to the question on which this Court voted to grant [review]."

Rehnquist, whose job it is to keep the process moving at the Court, has also been known to find Scalia's constant search for first principles exasperating.

Scalia's penchant for enunciating the clearest guidelines for lower courts and the justices themselves is something he has arrived at through long reflection. In speeches and opinions he has argued that a case-by-case approach is inappropriate for the nation's highest court because it leaves too much wiggle room for the next time.

As he said at Harvard University in 1989: "When one is dealing, as my court often is, with issues so heartfelt that they are believed by one side or the other to be resolved by the Constitution itself, it does not greatly appeal to one's sense of justice to say, 'Well, that earlier case had nine factors, this one has nine plus one.' Much better, even at the expense of the mild substantive distortion that any generalization introduces, to have a clear, previously enunciated rule that one can point to in explanation of the decision."

But finding a majority for an overarching approach is always much harder than finding one for a narrow, facts-of-the-case one. It may make Scalia seem more "principled" for some that he tries, but for others—liberals especially—he takes the wrong tack for the mucky real world.

"He has trouble realizing that everything isn't beautiful, sharp, and clean," complained a judge who follows his work closely and generally disagrees with him. "He is insensitive to the fact that a lot of people aren't living good lives. They have messy lives filled with conflict which are not going to be solved by maintaining the rigid structure of government and the relations between the branches.''

Laurence Gold, general counsel to the AFL-CIO, says that Scalia's approach would be fine in a perfect world but is inappropriate for the one in which we live.

''This is an example of the best being an enemy of the good,'' he says. ''When Scalia is at full steam, he produces good polemic but not necessarily a full and fair explanation of the problems inherent in an issue.''

What remains to be seen is how long Scalia will play the role of preacher of first principles. He is young, and the institutional power of the Court rests with an older, entrenched generation. Once that changes and Scalia finds himself coming upon the same constitutional question for the third time—still unresolved to his liking because other justices have refused to go along with him—he may change tacks and seek to build majorities on narrower grounds.

He has done that in his work in government. In his time, he has been a champion schmoozer, someone able to develop consensus through sheer personality. Over time, his purist's sense of the Court's role may yield more to such tendencies.

''For me,'' said an admirer who often feels Scalia is too rigid, ''the big question is, here you have a man of such charm, such rapport, such collegiality. Why is he letting himself become a sole dissenter in so many cases? Here's a man who could bring people together. He has done it in the past. He knows how to win. Right now, he doesn't give the impression he wants to win. But, knowing Nino, that could well change.'' ❏

Article 3. The Swing to the Left in State Courts
by Ted Gest

Ted Gest argues that while the U.S. Supreme Court may be becoming increasingly conservative, state jurists are fast embracing judicial activism. Specifically, he contends that state courts are rapidly expanding the rights of citizens by invoking the powers and protections of state constitutions—not the U.S. Constitution. This trend, which is relatively new, is clearly evident in such areas as discrimination and privacy, where the state courts have struck down unconstitutional school financing schemes and anti-abortion legislation. Conservative court-watchers decry this trend, insisting that many state courts—whose members are either appointed for life or who stand for election only infrequently—are "legislating" from the bench with near impunity.

Forget the Supreme Court. The real hot spot for judicial activism these days is state courts, where jurists in increasing numbers are expanding the rights of citizens at the same time the Supreme Court is limiting constitutional protections in such areas as privacy and discrimination. And the tool the state courts are using is not the U.S. Constitution but state constitutions that until recently had been relatively ignored. The striking power of state high courts was evident in two cases from Southern tribunals this month. The Texas Supreme Court, pointing to extreme disparities between rich and poor school districts, ordered a statewide overhaul of school financing. Three days later, the Florida Supreme Court invoked a privacy-protection clause in the state constitution to strike down a law that required girls under 18 to receive parental consent before obtaining abortions.

New judicial activism. Crime suspects, workers challenging drug or lie-detector tests and shopping-mall pamphleteers are among many beneficiaries of this judicial activism. "State constitutions that had been dormant for a century or more now are getting attention," says Vermont Atty. Gen. Jeffrey Amestoy, who heads a committee of legal experts monitoring the trend. About 400 state decisions in the 1980s have gone further than the U.S. Supreme Court in protecting individual rights, three times the number of similar cases in the 1970s, reports Prof. Ronald K. L. Collins of Temple University School of Law. Among major criminal-law decisions, courts in New York State and Mississippi rejected a doctrine the U.S. Supreme Court upheld for federal cases that juries may consider evidence that police officers seized illegally but in "good faith." Judges elsewhere have used state constitutional guarantees to privacy to protect workers from being forced to take random drug tests or polygraph exams when suspected in thefts—rights that had been curtailed by federal courts. A half-dozen state courts have gone beyond the Supreme Court by requiring shopping-mall owners to allow leafleting, reasoning that freedom of speech outweighs guarding private-property rights.

This "New Federalism" in state courts rests on a longstanding principle of the Republic that allows states to enact stricter protections of individual rights than the federal Constitution. Over the years, many states have done just that. Nearly three dozen explicitly bar public support for religion, 18 prohibit sex discrimination and 9 guarantee a right to privacy.

Much of the judicial trend is encouraged by civil libertarians, who have been quick to shift their lawsuits to state courts to avoid unfavorable rulings by conservative federal judges appointed by Ronald Reagan. "Texas courts are much more receptive than local federal judges on equality and privacy issues," says Jim Harrington, legal director of the Texas Civil Liberties Union, who now files virtually every case raising a constitutional issue in state courts. "Western states have a real egalitarian, individualist tradition." Harrington notes that even courts in normally conservative Montana and Utah have handed down decisions favoring women's or criminal suspects' rights. One liberal applauding the trend is Justice William Brennan, who has lately been on the losing end of many of the High Court's constitutional-rights decisions. Brennan said in a 1986 speech that state courts are assuming "a leadership role in the protection of individual rights and liberties."

Conservatives and some state attorneys general decry the emergence of state-court activism. "State courts are in various stages of radicalism," complains James McClellan of the conservative Center for Judicial Studies, which recently issued a report denouncing the trend. The record of critics in trying to stem the activism is not great. Though California conservatives were able to organize a drive to oust state Chief Justice Rose Bird and two of her liberal colleagues in 1986, her defeat was an exception. Most state judges either serve lifetime terms or face voters only infrequently, so many liberal activist judges are immune to conservative attacks. They are free to issue the kind of freewheeling decisions conservatives will be battling for years. ■

SELECTED BIBLIOGRAPHY

Abraham, Henry J. *The Judiciary: The Supreme Court and the Governmental Process.* Needham Heights, MA: Allyn & Bacon, 1987.

Barber, James D. *The Presidential Character: Predicting Performance in the White House.* Englewood Cliffs, NJ: Prentice-Hall, 1985.

Barone, Michael, and Grant Ujifusa. *The Almanac of American Politics.* Washington, D.C.: National Journal, 1990.

Bryner, Gary. *Bureaucratic Discretion: Law and Policy in Federal Regulatory Agencies.* New York: Pergamon Press, 1987.

Carp, Robert A., and Ronald Stidham. *The Federal Courts.* Washington, D.C.: Congressional Quarterly Press, 1985.

Cronin, Thomas E. *The State of the Presidency.* Boston: Little, Brown, 1980.

Davidson, Roger, and Walter J. Oleszek. *Congress and Its Members.* Washington, D.C.: Congressional Quarterly Press, 1990.

Downs, Anthony. *Inside Bureaucracy.* Boston: Little, Brown, 1967.

Edwards, George C., III, and Stephen Wayne, Jr. *Presidential Leadership.* New York: St. Martin's, 1990.

Elliot, Jeffrey M., and Sheikh R. Ali. *The Presidential-Congressional Political Dictionary.* Santa Barbara, CA: ABC-Clio, 1984.

Fenno, Richard F. *Home Style: House Members in Their Districts.* Boston: Little, Brown, 1978.

Green, Mark J. *Who Runs Congress?* New York: Dell, 1984.

Greenstein, Fred I. *Leadership in the Modern Presidency.* Cambridge, MA: Harvard University Press, 1988.

Hart, John. *The Presidential Branch.* Elmsford, NY: Pergamon Press, 1987.

Jacobson, Gary C. *The Politics of Congressional Elections.* Boston: Little, Brown, 1987.

Levy, Leonard W. *Original Intent and the Framers' Constitution.* New York: Macmillan, 1988.

Neely, Richard. *How Courts Govern America.* New Haven, CT: Yale University Press, 1981.

Neustadt, Richard E. *Presidential Power: The Politics of Leadership from FDR to Carter.* New York: John Wiley, 1980.

O'Brien, David M. *Storm Center: The Supreme Court and American Politics.* New York: Norton, 1990.

Oleszek, Walter J. *Congressional Procedures and the Policy Process.* Washington, D.C.: Congressional Quarterly Press, 1989.

Rieselbach, Leroy N. *Congressional Reform.* Washington, D.C.: Congressional Quarterly Press, 1986.

Riley, Dennis D. *Controlling the Federal Bureaucracy.* Philadelphia: Temple University Press, 1987.

Rosen, Bernard. *Holding Government Bureaucracies Accountable.* New York: Praeger, 1984.

Rourke, Francis E. *Bureaucracy, Politics, and Public Policy.* Boston: Little, Brown, 1984.

Tribe, Lawrence. *God Save this Honorable Court.* New York: Random House, 1985.

Wilson, James Q. *Bureaucracy: What Government Agencies Do and Why They Do It.* New York: Basic Books, 1989.

Woodward, Bob, and Scott Armstrong. *The Brethren: Inside the Supreme Court.* New York: Simon & Schuster, 1979.

PUBLIC POLICY

For our purposes, *public policy* can be defined as a deliberate course of action adopted by a government institution or public official for resolving a particular issue or problem. This section focuses on a variety of public policy questions, among them economic and regulatory matters, social welfare concerns, environmental and energy initiatives, and foreign and defense considerations. Public policy significantly affects the lives of every citizen in numerous ways, some of them obvious and some less so. The study of public policy is important; it helps us to make intelligent policy choices.

Specifically, policy analysis is primarily concerned with the description and investigation of how and why particular policies are proposed, adopted, and implemented. It eschews prescription in favor of explanation, preferring to search for the causes and consequences of various policy proposals. At the same time, we cannot dismiss the importance of policy advocacy, which seeks to examine public policy in the context of discovery and recommendation. In this regard, policy advocacy is an outgrowth of ethical principles and ideological predispositions. Thus, we cannot sharply separate the two, as any policy option must be evaluated in the context of its chances of adoption, the probable effectiveness of the option, and the difficulties of implementation.

In order to assess public policy, political scientists, among others, have developed several theories and models to help understand and explain the decision-making process. These include systems theory, which views public policy as the response of a political system to demands arising from its environment; group theory, which views public policy as the product of the group struggle; elite theory, which views public policy as a reflection of the values and preferences of the governing elite; and institutionalism, which views public policy as the result of institutional structures, functions, processes, and relationships.

Clearly, the creation of public policy is a dynamic process, involving a wide variety of actors, events, and institutions, which cooperate and conflict in a host of predictable and unpredictable ways. Generally, policy issues are raised by public officials, the mass media, interest groups, and the bureaucracy, who may work alone or in combination in their efforts to place issues on the public agenda. Despite this fact, public policy cannot solely be explained by examining the decisions that result from government actions. Policy makers may be major catalysts for social change, but the public agenda is shaped—to a large extent—by the goals and objectives of the citizenry.

In our society, most people approach public policy with a problem-solving mentality—that is, for every problem, there must be a solution. Unfortunately, this is not always the case, as a public policy may fail to achieve its desired result. This may occur for several reasons, among them: there is no general agreement on what the issues are; when perceptions of issues differ, it is likely that the policies will reflect conflicting goals or prove inadequate to address the problem; the costs of a total "solution" may be too high or resources too few, even if such a solution was theoretically possible; the problem itself may change before a policy has had time to achieve its desired result, or a new problem may intervene, thereby drawing attention and resources away from the first; and some "problems" are, by definition, inherently unsolvable.

In his book, *Public Policy-Making,* James E. Anderson, a well-known policy expert, provides a conceptual framework that should assist you in analyzing the articles in this section. Anderson's model consists of five main steps: (1) Problem identification and agenda formation. What is the policy problem? What makes it a public problem? How did it get on the government agenda? (2) Formulation. How are alternatives for dealing with the problem developed? Who participates in policy formulation? (3) Adoption. How is a policy alternative adopted or enacted? What requirements must be satisfied?

Who adopts policy? What processes are used? What is the context of the adopted policy? (4) Implementation. Who is involved? What is done, if anything, to carry a policy into effect? What impact does this have on policy content? (5) Evaluation. How is the effectiveness or impact of a policy measured? Who evaluates policy? What are the consequences of policy evaluation? Are there demands for change or revocation?

In assessing a policy, you should do so in terms of its impact on the target situation or group; its impact on situations or groups other than the target; its impact on future as well as immediate conditions; its direct costs, in terms of resources devoted to the program; and its indirect costs, including the loss of opportunities to do other things. Obviously, all these aspects of public policy are very difficult to identify, describe, and measure. Still, in order to understand and evaluate a public policy, it is important to weigh the goals, means, and methods of a policy option. This will help us to simplify and clarify our thinking about politics and public policy, identify important aspects of policy problems, allow us to communicate with each other by focusing on essential features of political life, enable us to distinguish that which is important from that which is less so, and suggest explanations for public policy and aid us to predict its consequences.

Chapter 15, *Economic and Regulatory Policy,* begins with a discussion of America's debt burden. The author suggests that the long-term consequences of the debt debacle could prove infinitely worse than initially anticipated. The powerful combination of excess consumption, reduced savings, and high debt suggests that the economic recovery may be less vigorous than previous comebacks. The second article explores the myth of an independent Federal Reserve Board. In reality, the Fed is beholden to the nation's large commercial banks, which may explain many of its misguided monetary policies. The time has arrived, concludes the author, to end the Fed's autonomy, and transfer its money-creating functions to the Department of the Treasury or some other cabinet agency. The final article analyzes the causes and consequences of the savings and loan scandal, which can be attributed, in large part, to corrupt campaign financing practices and inaccurate accounting procedures.

Chapter 16, *Social Welfare Policy,* focuses on the nation's poor, beginning with an article that attempts to define the underclass, identify its members, and explain its behavior. In this piece, the author draws a distinction between those who are merely poor and those who belong to the underclass, which includes those people who are found at the bottom of both the legal and illegal class systems. The second selection suggests that current discussion of the underclass reflects the assumption that government social programs are doomed to failure, a view that the author contends is oversimplified, exaggerated, or untrue. The article disputes the view that, first, the situation is completely hopeless and that, second, the underclass can be healed from within black America, through black leadership. In the third piece, the author describes America's growing impatience with the homeless, arguing that public disfavor may be the result of changes in the numbers, makeup, and behavior of the nation's homeless.

Chapter 17, *Environmental and Energy Policy,* starts with a hard-hitting exposé of the Environmental Protection Agency, which ignored independent and agency findings concerning the dangers of dioxin—one of the most deadly substances known to science—in response to political pressure from the chemical and paper manufacturers, which mounted an aggressive lobbying campaign to prevent a possible ban by the agency. The author documents the dangers of dioxin, as well as the political wheeling-and-dealing by industry representatives. The next article examines the Superfund legislation, which has unfairly strapped banks and insurance companies with the staggering costs of environmental cleanups, regardless of their true liability. The last article discusses President Bush's National Energy Strategy, which encompasses over 100 proposals aimed at increasing the nation's domestic energy production—a strategy that places heavy emphasis on nuclear power, energy conservation, and deregulation of the natural gas industry. The article also presents an alternative national energy strategy, which calls for improving automobile fuel efficiency, raising the federal gasoline tax, and increasing funds for research on energy conservation and renewable energy.

Chapter 18, *Foreign and Defense Policy,* assesses the decline and fall of the Soviet Empire and the nature and direction of American foreign policy in a post-Cold War world. The United States, the author believes, should develop a new foreign-policy consensus, one that will inevitably involve a spirited debate over strict adherence to national interest, a desire to export American democracy, and a commitment to global partnership. The second selection examines the Bush foreign policy, concluding that in the post-Cold War era, the international interests of the United States, as well as its own economic well-being, will require the president to develop a set of new ideas, skills, and approaches to the conduct of foreign relations. The final article highlights the perils of Pentagon politics, showing how an important aircraft review failed to consider serious flaws in the programs, bowing instead to the demands of political expediency.

DISCUSSION QUESTIONS

1. How has the nation's debt burden affected its economic recovery?
2. What are the long-term implications of today's debt crisis?
3. To whom is the Federal Reserve Board accountable and responsible?
4. Should the Fed be stripped of its "independence"? Why, or why not?
5. Who is to blame for the savings and loan scandal?
6. What steps should Congress take to deal with the S & L crisis?
7. Why is it so difficult to define the underclass?
8. How does the underclass differ from the merely impoverished?
9. Is it possible to revitalize the nation's ghettos? Why, or why not?
10. What explains the growing resentment against the homeless?
11. Why should the middle class care about the homeless?
12. Is the Environmental Protection Agency really "independent," or is it a tool of the very industries it is supposed to regulate?
13. In what way, if any, has the Superfund failed?
14. Is America headed toward a post-petroleum society?
15. What are the essential components of President Bush's National Energy Strategy?
16. Why are many environmentalists opposed to nuclear power?
17. What path should the United States follow in a post-Cold War world?
18. Will the United Nations play an expanded role with the end of the Cold War?
19. What explains the collapse of the Soviet Union and the liberation of Eastern Europe?
20. Are economic questions likely to assume a new international importance?
21. To what extent, if any, does Pentagon politics affect major weapons reviews?

KEY TERMS

AID TO FAMILIES WITH DEPENDENT CHILDREN   Financial assistance provided under the categorical assistance program of the Social Security Act of 1935 for children who lack adequate support but are living with one parent or relative.

ARMS RACE   The competition between nations to maintain their real or perceived military superiority.

BALANCE OF POWER   A relationship in which countries attempt to achieve national security in an environment of shifting alignments and alliances by maintaining an approximate power equilibrium in the state system.

COLD WAR   The post-World War II period of global tensions between the United States and the Soviet Union.

DEPARTMENT OF DEFENSE   The branch of the U.S. government responsible for managing the nation's military forces and materiel.

DEPARTMENT OF ENERGY   A department created in 1977 that exercises primary responsibility for policies, programs, and administration in the field of energy.

ENTITLEMENTS   Benefits provided by government to which recipients have a legally enforceable right.

ENVIRONMENTALISM   A social and political movement that seeks to inform the public about ecological dangers and to encourage action to achieve basic environmental goals.

ENVIRONMENTAL PROTECTION AGENCY   An independent agency set up in 1970 to help protect the environment, which is concerned with air and water pollution, pesticide research and control, radiation dangers, and ecological study and investigation.

FEDERAL RESERVE SYSTEM   The central bank of the United States, including the Board of Governors and the Federal Reserve Banks located throughout the United States, with broad powers to regulate the money supply and interest rates.

FEMINIZATION OF POVERTY   The increasing tendency of the poverty population to consist of women and their children.

FISCAL POLICY   The use by government of its taxing and spending powers to influence the nation's economy.

FOREIGN POLICY   A strategy or course of action developed by a country to enhance its international position.

GROSS NATIONAL PRODUCT   The total value of goods and services produced by a nation in a particular period.

INFLATION   An economic condition marked by a rise in price levels for goods and services, accompanied by a decline in purchasing power.

MONETARY POLICY   Government policy that seeks to affect the amount of currency in circulation and the availability of credit.

NATIONAL SECURITY   The freedom—relative or absolute—of a country from possible armed attack or political or economic sabotage, along with the nation's ability to strike back with deadly effectiveness if attacked.

PENTAGON   The headquarters of the Department of Defense, which includes the departments of the Army, Navy, and Air Force.

PUBLIC POLICY   The body of laws and rules that determine the distribution of benefits and burdens of social programs.

RECESSION   An economic slowdown characterized by declining output and rising unemployment.

SOCIAL SECURITY   A public insurance program, financed by taxes on wages paid by workers and employers, that provides assistance to retired people and surviving dependents of deceased workers.

UNITED NATIONS   An international organization, established in 1945, to foster world peace and global understanding.

WAR ON POVERTY   The "Great Society" programs of the 1960s that attempted to address the long-term causes of poverty.

WELFARE STATE   A concept that emphasizes the role of government as the chief provider and protector of individual security through governmental social and economic programs.

WORKFARE   A governmental income-maintenance program that requires employment as a condition of assistance.

Chapter 15

Economic and Regulatory Policy

Article 1. Heavy Lifting: How America's Debt Burden Threatens the Economic Recovery
by Robert F. Black, Don L. Boroughs, Sara Collins, and Kenneth Sheets

The authors examine the nation's budget deficit, noting that the present recession shows little sign of abating. The debt crisis not only threatens the governmental sector, but poses dire consequences for the business community and the nation's consumers. For example, the budget deficit has contributed to a dramatic reduction in net national savings, which have plummeted in recent years. At the same time, the real net worth of American households has similarly declined, in part due to the fall in real estate values. The corporate world has also been hard hit, with interest payments at an all-time high. This has led many economists to predict a decline in future investment and potential growth. Likewise, Washington has been plagued by its own debt problem—a record $300 billion deficit in 1991—which has led to additional federal borrowing at record levels and major cutbacks in essential social programs.

Living in a mobile home in Michigan, Doug and Mary Schartzer have almost nothing in common with global media tycoon Rupert Murdoch. Or so it seems. But both the Schartzers and Murdoch gorged themselves on debt in the 1980s — the Schartzers by running up thousands of dollars on credit cards, Murdoch by piling on $8.2 billion in loans as he rapidly built News Corp., his empire of newspaper, magazine and television properties. And in the bleaker, less forgiving 1990s, both are now paying the price.

By last year, the Schartzers, with a combined income of $32,400, had amassed debts of $24,379 not including a mortgage. But after staring into the abyss of personal bankruptcy, the couple pulled back from the brink, tore up their plastic and began seeing a credit counselor. Murdoch's credit counselors are his bankers, who refinanced most of his debt and then pushed him to shrink his dominion to lighten the financial load. Last week, the Australian-born publisher agreed to sell most of his American magazines for $600 million to a partnership controlled by Kohlberg Kravis Roberts, the New York leveraged-buyout firm. Publications in the deal include *The Racing Form, New York, Seventeen* and *Soap Opera Digest.*

Signs of life? With the nation still mired in recession, impatient Americans are anxiously searching for signs of economic life, but they aren't finding many. Last week, for example, the government announced that the gross national product plummeted by 2.8 percent in the first quarter of 1991. As the gloomy statistics mount, it has become increasingly clear that debt-ridden families like the Schartzers and heavily leveraged companies like Murdoch's News Corp. are unable to generate the massive consumer and business spending needed to spark a meaningful recovery this year. Nor will the federal government, awash in red ink, ride to the rescue in its traditional role as fiscal catalyst of last resort.

Analysts such as Harvard University's Benjamin Friedman, author of "The Day of Reckoning," warned in the late 1980s that America's dance with the debt devil would end up destroying the soul of the U.S. economy. The debt crisis in this country has deepened since then, and now, as fresh data and new studies emerge, the full and frightening dimensions of the problem have become clear.

For starters, America's $10 trillion debt load — from the consumer, corporate and governmental sectors — is now double the nation's $5 trillion GNP. This burden is one-third higher than the historical debt-to-GNP ratio of the past 30 years. Household debt as a percentage of income after taxes, interest and pension contributions rocketed from just over 80 percent in 1980 to almost 110 percent in 1989. Corporate debt climbed during the same period from 30 percent to 40 percent of America's GNP. And U.S. government debt rose from 27 percent to 45 percent of GNP.

The current recession isn't the worst on record, but it does represent a number of important milestones. For example, after positive growth for 15 years, the amount of bank lending in this country declined in 1990. This is the first slump in which real consumer spending has dropped since 1973-75. And, for the first time, real incomes and real spending slowed prior to the economic downturn.

A number of analysts believe the United States may also be experiencing a different kind of recession — a balance sheet downturn brought about by the huge debt overhang that has left big borrowers too weakened to borrow more and big lenders too scarred to lend again. Some analysts, on the other hand, cling to a more traditional explanation and attribute the recession to the gulf-war oil shock or the Federal Reserve Board's tightfisted grip on the money supply in 1989. In a typical business cycle, the economy slows and the Federal Reserve stimulates spending by lowering interest rates. The object is to turbocharge growth without triggering inflation. However, according to David Stockman, the former Reagan administration budget director who is now a partner at the Blackstone Group, a New York-based investment banking firm, "If this is a balance sheet recession, it's not clear that the Fed's stimulus will make lenders any healthier or borrowers more eager to assume new credit."

Indeed, banks are already enjoying a sharply lower cost of funds, but several recent surveys show they are failing to pass along declining interest rates to borrowers, in order to bolster sagging profits and compensate for the rash of bad loans made in the 1980s. In fact, Bank of America last week raised its prime rate to 9 percent, the interest it charges its best corporate customers.

As Stockman points out, falling interest rates might not motivate overly leveraged shoppers anyway. Many who splurged on cars, compact disc players and VCRs during the 1980s now find their households overstocked from a consumer spending spree that was $1 trillion greater than normal purchasing trends anticipated, according to the Blackstone Group.

With many banks reluctant to lend and debt-laden consumers and corporations slashing their borrowing, the economic comeback in 1991 could be far more sluggish than the average post-World War II recovery. According to Henry Kaufman, president of Henry Kaufman & Co. in New York, "The impact of debt on corporate spending will result in a weak recovery with an annual growth rate of 2 to 2.5 percent, compared to a more normal 5 to 6 percent rate." With the economy still sinking, many economists are concerned about where near-term growth will come from. Exports, which have been a bright spot in the economy, may dull because of the dollar's rise and slumping overseas demand. In the first quarter of 1991, real exports declined by 0.4 percent after growing at an 11 percent clip in the fourth quarter of 1990. Says Nariman Behravesh of Oxford Economics USA: "There is no locomotive on the horizon now that would get the economy going at anywhere near a 6 percent growth rate."

Savings slide. The long-term implications of today's debt debacle are just beginning to be understood, but they could prove far more destructive than initially expected. A new study by the New York Federal Reserve Bank indicates that America's growing debt burden helped to dramatically reduce net national savings, which plummeted from a peak of 7.9 percent of GNP in the 1960s to a historically low level of just 2.2 percent in the latter part of the 1980s. Without this savings decline, the U.S. economy could have added 15 percent more machinery, equipment and plants, which would have tacked on a full 5 percent to GNP. If the nation remains unable or unwilling to save, growth opportunities will continue to be missed. According to the New York Fed, the economy will lose 10 percent of GNP over the next nine years unless the savings rate picks up.

At the same time, the Fed economists point out that because the country is saving less, it is creating less wealth. Recent data show that from the end of 1989 to the end of 1990, the real net worth of American households actually declined by 4.3 percent, or $800 billion. This sharp drop-off, which is partially due to the fact that the nation's real-estate assets have fallen in value, is the largest since World War II. Last year, home-mortgage debt increased 12 percent but the value of family residences decreased 1 percent and residential net worth was sliced by 11 percent.

Tapped-out. With residential net worth declining and debt eating up household cash flows, consumers aren't likely to go on a shopping spree anytime soon. "Consumer spending will continue to be dampened by existing debt," predicts Bruce Steinberg, an economist at Merrill Lynch. Orders for appliances, equipment and other factory-made items dropped by a dramatic 6.2 percent last month, following declines in both January and February. And sales of domestically built cars and trucks plummeted by nearly 12 percent in mid-April. Since World War II, recoveries have been driven by a renewal of consumer outlays, which now account for 67 percent of the nation's GNP. According to DRI/McGraw-Hill, spending by consumers is expected to rise by 0.1 percent in 1991 and 2.4 percent in 1992, a far cry from the post-recessionary spending rate of 4.8 percent in 1983-84.

The consumer spending drought is expected to take its heaviest tool on two key sectors of the economy: housing and autos. The WEFA Group, a Philadelphia-based economic consulting firm, predicts that housing starts will not reach 1.4 million units a year through 1993. By contrast, at the end of the last recession, new-home building rose from 1.1 million units in 1982 to more than 1.7 million in 1983. Similarly, the automobile industry, which sold 10.6 million cars a year after the 1981-82 recession, will probably sell just 9.7 million vehicles once the current downturn draws to a close. These numbers could worsen if the banks, which are now turning down 40 percent of all new-auto loan applicants, fail to open up credit conduits.

Changing consumption patterns among gradually graying baby boomers could further smother consumer spending far into the decade. Between 1990 and 2000, the number of Americans between 45 and 54 will grow by an astounding 46 percent. As they age, "they will spend less money on such big-ticket items as autos and household appliances," says Oxford Economics's Behravesh, "and more on health care and retirement related purchases." Another demographic trend working against consumer demand in the coming decade is the shrinking size of the U.S. population that is age 25 to 34. This segment of society will contract by about 15 percent over the next nine years, which means that there will not be a new influx of buyers into the market. "The quantity of goods out there at any one time is just not going to change that much," says David Wyss of DRI/McGraw-Hill.

Like U.S. consumers, corporate America assumed debt with abandon in the 1980s. Interest payments currently account for 28 percent of corporate cash flow, a post-World War II record. Many analysts now fear that the high level of business leverage will prevent future investment and stifle potential growth.

The nation's economic prospects are shakier still, because battered banks are hesitant to make corporate loans that would create jobs, stimulate demand and help propel the economy out of recession. Prior to the 1981–82 downturn, U.S. banks wrote off just $3.8 billion in bad loans. Last year, they wrote off a record $29 billion in lending commitments and are currently coping with nearly $78 billion worth of delinquent loans, a 25 percent increase over 1989. These growing losses are sending many money-center banks like Citicorp scurrying to equity markets, where they hope to raise needed new capital.

The bond markets have become even more inhospitable to the growing number of debt-heavy companies. As these firms watch their credit ratings lowered, their borrowing costs rise. Over the past year, for example, Standard & Poor's, the debt rating agency downgraded 768 long-term corporate debt issues while upgrading only 189. James Grant, editor of *Grant's Interest Rate Observer,* says riskier companies able to get funds in the 1980s fueled much of the decade's growth. "If borrowing becomes too costly for them in the '90s," says Grant, "it could slow the economic recovery."

As the window on debt financing closes little by little, the door to equity financing is opening wider. With stock prices soaring in recent months, a number of debt-burdened firms, such as RJR Nabisco, Duracell and McCaw Cellular, have been raising equity in order to trim financial liabilities. Leverage used to be the key to success on Wall Street, but the recession has cruelly reminded investors that equity-dependent firms can cut their dividends to muddle through tough times, but interest payment must always be met.

Companies with strong balance sheets have the financial flexibility to invest in new plants, equipment and research and development without being encumbered by high interest-to-cash-flow ratios. However, with capacity utilization rates dropping below their 20-year average, capital spending in the United States has already dropped 14 percent in the first quarter and is likely to shrink further this year, which could hurt U.S. competitiveness with Japan. "Debt-laden companies don't have the capacity to make long-term commitments," says economist Henry Kaufman. "They cannot pursue aggressive marketing plans, they cannot forgo near-term profits for long-term growth."

Broken pump. Washington has its own debt problem—namely a $300 billion deficit in 1991—that prevents it from easing the downturn by spending more on unemployment insurance, food stamps and other social-welfare programs. At this point, all the politicians can do to prime the pump is to jawbone the Fed into lowering interest rates.

During the fourth quarter of 1990, the federal government was able to borrow $328 billion—more than all the new debt amassed by home buyers, credit-card holders, small business, real-estate developers and nonfinancial corporations. For the moment, such a large debt offering is not a concern. "Private borrowing has collapsed," says Merrill Lynch's Bruce Steinberg. "It's the slowest it's been since statistics were kept, so the government could keep going to the till without putting pressure on the capital supply." But as the recovery begins and companies need to expand, they could find themselves bidding up interest rates and competing with Washington for precious capital. Another vexing worry is paying the interest on the mushrooming federal debt, which will claim an ever increasing chunk of the government's budget in the 1990s.

Despite these potential obstacles, many analysts now believe that Washington's massive budget deficits won't present a long-term problem for the economy. They claim that the new budget process, as well as last year's big fiscal package, could reduce the deficit-to-GNP ratio from 5 percent today to 2 percent by 1996.

During the 1980s, Ronald Reagan and junk-bond king Michael Milken argued, in very different ways, that boosting debt would speed the creation of wealth in America. Consumers and corporations listened and then leveraged themselves. But as household, corporate and government liabilities climbed to record levels, the national savings and wealth accumulation rates declined.

The potent combination of excess consumption, low savings and high debt means that the recovery following the recession will be less vigorous than previous comebacks. And American business and consumers will have to struggle as they attempt to shed the credit excesses of the 1980s. But with aging baby boomers starting to tuck money away for retirement and chastened government leaders starting to grapple with the nation's fiscal woes, there is at least some hope that the debt drama currently being played out all across America will have a happy ending.

Article 2. Money and Democracy: The Myth of an Independent Fed
by Bernard D. Nossiter

Bernard D. Nossiter explores the inner workings of the Federal Reserve Board and its battle for price restraint. Nossiter argues that the Fed's role should be redefined, such that its money-creating functions be transferred to an office in the Treasury or some other cabinet agency. In addition, it should be divested of its commercial bank control. These reforms would allow economic policy to be made by the Treasury Department, the Office of Management and Budget, and the Council of Economic Advisers—whose members owe their jobs to the president—as opposed to the Fed, which is controlled by the banking industry. In the author's view, it is essential that the Fed be stripped of its much vaunted "independence."

As the economy sinks deeper into a slump, the Federal Reserve Board, governor of the nation's money supply, makes feeble gestures of disapproval. Interest rates are sliced in cheese-paring steps; a token cut in required reserves swells profits for big banks by $1 billion. The Reserve resists economic expansion with all its considerable force. Its chair, Alan Greenspan, a onetime follower of Ayn Rand and more recently a stock tipster on Wall Street, concedes that jobs, incomes and output are falling. But he fears that if he does anything useful—swiftly increasing the money supply, sharply lowering interest rates to spur borrowing—things will get worse. In the Fed's world, rising prices are always worse than falling jobs or output.

Greenspan serves a critical constituency: the nation's large commercial banks. Since the Fed was established in 1913, his predecessors have also recognized that their allegiance is to the big commercial banks, the giants like Chase, Citibank and Manufacturers Hanover, which collect tens of billions in deposits and make tens of billions in business loans. They alone are secure in the knowledge that no matter how recklessly they behave, whether in loans to Latin America or in real estate, the Reserve will always bail them out of their folly, turning on its money spigot to rescue them, if not the economy.

The Federal Reserve System was created by the big banks (Woodrow Wilson was merely an adventitious midwife), and they have never lost their grip. Nelson Aldrich, father-in-law to John D. Rockefeller Jr., was its key architect, and he and his fellows proposed that it be run entirely through regional banks, completely in the commercial banks' grasp. Such a proposal might have been approved today, but populist pressure at the time led to the creation of a seven-person board—now Greenspan's board—with overriding authority. Since some of its members are tame academics, this was a concession to popular control. So was the granting of an ex officio seat on the board to the Treasury Secretary. But that was too democratic for the bankers, so the Treasury Secretary lost his seat. Since board members serve a luxurious fourteen years, no elected President can interfere with anything so important as the creation and liquidation of money.

Today, the commercial bankers maintain their grip largely through their selection of a majority of the directors of the twelve regional banks and their control of five of the twelve places on the vital Open Market Committee. Every few weeks, this powerful body determines whether credit shall be eased or tightened—whether bank reserves, the basis of loans, shall expand or contract. Greenspan's board fills the other seven seats on the Open Market Committee. The bankers and academics on the board mostly echo the commercial bank view.

All this might be a mere curiosity, another example of a regulatory agency captured by those it regulates, except that the Reserve is in a serious business. No agency is more powerful in the economic life of the country. The central bank, with appropriate support from taxes and government spending, can literally determine prosperity or misery, inflation or deflation, boom or slump. Flood the banks with the Fed's high-powered money reserves, and a boom is triggered, even inflation and high employment. Starve the banks, as the Fed in its wisdom did at the bottom of the Great Depression, and business, incomes and jobs wither.

Greenspan, like his notorious predecessor, Paul Volcker, piously claims that he merely responds to the broad needs of the economy. William McChesney Martin, the Fed chair in the Eisenhower-Kennedy era, characterized the policy as "leaning against the wind." That simply isn't so. Fed chairs try to direct the economy as Greenspan did this fall when he urged deflationary cuts on the Congressional budget negotiators in return for some easing of credit. Since his advice came at the start of a slump, Greenspan was prescribing precisely the wrong medicine. In the same way, Volcker threw the country into its worst postwar recession in 1980–82. He actually persuaded President Carter to accept political suicide on behalf of some higher economic good.

"I'm the guy who spoils the party by saying, 'That's enough,'" one former Reserve chair boasted. This is neat but deceptive. The Fed does not simply curb monetary excess; it executes the narrow agenda of the commercial bankers. Bankers have a natural bias against growth and a natural predilection for slowdown. It is built into all loans. Bankers lend hoping they will be repaid in dearer dollars. If

From *The Nation,* December 31, 1990, pp. 837–838. *The Nation* magazine/The Nation Company, Inc., © 1990.

I lend you $1,000 at today's prices, I'll enjoy a windfall of $100 if prices fall 10 percent. In the real world, prices seldom fall. But the more they are restrained, the greater the bankers' profits. Inflation has the opposite effect on profits, because bankers will be paid in cheaper dollars than they loaned, which is why inflation is so detested. To maximize gains, bankers always favor curbing credit, cutting government spending and resisting expansion, regardless of whether the economy is in a boom or a slump.

It is to this pressure that Greenspan, Volcker and all the rest respond. The overriding goal of Fed economics is price restraint. All hail the profit-and-loss statements of large commercial banks! To be sure, there are times when inflation is a serious problem and needs to be dealt with. But it is not clear that the Fed is the proper instrument. The Reserve was neutered in World War II and compelled by the Treasury and Congress to keep interest rates down. Inflation was splendidly checked by price controls.

Despite this record the Fed can now be liberated from commercial bank control with the establishment of some kind of democratic governing of money. The key step is to end the Reserve's much vaunted "independence," the formula that says the central bank's integrity depends on its divorce from politicians. This simply insures that the central bank is a handmaiden of the banking industry. Control by deflationist private bankers is far less preferable than control by elected politicians. Indeed, this is the way central banking is conducted in much of the developed world.

Each morning in London the Bank of England, the British central bank, politely calls over to its master, the Exchequer, and asks for instructions on whether to increase or decrease the reserves of banks. In Paris the Banque de France and the Finance Ministry enact a similar ritual. Both central banks are agents of a ministry that is part of an elected government. If you are angry with Greenspan, there is not much you can do. Wrongheaded money policy in France or England can be traced by voters directly to an elected government. Unlike the Fed, European central banks are responsible and accountable. That is, except for the German Bundesbank, which is fiercely independent of government. This autonomy reflects Germany's horrific history of inflation and Nazism. In her last great fight Margaret Thatcher, a Tory democrat, bitterly resisted attempts by the Common Market to swallow up the Bank of England and deprive Britons of popular control over money, jobs and prices. She understood the critical link between money and democracy.

The central reform, then, would end the Fed as an autonomous agency and give its money-creating tasks to an office in the Treasury or some other agency in the Cabinet. Other reforms could further strip commercial bank control of the Fed. If a board is to survive, Greenspan and his fellow members should serve at the pleasure of the President. In a modern electronic world there is no need for regional banks. Make them Treasury substations. We should abolish the cials take its place.

With these reforms, economic policy would be fixed by a triad — the Treasury Department, the Office of Management and Budget and the Council of Economic Advisers. These are not populist bodies, but, unlike the Federal Reserve Board, their members owe their jobs to the President and they are charged with executing the President's policy. Apart from trading quips with Congressional committees, the Fed chair now reports to no one. His constituents, the commercial banks, neither know enough nor are infused with enough public spirit to run anything. It is time to admit that the seventy-seven-year experiment has failed. □

Article 3.   Who Really Made the S&L Mess?
by Lenny Glynn

The facts are widely known. Spawned by deregulation, the oil boom, high-interest money market funds, and run-away speculation, the savings and loan scandal threatens to bankrupt the federal budget and strap the taxpayers with billions of dollars of additional debt. The article surveys the origins of the crisis, concluding that blame rests with the S & L industry, the Federal Home Loan Bank Board, the Carter and Reagan White Houses, the Federal Reserve Board, Congress, the S & L lobby, and assorted other "villains." In grappling with the crisis, the nation must resist the tendency to blame the crisis on a handful of "crooks" rather than reexamine the institutional failings that made the scandal possible.

During the mid-to-late-1980s much of the American Southwest came to resemble the closing scenes of *The Last Picture Show*, with the prairie winds blowing dry leaves and tumbleweeds past the filmtown's dilapidated stores and shuttered movie house. Along a fault line running roughly from Tulsa to Dallas and Houston, the decay spread east, west, and south as far as Louisiana, Arizona, and Colorado. Throughout the region, once-busy oil rigs lay rusting, empty "see-through" office buildings stippled big-city downtowns, tawdry malls and unsold condos flaked and peeled along the interstates and feeder roads. Spawned by the late seventies' oil boom and the speculative frenzies that followed, the derelict structures are the visible legacies of the savings and loan (S&L) "mess." Roughly half the $150 billion plus in failed assets (aka "loans") now in the Resolution Trust Corporation's hands are in Texas and Oklahoma alone.

The most grotesque, still metastasizing financial scandal in American history, the S&L collapse has already busted this year's federal budget, forced George Bush to renege on his fatuous "no-tax" pledge, undermined foreign confidence in U.S. finances, and derailed the careers of the politicians—Jim Wright, Tony Coehlo, the "Keating Five"—so far identified as willing tools of the S&L lobby. There will be plenty more casualties, financial and political. The current recession will be deepened both by higher taxes and the lost liquidity that now-defunct S&Ls provided. The dream of home ownership that the S&Ls were designed to finance may recede beyond the grasp of millions of Americans. The full cost of the S&L "rescue" will likely surge past current estimates of $500 billion or $2,000 per capita. And if the past is prologue, the "rescue" will itself generate "Son of S&L" scandals.

That's because the S&L mess was born under, analyzed by, and is being "solved" through the lenses of a uniquely American optic. Call it "Sunbelt ideology," though it's hardly unique to the region. It is, in fact, the dominant ideology of the Nixon-Carter-Reagan-Bush era. Sunbelt ideology is pseudo–laissez-faire, shamelessly combining a drive to get government "off the backs" of business with a huge appetite for government spending and guarantees—currently, of course, for the S&Ls victim/depositors. It's party-time ideology, bereft of accountability.

In its original manifestation, the Goldwater campaign of 1964, Sunbelt ideology had the virtue of some libertarian consistency. Goldwater bluntly proposed privatizing Social Security and selling off the Tennessee Valley Authority to private business. But in the sixteen years before the ascension of Ronald Reagan, the ideology mutated, dropping its politically suicidal honesty while retaining its deregulatory core. Most farm supports, water projects, loan guarantees, deposit insurance—the bulk of New Deal financial and infrastructure programs—would be inviolable; only the regulations meant to monitor them would be scrapped and the regulators degraded. The unspoken aim was a "free market" with risks guaranteed or underwritten by the state.

It's hardly surprising that such a stew simmered best over the ideological campfires of the Southwest and Southern California, the adopted homelands of Richard Nixon, Ronald Reagan, and George Bush. This Wild West of raw "individualism" is not only dominated by vast federal landholdings but historically more dependent on federal spending than any other region. From the Grand Canyon to the sprinkler systems of Beverly Hills and the irrigation ditches of the San Joaquin Valley, a vast hydraulic civilization has been built on taxpayers' money. The allegedly rip-roaring capitalism of the whole region has been underpinned by a multibillion-dollar tide of federal cash for dams, water projects, farm supports, interstates, defense plants, and bases.

The Southwest's resulting love-hate relationship with the federal government has been compounded by the get-rich-quick mentality of resource booms in land, gold, uranium, and, above all, petroleum. Little wonder, then, that when Sunbelt ideology came to power with Reagan's 1980 victory, the removal of all oil and gas price controls, indeed, the dismantling of any serious federal energy policy at all—save for filling the Strategic Oil Reserve—was as high on the new regime's agenda as tax cuts and the defense spending surge. That the United States is paying for the Reagan-Bush decision to "get government off the backs" of the energy industry is painfully obvious as Saddam Hussein squats atop Kuwait. But that Washington has to go hat-in-hand to allies to finance Desert Shield is largely a result of the deregulatory moves that "freed" S&Ls from 1982 to the present from the controls and supervision that had made them secure institutions for half a century.

Origins of the Crisis

To be fair, the Reagan administration did inherit an S&L industry in its first major crisis since 1932. It had begun, subtly, with competition for deposits from high-interest money market funds in the inflationary 1970s. As inflation hit double digits, billions of dollars drained out of S&Ls and commercial banks barred from paying more than 5.25 percent. The result was a slow-motion bank run stanched only when Congress lifted the interest rate ceilings in March, 1980 and raised the levels of federal deposit guarantees to $100,000. That enabled banks and S&Ls to bid against the money funds for depositors and spawned a new "industry" on Wall Street—brokering "hot money"—packaging deposits close to the $100,000 insurance limit into S&Ls desperate for cash flow.

In a more subtle regulatory shift, the Federal Home Loan Bank Board in 1980 also deleted a long-standing rule limiting brokered deposits to 5 percent of an S&L's total. By the late 1980s some of the largest, most disastrous failures would strike S&Ls with up to half their deposits in "hot money."

Consider the American Diversified Savings Bank of Lodi, California, one example cited by Martin Mayer in the best book so far on S&Ls, *The Greatest Ever Bank Robbery*. From 1983 to 1988, when it was finally shut down, American Diversified held from $11.7 million to over $1.1 billion in assets, all of them federally insured, $800 million of them worthless loans to be made good by the Feds—"Roughly as much," Mayer notes, "as the Federal government had at risk in the much-debated bail-outs of New York City, Chrysler and Lockheed combined."

Pyramiding on a tiny capital base, American Diversified's growth was almost exclusively fueled by "hot money." At collapse, the bank's average deposit was $80,807. Mayer cites Jonathan Gray, a Wall Street researcher who reported to the Federal Deposit Insurance Corporation on American Diversified: "[W]ith perhaps $500,000 in equity, it destroyed $800 million in insured deposits, a kill ratio of 1,600 to 1. . . . This anecdote is tantamount to a news report that a drunken driver has wiped out the entire city of Pittsburgh."

But that's hindsight. In 1981, the "Father" of the brokered deposit business, former Merrill Lynch chairman Donald Regan, became Ronald Reagan's secretary of the treasury.

By then, the first S&L crisis was already well underway, compounded by Federal Reserve Board Chairman Paul Volcker's 1979 decision to crush inflation by letting interest rates drift to stratospheric levels. The prime rate climbed as high as 20.5 percent by 1981. That plunged the bulk of the S&Ls into a bind: they might be able to attract deposits by paying high interest rates, but the bulk of their outstanding loans was tied up in low-paying mortgages, they still faced mandatory interest-rate "caps" on new mortgages, and they were virtually barred from lending to riskier, more lucrative industries than home buying. Not suprisingly, the net worth of American S&Ls plummeted from $32 billion in 1980 to $3.7 billion by December 1982.

The S&L industry seemed on the verge of extinction; but there were grounds for hope. Volcker's brutal money squeeze had broken the back of inflation. Interest rates were easing, and much of the S&L industry could look forward to a return to health once the rates fell enough to make mortgages profitable again. As L.J. Davis noted in a brilliant *Harper's* article ("Chronicle of a Debacle Foretold," September 1990), all that would have been required was to let the worst S&Ls fail at the cost of a few billion dollars from the Federal Savings and Loan Insurance Corp. "This would strain the fund," Davis wrote, "a fund, remember, built of moneys from the thrifts themselves—but not destroy it. Were the industry to take its losses now [1982–83], it would cost the taxpayers nothing."

Alas, the S&L lobby in Washington, the U.S. League for Savings Institutions, didn't see it that way, and, in the supercharged laissez-faire ambiance of Reagan's Washington in 1982 it was able to get a series of legislative and regulatory changes that created a disaster our children will be paying for. The League's already legendary clout was greatly enhanced by the bipartisan bidding for business favor—and campaign contributions—that marked the early Reagan years. S&Ls are estimated to have contributed more than $11 million to politicians during the 1980s.

The Reaganauts' disparaging and starving of regulatory bodies went hand-in-glove with the league's efforts. As Stanford Law School's Joseph Grundfest notes, the League was better able to override the public interest than most of the more narrowly based lobbies. The balance of special-interest demands that Congress brokers "is vulnerable to a rogue constituency that has a broad geographic base, pursues a noncontroversial ideology popular with the middle class, actively finances congressional campaigns and is willing to exploit Congress' fiscal blind spots," Grundfest argues.

Cloaked in the mantle of "home ownership," with bases nationwide, the League was able to extract changes that effectively freed S&Ls from the very home-lending mandate that gave them legitimacy. It also pressed for sublte but far-reaching shifts from pliant Reagan-era regulators—then drove truckloads of lucre past Congress's fiscal "blind spots" through rulings so obscure they made even financial journalists yawn.

For its part, the Federal Home Loan Bank Board lowered the reserves that S&Ls were required to hold from 5 percent of outstanding loans to 3 percent, nearly doubling S&Ls' lending power. (Instead of lending $100,000 with $5,000 on reserve, an S&L could now float loans of nearly $170,000 on the same $5,000 safety margin.) A series of arcane accounting changes followed, essentially allowing S&Ls to depict themselves as financially sound while the real value of their balance sheets deteriorated.

The Federal Home Loan Bank Board also opened the once tightly regulated S&L business—formerly dominated by locally based "mutual" associations of depositors—to virtually anyone with the capital to buy or found an S&L. With hundreds of S&Ls still under water financially, that opened the way for cheap takeovers and start-ups by poorly capitalized, even shady "entrepreneurs." The script that cast Jimmy Stewart as a benevolent S&L owner in *It's a Wonderful Life* was being rewritten as film noir.

It was left to Congress, faithfully stenographing the S&L wish list, to complete the rewrite. It's called the 1982 Depository Institutions Act, sponsored by Representative Frederick St. Germain of Rhode Island and Senator Jake Garn of Utah. "Freeing" S&Ls to invest up to 40 percent of their lending in nonresidential real estate and 30 percent in high-interest consumer loans, the act relieved S&Ls of the chore of financing home construction and sales. The greener pastures of commercial real estate speculation were now open to them—and they, in turn, were up for grabs by canny developers. With no trace of irony—or any sense of what he was signing—Ronald Reagan called it "the most important legislation for financial institutions in the last fifty years."

All too right! In a competitive bidding war that quickly followed, California, Texas, and Florida soon adopted even more liberal legislation for their state-chartered—but federally insured—S&Ls, allowing them to lend to any venture they wanted, even to take equity stakes. The S&L sheep, in short, were now free to play with the wolves of Sunbelt real estate or to be taken over by those very wolves who could then bid up for vast amounts of "brokered" deposits to loan to each other. This foul mix explains why the vast bulk of S&L losses so far is concentrated in Texas and a few neighboring states that spent the middle 1980s in an insensate burst of real estate speculation.

It should be no surprise that the mix of government deposit guarantees, unlimited access to brokered deposits, freedom to speculate, and demoralized, intimidated regulators would breed scams among the Sunbelt S&Ls. There is, after all, a long tradition of confidence men in both American life and literature and a free-floating population of loan kiters, financial con men, and "boiler-room" land and commodity hustlers separating fools from their money. (See: Florida, History.) These folks were drawn like jackals to the Sunbelt S&Ls in the middle 1980s and doubtless stole far more with their fountain pens than in any pistolero's wildest dream.

The complex daisy chains of property "flipping" practiced by the new breed of "rogue" S&L operator was captured by Curtis J. Lang in the July 10 *Village Voice*:

In October 1983, one Dallas real estate investor, Louis G. Reese III, bought 2145 acres of cow pasture from a Vancouver S&L called First City Investment, which loaned him $17.25 million, or $8,014.51 per acre. That same day, Reese sold the property to Jerry Parsons, who worked out of Reese's Dallas office. Parsons borrowed the money from State Savings in Lubbock. The price per acre had soared to $11,188.19 and the debt on the cow pasture had now climbed to $24 million.

Three days later, Parsons sold the land to a shell company called 2138 Joint Ventures controlled by himself and Louis Reese, simultaneously using part of the original loan as collateral to get a $5.3 million loan from a Fort Worth bank. Four months later, in March, 1984, Parsons and Reese sold the property to two developers who borrowed money from Sunbelt Savings in Dallas to buy it. A few hours later, the developers sold one-quarter of the land, which was now encumbered with a debt of $44.7 million, at a price of $20,915.77 per acre.

In November 1984, the developers sold the remaining three-quarters of the land back to the Reese Children's Trust No. II. The Reese family used money borrowed from Stockton Savings in Addison, Texas, to buy the land back and then defaulted on the loan, forcing Stockton to foreclose. The price per acre was now $23,995.34. Three weeks later, Reese's Children's Trust sold the foreclosed property to Monticello Investments, a shell company whose president and treasurer was Louis G. Reese III. Three days later, the Reese family paid Stockton $2 million in overdue interest to get a loan extension. That same day, Reese sold the property to five developers, who borrowed more money from Western Savings in Dallas to purchase the property at a price of $41,578.86 per acre—total cost, $65.737 million. Nine months later, Western Savings went broke and the developers filed for bankruptcy. No one had ever put brick to a stick. U.S. taxpayers will have to make up for all the "missing deposits."

Sunbelt Savings, Western Savings, and State Savings have all been named by the *Houston Post* as members of a daisy chain of failed thrifts with links to organized crime and even, perhaps, to the CIA. All three have collapsed, at a cost to taxpayers of over $3 billion. And they were hardly unique. Indeed, popular myth by now ascribes the S&L crisis to outright fraud, embezzlement, and con artistry. That sentiment is being assiduously fostered by Congress and the Bush administration in search of politically juicy scapegoats.

Not surprisingly, their targets vary. Bush, who headed a Reagan administration task force on deregulation, now professes himself shocked, frankly, *shocked* by the "S&L crooks" he failed to notice a few years back. Congressional Democrats, up to their eyeballs as a party in the S&L mess, prefer to keep the spotlight on the President's son Neil Bush, the "poster boy of the S&L crisis." Neil Bush was a tender thirty years of age when named director of a Denver S&L called Silverado—local nickname: Desperado—later shut down at a cost to taxpayers of over $1 billion. Like many spawn of the Sunbelt's salad days, Silverado managed before collapsing to breakfast on the new morning in America—swelling from under a hundred million dollars in loan assets in 1980 to billions of dollars by the time federal regulators were given a green light to stop the hemorrhaging. That permission came, conveniently, just weeks after Dad George secured his 1988 election victory. Son Neil has been accused of conflicts of interest for his role in recommending loans from Silverado to some

of his own, generous business partners. This bears watching.

However sleazy the Reagan-era S&L industry became, fraud per se explains only a fraction of the losses—perhaps a mere $10–$20 billion. The exuberant greed so often featured in the winning of the West—combined with the rank stupidity of S&L managers weaned in a protective regulatory atmosphere—accounts for the bulk of the losses. The region was simply swept up in a speculative bubble in which greedy developers and dumb bankers reinforced each others' propensity to gamble. The psychology worked like this: bankers would lend to dubious projects because developers had had successful track records, while developers would take the bank's confidence in them as a sign that their intuitions were valid. Together with the incentive structures that newly lax S&L regulations set up, the combination was highly combustible.

Bankers began earning more money on "origination" fees for loans than on the loans themselves, while developers were often able to sell projects to other speculators for a heady profit. It was a classic Ponzi scheme in which the latest investors were paid off by new incoming funds, fresh "hot money" deposits fueling new waves of speculation. For real estate brokers and investors, construction firms, lawyers, auditors, title companies, surveyors, and so on, it was in those days heaven to be alive. Brokers raked in commissions, auditors inflated values, bankers booked "origination" fees, lawyers battened on fighting off regulators, regulators sometimes sold out for plush jobs at the S&Ls, journalists largely missed the story, and some toadying economists blessed the new S&L "entrepreneurs" as a godsend.

Alan Greenspan, now chairman of the Federal Reserve Board, was one of those who testified before Congress on behalf of Charles Keating, the egregious owner of Lincoln Savings in California. Keating paid himself and close relatives about $34 million in salaries for running up losses of $2.5 billion. Of seventeen S&Ls Greenspan cited in his testimony, sixteen have failed. With blue-chip opinions blatantly up for sale, half a dozen professions prostituted themselves. The worst outrage in the S&L mess, Mayer writes, "is not the hundreds of billions of dollars, but the demonstration of how low our standards for professional performance have fallen in law, accounting, appraising, banking and politics."

Still, it was a hell of a party. When the music stopped in 1986–87 and land values began plunging fast, only the very last speculators and the S&Ls that lent to them were hurt—Uncle Sam was left standing, guaranteeing all those deposits.

The S&L mess, then, wasn't mainly fraud, just a magic-realistic collective delusion played out by Babbitts in cowboy boots. Sunbelt banking was a weird, weird scene. Too bad if we couldn't be there for the fun, but we're all in on the action now.

Regional Favoritism

Professor Edward W. Hill of Cleveland State University was the first to tote up the interregional resource transfers the 1989 S&L rescue will demand. By his conservative calculation of $150 billion for the initial bailout—not counting interests costs that will triple the bill by 2020—thirteen states, mostly in the South and Southwest, will be "net winners" as depositors are made whole, while thirty-seven other states "lose" on balance, despite having some failed thrifts. Residents of one of George Bush's home states, Connecticut, will "lose" $882 per capita; those of his other home state, Texas, will "win" $3,510 per man, woman, child. Count interest payments and those sums will roughly triple. Hill calls it "the largest Corporate Welfare program since the Great Depression. Individual and corporate taxpayers in 37 states and the District of Columbia will be shipping vast sums of money to 13 states over the next 30 years."

That argument is already causing fissures among regions as the full cost of the S&L crisis bites. "We're looking at resources we desperately need," said Ohio Governor Richard Celeste last summer, "and see them being dished out to deal with this problem—with no real sense that we have a tourniquet to stop the hemorrhaging. Part of this is regional sentiment, but there's a real sense that Head Start and other programs for children and the poor will pay for this."

Of course they will. Yet Hill's seductive thesis is badly flawed. For starters, the insurance is being paid legally. It couldn't be revoked without expropriating depositors' funds, wrecking the government's credit globally, and triggering massive runs on remaining S&Ls and banks. And if nationally financed deposit insurance is, indeed, reimbursing depositors in Sunbelt S&Ls, those depositors don't necessarily live in the Sunbelt, nor are they likely to re-invest there soon.

Instead, thanks to the vast flows of "brokered" money, S&L depositors in, say, Lubbock, Texas, may hail from Boston, Chicago, Osaka, or Medellin. Making good their deposits promises small comfort for Texans who've lived through boom, bust, layoffs, foreclosures, and the collapse of home values. A more relevant point is that the "distressed" office buildings, malls, and condos the feds are now trying to sell in the "winning" Sunbelt states will serve for years to come as lures for companies in other regions to relocate in what amounts to financial free-fire zones. And because taxpayers as a class are far poorer than savers as a class—especially savers who telex wads of $100,000 to desperate S&Ls—the bailout will effect a classically Reaganite "trickle-up" of wealth from poor to rich.

So may the selloff of S&Ls and their assets, if the government persists in rushing what ought to be a slow, deliberate process. Haste in vending off a posse of Texas S&Ls in late 1986—the so-called Southwest Plan—led to poorly structured deals that promise a virtually risk-free windfall for investors like Revlon chairman Ronald Perelman. Perelman picked up five dead Texas S&Ls for $161 million in cash while receiving $1.2 billion in tax benefits and dumping the riskiest assets onto the government's balance sheet.

That package of deals was rushed through by the incompetent Danny Wall, Reagan's head of the Federal Home Loan Bank Board (FHLBB), which was due to be replaced in 1989 by the Resolution Trust Corporation. The cost of the "Southwest Plan" fire sale has since soared from Wall's estimate of $39 billion in taxpayer losses to over $90 billion. Made as the FHLBB was running out of both time and money, these eleventh-hour deals are a paradigm of what the government should not do as it unloads its massive S&L portfolio.

"When you have an imposed deadline, no cash, and doubtful credit, you are going to pay through the nose," says William Seidman, head of the Resolution Trust. "The real question is whether they should have undertaken the transactions at all." The real answer is no. As William Greider, author of *The Secrets of the Temple*, argues, "The greatest hypocrisy of the era is that despite its laissez-faire pretensions, the Federal government is now more deeply engaged in the affairs of private finance—both as owner and manager and as generous beneficiary—than at any other time in the nation's history . . . they are buying and selling and subsidizing—and virtually giving away—financial assets and property on a scale that would have made New Dealers tremble."

It's time, in short, to drop the "free market" cant, admit that we've nationalized a vast chunk of our banking and real estate system, and control its reprivatization over many years. The aim would be to capture for the public the very capital gains that motivate speculators to buy what the government now plans to dump fast and cheap. Selling the assets we've bought collectively to private speculators now promises a final "trickle up" windfall.

We've already paid enough as a nation for this debacle—in global standing as well as in cash. Foreigners are amazed that waste on this scale could be allowed to occur. The S&L mess is fueling a general crisis of confidence in U.S. financial management. The dollar's 1980s peak, in fact, came with a March-April 1985 run on Ohio and Maryland S&Ls, not the famous Plaza Accord to lower the greenback in September.

That 1985 warning shot was only a foretaste for foreigners of the bizarre budget wrangles that paralyzed the government last fall when the cost of the S&L rescue busted the budget. It's difficult to exaggerate the sense of incompetence and decay that the government's near paralysis caused abroad. One measure is that the dollar, once a "safe haven," continued to slump through most of the Iraq-Kuwait crisis.

With the former Evil Empire and its satellites imploding economically at year-end 1990, the United States looks increasingly like a marginal player in resolving the cold war it paid so dearly to "win." Nervous foreigners view the S&Ls as harbingers of disasters that could come in commercial banking, insurance, and other financial industries operating under the umbrella of government guarantees. Outside the banking sector, where it guarantees $2 trillion in commercial bank deposits, the government has underwritten at least $750 billion in other loans to farmers, homeowners,

students, and so on. Given its S&L record, these are some very large beads to worry with.

Indeed, this year, foreign investors have begun a massive capital flight from the United States, selling billions of dollars in stocks and bonds and sharply curbing direct investment. The result will be slower recovery from recession and less room for the Fed to ease credit without triggering a full-scale collapse of the dollar.

It's probably too much to expect that Congress will effectively grapple with the corrupt campaign financing that lies at the root of the S&L disaster. It's far easier to pontificate about S&L "crooks" than to admit that it was the whole degrading system of fund raising that had a Republican administration wooing S&L contributors with lax regulations while Democratic lawmakers awash in S&L dough lobbied and intimidated the few regulators who tried to slow the rot.

A far simpler measure might be for Congress and the administration to craft legislation mandating accurate accounting—that is, market-based pricing of the risks the feds routinely assume in loan guarantees and other programs hidden off the books. Right accounting might be easier to get through Congress and the regulatory bodies than any package of campaign reform. Forcing the hidden costs of loan insurance and guarantee programs out into the open, argues Grundfest, would have an immediate budget impact. These seemingly "costless" financial time bombs would then have to compete—up front—with Defense, Head Start, and so on rather than festering for years before erupting. "Budget-based, mark-to-market accounting," he warns, "is not an iron-clad guarantee against a recurrence of an S&L-type failure. It is, however, a necessary and feasible first step toward restoring integrity to the political and financial process."

It may also be the quickest way to detect where in the morass of federal obligations the next disaster is incubating. There really is no time to waste. For the $5 trillion U.S. economy, the S&L mess is a painful if affordable farce. Given the shaky state of the nation's finances, the next "discontinuity" could be a tragedy. □

Chapter 16

Social Welfare Policy

Article 1. Who Is the Underclass?
by William Kornblum

This article discusses the plight of America's underclass, noting that mere poverty is only one characteristic of the nearly thirty-two million people who comprise this netherworld. A heterogeneous group, the underclass includes many elderly persons on fixed incomes, households composed of graduate students, Native Americans on impoverished reservations, and households with a full-time low wage earner, among others. The underclass is trapped both below the legitimate class system of capitalistic society and the lowest runs of the criminal class system as well. Plagued by addiction, mental illness, homelessness, and deprivation, the nation's underclass is growing steadily, especially in the central cities and segregated ghettos.

The possible arrival of a new social class evokes grand blasts of imagery. Across history's bookish stage roll bourgeois Christian soldiers, boxcars of workers (trailing haunting specters), limos carrying commissars of the *nomenklatura*, electricians in white coats (breathing soul into new computers). On they parade until, at what we thought must be the end of the social-class spectacle, there appears the latest entry: a ragged urban underclass.

For the class parade to be a full success it seems there must be one class that highlights in its evil all the virtues of the others. The proletariat no longer provokes fear and reaction? Then send up a fearsome underclass. What could be more frightening to the precariously comfortable than drug-crazed, poverty-incensed hordes, led by Willie Horton and Central Park Wilders, legions of dark people with strong backs and weak intellects, who, it is said, do not want to work in "available jobs." The underclass is also said to be breeding generations of feral children. If they reach adulthood, their underclass culture will make them unsuitable for whatever jobs will be available in these waning years of "The American Century."

George Orwell would have recognized this as old-fashioned "fear of the mob" and as weak excuses of the rich for their own excesses. In 1988, however—in our era of trickle down and gush up—George Bush hit on underclass imagery (with its implicit appeal to bigotry) for campaign paydirt. Attention is easily shifted to the moral qualities of the poor and away from those responsible for much of the neglect we see around us. Social scientists (myself included) and journalists write reams about the underclass while the psychology and sociology of savings and loan supercrook Charles Keating and other buccaneers go relatively unexamined.

But, real or not, the idea of the underclass cannot be wished away. There are too many issues in the underclass debate that have immediate bearing on the crisis of our cities. As with all stereotypes there are elements of truth in the imagery. The risks of criminal victimization by people who resemble underclass types are increasing for those who live in the big cities. The rise of homelessness and AIDS, the despair of crack and heroin, the proclaimed (but not factual) failure of public institutions (education, housing, criminal justice, public health): all these are demoralizing and cause people to wonder if the segregated poor have become redundant. Even worse is the claim that the very institutions of the welfare state have failed and in fact have helped to create this new underclass. A convenient charge, this one, for it serves to excuse the nation's ever greater neglect of its have-nots.

I write at a moment of despair over the fate of urban America and New York City in particular. Brutal violence and random slayings, mayhem in public parks and commercial neighborhoods, roving "posses" of violent, alienated teenagers, all seem to be symptoms of an ever more dangerous underclass. But the facts revealed in the aftermath of the violence frequently contradict our assumptions. The murderers or rapists often turn out to come from relatively stable families and to have jobs and educational aspirations. I think the evidence of declining respect for human life and our failure as a society to inspire our young people are urgent problems. But they are not a unique feature of the poor or down-and-out.

To understand why the idea of the underclass is of limited value we need to separate the arguments over definition from those concerning facts. We need, above all, to locate discussions of the underclass within a broader understanding of continuities and discontinuities in poverty. It may be that permanent poverty is to be a lasting feature of the postindustrial society. As Katherine Newman points out in *Falling From Grace,* downward mobility is threatening to become as much a part of the late twentieth-century American experience as success and affluence. But the idea of the underclass inevitably, and I think wrongly, raises the question of whether the people most in need are redeemable or worthy of redemption. Who, then, are these so-called underclass people?

The Underclass and the Merely Impoverished

All writers on the underclass agree that no matter how defined, its numbers are smaller than those of the poor. The most often used "official" U.S. government definition of poverty nets about thirty-two million Americans (13.1 percent of the population) who live below the threshold annual income of about $12,500 for a family of four. But included among these 32 million (and among the millions of others whose incomes hover just above this low figure) are Native Americans on impoverished reservations; people in households where there is a full-time (low) wage earner, where the household is composed of graduate students, where the household is composed of elderly persons on fixed incomes; and many others. So mere poverty, no matter how calculated, may be a necessary qualification but is not a sufficient measure of what the underclass might be.

The leading cause of poverty in the United States is low wages. Throughout the entire decade of the 1980s and continuing into the 1990s (despite the rather paltry 1990 increase in the minimum wage), a family of four with one full-time wage worker earning at or slightly above the minimum wage did not come even close to bringing home enough to exceed the official poverty threshold. Among the fifty million two-parent families in which one or more parents works full time, there are about three million families below the official poverty threshold. Much is written about the dramatic rise in poverty among single-parent families, and the large majority of children in single-parent families are living in poverty; but there are still far more children growing up in two-parent families and many of these are quite poor. In his book *Poor Support,* an invaluable study of contemporary poverty, David Ellwood shows that at least half the children in poverty in the United States are living in two-parent homes suffering the hardships of low wages and lack of employment. And an additional heavy proportion of the children growing up in single-parent homes once lived in two-parent homes that disintegrated because of severe economic hardship.

Separate the working poor, the unemployed, and the handicapped from the underclass, and what remains are people whose behavior, rather than unemployment or low wages, seems to some observers to be the cause of their woes. In *Science* (April 27, 1990), the nation's most prestigious scientific journal, economists Ronald Mincy, Isabel Sawhill, and Douglas Wolf point out that if one subtracts only those among the impoverished in America who have been down for a long count—eight years or more—"then about one fifth of the poor or about 6 million people could be considered members of the underclass." And if one considers the underclass as only those who have been impoverished over their entire lifetimes, the total would be perhaps no more than one or two million (their "educated guess"). But these authors go further and choose, as many who write on this subject do, to define the underclass in "behavioral terms." This "behavioral underclass" could be measured, they assert, by counting "the number of people who engage in bad behavior or a set of bad behaviors." Crime (especially in the drug industry), failure to work when not physically or mentally handicapped, teenage pregnancy, dropping out of school, and long-term welfare recipiency, are the actual bad behaviors they cite, arguing that these are typical of people who do not conform to norms of work, family, and morality. Using a methodology developed by Erol Ricketts and Isabel Sawhill, which counts the population in neighborhoods predominantly composed of people with such "bad behaviors," the authors come up with an estimate of a "behavioral underclass" composed of about 2.5 million people (based on the 1980 census) who live in 880 neighborhoods in American cities where there are high concentrations of other such ill-behaved people.

William J. Wilson's Postindustrial Chicago Underclass

These behavioral definitions of the underclass do not please University of Chicago sociologist William J. Wilson. The most influential writer on persistent poverty and the ghetto poor in the United States (and a dedicated social democrat), Wilson defines the underclass somewhat more broadly as "that heterogeneous grouping of families and individuals who are outside the mainstream of the American occupational system." Wilson's definition includes people who lack training and skills and are thus out of the labor force or at best experiencing long periods of unemployment, individuals engaged in "street crime and other forms of aberrant behavior, and families that experience long-term spells of poverty and/or welfare dependency." These are the populations Wilson refers to when he speaks of the underclass, a term he uses to "depict a reality not captured in the more standard designation, lower class." Although his conception of the underclass clearly has much in common with the behavioral measures of the economists, it encompasses a larger population of people who are excluded from the legitimate occupational world and whose behavior in response to that exclusion may further remove them from legitimate economic competition.

Wilson writes mainly about "the ghetto underclass," which he sees as a new phenomenon. His arguments are presented in his book *The Truly Disadvantaged* (University of Chicago Press, 1987), but his more recent data and analysis of the underclass in Chicago appear in a special issue of the *Annals* (American Academy of Political and Social Science, January 1989). This issue contains a number of important empirical articles by Wilson and his students and colleagues that further develop the theme of social isolation in the "ghetto underclass," especially in Chicago, where their door-to-door research is conducted. This social-isolation thesis has also influenced the work of many other authors, including those who wrote the *Science* article.

Wilson and his coworkers in Chicago strive mightily to avoid the pitfalls of labeling (terms like "bad behaviors") and also seek to avoid having their research appear to blame the victims of poverty for evolving a self-fulfilling "culture of poverty." On the contrary, for Wilson and his student Loïc Wacquant (in the *Annals* article), the central theme

is that the interrelated set of phenomena captured by the term "underclass" is primarily social-structural and that the ghetto is experiencing a "crisis": not because a "welfare ethos" has mysteriously taken over its residents but because joblessness and economic exclusion, having reached dramatic proportions, have triggered a process of hyperghettoization.

The terribly depressed Chicago ghetto is their primary example. The authors describe a racially segregated population on Chicago's South and West sides where between 1970 and 1980 the proportion of African Americans living in "extreme poverty areas" (neighborhoods where 40 percent or more live in "official poverty") increased from 24 percent to 47 percent and continued to rise during the 1980s. Over the same period in the ten largest U.S. cities, the proportion of poor blacks living in such highly concentrated poverty neighborhoods increased from 22 percent to 38 percent. Wilson could have extended this observation to scores of smaller cities such as Newark, Gary, Camden, and Bessemer, Alabama (once a thriving and largely black industrial satellite of Birmingham, now a dusty slum).

In Chicago, as in other large cities, the exodus of jobs and stable families with steady work has amounted to a social hemorrhage. Today's ghetto residents, Wacquant and Wilson argue, "face a closed opportunity structure." They are increasingly closed off from the opportunities afforded others in the society by the "rapid deterioration of housing, schools, businesses, recreational facilities, and other community organizations"—a deterioration greatly aided by government policies of industrial and urban laissez-faire that have channeled a disproportionate share of federal, state, and municipal resources to the more affluent."

Jobs for people in Chicago's black metropolis were always more difficult to obtain than for others in the city, but Wilson and Wacquant show that deindustrialization of the city has hit ghetto residents particularly hard. From 1950 to 1980 the overall proportion of adults (including people over sixty-five) of all races not employed in the city remained rather steady, around 43 percent. For ghetto blacks entering Chicago smokestack industries in the 1950s, the proportions outside the labor force were only slightly higher than for the city overall. By 1970 rates of nonparticipation for ghetto residents were ten to fifteen percentage points higher, and by 1980 anywhere from two-thirds to three-quarters of ghetto adults were not in the labor force. As a further measure of how far the American Dream is slipping away from the inner-city black poor, Wilson's research shows that in the extreme poverty neighborhoods of Chicago's ghetto, over half (51 percent) of all residents live in households where the annual income is less than $7,500. Three-quarters had "none of six assets" (personal checking account, savings account, IRA, pension plan, money in stocks or bonds, prepaid burial), and 97 percent owned no home, no business, no land.

Some of Wilson's critics, especially conservatives like Charles Murray and Lawrence Mead, think blacks themselves are more to blame for their hardship than Wilson does. They counter his "structural" arguments by noting that despite years of economic growth in the 1980s, when millions of jobs were added to the economy, ghetto blacks, and especially males, did not seem to benefit proportionately. Blacks are too quick, the conservative argument essentially states, to accept opportunities in the illegal economy, or too lazy or proud to accept unskilled work, and prefer to sponge off others (for example, AFDC women from the government, black men from AFDC women). They are, from this vantage point, the ill-behaved bulwark of the ghetto underclass. Lest the onus fall on ghetto blacks alone, there are the equally important examples of the Puerto Ricans and Native Americans, whose fate is especially like African Americans. But it is just these examples that help give the lie to the conservatives' blame-the-black-victim arguments.

The Strategic Example of the Puerto Ricans

In the twenty-five years between 1959 and 1984 no minority group in the United States fared worse economically than the Puerto Ricans. Native Americans experienced dramatic declines in their high rates of poverty during the 1970s but still ended the eighties with the highest rates (about 41 percent) of any minority. But Puerto Rican mean family income (measured in constant dollars) decreased by 25 percent over the period, more than double the rate of decline among blacks. In their research on U.S. Hispanics and poverty, Marta Tienda and her colleagues at the University of Wisconsin show that rates of increase in female-headed families and drastic declines in Puerto Rican men's and women's access to decent jobs account for much of this loss. Single-parent (largely female-headed) families increased among Puerto Ricans from 10 percent in 1959 to 35 percent in 1984. The bulk of this decline came, Tienda shows, after 1979, when wealth and opportunity were supposedly beginning to "trickle down."

Declining fortunes in Puerto Rican and black ghettos lend particular support to Wilson's "structural" arguments. The shared experience at the bottom of the American working class for Puerto Ricans and African Americans begins during the (relatively) booming 1950s, in New York, Philadelphia, Boston, Chicago, and other metropolitan centers and their industrial satellites (like Newark and Camden and more obscure places like Brightwaters in New York's Suffolk County). Blacks and Puerto Ricans have their own versions of colonial domination to surmount, but in their early experience with industrialization each group did rather well—not, of course, without great hardship. In the 1970s and more precipitously and cruelly in the 1980s, the industrial opportunity ladder for Puerto Ricans had its legs snapped. Call it deindustrialization, restructuring, the Great U Turn, or whatever you want, the result was disaster for brown people on the social-mobility queue in urban and industrial America. To make matters far worse, the Reagan years brought drastic cuts in public-sector employment, cuts in hospital work, cuts in the social safety net, cuts in the quality of education. Like the African Americans, many Puerto Rican ghetto men are demoralized and marked for early graves. Puerto Rican women are left with children and declining employment opportunities. The Puerto Rican experience helps to demonstrate once again that what matters is where you lived and where you had previously hoped to work, as well as the economic and social capital of your parents, not the culture or the particular colonial history of your people.

Demographer John D. Kasarda notes that from 1975 to 1985, "more than 2.1 million nonadministrative jobs were added in eating and drinking establishments, which exceeds the total number of production jobs that existed in 1985 in America's automobile, primary metals, and textile industries combined." And almost all the net gains in jobs with low educational entry requirements have been on the edges of the metropolitan areas, "far removed from large concentrations of poorly educated minorities." Puerto Ricans and African Americans in the rustbelt cities are particularly hard hit by these changes, but innumerable studies around the nation show that there has been a dramatic increase in temporary, part-time, and casual labor and even, in the farming states, a renewed increase in tenant farming as a means of escaping unionized farm labor. Runaway shops, tenant taxis (leased) in the cities, and sharecroppers and tenant farmers in the countryside are evidence of the real meaning of trickle-down economics and the vicious assault upon unions.

A Mirror for the Middle Class

Wilson, Tienda, Mincy, and others serve us well by documenting trends in American poverty, but there remains the problem of separating the poor from those who continue to be lumped in the underclass. In this we are helped by the clear-headed analysis of Christopher Jencks.

In recent articles Jencks traces the ambiguity surrounding the term "underclass" to Ken Auletta's 1982 book of that title. While surely not the first to describe an underclass, Auletta is "largely responsible for making it part of middle-class America's working vocabulary." Auletta included in that description chronically jobless men, long-term welfare mothers, alcoholics, drug dealers, street criminals, deinstitutionalized mental patients, "and all the other walking-wounded who crowded New York City's sidewalks in the later 1970's." The term was convenient for a journalist, Jencks believes, because it "focuses attention on the basement of the American social system (those who are 'under' the rest of us), without specifying what the inhabitants of this dark region have in common." But once the idea of the underclass took hold among journalists and policymakers, they in turn demanded of social scientists the usual studies of definition, size, and trends. In time-honored fashion we social scientists came up with at least twelve ways of defining the supposedly new class, including some of those described in this essay.

To clear things up somewhat, Jencks compares definitions of the underclass to those of the "middle class." The term "middle class," he notes, has a number of meanings in the United States, each of which "implies a mirror-image for the term underclass."

As Americans often define the middle class in terms of relatively stable white- and blue-collar occupations, then there may be an "economic underclass" composed of "working-age men and women who cannot get or cannot keep a steady job." But we frequently think of the middle class as those whose behavior affirms such norms as respect for the law, marriage before parenthood, moderation, and so on. If one defines the middle class this way, then perhaps there is a "moral underclass" of those without economic means (to eliminate the Mick Jaggers, Charles Keatings and Ivan Boeskys) who regard these moral tenets "as impractical or irrelevant." Sometimes, however, we think of the middle class in cultural terms, as people who are educated and have social and cultural skills, people who "talk, think, and act like professional and managerial workers" regardless of whether they actually have such jobs. We may also think of the working class as "composed of people who talk, think and act like blue collar workers." Below both the cultural middle class and the blue-collar class there may be an "educational underclass" of people "who lack the information and skills they would need to pass as members" of either class.

Only a social scientist could claim to clarify a debate by replacing one term with three. Jencks points out that a problem with the underclass concept is that it always requires adjectival acrobatics, as we have already seen with Wilson's use of the term "ghetto underclass" and the Mincy-Sawhill notion of a "behavioral underclass." But to postulate the economic underclass, the moral underclass, and the educational underclass helps define whom we are talking about and permits some measurement of possible growth in recent decades.

It will be no surprise that the data Jencks reviews on work and idleness demonstrate real growth in the "economic underclass." The percentage of joblessness among men aged 25 to 54 between 1954 and 1988, for example has crept upward since the 1950s. Joblessness reached a peak about 1984 but still has not declined to levels that were usual in the previous decades. And as always in this century, black joblessness was twice that of whites. Part-time work, casual labor, and long stints of unemployment are routine for youthful workers and those with lower levels of education. Wages also have eroded significantly among hourly workers and those with lower levels of education. Census data that Jencks summarizes show that in constant dollars income between 1967 and 1988 declined by 29 percent for working men with eighth-grade educations or less, by 23 percent among men with some high school, by 10 percent among men with high school diplomas, and by about 4 percent among men with some college. Income rose over the period only for men with college educations.

It may surprise many, however, that Jencks finds no evidence of growth in a moral underclass or in an educational underclass. Ask a sample of taxi drivers or sociology students what has happened in the past decade to crime rates, Jencks suggests, and they will be almost unanimous in asserting that crime has skyrocketed. But they will be wrong. In comparison with the high rates sustained in the 1960s and early 1970s, murder rates are down, as are other victimization rates (although they have increased in some inner city areas—for instance, the New York City Police Department reports that murders and robberies, many associated with the vicious crack epidemic, in the city rose sharply, to near-record levels, during the first six months of 1990). Aggravated assault with injuries (often associated with muggings) declined among whites from 310 per every 10,000 Americans in 1960 to 270 in 1986. Among blacks the decline was from 550 in 1965 to 420 in 1986. These rates are unconscionably high, but offer little evidence for a growing criminal underclass among blacks or whites.

Middle-class Americans often cite the growth in teenage pregnancy and illegitimacy as indicators of the growth of a moral underclass, but here too Jencks finds little support in the data. Between 1960 and 1986 expected births to teenage females actually declined by 50 percent among whites and by almost that much among blacks. Illegitimacy, however, has increased dramatically in the same period, so that about 16 percent of white babies and about 60 percent of black babies will be born to unmarried women. Much of the precipitous increase in illegitimacy among blacks can be attributed to joblessness among men. There is even evidence among whites and blacks with jobs and income of an increase in male unwillingness to take on family responsibilities; but, as Jencks also notes, "as women earn more they become less willing to marry and more willing to divorce men who are hard to live with." In any event, because illegitimacy is increasing among middle-class people as well as among the poor, it is difficult to make the case that the increasing prevalence of illegitimacy is evidence of growth in a moral underclass.

In education, finally, trends in school achievement offer little support for the idea that there is a growing educational underclass, especially among African Americans. In 1960 almost 44 percent of whites and 76 percent of blacks between 25 and 27 years of age had not finished high school. By 1985 the proportions had declined to 13 percent for whites and 17 percent for blacks, and in fact white graduation rates have leveled off since the mid-1970s while black graduation rates continue to improve steadily. The same trends apply to college completion. In 1960 only 8.2 percent of whites and 2.8 percent of blacks (aged 25 to 29) had completed college. By 1985 the proportions were 23.2 percent for whites and 16.7 for blacks. Considering their extremely low "cultural capital" at the start of desegregation (as economists like to say), blacks made extraordinary gains in this period, and their rate of gain is now faster than that of whites.

These figures do not lend support to the idea of an educational underclass (especially not a black one), but neither are they cause for celebration. If rates of college completion have been increasing (only slowly, if at all, for whites), we still have far to go before we will be educating enough young people with the technical and cultural capabilities required in a rapidly altering economy.

So Jencks finds that only the economic underclass is growing and that "the term underclass, like the term middle class," lumps together so many different populations that social scientists must use it with extreme care. "They should probably avoid the word altogether unless they are prepared to make clear which of its many meanings they have in mind." Still, he admits, the idea will continue to hold great appeal outside academic circles, and "If the term underclass helps put the problems of America's have-nots back on the political agenda, it will have served an extraordinarily useful purpose." This is a sentiment almost everyone can share, but it still leaves some confusion. The underclass is either a political slogan that may be shaped to the advantage of the all-inclusive have-nots of society, or, more accurately from the Jencks analysis, it is a poor surrogate for the lowest, most insecure ranks of the working class.

Falling into the Underclass

Men who unload trucks for daily cash and other casual laborers and those who still seek to become part of the more stable working class (the Jencks "economic underclass") ought not be included, I believe, in a general definition of the underclass. If we must speak of an underclass I hope the term may be narrowed to include only people who barely survive below the legitimate class system of capitalist society and below the lowest ranks of the criminal-class system as well. Most writers agree that the term will be with us despite its difficulties, although Wilson has recently decided to abandon the term as a description of the isolated ghetto poor. He believes, as I and many others do, that the term risks the negative effects of "blaming the victims." If it must be used at all, I think the term underclass ought to refer to people who have fallen or been pushed into a world of suffering they can escape only *with help from others* in the larger society. We can reasonably use the concept of the underclass, for example, to understand such familiar scenes as this:

It is about midnight, on a wintry early spring night, quite near the beginning of the twenty-first century. A line of sedans and taxis, here and there a stretch limo, inches across Manhattan from the Midtown Tunnel toward the Lincoln Tunnel on the West Side. I am in the fitful procession on my way to a college lecture scheduled for early the next day. Once past Fifth Avenue and into the garment center, the cars stopped at red lights are approached by gaunt men holding cans of window spray. They do not wait to see if the *drivers want their windshields cleaned but immediately begin their sullen work. Some drivers wave them away, others are more offended. Shouts and insults fly. I take either the more socially conscious or cowardly path (depending on your politics) and spend a few quarters to have my window washed over and over again. Three times in three blocks I put coins in a man's hand. Each time I touch well-calloused fingers or a work-hardened palm.*

The windshield washers are not the street urchins who ply this annoying trade uptown. They are adults who haunt the streets of midtown below the bus terminal. In cold weather they sleep in packing crates and cardboard boxes. By day they may seek casual labor, unloading trucks, moving merchandise, sweeping up, anything for immediate pay. At night many drink themselves to sleep. Some have crack or other dope habits to support. Most, but not all, are black or Puerto Rican.

If, then, we must have an underclass category, these men and others like them are good candidates for it. The bottom ranks of the working class always have men and women who are the most exploited and who, despite their hard work, cannot keep body and soul together. Sometimes such people are called wage slaves (Alec Wilkinson's book *Big Sugar* is a moving account of rural and migrant wage slavery). But homelessness and destitution in addition, as George Orwell showed in *Down and Out in Paris and London,* become a form of prison (with wage slavery) in the bosom of civil society. The homeless person can become locked into a round of daily survival behaviors, the search for food, for coins, for warmth, for an anodyne, for sleep. Increasingly most kinds of work except the most casual come to be out of reach for one reason or another, apart from how well the economy is doing. Life on the street soon destroys most people. Sleep deprivation, hunger, cold, sickness, and depression quickly take a toll. Men (and women) like these windshield wipers inhabit a despised street world intimately tied to the "regular economy," which that economy in fact produces in the backs of restaurants and in all the growing markets for casual labor and "lower overhead."

What about the children these men may have fathered along the way to their precarious adulthoods? Are they also to be thought of as part of the underclass? Suppose, as is often likely, the children are living with mothers who are on welfare. Some of their mothers may have had a few children by different fathers and been on welfare for years. Are "chronic" welfare mothers and their children also part of the underclass?

In most definitions of the term, welfare mothers who are on public assistance for more than three years and have additional children while on assistance are classified as "chronic welfare recipients" and are considered as part of the underclass. I reject this idea.

A mother of dependent children has real work to do and a mother with no regular male help has even more work. This should not be a controversial assertion. Middle-class mothers who choose to stay home in order to raise children often zealously defend their choice. They do not look kindly on suggestions that their lives are leisurely even if they also admit their good fortune in not "needing to go to work right away." Welfare mothers have even more obstacles to surmount since just existing on welfare is hard work itself. And few welfare mothers can actually exist on AFDC benefits, Medicaid, and food stamps. Almost all seek additional income, from off-the-books work, like caring for others' children along with their own, or in innumerable "hustles." And if receiving welfare payments was such a cushy way of life, welfare mothers would be expected to migrate from states with lower benefits to those with higher ones. But there is no evidence that such migration occurs. Instead, the women typically plan ways of improving their education or finding a decent job or forming a stable relationship, all the things any of us would try in order to "get on our feet." Now the welfare laws increasingly push women to get back into the labor market when their children are old enough to be in day care, but of course we have yet to develop anything like an adequate day-care system.

Yet to exclude all mothers on welfare from even my narrow and reluctant definition of an underclass would not well reflect the suffering and neglect we see around us in cities like New York and Chicago and in hundreds of other American communities large and small. Women without homes, mothers and children without homes, all run the risk that homelessness itself becomes an insurmountable and debilitating obstacle. Welfare mothers who become addicted or who become entrapped in a world of prostitution and unsuccessful petty crime, or whose material and emotional lives have disintegrated to the point that they neglect and abuse their children, all can be thought to have fallen into the lowest ranks of poverty and misery. AIDS workers like Victor Ayala (see box) would agree that indigent AIDS patients, surely down and out, might also be counted among an underclass, but he believes the term serves little purpose except to excuse our ignorance of the AIDS epidemic.

There are also children who fall into extreme poverty and risk living out brutally shortened lives at the bottom. One of the best recent books about this subject is Terry Williams's *Cocaine Kids,* a detailed ethnography of the lives of teenagers in upper Manhattan who become involved in the world of crack dealing. Williams and others have shown that existing drug laws encourage adult dealers to recruit children into the underground drug industry. There are a few cases of teenagers who become wildly successful and even more cases of teenagers who make some money for a while before getting into trouble with the authorities or within the drug underworld. Williams shows that those who begin using drugs, other than marijuana, quickly decline and are cast out, often to drift into trouble or violence. Kids with records of arrest, failure in school, histories of drug abuse and depression, and with only limited training for employment and few contacts in labor markets are prime candidates for lives as windshield washers and street-corner junkies. But if they are not trapped into such lives because of homelessness or severe debilitation, they should not be counted among those who are down and out. Though at risk of falling, they have not yet dropped into the underclass. Whether they do so or not will depend a good deal on the opportunities our society makes available to them to help themselves. It will also depend on the kind of adult mentors it provides them.

In sum, as I use the term, the underclass includes those people who are trapped in a netherworld at the bottom of both the legal and illegal class systems. The major traps are addiction, homelessness, mental illness, destitution, and usually a combination of these conditions. Although their numbers are growing steadily, especially in central cities and segregated ghettos, the size of this population is far lower than the overall poverty population (which has also been growing). As a spur to social policy a narrow definition of the underclass does not detract from the argument by Wilson and others that we urgently need industrial policies targeted toward economically depressed communities. The idea that the underclass is relatively small and is composed of people who have fallen out of the working or criminal classes (or who never made it up before becoming trapped at the bottom) will help emphasize the special programs of emergency housing, supported work, drug rehabilitation, enhanced schooling in low-income communities, and other measures that could reduce destitution and homelessness. If the down-and-out make up no more than three million people (including the nation's present homeless population), we ought to be able to immediately reduce that number.

We ought to be able to help, that is, if we can ever overcome the consequences of all the theft of public funds and the vicious attacks on our social institutions that has marked the past decade. In fact, by my definition of the underclass there is not a major new social class to trumpet about or to blame on welfare institutions. There is instead a significant growth in old-style misery, due in some part to industrial restructuring and in another and more evil part to the cupidity of the nation's elite. History will show that for some time toward the end of our American Century the nation's upper class, or the part of it in power, embraced a philosophy of narrow self-interest first elaborated by Bernard Mandeville in his tract of 1705, *The Grumbling Hive* (later expanded into *The Fable of the Bees*). Mandeville coined the phrase, "Private vice makes public virtue." Someone might want to offer this profound insight to the corner windshield washers or to the homeless people huddled outside the gates of the White House.□

Article 2. Making It: The Underclass Cycle
by Nicholas Lemann

Nicholas Lemann debunks the view that the underclass is doomed to permanent poverty, questioning those who maintain that the government can do little if anything to ease their condition. Noting that short-term, one-shot programs are destined to fail, the author urges the government to intensify its efforts, beginning with prenatal care. The government should also intensify its commitment to Head Start, special-education programs, job training, and crime fighting. In addition, the welfare system should be completely overhauled to include a new emphasis on workfare.

Mr. Lemann is national correspondent of The Atlantic Monthly. *From "The Underclass Cycle: Making It— Then and Now" by Nicholas Lemann,* The Washington Post, *May 21, 1989, pages C1, C4:*

The Irish, crowding into the cities, posed problems in housing, police, and schools; they meant higher taxes and heavier burdens in the support of poorhouses and private charitable institutions. Moreover, the Irish did not seem to practice thrift, self-denial and other virtues desirable in the "worthy, laboring poor." They seemed drunken, dissolute, permanently sunk in poverty.
—*William V. Shannon, The American Irish*

Hardly less aggressive than the Italian, the Russian and Polish Jew . . . is filling the tenements of the old Seventh Ward to the river front, and disputing with the Italian every foot of available space in the back alleys of Mulberry Street. The two races, differing hopelessly in much, have this in common: They carry their slums with them wherever they go, if allowed to do it. . . . The Italian and the poor Jew rise only by compulsion.
—*Jacob Riis, How the Other Half Lives*

The present always imputes a degree of innocence to the past. One of many possible examples is our attitude toward the underclass, which is, essentially, that no similar social problem has ever existed in urban America— and that therefore the problem can't be solved. An ethnic group living in isolated slums in the very heart of our prosperous cities; fatal disease spreading as a result of irresponsibly licentious behavior; rampant welfare dependence; out-of-control violent crime; abuse of lethal intoxicants; rampaging youth gangs; rich, swaggering criminals who sit atop the society of the slum; a breakdown of family values; a barely disguised feeling among the prosperous classes that perhaps the poor are inherently not up to being fully functioning Americans—the whole picture has been around, intermittently, in this country since about 1850.

Historically, alarm about urban ethnic poverty arises with the arrival in our cities of a large group of immigrants who are visibly very different from middle-class America. The first such group was the peasant Irish, who began coming here in the 1840s. Within a decade, there were large Irish slums; the Irish dominated the resources of the jails, public hospitals and social-welfare agencies; and the fear of where all this would lead was an important factor in national politics. In the late 1880s, after immigrants from eastern and southern Europe had established their own urban slums, another substantial wave of concern about the underclass began, and one of its many consequences was a major political realignment that led to the heyday of Progressivism.

Worries about the turn-of-the century underclass led to strict limits on immigration, and this created labor shortages in the cities. The abundance of unskilled jobs began attracting large numbers of southern blacks to the cities starting around the time of World War I. This black migration intensified with World War II and the boom years that followed it, which vastly increased the demand for labor and coincided with the mechanization of agriculture in the South. The number of black migrants from South to North in the '40s, '50s, and '60s was greater than the number of Irish, Jews, or Italians or Poles who came to the cities during their peak years of migration. It should not be surprising that, like the earlier migrations, the black migration, which lasted until about 1970, should have brought the issue of slum life back to the fore, and contributed to another political realignment—the shift of the presidential electorate to the Republican Party in the late '60s.

SLUMS IN THE 1890s

It is impossible to read Jacob Riis's How the Other Half Lives, published in 1890, without noticing the parallels between Riis's concerns and those of middle-class reformers in the big cities today. Rotgut liquor seemed every bit as dangerous then as crack does today; in fact, his chapter called "A Raid on the Stale-beer Dives" is an eerily precise parallel to those television shows in which a camera crew accompanies the police to a crack house. The saloon-keeper was the equivalent of the drug-dealer, the only visibly affluent male in the slum (except for the numbers king, whose function in recent years has been taken over by local government lotteries). Teen-age gangs were even worse than they are now, in the sense that one of their usual activities, according to Riis, was assaulting police officers.

Riis even shared some of the suspicions of present-day conservatives that social programs may add to, rather than diminish, the conditions they seek to alleviate. "Ill-applied charity," Riis feld, was creating a class of poeple

who didn't bother to look for work. Cholera, bred by willfully unclean living, played the role AIDS does now. Teen-age girls were having babies and letting them run wild. Illiteracy was rampant. Murder was an "everyday crop."

In Riis's work, as in that of the other great liberal reformers of the day, there lurks just beneath the surface the idea that ethnicity is destiny. Obviously the same idea, again barely submerged, is around today, though it is reassuring to see how silly Riis's stereotypes seem after less than a century. "Penury and poverty are wedded everywhere to dirt and disease, and Jewtown is no exception," he wrote. "It could not well be otherwise in such crowds, considering especially their low intellectual status."

Riis saw the relatively small black population of New York as occupying a much higher plane: "Cleanliness is the characteristic of the negro in his new surroundings, as it was his virtue in the old. In this respect he is immensely superior to the lowest of the whites, the Italians and the Polish Jews . . . ." As late as World War I, blacks living in the North outscored Jews on the Army intelligence test.

I don't mean to argue that all the problems of the ghettos are simply going to go away over time—only that the current atmosphere of fatalism is unwarranted. What will happen is similar to what has happened in the past: The ghettos will become depopulated as everybody who can get a job moves out. This has been going on for two decades in the big-city black ghettos, virtually all of which were badly overcrowded in the mid-'60s and have an emptied-out look today. In the 1970s, the District of Columbia lost 16 percent of its population while its black-white ratio stayed almost exactly the same; there was a lot of black flight going on, too. If you define the underclass as people living in majority-poor inner-city neighborhoods (and social scientists are moving toward this kind of geographical definition), then instead of being the "growing problem" that everyone says it is, the underclass is a shrinking problem.

Of course, the more the employed migrate out of inner cities, the worse ghettos will become as neighborhoods: There will be still less of a social check on crime, less institutional structure, fewer intact families. (The main difference between today's ghettos and those that Riis wrote about is that there are so many fewer poor husband-wife families today—a difference that does make today's underclass more intractable but still not totally so.) Eventually, the out-migration will stop—though it hasn't stopped yet—and a dispirited core of people will be left behind to live in what will be, functionally, the urban equivalents of Indian reservations.

SOCIAL PROGRAMS

We should not sit around and watch this happen. External events have a tremendous effect on the ability of poor people to get out of the ghettos. The Irish middle class began to emerge when Irish political machines took over city halls and got access to the many thousands of decent-paying municipal patronage jobs. The immigrants Riis wrote about had the good fortune to arrive in the United States early in a long period of industrialization, in which unskilled jobs were plentiful and the economy was expanding.

The black migration out of the ghettos was spurred by the domestic initiatives of Lyndon Johnson, such as the Civil Rights Act, the Fair Housing Act, affirmative action and the large increase in black employment in government that began with the declaration of the War on Poverty. The proportion of the poor who escape poverty, and the speed with which they escape, are variable and depend greatly on economic trends and on what the government does.

Today, most discussion of the underclass is strongly influenced by the idea that government social programs can't possibly help. We believe we've tried everything; we believe none of it worked; we believe that if the programs that began in the late '60s had any effect at all, it was to make things worse. Most of this is wildly oversimplified, exaggerated, or untrue. The government's anti-poverty efforts were of limited size and duration—the heyday of poverty programs, as opposed to welfare programs, lasted only five years, from 1964 to 1968—and were built around a new, unproven idea: community action.

Moreover, progress was made: The percentage of Americans who are poor decreased substantially during the '60s, then leveled off in the '70s and rose in the '80s, when the government was cutting back its efforts. It's hard to find individual members of the underclass who are downwardly mobile—mostly they come from families that have always been poor.

Now we know a lot more about what kinds of poverty programs work. In general, what works is intensive efforts—not short-term, one-shot aid injections—to help poor children arrive at adulthood well-educated and trained for employment. These efforts ought to begin with prenatal care and continue through Head Start, special-education programs during the school years and job training of sufficient duration and intensity to teach real skills and good work habits. Ridding ghetto neighborhoods of crime would help, too. So would making long-term welfare recipients get jobs. All this is both expensive and intrusive, so it lacks a certain mom-and-apple-pie appeal. But it would do a lot of good.

Since the ghettos have deteriorated so much as places, it's tempting to say that the answer is to improve them as places. But this works only up to a point. Public safety, education and the housing stock in ghettos can and should be improved, but the idea of creating an independent economic base and a class of successful role models there is a persistent fantasy. This idea has a respectable ancestry in Booker T. Washington's vision of a black America made up of yeoman farmers and skilled artisans. But remember that Washington formulated his views during the height of Jim Crow and foresaw a totally segregated black America.

The vision of a self-sufficient ghetto doesn't work in a world in which, happily, successful blacks have the option of entering the mainstream economy and making much more money. There is no reason to hope, or to expect, that when people in the ghettos become successful enough to be role models, they won't leave. The idea that people who have already left will move back is even more unlikely absent a total overhaul of inner urban areas in which the ghettos themselves are displaced.

Economic development efforts in poor neighborhoods have been one of the conspicuous failures of the past generation, because it's murderously difficult to build businesses in neighborhoods that are rapidly losing population. The most publicized success stories involving ghetto development, such as Bedford-Stuyvesant in Brooklyn and South Shore in Chicago, really involve the residential stabilization of working-class neighborhoods, not the establishment of a neighborhood economic base.

Two sentiments about the underclass seem to prevail these days: First, the situation is completely hopeless; and second, the underclass can only be healed from within black America, through black leadership. The best answer to the first point is to look at the history of previous immigrant ghettos, which should lead to the conclusion that the situation is exactly as hopeless today as it has always been—which is to say, not hopeless at all. The second point is really an attitude, not a program. Does anyone really believe that if Benjamin Hooks of the NAACP—an organization of, by and for middle-class blacks—made daily speeches about drugs, crime and teen-age pregnancy, it would turn the ghetto around?

Jesse Jackson, to his credit, has been making such speeches for years. He is a hero in the ghettos, but he hasn't made the problems go away. The underclass is cut off from the rest of America, and what it needs is the direct intervention of the whole society, not just black society. A generation from now, the wild pessimism now prevailing about the underclass will seem dated; and so will our disinclination to see that the problem exerts a call to which the whole country must respond for both moral and practical reasons.

Article 3. Us Vs. Them: America's Growing Frustration with the Homeless
by Sarah Ferguson

Although America was initially sympathetic to the plight of the homeless, recent developments suggest
a growing backlash, which is reflected in the increasing number of cities that have passed
antiloitering ordinances. This frustration is due, in large measure, to their sheer numbers, as well as
changes in the composition of the homeless population, which has grown significantly younger. The
stereotypical image of the old skid row bum has been replaced by young black and Hispanic men,
angry at themselves and the system, who frequently use and sell drugs, and insult or accost passersby
demanding money. Regardless of the reasons, there is ample evidence to suggest that a class war is
brewing between the homeless and disgruntled citizens who are forced to endure them.

Most of us are quick to sympathize with the lot of the homeless. But our reaction might not be as charitable after we're aggressively and repeatedly panhandled on the street. As Sarah Ferguson reports, a public already overwhelmed by the ever-growing presence of the homeless is increasingly receptive to government proposals to get the homeless out of our face, with restrictions on where they can solicit or sleep. Yet the homeless can't disappear—a lack of decent housing, health care, jobs, and education are daily driving more out on the streets. And as a posthumous report from a homeless woman shows, the street is indeed a dreaded last resort.

In streets and doorways across the country, a class war is brewing between angry indigents and disgruntled citizens forced to step out of their way. Tompkins Square, the Manhattan park that spawned New York's first love-in in the '60s, has become symbolic of what happens when a liberal community loses patience with the homeless. It was neighborhood tolerance that allowed the encampment of homeless men and women to swell to a shantytown of more than 300 indigents last summer. But it was the rising outcry from neighbors who claimed that the homeless had "taken the park hostage" that finally forced the city to tear the shanties down. Police raids on Tompkins Square Park over the past year, however, have done nothing to abate the flood of homeless people camped out in public spaces. Because, of course, the homeless keep coming back. In Tompkins Square, construction crews have already plowed away the patches of scorched earth that remained after a raid last December, during which many of the homeless burned their tents in protest. But a dozen or so homeless people, mostly African-Americans, remain huddled around the Peace, Hope, Temperance, and Charity gazebo. Another 15 are sprawled on piles of sodden blankets in the band shell, and maybe 20

From *Utne Reader,* September/October 1990, pp. 50–55. Excerpt from Pacific News Service, April 16, 1990. Copyright © 1990
by Pacific News Service. Reprinted by permission.

more are jammed in the bathrooms, sleeping in the stalls and sometimes charging 50 cents to move their bedding before you can enter. Fed up with such seeming intransigent masses, their budgets squeezed dry by the Reagan Revolution, cities across the nation are starting to adopt a closed-door attitude toward the displaced:

•In New York City, the Transit and Port Authority has banned panhandling in subway stations and bus terminals.

•In Washington, D.C., the city council recently slashed $19 million from the homeless budget and is seeking to roll back Initiative 17, the referendum that required the city to provide shelter to all those in need.

•In Atlanta, Mayor Maynard Jackson has proposed a policy of licensing panhandlers as part of an intensified campaign to drive the homeless out of the center city business district.

•In Berkeley, the University of California has ordered repeated police sweeps of People's Park, long a holdout for vagrants and the dispossessed,

There's a growing rift between the homeless themselves and the advocates who represent them.

and has evicted People's Cafe, a soup kitchen set up this winter by the Catholic Worker.

There have been periodic outcries against the homeless since the media first discovered the "problem" in the early 1980s. But today's growing disfavor bodes ill at a time when the economy worsens and the line between the middle class and the poor becomes ever more precarious. Many people's need to maintain an "us versus them" mentality seems all the more urgent.

"The tension level is definitely rising," says Wendy Georges, program director for Berkeley's Emergency Food Project. "With more homeless in the streets, people are starting to lose patience—even in Berkeley. If a city like this successfully attacks homeless people and homeless programs, it will set precedents. The homeless backlash will become a popular thing—so that nobody has to feel guilty about it."

Part of the reason for the growing backlash is sheer numbers. The U.S. Conference of Mayors annual survey found that the demand for emergency shelter in 27 cities increased an average of 13 percent in 1988 and 25 percent in 1989. Some

22 percent of those requesting emergency shelter were turned away.

Public disfavor may also be spurred by changes in the makeup of the homeless population. Although figures are scarce, anyone who walks the streets can see that the homeless population has grown younger. A 1960 survey of Philadelphia's skid row by Temple University found that 75 percent of the homeless were over the age of 45, and 87 percent were white. In 1988, 86 percent were under 45, and 87 percent were minorities.

As the population shifts, the stereotypical image of the old skid row bum meekly extending his palm for change has been replaced by young African-American and Hispanic men, angry at the lack of good-paying jobs, often taking drugs or selling them—or demanding money from passersby with a sense of entitlement that the passersby find enraging.

In front of the Tower Records store near Greenwich Village in Manhattan, a group of brazen panhandlers confront shoppers with cardboard signs that read "Homeless Donations: $1 or token." "Cheap bastards," mutters one of the beggars, an

A class war is brewing between angry indigents and disgruntled citizens forced to step out of their way.

African-American man named Flower, as he dumps on the sidewalk a handful of pennies that a passerby just gave him. "What am I supposed to do with that?"

"Look, corporate criminals!" shouts his companion, Paradise, who sports preppy clothes and seashells woven in his short dreadlocks, pointing to a group of businessmen picking up their Lincoln Continental in the parking lot next door. "Hello Mr. Executive, how you doing? You remember how to be human, don't you?" Paradise asks him mockingly, shoving a cardboard box in his face. "Come on give me a dollar man, I bet you make $50,000 in 10 minutes," he shouts. In response, the driver edges his window down a crack and mutters, "Get a job, will you?"

Meanwhile, Flower is chasing a frightened-looking man on the street. "Help me out. I know you're afraid of black people, but I won't bite."

"Get away from me," says John Kroeper, a young Jersey City resident in a business suit, who passes the panhandlers with contempt. "It's an invasion of my privacy. I don't want to be forced to give. Just because I have a suit on doesn't mean I'm a yuppie. I just lost my job."

"I'll give when they're just sitting there on the ground, but not when they come on to you like that," adds his sister Jean. "If you give money to people on the streets, you never know if they're really going to buy food with it or just buy liquor or drugs. I like to give to organizations like the Salvation Army or Covenant House, where I know the money will go to good use."

"It's just too overwhelming," says one woman, shaking her head. I ask her why she didn't give anything and she responds, "I think there's plenty of services in the city for people who want help."

The sometimes belligerent attitude of street people goes along with a growing shelter and welfare rebellion. In New York, the growth of the tent city in Tompkins Square reflected the refusal by many homeless to enter New York's degrading shelter system, where as many as 1,000 people may be housed in armories nightly. Moreover, a substantial number of homeless people refuse to sign up for welfare and other entitlement programs, preferring to fend for themselves on the streets rather than get caught up in a "dependency mentality" and suffer the degradation of long welfare lines and condescending caseworkers.

Instead, homeless people have begun banding together in support networks and tent encampments, demanding political recognition, and fighting back when they don't get it. Their resolve is seen in Santa Cruz, where a dozen vagrants have been arrested repeatedly for sleeping outside the local post office, and in San Francisco, where more than a hundred people continue to camp in front of City Hall, adamantly protecting their belongings as police patrol the area daily to sweep away unguarded possessions.

"I see this as a form of anarchy," says Jake, a 30-year-old blond woman with tattoos decorating her chest as she lies back in a bed of blankets and heavy-metal tape cassettes next to her two companions, Red, 29, and Gadget, 24. "We're not going to hide somewhere. Just us being here is a protest." When pressed about why they don't go out and get jobs, Gadget responds, "I'm not going to go flip burgers at some McDonald's so I can share a tiny apartment with a bunch of crazy a———s. I've got friends and family here."

Such comments are grist for the mills of newspaper columnists who justify their new hard-line attitude toward the homeless with the argument that little can be done for people who don't want to help themselves. "Enough is enough," proclaims the editorial board of the *Philadelphia Inquirer*, which has called for a law to prohibit camping out in public places. Similarly, the *San Francisco Examiner* recently ran an editorial calling for the "benign incarceration" of street people.

On Manhattan's Lower East Side, a group of merchants called BEVA (Businesses in the East Village) formed last year to respond to the growing number of street people and peddlers clogging the parks and sidewalks. "All of us are liberal people," says BEVA president Kathleen Fitzpatrick, owner of a local cafe. "Our doors are open. But many well-meaning acts, when they go unregulated, turn sour. Look at Tompkins Square—it's the only park without a curfew and that [allows] open fires [fire barrels]. But look at what's happening. It's uncontrolled. It's a toilet. The other day they found 20 needles in the playground area.

"We want to do something to re-establish a community presence in the park—not to kick the homeless out—to try and regulate it," Fitzpatrick continues. "I'm a victim of this. What happened to all the government programs? It all filters down to the community—all of us little people who are now forced to contribute our income, our time, our energy and money to finally do something. I guess that's what Reagan wanted."

It is 11 a.m. in October outside the Center for Creative Non-Violence—the famous shelter that the late homeless advocate Mitch Snyder built in downtown Washington, D.C.—and the homeless are angry. Here as elsewhere in recent months, it is possible to see another growing rift concerning the homeless—this one between the homeless themselves and the advocates who represent them.

More than 400 homeless people have walked from as far away as New York City and Roanoke, Virginia, to take part in a Homeless Now! march on the capital. Now half are milling outside the shelter, still waiting for breakfast. Several march leaders try to push their way into the Second Street entrance, temporary headquarters for Housing Now!'s shoe-string operation, but the doors are barred. Only "organizers" get admitted.

The crowd surges forward and scuffles break out. As the CCNV guards try to wrestle back the marchers, a pregnant woman is struck to the ground. Sirens flash as a riot squad plows through the crowd, followed by a dozen cops on motorcycles.

The fight outside CCNV reflects the class dynamics of a movement that has yet to find its indigenous voice. Although more and more homeless people are organizing and speaking out for themselves, most advocacy groups continue to be dominated by professional and volunteer organizers.

"All too often, services and events are developed by white, middle-class people," says Mike Neely, a 41-year-old Vietnam vet who founded the Homeless Outreach Project in Los Angeles after sleeping on the streets for 18 months. "But when you look out there, the majority of the homeless are black or brown and have never been middle class and are never gonna be."

Of the 65 board members of the National Coalition for the Homeless, only 10 are currently or formerly homeless. Executive director Mary Ellen Hombs says that the coalition actively encourages homeless people to serve on its board.

Another advocacy group, the National Union of the Homeless, maintains that only the homeless can speak for the homeless. It's not an easy route. Since 1985, the union has been trying to develop a national organizing framework. From a high point in 1987, the number of active locals has fluctuated downward. But this year has seen a resurgence in organizing. This spring, union activists in Oakland, Minneapolis, Tucson, Detroit, Dallas, New York City, Philadelphia, and Santa Monica took over abandoned federal properties, aiming to force the government to turn them over to homeless families. Although the union had staged similar housing takeovers in 1988 with the aid of the coalition and CCNV, this time they've struck out on their own.

This rift is partly the result of an increased radicalization of homeless organizers. "Homeless people are saying they don't want any more stop-gaps. They don't want shelters, they want houses. They don't want welfare, they want jobs. That's a profound threat to people who say they want to enable, but really want to control," says union member Alicia Christian.

Professional homeless and housing lobbyists are quick to offer statistics on the numbers of homeless children and intact families on the streets. They say that single homeless men, particularly young, angry minorities, are not going to move politicians or the public. But by minimizing substance abuse problems and the swelling ranks of able-bodied, yet unemployable men among the homeless, some activists may be practicing politics of denial.

In response, activists like Mike Neely have begun forming their own service agencies, run for and by the homeless. Yet even as more homeless organizers move into service provider roles, the lines of conflict become blurred. "People say, 'How can you speak about being homeless when you're not even homeless yourself?'" Neely says. "It's a double-edged sword." ∎

Homeless people have begun banding together in support networks and tent encampments.

Chapter **17**

Environmental and Energy Policy

Article 1. The Dioxin Deception
by Joe Thornton; additional reporting by John Hanrahan

This article discusses the failure of the Environmental Protection Agency to ban dioxin, a group of some seventy-five chemicals, but used most often to refer to its most toxic form. Despite its dangers, the agency bowed to the pressure of the special interests—led by the chemical and paper manufacturers—and refused to prohibit its use. The author contends that EPA's own studies revealed that dioxin not only causes cancer in humans, but encourages cancers started by other carcinogens. In fact, the agency found that human exposures to dioxin were greater than EPA's own dose. As a result of its action, many states have already lowered their standards to allow greater dioxin levels. The author reviews the research on dioxin, the EPA's own experiments, and the behind-the-scenes actions of the pro-dioxin lobby.

In the 1960s, when scientists discovered that the pesticide DDT was causing reproductive problems among birds and fish, and that the same chemical was building up in the environment and the tissues of U.S. citizens, the government banned it.

In the mid-1970s, scientists found cancer-causing PCBs, chemicals used in electrical transformers, accumulating in the tissues of marine mammals, birds, fish and humans. Although Monsanto, the only U.S. producer of the chemicals, released studies saying PCBs were harmless, Congress banned them.

In the 1980s, scientists discovered the same, and worse, about a class of chemicals called dioxins. But the Environmental Protection Agency (EPA) has allowed dioxin pollution to continue while cooperating with the industries most responsible for it, in an attempt to roll back regulations and reduce public fears.

Why the break from tradition? Dioxin (shorthand for a group of 75 chemicals, but most commonly used to refer to the most toxic form, also known as 2,3,7,8-tetrachlorodibenzo-p-dioxin, or TCDD) is no less dangerous than PCBs or DDT; on the contrary, dioxin is more toxic, longer-lived and even more likely to accumulate in living organisms. But dioxin has many powerful friends. While only a handful of industries were dependent on PCBs and DDT, dioxin is the unintended by-product of dozens of chlorine-based industrial chemicals and processes, including pulp and paper bleaching, garbage and hazardous waste incineration, the manufacture of many pesticides and industrial chemicals, and certain types of wood preserving, oil refining and metal smelting.

An industrial coalition, with U.S. chemical and paper manufacturers in the lead and EPA and lesser industries in tow, has conducted a decade-long campaign to "detoxify" dioxin's image in the public eye. And it is succeeding. "We're failing to deal with dioxin not because of any lack of information about its dangers to human health, but because of political and economic considerations," says Dr. Samuel Epstein, professor of Occupational and Environmental Health at the University of Illinois.

DIOXIN HAS BEEN BUILDING UP IN THE ENVIRONMENT since the rapid growth of the chlorinated chemicals industry after World War II. But controversy over the contamination didn't erupt until 1979, when EPA suspended use of the dioxin-contaminated herbicide 2,4,5-T on forests, rights-of-way and pastures. The sudden decision was prompted by an EPA study correlating spraying patterns of the herbicide with human miscarriages in western Oregon. Despite a flurry of protests from the chemical industry, EPA then began the long process of canceling 2,4,5-T's registration permanently, arguing that no safe level of exposure to dioxin could be demonstrated and that a ban on the herbicide was necessary to protect the public.

At that point, the agency was on firm scientific ground. Tests on laboratory animals showed dioxin to be among the most poisonous substances known to science. Doses as low as one one-trillionth of an animal's body weight have correlated with cancer, birth defects and reproductive problems. At higher but still tiny doses, it has produced those same effects, plus developmental and nervous and immune system abnormalities, and damage to the kidneys, liver and skin. A 1985 EPA document regards TCDD as "the most potent carcinogen ever tested in laboratory animals."

Even worse, dioxin not only causes cancer itself, but also promotes cancers started by other carcinogens. Since TCDD always occurs in combination with other pollutants, the implications of this "cancer enhancement" are

sobering. "Thirty years ago," Dr. Epstein says, "one in four Americans was getting cancer and one in five was dying from it. Today, one in three Americans gets cancer, and one in four dies from it. I have no doubt dioxin must be given some credit for this."

While EPA's pesticide regulators moved to ban 2,4,5-T, other EPA officials realized that a "no safe level of dioxin" policy would have broad implications. For instance, EPA was advocating incinerators for garbage and toxic waste, despite evidence that dioxins were formed and released in the burning process. An EPA memo described the quandary: "What should EPA do—regulate [dioxin] using the Clean Air Act—which could result in closing all resource recovery [garbage incineration] facilities?" Other federal agencies were threatened as well: Waiting in the wings were perhaps billions of dollars in claims from Vietnam veterans exposed during the war to dioxin (as 2,4,5-T) in the defoliant Agent Orange.

While EPA tore itself in two, Dow and Monsanto, the nation's major 2,4,5-T manufacturers, began a scientific and political battle to salvage their herbicide and soothe the public's fear of dioxin. At the same time, the federal government began a research program into Agent Orange's effects on veterans.

In 1980, Monsanto released the first of three studies of workers exposed to dioxin at its 2,4,5-T factory in West Virginia. It concluded that the workers suffered no dioxin-related effects except for chloracne, a painful skin disease. Along with studies conducted by Dow, the German chemical company BASF and the government's Agent Orange project, the Monsanto research laid the foundation for claims that humans were somehow immune to the extraordinary toxicity dioxin had shown in animal tests.

This position was reported approvingly in the media throughout the 1980s, and it soon became accepted wisdom. The Monsanto studies were influential in EPA's dioxin policy, and they played key roles in legal decisions denying compensation to American and Australian Vietnam veterans.

In 1990, information surfaced showing that the Monsanto, BASF and Agent Orange studies were manipulated and scientifically invalid. In each case, the data or methods of the studies appeared to have been massaged to obscure dioxin's effects on exposed workers and veterans. Dr. Cate Jenkins, a chemist in EPA's Regulatory Development Branch, calls Monsanto's research "fraudulent" and refers to "flawed data and the knowing, inappropriate use of such data" in the studies. EPA is now conducting a criminal investigation of Monsanto's conduct, but the policies based on these studies remain. Despite ongoing revelations of this kind, EPA continues to rely on information prepared by industry. "Industry studies are always

Reprinted with permission of *Greenpeace* magazine, May/June 1991.

suspect," says Epstein. "The people who profit should not do the testing."

And, in August 1990, the House Government Operations Committee charged that the Agent Orange study, conducted between 1982 and 1987 by the government-run Centers for Disease Control (CDC), amounted to a "cover-up." According to the report, the CDC study embodied "flawed science" and "political manipulation" by the Reagan White House, which "controlled and obstructed" the study to ensure that Agent Orange was not linked to the veterans' health problems. Representative Ted Weiss (D-NY), who chaired the subcommittee investigation, termed the CDC study "a sham."

THROUGHOUT THE 1980S, WHILE INDUSTRY MAINTAINED that dioxin was safe for humans, some EPA officials lent a hand by suppressing information to the contrary. In late 1980, the Canadian government began to urge the U.S. to investigate the source of high TCDD levels found in the Great Lakes, and the U.S. and Canada agreed to conduct a joint investigation. Internally, EPA scientists had already predicted increased cancer rates as high as 1 per 100 among people who ate just one meal of Great Lakes fish per week contaminated with dioxin at levels of 10 parts per trillion. Such an estimate, however, would require that the U.S. Food and Drug Administration (FDA) declare a quarantine on Great Lakes fish. EPA kept these figures quiet and successfully pushed FDA to recommend only that people limit their consumption to two meals per month of fish contaminated at a 25-50 parts per trillion "level of concern."

But EPA's Region 5 office, which serves the Great Lakes states, took a harder line. In the spring of 1981, EPA Region 5 prepared a draft report rejecting FDA's "level of concern" and concluding that dioxin in the Great Lakes constituted a grave cancer threat to persons eating fish from the lakes. The report named Dow, manufacturer of 2,4,5-T, as the primary dioxin source and recommended that consumption of fish caught in the region of Dow's Michigan plant "be prohibited."

When EPA released the report, all the damaging information had been deleted. A 1983 congressional investigation found that EPA officials John Hernandez and John Todhunter had forced Region 5 to delete all references to Dow as well as any discussion of health risks posed by eating Great Lakes fish. Also deleted were all mentions of other studies pointing to dioxin's toxicity, including miscarriages in Oregon and the effects of Agent Orange exposure. Both Hernandez and Todhunter resigned in the wake of the scandal.

In addition, documents leaked to the press in 1983 showed that EPA officials had concealed evidence conclusively linking dioxin to the miscarriages in Oregon and had

forbidden its scientists to discuss the project with the public or the media. Within two months after the suppressed link came to light, EPA began an internal investigation, Dow "voluntarily" withdrew its opposition to the ban on 2,4,5-T and EPA quietly canceled the herbicide's registration without having to ratify a "no safe level" position.

WHILE INDUSTRY PUSHED ITS POSITION THAT DIOXIN WAS safe for humans, EPA regulators had to take another tack to avoid action because the agency's own science made clear that *any* dioxin exposure was a threat. The new strategy was based on elaborate studies called risk assessments, which attempted to measure the number of cancers in humans caused by dioxin. With these, EPA could make the political judgment that the threat posed by low-level dioxin exposure, while undeniable, was "acceptable." (For a comprehensive look at the politics of risk assessment, see "At Our Peril: The False Promise of Risk Assessment," *Greenpeace*, March/April 1991.)

EPA Chief William Ruckelshaus put the issue in stark terms in a 1983 speech to the National Academy of Sciences, while the 2,4,5-T controversy still raged. "The administrator of EPA," Ruckelshaus insisted, "should not be forced to represent that a margin of safety exists for a specific substance at a specific level of exposure where none can be scientifically established." Instead, he urged the use of risk assessment to calm public "hysteria" and "resolve the dissonance between science and the creation of public policy."

For EPA, this meant fine-tuning the science to harmonize with its political agenda. From this point on, according to Paul Merrell and Carol Van Strum, who have written exhaustive analyses of EPA's dioxin policy for Greenpeace, "Government scientists were expected to tailor their risk assessments to support already-made management decisions on dioxin."

One of the agency's first risk-based dioxin decisions involved the government-financed cleanup of Times Beach, Missouri. Emergency action was clearly necessary, but a no-safe-level position would have set a dangerous precedent. EPA thus declared a one-part-per-billion "level of concern"—requiring cleanup and evacuation at Times Beach but setting the stage for ignoring future sites contaminated below this level.

In an internal briefing document, EPA officials admitted that the level was "based on cost and need for immediate action, not total health protection." But, the document said, this position "allows immediate action for agency, and good press. Buys time: allows time for reassessment of agency risk analysis methods and policies....Allows preparation of public for possible change in policy. Intermediate cost option....Easily implemented, sampling is relatively inexpensive and easy."

Meanwhile, EPA was developing its official cancer potency estimate for dioxin under a court order forcing the agency to issue water quality regulations for dozens of chemicals, including dioxin. The estimate, finished in 1984, used standard methods to extrapolate from tests conducted by Dow on laboratory rats the cancer threat to humans posed by any exposure to dioxin. Once again, the tests showed that dioxin was the most potent synthetic carcinogen ever tested.

But EPA policymakers turned the study on its head, using it to set levels of dioxin exposure they considered "acceptable." Throughout the rest of the 1980s, then, EPA regulators could tell concerned communities that dioxin discharges from an incinerator or chemical factory were "acceptable" on a scientific basis. This risk-based policy also suited the affected industries, who could point to EPA regulations that reflected this new standard of "safety."

Just after EPA policymakers had finished their risk assessment policy, however, new information emerged that sparked the call for emergency action once again. Scientists around the world were finding that dioxin contamination was not limited to those who worked in chemical factories or were sprayed with 2,4,5-T; on the contrary, dioxin was literally everywhere in the environment in alarming quantities.

The findings undermined EPA's "acceptable risk" position. Dioxin exposures were not only universal but they were already greater than EPA's "acceptable" amounts. The entire food supply—especially animal products—now contains so much dioxin that the average American is ingesting from 150 to 500 times EPA's "acceptable" dose on a daily basis. A single meal of Great Lakes fish can contain the "acceptable" dioxin dose for an entire year.

These results are no surprise to anyone familiar with dioxin's behavior in the environment. The chemical is extraordinarily long-lived, resisting natural breakdown processes for many years, even decades. And dioxin's tendency to collect in fatty tissues means that it is found in frightening concentrations in species near the top of the food chain. As a result, fish, birds of prey, marine mammals and people act as living reservoirs for dioxin at levels thousands of times higher than those found in the environment.

Since nursing babies occupy a place even higher on the food chain than adults, they receive the greatest dioxin doses of all. Surveys of mothers' milk in industrialized countries, including the U.S., have found dioxins in alarming quantities. EPA's latest estimate is that breast-fed infants are subject to dioxin doses about 11,000 times greater than the "acceptable" amount daily.

This information put EPA in an impossible position. Suddenly, the agency's level of "acceptable risk" was exceeded by levels of dioxin found in the general public. In response, EPA moved quickly to revise its risk assessment to declare these new, higher doses "acceptable." By July 1986, EPA administrative staff convened a panel to assemble evidence justifying a downgraded estimate.

The pulp and paper industry, whose use of chlorine was just being revealed as a major dioxin source, joined the chemical companies in pressuring the agency. According to paper industry documents leaked to Greenpeace in 1987, the industry mounted a campaign to "forestall major regulatory and public relations difficulties" by pressuring EPA to keep alarming information from the public and to relax the present risk estimate. The briefings said the industry's "short-term objectives" were the following: "Get EPA to 'rethink' dioxin risk assessment....Get EPA to issue statement 'no harm to environment or public health.'"

EPA complied, agreeing to highly unorthodox arrangements with the American Paper Institute to limit access to information on the industry's contribution to dioxin pollution. At the same time, the agency's risk panel had developed a risk proposal that said dioxin's cancer potency was only one-sixteenth what the agency had thought in 1985. The panel was surprisingly frank about the dubious basis of the proposal, noting that "there is considerable uncertainty and controversy about the mechanism by which 2,3,7,8-TCDD causes cancer," and admitting there was "no definitive scientific basis" on which to choose one risk estimate over another. Nevertheless, EPA said its downgraded estimate was "rational, prudent science policy."

The reassessment drew immediate fire. "I believe that the new draft report on dioxin health risk fails to meet the rudimentary requirements of scientific discourse," Dr. Barry Commoner, of the Center for the Biology of Natural Systems at Queens College, told an EPA audience in 1988. "Politics should not hide behind the skirt of bad science." EPA's Science Advisory Board, too, rejected the new risk assessment, finding "no scientific basis for such a change." The proposal was canceled—for the time being, at least.

While EPA and the industry assured the public that dioxin was not a cancer danger, new information emerged that suggested just the opposite. For instance, a 1989 study of a dioxin-exposed community near a chemical factory in Italy found increased rates of brain cancer, leukemia and other cancers. A 1990 study of Swedish pesticide applicators conclusively linked dioxin to high rates of specific, rare cancers. The same year, a panel of eight independent scientists, including Dr. Epstein and Dr. Commoner, surveyed all the information to date and found links between dioxin-contaminated Agent Orange and 10 different kinds of cancer, neurological effects, reproductive problems, immunological abnormalities and liver damage.

The final nail in the coffin for industry's argument came in January 1991, when the National Institute for Occupational Safety and Health (NIOSH) published the results of a 10-year study of thousands of dioxin-exposed workers in the United States, including the same group studied by Monsanto. This, the most comprehensive epidemiological study of dioxin ever conducted, found conclusive links between dioxin exposure and elevated cancer rates.

With a final gasp, industry tried to dismiss the study. "This is very reassuring," said George Carlo, an epidemiologist who heads a consulting firm that has been retained by the Chlorine Institute. Because the link between cancer and dioxin was clearest at high exposure levels, Carlo asserted that lower levels were safe.

But that conclusion was clearly indefensible. "It doesn't say there is no risk," Marilyn Fingerhut, the study's chief author, says flatly. The study will cause "some weakening of the position of those who believe low levels of [dioxin] exposure are entirely safe for humans," epidemiologist John Bailer wrote in an editorial in the *New England Journal of Medicine*.

Now, according to a flood of new dioxin studies, cancer may prove to be only one of our worries. Because dioxin imitates naturally occurring sex and growth hormones, it can promote the growth of cancers in fledgling stages throughout the body, according to a 1988 EPA document. Even worse, dioxin-altered hormone levels can disrupt the development of the immune system and interfere with fetal development, according to Ellen Silbergeld, a University of Maryland toxicologist who is a staff scientist with the Environmental Defense Fund. A damaged immune system can make people vulnerable to a variety of diseases, none of which can be traced to dioxin exposure exclusively.

Above all, hormonal disruption impairs reproduction. Dioxin's effects on sex hormones can inhibit sperm formation, suppress ovulation and decrease libido, Silbergeld says. Michael Fry, a biologist at the University of California, told the *New York Times* in May 1990 that male birds exposed to dioxin-like compounds failed to exhibit normal courtship behavior, developed malformed testes and even began to grow ovaries. "Essentially they were chemically castrated," he said. Vietnamese villages sprayed with Agent Orange are showing high rates of infertility and birth defects years later, and Monsanto workers have reported impotence and decreased libido.

Some of the most sobering of recent research involves dioxin's effects on the development of children. Observation of rhesus monkeys exposed to dioxin prenatally and through mother's milk showed that the infant monkeys were unusually dependent upon their mothers and that the mothers, in turn, treated them as if they were ill or injured. Years later, the dioxin-exposed young had behavioral and mental difficulties. Their performance in memory and other mental tasks was poor, and they seemed unusually apathetic about learning. In peer groups, the dioxin-exposed young were unusually aggressive, initiating violent behavior more often than unexposed monkeys.

"It took us centuries to recognize that lead was impairing our children's mental development," says Pat Costner, Greenpeace's research director. "There's no excuse for sitting back while the same—or worse—happens with dioxin."

YET EPA's EFFORT TO DETOXIFY DIOXIN PERSISTS. IN A 1990 internal memo, EPA official Donald Barnes—one of the earliest advocates of slashing the risk assessment by a factor of 16—wrote that if the agency could find a way to adopt the level proposed in 1988, EPA could make a "risk management decision" to allow risks of one in 100,000 instead of one in a million. "EPA's number," Barnes wrote, referring to the "acceptable" dose that would result, would then be "comparable with the 'background' dietary intake level." In other words, levels of dioxin already present in the environment would abruptly, and conveniently, be labeled "safe."

The day NIOSH's 1991 study linking cancer to dioxin exposure among chemical workers was released, an EPA memo leaked to Greenpeace expressed the agency's plan to use the study to reduce the risk assessment. Though NIOSH's research involved no measurement of dioxin doses in any of the workers examined—and, according to the memo, EPA had not yet received the study's data from the author—the agency's intent was clear: "EPA will attempt a new quantitative risk assessment if the data allow (which is likely)."

Also in 1991, a dioxin conference hosted by the prestigious Banbury Center exploded in controversy when the Chlorine Institute declared, in a press packet put out with the help of a public relations firm, that a "consensus" had been reached on a new downgraded estimate of dioxin's danger. Independent scientists who attended the conference bristle at the assertion. "It was not a consensus conference," says Jan Witkowski, Banbury's director. Silbergeld, who gave the meeting's central address on dioxin and risk assessment, says she is "astounded" that anyone is suggesting there was agreement to reduce the cancer potency estimate. "I did not expect to be manipulated by industry or government spokespeople," Silbergeld told *Science* magazine in February.

But EPA apparently is already pushing the fake consensus. Linda Birnbaum, an official in EPA's Health Effects Research Laboratory, is telling the agency that "back of the envelope calculations led to agreement" at the conference that EPA's dioxin risk assessment could be weakened by a factor of as much as 500.

While it prepares to alter its risk assessment, EPA is allowing states to weaken their own dioxin positions. Regulators in seven states have already changed standards to allow greater dioxin levels. The Environmental Defense Fund is now suing EPA for its failure to implement the Clean Water Act.

SOME 17,000 STUDIES EXIST ON DIOXIN'S HEALTH EFFECTS. The controversy over the best way to measure its toxicity will continue. But alternatives are available now for industrial processes that produce dioxin. Paper manufacturers can substitute oxygen-based processes and other methods to eliminate the use of chlorine. Recycling and other waste-reduction strategies can eliminate any need for incinera-tors, and chlorinated pesticides, plastics and industrial chemicals can be replaced with safer materials and processes.

Protecting the environment from dioxin means eliminating chlorine from a whole range of industries, and the transition will require major investments from industry and ambitious action from government. For the makers of chlorine and chlorinated chemicals, it means making different products. These are serious changes that will not come easily or, judging from the various industries' questionable efforts, voluntarily. But focusing on lengthy disputes over science and risk assessment has diverted time and money from action and jeopardized public health.

Since PCBs and DDT were banned, their levels in the environment have steadily dropped. There is more than enough information now to justify emergency action to ban dioxin sources, if only the government had the political will to do so. "EPA has been asleep at the wheel on dioxin for far too long," Greenpeace's Costner says. "It's time for the country to wake it up." ❑

Article 2. Superfund Has Failed
by Paul Craig Roberts

Paul Craig Roberts contends that in its zeal to protect the environment, the Environmental Protection Agency's Superfund is saddling the nation's banks and insurance companies with the costs of environmental cleanups. The Superfund law does not provide government funds for such purposes, leaving it to the courts to decide issues of liability. In many cases, notes the author, banks and insurance companies have been forced to bear the costs in cases where they have foreclosed on borrowers or work out rescue plans for failing companies. This has resulted in a huge loss of jobs, since many firms are unable to shoulder the high cost of environmental cleanups. Sadly, the Superfund has done little to protect the environment or promote human health.

The Superfund environmental legislation is failing to clean up the environment, but it is wiping out jobs and banks and is threatening our insurance companies.

When S&Ls go bankrupt, depositors are protected by the general taxpayers. However, there is no federal insurance to protect us if insurance companies cannot pay our life insurance policies or make good on our liability coverage.

The problem with insurance companies is not crooks stealing our premiums. Rather, it is the 1980 Superfund legislation, renewed in 1986, that was supposed to clean up the environment.

Instead, Superfund is wiping out financial institutions that the Environmental Protection Agency and courts decide have deep enough pockets to bear cleanup costs, even though they are not responsible for any acts of environmental pollution. The Superfund law provides no government funds for cleaning up the environment. Instead, it requires courts to assign retroactive liability for waste disposal that in many cases occurred decades ago and was perfectly legal at the time.

Since waste disposal sites are the historical results of many users, some of which no longer exist or have gone broke, the EPA and the courts have implemented a policy of sticking the liability on any profitable businesses that could be remotely connected with the site. In practice, this has meant banks and insurance companies, even though the original legislation had a provision prohibiting the assignment of liability to financial institutions.

The EPA and the courts simply ignored this provision of the law. Someone had to pay, and the lawyers went after those with money. This meant banks that had lent money to companies whose waste disposal practices have been retroactively declared illegal, and it meant insurance companies that insured aspects of a retroactive polluter's business, even though they might never have collected a penny in premiums for pollution coverage.

Banks were stuck with liability in cases where they were forced to foreclose on borrowers or work out rescue plans for failing firms. This allowed lawyers and courts to argue that the lenders had become the owners or managers and, therefore, were responsible for decades-old acts of waste disposal.

And this, in turn, is part of the reason for the credit crunch that helped to push the U.S. economy into recession. Small banks can no longer stand the risk of lending to any company or farm that might have a waste disposal problem somewhere in its past since the bank may ultimately be stuck with the cost.

The cost estimates for environmental cleanup range from $150 billion to $700 billion—the harshest figure several times higher than the total capital of the insurance industry. The policy of sticking the insurance industry with the full cost means, of course, the destruction of the industry and the loss of our life insurance savings and liability protection.

The government, however, could not care less. After first violating our legal traditions by creating retroactive crimes and then mandating cleanups, the government is sticking the financial blame on whoever it deems has money.

Also as a result, as much as 60 percent of the billions of dollars spent under the guise of environmental cleanup has gone to lawyers for legal expenses. Consequently, only 27 of the 1,000 most hazardous waste sites have been cleaned up.

Two years ago the U.S. Office of Technology Assessment issued a report that the Superfund legislation was ineffective and inefficient: that it has turned out to be a bonanza for law firms at the expense of innocent parties and the environment.

The government estimates that there are 425,000 potentially hazardous waste sites that need to be investigated. If the Bush Administration and the courts continue with their current policy of sticking insurance companies with the bill, the insurance companies will be the next S&Ls.

Superfund has failed. It has directed the action to the courtroom and the money to the lawyers, while leaving the hazardous waste sites unattended. Now it is threatening the viability of our life insurance companies and curtailing bank lending to industry.

We urgently need a more effective and less costly approach to environmental cleanup.■

Paul Craig Roberts is the William E. Simon professor of political economy at the Center for Strategic & International Studies in Washington and is a former assistant secretary of the U.S. Treasury.
Distributed by Scripps Howard News Service

Article 3.   Energy for the Next Century
by Will Nixon

This article examines the need for a national energy strategy, reviewing President Bush's major proposals for domestic energy production. It also discusses a variety of alternate energy proposals that its proponents claim will be cleaner, faster, and cheaper than increasing the nation's energy production. Special attention is paid to the debate over the merits of solar power versus nuclear energy, which are, of course, related. Many experts, including the author, believe that the United States is moving toward a post-petroleum society. The choices America makes in the next decade will, to a large extent, determine its energy future.

Just when the peace movement had run low on placard slogans—"No Blood For Oil" having lost some of its octane as the Gulf War wound down—George Bush announced his long-awaited National Energy Strategy (NES) at lunchtime on February 20. Not since Jimmy Carter had a president decided that energy planning should involve more than checking the gas gauge before heading off

From *E Magazine,* May/June 1991, pp. 30–39. Copyright © 1991 *E—The Environmental Magazine,* 28 Knight St., Norwalk, CT 06851.

on a long trip. Indeed, Carter had donned a cardigan sweater, turned the White House thermostat down to 68, and solemnly told the nation that his energy policy was "the moral equivalent of war." Cynics now quipped that George Bush had dropped the equivalency part. But the NES was much more than that. It admitted that the United States couldn't kick the foreign oil habit, which was the great dream of presidents in the 70s, but offered almost 100 ways to increase our own energy production. It recommended opening up Alaska's Arctic National Wildlife Refuge for oil and gas exploration, reviving the nuclear energy industry by eliminating some of those pesky public hearings, freeing the oil and gas industries from some cumbersome regulations, and burning more garbage for energy. As for encouraging us to use less energy to begin with, well, better luck next time. The NES virtually ignored better car mileage standards and mass transportation. It dropped tax breaks for renewable energy and federal lighting standards. And, perhaps most negligent of all, it never got around to the reason we need an energy policy in the first place—to stop the flood of carbon emissions into our atmosphere which cause global warming. "When people talk about the need for a national energy policy, they don't mean writing down the mistakes of the past 10 years, which is what the Bush Administration has done," said Alexandra Allen of Greenpeace.

The next morning, a handful of Greenpeacers went to the Senate offices where Admiral James Watkins, secretary of the Department of Energy (DOE) was due to appear before the Energy Committee. Senator Albert Gore of Tennessee had already promised a "battle royal" on Capitol Hill over Bush's energy plan. The Greenpeacers arrived at 7:30 AM, but the Washington media pack had already claimed the room. So they stood out front, holding a "Reality Check" for Bush and Watkins. It was made out for "Untold Billions" for "Oil Wars, Oil Spills, Global Warming and Nuclear Waste."

In the gray and white world of Washington, Greenpeace provides the most color, but they were hardly alone in their outrage at the President's energy plan. Only a year ago the DOE had suggested that its plan would be almost the reverse of what Bush finally announced. Deputy Secretary Henson Moore had said, "Energy efficiency and renewables are basically the cleanest, cheapest and safest means of meeting our nation's growing energy needs in the 1990s and beyond."

"Based on comments by the DOE last year," said Scott Denman of the Safe Energy Communications Council, "and based on George Bush's claims in his State of the Union address that his strategy would support conservation, efficiency and alternative fuels, what we've been given is a cruel hoax. It's not an energy strategy, it's an energy tragedy."

Out in San Francisco, Chris Calwell of the Natural Resources Defense Council (NRDC) said, "The themes that emerge are simple and familiar: drill more, nuke more, pay more, save less." His group released an analysis entitled: "Looking for Oil in All the Wrong Places," with some math to show just how wrongheaded the NES was. If we drilled the Arctic Refuge and the Outer Continental Shelf, as the NES proposed, we might produce a little more than six billion barrels of oil or its equivalent in natural gas, and these areas would be drained dry by the year 2020. But if we used our renewable energy supplies—the sun, wind, rivers that flow into hydroelectric dams, and plants and trees that can be turned into biomass fuels—and we made our world far more energy efficient, we would have the equivalent of 66 billion barrels of oil. As Robert Watson, the author of this report says, "We *will* have a post-petroleum society. The question is whether it will be like Mad Max or Ecotopia."

The NES hadn't always looked so grim. For more than a year, the DOE had held hearings across the country, patiently listening to an army of experts who hadn't found a sympathetic ear in the executive branch since Ronald Reagan took office and put the DOE under the sleepy care of dentist James Edwards. Admiral Watkins had made his name in Washington, DC by taking over Reagan's troubled AIDS commission and producing a good report. "He showed he has a good ear. He's receptive to contrary points of view," says Scott Denman, who spoke at two hearings late in 1989. "He heard from every energy expert in the country."

These experts had a remarkable story to tell: the United States, with what scrambled energy policies we do have, already saves an estimated $160 billion a year in energy costs compared with 1973. "The really interesting thing is that total energy consumption was virtually identical in 1973 and 1986," says John Morrill of the American Council for an Energy-Efficient Economy. "And yet our GNP grew by 40 percent during those years."

Until the 70s, conventional wisdom had insisted that energy growth was synonymous with economic growth, but changes wrought by the oil shocks of 1973 and 1979 tied that thinking in a knot. The Corporate Automobile Fuel Efficiency (CAFE) standards passed in 1975 pushed cars from 13 miles per gallon to 27.5 in 1986, and now save us five million barrels of oil a day. Utilities dropped oil for cheaper coal. Homes were weatherized. Some states took action, such as California, which required 1980 refrigerators to use 20 percent less electricity than the 1975 models, causing an entire industry to change. (By the mid-80s refrigerators, the biggest energy drains in most homes, had improved by 35 percent.) Not until 1985 when President Reagan rolled back the CAFE standards and oil prices dropped, did our energy savings stall.

One after another people appeared before the DOE with ideas on how to get us back on the savings track. After all, we still have a ways to go—Japan and Germany use half as much energy per dollar of economic output as we do. "The message from elect-

"There are all sorts of incentives for fossil fuels which, to be fair, should be eliminated or applied to energy efficiency and renewables."

ed officials, citizens groups and energy related businesses was conservation, conservation, conservation," Denman says.

The DOE listened. "Admiral Watkins looked at the issue, and he began to say the one thing that's loud and clear is that improved conservation and energy efficiency are where the most gains can be made and the government can do a lot more than it has," said Christopher Flavin of Worldwatch who testified at the first hearing in August 1989. In April 1990 the DOE released an interim compendium of what it had heard so far which was dominated by conservation and energy efficiency. But then the report left the DOE for the White House.

"President Bush knows as much about energy as anyone we've ever had in the White House," says one DOE official. What Bush knows, though, is producing energy, not saving it. His home state, Texas, is the worst energy hog in the country. It can't even fill up its own gas tanks, importing 48 thousand barrels of oil in 1989 on top of 736 thousand barrels from its own wells. "Texas has 42 percent fewer citizens than does California," reports a study by the consumer advocacy group, Public Citizen, "but it uses 37 percent more energy." California has a state energy department and Texas doesn't, which just shows what a little planning can do.

"The implicit assumption of the NES is that the market runs at top efficiency," says Michael Brower of the Union of Concerned Scientists (UCS). "Any conservation or renewable energy we have is the amount we should be getting because we have a free market. Our point is that the market is not really free. There are all sorts of incentives for fossil fuels which, to be fair, should be eliminated or applied to energy efficiency and renewables. And the free market doesn't take into account the cost to the environment." This spring the UCS, NRDC, and the Boston-based nonprofit environmental research group, the Tellus Institute, released an alternative national energy strategy to show what we can do by taking conservation and efficiency seriously. "Nobody has ever made this serious an effort to meet the skeptics on their own ground," Brower says.

More than a dozen states now give serious consideration to energy efficiency and the environmental costs of fossil fuels when planning out their needs. Rather than simply worrying about energy supply, they consider demand, and often find that the cost of reducing the demand is a lot cheaper than increasing supply. This new approach, labeled "demand side" or "least cost" planning, now dominates on the West Coast and in New England where states have to import fossil fuels. States that produce coal and oil, though, tend to stick to the "supply side" view.

"If every state took the least cost approach there would be no reason to build any new power plants—coal or nuclear—in this decade," says Michael Totten

of the International Institute for Energy Conservation. And if we took this approach in all of our energy decisions, we could be using seven percent less energy by the year 2000, instead of 34 percent more, as we would on our present course. In the next century, after we've captured these savings, renewable energy sources such as windmills, photovoltaics that turn sunlight into electricity, and turbines that run on biomass fuels could be competitive with fossil fuels.

But the NES took the supply side view. And many observers laid the blame on John Sununu more than on George Bush. "Sununu has always been hostile to demand side measures," Robert Watson says. "We both think the other's solution is a drop in the bucket. He dismisses conservation out of hand as being irrelevant. We dismiss nuclear power as largely being irrelevant. But I think we have the better basis for dismissing it."

After President Bush's announcement, the NES became just another influential sheaf of paper on Capitol Hill where Congress was moving into full gear to make 1991 the year for energy. The President was doing his part in the Persian Gulf, said one Republican staffer, now Congress had to do its part at home. The legislators introduced some 80 bills on energy, including one by Senators Bennett Johnston (D-LA) and Malcolm Wallop (R-WY) that was an oil and gas industry dream. But Senator Richard Bryan (D-NV) reintroduced his bill to improve auto fuel efficiency standards by 40 percent to 40 miles per gallon by 2001. It had been defeated the previous year, but now he had 35 co-sponsors. In the House, Representative Barbara Boxer (D-CA) offered an even better bill to push the standards to 45 mpg. And Representative Philip Sharp (D-IN) came up with a bill to make the federal government a major champion of energy efficiency. The battle had indeed come home.

One More Final Showdown at the Arctic Refuge

The Exxon Valdez spill seemed to save the Arctic Refuge, but the Gulf War put it right back into play. To the oil and gas industry, the Refuge could provide one tenth of our country's future production. To environmentalists, the Refuge is the last untouched corner of North America with the full spectrum of arctic and subarctic ecosystems.

"It's the only one up there," says Mike Matz, of the Sierra Club office in Washington, DC. "The oil industry has the rest of the North Slope, and all of the offshore areas, so there's no reason they need it." In fact, nearby Prudhoe Bay has 27 billion barrels of oil of which nine billion can be recovered, but another field nearby has 15 to 20 billion barrels. The oil industry is simply waiting until it is more profitable to drill. The Department of the Interior has done seismic testing of the Arctic Refuge and estimated a one in five chance of finding oil. They then estimated that *if* oil is found the field could yield maybe 3.2 billion barrels.

"We use 18 million barrels a day, so that's about a 180 day supply," Matz says. And it would take a minimum of seven years to begin shipping oil from the Refuge. So why do the oil companies want it so badly? "The financial health of the oil companies depends not on production, but on how much oil they have access to," Matz says. A gusher in the Arctic Refuge would immediately improve any company's financial standing even if they didn't drill it for years. "So all of this shouting about needing it for our national energy security is bogus," Matz concludes. He believes that, after a close debate, the Senate will kill the idea.

Arctic Refuge or not, the United States remains an oil power on its last legs. The average Saudi oil well pumps 9,000 barrels a day, while ours pump 15. Our domestic reserves could easily be dry by 2020 at our present rate of consumption. But the world's known oil reserves jumped from 615 to 917 billion barrels between 1985 and 1990, mostly in the Persian Gulf where it's cheaper to drill. During the late 80s we stopped producing two million barrels a day—as much as we imported from Kuwait—because the price fell too low. "A lot of the stripper wells, ten barrels a day or less, were shut down because they were just not economical," Watson says. "But if we kept eking out that stuff from already existing fields we'd have a lot of little wells that could add up to something big. We'd prefer that to sinking new wells in Alaska. But we'd need incentives for oil recovery in these fields because things like injecting steam to melt the thick globby oil or sideways drilling add five or ten bucks for each barrel of oil recovered."

"The fact is, oil is too cheap in this country," he continues. "It's simultaneously one of the most valued and one of the least valued commodities we have. It's valuable enough to send half a million people over to the Middle East—and our citizens are probably the most precious resource we have—yet we're not willing to spend an extra buck per gallon, or to require the auto industry to increase its fuel economy."

Car Wars

"The biggest untapped oil field in America is riding 18 inches off the ground in our gas tanks," says Paul Allen, communications director of the NRDC. Allen didn't invent this wonderful soundbite, nor will he be the last to use it as Congress begins debating new CAFE standards in one of the major energy battles of the session. "CAFE was one of the best energy policies we ever had," Watson adds. Passed in 1975 when new cars averaged 13 mpg, these standards pushed the standards up to 27.5 mpg in 1985 when Reagan rolled them back to 26 mpg, basically because Ford and GM couldn't make the higher standard and wanted to avoid the fines.

New standards have been contemplated for a while, but the Persian Gulf War gave momentum to the issue. After all, two thirds of our oil goes to transportation. "It's become much more politically mainstream," says Deborah Bleviss, author of *The New Oil Crisis and Fuel Economy Technologies*. "It has a good chance in the House, but in the Senate it's much more iffy because of John Dingell, who single-handedly held up the Clean Air Act for years." Dingell, who runs the Energy and Commerce Committee, represents Dearborn, Michigan and the auto industry. A new CAFE law would cost Detroit billions and probably add $500 to the price of a new car.

Detroit's old counterattack against CAFE is safety: when the head-on collision comes, do you want to be in a 27.5 mpg tank or a 40 mpg sardine can? "The real irony is that they've never really cared about safety," Bleviss replies. As for the big car/little car scenario, nobody really knows, she adds. The only tests we have, crashing a speeding car into a flat wall, simulate the impact of a car hitting its own weight. And the land rovers and mini-vans that are selling so well these days do poorly in these tests. Smaller cars can be built more safely, but Bleviss says, "The question is, do we want to?"

"If Detroit was really smart they'd go into the mass transit business," Watson says. "Our roads just won't be able to handle many more cars. And in many places there's no more room to build new roads." Our cars are indeed crowding in on themselves like lemmings—each day Californians lose a total of fifty years in traffic delays. Many feel we need to forgo the old suburban ideal of a quarter acre for every home and a car in every garage, and adopt a clustered, European style of life. But Watson warns, "What we're talking about is changing the American Dream, and that isn't going to happen anytime soon. Our conception is still of your big tailfin car driving out to your suburban home on empty freeways. But we haven't seen that since 1965, if we ever really saw it at all."

Power to the Future

Some say our energy future will become a showdown between solar power and nuclear energy. They're related, of course, since the sun is a giant fusion reactor—but solar power leaves the problems with fusion 93 million miles out in space. But all the problems we've created with fossil fuels have revived the nuclear alternative. The NES calls for increasing our nuclear power capacity by 30 to 80 percent over the next three decades.

Dr. Jan Beyea of the National Audubon Society, sometimes cast as an apostate for not rejecting the nuclear idea out of hand, says, "When we talk about global warming, we mean that if we don't take steps now, in 50 years the die will be cast; there will be no hope of preventing global warming from then on." Our planet releases six billion tons of carbon into the atmosphere each year; Beyea and many other scientists believe we must cut back by 20 percent by the year 2010 to avoid the greenhouse crisis.

> "If Detroit was really smart they'd go into the mass transit business—most of our roads will not be able to handle many more cars. And in many places there's just no more room to build new roads."

"We need energy conservation in the short run, but in the long run we have solar and nuclear," Beyea continues. "Both are problematic. The price of solar power during the day isn't bad, but at night it gets very expensive because of storage. Although I'm skeptical, Dr. Larry Lidsky at MIT says that an 'idiot proof' nuclear reactor can be built, so I think we should give him the dollars to see if that's true."

Unlike the nuclear proponents of the early 50s who promised energy "too cheap to meter" Beyea comes to his view out of pessimism. "The public has a choice," he says. "They can choose solar, or they can slip back into nuclear. I detest nuclear power, but I don't think one stone can be left unturned. This is no joke. This is the final environmental battle."

For now, though, nuclear power is one of the great white elephants of our industrial history. The United States has 111 plants which produce 25 percent of our electrical power, but nobody has ordered a new plant since 1978. The NES includes some band-aids for the industry, such as speeding the post-construction approval process, but one Congressional staffer doesn't take them seriously. "Even if they had a majority in Congress, which they don't, the industry still wouldn't get an order."

"You show me one utility that is really hot about nuclear, and I'll show you two dozen that wouldn't touch it with a ten foot pole," says NRDC's Watson. "When we've got reams of material that show the cost of saving electricity is one or two cents per kilowatt hour, why would anyone spend ten cents—25 in the case of Seabrook—for electricity from nuclear power?" These days many utilities meet their needs with energy savings campaigns supplemented by new 250 megawatt combined cycle plants that use oil or natural gas. Like many, Watson believes that natural gas will be our transition fuel to a renewable energy future.

The United States—so huge, so sunny, so windy, and so dotted with geothermal hotspots like those already heating homes in Boise, Idaho—has renewable energy supplies that dwarf our oil and gas reserves. And renewable sources, mostly from hydroelectric dams and wood burning power plants, already produce eight percent of our energy compared to the seven percent from nuclear power. Back in the late 70s the DOE created great expectations, confidently predicting that by the year 2000 twenty percent of our power would come from the sun. But Ronald Reagan wasn't interested. He took down the solar panels Carter had installed on the White House roof. He slashed the DOE's research and development budget for renewable energy from $557 million in 1981 to $78 million in 1989. And in 1985 he let the 40 percent solar tax credit for homeowners expire. A $700 million solar industry, which had installed solar water heaters in a million homes, preventing the need for a 1,000-megawatt power plant, rapidly became a $70 million one. Scott Sklar of the Solar Energy Industries Association says, "We lost 35,000 people in 1985, which was more than the U.S. auto industry."

California alone refused to give up the dream. Today it has become the world's showcase for solar and wind power. The parabolic mirrors of Luz International in the Mojave Desert produce 90 percent of the solar electricity generated in the world today—194 megawatts a day—or one percent of Southern California Edison's peak supply. The wind farms that stretch across the passes at Altamont, Tehachapi, and San Gorgonio, looking like crops of airplane propellers, can generate 1,500 megawatts. The first wind farm built in 1981 was quickly dubbed a "tax farm" because it seemed to produce more writeoffs than electricity. But Randall Swisher, executive director of the American Wind Energy Association, says those bad old days are long gone. "The cost of wind energy was 25 cents per kilowatt hour at the first wind farms in California in 1981, but it's between five and nine cents today, and we expect that to decline at least another 40 percent." And California is only the 14th windiest state in the country. Now that these technologies are proving themselves, proponents believe the federal government should get back in the business of supporting them with new tax breaks and research funds.

"If we get everything we think we can," Sklar says, referring to the energy legislation now pending in Congress, "solar and renewable energy could be producing 20 percent of our country's power by 2000."

"If we stop fooling ourselves that nuclear is only eight cents a kilowatt hour and coal four to six, instead of 12, 14, or 16 like it should be," says Robert Watson, referring to the environmental costs of those industries, "and we had the same level of effort going into solar and alternative technologies that we have going into the moribund nuclear industry, then we would have a very viable industry within ten years." **E**

WILL NIXON *is Associate Editor of* E Magazine.

"The United States—so huge, so sunny, so windy, and so dotted with geothermal hotspots like those already heating homes in Boise, Idaho—has renewable energy supplies that dwarf our oil and gas reserves."

A Brighter Idea

Compact fluorescent lightbulbs, those funny looking gadgets you find advertised in *E* and in mail order catalogs from the green regions of Vermont or Colorado, may soon sweep across America. A number of utilities have begun handing them out like low energy lollipops—and some distributors seem to be poised for a consumer explosion.

These miracle bulbs last 10 to 13 times longer than incandescents, use one fourth the electricity, and initially cost 15 to 30 times as much, but save double that by the time they die. They first appeared on the techno-freak market in 1983, but only in the past two or three years have they become available in all the shapes and sizes needed for homes and offices. "If compact fluorescents completely overtook incandescents," says Chris Myers of Rising Sun Enterprises in Old Snowmass, Colorado, "we'd make 120,000-megawatt power plants superfluous."

As we enter the 90s, blackouts, not gas lines, seem the energy crisis lurking in our future. Utilities on the West Coast, in New England, and elsewhere are running out of generating capacity to meet their growing demand. After dropping $100 billion on coal and nuclear plants that were never finished, utilities have grown shy about planning anything grand. Instead, they now spend $1 billion a year to encourage energy savings—and compact fluorescents make calling cards.

Earlier this year, New York City's Consolidated Edison area gave away 36,000 free bulbs to launch its $153 million "Enlightened Energy" campaign—a deal compared to the $300 million cost of new electricity. Southern California Edison has given out 800,000 compact fluorescents. But these bulbs are only a small part of the savings package. New England Electric goes door to door in poor neighborhoods, handing out compact fluorescents and shower head aerators, vacuuming refrigerator coils and air conditioner coils, and wrapping electric water heaters. But anyone can call for a full energy audit. They take off your front door and put up a "door blower" that sucks the air out of the house. With a smoke stick they then search out all the drafts that need caulking. It takes one to eight hours and costs you nothing. They also hand out several compact fluorescents, but Dick Morency, head of these programs, warns against mistaking them for a miracle cure. "If you go from an old model refrigerator to a new one, you'll save much more electricity," he says.

No utility has yet gone knocking with free refrigerators. "Utilities are looking at compact fluorescents as their panacea," says Robert Watson of the Natural Resources Defense Council (NRDC) in Manhattan. And in offices the utilities are absolutely right. The NRDC offices, built as an energy efficiency showpiece, use 70 percent less power than a typical building and, except for the foot high windows along the top of the office walls that let sunlight reach far inside, they don't even look that odd. Compact fluorescent lighting, superwindows that block much of the sun's radiant heat, and a cooling system that draws most of its air from the shady side of the building all add up to huge savings. "If every building was built this way we could probably shut down two thirds of the nuclear power plants in this country," Watson says. A brighter idea, indeed.   —*W.N.*

Chapter 18

Foreign and Defense Policy

Article 1. America Without the Cold War
by Charles William Maynes

This article explores the future of American foreign policy in a post-Cold War world. Although the future is by no means clear, the United States must begin to rethink its role in what President Bush calls the "New World Order." As the Cold War ends, the nation must build a new national consensus, which reflects a changing definition of America's security interests. At the same time, renewed attention must be given to major economic challenges, environmental concerns, and human rights issues. The Cold War's end will deprive America of its dominant organizing principle: anticommunism. In its place, the nation must debate the merits of a new foreign policy based upon national interest, democratic values, or global partnership.

The December 1989 Malta summit between Mikhail Gorbachev and George Bush opened on an unexpected, and thus far unreported, note. Gorbachev urged Bush to end his public suggestions that the East is now adopting "Western ideas." He argued that most of the ideas behind the East's reform efforts are not Western but universal. Bush later said to offi-

Reprinted with permission from *Foreign Policy 78* (Spring 1990), pp. 3–25. Copyright © 1990 by the Carnegie Endowment for International Peace.

cials in Washington that, never having thought about this problem before, he told Gorbachev that he would alter his language. After all, why make Gorbachev's task more difficult?

But semantic silence even at the presidential level cannot hide the reality that throughout the bleakest days of the Cold War it was the West that championed the ideas now being adopted in the East. It is understandable that Western leaders as well as their publics now regard the growing democratization of Eastern Europe as a vindication of Western policy.

So there is a sense of triumph in the air. The world has arrived at one of those rare moments in history when everything seems to change. Questions not seriously discussed since the end of World War II are now being constructively considered. But concern is also mounting that misjudgments in policy could return the world not to costly Cold War stability but to even more costly interwar instability.

It is time to consider in detail the consequences for American foreign policy of these profound changes. It is time to debate in earnest the very different paths the country might follow in a post–Cold War world.

In one fundamental respect the new world that is unfolding contrasts very sharply with comparable periods of major historical transition. Unlike those earlier periods, no major new military threat is likely to replace the old one anytime soon. In the last half of the nineteenth century, after the rest of Europe had finally crushed a politically and militarily dynamic France, a powerful Germany emerged to challenge the European security system. In this century, after the entire world united to defeat Germany and Japan, an ideologically dynamic and militarily overpowering communist superpower, the Soviet Union, emerged to challenge the global order.

Unlike Napoleonic France or Nazi Germany, the Soviet challenger to the established order has not been crushed but contained until its revolutionary dynamism has been exhausted. And this, too, may be a reason for believing that the future holds greater promise than the past. For then the world's immediate security problem was solved through war, which tends to create new resentments and insecurities. This time, if the West has "won," the Soviet Union has not so much "lost" as

changed direction. And for a variety of reasons, it seems unlikely that the Soviet leadership will or can reverse its current direction and revive the earlier revolutionary thrust. Yet without that impulse to revolution, the Cold War itself cannot revive; for it was this element of Soviet power that most frightened the West, which felt it was confronting not so much a nation-state as a radical ideology that could inspire the development of fifth columns around the world.

Meanwhile, efforts to find a new security threat in terrorism, Third World radicalism, or Japan's growing economic power do not persuade. Soviet officials have the power to destroy the American experiment. No terrorist, not even one in possession of a nuclear device, has comparable power. Nor does any Third World revolutionary state: Its only hope of acquiring such power would be to trigger a nuclear conflict between the Soviet Union and the United States. That contingency will remain but become progressively less likely as the Cold War ebbs.

Efforts to depict Japanese economic success as a security threat comparable to the Soviet military menace can succeed only if hysteria replaces common sense. For the Japanese do not challenge America's survival. Indeed, Japanese goods and capital, if they harm individual industries, do not harm the United States. They raise Americans' standard of living.

On the horizon perhaps there are other states that may someday pose new challenges to American power or pride. Perhaps states like Brazil or India will develop regional aspirations and capabilities that bring them into conflict with an America still trying to maintain a global reach. But it is difficult to spot a state that can challenge American preeminence in several dimensions at once—economically, militarily, and politically—as Great Britain, Germany, and the Soviet Union have done in different periods. So the sense of triumph or at least relief among American policymakers these days is in order.

The Lost Sextant

Yet if there is satisfaction, there is also anxiety. For more than 40 years the Cold War imparted a clarifying logic to American foreign policy that now will be missing. It reduced international politics to a zero-sum game that everyone could understand.

CHARLES WILLIAM MAYNES *is the editor of* FOREIGN POLICY *magazine.*

Both Cold War supporters and critics took advantage of this logic, which provided them a common language. Scholars could disagree about the importance for victory in the Cold War of the Western position in Laos or Zaire, but at least all knew they were discussing the same problem. As the Cold War ends, therefore, American foreign policy will lose more than its enemy. It will lose the sextant by which the ship of state has been guided since 1945.

The end of the Cold War will also have institutional consequences. Particularly in the postwar period, Americans have tended to believe that their system of government was a source of strength at home but a source of weakness abroad. The separation of powers provided an equilibrium to the system at home. But in foreign policy, it meant that the country could not speak with one voice. That hindered decisive action. It placed the United States at a disadvantage in dealing with those who could speak more coherently or act more expeditiously.

To compensate for this disadvantage, Americans willingly accepted severe limitations on their democratic freedoms. They tolerated, for example, a degree of secrecy and a lack of accountability in foreign policy that they would find unconstitutional at home. They allowed the nation's foreign policy elites a measure of control over policy that is permitted in no other area of public policy. These elites complain of congressional micromanagement; but only in the field of foreign policy does the Congress repeatedly permit one administration after another to ignore laws such as the War Powers Act, spend large sums in unvouched CIA funds, and deny the public information vital to a rational discussion of particularly sensitive issues.

For years most Americans have been unwilling to examine the consequences of such practices for the health of democracy itself. There was an establishment consensus that for security reasons political disputes should end at the water's edge. Evidence of the consensus can be seen in the way both left and right have reacted when moral leaders in the United States have taken their concerns into the field of foreign policy. The establishment left applauded Martin Luther King, Jr., when he assaulted racial barriers at home. When he turned against the Vietnam War as immoral and a barrier to social progress at home, concern mounted. The *New York Times* editors, for example, who praised

his civil rights campaign at home, complained that he was "fusing . . . two public problems that are distinct and separate." The establishment right defends the Catholic clergy when it speaks out against abortions. It criticizes that clergy when it questions the morality of nuclear deterrence.

But the essence of democracy is that the people should have a voice in the decisions that affect their lives and welfare, and the two most important things that any government can do to its citizens are to demand their money or their lives. In no area of government can officials ultimately spend more money or end more lives than in the field of international affairs. So from the standpoint of giving citizens control over the issues that truly count, debate about foreign policy should be even more vigorous than that about domestic policy.

The end of the Cold War should bring that debate. As it proceeds, there are likely to be important institutional consequences both at home and abroad. For example, as the conflict's intensity continues to ebb, so should concern about security policy, which will no longer remain undisputed as a form of high politics while economic policy or multilateral commitments or legal obligations are constantly relegated to the realm of low politics. That shift in turn will alter the balance of power within administrations and alliances, as well as between the executive branch and the Congress.

It is time to debate in earnest the very different paths the country might follow in a post-Cold War world.

Appointments within administrations are likely to be affected. Throughout the Cold War period the struggle within administrations between those hoping for a stronger America and those hoping for a better world has been an unequal contest. In administration after administration individuals like Harold Stassen, Adlai Stevenson, Elliott Richardson, or Cyrus Vance lost ground. Individuals like John Foster Dulles, Dean Rusk, Henry Kissinger or Zbigniew Brzezinski gained ground. Since the early 1970s, there has ceased to be much of a struggle. On five separate occasions individuals with a military background have been selected to serve as national security adviser—two generals (one appointed twice), one admiral, and one lieutenant colonel. Such patterns are unlikely to survive the Cold War's end. The definition of national security is likely to acquire new dimensions and those wielding power are likely to display a new set of qualities.

The balance of power between the executive and the legislature is also likely to shift with the Cold War's end. For as security policy receives less attention, economic policy, environmental concerns, and human rights should achieve greater salience. In all three areas Congress is likely to play a greater role than it has in security policy. Indeed, Congress constitutionally has a special role in foreign policy that the Cold War has helped to obscure. Precisely because of the importance that security policy has enjoyed in the postwar period, there is a widespread belief that the Constitution accords preeminence to the president in the field of foreign policy. But as Arthur Schlesinger pointed out in *The Imperial Presidency* (1973), the Constitution does not establish the president as more important than Congress in the field of foreign policy. The Founding Fathers thought that the most important foreign policy issue was likely to be commercial policy and they accorded primary responsibility for commercial policy to the Congress, not to the president.

For most of the postwar period, congressional leaders willingly allowed the president to seize leadership in this field as well. But in the face of a declining security threat and a mounting trade deficit, congressional restraint was weakening by the late 1980s.

Perhaps the most important consequence of the Cold War's end will be to deprive the American foreign policy establishment of its main organizing principle: anticommunism. For decades this principle justified every aspect of American foreign policy from the composition of its alliances to the size of its foreign aid program. Almost as important, it served as a tool to discipline critics, whether in Congress or alliance councils. Deprived of this principle, American foreign policy will lack direction. It is inevitable, therefore, that the country will face a major debate over the future course of American foreign policy.

That debate has only begun and it is difficult to anticipate all of the directions in which it might move. Nonetheless, the various participants in the debate seem to be struggling to maneuver into place three very different foundation stones on which a new foreign policy consensus might be built: national interest,

democratic values, or global partnership. Each approach could provide a new logic to discipline American foreign policy. Two questions, however, arise: Which one of them will allow the country to deal most effectively with the real problems it faces abroad? And can any one of them develop and sustain the popular support necessary for an effective foreign policy?

A World without a Great Enemy

A foreign policy based strictly on national interest would permit a sweeping retrenchment of the American presence in the world. With the Cold War over, no nation threatens American survival in any direct way.

There are five power centers in the world that, at least in the near term, determine the fate of the globe—China, Japan, the Soviet Union, the United States, and Western Europe. A major goal of U.S. foreign policy since the end of World War II has been to block the two great communist powers, but primarily the Soviet Union, from achieving a dominant position in either Europe or Japan. In the 1970s China evolved from a hostile into a friendly power. Now in the 1990s the Soviet Union is following a similar evolution.

Neither communist giant is likely to become an enemy of the United States in any foreseeable time frame. Even the tragic events in Tiananmen Square in June 1989 do not threaten a return to U.S.-Chinese hostility. Estrangement, perhaps, but China's long-term interests require it to develop a cooperative relationship with the United States and other major Western powers. Otherwise, China's efforts to modernize will fail and, if they fail, China's relative power position will decline steadily. Now with the dramatic reforms that have swept over Eastern Europe, the Soviet Union can no longer be regarded as a hostile power. It is in neither a position nor a mood to threaten Europe or Japan. Periods of greater tension may recur but the Cold War itself with its global character is over.

A post-Cold War foreign policy based strictly on national interest would also sharply decrease American involvement in the Third World. After all, for most of the postwar period the majority of Third World countries were of immediate interest to the United States only because of Cold War considerations. The most persuasive official defense of American involvement in the conflict in Vietnam was its relationship to the bipolar struggle; to the degree administration figures could plausibly link events in Indochina to the global struggle with the Soviet Union, critics were cowed. Hence the political value of touting the so-called domino theory. (Perhaps one reason that critics did not remain cowed is that international realities compelled U.S. officials to send mixed signals. President Richard Nixon found himself promoting détente with Moscow at the same time that he was warning Americans of Soviet expansion.)

American involvement in such different and insignificant states as Chad, Grenada, and Laos can only be explained by reference to the larger global struggle. Even America's fixation with many Third World radicals is primarily explained by their security ties to the Soviet Union. Without these ties such figures would regain the obscurity they merit. If the Cold War ends, therefore, it seems to follow that most of America's security concerns in the Third World will disappear. American ties to the Third World can be determined by economics, proximity, and sentiment.

Even some of the areas in the Third World considered strategic lose much of their significance in the absence of the superpower struggle. The United States has long feared the possibility of Soviet domination of the Persian Gulf states, which have nearly 60 per cent of the world's oil reserves. But if the Cold War is over, American concern should recede. Perhaps vehemently anti-Western Iran is a candidate to replace the Soviet Union as the principal threat to Western interests in the area. Certainly Iran will remain a thorn in the U.S. side for some time to come; but without a highly developed air force or navy, Iran does not have the reach of the Soviet Union even in its own region. Indeed, the outcome of the Iran-Iraq war demonstrated that control of the Gulf is beyond Iranian power. Moreover, even if Iran does seem to pose a threat to U.S. interests, an end to the Cold War should erase U.S. objections to a joint U.S.-Soviet agreement to protect the security of Gulf states.

Central America has always been considered an area of critical importance to the United States. But with an end to the Cold War, the question arises: From the standpoint of strict national interest, why does the United States care what kind of government the people of Nicaragua or El Salvador have or select? The only vital American interests would seem to be whether the new authority in either country can create a domestic order sufficiently attractive to persuade most of the inhabitants to remain in place instead of heading for the United States. Protection of American economic interests in the region would be secondary since it plays such a small role in America's economic prosperity.

The rest of the Third World becomes a matter of United Nations policy or domestic politics, which includes such health-related issues as drugs or AIDS. Like other major countries the United States would have to continue to employ diplomatic resources to earn the support of a majority of the Third World on multilateral issues of concern to the United States. And it would have to remain active in many Third World states to pursue goals that affect its domestic welfare. But these would be concentrated in particular countries. Few of these interests would seem to require that the United States have the capability to intervene militarily or covertly. American policies regarding most Third World states would begin to resemble those of other major developed countries.

A foreign policy of strict national interest could also permit a drastic retrenchment of the U.S. military presence in the world. Over half of the American defense budget is designed to defend against a Soviet attack on Western Europe—the probability of which has never been high and is now effectively zero. From the standpoint of strict national interest, the American army could be slashed back to an expeditionary force designed to meet the modest military requirements involved in protecting American lives abroad, combatting terrorism, and maintaining a deterrent force suitable for emergency deployment. As a hedge against Soviet recidivism, the United States might reach agreement with key European states for the pre-positioning of U.S. equipment on European soil. It could cooperate with its allies in providing sea and air support for Europe's defense. And perhaps even a token U.S. army presence could remain on European soil. But virtually all the American troops on European soil could be brought home and disbanded.

The same point applies to Japan. Again for reasons of prudence, the United States might maintain a military alliance with Japan and reach certain understandings regarding the future. But most of the bases could be closed and the troops brought home.

The country's nuclear forces could be pared back to a minimum deterrent since no other country's nuclear force now threatens the survival of the United States as a political entity.

The size of the U.S. deterrent and the vigor of weapons research would depend upon the co-operative measures Americans and Soviets could devise to reassure each side that the other was not cheating or on the verge of a breakout. But under almost any arrangement the number of nuclear warheads on each side could be far below the 9,000 or more that the United States and the Soviet Union could end up with should the deep cuts of START be accepted.

One possible goal might be to aim at a limit on U.S. and Soviet warheads close to the total number of warheads the French or British will jointly achieve after their current moderniza-tion—somewhere in the neighborhood of 1,500 warheads. (China is reported to have 200 war-heads.) This number, in the case of the French, will still be enough to destroy two-thirds of all Soviet industrial capacity. Accepting a number like 1,500 warheads, mounted on single-war-head launchers, would still leave each super-power with vastly greater conventional and nu-clear power than any other nuclear state yet it would put a cap on the nuclear arms race, provide it with a certain symmetrical stability, and permit the five nuclear powers to begin negotiations to drive the limit even lower.

It is necessary to deal with the suggestion that if the Soviet threat recedes, the United States should maintain a high military profile in Europe and Asia in order to restrain Ger-many and Japan. Retired General and former Army Chief of Staff E. C. Meyer has sug-gested that in the event the Cold War is over, "the two biggest threats" become a united Ger-many and a militarized Japan.

Certainly one unstated purpose of the Amer-ican defense arrangements after World War II was to restrain Germany and Japan. But just as the Cold War has faded, so should the fear of West Germany and Japan. Both have been among the world's most responsible states for more than four decades. Not to acknowledge this achievement risks a popular backlash in either or both. Moreover, each has demon-strated that economic success in today's world is a surer path to influence than a large military establishment. Without the asset of nuclear weapons, there is no way that Germany and Japan—nations of approximately 80–120 mil-lion people each (assuming Germany is united) —can pose a serious threat to the security (as opposed to the pride) of the postwar interna-tional order dominated by states with popula-tions two and three times as large and with a land expanse many times greater. Because Ger-many and Japan are worried about the reaction of their neighbors, each is probably willing to accept certain limitations on its freedom of ac-tion: Each should stick to its commitments under the nonproliferation treaty. Each should remain part of an alliance structure designed not so much to counter a real threat as to offer reassurance to all parties about the future. But unreal fear of these two constructive members of the international community should be put to rest.

The critical question is whether the United States is capable of following a foreign policy grounded in a strict definition of national inter-est. America's relatively open political system ensures that public opinion will play a major role in the field of foreign policy. Given that role, it seems almost inconceivable that the United States could follow a foreign policy resting on a strict view of the national interest. Ethnic empathy toward various parts of the world, popular sympathies for the underdog, the political impact of economic issues activat-ing new constituencies to press Congress to become more involved in the details of foreign policy—all will make a foreign policy resting solely on national interest difficult to carry out.

There is a final objection to the first grand option. Even though the Cold War is over, history and prudence dictate that at least in its early stages the coming retrenchment not be too sweeping. Just as individuals prudently purchase insurance, so should nations.

Planting the Flag of Democracy

Some analysts argue that the export of de-mocracy should replace anticommunism as the guiding principle of American foreign policy. The operative word is "export." Virtually all American foreign policy analysts would agree that the United States should support the growth of democratic values and practices abroad. To this end they would deploy a con-siderable portion of the resources of American diplomacy, including financial support. Amer-ican administrations have spoken and will speak out in favor of democratic values and practices in other countries, have provided and will provide political backing and financial help to democratic leaders abroad, and have tended and will continue to develop closer intergov-ernmental ties with states that benefit from a democratic domestic order.

But the proponents of a new crusade for democracy are not content with mere diplomatic or financial support for democratic forces abroad. Such a policy is too passive and it does not have the same expansionary impact on the defense budget. Ben Wattenberg, chairman of the Coalition for a Democratic Majority, a group that presses the Democratic party to adopt more conservative positions on defense issues, argues, for example, that embarking on a crusade for democracy can help persuade the American people to keep defense budgets high "to prevent Soviet imperial recidivism." For most of this school of thought the American invasion of Grenada or Panama, covert operations to overthrow undemocratic governments, or direct subsidies to opposition parties in other countries are all appropriate tools in a new crusade to plant democracy's flag around the world. Burton Yale Pines, senior vice president of The Heritage Foundation, suggests that even in the new conditions of détente between the United States and the Soviet Union, "America must be engaged or have the ability of engaging militarily almost everywhere in the world—including, obviously, Europe."

For 40 years fear of Soviet intentions persuaded America to maintain a gigantic military machine. Will hopes for the spread of democracy now persuade Americans to retain a large military machine and to use it to pursue a crusade for political change?

Most Americans probably would be willing to defy international law and to support the use of military force to spread the cause of democracy if the cost were low. The American invasion of Grenada was popular with the American people. Only 18 Americans died in that invasion, the people of Grenada seemed to welcome their sacrifice, and the island has not been heard from since. Perhaps the U.S. invasion of Panama will work out in a similar fashion. The use of military force to overthrow a dictator and permit the development of democracy can violate international law yet not violate a basic code of decency understood by anyone in favor of democratic choice. Much depends on the casualties inflicted, the form of government implanted, and the degree of future freedom permitted. The U.S. invasion of Grenada would clearly have met these criteria if the U.S. government had not so distorted law and fact in seeking public support for its action. The jury is still out in the case of Panama, but U.S. government unwillingness to confront energetically the issue of civilian casualties can only raise troubling questions certain to linger. In any event, even defenders of the invasion seem to agree there are few such opportunities for success in the world.

Americans probably will also accept covert efforts to promote democracy, that is to say, other forms of interference, including violence, that are barred by international law. Specialists may point out that the cause of democracy suffered some long-run setbacks in such places as Guatemala and Iran because of earlier CIA "successes" in overthrowing governments there that happened to displease authorities in Washington. The views of such specialists will carry little political weight. Most Americans, like ordinary citizens everywhere, do not have the time or background to become terribly troubled over long-term costs. If the end is democracy, officials can persuade them that the end justifies the means. The average American will rely on his government to exercise good judgment in carrying out this policy. The more important question, therefore, is not whether the United States can embark on a democratic crusade but whether it should. There are several reasons to harbor doubt:

• For the first time since 1945 there appears to be a possibility of reaching an agreement with the Soviet Union about a meaningful and constructive code of conduct for the superpowers in international relations. To this end the Soviet Union has submitted several constructive proposals to the United Nations on measures to "enhance the role of international law." It would be worse than ironic if the opportunity to enter into a constructive agreement with the Soviet Union in the field of international law were lost because, at the very moment that the Soviet Union became more lawful, the United States decided to become more lawless.

• Direct intervention in a country to favor one political party or personality over another cannot be undertaken without incurring obligations that may prove difficult to fulfill. No single act did more to draw America into its disastrous commitments to the various regimes that took power in Saigon than the U.S. decision to assist forces that were planning the overthrow and assassination of President Ngo Dinh Diem. Recent CIA efforts, ultimately successful, to end the prohibition against U.S. involvement in coup attempts that might end up in the assassination of another head of state bring back troubling memories.

- A majority of the American people may support a crusade for democracy that resorts to force or covert action; but unless administrations are careful to support only real democracies rather than façade democracies, significant groups within the United States will object vehemently. A bipartisan consensus will prove impossible. America's current involvement in Central America is an example. There is not a single true democracy in Central America except Costa Rica. All the rest are what might be called façade democracies. Those elected do not exercise power. In each country except for Costa Rica the army maintains control through intimidation and violence. When administration officials invoke democratic values in urging continued U.S. support to such governments, Americans who are knowledgeable about local conditions hesitate to support their own government. A divisive debate opens up that may paralyze U.S. policymakers.

- A crusade to promote democracy assumes a degree of American omniscience that is lacking. Even the most knowledgeable Americans usually do not know enough about local conditions in other parts of the world for the United States to intervene effectively. (The recent democratic surge in Eastern Europe should humble all specialists, virtually none of whom predicted it.) Democracy, after all, is a social plant that adapts to the local political climate and tradition. As Richard Cobden, one of history's most perceptive thinkers on the issue of intervention, warned in a historic speech to the House of Commons in 1850: "[A] people which wants a saviour, which does not possess an earnest and pledge of freedom in its own heart, is not yet ready to be free." In international affairs there are always dangers lurking in categorical judgments. It is possible that on rare occasions a people may need a savior. Cambodia may need one to prevent the genocidal Pol Pot from returning to power. But, in general, the variety of democracy that America implants by force in other countries is likely to wither there. America can avoid serious mistakes if it responds with financial and political help to requests from local democratic forces, which presumably know their own country better than outsiders, rather than attempting to impose its model on people who may find it inappropriate or irrelevant.

An Unexpected Partnership

To be fair to the proponents of a democratic crusade, however, it is necessary to acknowledge one advantage often passed over in silence. It would help bind the country together. For one curious feature of the superpower relationship is the role that a combination of ideology and economic success plays in the internal cohesion of both societies. People of many nationalities chose to come to America; people of many nationalities were forced to become part of the Soviet Union. The myth in both societies has been that the American way or the socialist model justifies the allegiance of diverse nationalities. The clear evidence that the West is increasing its economic lead has been extremely damaging to the socialist model. Evidence that the Japanese form of guided capitalism or the German path of the social market economy continues to outstrip the American economy will be very damaging to the American faith in the "city on a hill."

Because of these important myths and their role in maintaining national cohesion, both the Soviet Union and the United States have been strong ideological powers. For it is difficult to develop an ideology that one claims is appropriate to various nationalities brought together inside one country's borders and not conclude that those living outside these borders, who may even share the same language and culture, would not be better off if they, too, had the benefit of the same ideology and system of government.

Gorbachev has announced that his goal is to de-ideologize international affairs. But it seems unlikely that he can ever be completely successful unless he fails at his own reform efforts. For if the Soviet Union is able to surmount its current internal crisis, it will again believe that it has a unique message, now freshly reformulated, to carry to the rest of the world. It is likely to convey that message much more benignly in the future than in the past, but it will be unable to ignore its ideological obligations completely. Nor is the United States dissimilar in this regard. Senator Bill Bradley (D-New Jersey), for one, has argued that the United States cannot be a country of small ambitions. But can any political system have a large ambition that does not involve others?

Today both the American and the Soviet people are having to come to terms with their own limitations. The 1970s were a difficult decade for the United States and the 1980s were difficult for the Soviet Union. Each superpower has emerged from its decade of trial somewhat chastened. Each is increasingly recognizing that the priority of the 1990s is to concentrate on domestic affairs. Each understands that as great as its power may be, in different ways each is falling behind others in critical areas, the Soviet Union quite a bit faster than the United States.

Despite this need to concentrate on domestic affairs, for the reasons already cited, each probably will be harmed internally by a total abandonment of the effort to project its values externally. Each needs to assure its citizens that their state stands for values and ideals worthy of emulation by others.

What then could satisfy the ideological need of each state yet present a constructive face to the outside world? Perhaps a partnership for peace resting on the pillars of disarmament, development, and democracy would provide the grand ambition each seems to need. Such a proposition at any time in the last 45 years would have seemed preposterous. But Gorbachev may have made just such a partnership possible with his extraordinary address to the United Nations in December 1988. In that speech he embraced concepts of individual rights and the rule of law that make true cooperation between the United States and the Soviet Union possible for the first time since World War II. His representatives have followed up with a series of remarkable documents proposing steps within the United Nations that would permit the creation of a more stable and just international order.

It also may be a hopeful coincidence that, with the possible exception of Japan, all of the states in the world that can either protect or endanger world peace are entering what might be called an internal phase. China and the Soviet Union face daunting internal problems that are likely to siphon off their energies and attention for several decades. The United States must finally face up to social and demographic divides—sometime in the next century the United States will cease to have a white majority—that will pose the greatest test to national unity since the Civil War. Europe must concentrate on creating a more united continent and raising Eastern Europe to the level of the West. Japan with its enormous wealth must carve out a new international role for itself but that role will be less threatening to others if Japan also attends to the major social problems it faces at home—a rapidly aging population, a deficient infrastructure for a country of Japan's capabilities and prosperity, and a large, unabsorbed Korean minority.

This period of internal focus could be used to draw the world back to more reasonable levels of armed defense and to develop more enduring patterns of political and economic cooperation. Because of the Cold War, many countries have conducted their affairs since 1945 as though they were in a permanent state of siege. Armies have reached sizes unprecedented in peacetime. Almost as important as the resources wasted has been the political burden of having adopted policies capable of confronting the enemy both at home and abroad. The fact that a paranoid sense of national security in the Soviet Union has imposed barbaric sacrifices on the Soviet people should not obscure the very heavy price paid by the American people during the Cold War in terms of excessive secrecy and lost liberties. The powers assumed by the KGB were grotesque, but those granted the CIA and the FBI were often outrageous, as decades of scandal from Watergate to Irangate attest.

With the Cold War over, therefore, each side has an opportunity to engage in a significant degree of disarmament at home as well as abroad. Abroad, many bases can be closed, a large number of troops withdrawn, and key weapon-free zones created. At home, secrecy regulations can be reexamined, transparency promoted, and rights made more secure.

The U.S. political system, for example, should reexamine the discarded recommendations of several important commissions or congressional committees regarding national security, covert activities, or individual liberties. In 1970, for example, a Pentagon task force reviewing the government's security classification system concluded that "more might be gained than lost" if the United States unilaterally were to abolish all classifications. Although task force members ultimately concluded that implementation of their own recommendation would not be "practical," those making this astonishing judgment about U.S. classification systems included such prominent conservatives as Frederick Seitz, a former president of Rockefeller University, and Edward Teller, who helped develop the hydrogen bomb.

In the post-Cold War era both superpowers need to take steps to subject to a much greater degree of accountability and democratic control the activities of their national intelligence and internal security services. CIA and KGB budgets should be made public, surveillance files on individual citizens sharply restricted or destroyed, and rules of the road negotiated to curb CIA and KGB excesses in the field of intelligence collection and covert operations.

Internationally, the two superpowers should recognize that their opportunity to remain politically preeminent well into the next century may lie in shoring up the very institution that at different points in the Cold War each has done so much to tear down—the United Nations. For the established patterns of the Cold War and the U.N. Charter accord the two superpowers unusual opportunities for influence in the management of a new post-Cold War security system. While three other states enjoy the privilege of veto power in the Security Council, only the two superpowers have the global reach and the technology in the skies, on land, and at sea to play a leading role in a new world security system that could be based on the U.N. Charter. The general staffs of the two superpowers, therefore, should begin discussing the future role of the superpower militaries in a post-Cold War order involving peacemaking, peacekeeping, and international arms control verification under a U.N. umbrella.

The end of the Cold War may also make possible the imposition of certain qualitative restraints on the arms race in regions of the world like Africa and the Middle East. While the Cold War lasted, the interest of each superpower was usually to exploit each regional conflict to achieve some gain globally. With the Cold War over, the interest of each superpower should be to end each conflict in order to eliminate the possibility that it could evolve in a manner that would jeopardize the central relationship. Here, if one is to judge by U.S. policy toward such regional disputes as Afghanistan, Angola, Cambodia, Central America, and the Middle East, the United States seems more frozen in the thinking of the past than the Soviet Union.

As the East-West axis in world politics ceases to have the importance it once did or at least acquires a more constructive character, the key division in world politics is likely to become the North-South divide. The reasons are the relationship between poverty and people and the clash between economics and demographics.

As goods and money move among states, so will people. Borders will become more porous, not less; knowledge of others will get more accurate, not less; travel opportunities will go up, not down. Birthrates in the developing world will remain high while those in the more developed states will stay low. Opportunities will emerge where there are few people, and people will be born where there are few opportunities. One way or another the people and the opportunities will come together—through migration of people toward the North or the creation of more opportunities in the South.

A partnership between East and West can make it more likely that the international system will create opportunities rather than experience disruptive demographic movements. Centralized planning at the microlevel of a national economy, replacing the resource allocation function of market pricing, has been demonstrated to be a spectacular failure. But judicious planning at the macrolevel has proved to be a spectacular success. The economies that have made the most progress in the world in the last several decades have generally been states that have allowed a significant role for the state (or its central banking system) in developing the national economy—France, Italy, Japan, Singapore, South Korea, Taiwan, and West Germany.

Yet on the global scale today little serious planning is done. Each developing nation remains on its own. Often at the urging of aid officials from the developed world, each undertakes efforts that may prove futile because too many others are planning the same strategy.[1] The challenge of the 1990s is for East and West to cooperate not only in a program to bring the living standards of the East up to those of the West but to begin the very difficult conceptual work that will be required to construct a global plan for development—one that can provide the kind of information and infrastructure that permits private and public enterprise to thrive everywhere. Initially, the largest contribution in terms of energy, money, and expertise will have to come from the West but the ultimate task will require the efforts of all the world's major countries.

The peace dividend is not just the money that will be freed up. It is also the categories of thought that will finally be opened up.

---

[1]See Robin Broad and John Cavanagh, "No More NICs," FOREIGN POLICY 72 (Fall 1988): 81-101.

Is it conceivable that there could be an East-West consensus on democracy? Until Gorbachev, the answer could only have been no. Today the answer is less certain. The future of democracy in Eastern Europe and the Soviet Union is far from assured. Even if a return to the Cold War seems highly unlikely now that the communist ideology has lost its magnetic power, a return to authoritarian or military rule cannot be excluded. But the forces of democracy in communist countries have displayed remarkable resilience and energy. Steady acceptance in the East of the universal ideas Gorbachev discussed with Bush at Malta suggests that a convergence of views is possible even here. For it to be complete, however, the West will have to give greater prominence to economic rights than it habitually has. Americans in particular have defined democracy in recent years in a way that is too narrowly political and mechanistic. It is almost as though periodic and secret elections alone can bestow democracy on a people. But Americans are born in a rich and blessed land that has provided a relatively decent living to most of its citizens. For much of American history those who found that they could not make an adequate living where they were had only to move West or to appeal to the government for free land under the Homestead Act.

In other words, one essential element for democracy—an economic and social order that does not intimidate and subdue—was for much of American history provided free by government or nature to all who sought it. Yet in recent years, as the human rights debate has moved up on the international agenda, most Americans have forgotten the economic and social dimension of freedom.

The approach of the socialist countries to democracy, of course, has been far worse. The regimes in power appropriated the language of democracy while denying its reality. Freedoms were constitutionally guaranteed but never granted. And in return for this infringement of political liberty the population gained officially sanctioned economic rights but, over time, relative impoverishment because the system did not work.

It is time that East and West unite around a common definition of democracy, and Franklin Roosevelt's Four Freedoms—freedom of speech and expression, freedom of every person to worship God in his own way, freedom from want, and freedom from fear—are a good place to start. All four of these freedoms are stated or implied in the Universal Declaration of Human Rights.

A commitment by all to the provisions of the Universal Declaration and a pledge to work for their realization through the various bodies of the United Nations could provide the grand ambition that both the American and Soviet people seem to need. It could fulfill their missionary impulse constructively and peacefully. It could enrich the lives of others and prevent the return of the Cold War not simply for the next decade but for those that follow.

On which foundation is America likely to erect its post-Cold War consensus? In any age foreign policy tends to be an accumulation of nuance and emphasis. Americans may prefer one of the three options discussed but they will construct their approach to the world with elements of all three. Even during the height of the Cold War, rigorous anticommunism was not the only guide to American foreign policy. The United States provided economic assistance to communist Yugoslavia when it defied Stalin to embark on an independent course. It entered into a tacit strategic alliance with China in the early 1970s although the political order in China was, if anything, far more repressive than the regime of Leonid Brezhnev.

Nevertheless, preferences are important. So are paradigms. Together they provide direction to a nation's citizens, who need a framework with which to understand the world. Together they provide a standard to its policymakers, who must struggle to explain departures from the norm. Together they provide a guide for the media, which then have a clear benchmark against which to measure an administration's words and deeds.

Preferences shown or paradigms selected also have political consequences. A foreign policy based on a strict adherence to national interest could bring security at a lower cost in terms of money but perhaps a higher cost in terms of reduced vision and hardened hearts. A foreign policy based on a desire to export democracy might enhance American power in the short run, but it could lead to acting with arrogance abroad that might be dangerous in the long run. A foreign policy based on a global partnership could bring cooperative efforts in the best interests of the American people, but it would come at a cost. The two patterns of

[1]See Robin Broad and John Cavanagh, "No More NICs," FOREIGN POLICY 72 (Fall 1988): 81-101.

diplomacy Americans have known are isolationism and preeminence. Either maximizes America's ability to decide its own fate alone. Will Americans be comfortable with an approach that requires them to allow others a voice in America's future?

Some might prefer to avoid a choice. They might argue for further attempts to shore up the status quo, a version of the "status-quo plus" approach to foreign policy that the Bush administration initially hoped to pursue. But such caution would waste an extraordinary opportunity. For the peace dividend is not just the money that will be freed up. It is also the categories of thought that will finally be opened up. It is time for a great debate on American foreign policy, and it is not possible to have a great debate without a discussion of clear options. The most precious peace dividend is precisely the legitimacy of this debate. The country must make the most of it.

Article 2. The Bush Foreign Policy
by Michael Mandelbaum

Michael Mandelbaum argues that George Bush—and the values he represents—served the United States well at the end of the 1980s. Like other presidents before him, Bush is a product of the Cold War; his ideas, skills, and constituency represent the political realities of a bygone era. To meet the challenges of the future, the president must be willing to forge a new foreign policy consensus—one that will require a new definition of world leadership. Unless Bush is able to seize the moment, and recalculate the nation's economic, political, and military requirements, he may find it difficult, if not impossible, to shape the new post-Cold War era.

In 1989 the greatest geopolitical windfall in the history of American foreign policy fell into George Bush's lap. In a mere six months the communist regimes of eastern Europe collapsed, giving the West a sudden, sweeping and entirely unexpected victory in its great global conflict against the Soviet Union. Between July and December of 1989 Poland, Hungary, East Germany, Czechoslovakia, Bulgaria and Romania ousted communist leaders. Their new governments each proclaimed a commitment to democratic politics and market economics, and the withdrawal of Soviet troops from Europe began. All this happened without the West firing a single shot.

The revolutions in eastern Europe ended the Cold War by sweeping away the basic cause of the conflict between the two great global rivals: the Soviet European empire. They did so on George Bush's watch, a term that seems quite appropriate. As the revolutions occurred, he and his associates were more

Michael Mandelbaum is the Christian Herter Professor of American Foreign Policy at the Paul H. Nitze School of Advanced International Studies of The Johns Hopkins University, and the director of the project on East-West relations at the Council on Foreign Relations.

From *Foreign Affairs*, Vol. 70, No. 1, 1991, pp. 5–22. Reprinted by permission of *Foreign Affairs*, America and the World 1990/91. Copyright 1990/91 by the Council on Foreign Relations, Inc.

spectators than participants—a bit confused, generally approving, but above all passive. The president kept the United States in the background. In response to the most important international events of the second half of the twentieth century, the White House offered no soaring rhetoric, no grand gestures, no bold new programs. This approach served America's interests well. Events were moving in a favorable direction; staying in the background, taking care not to insert the United States into the middle of things, was the proper course of action. The qualities most characteristic of the Bush presidency—caution, modest public pronouncements and a fondness for private communications—were admirably suited to the moment.

The end of communism in Europe need not have proceeded so smoothly. There were pitfalls and blind alleys, alternative policies that had serious advocates. The Bush administration steered clear of them all. In so doing, it steered the United States into a new world.

But with the end of the Cold War the familiar guideposts of American foreign policy have disappeared. The revolutions in eastern Europe, taken cumulatively, were a revolution in international politics, and they have had a revolutionary impact on America's relations with the rest of the world. There will be greater discontinuity in foreign policy between the first and second halves of the Bush presidency than between any two administrations in the postwar period.

The post-Cold War international agenda is beginning to take shape. It is not likely to be dominated by military confrontations between great nuclear powers, or even by crises like the one in the Persian Gulf. Instead, economic issues will predominate, particularly as formerly communist Europe and countries in other regions move toward market institutions and practices. For these challenges President Bush's style of leadership seems less appropriate. The attributes he lacks—the capacity to define clearly American interests abroad and the policies necessary to pursue them, a mastery of the intricacies of economic affairs, and a determination to redress the chronic imbalances of the American economy—may well be the qualities required for effective leadership in the post-Cold War era.

II

The end of the Cold War took place in two stages. In the last half of 1989, the communist governments of eastern Europe fell; in the first half of 1990, the fate of Germany was decided. In both stages, plausible alternatives existed to the approaches adopted by the Bush administration; at each stage, the administration chose the proper policy.

The president could have done what many wanted him to do: exult in the West's triumph. He could have celebrated victory more publicly, more frequently and more emphatically. Doing so, however, would have jeopardized the necessary condition for the revolutions of 1989: Moscow's willingness to tolerate them.

There was no doubt more than one reason that the Soviet leaders decided not to stop the process of political change in eastern Europe in 1989, as their predecessors had done in Hungary in 1956, in Czechoslovakia in 1968 and, indirectly, in Poland in 1981. Mikhail Gorbachev and his colleagues were aware of the weakness of their country's international position. They were preoccupied with internal affairs, especially deteriorating economic conditions and the rising rebelliousness of the non-Russians. Whether or not they recognized that they could end their conflict with the West only by relinquishing eastern Europe, they were plainly convinced that they could give up the empire that Stalin had acquired without putting Soviet security in mortal jeopardy.

That conviction might have wavered had the West ostentatiously celebrated the retreat of Soviet power. By what it refrained from doing publicly, as much as by whatever private messages it may have conveyed to Moscow, the Bush administration avoided embarrassing, threatening or otherwise provoking the Soviets. This was the most important contribution to the events of 1989 that the United States was in a position to make.

The administration might also have followed the opposite policy. It could have made common cause with the Soviet Union to try to control the process of change in eastern Europe. Secretary of State James A. Baker was reported in March 1989 to be favorably disposed to discussing that subject with Moscow.[1] The idea was far from absurd. When communist governments in eastern Europe were challenged in the past, the Soviet Union intervened to keep them in power, bringing bloodshed and repression and poisoning relations with the West. There was every reason in 1989 to try to avoid a similar sequence of events.

The Bush administration acted wisely in not making the political future of eastern Europe the subject of Soviet-American negotiations. Such negotiations would have severely damaged relations with the Europeans themselves, both east and west, who objected to what they termed a "second Yalta"— the two great powers deciding Europe's fate without European participation. Negotiations, as it turned out, were unnecessary. The Soviet Union did not intervene. The Bush administration correctly calculated that the interest of the United States lay in allowing the authentic, peaceful, democratic revolutions to run their course. Washington encouraged this process by reassuring Moscow that the course of events did not jeopardize legitimate Soviet interests. This middle course with the Soviet

---

[1] Thomas Friedman, *The New York Times*, March 28, 1989.

Union, between collaboration and confrontation, was an important and underappreciated achievement of American foreign policy. If one of the tests of each presidency after 1945 has been the capacity to manage crises, the president deserves high marks for his policies during the six eventful months that may be seen in retrospect as the final crisis of the Cold War.

No sooner had the last east European revolution been completed—in Romania—than Europe and the two great nuclear powers had to confront the issue of German unity. The march toward the merger of the two Germanys—or, rather, toward the collapse of East Germany and its takeover by the West—was not initially intended by any government, including Bonn. It was the product of the spontaneous initiative of hundreds of thousands of East Germans. By moving to the West in large numbers, even after the opening of the inner-German border, they voted with their feet against the continued existence of a separate state. They also voted for the end of East Germany in March 1990 in a more familiar way: the first free elections ever held in the G.D.R. yielded a resounding majority in favor of rapid unification.

In light of the four decades of peace that a divided Europe had enjoyed and the havoc that Germany had wrought when it had been powerful and independent, it was hardly surprising that German unity was not universally welcomed. British Prime Minister Margaret Thatcher and French President François Mitterrand each indicated that they were not happy at the prospect. Commentators in the United States were not wholeheartedly enthusiastic either, and for the same reasons: the Germans could not be trusted; or, even if they could be, discarding the security arrangements that had served so well for so long was unacceptably risky. Had Washington also shared and acted on these reservations, it could have slowed and perhaps even blocked German unification. The United States—as well as Britain and France—would have in effect declared that, while every other nation in Europe, and all peoples elsewhere, were entitled to choose their own political arrangements, the Germans were not. Such a declaration would have stirred the same kind of resentment at unequal treatment that Hitler exploited in the 1930s in order to win power and launch his ruinous policies. Although it would not have pushed Europe into war, it would have discredited in the eyes of Germans the important roles the Federal Republic played in the postwar period—in NATO, in the European Community and in other international organizations.

The Bush administration declined to place obstacles in the path of German unity. Without American support no other country, or combination of countries, could have hoped to block German unification. But Washington was no more prescient than any other capital about the pace of events in Germany. It was motivated in part by a short-term concern that a fight over unification between West Germany and its allies would bring to power Germany's Social Democrats, who might adopt a dangerously neutralist foreign policy. Support for Chancellor Helmut Kohl was nonetheless consistent with the proper long-term American approach to the German Question: that is, support for the right of Germans to decide their own fate, combined with efforts to create conditions in which the German decision, especially if in favor of unity, would not make others, or Germans themselves, feel insecure.

The key to maintaining a secure Europe was to keep the newly united Germany firmly anchored in an American-led security community. The Bush administration waged a successful diplomatic campaign on this issue within the framework of the "two plus four" negotiations. These talks involved the two Germanys plus Britain, France, the Soviet Union and the United States—the four powers whose victory in World War II gave them special prerogatives in Germany. In the first half of 1990 the administration used this forum to obtain Soviet acquiescence on Germany's continuing membership in NATO.

The final details of the terms of German unity were worked out without the United States, Britain or France, in the summer of 1990 in a meeting between Chancellor Kohl and President Gorbachev at the Soviet leader's home in Stavropol. The meeting raised the specter of Soviet-German collusion against the interests of the rest of Europe. Without reconciliation between Germany and Russia, however, there could be no end to the Cold War. Peace in Europe was impossible without an accommodation between its two largest powers. For most of the hundred years between the fall from power in 1890 of Bismarck, the original architect of German unity, and the 1990 unification of the two German states, Germany and Russia had defined their interests in Europe in ways unacceptable to each other. This ongoing Russo-German antagonism caused much of the tension, rivalry and war on the continent in that period. It now may be hoped that the events of 1990 have brought that era to an end.

The Soviet-German rapprochement is not dangerous to others, provided it takes place within a European security framework that includes a continuing American presence. It is just such a framework that the Bush administration was instrumental in designing, and is apparently committed to maintaining.

III

Just as America, the Soviet Union and the European nations were beginning the task of constructing a new post-Cold War Europe, Saddam Hussein interrupted them. His invasion, occupation and declared annexation of Kuwait—and the American response—dominated U.S. foreign policy in the latter half of George Bush's second year as president.

President Bush dispatched to the Middle East the largest expeditionary force since the Vietnam War and organized an impressively wide coalition against Iraq. The American intervention in the gulf, whatever its outcome, will exert a major influence on future American policy in the region. It may also prove to be the decisive event of George Bush's presidency. Success could assure his reelection and strengthen his hand at home and abroad; failure could have the opposite effects. Even a limited victory for Saddam Hussein would increase the power of forces opposed to the United States and its friends, and have adverse and perhaps disastrous consequences for the entire Middle East.

The gulf crisis is not, however, a preview of international politics beyond the Cold War. It is an important development, to be sure, that cannot help but influence American foreign policy in years to come. But it is not the seminal event from which America's new international role will emerge.

The Iraqi invasion demonstrated that some features of the Cold War persist, even in the absence of the Soviet-American rivalry. There are still dangerous people abroad who have the power to jeopardize Western interests. It also demonstrated that when those interests must be defended by force the principal responsibility continues to rest with the West's leading military power, the United States. The gulf crisis also illustrates the changes that the end of the Cold War has produced in international politics. The United States and the Soviet Union find themselves on the same side of the conflict. In part because of this harmony, it proved possible to assemble an international coalition of unprecedented breadth to oppose Saddam Hussein.

Soviet-American cooperation also made possible a prominent role in the gulf crisis for the United Nations, whose machinery, especially the Security Council, had for most of its history been paralyzed by the great schism between its two strongest members.

Most important of all, the end of the Cold War and the newfound solidarity between Washington and Moscow allowed the United States to undertake military operations on a large scale in the Middle East, without the fear of triggering a larger conflict with the Soviet Union and uncontrolled escalation to World War III. This was an enormous military advantage for the United States.

The gulf crisis, however, does not offer a reliable guide to the post-Cold War world. The United States sent forces to the Middle East for two reasons: to support the principle that stronger powers must not swallow up weaker neighbors; and to prevent a large fraction of the world's oil reserves from coming under the control of a brutal, aggressive and unpredictable tyrant. The principle of sovereign independence is important. Where it is challenged in the years ahead the United States will surely support beleaguered small states— but not by sending 400,000 troops to liberate them. Oil is a uniquely valuable resource, one that makes the Persian Gulf the only part of the Third World where Western interests are sizable enough to justify a large war.

In the minds of American policymakers, the various conflicts of the Cold War were all connected. The Greek civil war, the Korean War, the Vietnam War and others were seen as part of a global struggle against communism. Each was consequential not only for what was directly at stake, but for its effect on the Western position in other parts of the world. The confrontation with Iraq, by contrast, is not connected to anything beyond the Middle East. Important as the Middle East is to the United States and the rest of the West, it does not provide the basis for a global foreign policy, as did the conflict with the Soviet Union.

During the Cold War, wars and conflicts outside Europe derived their importance for the United States from their connection to the Soviet Union. With the end of the Cold War, they will be far less consequential for American foreign policy. The Persian Gulf excepted, the United States is considerably less likely to dispatch forces abroad in the post-Cold War era. In this sense the gulf crisis belongs to the past, not the future, of American foreign policy.

There is still a military role for the United States to play, but the regions where American forces will remain useful are those where they were concentrated during the conflict with the Soviet Union: Europe and East Asia. Their mission, however, will be different from those they have become accustomed to carrying out.

IV

Deterrence of the Soviet Union has ceased to be the all-consuming international concern of the United States. Moscow is withdrawing its troops from Europe, and drawing down its forces in East Asia as well. Equally important, the sources of an expansive Soviet foreign policy—the commitment to the principles of Marxism-Leninism and the determination to spread them abroad—have all but disappeared.

The end of the Cold War, however, does not bring an end to the system of relations among sovereign states in which threats can arise. The difference is that, henceforth, the dangers to the security of America's friends in Europe and Asia are likely to be more distant and nebulous than the sharply defined threat the Soviet Union was seen to pose over the last four decades. Dangers could still arise, and there is still a role for the United States to play in dealing with them. West Europeans will continue to share a continent with a Soviet Union that, whatever form it ultimately takes, will be both large and heavily armed. Europe will need to counterbalance that military power; perpetuating the American commitment is the best way to do so.

The newly united Germany in particular will need some form of protection. German-Soviet relations are now cordial.

But Soviet military force, particularly Soviet nuclear weapons, give Moscow considerable potential for leverage over Germany should new disputes arise between them. Without some form of protection, Germans will be vulnerable to Soviet pressure. A Germany without a security tie to the United States might well feel the need to strengthen its own armaments, perhaps even with nuclear weapons. A German nuclear arsenal would not arise from aggressive impulses. Rather, it would be a prudent, defensive response to a new set of geopolitical conditions. But however benign its motives, a Germany armed with nuclear weapons would create uncertainty, alarm and instability in Europe. Perpetuating the American commitment to western Europe is a hedge against this undesirable and potentially dangerous sequence of events. This is why the Bush administration's determination to maintain the basic structure of NATO is well advised.

Such a commitment would be designed not so much to deter an immediate threat from the Soviet Union as to reassure all of Europe—including Germany and the Soviet Union—that it need not fear a power vacuum. Such a vacuum might compel European nations to recalculate their military requirements, perhaps in ways others would consider as threatening.[2]

In East Asia, as in Europe, the Soviet threat to America's principal ally, Japan, has diminished considerably. Yet the American military presence there remains useful for the same reason. If the United States were to withdraw completely from the region, Japan, like Germany, might feel the need to adopt a more independent military role, including the acquisition of a nuclear arsenal. A nuclear-armed Japan would likewise alarm neighboring countries. In the post-Cold War era, American military forces in East Asia, as in Europe, can serve as a buffer among countries that, while no longer avowed adversaries, continue to be suspicious of one another and might conduct more aggressive foreign policies without a reassuring American presence.

Providing reassurance will require America's continued military cooperation with other countries, which may prove difficult. The United States may not retain all the overseas military facilities and basing rights of the Cold War. The American presence in the Philippines, for example, is already contracting; the United States has agreed to withdraw its fighter aircraft from Clark Air Force Base. Similarly, although the German government will welcome the continuation of an American security guarantee, the German people may be increasingly reluctant to play host to American forces, especially American nuclear weapons. If the political difficulties of deploying armed forces abroad will multiply in the wake of the Cold War, however, the forces that the United States will need to deploy will be more modest. The military requirements of

---

[2] On the distinction between deterrence and reassurance see Michael Howard, "Reassurance and Deterrence: Western Defense in the 1980s," *Foreign Affairs*, Winter 1982/83.

reassurance in Europe and Asia will surely be less demanding than those of deterrence.

The greatest difficulty in sustaining a policy of reassurance, ironically, may lie in winning support for it in the United States. The forty-year rationale for stationing American troops abroad is gone. The Cold War provided a succession of American presidents with a powerful justification for stationing troops overseas and occasionally sending them into battle. The simple, compelling purpose of the nation's global military deployments was to check the Soviet Union. To the American public, the new purpose—reassurance—is liable to seem vague, implausible, the product of tortured logic, or simply not worth the risk.

In the absence of a Soviet threat the Bush administration floundered in finding a public justification for its military buildup in the Persian Gulf. This president and his successors may well encounter comparable difficulties in persuading the public to continue to support an American military presence overseas. The same question that was raised about troops in the gulf is likely to be directed at the continuing American deployments in Europe and Asia: Why are they there?

To answer that question, and to rally public support for a continuing American military presence abroad, what is needed is what this administration notably lacks: vision—the capacity to paint a vivid, convincing picture of the new world and America's interests in it. Vision requires the ability to communicate not only privately to other leaders, but publicly to the American people. If this president and his successors are able to present the appropriate vision, if they are able to make a persuasive case for keeping enough forces in Europe and Asia to reassure the countries of both regions, then political and military disputes of the kind that dominated the Cold War era are likely to recede. For with the end of the Soviet-American rivalry and the retreat of Soviet power, the basis for many, though by no means all, of these conflicts has vanished. And as security issues lose some of their previous significance, economic questions will assume a new international importance, particularly those that have arisen out of the end of the Cold War.

v

The Cold War ended in victory for the West. It was a victory not so much of Western arms, although they were certainly important in checking Soviet expansion in Europe. It was, rather, a victory of Western ideas, Western political institutions and, above all, Western economic practices. All three are now ascendant throughout the world. The rejection of socialist economic practices and the adoption, at least in principle, of market forms of economic organization is perhaps the broadest and most important ongoing global trend at the outset of the 1990s. It is a development that is bound to affect America's relations with the rest of the world.

The trend is most dramatically evident in the former communist countries of Europe. Having deposed their old-guard communist leaders, all of the east European nations now intend to embark on transitions from centrally planned to market economies. They have announced that they will eventually eliminate the cumbersome planning apparatus that dictated targets for production, gradually allow prices to be set by supply and demand, restore the right to own private property, and sell state-owned enterprises as quickly as possible to private owners, including foreigners. Some east European countries, notably Poland, have already begun this process. In the Soviet Union, too, the transition to a market economy is high on the political agenda, although the commitment there is more equivocal, and the steps taken so far more modest and hesitant.

The rise of the market is evident as well in communist countries outside Europe, even in those where political change has come slowly or not at all. Although the communist party still holds a monopoly of power in Vietnam, it transformed the country almost overnight from an importer to an exporter of its staple food, rice, largely by freeing agriculture from state control. The Vietnamese communists followed in the footsteps of the successful market reforms in agriculture that began a decade ago in China, which also dramatically increased its food production.

Nowhere have governments controlled economic activity as thoroughly as in communist states, but after achieving independence from colonial rule many noncommunist Third World countries practiced their own brand of socialism. They emphasized the protection of domestic industries, generous government subsidies for consumers and producers, and considerable public ownership of the industrial sector. The popularity of this milder form of socialism has also faded. In India, for example, socialism was an article of deep political faith for decades, but in the 1980s its leaders took tentative steps to liberalize the economy. Much of Latin America has recently turned in this direction as well, Mexico being a particularly dramatic example.

The collapse of communism in Europe is thus part of a broader trend. As the distinguished economist Robert Heilbroner has observed, "In the materially more advanced nations, 'socialism' as a distinct social objective has disappeared. Nothing is left of it but a better-run capitalism."[3] Promoting capitalism, then, is a plausible goal for American foreign policy in the post-Cold War world, especially if the impetus for it comes from foreign countries themselves. Americans have a long history of faith in free enterprise, free markets and free commerce. They have, it is true, an older, deeper attachment to political freedom. But fewer governments would welcome an American role in fostering democracy in their countries

[3] "The World After Communism," *Dissent*, Fall 1990, p. 429.

than would seek Western help in establishing market institutions and practices. China's current leaders, for example, are open to the second but opposed to the first.

Even where a people and its government are dedicated to establishing working parliaments, competitive elections and a free press, other countries can be of only limited assistance. Political institutions are, after all, built from within. Outside assistance is of course not irrelevant. Democratic structures are in place in Japan, Germany and the Philippines in no small part because the United States, having occupied those countries, helped to build them. Such an American role, however, is no longer plausible in the post-Cold War world.

Installing a market economy, by contrast, lends itself more readily to technical and economic assistance from the outside. The promotion of market practices, moreover, indirectly fosters democracy in at least two ways. First, functioning markets restrict the power of the state because, by operating independently of governing authorities, they expand the political space available to the individual. Public space independent of the state, in which citizens can organize themselves, is a necessary condition for democratic politics. This is the sense in which, as the old saying goes, "free markets make free men." Second, democratic government seems to flourish most readily in conditions of economic success. In eastern Europe, in particular, the new democracies are fragile. Their communist predecessors were overthrown in part because they presided over economic stagnation. Democratic politics will accumulate popular support to the extent that they are identified with prosperity.

The trend in favor of market institutions and practices, although strong, is not universal. It is weak in Africa and the Arab world, and virtually nonexistent in countries such as Burma. But even where it is strong, it may not prevail. Market reforms are often painful to implement. Removing subsidies on basic commodities can trigger political unrest, as governments from Egypt to Poland have discovered to their dismay. Restructuring a country's industry along more economically rational lines inevitably throws people out of work. In a market system those with skill, initiative or just good luck prosper; others who do less well often resent the prosperity of the fortunate.

Finally, even where market reforms are initiated, the reformers will not necessarily use the United States as their model. The American economy is but one version of a market system, and not necessarily the most attractive. The formerly communist countries of Europe are likely to be drawn to the west European "social market" style of capitalism, as exemplified by the German Federal Republic, which provides more generous welfare benefits than the United States. In East Asia the great economic success stories of the 1970s and 1980s— Taiwan, Singapore and South Korea—have followed the path pioneered by Japan. This model features far closer relations between the government and the private sector, especially in the allocation of capital, than are found in the United States.[4]

The American, West European and East Asian varieties of capitalist economic organization are nonetheless closer in form to one another than any one of them is to the centrally directed economic systems of orthodox communism, or even to the milder versions of socialism that have appeared elsewhere during the last thirty years. At the end of the Cold War, in part because of the manner in which it ended, these three versions of capitalism stand as the models that much of the world now aspires to adopt. This is perhaps the greatest achievement of Western policy over the last forty years.

There is a parallel with the immediate aftermath of World War II. What the United States helped western Europe and Japan to do in the late 1940s, much of the rest of the world is seeking to do at the beginning of the 1990s. There are, to be sure, important differences between these two periods. The task of economic construction is today more complicated. World War II left the nations of western Europe with ruined farms and factories, but also with long experience with functioning market economies. West Europeans had the skills necessary to operate such an economic system. They needed capital, which the United States supplied. In formerly communist Europe, by contrast, almost no one has any experience in buying, selling, investing and producing in conditions of economic competition. The citizens of these countries must start virtually from scratch to learn the techniques of modern economic activity. They must also build the relevant institutions; none has a private sector in manufacturing or services, a financial system or a labor market. All this requires technical, but not necessarily economic, assistance from richer countries.

Eastern Europe, the Soviet Union and much of the Third World are not yet in a position to benefit from Western capital. They must first create economies that can make productive use of it. The Bush administration is thus not under immediate pressure to undertake a policy that it would, in any event, have great difficulty in launching: a program of large-scale economic assistance to countries adopting liberal economic practices.

There is another important difference between 1990 and 1947. Then, only the United States could offer support to struggling democracies. Now, there is a thriving community of capitalist democracies, encompassing western Europe and Japan, which can share the task of promoting market systems the world over. The United States need not, and indeed should not, be the sole source of support. Here, too, President Bush's inclinations are in harmony with international condi-

---

[4] This typology is drawn from Paul Marer, "Roadblocks to Economic Transformation in Central and Eastern Europe and Some Lessons of Market Economies," in *United States-Soviet and East European Relations: Building a Congressional Cadre/Eighth Conference, August 25–31, 1990*, Dick Clark, ed., Queenstown (MD): The Aspen Institute, 1990.

tions. The Bush administration is happy to deal with reform-minded economies on a multilateral basis, working through international organizations such as the International Monetary Fund and even the European Community, of which the United States is not a member.

There is, however, one important feature common to the period of the Marshall Plan and the present, to which the Bush administration's response is not encouraging. To create successful market economies, the countries of eastern Europe and the Third World will need in the future what the countries of western Europe enjoyed in the past: a hospitable international economic environment. Once in place, market institutions in these countries will need access to capital. This is a particularly complicated problem for those nations with large external debts. They will need more extensive debt relief—indeed, debt forgiveness—than they have thus far received. Even with their debt burdens lightened, they will be affected by the price of capital. The lower world interest rates are, the greater the chances for economic success.

These nations will also need access to markets in order to sell what they produce for hard currency—the lifeblood of any healthy economy. In the first year of the post-Cold War era, world interest rates were uncomfortably high. The trend in the international trading system, especially among the advanced industrial countries to which the new practitioners of market economics will look for export opportunities, was at best uncertain. The Uruguay Round failed to move that system decisively toward greater openness. The reasons for these trends are varied and are hardly the result exclusively of American policies—the Europeans are the chief culprits on trade. Over the last ten years, however, the American contribution to the worldwide cost of capital and the status of global markets has not been constructive. Its fiscal imbalances have had quite harmful effects.

At the end of World War II, the United States took the lead in launching international economic initiatives, beginning with the establishment of the International Monetary Fund, the General Agreement on Tariffs and Trade, and the Marshall Plan. West Europeans benefited not only from American generosity, but from American leadership. In keeping with that tradition, America has initiated recent international efforts to lighten the burden of the world's principal debtors and to lower barriers to trade: the Brady Plan and the GATT's Uruguay Round.

But deficits reduce America's capacity to lead. They limit its scope for reducing the debt held by its own banks and for increasing imports from other countries. This, in turn, diminishes American leverage with western Europe and Japan to help solve the debt problem and expand trade. Not only is the United States historically the leader of the international economic system, it is also its biggest member. Its policies have a considerable effect on the system, apart from any efforts it may make to guide others in a particular direction. America's reduced capacity to lead, due to the fiscal imbalances of the 1980s, has obstructed the creation of international conditions favorable to the flourishing of market economies around the world.

The United States has also pushed up the cost of capital by running large, chronic budget deficits and financing them by borrowing in international capital markets. These budget deficits were not the only cause of the historically high real interest rates in the 1980s, but they were certainly among the most important. The budget deficits and the effort to finance them also raised the value of the dollar. This, in turn, depressed American exports, leading to a series of large trade deficits. Exports declined, imports rose and American industries dependent on selling abroad, or in competition with foreign products at home, suffered. These industries demanded protection. The United States retreated farther from free trade during the 1980s than in any comparable period since World War II. American protectionism imposed a particular hardship on Third World countries; the United States has historically taken a far greater share of their exports than Japan or western Europe.

VI

If economic issues will be ascendant in the post-Cold War era, if an important American goal will be to assist in the establishment of market economies, and if the most immediately useful way to promote market reforms is to reduce America's own economic imbalances, then the 1990 budget negotiations were as relevant to the long-term future of American foreign policy as the Persian Gulf crisis.

Those negotiations finally did produce a budget agreement. The way the president went about securing it, however, did little to convey a strong commitment to the kinds of policies required to pursue America's international political and economic interests in the post-Cold War world. President Bush failed to draw the necessary connection for the public between the nation's fiscal soundness and its international interests, even in the Persian Gulf. He could have appealed for modest economic sacrifice at a moment when American troops were at risk in the Arabian desert. A budget agreement, he could have argued, would send a signal of resolve at a time when the United States was trying to project an image of determination against a foreign tyrant. He delivered no such message.

If the United States is to play a useful, let alone a leading, role in the reconstruction of the world's economies according to market principles, a far greater public appreciation of the importance of particular economic policies will have to be developed. What is required to rally support for such policies is a credible political explanation of the connection between them and America's international interests. Perhaps such an explanation can be provided, but it seems unlikely that this president will do so.

President Bush has proclaimed his distaste for the details of economic policy and for the task of bringing spending into line with resources. "When you get a problem with the complexities that the Middle East has now, and the gulf has now, I enjoy trying to put the coalition together and keep it together," he said in the fall of 1990. "I can't say I just rejoice every time I go up and talk to [House Ways and Means Committee Chairman Dan] Rostenkowski about what he's going to do on taxes."[5] But the way Rostenkowski and his colleagues vote on taxes will have as much to do with the pursuit of American international interests in the post-Cold War era as the way foreign governments, with whose leaders the president has dealt so artfully, vote at the United Nations.

Apart from his personal inclinations, Bush's presidency rests on a coalition of forces and interests that offer no political basis for economic policies in support of the international trends favored by the United States. For twenty years Republican presidents have supported American Cold War security commitments, while avoiding the costs of sustaining the international economic order designed after World War II. They have been simultaneously scrupulous in fulfilling the nation's security obligations and delinquent in observing standards of international economic propriety.

Richard Nixon inaugurated this two-track foreign policy by going to great and expensive lengths to vindicate the American commitment to Vietnam and, at the same time, abandoning the gold-exchange standard and destroying the international monetary system crafted in 1944 at Bretton Woods. Ronald Reagan continued the pattern by presiding over both substantial increases in defense spending, the better to confront the Soviet Union in the early 1980s, and large budget deficits, with all the attendant international economic dislocation. The combination proved to be a formula for electoral success for them and for their political heir, George Bush.[6]

In the post-Cold War era, the international interests of the United States, not to mention the nation's own economic well-being, depend on reversing this approach and giving priority to what most economists regard as sensible economic policies. Such a reversal will be politically difficult to accomplish, as the protracted wrangling over the budget in 1990 demonstrated. It is, moreover, a reversal that this president is unlikely to achieve. This is so ultimately because George Bush is, personally and politically, a product of the Cold War. He could hardly be anything else. His skills, ideas and political constituency were acquired in a time when the great rivalry

[5] Quoted in *Time*, Oct. 22, 1990, p. 27.

[6] This combination of policies arguably originated in a Democratic administration, with Lyndon Johnson's decision to escalate American involvement in Vietnam without increasing taxes or reducing domestic spending.

with the Soviet Union dominated America's relations with the rest of the world. These qualities served him and the nation well at the end of the 1980s, but they are likely to be far less useful in the era ahead. In historical perspective, George Bush may come to enjoy the ironic distinction of having presided, adeptly, over the disappearance of the kind of world in which he was best able to guide the foreign policy of the United States.

Article 3. Pentagon Charade
by David C. Morrison

In this article, the author discusses a recent Pentagon aircraft review, which raises serious questions about the programs and underscores the pitfalls of Pentagon politics. After a much-touted two-month review, the Pentagon dodged the difficult question of program cancellations, opting instead to forego or delay the building of some 450 new aircraft. Bowing to political pressure, the Pentagon merely rubber stamped the programs in question, while ignoring many of the concerns raised by leading congressional and defense critics.

On the surface, the presentation that Defense Secretary Dick Cheney gave in unusual back-to-back testimony to the House and Senate Armed Services Committees this spring seemed the very model of a post-Cold War cost-cutting exercise.

During a much-heralded "major aircraft review," the Pentagon had spent more than two months scrutinizing the whys, hows and wherefores of the B-2 bomber, the C-17 airlifter, the Air Force's Advanced Tactical Fighter (ATF), the Navy's A-12 medium bomber and cross-service variants of the ATF and A-12. All told, these projects were slated to encompass about 3,000 planes costing more than $400 billion to build.

And now Cheney was unveiling the long-awaited results. Some critics felt that the review should have yielded a program cancellation or two. But the message still sounded reasonably sweet to Members of Congress desperate for defense savings: Thanks to decisions to forgo 450 aircraft and to delay others, Cheney announced, $34.8 billion could be saved through fiscal 1997.

"Thank you, Mr. Secretary," Senate Armed Services Committee chairman Sam Nunn, D-Ga., intoned as Cheney wrapped up his April 26 briefing. "I know this reflects an awful lot of hard, long hours of work by you and everybody on your staff and the [military] services involved. This review is going to be very helpful to us."

Not very, as it turned out. In no time at all, the review came unglued in a rush of revelations that the projects that supposedly had been scrutinized at such length would cost much more, and be ready much later, than advertised. Most notoriously, it was disclosed in early June that the A-12 was running a year or so behind schedule and way over budget.

A *National Journal* review of the review—based on not-for-attribution interviews with a range of participants and observers—finds that the vaunted aircraft studies, in fact, amounted to little more than a prototypical Pentagon logrolling exercise.

Formal operational and technical requirements for the weapons were basically rubber-stamped by the Joint Chiefs of Staff (JCS). Contractors' assurances that programs were on track were accepted on faith, even after Pentagon examiners had waved red warning flags. Lower program cost estimates were substituted at the last minute for more credible, higher numbers. And plans for formal reports on the aircraft were jettisoned: The only paper trail left by the review is a batch of Vugraph transparencies.

"The whole thing has been a green-light exercise from Day 1," a Pentagon official said in disgust. "There was no text, no report at any stage. It was just forwarding Vugraphs through different committees. And they massaged the Vugraphs until they got the answers they wanted."

In one case, the review even prompted a service to *increase* the number of aircraft it projected buying. The Air Force last spring, in drafting its "program objective memorandum" for the fiscal 1992-97 budget-building process, recognized that it could never finance all of its planned projects. So, it provisionally cut back on the total number of ATFs it wanted. But after Cheney, in the review, endorsed the original plan for 750 ATFs, the Air Force revised its spending blueprint to reflect that higher number.

As that outcome suggests, the aircraft review was something of an oddball exercise—if only because it seemed largely disconnected from the regular biannual budget process that consumes so much of the time and energy of the Defense Department.

A related anomaly: Even as the Pentagon was busily charting long-range plans for major aircraft programs in the review, Defense officials were deflecting budget cutting pressure from Capitol Hill with the assertion that they were deferring judgment on major issues until the internal 1992-97 budget planning process was done. But that won't happen until late this year.

"How can you make a policy decision to reduce the number of C-17s you want to buy while you're admitting in other rooms that you're very uncertain about the post-Cold War environment and thus uncertain about, among other things, what lift requirements would be?" a congressional analyst wondered with exasperation.

"It is kind of a strange way to go about it," House Armed Services Committee chairman Les Aspin, D-Wis., agreed in an interview. "It's an unusual process, doing this kind of thing piecemeal like this. It was weird."

Any account of how the review process went awry is thus also a story about how decisions tend to get made—or not made—in the Pentagon. As in many other agencies, bad news has a hard time getting a hearing at the Defense Department and officials and officers typically go along to get along.

Thanks to these bureaucratic phenomena, the aircraft review "was just a big contrivance to justify the programs," another Pentagon analyst charged. "They really had an opportunity to do something, to react to lower budgets. But they didn't structure any kind of reasonable program. They reduced the [planned aircraft] buys, but did they really get anything under control?"

This is also a story about the perils of stealth. The gigabuck, super-sophisticated aircraft hatched under the top-secret cloak of the "black" budget a decade ago are proving far more difficult to bring on line than blithe early assurances suggested.

"I don't think there's a full appreciation at the higher levels of [the Pentagon]—and that's true, I would think, at the higher levels of the management of these corporations," a Pentagon employee said, "of the type of technical problems that are out there ahead of us."

OPEN TO CHALLENGE

The aircraft review began unraveling only four days after Cheney's widely reported appearance on Capitol Hill. Revising his testimony, Cheney stated in a quiet memo to Congress—first reported by *Defense Week*—that total costs for the A-12 Avenger II were not $51.9 billion, as the data sheet had said, but $57 billion. That was simply a paperwork "mixup," a Navy spokesman said at the time.

Of far graver import, it became public knowledge on June 8 that the A-12 was in deep trouble. The planned first test flight for the stealthy, wedge-shaped bomber had slipped by more than a year, to late 1991 at the soonest. Moreover, it was revealed, the contractors teamed on the top-secret project—McDonnell Douglas Corp. and General Dynamics Corp.—had overrun their $4.8 billion development contract by at least $1 billion.

"If the A-12 received the highest marks of any aircraft during the major aircraft review," House Energy and Commerce Committee chairman John D. Dingell, D-Mich., asked Cheney in an irate mid-July letter, "what is the real status of the other aircraft procurements involved?"

Not very good, as it happened. Cheney had stuck a $61.1 billion price tag on the revised B-2 program, which called for building only 75 of the bat-winged bombers instead of 132. Before long, however, the Air Force came in with what promised to be the first of a series of price revisions: $62.8 billion. More recently, the B-2's prime contractor, Northrop Corp., has been harshly accused of sloppy management by the Air Force, the firm's usually protective customer.

The C-17 program, which Cheney cut from 210 airlifters to 120, has also been buffeted by programmatic turbulence. In July, citing management concerns, the Air Force cut off all progress payments to the C-17 prime contractor, McDonnell Douglas's subsidiary, Douglas Aircraft Co. Late last month, Dingell released an internal report from Douglas suggesting that as of last April, when the review was being completed, the company was projecting an $837 million overrun on its $4.9 billion C-17 development contract. *(For a report on the C-17, see NJ, 2/24/90, p. 434.)*

A Douglas spokesman said that the company should come in under a $6.6 billion aggregate cost ceiling for the development contract and the first two lots of aircraft. "There is not a financial crisis at McDonnell Douglas, and we're not going bankrupt," he insisted, responding to Dingell's charges.

A Pentagon official with knowledge of the C-17 program contended that the actual situation "is probably worse" than even that portrayed by Dingell. It can be hard for outsiders to judge such conflicting assertions. But, clearly, the picture Cheney painted in April, based on the review, was considerably out of focus—as Nunn and others came to see as the summer wore on.

"The various revelations so close upon completion of the [aircraft review] means that the staffs of the various military departments may not have taken the reviews seriously," the Senate Armed Services Committee complained in its fiscal 1991 defense authorization report, published in July.

The welter of woes that have come to light, the panel continued, "most certainly indicates that [Pentagon aides] provided inadequate support for the Secretary that calls into question many of the decisions he made."

The many problems that have cropped up with the aircraft review have also left the department's subsequent reviews of two major Navy ship projects and the Army's Light Helicopter program open to challenge. *(For more on the review results, see box, p. 2520.)*

That vulnerability underlines the broader political failing of the reviews as they were conducted. Cheney "has been embarrassed by revelations about programs after the review; he has not been taken seriously; his numbers have been questioned," Natalie J. Goldring, a senior analyst with the private Defense Budget Project, said. "What I think the Defense Department hoped was that the [review] would stop debate in the Congress, that they would accept the expertise of the Department of Defense and these numbers would become the starting numbers. Instead, they've become the starting point for renewed debate."

RUBBER STAMP?

The starting point for the aircraft review came early this year when the Pentagon sought the intelligence community's view on what the world and "the threat" might look like from now until 2015.

"And, with that view, we went to the war fighters," Defense undersecretary for acquisition John A. Betti, who headed up the weapons reviews, explained during a Sept. 27 breakfast interview with a small group of reporters. "They came up with what the requirements would be to meet those threats," he said.

The uniformed "war fighters" were represented by the Joint Requirements Oversight Council, a panel of officers chaired by the JCS vice chairman, Adm. David E. Jeremiah.

But "the JCS has never been staffed with the right level of expertise to play in these games," a review participant explained. "So it does get to be a rubber-stamp type of operation. And that was pretty blatant, I can tell you candidly."

During meetings on the various aircraft, for instance,

officers on the JCS requirements council tended to parrot, word for word, the views of senior officers in their service's acquisition directorate. And, when the Air Force needed the Navy to back up its views—and vice versa—a helping hand was freely forthcoming.

"The Army played nothing in this," the participant recalled. "It was run by the Air Force and the Navy, and they played it tit for tat. And this was a major part of the review."

Another major part of the review involved examining alternative approaches to satisfying the military requirements that the JCS council endorsed. Many observers and participants are also unhappy with this segment of the exercise.

A problem, a Defense official said, was that any alternative that "didn't somehow come very, very close to meeting those requirements"—which were pegged directly to the costly new aircraft under review—did not make the grade.

In its July report, therefore, the Senate Armed Services Committee rapped the "limited scope" of the review, which, it said, looked at the Air Force's ATF "in isolation from the broad question of modernizing tactical aircraft" and focused instead on acquiring entirely new planes.

While restricting the Air Force from proceeding with full-scale development of the ATF, the Senate committee urged the Defense Department to perform "a more comprehensive evaluation" of Air Force and Navy tactical aircraft that would not be limited to "ATF performance requirements only." In other words, it directed the department to repeat a central task of last spring's major review. *(For a report on the ATF and A-12, see NJ, 10/7/89, p. 2448.)*

Another problem was the way in which consideration of alternatives—which largely involved possible changes in acquisition rates, apparently—became the be-all and end-all of the review. As a result, basic management questions about the programs fell through the cracks.

"A lot of the time was spent on alternatives, boogering them up and costing them, without looking at the focus of the [review]," a Pentagon analyst said. "Fifty people did not descend on these programs and analyze the shit out of them. What they did was run thousands of alternatives. So time and energy was just bled off doing that."

In the process, the Pentagon's cost analysis improvement group (CAIG) spent a lot of time working up total price figures under many differing buying scenarios for the programs under review.

The CAIG's mandate is to develop independent cost estimates, as a counterbalance to the military services' generally rosier estimates. But critics complain that the CAIG too often does not serve as an adequate counterweight to service optimism and that its estimates are neither sufficiently realistic nor independent. Consequently, the Pentagon inspector general's office is currently running a management review of the department's independent cost-estimating.

Acquisition czar Betti, arguing that "no estimates are perfect," strongly defended the CAIG's work on the review. "As a matter of fact," he said, "wherever there was a difference of opinion [on cost estimates] between the CAIG and the services or the contractors, the CAIG was higher, and we always used the CAIG numbers."

When Cheney was briefed on the aircraft review, he saw a mix of CAIG and service cost figures, Betti's office confirmed. But the numbers that went up to Capitol Hill, to the amazement of many participants in the review, were not the CAIG figures. Instead, they were estimates worked up by the office of Pentagon comptroller Sean C. O'Keefe. The same cost switch occurred later when the Light Helicopter and the Navy ships were reviewed.

"Coincidentally," Betti's office said in a written response to *National Journal*'s query about the source of the numbers presented to Congress, the comptroller's estimates "tracked more closely with the lower estimates received for each program." That "coincidence" could only ease sticker shock in Congress. The CAIG came in $7.6 billion higher than the Navy figures on the A-12, for instance, and a whopping $10.7 billion higher than the Air Force numbers on the ATF.

In that light, the aircraft review further illuminates "a generic problem" at the Pentagon, said Sen. Jeff Bingaman, D-N.M., who chairs the Armed Services Subcommittee on Defense Industry and Technology.

"They make decisions based on wildly optimistic projections that seldom turn out to be true," he said. "They're supposed to have people over there who ask the hard questions and make people be realistic about projections. But it doesn't seem to have worked."

Anyone wishing to track exactly what happened with the aircraft cost estimates will have a hard time; atypically for an exercise of this supposed rigor, there is no formal documentation, no audit trail, no "stake in the sand," as a critic put it.

"We didn't do a detailed report with a detailed recommendation," Betti explained. "What we did, we did a study, we tried to capture the essence of the results on things like Vugraphs and tried to present that to the Secretary, to say, 'Here are your viable options.' "

But Pentagon sources say that there were originally supposed to be reports. And, in fact, reports were written. Among them, the ever-controversial program analysis and evaluation office had drafted a report on the Air Force's tactical projects. *(For more on that office, see NJ, 11/11/89, p. 2740.)*

That draft report asserted that the Air Force had failed to provide sufficient technical data for the review working groups to pass realistic judgment on its projects. Unhappy about the draft, the Air Force appealed to Frank Kendall III, the deputy director for tactical warfare programs. "Some point in time after that," a participant said, "the decision was made that there would be no reports."

POLICY BOMBSHELL

This and other questionable aspects of the review process have been little noted outside the Pentagon. But, coming a little more than a month after Cheney and other officials praised the review's progress to Congress, the revelation that the A-12 was in big trouble detonated like a bombshell in Washington's defense policy community. Since then, the A-12 flap has sparked a round of investigations and embarrassed recriminations.

"The A-12 is turning into a gumshoe detective story," a congressional naval analyst joked: "Who knew what, and when did they know it?"

Numerous sources, including acquisition chief Betti, in fact, assert that Cheney was explicitly told of problems with the A-12 when he was briefed last spring on the findings of the review.

But that wasn't evident from the Secretary's testimony on Capitol Hill. "Every alternative we looked at, basically, led us back to saying, 'We think we ought to go forward to the

A-12, that it's a good system, that the program appears to be reasonably well handled at this point,'" Cheney told the Senate Armed Services Committee on April 26.

That assessment was clearly reflected in the changes the Defense Secretary endorsed for the program, which were minimal compared with those for most of the other aircraft reviewed. Though Cheney cut 238 A-12s from the initially planned buy of 858, about half of that reduction resulted from the Marine Corps's having bailed out of the project (which the service had made clear last year that it planned to do). The balance of the reduction was facilitated by an unrelated decision to cut back eventually from 14 to 12 aircraft carriers.

Cheney was not the only one to cheer on the Avenger II. "The A-12 program is on schedule," Vice Adm. Richard M. Dunleavy, the assistant chief of naval operations for air warfare, confidently told the Senate Appropriations Subcommittee on Defense on May 8. "We're very, very pleased with it. We had a review in St. Louis just a week ago this past Thursday by the program managers for both McDonnell Douglas and General Dynamics and the Navy."

When it became public a month later that the A-12 was at least a year off schedule and at least $1 billion over budget, exclamations of shock and dismay echoed along the Pentagon's E-Ring.

"I was not happy to discover that the contractors were having problems with the A-12," Cheney told reporters on June 19. "Listen!" Betti erupted during the late-September interview. "Nobody was more embarrassed than I was."

But there is little reason why anyone should have been particularly surprised. As early as last year, an examiner in the Pentagon comptroller's office had circulated a position paper arguing that the A-12 program should be slipped by two years because the contractors were falling so far behind. That paper quickly vanished from sight.

Another obvious clue that something was amiss turned up early this year, when members of the Pentagon staff working on the review toured the A-12 final assembly plant in Tulsa, Okla. "It looked like a basketball court," someone familiar with that visit said. "All there were were chalk marks on the floor where tooling was supposed to go."

Profound concern was voiced at a meeting at which Cheney was briefed on the program, officials say. "We said, 'There are concerns over the schedule, and we have reason to believe that there's some cost overruns, a little less than a billion dollars,'" a defense official said.

That apparently did not elicit an alarmed response. "But you have to understand the building," this official said. "In order to get somebody's attention at the Pentagon, you have to mention numbers in the neighborhood of $10 billion."

A PIG IN A POKE

Though that was hardly the uncertain light in which the A-12 review was presented to Congress, Betti acknowledged in the Sept. 27 interview that his team had informed Cheney that "out of the programs we have, the one that seemed not as firm as the others is the A-12."

After that meeting with Cheney, Betti was prompted by the worries that had been vented to telephone the chief executive officers of McDonnell Douglas and General Dynamics. He asked if there were any problems that he should know about. He was reassured, he said, that if there were, they were manageable.

"The fundamental issue with the A-12 was that neither the [Navy] program manager nor the contractors knew the kind of problems that were developing at the working level," Betti contended. "There was a disconnect between what was going on at the working level and the management of the contractors, and also of our program management."

In an interview, the question was put to retired Vice Adm. Robert F. Dunn, Dunleavy's predecessor as naval air warfare chief from 1985 to mid-1989: Had he had any inkling of these problems during his tenure? "Absolutely not," Dunn said. "That was a complete surprise. Unfortunately, I think the contractors let us down; McDonnell Douglas and General Dynamics let us down."

Neither company is willing to discuss A-12 issues on the record in any detail. But General Dynamics has shaken up the management at its Fort Worth A-12 plant. And both firms have recently taken large write-offs against earnings thanks to losses on the A-12—$450 million for General Dynamics and $89 million for McDonnell Douglas.

Both companies are also preparing to file claims against the Navy to recover money lost on the project. "We have not yet announced any action, but there will be a claim filed," a General Dynamics spokesman said. The two firms are expected to file claims totaling $1 billion.

Meanwhile, the Avenger II is flying into severe down drafts over the Pentagon and Capitol Hill. The project is expected to encounter some very deep skepticism when it is reviewed next month by the high-level Defense Acquisition Board. Some believe the board may vote to put off or even terminate the A-12.

The Navy wants an estimated $1.6 billion to buy A-12s in fiscal 1991. In an illustration of congressional unhappiness with the program, the Senate Armed Services Committee wants to cut that request by $1.5 billion, and the House Armed Services Committee, by $1.15 billion.

The House committee cited "financial and technical difficulties that will result in significant delays to first-flight and operational testing." The panel added that it was "troubled that these A-12 issues have come to light just weeks after the Department of Defense concluded its major aircraft review."

The committee also cited an aspect of A-12 program management that many believe has contributed to its current woes: its closely held status as a tightly compartmented "special-access" program, which "may have inhibited rigorous departmental review," the panel said. Cheney must declassify the A-12, the committee ordered, before any further procurement money would be considered.

"This program has been in the special security arrangement far longer than it should be," Adm. Dunn agreed. "Nothing was kept from Dunleavy, nothing was kept from Congress," he argued. "But you don't get to the full discussion" when programs are so thickly veiled under the black cloak, he said. "It makes it a little bit harder, and I think that's a problem."

In a bid to address this issue, House Armed Services Committee member John R. Kasich, R-Ohio, has introduced a bill stipulating that total costs and program schedule data must be clearly reported to Congress after outlays for a special-access project have exceeded $50 million.

Kasich does not expect action on his proposal this session, but he expects hearings to be held next year. "Nobody should be asked to buy a pig in the poke," he said. "We're being told to approve these programs. And then, if you [change your mind], we're told, 'We've put all of this money up front.'"

There is more to the matter than just money, however. The A-12's woes have broader implications for the many stealth projects under way. Constructed of novel "composite" materials, these are not the aircraft the U.S. aerospace industry has had long practice "bending metal" for.

A major A-12 snag late this spring, for instance, was the manufacturers' difficulty in producing a certain "critical-path component," a large structure to which other components are attached. That technical obstacle was eventually overcome. But new ones are sure to crop up.

"They are literally, no kidding, writing the book on how to do this as they go, because nobody has ever done it before," a Defense official said. "I'm a real skeptic now. I used to be a real believer. Then I started to see it come unraveled. There are major roadblocks to overcome along the road here before we get the first one out and fly it."

Another A-12 shortcoming sends out even wider policy ripples. Though teamed on the Avenger, McDonnell Douglas and General Dynamics are on competing teams in the impending fly-off for the high-stakes Air Force ATF. That doesn't make for the healthiest of partnerships.

A company is "not going to share with their competitor a better way to do something if they could use that same technology to compete with them on another project," a Navy officer said. "We've learned a lesson here—in the future, not letting the different corporations that are teamed on one thing compete on another, if we can help it." But, he added, "it may be too late."

SEEKING A SCAPEGOAT

Many people in Washington want to know how something like the A-12 review snafu could happen. "If we can have programs floating around that can get this kind of attention and yet have problems that don't surface," acquisition chief Betti said, "then you have to worry about what that means in the control process."

This summer, the Pentagon inspector general's office launched an investigation of the A-12 review. Just as it got started, however, Navy Secretary H. Lawrence Garrett III asked his own inspectors to look into the Navy's management of the program and its role in the review. Betti then asked Garrett to broaden that investigation into an examination of A-12 oversight in the Office of the Secretary of Defense. That Navy investigation is supposed to wind up any day now.

"We're sitting back here and waiting to see what they do," deputy Pentagon inspector general Derek J. Vander Schaaf explained. "Then we'd decide whether we want to do more work, or whether we were satisfied. I want to make sure that this gets adequate and appropriate coverage."

Rampant rumors that senior officials who worked on the aircraft review will be given government cash bonuses are unfounded, according to Betti's office. But, having taken a raincheck on a ceremony originally scheduled for Oct. 9, Betti is planning to give Defense Meritorious Ci-vilian Service awards to three review over-seers: CAIG director David L. McNichol, tactical warfare deputy director Kendall and George R. Schneiter, the deputy director for strategic and theater nuclear forces.

"Something's wrong!" Rep. Andy Ireland, R-Fla., exclaimed. A member of the Armed Services Subcommittee on Investigations, Ireland filed the initial request for an inspector general's investigation of the A-12 review. He is now worried that the investigation might turn into simply a search for a uniformed scapegoat.

"Something's wrong when you're rewarding people, and when the snooping around that we've done suggests that [the A-12's problems] were known all the way up into the office of the Secretary," Ireland said. "Their fingerprints are all over the damned thing.

"We're really afraid that they will, in another classic bureaucratic thing, slam dunk some low-level people in the Navy," he said. "And the people who should take responsibility for a foul-up like that will go on to live another bureaucratic day." ∎

SELECTED BIBLIOGRAPHY

Birnbaum, Jeffrey H., and Alan S. Murray. *Showdown at Gucci Gulch.* New York: Random House, 1987.

Bremer, Stuart A., and Barry B. Hughes. *Disarmament and Development: A Design for the Future?* Englewood Cliffs, NJ: Prentice-Hall, 1990.

Chisman, Forest, and Alan Pifer. *Government for the People: The Federal Social Role.* New York: Norton, 1988.

Day, David. *The Environmental Wars.* New York: Ballantine Books, 1989.

Derthick, Martha. *Policymaking for Social Security.* Washington, D.C.: Brookings Institution, 1979.

———, and Paul J. Quirk. *The Politics of Deregulation.* Washington, D.C.: Brookings Institution, 1985.

Ehrlich, Paul R., and Anne H. Ehrlich. *Healing the Planet: Strategies for Resolving the Environmental Crisis.* Reading, MA: Addison-Wesley, 1991.

Elliot, Jeffrey M., and Sheikh R. Ali. *The Trilemma of World Oil Politics.* San Bernardino, CA: Borgo Press, 1991.

Friedman, Benjamin. *Day of Reckoning: The Consequences of American Economic Policy.* New York: Random House, 1990.

Garfinkel, Irwin, and Sara S. McLanahan. *Single Mothers and Their Children: A New American Dilemma.* Lanham, MD: Urban Institute Press, 1986.

Greider, William. *The Secrets of the Temple: How the Federal Reserve Runs the Country.* New York: Simon & Schuster, 1989.

Hadley, Arthur T. *The Straw Giant.* New York: Random House, 1986.

Harrington, Michael. *The Other America.* Baltimore: Penguin Books, 1981.

Katz, Michael B. *The Undeserving Poor: From the War on Poverty to the War on Welfare.* New York: Pantheon Books, 1989.

Kegley, Charles W., Jr., and Eugene R. Wittkopf. *American Foreign Policy: Pattern and Process.* New York: St. Martin's, 1987.

Kozol, Jonathan. *Rachel and Her Children: Homeless Families in America.* New York: Fawcett Columbine, 1988.

Leone, Robert A. *Who Profits: Winners, Losers, and Government Regulation.* New York: Basic Books, 1986.

Markovich, Denise, and Ronald E. Pynn. *American Political Economy: Using Economics with Politics.* New York: Brooks/Cole, 1988.

Mead, Lawrence. *Beyond Entitlement: The Social Obligations of Citizenship.* New York: Free Press, 1986.

Mueller, John. *Retreat From Doomsday: The Obsolescence of Major War.* New York: Basic Books, 1990.

Nance, John J. *What Goes Up: The Global Assault on Our Atmosphere.* New York: William Morrow, 1991.

Rifkin, Jeremy. *Biosphere Politics: A New Consciousness for a New Century.* New York: Crown, 1991.

Rosenbaum, Walter A. *Energy, Politics, and Public Policy.* Washington, D.C.: Congressional Quarterly Press, 1991.

Scarce, Rik. *Eco-Warriors: Understanding the Radical Environmental Movement.* Chicago: Noble Press, 1990.

Schumacher, E. F. *Small Is Beautiful: Economics as if People Mattered.* New York: Harper & Row, 1989.

Spanier, John, and Eric M. Uslaner. *American Foreign Policy Making and the Democratic Dilemmas.* Pacific Grove, CA: Brooks/Cole, 1989.

Sweet, William. *The Nuclear Age: Atomic Energy, Proliferation, and the Arms Race.* Washington, D.C.: Congressional Quarterly Press, 1988.

POLITICS AND POLICY IN PERSPECTIVE

This section is about political access: the right to participate in decisions about the way our society is governed. Political access is basic to the right of a free people to govern themselves and to shape their society and its policies. Political access includes the right to vote, the right to elect people who are accountable and responsible, and the right to influence public policy decisions at all levels of government.

Simply stated, *government* can be defined as "the individuals, institutions, and processes that make the rules for society and possess the power to enforce them." Political scientist Harold Lasswell contends that the "government makes rules to decide who gets what of valued things in a society." The process by which this is accomplished is called *politics*. According to Benjamin Disraeli, the distinguished nineteenth-century British statesman, *politics* can be defined as the acquisition and distribution of power.

This section is about power—how people get it, keep it, and use it. Specifically, it examines the opportunity to acquire and exercise political power. Clearly, power is not distributed evenly throughout our society. Certain groups have often been unrepresented or underrepresented in exercising power. Indeed, for much of America's history, many groups were even prevented from voting in various sections of the country. For example, although the Fifteenth Amendment, adopted in 1870, gave all citizens—regardless of race, color, or past slavery—the right to vote, blacks continued to be denied that right in many sections of the country, through ingenious devices such as literacy tests, poll taxes, the white primary, and grandfather clauses. Over the past several decades, the Supreme Court has declared such practices unconstitutional and ordered them halted.

There are two kinds of political access: formal and informal. Formal access includes the right and/or privilege to vote, to run for office, to take part in political activities, to communicate directly with legislative and judicial officials, and to serve on juries. It also includes those rights specified in the Bill of Rights: the freedom of speech, association, and assembly. Together, all these rights and/or privileges enable citizens to influence government officials and actions directly.

Having the legal right to participate is, however, no guarantee of power or influence. One must also have "informal access"—that is, access to government officials, family and job connections, school and friendship ties, and certain capacities such as the ability to speak the "majority" language. It is necessary not only to have the right to participate, but also the means to do so. This often requires time, effort, money, connections, and know-how.

Group influence and/or power are also important. People identify with—and act in—groups, and government makes policies that affect groups. Groups wield real power. Individuals, acting alone, are limited when it comes to influencing government policy. Group action, therefore, is extremely important. But not all groups are equally effective. Skills, resources, numbers, and geographic location all affect voting outcomes. Groups that possess these advantages are the most likely to be effective in politics.

Chapter 19, *The Democratic Promise,* begins with an examination of American decline and the prospects of revival. The author concludes that if this decline is to be reversed, the public will have to renounce the ethic of "borrow and spend," emphasize growth and investment, and reassess domestic priorities. The second article analyzes the nature and extent of participation in the United States and offers various explanations for the patterns that have emerged. Special attention is devoted to the lack of political trust, voter efficacy, civic duty, political interest, and government ethics. The author describes an experiment in democracy in Vermont, which places strong emphasis on citizen participation and local autonomy. The third selection calls for the establishment of a new order at home, one that seeks to build a more just, prosperous, and lawful society. To do so, the nation must reject the military model, which calls for more command and less participation.

Chapter 20, *Making a Difference,* starts by chronicling the efforts of a gritty New Orleans woman who, upon finding herself homeless, took possession of an abandoned house—which had been vacant for two years—and made it livable. The author recounts her unsuccessful duel with the government to purchase the house, and the bureaucratic nightmare she faced in persuading the Reconstruction Finance Corporation—which was created to help people like her—find decent housing. The next article reveals how personal tragedy can transform ordinary citizens into political activists. It focuses on four special individuals: Wayne Bates, the "guru" of railway safety; Bonnie Sumner, who challenged the all-terrain vehicle industry; Phil Sokoloff, a critic of the fast-food industry; and Mitch Kurman, who led a campaign for summer-camp safety. The final article describes the efforts of Jim McCloskey, a Protestant clergyman and super-sleuth, who has championed the cause of dozens of individuals wrongly convicted of crimes. Although experts contend that the error rate is less than 1 percent, a mistake rate even that high would result in 6,000 wrongful felony convictions a year in the United States. In McCloskey's view, the rate is considerably higher. Half of his cases, for example, have involved false confessions that never took place.

DISCUSSION QUESTIONS

1. In what sense, if any, has America declined?
2. How will the United States be different in the twenty-first century?
3. What, if anything, can be done to revitalize American democracy?
4. Why are so many people turned off to the political process?
5. Does America's success in the gulf war threaten democratic rule at home?
6. Is there a danger that the combat culture will be extended to the domestic sphere?
7. Has the Reconstruction Finance Corporation dragged its feet on affordable housing? If so, how?
8. How, if at all, do banks discourage low-income families from purchasing their own homes?
9. Is it possible to restore public trust in government? If so, how?
10. Why are so few people willing to blow the whistle on government waste or corruption?
11. What explains the courage and persistence of those citizens who challenge the system?
12. Is American justice, as it is often claimed, really blind? Why, or why not?
13. Do adequate safeguards exist to protect the rights of those falsely accused of crimes?

KEY TERMS

ACTIVISTS   Individuals who are highly involved in politics, either within or outside the party system.

AGENDA SETTING   The power to decide which policy questions will be considered worthy of a political response.

ATTENTIVE PUBLIC   The proportion of the voting public that pays attention to political issues.

CRIMINAL JUSTICE SYSTEM   An interrelated set of agencies, organizations, and law-making bodies established to detect crime, control criminal behavior, and apprehend, process, prosecute, punish and/or rehabilitate criminal offenders.

DECENTRALIZATION   The distribution of administrative functions or powers among several local authorities.

DIRECT DEMOCRACY   A system of government in which political decisions are made by the people directly, rather than by their elected representatives.

ELITE   Those people who wield disproportionate influence in the political arena as a result of money or power.

OPINION LEADERS   Individuals able to shape the views of others because of position, expertise, or personality.

PARTICIPATORY DEMOCRACY   A system of government in which all or most citizens participate directly either by holding office or helping to make policy.

POLITICAL EFFICACY   The belief that citizens can affect the behavior of government or that government considers citizen opinions in making its decisions.

POLITICAL PARTICIPATION   The involvement of citizens in the political process of a nation.

POLITICAL REALISM   A philosophy that sees individuals acting principally in their own interest.

POLITICAL TRUST   The degree to which people express trust in government and political institutions.

POWER   The ability to affect the behavior of others and to influence political outcomes.

PUBLIC HOUSING   Government construction and maintenance of dwellings for low-income families, usually in depressed areas.

PUBLIC INTEREST   The best interests of the nation, rather than the narrow interests of a self-serving group.

SQUATTING   To settle on unoccupied public land in order to acquire title to it.

WHISTLE BLOWERS   Government employees who publicly expose evidence of official waste, misconduct, or corruption that they have discovered in the course of their duties.

Chapter 19

The Democratic Promise

Article 1. Must America Decline? American Renewal
by Richard Rosecrance

Disputing the prophets of American decline, Richard Rosecrance argues that while the United States has demonstrably declined, there is every reason to believe that it can and will reemerge. Challenging the historical view that nations, like biological organisms, rise to power and then age and wither, he points out that decline can be the impetus to renewal. This will necessitate a new national strategy—one that emphasizes the need to reduce military spending and consumption, while pursuing industrial modernization and the expansion of exports.

Mr. Rosecrance is professor of political science at the University of California, Los Angeles. From "Must America Decline?" by Richard Rosecrance, The Wilson Quarterly, Autumn 1990, pages 67–83:

*T*here are today three fundamental views of the American future. One is that the United States, like 19th-century Britain before it, has lapsed into a terminal condition of economic lethargy and decline. A second view is that while the nation has experienced its ups and downs, its position has not appreciably changed. The third view, which I share, is that the United States has demonstrably declined but that it can and will come back.

PROPHETS OF DECLINE

The "declinists"—a group which includes academicians such as David Calleo and politicians such as Colorado's former governor Richard D. Lamm—point out that while shortly after World War II the United States accounted for 45 to 50 percent of world gross national product (GNP), it now claims only 21 percent, and its share could soon shrink below 16 percent. Part of this decline was to be expected as Western Europe, Japan, and East Asia recovered after World War II. But the declinists argue that the reversal of American fortunes is greater than these figures indicate. From being the leading industrial exporting country, the United States has fallen to third place behind Germany and Japan. It has run a trade deficit every year since 1975. (Today's current account deficit is about $109 billion.) To satisfy Americans' hunger for imports of everything from autos and mineral water to machine tools and computers, the country has become the world's largest debtor. U.S. foreign debt now exceeds $600 billion and at current rates will reach $1 trillion during the early 1990s. All told, the national debt—which the Reagan administration ran up to unprecedented heights—and the private debt accumulated by U.S. companies and consumers has soared to some $7 trillion. That represents nearly 140 percent of the nation's total annual output, or more than one-third of world GNP. Thus, even if America regains its equilibrium in trade in five years, which it may be able to do if it is moderately lucky, ballooning interest and dividend payments to foreigners could wipe out much of its progress.

In industry after industry, U.S. companies have lost their lead. The *Wall Street Journal* recently put the matter with stark clarity: "While U.S. manufacturers in 1969 produced 82 percent of the nation's television sets, 88 percent of its cars and 90 percent of its machine tools, [in 1988] they made hardly any TVs, and gave up half the domestic machine-tool market and 30 percent of the auto market. Even in a new industry like semiconductors, this country's world market share has shrunk to 15 percent from 85 percent in 1980."

LOSING GROUND

When America lost its lead in cars, consumer electronics, and advanced machine tools, people consoled themselves with the thought that the United States was tops in finance and services. But in each realm Japan and other nations have caught up. Now, there is not a single American bank among the world's top 10; all of them are Japanese. In biotechnology, civilian aircraft, and advanced semiconductors and computers, Japan is beating at the U.S. door. Even the American farmer's once unassailable boast that he was the world's most efficient producer of food is being challenged. Wheat growers in Argentina are already more efficient than their American counterparts, and farmers in Australia and Thailand are rapidly improving.

The prophets of American decline believe that Yale historian Paul Kennedy's somber study, *The Rise and Fall of the Great Powers* (1987), foretells the American future. They point out that intelligent Dutchmen of the 17th century and prescient 19th-century Britons were well aware of the plight of their nations yet were unable to halt the decline. What awaits the United States in the 21st century?

Kennedy writes: "The only answer to the question increasingly debated by the public of whether the United States can preserve its existing position is 'no'—for it simply has not been given to any one society to remain *permanently* ahead of all the others, because that would imply a freezing of the differentiated pattern of growth rates, technological advance, and military developments which has existed since time immemorial."

CRITICS OF DECLINE

The second school of thought on American decline offers a much more reassuring view. The thinkers in this camp maintain either that the United States has not declined or that any decline is temporary and explicable, harmless, or easily remedied.

Some conclude that America has suffered only minor reverses and that there is no project it cannot accomplish if citizens are willing to pay for it through new taxes. In *Can America Compete?* (1984), Robert Z. Lawrence of the Brookings Institution speaks for a group that maintains that the manufacturing sector is as vibrant as ever. And even if manufacturing has declined, others argue, the United States can compete as effectively as ever in services. Still others observe that there is nothing dramatically new in America's relative economic situation. During the mid-1960s the United States produced about 24 percent of world GNP; today the figure is about 22 percent. In fact, the U.S. share of world GNP is not much smaller than it was in 1938.

To the degree that America has measurably declined, defenders of the status quo argue, this is because of, not despite, American policy. Thus, Harvard's Joseph Nye notes that, during the late 1940s, "rather than seeking hegemony over its allies, the United States opted to stimulate their economic revival and create a strategic partnership balancing Soviet power."

Still another explanation advanced for waning American influence is that we now live in a more complicated and obdurate world. The latent, unmobilized populations that passively yielded to British imperialism during the 19th century have been transformed into prickly and tough new nations. Small, formerly weak powers are now quite influential—or even, as in the case of Iraq, threatening—as are such new "players" on the international scene as multinational corporations and multilateral institutions. Even the strongest power cannot always expect to get its way in such an interdependent world. What matters now, in this view, is not military and economic power but the power to persuade.

Furthermore, the argument goes, if the United States has declined, so has Japan. During the 1960s Japan grew by more than 10 percent per year. Since then it has been averaging around 4 percent annual growth. The result is a comfortable sort of "convergence." Harvard's Samuel Huntington writes: "There is little reason why the Japanese economy as a whole should grow much faster than the U.S. economy, and there is little reason why an individual U.S. worker should be significantly more productive than a Japanese worker. On such indices of economic performance, one should expect long-term convergence among countries at similar levels of economic development and with economies of comparable complexity."

Converging rates of growth, however, mean that the United States can maintain its lead. *Discriminate Deterrence* (1988), a major study by a panel of experts (including Huntington) convened by the U.S. Department of Defense, plots U.S. economic growth for the next two decades at 2.6 percent annually and Japanese growth at 2.8 percent. By the year 2010, U.S. GNP will reach nearly $8 trillion (in 1986 dollars); China and Japan will be next at nearly $4 trillion each; the Soviet Union will follow at $2.9 trillion.

Still other writers who are content with American economic performance take a "so what?" attitude toward decline. In the new "one world" economy, U.S. trade deficits with Japan and South Korea don't matter any more than Maine's trade deficit with California. Capital travels freely across national frontiers, and the fortunes of one entity do not mean much so long as the system as a whole works.

Federal budget deficits? As a percentage of GNP the deficit has declined from a maximum of 6 percent of GNP in 1983 to only 3.5 percent today—less than that sustained easily by Japan during the mid-1970s. In any event, the argument goes, the deficit will continue to decline for the next few years. Robert Eisner, a prominent economist from Northwestern University, insists that the deficit is actually a plus, a stimulus that we cannot do without.

Not surprisingly, those who deny that America has declined believe it can continue to shoulder substantial military and diplomatic commitments. Since the United States could afford to devote 10 percent of its GNP to national security during the 1950s and 9 percent during the Kennedy administration, it can certainly spend 6.5 percent or perhaps a bit less now that the Cold War is over. If the deficit eventually must be cut, a one-third reduction might be effected simply by imposing, say, a higher tax on gasoline. And as Valéry Giscard d'Estaing, the former president of France, commented to the *Wall Street Journal*, "It's hard to take seriously that a nation has deep problems if they can be fixed with a 50-cent-a-gallon gasoline tax.''

A subgroup within the second school accepts part of the ''decline'' thesis but believes that the argument has been carried too far. Princeton's Aaron Friedberg, for example, contends that military spending was not responsible for the decline of the great powers of the past. At worst, defense burdens accentuated the problems of countries already facing economic weakness. Friedberg believes that increases in consumption or in social-welfare spending are at the bottom of most stories of decline, including that of the United States today.

OVERCOMING DECLINE

The third possible perspective on decline, and the one I hold, is that the United States *has* demonstrably declined but that it can and will come back.

The evidence of American decline is irrefutable. In 1929, well before it reaped the artificial advantage of victory in World War II, the United States claimed more than 43 percent of world manufacturing production. Today, it claims only 22 percent. Assuming no change in current trends, one can foresee a much less comfortable future for the United States than the one outlined by the Pentagon's experts in *Discriminate Deterrence*. Twenty years from now, Japan will be a close second to the United States, with the momentum to pull ahead during the decade of the 2020s. China will have ousted the Soviet Union from third place and will be growing rapidly. And if the European Community achieves its goal of thorough political and economic integration after 1992, it could challenge U.S. leadership. The resulting multipolar world will be a much more uncertain place than today's relatively simple world order. The result easily could be a return to the conditions of the 1930s: not necessarily war but momentous conflicts over trade and the creation of hostile tariff blocs. Only a continuously growing American and world market will prevent such economic conflicts.

A vast literature exists on what happens when a previously dominant economic power declines. Many scholars conclude that without a single leader, the international order founders. Rising challengers refuse to pay the costs—such as providing loans or markets to nations in distress—of keeping the international economic system open. The three or four successor nations tend to implement high-tariff policies, stunting world trade, as happened in the Great Depression. History is conclusive on this score: It is far better to have one large power at the helm of the international economy. The United States, however, may not be able to continue its leadership role. Even today, the United States and its closest allies in Western Europe cannot agree on many important measures of economic and trade policy. Will a triumphant Japan and a resurgent China feel any greater compulsion to reach an accommodation with the United States 20 years from now?

In the future, it will take a higher U.S. growth rate—an eminently attainable 3 percent or more per year—and a dynamic American marketplace to convince others that they need to respond to U.S. policies and open their economies to foreign trade. To achieve faster growth, however, there must be a massive change in American priorities. National security must be redefined to include the strength and productivity of the economy, which is after all the base on which military capability rests. Some budget savings from reduced U.S. commitments overseas—plus, perhaps, domestic budget cuts and tax increases—will be needed to promote an economic resurgence that will eventually allow the United States to return to its leading role on the world stage.

If American fortunes are to be revived, the nation's leaders will have to challenge Americans to renounce the ethic of ''borrow and spend.'' Special incentives ought to be extended to Americans who save for retirement or for the education of their children. Rampant inflation during the 1970s schooled a generation of Americans to buy rather than save, to borrow rather than invest. History suggests that great civilizations have been fatally weakened through such self-indulgence. David Landes, the great historian of the Industrial Revolution, rendered the pattern in generational terms:

> Thus the Britain of the late 19th century basked complacently in the sunset of economic hegemony. In many firms, the grandfather who started the business and built it by unremitting application and by thrift bordering on miserliness had long died; the father who took over and, starting with larger ambitions, raised it to undreamed-of heights, had passed on the reins; now it was the turn of the third generation, the children of affluence. . . . Many of them retired and forced the conversion of their firms into joint-stock companies. Others stayed on and went through the motions of entrepreneurship between the long weekends; they worked at play and played at work.

The pattern Landes describes sounds eerily familiar. Great Britain went through its decadent phase during the Edwardian period, before World War I. The United States appears to have entered a similar phase today. Financial strategies maximizing short-term profits replace the long-term goals of increasing industrial competitiveness and market share. The industrial pioneers' ethic of hard work and team effort degenerates into the selfishness and conspicuous consumption of the grandsons and granddaughters. In sum, if critics of the contemporary American situation are correct, the United States has now entered a well-nigh irreversible decline.

But pessimists, even historically trained ones, are not always right. Nations can decline and rise again. Both Germany and Japan appeared to have reached their economic summits during the 1930s. Yet, after sharp declines, both experienced a remarkable renaissance after World War II. Tsarist Russia reached a major economic peak in 1913, but Stalinist Russia grew rapidly through the late 1920s and 1930s. True, Russia had to experience a revolution and Japan and Germany had to be defeated in war to trigger the economic transformation. And it also seems to be true that no declining power of hegemonic rank has ever made a real comeback. Spain, Holland, and England never came close to regaining their former status.

A UNIQUE CASE But with the possible exception of Russia, none of these nations was a continent-sized power endowed with enormous resources and a large, well-educated population. None, including Russia, possessed, as the United States does today, a vast and sophisticated industry and the ability to create technology of the highest order. Despite certain parallels with the past, the United States remains in a distinctive position. No hegemonic state in other periods of history remained far ahead of its competitors in the total production of goods and services. None of the imperial predecessors had almost unlimited investment funds available through the contributions of other nations. No other state was dominant in research in pure science.

Furthermore, the United States, unlike its hegemonic counterparts of yesteryear, is bargaining to maintain its position. Britain failed to negotiate an opening of German or American markets at the end of the 19th century, when economic decay had begun to undermine British industry. Holland could not persuade Britain to reduce its prohibitive tariffs during the mid-17th century. The United States, however, in tough trade negotiations with the Japanese and others, has shown that it is not willing to offer an unlimited market to nations that are closed to American goods.

In history, it is traditional to chart rise and then decline. Historians have assumed that nations, like biological organisms, rise to power and then age and wither. But decline can be the prelude to rebirth. Indeed, for important

countries (though not yet for the greatest powers) decline and loss have frequently preceded economic revival. In *The Rise and Decline of Nations* (1982), economist Mancur Olson argues persuasively that countries need a jarring shock to free themselves from old habits and institutions and to regenerate growth. Countries that have not declined enough, that have not been subjected to the national shock of defeat and despair, have had more difficulty maintaining economic growth than those that have. Japan, West Germany, France, the "little dragons" of East Asia, and the small democracies of Western and Central Europe —these gained a powerful economic impetus from defeat and occupation in war. By contrast, Britain, Canada, Australia, New Zealand, and the United States—victors all—were not prodded to strive for economic resurgence and revival.

Rather, the victors chugged along on a curve of moderate military and tepid economic success, spending (in the British and American cases) large amounts on arms and ultimately enfeebling themselves. The worst outcome of a challenge, therefore, is an expensive but narrow triumph.

Victory in two world wars sanctioned a history of indolent economic efforts and impaired social progress in Britain. In the United States, the Cold War failed to produce the needed reevaluation of economic strategies. (The loss in Vietnam was not a sufficient social shock; in fact, Vietnam was a reverse shock that caused Americans to become alienated from their government and to distrust authority.) The superpower arms race inhibited needed reinvestment in the civilian economy of both adversaries. In Paul Kennedy's words, military "overstretch" and heavy defense spending captured the very investment capital that was needed to regenerate economic growth.

THE QUESTION OF DEFENSE SPENDING

Yet the matter is not so simple, for military spending may not disable an economy if domestic consumption is held in check. This was undoubtedly the case in Britain's costly wars with Napoleonic France between 1795 and 1812, which did not shortcircuit the Industrial Revolution in Great Britain. Military spending may even spur industrial growth if there is a great deal of idle industrial capacity. It was chiefly through rearmament outlays, not New Deal social spending, that President Franklin D. Roosevelt finally got America out of the Great Depression. The surge of defense spending during the Korean War did not create inflation or divert civilian investment; it reversed the recession of 1949 and stimulated a boom. Likewise, there appears to be little question that military spending under the Reagan administration helped lift the nation out of the recession of 1981–82.

Excess capacity and civilian consumption, then, have to be included in any account of the effect of military spending upon economic growth. In Britain during the first half of the 19th century, investment and savings remained very significant, while consumption was modest. After mid-century, however, investment began to decline and the British economy was propped up by increased consumption. Military spending was not destructive because from the Crimean War (1854–56) until the very end of the 19th century (with the Boer War and the beginning of the naval race with Germany) England did not need to re-arm. Its navy was antiquated but still much larger than that of any possible foe, and its overseas empire was quiet, needing little policing. Even after 1897, there was no initial disadvantage because England had excess capacity remaining from the depression of 1873–96. It was not really until World War I that military spending displaced civilian investment. And it was not until the 1920s, and particularly the 1930s, that British governments began to worry about the trade-off between military preparedness and industrial rejuvenation.

BALANCE NEEDED All imperial powers have had to balance consumption, investment, and the costs of empire. During the early 17th century, the Spanish indulged in an orgy of consumption which raised the prices and wages. Military demands pushed inflation up more, but the remaining price increases stemmed from the inflationary effects of the vast inflow of bullion from Peru and Mexico. As a result, Madrid lagged behind in productive investment in new products. Spain's traditional wares—silk, textiles, leather, wood, wool, and iron—were priced out of their customary markets in Europe.

A century later, Holland imposed confiscatory taxes to finance its wars against Louis XIV of France. Prices surged, reducing the competitiveness of Dutch goods. In the later stage of the Dutch Empire, inflation encouraged lavish spending by the once somber burghers. Dutch merchants failed to reinvest sufficiently in the now less profitable foreign trade, preferring to send their money to London, where the return was higher. Meanwhile, the streets of Holland's towns and cities were filled with the destitute. In this phase, short-term economic profits for the upper and middle classes took precedence over building a strong national economy at home.

SAVINGS AND INVESTMENTS

Thus economic growth appears to require both heavy savings and investment, with consumption remaining at a relatively fixed share of GNP, and low military and foreign-policy outlays, except during economic downturns. Rising powers typically find these conditions easier to meet than mature ones. The rising power, however, eventually confronts either rival military powers or the necessity to provide consumers with rewards for their past sacrifices. If both occur at the same time, the nation is forced to deplete its productive assets.

When Great Britain was on the rise, its people invested and saved and aimed for long-term growth. As the British achieved preeminence, however, they began to yield to the temptation to relax and enjoy their position. Short-term returns became important to appease stockholders and investors and to minimize risk. Factory owners hung on to aging equipment and frequently neglected to make new investments unless they were justified by immediate profits. Thus, after 1870, British manufacturers spent less to create new products than did their counterparts in Germany and the United States. They did less to improve worker productivity, and they acquiesced in a less educated and less technically proficient labor force than that of their rivals. When they found fewer profitable investment opportunities at home they increasingly chose to send their money overseas.

This worked so long as foreign investments and the British money market provided for a balance-of-payments surplus. When those overseas investments were sold off to finance two world wars, however, Britain had to fall back on merchandise exports at just the time when its past comparative advantages were disappearing.

The first indications of decline showed up in productivity. At the peak of its economic power during the third quarter of the century, Britain's labor and capital productivity grew at the solid rate of 1.2 percent per year. For the next 40 years, however, it fell to only 0.4 percent. During the same period productivity rose by 0.9 percent in Germany annually and by 1.2 percent in America. Some economic historians have explained the dynamics of national decline by claiming that the "advantages of backwardness" accrue to rising economies, which can simply exploit the industrial lessons and technologies already created by others. This is no doubt true. But Britain during this period slowed down relative not only to its rising competitors but to its own past performance.

The failure to invest was complicated by conflicts between labor and management. Increasing unionization led to worker demands for higher wages and shorter hours. If these had been offset by higher productivity, there would have been no disadvantage, but they were not. Unlike some of its rivals, Britain did not offer enough incentives to improve the performance of labor. Under pressure to reduce costs, British managers were likely to trim wages rather than install labor-saving machinery. But wage reductions alienated workers and further reduced productivity.

NO INCENTIVES   The result was that the British worker was neither as well trained nor as motivated as his opposite numbers in Germany and the United States. Britain did not even introduce compulsory primary education until 1880. In steel and engineering, Britain tended to rely on the talented "tinkerer" rather than the trained engineer or scientist. The British generally confined their research activities to areas that would return an immediate profit, while German managers made painstaking efforts to discover and create new products in chemicals and other lines. Finally, British scientists and engineers were paid less than their American or German counterparts. At the Woolwich Arsenal, for example, chemists earned £100 a year, the same as workers.

Perhaps Britain could have compensated for deficient labor productivity with more investment. But after 1900 it sent an even greater proportion of its capital abroad. By the last decade before World War I, domestic investment had declined to 8.7 percent of GNP and more than 5 percent was invested abroad. At a time when the United States was devoting more than 21 percent and Germany 23 percent of GNP to investment at home, the British failure to reinvest was fatal.

How could this have occurred? Economic historian Arthur Lewis contends that the productivity of the British working man was already so much lower than that of his American counterpart that businessmen could not even make automatic looms, mechanical coal cutters, and other labor-saving machinery pay for themselves, at least in the short term.

Britain's inability to make headway in the markets of its principal rivals—Germany and the United States—confronted it with several possible responses. It could have moved to higher-quality products (enhancing profits); it could have tried to reduce costs (through labor-saving devices); or it could have directed traditional products to new markets. Largely, it adopted the third alternative. As late as 1870 Europe bought 42 percent of British exports, but by 1910 the figure had declined to 35 percent. Meanwhile, the total purchased by Africa, Asia, and Australasia rose from 29 percent to 43 percent. But this palliative would work only until Britain's competitors turned their sights on the same markets.

A fourth tack might have led Britain to innovate and introduce new industrial products. America and Germany were rapidly turning their attention to electrical appliances, automobiles, and chemicals. Like the United States today, Britain had initial advantages in many of the new technological fields of the day. The British made the essential discoveries in steel-making, but they often found that their designs were put into service by others. Britain built the world's first functioning electric power station, but America and Germany spread urban electrification more quickly and then applied electric motors to industry.

Ultimately, however, it was the cost of two world wars that destroyed British economic illusions. In the first great encounter, Britain was forced to borrow nearly two-thirds of war costs from its citizens and from the United States. This might have posed no problem had British exports remained competitive, but they did not. During World War I, Britain lost its primacy in shipping and textiles and had to sell off half its foreign investments. John Maynard Keynes managed the Treasury portfolio during the war with remarkable dexterity, but on February 22, 1917, he calculated that Britain's gold stock would not last "for more than four weeks from today." Only America's entry into the war saved Britain from bankruptcy. It was true, as Paul Kennedy wrote, that "The harder the British fought, the more they bankrupted themselves."

What does the British example tell us about economic ossification and decline? From 1860 to 1913, Britain invested too little in its home industry and consumed too much. The record does not demonstrate that military spending was the cause of British decline. Britain was failing to invest at German and American rates long before it was forced to divert funds from the civilian economy to rearmament. The war merely completed the process.

MAINTAINING MILITARY LEADERSHIP

Not surprisingly, the Dutch Empire, Britain, and the United States all confronted the twin problems of high consumption and large military outlays, though the sequence differed in each case. Holland had to fight Louis XIV on land and, for a time, Britain at sea. During World War I, England had the burden of maintaining its dominance at sea at precisely the .same time that it had to raise an expeditionary force to resist the German challenge on the continent. It did this carefully, always husbanding its forces and hoping to keep France at the forefront of the continental military effort. But the role left for Britain was still too much for it.

By comparison, the United States today not only seeks to maintain superiority at sea but also seems likely to try to keep a substantial force on the land in Europe despite the dissipation of the Soviet threat. The Iraqi challenge could even elicit a new long-term commitment of forces in the Middle East. Even with the reduced priority given to the Strategic Defense Initiative, America continues to aim at military dominance in space. Although the United States spent heavily on defense after World War II, U.S. decline did not reach exaggerated proportions until the defense-spending binge of the Reagan administration. That was because, even more than in the Vietnam War buildup, defense expenditure was not allowed to reduce civilian consumption but was financed by domestic and international borrowing.

INCREASE
IN DEBT

That strategy created no great difficulty for post-Napoleonic Great Britain, because the country maintained a solid surplus in its balance of payments. By contrast, during the 1980s American exports were allowed to fall well beneath imports, and there was no immediate way to repay the nation's growing foreign debts.

The timing of big increases in military outlays can be just as important as their amount. During the Napoleonic Wars, Britain restrained domestic consumption by raising taxes, while borrowing heavily to finance its military effort. By World War I, however, consumption was already too great. Civilian investment had to be sacrificed to pay for guns and soldiers. By the time the war was over, Britain had already lost many markets; it was nearly too late to redeem its industrial future.

The yet unanswered question for the United States is whether it can increase national savings and investment in time to achieve higher rates of productivity growth. Can America surmount the limitations that history seeks to impose upon great powers?

We have already seen that no truly hegemonic power of the past has ever been able to bring itself back. The powers that have made a return (such as Japan and Germany) did so under the beneficent protection of others. But history does not lend us enough perspective to predict the consequences of America's current condition. In certain respects our situation is unparalleled. The military load on the great powers of the past was never lightened. For the United States today, a reduced military burden seems possible if we can avoid a costly permanent commitment in the Middle East. Every earlier hegemonic power had to keep looking over its shoulder to see who might be gaining on it. Spain had to worry about France and the Netherlands; Holland had to contend with France and England; and Britain could not neglect the German challenge.

During the 1990s, however, the world will confront an entirely new situation. There is and will likely be no hegemonic successor to the United States. Though there will be military threats to guard against, as the Iraqi invasion of Kuwait reminds us, no single military challenger will be capable of wresting leadership from the United States. As America looks over its shoulder, the country gaining on it is not a great military power but rather a "trading state," Japan. There is no great and sustained territorial threat to the existing order. Thus the choices that world leaders faced in the past were different from those confronting the United States. In the past, the choice was to continue to struggle for primacy, with disastrous economic consequences, or to drop out of the great-power race. Every other great power has been forced to give up. The United States does not confront such a dilemma. It can continue, though in a slightly diminished role, because there is no combined military and economic challenger.

History shows that a shock usually is needed to bestir the complacent social and economic system of a great power. But there are several reasons to believe that a shock short of total war will suffice to arouse the United States. First, a major economic challenge in the form of a sharp recession is sure to confront the nation in the near future. Second, there is the challenge of foreign trade. In the past, other world leaders, particularly Holland and Britain, were major trading powers, but military preoccupations prevented them from fully pursuing their trading vocation. For too long, they limped along, attempting to combine their great-power role with a flourishing export sector. By the time they realized that they could not do both, they had lost their trading advantage. The Dutch even missed the first installment of the Industrial Revolution, thereby postponing industrialization until the late 19th century. Britain still has not regained the markets and market share that it lost in World War I. The end of the Cold War spares the United States a similar fate. Unlike its predecessors, it will increasingly be able to concentrate on foreign trade.

FOCUS ON
TRADE

At the same time, the international economic and financial system is now uniquely favorable to an American revival. Support for foreign trade has risen not only in the United States but around the world. Always before, there were major conflicts between countries in which capital was scarce and those in which capital was abundant. Broadly speaking, capital-abundant countries wanted low tariffs and benefited from expanding trade. By contrast, capital-scarce and land-scarce countries favored protectionism. As nation after nation (most recently South Korea) has entered the phase of capital abundance since World War II, dominant economic interests within these countries have also acquired an interest in low tariffs. This may well be the reason why there has been no general move to higher tariffs in the United States, despite the nation's vexing trade deficits. Certain sectors of industry have asked for and received relief, but Japan continues to sell 36 percent of its exports in the American marketplace. During the 1930s, the United States retreated behind high tariff walls; today, it remains in the international marketplace. And there are few greater incentives to modernize industry than the challenge of foreign trade.

In summary, given a major shock or stimulus and a favorable international environment, nations can alter a trajectory of decline. Resurgence becomes possible when the fact of failure can no longer be denied, and when new resources become available to finance an alternative strategy. Then the challenge to the national psyche shatters past assumptions and breaks conventional patterns of behavior. The chastened state can retrench and regroup, cut military spending and consumption, and dedicate itself to a new strategy combining industrial modernization and the expansion of exports.

To be sure, too great a delay in returning to such a strategy can do irreparable harm to domestic economic institutions, making it impossible to catch up. American scientific and technical research still sets the standard for the world. Major U.S. industries, such as civil aviation, chemicals, pharmaceuticals, computers, and software, retain their leading edge. But if there is to be an American renaissance, our national neglect of these assets must end soon. There are no mysteries about what needs to be done: Layers of bureaucracy must be stripped away from the public and private sectors; tax policies that encourage corporate indebtedness must be reversed; government deficits and other policies that raise the cost of investment capital must be erased; and it may be necessary for government to channel capital directly to industry. Above all, improvements are needed in American schools to keep U.S. workers competitive internationally.

There are two major reasons to be confident that the United States will regain its equilibrium. For perhaps the first time in modern history, international relations—in this case, international economics—is the stimulus to domestic change. In the past, international relations was governed by epoch-shaping events in individual countries—the French Revolution, the Bolshevik Revolution. Now the central realities are the rise of Japan, the archetypical trading state, and the paramount importance of international economic competition. As the Soviet Union, Eastern Europe, and China liberalize their economies, these new challenges are certain to spark a resurgence of American industry.

The new emphasis on economic competition will also create a more favorable environment for an American renaissance. Because the growth of one nation does not impede that of another (and may even aid it), the pursuit of economic growth will reduce international conflict, providing the United States with the opportunity to reduce its costly foreign burdens. The challenge of international politics becomes economics and foreign trade, not warfare. Under these new conditions, the decline of nations is no longer final. Great powers can recover and ascend.

Article 2. From Vermont, A Radical Blueprint to Reinvigorate American Democracy
by Frank Bryan and John McClaughry

This article assesses the state of American democracy, which, according to the authors, is in desperate need of reinvigoration. After chronicling the failings of the system—and reviewing several of the reform proposals advanced over the past twenty-five years—they propose a return to the roots of democracy. Their focus, in this article, is on the state of Vermont, which has launched a radical plan to increase citizen participation by returning political choice to the local level. This approach, which emphasizes local autonomy, has already begun to restore liberty, community, and democracy to the state.

Vermont was once thought to be the most conservative state in the union. It was one of only two to reject FDR's reelection bid in 1936. Now it's considered one of the most progressive—this fall Vermonters elected socialist Bernie Sanders to Congress and in 1988 Jesse Jackson claimed the largest share of the state's Democratic convention delegates. Is it Vermont that's changed or people's view of what's progressive? It seems that Vermonters' traditional emphasis on local autonomy now appeals to many on the left. John McClaughry (a Republican state senator and self-proclaimed conservative) and Frank Bryan (a political science professor) propose to take Vermont's tradition a few steps further with a radical plan to bring greater democracy to the state by dividing it into semi-independent political units called shires.

For all its inspiring success, the American dream still lies beyond our reach. America stands as a beacon to liberty, democracy, and community. But that tradition is under challenge from the forces of centralized power—both big government's indifference to individual people's needs and big business' willful disregard of people's welfare. ■ Elections—the pulsing heart of American democracy—have become empty, even disgusting, spectacles. National campaigns today are issueless soap operas feasting on scandals and trivia. Their language is the language of horse races and sporting events, with commentators awaiting the next play. Disgusted voters are opting out of the whole process. If the gross national product had fallen the way voter turnout has since 1960, there would be panic in the streets. In 1990, barely a third of Americans bothered to vote in Congressional elections. Most were disgusted with the entire political process. ■ Over the past quarter-century there have been many recommendations to save American politics, but they have been superficial, like giving smelling salts to a fighter whose legs have gone. We propose that American politics return to the roots of democracy. We propose that government look for a new model of politics that prizes citizenship. We propose to build a new, decentralized government structure that returns political choices to the local level, where more people can participate. As the place to build this new political process that will inspire allAmerica we suggest

Vermont. This green—old-fashioned and progressive at the same time—state may well become the place to show us how liberty, democracy, and community can be restored to American politics.

At the very time America's democracy seems most endangered, Vermont is well-positioned to demonstrate how it can be rescued. Vermont's politics are bubbling like early sap over a new-fired arch: Conventional two-party politics have become obsolete in the state. Last November, Bernie Sanders, an independent socialist, startled the nation by defeating the Republican incumbent for the state's single congressional seat. He's the first socialist elected to Congress since the 1940s. The state is

From *Utne Reader*, January/February 1991, pp. 50–57. Copyright © 1989 by Frank Bryan and John McClaughry. Reprinted from *The Vermont Papers: Recreating Democracy on a Human Scale*, Published by Chelsea Green Publishing Company.

brimming with non-party political organizations: the Vermont Greens, independent progressives, the American Freedom Coalition, the Rainbow Coali-

Vermont can't save the world, but it can save itself and by example show the U. S. how to regain democracy.

tion, the Vermont Republican Assembly. Two independent progressives won seats in the state Senate in November.

Vermont ranked second in the nation in supporting the independent presidential candidacy of John Anderson in 1980, and Burlington elected Sanders mayor four times. He has now been replaced by Peter Clavelle, elected on the same independent Progressive ticket. In 1988 Vermont, the whitest state in America, sent to the Democratic National Convention more delegates committed to Jesse Jackson than to any other candidate. Walter Shapiro, a senior editor of *Newsweek*, has written that Vermont's politics are clearly different and that what makes them different is not conservatism. Yet "liberal" or "left" doesn't exactly sum up Vermont's new politics either.

Vermont is physically in the past and technologically in the future. It leapfrogged America's urban-industrial period and landed smack in the Information Age. It is still green. Unfettered by the baggage of urban-industrialism and free of the problems associated with it, Vermont nevertheless is among the leading states on measures of technological advancement. Those who live here enjoy a blending of past and future. We can feel the spirit of earlier Yankee and Iroquois inhabitants. We can imagine the merging of old values and new technologies.

Vermont is an ideal setting, too, because it is still a governable place. With half a million people scattered over a granite wedge of field and forest about twice the size of Connecticut, it is small enough to be politically manageable. Vermont can't save the world, but it can save itself and by its example show the United States how to get its democracy back. Working things out in a small place first is far preferable to banging one's head against the wall in a larger system.

In Vermont, community still lives. There is no agreement, of course, on what is actually meant by the often-used term *community*, but some characteristics appear in nearly every discussion of the subject. Community generally means people who interact at a personal level; have shared identity, values, and traditions; sense an organic bond to one another; possess the power to make many decisions about their common lives; and feel a responsibility

for extending mutual aid to their fellows in need. Community, in its geographic sense, requires human

Aristotle observed that the scale of a state should not be so great that its inhabitants cannot know one another.

scale—a scale that human beings can understand and cope with. As Aristotle observed, the scale of a state should not be so great that its inhabitants cannot know one another's character. Most important, the preservation of community requires that decisions about things that matter be made by the people affected.

In Vermont, as in the rest of the country, the idea of community has recently been weakened by trends toward centralization, mobility, mass culture, and social disintegration. But even so, Vermont remains the first place in America to go for those seeking to discover and preserve what remains of authentic community life in the 20th century. The hills are still alive with the sound of town and village, of neighborhood, corner, and place.

Vermont has largely maintained its democratic institutions. The state legislature is large and nonprofessional. Fewer than 10 percent of its members are lawyers, one of the lowest ratios in America. The judiciary has maintained its tradition of including citizen "side judges" on the bench. The most important institution of Vermont's democracy, however, is town government. Two hundred thirty-six of Vermont's 246 units of government are towns in which the "executive" is a three- or five-member board and the "legislative branch" is the legendary town meeting.

To combat giantism, preserve our liberties, reinvigorate our democracy, and reunite our communities, we propose the creation of *shires* throughout Vermont—new units of local government to which most of the powers of the state will be handed over. The shires—a name borrowed from the small-scale governing units of Old England—will allow people an accessible forum to express their most heartfelt ideas on community needs.

To achieve this, Vermont must change more radically than any other American state has ever changed. The state government will become unrecognizable by present standards. While the authority for laws that must be uniform (environmental and civil rights regulations, for example) will continue to be administered on the state level, the great bulk of spending programs (education, welfare, mental health, and even roads) will be handled by the new shire governments.

These shires are not designed as *more government*. They will represent the same amount of government we have now, but redistributed from Montpelier (our capital) to St. Johnbury, Rutland, Wilmington, Canaan, etc. We want more democracy in the government, not more government in the democracy.

The shires will be independent political units, accountable directly to their own people. They will be governed by a body elected by the people, and each one will have an independent revenue base that is adequate to its needs.

These new shires will embody many key principles of democracy, many of which are currently missing from U.S. government at the local, state, and national levels.

•Government efficiency must never be pursued in a way that inhibits input from local citizens. All too often, when democratic control conflicts with plans for administrative efficiency, democracy is *automatically* precluded.

•The size of governing bodies must be permitted to float free and seek its own best level. At present, governments are encouraged (and often forced) upward in size but never allowed downward. The question of whether a locality is *big* enough to provide a welfare *system*, for instance, must be changed to this: Is the unit *small* enough to provide the human *context*, without which attempts to care for the needy fail due to bureaucratic depersonalization?

•Democracy depends on people well-versed in the principles of citizenship. These can only be learned through taking part in human-scale institutions. Direct democracy is a requirement, not a luxury.

•Subdividing policy-making institutions into a multiplicity of one-purpose bodies (school boards, solid-waste authorities, planning commissions) creates a puzzling web that discourages people's participation. Democracy is lost to the tyranny of complexity. The size of jurisdictions must be reduced to the point where the connections between, say, highways and schools become understandable and manageable.

This decentralized political system abandons the way of government currently in favor: education by standardized tests, welfare by mailbox, police protection by radio, and health care by strangers.

The power of the state and national government as the protector of the environment and guarantor of basic civil rights and liberties will be preserved. There is also a need for state presence in other concerns that transcend local boundaries, such as transportation, disease control, information gathering, and technical assistance. But even in

areas such as transportation there should be a substantial shift of power to the shires. If when

To reinvigorate democracy we propose the creation of new small-scale government units called *shires*.

traveling through Vermont one encounters variations in the quality of the roads, that is the price one pays for democracy.

In all areas where lawmaking is shared between state and shire, the *administration* of policy should be at the shire level. In this way citizens will be required to do the *work* of government as well as make the decisions. An example of how this might work would be the creation of a new local post in most communities—the environmental constable, a local citizen with the power to poke around the shire and make sure laws designed to keep the countryside clean are being obeyed. With the shires in place, a whole range of administrative services now run by the state will become the work of local people.

Beyond the emotionally satisfying activity of self-government itself, several steps can be taken to establish a strong community identity in the new shires. Foremost among these steps is the creation of shire symbols. In front of the shire's public buildings, its assembly halls, town halls, schools, and community centers, will fly the unique and colorful shire flag. The shire colors will be emblazoned on its road signs and on the shirts of the shire athletic teams.

Symbols of proud local history will abound. Each shire will have its monuments to commemorate shire residents or even sad events in the shire's history. Small corner parks or crossroads commons will bear the names of citizens distinguished for their learning, achievements, or long service to the shire community.

We hope that shire citizens will enthusiastically volunteer to hold positions of civic responsibility or community self-help. It might be as an apprentice to the pound keeper, or as a trumpeter in the shire band, or manager of the shire computer bulletin

If the gross national product had fallen the way voter turnout has, there would be panic in the streets.

board. It would not be compulsory for a new citizen to choose a mode for making a contribution to the shire, but it would be expected that he or she do so.

With domestic affairs returned to the people in their shires, Vermont's state government will be free to address the other issues that must have its attention in the coming century. The *range* of state government activities will be drastically curtailed, but not necessarily the *amount* of activities. The new state government—crisp, efficient, and innovative—will maintain the purity of the environment, establish Vermont as a new actor in global affairs, and help coordinate relations among the shires, and between the shires and itself.

A new Agency of Vermont Affairs will take bold steps to increase Vermont's influence—including its emphasis on decentralized government—beyond its own borders. Within this agency, the Office of Global Involvement (OGI) will administer policy set by the state legislature in world trade, international cultural exchanges, technology sharing, and initiatives to promote world understanding and development. A prime responsibility of OGI will be the management and expansion of programs like Vermont's people-to-people project with Honduras, begun many years ago.

As Vermonters restore their liberty, community, and democracy, perhaps others can learn from us. Our dream is that Vermont will meet its own challenge and thereby provide the nation with the hope it now so desperately needs. ∎

Article 3.   The Warrior State: Imposing the New Order at Home
by Andrew Kopkind

Fresh on the heels of a massive foreign policy triumph in the gulf, many observers believe that the time has come to wage a similar attack on the problems that grip American society. According to the author, the nation should take little comfort in the Iraqi campaign. It is one thing to liberate Kuwait, it is quite another to create a more just society at home. Although the war model boasts its own rationale, it cannot and will not work at home. A free society, warns the author, can ill afford to choose command over participation, obedience over agreement, hierarchy over equality, repression over liberation, uniformity over diversity, secrecy over candor, and propaganda over information. The nation must avoid the temptation to apply the dictates of war to the problems of a democratic society.

War creates consent. The best wars—those that are fought decisively, are won quickly and cost little—deliver so much approval to those who wage them it's a wonder strong leaders allow so much time to pass between campaigns. And in the case of the United States, they don't. America has been in a state of war—cold, hot and lukewarm—for as long as most citizens now living can remember. The epic struggles against fascism, communism, nationalism and tin-pot tyranny have been used effectively to manufacture support for the nation's rulers and to eliminate or contain dissent among the ruled. Now, after a half-century of construction, the warrior state is so ingrained in American institutions, has so saturated everyday ideology, is so essential to prosperity—in short, is so *totalitarian*—that government is practically unthinkable without it. And from the look of things, that past may be merely prologue to a future dressed in khaki and marching in lockstep.

The late gulf war was a paradigm of modern militarism mobilized in the service of political command. The *casus belli* may have been Iraq's invasion of Kuwait, but the context was a long history of ambiguous military engagements as well as the current paralysis of U.S. government. The malignant post-Vietnam syndrome (disease metaphors recur in political discourse like a stubborn fever) was as much on the war planners' minds as the threats of Saddam Hussein. The enemies within and without were targeted for ordnance or propaganda, whichever was appropriate.

From the start, the multistage and richly layered U.S. response in the gulf was strategically directed against the syndrome and all its symptoms: anti-interventionism, progressive political action, black and minority alienation and separation, Third World solidarity consciousness, radical environmentalism, cultural "permissiveness," feminist and gay activism, class and labor demands—all those movements, tendencies and patterns of thought and behavior that seemed to take hold in the American civitas and psyche from the Vietnam era. Victory in the gulf was supposed to produce the kind of harmony and unanimity that had not been seen in America since World War II—a model in many ways for this desert battle.

But there were pressing failures on the home front last summer as the gulf was simmering. The pathetic performance by both the Bush Administration and Congress during the long budget negotiations convinced many die-hard democrats that the political system of their dreams didn't work anymore in the real world. Talk shows and Op-Ed pages were full of discussions about the "excess of democracy" that had led to political paralysis. President Bush's popularity plummeted. Several states held referendums on limiting the terms of public officials, and voters in California and Colorado passed them with relish. Vice President Quayle rode the limitations idea for the Republican right and Bush endorsed it at the opportune moment, his favorite time of day.

What better antidote to excessive democracy, then, than war—its absolute antithesis? War implies command rather than participation, obedience over agreement, hierarchy instead of equality, repression not liberation, uniformity not diversity, secrecy not candor, propaganda not information. And the war state is so much more *efficient* than the quasi-democratic model practiced here, with its paralyzing quarrels, its contentious factions (also known during recent election campaigns as "special interests"), its occasional ideological loop-de-loops and its famous bad bargains.

"One reason the war was so popular," Vermont's Independent/Socialist Representative Bernie Sanders said recently, "was that something real happened over there—the military mobilization, moving half a million troops in a few weeks or months, was staggering; the war was fought quickly, effectively. Contrast that with politics, where you can't do anything, where nothing real seems to happen. And especially with last October, when the political structure was seen to be unmovable."

What's more, the war allowed Bush to clear the national political forum of all arguments that interrupted his monologue before the American people. There would be only one item on the agenda. The budget debacle was dismissed. The S&L mess disappeared. Civil rights, child care, drugs, health and education, recession and economic competitiveness were dropped for the duration. Yellow ribbons replaced democratic dialogue. The media defined the good fight and then enlisted as loyal lieutenants of the warrior *kommando*.

Of course, much of Bush's success in waging war and managing consent was dumb luck. As someone wrote last winter, "Even a blind pig will finally find his feed." Saddam was an unambiguous villain, a stupid strategist, an incompetent statesman—and a military weakling, whose vaunted arms and armies were never a match for those of the world's sole surviving superpower. It didn't matter that the air war took longer and did less than was expected, or that the heroic Patriots sometimes hit Scud rockets and let the lethal warheads get through. The doctrine of overwhelming force allowed for a large amount of wasted weaponry and effort.

But luck wasn't all Bush had. Since Vietnam the U.S. military has indeed been learning its lessons and perfecting its management, and not only in the artistry of death. The Pentagon's public relations campaign—of which straightforward press censorship was only a small part—has yet to be fully exposed, but when it is, we will see how brilliantly the propagandists performed according to plans drawn over a decade. Every P.R. ploy was planned and executed like—well, like a Republican presidential operation in the age of Deaver, Teeter and Hill and Knowlton. This time, there would be no media-dumb generals blinking at cameras and lamely discerning lights at the end of tunnels. Heeeeere's Stormin' Norman! Color! Laughs! Emotion! Home video sales (forty-five minutes of the general's "final briefing") are brisk.

Even before the 100-hour ground rout and subsequent cease-fire, admirers of the gulf campaign began to think about ways to bring the war home. If America could be so successful in the desert (and in the P.R. effort), why not harness those arts and crafts to domestic affairs? A key document was provided by Anthony Cordesman, ABC's on-camera android for strategic affairs. Square-jawed, tight-lipped and broad-shouldered, wearing clear aviator glasses that somehow seemed molded to his face, Cordesman looked as if he was chiseled from a mountain somewhere out West and wheeled onto the set of *World News Tonight* for his electronic chalk-talks and chilling military scenarios. On February 28, he dipped into print with a *New York Times* Op-Ed celebration of "America's new military culture," with its "implied . . . new civil-military relationship." In other words, America had won because politics was no longer in command—the warriors had taken over.

Cordesman worried that the wimps and appeasers and pound-foolish cheapskates in Congress would cut military spending after the war and thus throw the civil-military relationship off kilter. He did not, however, finish his thought. Money is a good way to keep the military in power, but it is not sufficient to militarize the entire political structure, to extend the combat culture to the social sphere. To accomplish that, heavy ideological work is required—starting, perhaps, with the destruction of the opposition (*any* opposition) as a legitimate political force. Republican water-carriers started that process while the bombs were still falling. As Bush made a show of bipartisanship and political generosity, the President's men tore into Democrats who had voted in January to postpone the shooting war. The media did their best to marginalize the antiwar movement (no big deal) and to bring the emotions of patriotism and militarism into every home with nonstop blather about our boys and girls at the front. Peace protesters never got their point across that the best way to protect our troops was to bring them home, for the goal was not protection but glorification.

Hovering over this landscape of authority, arms and ecstasy was a faint, familiar odor. "There's more than a whiff of fascism," Bernie Sanders said ruefully. More enthusiastically, columnists Rowland Evans and Robert Novak began to portray George Bush as a President from Valhalla: "There is something more," they swooned, "intangible and mystical, in the new relationship that now appears to bind the president and his country, affording him precious new strength." Further historical annotation seems superfluous.

For years there has been a small but influential intellectual lobby for limits on democracy. The Buckleyite, Birchist "New Right" of the late 1950s and early 1960s yammered about America as a *republic* instead of a *democracy*, and they haven't stopped yet—see columns by Pat Buchanan and his kind. They still awaken from nightmares of the French Revolution, with visions of mob rule and the tyranny of unpropertied classes. More sophisticated political scientists, many of them self-styled liberals on certain issues, became enamored of authoritarian rule when studying Third World development and "nation building." Democracy in corruption-ridden, slothful, underdeveloped lands simply didn't "work." Many of those types were designers of America's policy in Vietnam. In particular, Harvard's Samuel Huntington, widely known by his sobriquet "Mad Dog," is always pushing for more command and less participation (one of his favorite political parables involves the comparison of the efficient, military-run U.S. Military Academy with the sloppy, citizen-run neighboring town of West Point).

Bush's eagerness to criminalize Saddam, and his desire to bring him to trial, are part of the overall strategy of identifying the police and military functions of the state.

We will soon see how the mystical leader will use his precious new strength to impose a civil-military relationship—indeed, a new order—on his own country, as he says he will do for the rest of the world. It is not clear that America is ready for *Bushismus*. The elaborate antecedents of authoritarianism in the Axis countries before World War II, and in many Third World states today, are simply not present in the United States. There seems to be no historical logic nor, yet, an urgent economic need for a rigid new order.

But popular frustration is growing, and the structural faults in the political economy are widening. James William Gibson, author of the trenchant book on Vietnam *The Perfect War*, has been working on a new study about the post-Vietnam culture, with its "warrior dreams." He says, "This [the victory in the gulf] is the culmination of the dream, what we read in Tom Clancy's technothrillers that have been so popular, the rejuvenation of the system by high-tech systems. Well, they got it. It's a very magical time. Americans hope that this will return us to a pre-Vietnam past, that the wicked spell has been broken. It's another example of America being regenerated through violence. But how long can cheap oil prices keep the structural problems from coming to a head?"

An indication of what may be in store for the country came in early March, when Bush proposed that local police forces take a leaf from the gulf war book and "take back the streets and liberate our neighborhoods from the tyranny of fear." The Administration's crime bill that was then introduced would further emulate the style of war by eliminating a whole roster of civil liberties for "suspects" in criminal proceedings (i.e., enemy soldiers) and extend the death penalty as a way of institutionalizing state violence (i.e., indiscriminate bombing).

At the moment, such methods may be limited to minority ghettos at home and to Third World countries, while the middle classes and the elite enjoy the same kind of liberties they've always had. The show and threat of violence will still be used by America's leaders (mystical or mediocre) to impose order, only instead of communists the perceived enemy will be criminals—local hoods and international outlaws, like Manuel Noriega and Saddam Hussein. Bush's eagerness to criminalize Saddam, and his desire (now suppressed?) to bring him to trial, are part of the overall strategy of identifying the police and military functions of the state. There's a war on drugs, a war on crime and a war on international aggression. We are the world's military policeman. Los Angeles Police Chief Daryl Gates, who has instituted a repressive regime in minority communities as harsh as any police state in the world, is Bush's idea of an "all-American hero." According to the *Los Angeles Times*, Bush recently recalled that he stood with the Chief last year "looking out over a neighborhood where they reclaimed their streets, their kids, their future." So now may he stand with General Schwarzkopf, looking out over another neighborhood in the sand, where the U.S. world police have imposed another military reclamation.

The ghettos may be ungovernable now except by faux fascist methods, but the "talking classes" will not feel the jackboot or the lash until the need arises. Prosperity is a good guard against repression. But here the experience of war may not be so productive. Although in relative terms the gulf expedition cost little (one analyst thinks the Pentagon may "break even" on the operation, what with third-party contributions, creative bookkeeping and inventory depletion), over the long term it is part of a prescription for decline, not renewal. While America's competitors (Germany and Japan) continued to build their productive economies, America turned again to military concerns. If such tendencies persist and the policy managers go into world policing in a big way, any hope for economic reconstruction must be abandoned.

America learned that it can do war well. The temptation now is to apply that skill to areas where, of late, it has done poorly: the development of a prosperous, lawful and just society. That is precisely where militarism would be disastrously inappropriate. This may be a magical time for the warrior dreamers, but it is a moment of maximum danger for everyone else. □

Chapter 20

Making a Difference

Article 1. Squatter's Right
by Katrina Willis

The author describes the feisty exploits of Myrtis Clark, a thirty-seven-year-old woman from New Orleans who, after she was evicted by her landlord for complaining about a disagreeable neighbor, obtained a list of vacant government-owned houses on which she was eligible to bid. Aware that her next move was illegal, Clark picked a house that had been boarded up for two years, removed the planks from the dwelling, and staked her claim as a squatter. The author chronicles her struggle to buy the house, her skirmishes with the management firm that represented the Resolution Trust Corporation (which was charged with selling the house), and her unsuccessful battle with the RTC, which sold the house to another low-income family. The article explores the problems that many poor people face in attempting to buy affordable housing from the RTC.

New Orleans, La. —Eighteen years of moving from apartment to apartment, at the mercy of capricious landlords and real estate agents, had taken its toll on 37-year-old Myrtis Clark. When her last landlord evicted her for complaining about an abusive neighbor, she decided she'd had enough. As a member of ACORN, a grassroots organizing group, she obtained a list of vacant government-owned houses that she was eligible to bid on. Her next move was calculated — and illegal. On October 13, 1990, with the backing of ACORN, Clark tore the planks off a house that had been boarded up for two years and staked her claim. Clark had become a squatter.

With the help of friends and neighbors, Clark got down to work on the house, long ravaged by time and vandals. A dry-wall finisher by trade, she spent months hammering up holes, gutting internal walls, replacing gyprock and broken windows, and ripping out ceilings to expose the rafters for a light, airy look. The interior of the small woodframe house was a riot of planks, nails and cartons, out of which Clark fashioned a place she could call home.

Tall and slim, Clark stretched out her long legs as she sat at her kitchen table on a warm fall day last November. The drone of lawnmowers drifted through the open window. Clark had already been accepted by her neighbors on Pauline Street, located in a modest, quiet, predominantly black part of New Orleans. They were pleased to see the place occupied after standing vacant for two years. Ugly boards no longer covered the doors and windows, and the small lawn was neat and tidy. More important, the house no longer stood open to drug dealers, as did other abandoned houses in the neighborhood.

Clark felt lucky. "There are so many people who would love to move in and have a roof over their heads," she said. "I need this place. If I didn't have it, I'd be out in the street."

Uncle Sam, Realtor

The house Clark occupied is owned by the Resolution Trust Corporation (RTC), the massive federal agency created by Congress in August 1989 to sell off assets from hundreds of failed savings and loans. Now the largest real estate dealer in the world, the RTC says it has tried to sell properties as quickly as possible without disrupting the real estate market. It has been roundly criticized, however, for handing over many valuable assets to large financial institutions at bargain-basement prices, even *paying* some banks to take deposits worth millions.

By the time it's over, the bailout of the S&L industry is expected to cost every taxpayer at least $14,000. Even worse, the bailout is doing little to hold the industry accountable to its original purpose: helping ordinary Americans buy their own homes. As unemployment and real estate costs soared during the past decade, home ownership plummeted and homelessness reached crisis proportions. Many S&Ls, meanwhile, gambled deposits on junk bonds and other risky investments.

Pressured by the Financial Democracy Campaign, a national coalition of church, labor, and citizen groups like ACORN, Congress ordered the RTC to help ease the shortage of affordable housing by marketing its 37,000 residential properties to those who need them most. The agency has a clear mandate to offer discount prices and special financing to low-and moderate-income homebuyers like Myrtis Clark, and to non-profit groups like ACORN.

But in its first year and a half in the real estate business, the RTC has dragged its feet on affordable housing. Although the agency has given big investors cut-rate deals on real estate, it has shown little interest in providing discounts and seller financing for low-cost homes.

From *Southern Exposure,* Spring 1991, pp. 52–55. Reprinted by permission of *Southern Exposure* magazine, published quarterly by the Institute for Southern Studies, P.O. Box 531, Durham, NC 27702.

The result? "Untold thousands of eligible properties have been sold to speculators," says Tom Schlesinger, director of the non-profit Southern Finance Project based in Charlotte, North Carolina. "Poor and middle-income homebuyers, housing non-profits and public authorities have been locked out of the market."

U.S. Representative Barney Frank of Massachusetts is even more emphatic: "I've never seen a program administered less sympathetically."

The human cost of RTC stonewalling is apparent in New Orleans, where an estimated 8,000 people are homeless in a city full of vacant homes. Sixty-one percent of the city is black, and the neighborhood in which Clark staked her claim — like most black working-class areas of the city — is dotted with abandoned houses owned by the government. Among them are comfortable homes, architectural jewels built a century ago by German immigrants and sheltered by hundred-year-old oak trees lining the streets.

The housing trouble began when the domestic oil crisis struck New Orleans in 1984 and forced many renting families to move in with friends and relatives to save money. Absentee landlords who had borrowed heavily from savings and loans to get cash for their investments suddenly found themselves without tenants, and with no means to repay their debts. By the end of the 1980s, banks and S&Ls had foreclosed on many homes. Street after street was blighted by boarded-up homes falling into disrepair. New Orleans, the city never too poor to party, was looking mighty ragged.

Then the savings and loan crisis hit. Dozens of S&Ls failed, throwing hundreds of homes into the hands of the RTC. Only Texas suffered more than Louisiana, where, as of last September, the RTC controlled 19 failed S&Ls with $2.4 billion in assets. The agency lists 727 residential properties in New Orleans, all but 83 of which qualify for the affordable housing program. To date, only 10 properties in the city have been sold under the program.

Today almost every block of working-class neighborhoods in New Orleans is home to at least one vacant and vandalized property, ultimately owned by Uncle Sam. Sighs city housing official

Sheila Danzey: "Everything in New Orleans is 'for sale' or 'foreclosed.'"

HOME SWEET SQUAT

Despite the large number of vacant homes and the far larger number of homeless residents in New Orleans, few people have had the courage to simply take over abandoned houses. The day Clark began her squat, she recalls, the front door yielded immediately to reveal a dirty interior with broken windows and cracked walls. She placed a bid on the house with the RTC, hoping to have the $13,000 price tag reduced to account for the labor and materials she supplied.

Before long, an agent from the RTC's management company dropped by and asked Clark if she realized she was trespassing. The house was under contract from a buyer, he told her. She knew, she said. She was the buyer.

The agent told Clark that the police were on their way to throw her out, but a flurry of calls averted the move. Clark was permitted to stay, provided she take out insurance.

For Clark, squatting in the house meant more than asserting her right to a secure shelter. It was also an opportunity to help fix the damage done by wealthy investors who snapped up houses during the oil boom and walked away when times grew tough.

Indeed, the vacant houses left behind are drawing crime to neighborhoods where few people lock their doors. "Not too long ago one of the RTC houses on the corner was being used as a crack house, and a neighbor's little brother was robbed," says Sarah Dave, who has lived on the same street for 14 years. "Some city officials want to tear down the crack houses, but there are a lot of people here who would like to buy those homes. I really get upset, because the city wouldn't allow vacant houses like these to just sit in an elite neighborhood like the Garden District."

But those who need the houses the most may have the hardest time buying them. Seventy percent of New Orleans residents are renters, and 30 percent live below the poverty line. "We have a tremendous hidden homeless population — whole families of renters who have lost their homes and have moved in with

friends or relatives," says Beth Butler of ACORN. The federally owned properties could help ease the desperate housing crunch, she says, but the RTC has shown little interest in doing so.

ACORN, among the most active groups negotiating with the RTC, sued the agency last August for failing to live up to its affordable housing mandate. The group encouraged Clark to take over an RTC house to call attention to the federal footdragging — a strategy ACORN has used successfully in other cities.

Sitting in the Pauline Street house last fall, Clark was upbeat. ACORN officials, who were handling the legal dealings on her behalf, told her that the RTC had agreed to "freeze" all sales on the house and 99 other properties nationwide.

As neighbors dropped by, hearty New Orleans coffee with chicory brewed on the stove. Everything seemed fine. Still, aware of the uncertainty surrounding her acquisition, Clark hedged her excitement at the prospect of taking title to her own home.

"There is always that shadow that lingers when you're in negotiations," she said. "You just don't know what can happen."

"LANDLORD STATE"

With the risk involved in squatting, and the glut of rental property around New Orleans, why not give renting another try? Clark has an answer for that: If she buys her own home from the RTC, it will be the first place she will not face the constant threat of eviction.

Sitting amid a clutter of nails, tools, and furniture, Clark recalled the renting nightmare that drove her to squatting. "Everybody in my particular apartment complex got along fine, and then they moved someone in there who would beat his wife to a pulp," she remembered. "I was living right on the other side of the wall and would call and make complaints. Other neighbors would call, too, but the office didn't care."

When the man fired two shots at another neighbor, Clark called the Realtor and demanded action. She got it. The landlord evicted her, giving her five days to clear out of her apartment.

"I think I bucked the system too much," she said. "I was making too much noise about things."

When the landlord took Clark to look at another apartment, she couldn't believe her eyes. "The ceiling had literally fallen down, the cabinets were hanging, the place smelt like urine, the carpets were filthy — and he still expected me to take it."

Clark said such harsh treatment of renters is commonplace in New Orleans. "Renters don't have any rights. This is a landlord's state here; they have all the power. It's sad how they shift poor people around."

Clark said that she and her friends cannot buy their own homes because they don't fit the profile that banks require when making loans. "You have to keep in mind that you are in the Deep South. The people in power here are white and they tend to get the better jobs. It's hard. You don't make the money you do in California, New York. It's really hard to excel here and it's frustrating."

But Clark has not been discouraged. "If I get my foot through the door, it's going to open doors for other people. Right now, a lot of people are afraid to take the chance."

A DREAM DEFERRED

In the end, however, Clark's dream of owning the Pauline Street house proved short-lived. In early February, she learned that the RTC had decided to give the house to another low-income family. The agency evicted Clark, ordering her to clear out of the home she had made for herself. "I'm losing this place for good," she said. "It's so disappointing."

To add insult to injury, Clark said, ACORN officials had not called for weeks or offered to help her move. "I feel like ACORN didn't do its homework. They told me that everything was on track, that they had an agreement with the RTC. I assumed they were doing all the paperwork and had a written contract, and now I find out it was only a verbal agreement."

Beth Butler of ACORN said she was shocked that the RTC went back on its word. "A verbal agreement is binding in Louisiana. It was just unbelievable to us that RTC would sell the house to someone else, after the national officials had promised to freeze sales on that property." ACORN is trying to find another RTC house for Clark and has asked the agency to reimburse her for the time and materials she put into the property.

Muriel Watkins, coordinator of affordable housing for the RTC, said it turned out that the agency had received a bid on the Pauline Street house before it formally froze sales. "We want to provide low-income housing to people," Watkins insisted, saying the agency is working with ACORN to identify low-income buyers. The Pauline Street house, she added, is only "one property relative to all the properties ACORN is getting."

But to Myrtis Clark, the house on Pauline Street was more than one property — it was the chance to obtain her own home, and to reclaim a community asset. The obstacles she faced reflect the bureaucratic nightmare many low-income people confront in trying to buy affordable housing from the RTC. The nationwide cost of the agency's failure, like the cost of the S&L debacle itself, is borne disproportionately by the poor and middle-class, by people like Myrtis Clark — the millions of Americans for whom buying or renting a decent home is a fast-disappearing dream. ❑

Katrina Willis, a financial reporter, visited New Orleans while an associate of the Center for Investigative Reporting in San Francisco.

Article 2.   The Power of One
by Patricia Theiler

This article profiles the lives of four ordinary people, each of whom experienced a personal tragedy that transformed them into citizen advocates. It begins with **Wayne Bates,** whose brother, J. R., a railroad engineer for Southern Pacific, was blamed for a tragic accident he did not cause. In his quest to clear his brother's name, Wayne Bates became obsessed with railroad safety, to the point that he has been dubbed the "Ralph Nader of the Railways." **Bonnie Sumner** began her own crusade after her teenage son suffered severe injuries in an all-terrain vehicle. Sumner started monitoring the laws governing ATV sales and use, only to discover that her son's accident was not uncommon. She later became a lobbyist for ATV safety, testifying before a congressional panel on the subject. Unlike many citizen advocates who labor in relative obscurity, **Phil Sokoloff,** the multimillionaire founder and CEO of Phillips Manufacturing Corp., which produces metal fittings, became involved in 1985, after suffering a near-fatal heart attack twenty years earlier. He founded the National Heart Savers Association with $1 million of his own money, and launched a nationwide effort aimed at exposing the dangers of cholesterol and the foods that cause it. In 1988, his one-man association initiated a massive campaign, targeting by name food companies that used tropical oils, an ingredient high in saturated fats. Finally, there is **Mitch Kurman,** a retired wholesale furniture salesman who, for the past twenty-five years, has battled the summer camp industry, following the unfortunate 1965 death of his fifteen-year-old-son, who was killed in a boating accident. In the process of suing the YMCA, Kurman discovered what he considered to be a frightening lack of standards for summer camps, and has made camp safety a lifelong mission.

The papers are spread all over the kitchen table — transcripts of congressional hearings, countless letters and piles of accident reports marked with paper clips. The documents include a complaint about the Federal Railroad Administration lodged on the congressional General Accounting Office (GAO) hotline: "I indict the FRA for abuse of the public trust for their refusal to take action when presented with proof of improper accident reporting."

Wayne Bates, soft-spoken author of the complaint and outspoken critic of the FRA, thumbs through the documents. "I'm doing this for my country, for locomotive engineers and for my brother — not necessarily in that order," he says. A former electronic communications specialist for the U.S. Army, Bates, 68, has spent the last 12 years crusading for increased regulation of the railroads, citing evidence gleaned from his review of 500 accident reports from across the country. He has been called the "Ralph Nader of the Railways."

Bates's obsession with railroad safety began as concern over the FRA's handling of a 1978 accident involving his brother, J.R. Bates, who worked for the Southern Pacific. Bates was the engineer of a train that was heading from San Antonio, Texas, to Houston and collided with the caboose of another train on a side track. Bates's train derailed, causing injuries to his head, elbow and knee and more than $162,000 in damage.

As Wayne Bates tells it, the accident probably occurred because of a faulty green light — possibly caused by a sudden storm knocking out a signal. But the railroad blamed J.R. for the accident and fired him. The FRA backed up the railroad's finding.

After J.R. filed a grievance, a mediation board called on the railroad to reinstate him. In a separate trial, a jury awarded him $74,800 for his injuries. But, following heart bypass surgery in 1979, he was demoted, over his own and his doctor's objections, for "health reasons."

Patricia Theiler is a Washington writer and former managing editor of Common Cause Magazine.

Wayne Bates says the FRA has never fully exonerated his brother and he wants his "good name cleared — clean as a whistle."

In Bates's quest to clear his brother's name, he says he has found a pattern of flawed investigations by the FRA and unsafe practices by railroad companies that endanger railroad workers and the public.

Bates's opponents are more likely to characterize him as a Don Quixote tilting at windmills than a David packing a slingshot. But single-issue crusaders like Bates shouldn't be dismissed as dreamers. At a time when almost all conceivable interest groups — from the makers of chocolate to the consumers of packaged food — deploy sophisticated platoons of lobbyists, these lone warriors still play a vital role in the political process.

A personal brush with a senseless death or blatant injustice gives these citizen advocates a kind of credibility that can help them best an army of hired guns. And unlike many in the billable-hours world of professional lobbying, these self-styled citizen activists have plenty of time.

Motivated by belief in the justness of their cause, they may be willing to devote years, even decades, to exert pressure for change. They may sacrifice privacy, leisure time and family life to achieve results not for themselves but for the nameless others they believe at risk. Opponents may criticize their tactics and zeal, but it's hard not to admire their particular brand of persistence and courage.

PLEASE HOLD

Wayne Bates's interest in railroad safety grew exponentially as he looked into his brother's 1978 accident, then at accidents in San Antonio, Texas, and finally nationwide. "As I study the situation, I get more enthused," Bates explains.

A high-school-educated, self-described "country boy," Bates has mastered the art of filing Freedom of Information Act requests and reading between the lines of accident reports. He uses his findings to pound the FRA not only on his brother's behalf but on larger safety issues, such as railcars that are

overloaded or improperly carrying hazardous materials.

During the last Congress, Bates's documentation helped advance legislation to tighten weight distribution standards on railcars. The bill ultimately died but is expected to resurface.

Bates's activities have made him a familiar figure at the FRA. With a note of weariness, Mark Lindsey, chief counsel for the FRA, says Bates is "well known throughout the agency for making his views known," but hasn't brought "any major matters or great discoveries" to the FRA's attention that he is aware of. Lindsey defends the agency, which is small and has limited resources, as "responsible over the years."

Refuting this view of Bates is Lawrence Mann, a lawyer with the Railway Labor Executives Association, an umbrella organization for railroad unions and a Bates ally. Mann dubs Bates the "guru" of railroad safety and says he "has been a great assistance in uncovering [safety] issues." Mann says Bates is "a real thorn in the FRA because he's been so tenacious in holding them to the fire. He's been very effective — that's why they don't like him."

To say he's a thorn may be an understatement. The FRA's Lindsey says Bates's persistent barrage of letters and calls borders on harassment. "One day he tied up the telephone in the administrator's suite all day," Lindsey complains, adding that the FRA has "taken all the action we intend to take [on the J.R. Bates case]" and the matter should be dropped.

Bates claims he's merely doing what he has to do to get a response from slow-moving bureaucrats. If after 60 days he hasn't received an answer, from, say, J.W. Walsh, FRA associate administrator for safety, he starts calling his office. He may call three times a day until he speaks directly to Walsh. "If I don't get him, I call back," Bates says.

Bates's notoriety extends to the inspector general's office at the Department of Transportation, with which he has also frequently corresponded. This past May, Bates supplemented his usual phone calls and letters with a surprise visit. While waiting in the Transportation Department lobby, Bates noticed a number of people curiously poking their heads out of nearby doorways; staffers were trying to get a first-hand look at the man whose voice on the phone had become so familiar over the years. Finally, one official, perhaps emboldened by some vague sense of kinship, approached. "Are you Mr. Bates?" he asked. "I remember you from the 1981-Vulnerability-of-Assessment-by-the-FRA-study. . . ."

When Bates isn't on the heels of the FRA, he pursues two other hobbies that reflect his obsession with detail and sleuthing — genealogy (he's editor of a newsletter devoted to descendants of John Bates, who settled in York County, Va., in 1624) and ship reunions, an interest that developed after he and a fellow crew member spent three years tracking down all 400 shipmates of the destroyer they served on during World War II. "I got obsessed with the thing," Bates says characteristically.

It doesn't take long to get a sense of Bates's doggedness. During a single three-week period, he sent this reporter copies of more than a dozen letters from himself or the government, including ones he wrote on July 2, 9, 13, 23, 24 and 26.

"I'm interested in truth," he explains. "I'm interested in facts and figures, and I take pride in proving my facts."

LEARNING THE ROPES

The underfunded political weakling known as the Consumer Product Safety Commission (CPSC) is often the target of concerned parents, irate consumers, and health and safety professionals pushing for crackdowns on everything from hazardous stepladders to defective lawn mowers. A burn unit nurse recently drew attention to the dangers of children playing with cigarette lighters; a medical examiner identified an appalling pattern of infants accidentally drowning in five-gallon buckets; and an accident victim's father won a campaign to ban an outdoor game called lawn darts.

Then there's Bonnie Sumner, of Milwaukee, Wis., whose cause is the all-terrain vehicle (ATV).

Sumner became a critic of ATVs — three- or four- wheel recreational vehicles equipped with oversized tires — after her 14-year-old son Noah suf-

fered severe head, spleen, rib and facial injuries in a 1984 accident. "I literally didn't know what the thing was," says Sumner, whose son was hurt driving a friend's three-wheel ATV. Noah recovered, but following the accident, Sumner started tracking state and federal laws governing ATV sales and use. In the process, she discovered that her son's wasn't a freak accident but part of a pattern of serious injuries, particularly among children.

Sumner criticizes the continued lack of state and federal regulation of ATVs, which have been responsible for more than 1,400 deaths and thousands of accidents since 1982. According to ATV critics, the machines are especially dangerous because their high center of gravity makes it easy for operators to lose control or roll over.

Sumner plunged into lobbying at the national level when she was asked to testify at a 1985 congressional hearing. Back then, she had some trepidation, wondering, "Where do you sit? Who tells you what to do?" Now, after three appearances before congressional subcommittees, she's no longer nervous or unknown because, Sumner says, "I'm a pest." The label doesn't seem to bother her. It means "they're listening," she says.

In 1988, partly in response to pressure from consumer groups, health practitioners and others, ATV makers signed a complex agreement with the CPSC. The industry agreed to stop selling three-wheel ATVs and to prevent dealers from selling adult-sized four-wheel ATVs to children. But consumer groups challenged the agreement as weak and ineffective, claiming the industry was already phasing out three-wheelers. They also were critical because ATV dealers weren't legally bound by the agreement.

Subsequent studies have found that dealers are still encouraging adults to buy the larger models for their children. A 1989 survey conducted by the U.S. Public Interest Research Group (PIRG) found less than half of ATV dealers told potential customers the four-wheel vehicles were inappropriate for children.

Sumner supports not only a ban of three-wheelers but a government recall of ones previously sold. She also urges licensing and training requirements for users. Sen. Joseph Lieberman (D-

Conn.), a member of the Senate Governmental Affairs Committee, expressed support for the ban, recall and other measures during hearings in late July.

Sumner says her family has a long history of political involvement and activism on behalf of other people. "That's the way I was brought up," she says. She has "carried on a one-person crusade" in the last two Wisconsin state legislative sessions to win support for a bill that would ban ATV use for children, prohibit passengers and require helmets for operators.

It's clear that she brings a lot of energy to any task before her. Phone calls with this work-at-home mother of four are constantly interrupted by asides to her children, knocks at the door and clicks of her call-waiting signal ("that may be the CPSC"). While Sumner doesn't seem prone to excessive self-study, she says she's thought long and hard about her reaction to her son's accident and discovered that she "likes to be in control," especially when it comes to her children. Her crusade has allowed her to channel her anger toward a constructive goal.

James Baxter, executive director of the Wisconsin All Terrain Vehicle Association, says Sumner is "representative of parents of children who have been hurt and have a tremendous guilt complex because of it."

Wisconsin state Sen. Charles Chvala, sponsor of the ATV safety bill, says that Sumner's personal experience actually adds force to her arguments. He views her as "more rational than many people on the other side of the issue," who typically argue for personal freedom over the lives of children.

The emotional strain on Sumner, nevertheless, is high — whether it comes from painfully "having to retell and relive" her son's trauma or from having the memory rekindled when she hears of another accident. Because her advocacy work sometimes involves travel — she attended the PTA national convention in Indianapolis in July to successfully push for a resolution on ATVs — Sumner and her family pay a financial price as well.

Despite the costs, Sumner says, "I can't *not* do this. This isn't a job I'm going to quit." She now views her work as a calling, saying her commitment and personal experience uniquely qualify her to champion the cause. "No one else is doing this. If I don't do this, it won't get done," she says.

Lucinda Sikes, staff attorney with U.S. PIRG, says Sumner is an effective and articulate advocate and has more credibility than the average lobbyist. U.S. PIRG and the Consumer Federation of America have filed a petition asking the CPSC to ban ATVs for children and establish a mandatory safety standard for ATV stability.

Sumner is meanwhile buoyed by the small successes along the way. When one of her son's classmates volunteered that he and his parents decided not to buy an ATV after they heard her on local television, "that made my day," Sumner says. "I always think, if someone sees me and makes the decision not to buy [an ATV], I'm making headway."

MAC ATTACK

Most citizen advocates operate in relative obscurity. Not Phil Sokolof, the multimillionaire founder and CEO of Phillips Manufacturing Corp., which produces metal fittings. In 1985 Sokolof, who had suffered a near-fatal heart attack 20 years earlier at age 43, founded the National Heart Savers Association (NHSA) with $1 million of his own money. Since then, cholesterol and the foods that cause it to clog the arteries of Americans have been Sokolof's obsessions. ("I've been a workaholic all my life," Sokolof offers by way of explanation.)

In late 1988 his one-man association began a nationwide "Poisoning of America" campaign, targeting by name food companies that made their products with tropical oils, an ingredient high in saturated fat. The ads carried pictures of the offending products, including Pepperidge Farm Goldfish and Keebler's club crackers. Following the ads, a number of companies announced they would no longer use tropical oils.

Most of his targets say they were already converting their oils when the ads hit. Pepperidge Farm was reformulating its products eight to 10 months before the campaign, says spokesperson Tim Ouellette, and switched "in response to consumer demand," not pressure from negative advertising. But some industry experts give Sokolof credit for raising consciousness. "He has had a tremendous impact on

the industry," Joe Simrany, vice president of marketing at Sunshine Biscuits (makers of Hydrox cookies), told *Food Business* last year. "He's really stuck by his convictions. If he's to be criticized at all, it's for some of his tactics."

The silver-haired, pinstripe-suited Sokolof, who got his own cholesterol down to a healthy 150 compared to his pre-heart attack 300 level, obviously relishes the role of "America's No. 1 cholesterol fighter," an epithet used liberally in his press releases.

Because Sokolof has hitched his wagon to one of the trendiest issues of our time, he's generated more coverage of affairs of the heart than Donald Trump. Every phone call is another opportunity for him to gather converts. "Concentrate on pointing out the potential risk of cholesterol," he advised *Common Cause Magazine* at the end of a long conversation.

In April, Sokolof launched the "Poisoning of America, Part III" with plans for $500,000 worth of full-page ads in the *New York Times*, *USA Today* and other major newspapers. But the campaign hit a roadblock in the form of an American icon — the golden arches. Five major newspapers, including the *Los Angeles Times* and the *Chicago Sun-Times*, refused to run the ads, which charged that Big Macs had "too much fat" and criticized McDonald's for not cooking its French fries in vegetable oil. *Los Angeles Times* spokesperson Terri Niccum says the decision not to run the $30,000 ad was based on "legal" considerations (including the ad's use of the trademark golden arches) and "reasons of good taste." Niccum adds, "There were statements we believed were not true."

McDonald's spokesperson Melissa Oakley says there were a number of inaccuracies, including an incorrect calculation of the saturated fat in a burger and fries. A press release from McDonald's called the ad "reckless, misleading and intended to scare rather than inform. . . ."

"Was McDonald's mad about the ad?" the release asked. "Mad as hell."

Despite the Mac attack, on July 4 Sokolof struck again. In full-page ads in several national newspapers, NHSA charged: "McDonald's, your hamburgers still have too much fat and your French fries still are cooked with beef

tallow." The ads also criticized Wendy's and Burger King.

Three weeks later the three chains announced that their French fries would be fried in "cholesterol-free" vegetable oil. Any connection to Sokolof's media blitz? "The timing was coincidental," says a Burger King spokesperson. The switch was "in response to our customers' changing taste and lifestyle," adds McDonald's. "Our customers told us to," echoes Wendy's. Only Hardee's, which the July ad called "the industry leader" for already introducing a leaner hamburger and reformulating its fries, begs to differ. "Obviously he had some influence," observes a Hardee's spokesperson, who hastens to point out Hardee's switched two years ago, long "before Sokolof became the guru of saturated fat."

Sokolof isn't saying his ads were the sole motivation — he is quick to credit the fat-fighting efforts of the well-respected Center for Science in the Public Interest and others. But the ads "triggered the response of the public" in pushing for healthier fast foods, he says.

In contrast to the handwritten yellow "stickem" notes from Bonnie Sumner, Sokolof has a professional media kit, complete with a glossy black and white photo of himself, a "Poisoning of America" poster, several color reprints of articles in major newspapers and slick brochures on cholesterol.

Still, Sokolof claims he's "a little guy" when compared to the corporate giants he's battling. Referring to international press attention, he says, "Here I am in my office in Omaha, Neb., talking, literally, to the world. It shows one person can make a difference."

Despite Sokolof's maverick style, he's an old-fashioned philanthropist at heart. "I've been on two journeys," he told *Advertising Age* magazine. "On the first journey, I made a lot of money. On the second one, I realized that using that money on a good cause is better than making it."

THE NEVER-ENDING STORY

Most advocates operate out of spare bedrooms and basement studies on streets with names like Rocky Run and Lake Drive. News clippings and letters are stuffed in cardboard boxes or piled on desks in family rooms. Mitch Kurman of Westport, Conn., says you'd need a "U-haul truck" to move all the information he has collected.

For the past 25 years, Kurman, a retired wholesale furniture salesman, has battled the summer camp industry. In 1965 Kurman's 15-year-old son David died in a boating accident at a YMCA camp in New York. Kurman sued the YMCA and settled for $30,000. But Kurman's campaign didn't stop in court. When he discovered what he considered an appalling lack of state or federal standards for summer camps — among them no life preserver requirements for boats and no training requirements for camp counselors — he made camp safety his lifelong quest.

An estimated four to six million children attend summer camp. Regulation of the industry is largely left to the states, and only about 17 have licensing requirements, health and safety inspections or other standards.

"While there are excellent, wonderful camps," Kurman says, "there is also a very, very substantial number of downright dangerous camps," which don't protect kids against injuries from boating, riflery or other sports.

Kurman has been a crusader for so long that conversations with him are dotted with references to politicians of the past as well as names, middle initials and spellings of dozens of officials and parents he's encountered. He was initially able to build up his archives because of his work as a traveling salesman. Clients would pass on stories of accidents, and Kurman would make a detour to investigate.

In his stream of consciousness style, Kurman catalogs the dates, locations and details of tragic summer camp accidents — from drownings to sexual abuse — that he believes build the case for increased federal involvement in the industry. "This could happen to anybody," he says of his tragedy.

In 1971 Kurman helped win passage of a federal boat safety law, requiring manufacturers to post passenger capacity and safety features on boats. He also helped win passage of state laws in New York, New Hampshire and Connecticut requiring life preservers in camp boats. But Kurman and his wife Betty, whom he has enlisted as an aide-de-camp, have failed to catch the brass ring — establishment and enforcement of federal health and safety standards.

Kurman estimates he's spent $75,000 gathering information and visiting lawmakers. One letter from him included the practical request that the numerous articles, congressional statements and xeroxed letters be returned. In the same seven-page, handwritten missive Kurman admitted to being tired after having worked all night compiling a similar clipping file for a reporter doing a story for a small-town weekly. Despite the limited circulation, Kurman noted, his efforts "invariably have a snowball effect to bring me still more materials to prove the pattern of neglect that must be corrected."

"It's like a bone in your throat," says Betty Kurman. "He can't stop, and I can't either, until we accomplish what we want." While Mrs. Kurman concedes they have made sacrifices, their commitment also has built character. "I was amazed at the qualities that developed [in my husband]," she says.

Kurman had his 15 minutes of fame in the mid-1970s. He was profiled in the *New York Times*, put on page one of the *Wall Street Journal* and appeared on "Good Morning, America." Today he sets his sights closer to home, specifically the *Fairfield County Advocate* near Westport, Conn. Editor Jim Motavalli remembers reading about Kurman when he was growing up in the area. Now, says Motavalli, who recently wrote an article on Kurman, he "practically *lives* here." Despite Kurman's penchant for cornering busy editors, Motavalli firmly believes Kur-

man's "cause is just."

Justified or not, it's an uphill battle. As a 1989 GAO report notes, "Little information is available on accidents, illnesses and fatalities that occur in youth camps." Because the government doesn't require summer camps to file federal accident reports, Kurman says he's filling an important need by keeping files on "hundreds of cases."

Rep. Joseph Gaydos (D-Pa.), chairman of the House subcommittee with jurisdiction over the camping industry, says Kurman has done "yeoman's work on the issue" and "contributed valuable information." Nevertheless, Gaydos says the subcommittee concluded recently that the issue is "more of a state problem than a national" one and has no immediate plans to take action.

Kurman isn't likely to let one more politician deter him from the cause he's been fighting since he first persuaded former Sen. Abe Ribicoff (D-Conn.) to take it up in the '60s. "I would love to get this over with," Kurman says wistfully of his crusade, "I'd love to go back to my gardening, to my family. . . ." But Betty Kurman confirms it's unlikely the couple will let up any time soon.

A telling example of the grudging respect such dedication can stir even from adversaries comes from John Miller, executive vice president of the American Camping Association. Miller says that though Mitch Kurman is "misguided," he "has a very legitimate, heart-felt involvement in this issue."

"It's been Mr. Kurman, honestly, that keeps bringing this up at the federal level," inspiring repeated congressional hearings, GAO reports and newspaper editorials, says Miller.

Come now, Mr. Miller, can one person exert that much influence?

"When you're as single-focused and as committed as Mr. Kurman is. . . ," says Miller, "yes." ◆

Article 3. Minister of Justice
by Ted Rohrlich

Ted Rohrlich chronicles the efforts of Jim McCloskey, a clergyman and amateur detective, whose social conscience and moral outrage have led him to become an outspoken advocate of those wrongly convicted of crimes. A former business consultant, McCloskey gave up his $55,000-a-year job to study theology. As of today, his efforts have led to the release of dozens of inmates, several of whom were the victims of racial prejudice, perjured testimony, and witness intimidation. Despite the safeguards built into the legal system, McCloskey believes that one out of ten defendants whose cases go before a jury trial are wrongly convicted.

IN THE BASEMENT OF AN OFFICE building across the street from Princeton University, an iconoclastic Protestant minister is patiently searching through a box of files on a 17-year-old Los Angeles murder case.

The case was solved long ago to the satisfaction of the police and the courts. Two men were convicted and are serving life terms. But James McCloskey, the only full-time operative of Centurion Ministries, and not incidentally one of the nation's best detectives, thinks they are the wrong men. "This is a classic frame," he declares.

Finding what he was looking for in the box, McCloskey pulls out a letter written three years ago by one of the men.

"I've written numbers, numbers and NUMBERS of letters like the one I am going to write you now," it began. "I've written to newspapers, '60 Minutes,' NAACP, law firms, senators, '20/20,' Phil Donahue, magazines, the FBI, Jesse Jackson and other organizations trying to arrest someone's interest in my case, with hopes of getting them involved to the point of conducting a thorough investigation that would turn up crucial evidence to set me free.

"I couldn't have killed this guy . . .

"I was incarcerated in the custody of the L.A. County Sheriff's dept., IN JAIL!!! when this crime happened!"

McCloskey knows this sounds outrageous, but no more so than other similar claims that, astoundingly, have turned out to be true. A 48-year-old bachelor who considers himself a "radical disciple of Christ," McCloskey spends his days trying to redeem people who are not supposed to exist. They are the convicted innocent—people, who, because of police or prosecutorial mistakes or corruption, incompetent defense attorneys, faulty or coerced eyewitness identifications or simple juror misjudgments, are convicted of crimes they did not commit.

McCloskey calls his ministry Centurion after the Roman soldier who, the Bible says, was stationed at the foot of the cross, looked up and remarked of Christ, "Surely this one must be innocent."

He takes on only the most serious cases, involving people who have been sentenced to life imprisonment or condemned to die, whose appeals are exhausted or nearly so and who are too poor to hire investigative help.

Supported by scant contributions from foundations, churches and a few businessmen, Mc-Closkey promises the convicts that he will work for them, at no cost, until they are freed. But he also tells them he will abandon them in an instant if he discovers they have lied.

His extraordinary dedication and investigative skills have resulted in the freeing of eight men and women serving life sentences or awaiting execution for rape or murder in Texas, Pennsylvania and New Jersey.

His ministry is unique. And there is no secular organization in the United States that does similar work.

"He investigates like no one I've ever met," says Dennis Cogan, a leading Philadelphia defense attorney, "and I've come into contact with top-flight police investigators, federal investigators and private investigators. He's single-minded in his dedication, not taken in by a sob story and wedded to one thing—the truth."

Cogan helped McCloskey secure the release early this year of Matthew Connor, a Philadelphia man wrongly imprisoned for a decade for the rape and stabbing murder of an 11-year-old girl. The Philadelphia district attorney's office, which agreed to re-investigate the case at McCloskey's urging, wound up asking a court to free Connor, with the district attorney himself saying, "The evidence isn't there to say he is guilty."

Connor's release came during an extraordinary nine-month period in 1989 and early 1990 during which McCloskey obtained the releases of five inmates in three states.

One of them, Damaso Vega, was convicted of a 1980 murder of a teen-age girl in Monmouth County, N.J. He had stood in front of the trial judge who had sentenced him to prison for life in 1982 and declared: "I will eat a stone. I will eat dust. I will eat anything worse in the world for me to prove my innocence. I am not the man. I am innocent. I am not the man."

No one, of course, had believed him. But McCloskey dug up enough evidence to show that Vega had been framed by witnesses who had lied because of pressure from a detective. The officer had also hidden evidence that pointed to the guilt of another. Confronted with this new evidence, New Jersey Superior Court Judge Robert Figarotta said: "There are many aspects of this case which truthfully terrify me."

As for Vega, he says: "When I describe Mr. McCloskey, I always say the dictionary don't have words to describe how good is that man."

MCCLOSKEY, WHO usually smokes only when he is alone at night, needs a cigarette during the day to talk about his failures. In one case, he says, he had to give up when he was unable to turn up new evidence. In another, he became convinced that the man he thought was innocent was actually guilty. In the most disheartening, he lost a convicted murderer to the electric chair when the state of Louisiana decided to put him to death, despite new evidence McCloskey turned up at the last minute that pointed to his possible innocence.

In the Los Angeles case, the biggest frustration is not being able to prove conclusively that his correspondent was in jail at the time of the murder.

The murder occurred at 7 p.m. in the restroom of a South-Central Los Angeles gas station in 1973. Records show that Clarence Nathan Chance was indeed a prisoner at Men's Central Jail on the day of the murder, held on an assault charge. Records also show that the charge was dropped and that Chance was processed out of the jail downtown at 4:53 p.m. But no record has been found that shows how long it took for Chance to complete the processing and actually leave.

McCloskey tracked down the jailer who ran the tier on which Chance was housed, and the jailer recalled that pre-release procedures at the time would have meant an *actual* release anywhere from 45 minutes to four hours after 4:53 p.m.

If the procedures took two hours or more, Chance would not have had time to meet up with his friend, who was also convicted of the murder, and travel to the gas station to kill the victim—an off-duty Los Angeles County deputy sheriff whom he apparently had never met. But if the release procedures took significantly less than two hours, Chance could have had the time. The jailer who ran Chance's tier remembered Chance, who had been a trusty, but he could not remember how long the procedures took in Chance's case.

The issue of precisely when Chance was released was not explored at his trial. Chance's then-defense attorney, Charles Pope, says Chance told him he was released around 5 p.m., not that he was in jail at the time of the crime. But the transcript of the trial shows Chance saying, "But I was in jail when it happened. I was in the new county jail." Chance, who, at his lawyer's urging, did not testify, told that to the judge just before he was taken away to prison.

Because there is a possibility that Chance was released in time to commit the murder, McCloskey has focused on the way police built what even they admit was a weak case. The police, McCloskey says, used witnesses who told "such a concocted story it amazes me."

He began his investigation, as he does in every case, by making an exhaustive study of official records, looking particularly for witnesses' accounts that changed after repeated contacts with police. Such changes, he says, are often tip-offs that witnesses lied to get police off their backs.

After his study, he traded his customary sport shirt and suspenders for a black shirt and a clerical collar and hit the streets. "The collar can be a great door opener," he says. Then he "just parachuted in on" the witnesses—offering them a chance to redeem themselves by telling a lay minister the truth.

He found, as he often does, that two of the key witnesses, who said Chance and a co-defendant had confessed, were "broken human beings . . . absolutely alone in the world." They admitted to McCloskey that they had lied to police because they were frightened and wanted to say what the police wanted to hear. Over the years, they had told no one of their lies, McCloskey says, because "who would believe them?"

"Forgive me for sounding angry," McCloskey says as he recounts his findings, "but I am angry." He jabs at a table top with his finger. "I am [extremely] pissed when this happens!"

A former business consultant who turned to the ministry in mid-life, McCloskey has an easy way with people. He is a bald, round-faced man, with a double chin, a slight paunch and a hearty, ready laugh. But he says these kinds of witnesses "don't just plunk out the truth. They have to come to like you, respect you, trust you, know that you are well-intentioned and not conning them in any way." Then, he says, it is usually "a long, delicate walk" before they will tell their stories to a judge.

MCCLOSKEY'S MOST DRAMATIC breakthrough came in a Texas case, in which he was able to take a witness "back through the pain" of a police-inspired lie that put an innocent man on Death Row. McCloskey made sure he knew a lot about this witness—wiry, white-haired John Henry Sessum—by the time they met in early 1987 outside Sessum's two-room shack on the outskirts of Conroe, a small East Texas town.

Sessum was an alcoholic who had lost his driver's license for drinking. Every day, on his way home from his job on a highway road crew, he would stop to buy two six-packs of 16-ounce beers, put them in the wire basket of his bike, then peddle the 10 miles home.

Sessum, who is white, had been a key witness in 1980 against Clarence Brandley, who is black, in a racially charged murder case that had polarized the town. The murder victim was a 16-year-old white girl.

Days before fall classes started at Conroe High School, she had gone to the school to practice volleyball and had wandered off alone, apparently in search of a restroom. Her body was found a short time later. She had been raped and strangled.

The last people known to have seen the girl alive were school janitors—white janitors, including Sessum, who had been waiting at the bottom of a stairway for their next assignment. Authorities promised panicky parents that they would have the girl's murder solved by the time school started.

In a move a judge would later describe as "blind," they arrested Brandley, the only black janitor. Then they assembled Sessum and the rest of the white janitors for a talk. The white janitors, including Sessum, gave statements in one another's presence in which they said the girl had passed them and gone up the stairs to a restroom, that Brandley had then walked by and the white janitors had left.

The implication was clear. Brandley was the only janitor who could have been alone with the girl and killed her. Largely on that basis, Brandley was convicted and sentenced to die.

McCloskey had gone to Death Row to visit Brandley—he always visits inmates whose cases he may take—but was reluctant to become involved. Brandley already had advocates. A supportive family, lawyers and another private investigator were already working on his behalf.

McCloskey prefers to work alone for inmates who have no help. But he was impressed with Brandley and convinced that he was innocent. And Brandley's defense team convinced him that the case was stalled, with time running out.

McCloskey moved into a garage apartment at the house of one of Brandley's lawyers, where he studied the case's transcripts and police reports. He concluded that Sessum, who had once complained about the lead police officer's tactics, was most likely the weakest link in the prosecution's case. And with only 20 days left until Brandley's execution, McCloskey, along with Brandley's investigator, Richard Reyna, went to see Sessum.

They met him outside his shack. McCloskey remembers vividly because it smelled of urine.

"I said, 'John,'" McCloskey recalls, beginning in his slightly ponderous way, "'We think there's a good chance they got the wrong man. As you know, Clarence Brandley is going to be executed in two or three weeks. And we'd like to talk with you about whatever you might know about this.' We ended up standing in front of his house while he drank three or four 16-ounce cans of beers."

Then, after two hours of cat and mouse, Sessum made a stunning proposition. He offered to take McCloskey and the investigator to the high school and show them what had occurred. "I got chills," McCloskey recalls.

They met again, as agreed, in a few days. But when Sessum "got to the actual stairwell . . . [he] froze. He couldn't say a word." Later, at home, Sessum finally got a burst of inner strength and opened up.

He told how two of the other white janitors had grabbed the girl and dragged her off and about how he had stood by and done nothing, ignoring her pleas for help. "He said, 'I let one innocent person go to her death, and I'm not going to let two,'" McCloskey recalls.

But telling McCloskey that Brandley was innocent was not enough. McCloskey needed to get Sessum to tell his story to Brandley's lawyer on videotape, then to a judge. "It's like a sale now," says McCloskey. "You've got to close it."

McCloskey, Brandley's private investigator and his lawyer met at Sessum's house the next afternoon. The sale fell through. "John gives us a smile," McCloskey recalls. "'Come in.' We come into his shack. He turns the TV on. We all sit down on his bed. He goes into the kitchen and comes out with a butcher knife, and just says 'Get the [expletive] out of here!'"

McCloskey and the others left in despair but then thought of calling a friend of Sessum's—a neighbor who they thought might be able to calm him down. As it turned out, Sessum was already at the neighbor's trailer. "She convinced him to settle down, 'Nothing's going to happen to you. These are good people. If that's the truth, why don't you give a statement?'"

"We came back the next day and took a full 20-minute videotaped statement" in which Sessum said he had been intimidated into going along with the testimony of the other white janitors by the lead police officer, a Texas Ranger, McCloskey says. "He said the Ranger had told him, 'You go along with this or else you're going to jail.'"

"That's a common line. They're all afraid of the law. And they have absolutely nobody who they can confide in who will in any way help them." But why should anyone believe Sessum now? McCloskey's answer is to look at whether he has a motive to lie.

Perhaps he recanted, McCloskey acknowledged, because he wanted to be perceived as a hero. But "if he sees this as an opportunity to become the hero, why would he take a butcher knife and tell us to get out? Because, I'll tell you why, he's scared to death. He still doesn't want to do it. And why would he, sitting on the edge of his bed, have tears rolling down his eyes when he is saying to us that he's had nightmares all these years?

"His quote was, 'I guess I've got a little bit of the rabbit in me.' He runs away when there's trouble. . . . John Sessum had to stand up and tell a judge, TV cameras and an open public that he was a coward and let a girl go to her death without doing a thing. To me, there's a cost there.

"And not only that. He feels terrible for lying against someone he knows is innocent and sending him away to the chair. I mean, he's [Sessum] a human being. And this is a chance for redemption, in the most profound way."

A succession of Texas judges agreed with McCloskey. Sessum's videotaped statement was the beginning of the end of Brandley's troubles, leading to a stay of execution and then court-ordered freedom after 10 years behind bars. No one else was arrested.

After District Court Judge Perry D. Pickett reviewed the case, he called it an extraordinary miscarriage of justice. "In the 30 years this court has presided over matters in the judicial system," he wrote, "no case has presented a more shocking scenario of the effects of racial prejudice, perjured testimony, witness intimidation, an investigation the outcome of which was predetermined, and public officials who, for whatever motives, lost sight of what is right and just."

But for McCloskey, it was simply another case, the kind he runs into all the time. Despite this country's system of safeguards based on the philosophy that it is better to let a guilty man go free than to punish an innocent one, McCloskey believes that wrongful convictions occur with great regularity. Less than 10% of all criminal cases go before a jury; the vast majority are settled by pre-trial guilty pleas. McCloskey estimates "that one out of 10 who go to a jury trial are wrongly convicted."

He thinks a big reason is that some jurors place too much faith in the integrity and thoroughness of police investigations. They do not truly believe that criminal defendants are entitled to be presumed innocent until proven guilty. "People come together in a courtroom and the [defendant's] sitting there. They think, 'Where there's smoke, there's fire,'" McCloskey says. "'The police wouldn't have brought this person to trial unless there was good reason.' And a lot of times there isn't."

As for police in the cases he has investigated, he says, "I can't look you in the eye and say that [they] believed in their innermost person that these guys were innocent and set about to frame them. They built a case to fit their theory. A name [invariably that of someone with a criminal record] popped up as a suspect. And when information came their way that would lead them in a different direction, they ignored it. They hid it. And they also manufactured it to fit."

SOCIALLY SMOOTH WHEN he wants to be, McCloskey has a sense of priorities that one friend says would make him leave in the middle of a sentence if his schedule called for it. The eldest of three children, he grew up in an affluent, church-going family in suburban Philadelphia.

His father, a Presbyterian church elder, was executive vice president of the family business, McCloskey & Co., a large construction firm that changed much of Philadelphia's skyline and built one of the U.S. House of Representatives office buildings and Robert F. Kennedy Memorial Stadium in Washington, D.C. The firm was founded by McCloskey's great-uncle, Matthew, a powerful behind-the-scenes figure in the Democratic Party and a onetime U.S. ambassador to Ireland. But McCloskey had no interest in joining the firm.

After college at Bucknell University, Navy service in Japan and combat in Vietnam, he returned to Japan as a civilian, helping U.S. companies negotiate joint ventures there, then striking out on his own in a venture to market galoshes. Unfortunately, Tokyo experienced a drought the year he decided to become a galoshes entrepreneur. "It never rained," he says. "It was unbelievable."

Back home, broke and disappointed, McCloskey went to work for the Hay Group, a prestigious Philadelphia consulting firm, where he specialized in advising Japanese companies who were doing business in the United States. By 1978, he was making $55,000 a year and had bought himself a house in the Main Line Philadelphia suburb of Malvern. He was on his way to a partnership that year when he announced that, at the age of 36, he felt selfish and wanted to leave, to study for the ministry.

McCloskey had started to attend church for the first time since high school a few years before, and the minister's preaching gradually "drove me into the Scriptures. As I'm reading the New Testament, I'm really starting to feel that Christ was speaking to me."

"I was feeling an emptiness," McCloskey recalls. "The job and the business career were going well. But I didn't feel that I was doing anything really worthwhile. I've been a bachelor all my life. I [decided I] wanted to do something more with my life than just feed myself."

McCloskey deferred his departure from the business world for a year while he trained his replacement. Then he rented out his house and drove his Lincoln Continental to the Princeton Theological Seminary, where he checked into the dormitory. During his second year, he opted to do his field work by counseling inmates two days a week in the maximum-security section of nearby Trenton State Prison.

And there, in 1980, McCloskey, naive in the ways of the criminal justice system, met George "Chiefie" De Los Santos, an illiterate junkie from the streets of Newark, who put him on his present path.

Chiefie—the name tattooed across his chest—was in the sixth year of a life sentence for the murder of a Newark used-car salesman. He admitted to having earned heroin making deliveries for small-time dealers. But he claimed to be innocent of the murder.

After hours of conversation over a period of weeks, McCloskey agreed to review the transcript of Chiefie's trial. There it was, in black and white: Chiefie had confessed. He had admitted the murder to Richard Delli Santi, another petty criminal in jail.

Chiefie had played him for a fool. "It really shook me," McCloskey recalls. He confronted Chiefie. But Chiefie's explanation was simple: Delli Santi had made it up.

"Why would anybody do that to you?" McCloskey demanded. "Why would Delli Santi lie?"

"Well," Chiefie said, "he was in trouble with the law."

McCloskey thought that was pretty lame. But "I'd never been associated with the low lifes of the world," he says. "I'd never thought about police pressure."

Chiefie explained to him, and McCloskey came away convinced. He offered to take a year off from the seminary to investigate Chiefie's claims. "That was my Christmas gift to him," McCloskey says. "I was moved by his plight. So it seemed to me I couldn't just offer up prayers for him and move on."

Besides, McCloskey was tired of school. Living on his savings, he moved out of the dormitory and into the home of an elderly woman who allowed him to live rent free in exchange for doing her weekly shopping. Then he began his probe.

Delli Santi turned out to be a longtime jailhouse informant who repeatedly claimed that cellmates confessed serious crimes to him. Despite 40 arrests as a junkie and burglar, Delli Santi had managed to avoid being sent to state prison by trading the supposed confessions to authorities.

McCloskey persuaded a smart and cynical Hoboken defense attorney, Paul Casteleiro, to help him win Chiefie's freedom. Together, they convinced a federal judge that Delli Santi had "contrived the alleged confession."

What's more, U.S. District Court Judge Frederick B. Lacey said, the prosecution had known it and had suppressed evidence of perjury: Delli Santi had sworn that he had never before testified about confessions he'd supposedly heard in jail. "It is a virtual certainty that there would have been an acquittal if the jury had had all the evidence," the judge concluded.

It took McCloskey 2½ years to free Chiefie. By then, Mc-Closkey had given up his original plan to become a conventional church pastor. "I now know that I could never do that work," he says, "because you get sucked up into all this petty administrative handholding stuff that doesn't mean a hill of beans."

He had returned to the seminary and written his senior thesis on what he called "radical disciples"—men who challenged society's ways and obeyed Christ's teachings at great worldly cost. They were: civil-rights leader Martin Luther King Jr.; George Fox, a 17th-Century Englishman who was jailed for founding the Society of Friends; George Whitefield, an 18th-Century evangelist who died from exhaustion, and Toyohiko Kagawa, a 20th-Century Japanese labor activist repeatedly jailed for pacifist teachings.

These men, McCloskey wrote, "separated themselves from one life and blindly began another at the beckoning of Christ. Their work was both risky and revolutionary. Their personal inner knowledge of God and His Truth led them to challenge existing unjust structures, orders and systems. It led them to witness against and try to amend, reform, or eradicate terrible injustices. And in the end, except for God, their journey and work of discipleship was lonely. They were solitary and almost forlorn figures in trying to live out their faith."

McCloskey clearly saw himself as one of them. He incorporated his ministry as a nonprofit organization and went to work on the cases of two other convicts he had met through Chiefie. He had a three-year dry spell before his next client was freed. Wrongly convicted murderer Rene Santana walked out of a New Jersey prison in 1986, when McCloskey proved that the state's star witness, motivated by a secret deal with prosecutors to have charges against him dropped, had lied.

That year, McCloskey also won freedom for Nathaniel Walker, an Elizabeth, N.J., man who spent a decade behind bars for a rape he did not commit. The case rested on the blessed simplicity of physical evidence. McCloskey persuaded authorities to search for a vaginal swab that he knew had been taken but never tested. It turned up in a test tube, in a yellowed envelope, on a police property room shelf. FBI tests showed conclusively that Walker and the rapist had different blood types.

McCloskey's victory in the Walker case led to a burst of publicity. McCloskey, who had exhausted his own funds, had been getting contributions from friends and from the missionary fund of the church he had attended when he joined the seminary. But with the publicity came contributions from foundations and wealthy individuals, as well as an assistant.

Kate Hill, a born-again Christian who had operated restaurants, bars, inns, a soup kitchen, boutique and shoe store, was looking for work when she read articles about McCloskey who, in published photographs, had "piles of stuff around him." "I thought, 'I could organize this guy,'" she says. She began commuting by train from New York to Princeton.

Two years ago, McCloskey and Hill moved into their present office, across the street from the university, which a former Yugoslav prisoner of Tito rents to them at a below-market rate. The office consists of three rooms. There is a small storage area with boxes of letters from convicts labeled "no's and nuts." There is a much larger outer office, occupied by Hill and some volunteers, who mainly handle correspondence from inmates wanting help. And there is McCloskey's inner sanctum.

McCloskey lives monkishly, on about $22,000 a year, on the outskirts of Princeton. Far removed from the town's precious shops, his home is a studio apartment; the only decoration is a crucifix. But his office is cheery and shows a taste for the bizarre. Across from his desk is an oil painting given to him by Percy Foreman, the legendary Texas criminal defense lawyer. The painting is of a beautiful young woman posed seductively in the nude, a Foreman client who was accused of shooting her husband. There is a hole in the canvas—the fatal bullet must have passed through her image before it entered him.

McCloskey is overwhelmed with requests for help. He received 160 in the first quarter of this year alone. Initially, inmates who write receive a form letter in which he apologizes and says that there is only a remote chance he will take their case. A grease pencil board on the wall shows how slim the odds really are. It lists active cases. There are only six.

CHANCE MADE THE LIST in large part on the strength of his claim that he was in jail when the crime occurred. "That got my attention big-time," McCloskey says.

Although the jail claim remains unproven, McCloskey is convinced that Chance and his friend, Benny Powell, are innocent of the crime for which they were sentenced to life in prison: the murder of off-duty Los Angeles County Deputy Sheriff David Andrews, 24.

All that was known was that on Dec. 12, 1973, Andrews, dressed in civilian clothes, pulled into a service station at Normandie Avenue and Exposition Boulevard, parked his car at a phone booth, called someone, then went to the restroom. Two men entered behind him. Shots rang out. The men fled. Andrews was shot numerous times, and his gun was missing.

Police canvassed the neighborhood. Their best witness was an 11-year-old girl who said she had been riding her bicycle and had seen the two men enter and flee. Her descriptions did not fit Chance, whom she knew from the neighborhood, or Powell. She said one of the men had pimples and wore a Godfather-style hat. The other was short and wore a gold earring.

Moving methodically, detectives compiled lists of pimpled criminals, criminals who wore earrings and criminals who matched other facets of her descriptions. There was a lot of pressure to solve the case. Andrews had three brothers in local law enforcement, and, an investigator said, they wanted results. Police organizations offered thousands of dollars in rewards. But the police detectives assigned to the case were getting nowhere. They were removed, and a new team was instructed to work on the case full time until it was solved.

For reasons now lost to time, the new detectives decided that the answer to the crime was on 38th Street, where Chance lived, a block away from the station. Powell also sometimes lived on 38th Street, where he was known as a troublemaker.

Perhaps unwittingly, the investigators then constructed what McCloskey contends was a "classic frame."

They began with Powell. His name had already come up in the investigation. It appeared on a list of miscellaneous suspects compiled by the first set of detectives. And Powell hung around with Chance. Again and again, police visited the girl who had been riding her bicycle around the service station.

Could she recognize photos of Powell or Chance? No, she said, she could not. They took her to a lineup in which they had placed Chance. She said he was not the man. But the police kept coming, and finally she changed her mind.

McCloskey argues she succumbed to police pressure. Detective William Hall, a member of the team of new detectives, who now investigates officer-involved shootings, says the girl changed her mind on her own. He says she had not identified Chance at first because she had been afraid and that she finally decided to identify him because the Chance family house had burned down and the family had moved.

Whatever the truth, it is clear that shortly after the girl identified a photograph of Chance, police developed their best information on Powell. It came from another suspect in the case, Wayne Henderson, who now says he implicated Powell to divert attention from himself.

"I said things about [Powell] to throw the cops off me," Henderson told McCloskey. "I never thought [Powell] did it." Henderson led police to a woman who he knew "was a liar who would do anything for money and really wanted that reward."

She told police that Powell—whom she had known as a child but had not seen for many years—suddenly showed up at her house two weeks after the murder, told her he'd killed a man, needed to leave town and offered to sell her a gun.

Then she apparently put police in touch with two teen-age girls who sometimes stayed at her house and who provided most of the rest of the police case. One of them, 16-year old Bernadine Kelly, was confined to a juvenile hall for a robbery when she was interviewed by the police. She told police that Powell had casually confessed to her.

Tammy Jackson, 14, was on probation for the same robbery. After repeated visits from police and prompting from Henderson, who was acting at the behest of police, she said that, in a separate incident, Chance and Powell had confessed to her.

Based on the teen-agers' assertions—which they have told McCloskey they made up—in 1974, police arrested Powell, who had moved to Kansas City, and then Chance.

The 11-year-old eyewitness was taken to her second lineup.

She testified that police showed her pictures of Chance on the way to the lineup and suggested that they wanted her to identify the same man whose photo she had belatedly picked. She did.

But she said she still couldn't identify Powell. Then, suddenly a week before trial, Larry Wilson, a notorious jailhouse informant, claimed that Powell had proclaimed news of his guilt from the tier where he was housed in the county jail. Chance and Powell say they can't understand how a jury could have bought it.

"Put this on record," Chance says from Folsom Prison, "I would have preferred to have been judged by a computer."

But the jury did buy it, and persuading a court to overturn a jury conviction is tough. McCloskey has secured volunteer lawyers for Chance and Powell, and they expect to begin the slow process of petitioning courts for their release in the spring.

Meanwhile, McCloskey keeps talking to witnesses. Kelly, now a grown woman, says she lied "because the police, they kept on asking me all kinds of questions and like they was putting words in my head and so, I just went along with them and kind of made up stuff in my head."

Jackson says she lied because the police had threatened to take her away from her grandmother unless she told them what they wanted to hear. She says she made up three stories until she finally found one that satisfied them. "I just said anything," she told McCloskey. "I wanted them to get out of my hair."

To McCloskey this is a familiar refrain. Half of his cases have involved alleged confessions, ones that, as it turned out, never took place. For a long while, he couldn't understand how a human being could lie about someone confessing to murder. Then two recanting witnesses in two different cases explained it to him.

"'It's a matter of survival,'" he quotes them as saying. "'Either I go away or your guy goes away. And I ain't going away.'" ▬

SELECTED BIBLIOGRAPHY

Berry, Jeffrey M. *Lobbying for the People: The Political Behavior of Public Interest Groups.* Princeton, NJ: Princeton University Press, 1977.

Conway, M. Margaret. *Political Participation in the United States.* Washington, D.C.: Congressional Quarterly Press, 1991.

Dahl, Robert A. *Who Governs? Democracy and Power in an American City.* New Haven, CT: Yale University Press, 1961.

Friedman, Benjamin. *Day of Reckoning: The Consequences of American Economic Policy.* New York: Random House, 1990.

Horwitt, Sanford D. *Let Them Call Me Rebel: Saul Alinsky, His Life and Legacy.* New York: Knopf, 1990.

Judd, Dennis R. *The Politics of American Cities: Private Power and Public Policy.* Glenview, IL: Scott, Foresman, 1988.

Kiewiet, D. Roderick. *Macroeconomics and Micropolitics.* Chicago: University of Chicago Press, 1983.

Kingdon, John W. *Agendas, Alternatives, and Public Policies.* Boston: Little, Brown, 1984.

McFarland, Andrew S. *Common Cause: Lobbying in the Public Interest.* Chatham, N.J.: Chatham House, 1984.

Nader, Ralph. *Whistle Blowing.* New York: Bantam Books, 1972.

Polsby, Nelson W. *Political Innovation in America.* New Haven, CT: Yale University Press, 1984.

Present, Phillip E. *People and Public Administration.* Pacific Palisades, CA: Palisades Publishers, 1979.

Stone, Clarence N., Robert K. Whelan, and William J. Murin. *Urban Policy and Politics in a Bureaucratic Age.* Englewood Cliffs, NJ: Prentice-Hall, 1986.

INDEX

Article Evaluation Form

The Brown & Benchmark Reader in
AMERICAN GOVERNMENT 1992

We are very much interested in knowing your responses to the articles in this edition of *The Brown & Benchmark Reader in American Government*. Please rate the articles using the following scale:

1. Excellent: definitely retain this article
2. Good: possibly retain this article
3. Fair: possibly delete this article
4. Poor: definitely delete this article

Your ratings count! Please fill out this form and mail it back to us as soon as possible. Simply fold the form in thirds so the address is on the outside, staple, and mail. It's that simple! Thank you!

Rating		Article
_____	1.1.	The Declaration of Independence
_____	2.	The Constitution of the United States
_____	3.	The Size and Variety of the Union as a Check on Faction
_____	4.	Checks and Balances
_____	5.	The Judges as Guardians of the Constitution
_____	2.1.	Back to Our Roots
_____	2.	Waiting for Lefty
_____	3.	The End Is Near for U.S. Conservatism
_____	3.1.	Is the Bill of Rights in Danger?
_____	2.	Too Many Rights? Too Few Duties?
_____	3.	Human Needs, Human Rights: Time for a Second Bill of Rights
_____	4.1.	The Backlash Against Government Threatens Those Least to Blame
_____	2.	Now, Over to You, Fellas!
_____	3.	How State Governments Are Looking Ahead
_____	5.1.	A Crisis of Shattered Dreams
_____	2.	Cumulative Decisions that May Bury the Individual
_____	3.	Campus Madness
_____	6.1.	Is the Public Really Angry?
_____	2.	Where Have All the People Gone?
_____	3.	Give People a Choice: Let 'Em Vote for "None of the Above"
_____	7.1.	A Victim of Divided Government
_____	2.	Family Feud
_____	3.	Riding the Victory Train
_____	8.1.	The Keating 535
_____	2.	The Repackaging of Dan Quayle
_____	3.	Most Valuable Player
_____	9.1.	Can Democracy Survive the Media in the 1990s?
_____	2.	War Stories
_____	3.	TV News & the Neutrality Principle
_____	10.1.	King of the Road
_____	2.	As Clean Air Bill Took Off, So Did PAC Donations
_____	3.	Common Cause: A Watchdog that Barks at Its Friends

Rating		Article
_____	11.1.	Congress and Its Reputation: The Issue of Congressional Performance
_____	2.	Washington Gets to Mr. Smith
_____	3.	A Failure of Leadership
_____	12.1.	A Day in the Life
_____	2.	Why Great Men Are Not Chosen Presidents
_____	3.	How Bush Manages the Presidency
_____	13.1.	How to Cut the Bureaucracy in Half
_____	2.	The Education of Rockwell Schnable
_____	3.	To Live and Die in L.A.
_____	14.1.	The Siege of Yonkers
_____	2.	Bulldog Justice
_____	3.	The Swing to the Left in State Courts
_____	15.1.	Heavy Lifting: How America's Debt Burden Threatens the Economic Recovery
_____	2.	Money and Democracy: The Myth of an Independent Fed
_____	3.	Who Really Made the S & L Mess?
_____	16.1.	Who Is the Underclass?
_____	2.	Making It: The Underclass Cycle
_____	3.	Us vs. Them: America's Growing Frustration with the Homeless
_____	17.1.	The Dioxin Deception
_____	2.	Superfund Has Failed
_____	3.	Energy for the Next Century
_____	18.1.	America Without the Cold War
_____	2.	The Bush Foreign Policy
_____	3.	Pentagon Charade
_____	19.1.	Must America Decline? American Renewal
_____	2.	From Vermont, A Radical Blueprint to Reinvigorate American Democracy
_____	3.	The Warrior State: Imposing the New Order at Home
_____	20.1.	Squatter's Right
_____	2.	The Power of One
_____	3.	Minister of Justice

(Continued on next page)

NO POSTAGE
NECESSARY
IF MAILED
IN THE
UNITED STATES

2. (Fold Here)

Name: _____   Date: _____

_____ Instructor   _____ Student   _____ Full time   _____ Part time

Institution: _____   Department (if applicable): _____

Address: _____

City: _____   State: _____   ZIP: _____ - _____

Institution phone #: (_____) _____-_____

Course Information:

Course for which this book was used: _____

Was a text used with this reader? _____ Yes _____ No

If yes, which text(s)? _____

_____

Instructors, did you use the Instructor's Resource Guide? _____ Yes _____ No

Comments on the IRG:

1. (Fold Here)

Please rate the effectiveness of the following:

	Effective/ Useful						Ineffective/ Not Useful		
Abstract summaries that preceded the articles	1	2	3	4	5	6	7	8	9
Key Terms	1	2	3	4	5	6	7	8	9
Discussion Questions	1	2	3	4	5	6	7	8	9
Selected Bibliography	1	2	3	4	5	6	7	8	9
Instructor's Resource Guide	1	2	3	4	5	6	7	8	9

Overall comments: